The **General College Vision**

Integrating Intellectual Growth, Multicultural Perspectives, and Student Development

Editors

Jeanne L. Higbee

Dana B. Lundell

David R. Arendale

Associate Editor
Emily Goff

General College and the Center for Research
on Developmental Education and Urban Literacy

MINNEAPOLIS

2005

This book is dedicated to all of the General College

undergraduate and graduate students, staff, faculty, and

administrators, past and present, who have contributed

to the GC vision for access and excellence in higher

education. The synergy of the General College is the sum of

its parts. This book seeks to recognize the significance that

each individual's role has had in achieving an overall vision

for the General College community.

Contents

Editorial Board   ix

Acknowledgements   xi

PREFACE *Martha Casazza*   xiii

FOREWORD *Daniel Detzner, Robert Poch, and David V. Taylor*   xv

Introduction   1

The Vision and Purpose of the GC Book   3
Dana Britt Lundell and Jeanne L. Higbee

CHAPTER 1 An Introduction to the General College   7
Jeanne L. Higbee and Dana Britt Lundell

CHAPTER 2 Sharing Our Experiences: General College   17
Students Give Voice to Their Perceptions of GC
Joshua G. Schmitt, Mark A. Bellcourt, Khong Meng Xiong,
Amanda M. Wigfield, Inge L. B. Peterson, Sedrick D. Halbert,
Leah A. Woodstrom, Elizabeth Mai Tong Vang, and Jeanne L. Higbee

Honoring Our History   35

Introduction   37

CHAPTER 3 From the Beginning: The History of Developmental   39
Education and the Pre-1932 General College Idea
Allen B. Johnson

CHAPTER 4 Counseling Psychology and the General College: 61
An Implementation of the Minnesota Point of View
Cathrine Wambach and Thomas Brothen

CHAPTER 5 Fulfilling the University's Promise:
The Social Mission of Developmental Education   83
Katy Gray Brown

CHAPTER 6 The Politics of Transformation: 93
Development Education in a Postsecondary Research Institution
David V. Taylor

Promoting Multiculturalism   107

Introduction   109

CHAPTER 7 Students' Assessment of Their Multicultural   111
Experiences in the General College: A Pilot Study
Jeanne L. Higbee and Kwabena Siaka

CHAPTER 8 Creating Spheres of Freedom: Connecting 131
Developmental Education, Multicultural Education,
and Student Experience
Heidi Lasley Barajas

CHAPTER 9 Building Voice and Developing Academic 155
Literacy for Multilingual Students:
The Commanding English Model
*Laurene Christensen, Renata Fitzpatrick, Robin Murie,
and Xu Zhang*

CHAPTER 10 Multicultural Mathematics: 185
A Social Issues Perspective in Lesson Planning
Susan K. Staats

CHAPTER 11 Multicultural Writing Instruction 201
at the General College: A Dialogical Approach
Patrick Bruch and Thomas Reynolds

Embedding Skill Development in Content Courses 219

Introduction 221

CHAPTER 12 Integrating Best Practices of Developmental 223
Education in Introductory History Courses
David R. Arendale and David L. Ghere

CHAPTER 13 Aesthetic, Metaphoric, Creative, 247
and Critical Thinking: The Arts in General College
Patricia A. James

CHAPTER 14 Overview of the General College 287
Mathematics Program
D. Patrick Kinney, Douglas F. Robertson, and Laura Smith Kinney

CHAPTER 15 Learning Mathematics Through 299
Computer-Mediated Instruction
D. Patrick Kinney, Laura Smith Kinney, and Douglas F. Robertson

CHAPTER 16 Integrating and Enabling Skill Development 319
in a Symbolic Logic Class
Carl J. Chung

CHAPTER 17 Teaching Thinking and Reasoning Skills 333
in a Science Course
Leon Hsu

CHAPTER 18 Reading, Writing, and Sociology? 355
Developmental Education and the Sociological Imagination
Heidi Lasley Barajas and Walter R. Jacobs

Facilitating Development Through Student Services   369
Introduction   371
CHAPTER 19 General College Student Services: 373
A Comprehensive Model and How It Developed
Mary Ellen Shaw and Patricia J. Neiman
CHAPTER 20 Collaborative Learning Beyond the Classroom: 395
The Academic Resource Center
Donald L. Opitz and Debra A. Hartley

Integrating Theory and Research with Practice   415
Introduction   417
CHAPTER 21 Contributions of the General College   419
to Theory and Research
Dana Britt Lundell, Carl J. Chung, and Jeanne L. Higbee
CHAPTER 22 The Criterion Model of Developmental   449
Education in General College
Thomas Brothen and Cathrine Wambach

Using Assessment to Guide Practice   475
Introduction   477
CHAPTER 23 Reaching for the Standards, Embracing Diversity: 479
Students' Perceptions of the Mathematics Program
Irene M. Duranczyk and Donald L. Opitz
CHAPTER 24 Student Perceptions of General College: 519
A Student-Initiated Study
Mark A. Bellcourt, Ian S. Haberman, Joshua G. Schmitt,
Jeanne L. Higbee, and Emily Goff
CHAPTER 25 Pre- and Post-Admission Predictors of the Academic   527
Success of Developmental Education Students
Randy Moore

Conclusion   545
CONCLUSION   547
David R. Arendale
About the Editors   551
About the Authors   553
Bibliography of Developmental Education Publications   561
by General College Authors
Emily Goff

Editorial Board

Acknowledgments

The Editors would like to thank the following individuals for their efforts and dedication to the publication of this book. This book has taken over 2 years to come to fruition. Each person made an enormous contribution in meeting strict deadlines, making ongoing and demanding revisions, entrusting us to make this project happen, and supporting the project financially and administratively.

Foremost, we thank Dean David Taylor for his support and visionary leadership in General College. His presence and encouragement for students, staff, and faculty create a positive and productive working atmosphere that fuels projects such as this book. We also thank GC's administrators, Daniel Detzner and Robert Poch, for their support.

Central to this book, of course, has been its incredible and resilient group of authors. With political battles to fight, students to teach and support, research to produce, and other tasks that fill the hours of educators' time, this group rose to meet a challenge we could not have anticipated. They met all deadlines, respected our vision and dialogued effectively with our advice as Editors, acknowledged and incorporated the perspectives of the book's external reviewers, and turned in excellent finished chapters. It is both wonderful and hard to work so closely with in-house writers, and the General College provides a functional and exceptional space for doing this kind of work efficiently and in a synergistic way. To all the authors, thanks and congratulations!

The team of support staff from the Center for Research on Developmental Education and Urban Literacy (CRDEUL), including Robert Copeland and Emily Goff, helped in all phases of the project from organizing to communications to editing. Additionally, Laura Weber from the GC Communications office and Karen Bencke from the College of Liberal Arts offered editing support and technical assistance. We also thank Judy Gilats, who designed and typeset the book.

We thank our CRDEUL Editorial Board, especially Martha Casazza for her review of the entire book and constructive feedback she offered individually to the writers and Editors.

Finally, the Editors thank their friends and family and all of the General College as a community for offering support, humor, sincerity, and a constant source of inspiration during challenging and upbeat times in the field of developmental education.

Preface

Martha E. Casazza

We must create academies that are warm and nurturing and supportive learning communities that don't have biases that tend to exclude but rather are supportive of anyone who is willing to work hard and take the opportunities that are there. When we become more exclusionary, especially in an era where more students are not being prepared for the rigors of higher education, it is kind of self-defeating. (David Taylor, Dean, as quoted in Casazza & Bauer)

This statement was made during an interview for an oral history research project that is currently exploring access to higher education in the United States. The researchers are interviewing educators and students across the country to gather perspectives on how academic excellence is compatible with providing access to students who have traditionally been denied access to a postsecondary education. The supposed incompatibility between access and excellence has been debated for years across higher education, and the argument seems to gain strength during times of slashed budgets when institutions look for ways to cut services to students. Even though less than 1% of the public higher education budget nationally is spent on developmental education, decreasing support for underprepared students frequently heads the list of cutbacks, especially when it is accompanied by the rationale that it will help to raise academic standards. In addition, many states are limiting developmental instruction to 2-year and technical colleges. Since the mid-1980s, 30 states have proposed policies to limit this type of instructional support to these institutions. This concept, in effect, narrows the point of access to higher education and sets up rather exclusionary standards.

These trends are occurring when college enrollments are burgeoning. Between 1960 and 2001, they grew from 4.1 million to 14.8 million students. Ninety percent of high school seniors expect to attend college while only 47% of high school graduates have completed college preparatory curricula. Forty percent of students in 4-year postsecondary institutions takes developmental courses while the overall percentage for all institutions is 53%. Enrollment across colleges and universities is expected to grow, and by 2015 1 to 2 million additional young adults, many of whom will come from low income and minority families, will seek access to higher education (National Panel Report of the Association of American Colleges and Universities, 2002).

At the same time, employers today are increasingly looking for individuals who can process information and have good communication skills. A college education is no longer an option; indeed, it is becoming a requirement if one wants career choices. There are very few unskilled jobs left in this country. By 2008, 14.1 million new jobs will require a bachelor's degree or at least some postsecondary education, more than double those requiring high school completion or below (Association of American Colleges and Universities, 2002).

Access to higher education is a social imperative that we must take seriously. It is clear that the General College of the University of Minnesota has historically taken this mission with earnestness and centrality. It is also clear that the General College continues to serve as a national model for how access and excellence are not only compatible but provide a distinct and positive energy for the entire learning community in which they exist. No one can express this synergy more effectively than a student who has experienced it. The following words come directly from a General College student who is quoted in one of the chapters contained in this excellent historical document.

> As I continue to gain momentum in my pursuit of my degree, I wished to discredit the presumption that I have less academic potential than my peers in other colleges. Every success that I have had has been a direct reflection of ... General College's support and encouragement of them and lastly the application of hard work and persistency by myself. As a General College student, I seek to follow in the precedent set by the successful General College alumni that have traveled before us. One of which has won the Nobel Peace Prize ... Each student within the General College student body has it in them to succeed. By abstaining from the quicksand of mediocrity and pressing on towards our academic goals, we will harvest tomorrow's leaders from those society was content to let slip down society's proverbial cracks. (Joshua Schmitt, Chapter 2)

References

Association of American Colleges and Universities. (2002). *Greater expectations: A new vision for learning as a nation goes to college.* Washington, DC: Author. Retrieved May 11, 2005, at http://www.greaterexpectations.org

Casazza, M. E., & Bauer, L. (in press). *Access, opportunity, and success: Keeping the promise of higher education.* Westport, CT: Praeger.

Foreword

*Daniel Detzner, Robert Poch,
and David V. Taylor*

Over the past 15 years the General College (GC) has been the subject of inquiry from colleges and universities across the nation seeking to implement academic support curricula for "underprepared" students. The attraction of the General College experience is that it is a multidisciplinary program that embeds academic skills development into courses. This innovative concept has been presented at conferences and professional meetings and is nationally acclaimed.

The General College is the product of 73 years of exploration, experimentation, and refinement. It grew out of a curricular expression initially described as a general education experience; that is to say, introductory courses in the sciences, social sciences, and the humanities, designed to make the liberal arts curriculum of that day more accessible to the average first-year student. This approach, coupled with the use of academic advisors, another innovation stemming from the 1930s and 1940s, provided a more holistic approach to the then-burgeoning field of academic instruction and student services. Today, the General College mission statement reads as follows:

> The mission of the General College of the University of Minnesota is to develop, through teaching, research, and service, the potential for baccalaureate education in students who are serious about fulfilling their previous undeveloped or unrecognized academic promise. The General College seeks to generate and apply knowledge concerning how best to understand, broaden, and deepen academic achievement in our increasingly diverse, multicultural society. The General College selects for admission those students who can best benefit from their early integration into the total University community, who can demonstrate that they have the motivation and determination to achieve, and who are willing to direct their energy to a rigorous baccalaureate education at the University of Minnesota. (General College, 2005)

The impetus for this book is derived in part by explaining what it is that we do and to discern future directions for this work. It is also driven by definitions ascribed to our work, that is, "developmental education" and an even newer vision and vocabulary for the future that captures the integration of a variety of theories, pedagogies, and evaluation measures that fully support diverse and rapidly changing student populations. Given the demographic shift in Minnesota's population, the authors in this book have expressed an imperative that we look centrally at the experiences of the learner in higher education through a different set of lenses if we are to be successful in preparing all learners.

Defining What We Do

Practitioners of postsecondary developmental education and those professionals in higher education who are committed to supporting learning for all individuals entering colleges and universities have discussed what to call the work of programs such as General College. The outdated term "remedial" suggests deficits where students come to be fixed to acceptable standards of higher education. Remediation is not, and has never been, the work of GC, despite popular misconceptions that sometimes are applied in describing our work. The more recently accepted terminology of developmental education suggests a more comprehensive approach to serving and supporting the learning of all students. General College has provided a unique form of developmental education to students who demonstrate potential to be successful in college despite past academic measures. Some believe that the term developmental education is still widely misunderstood and confused with remedial education by those outside of the field, sometimes leading to ongoing misperceptions about the work of a college such as GC. That is why General College is in a unique position to redefine and continue to evolve definitions of what it means to support learners in higher education. Thus, what GC does is far more comprehensive than any standard term that has been applied yet to describe our work, though terms like "access," "developmental education," "learning assistance," "human development," and "multicultural developmental education" offer informative descriptions about our approach.

Instead of apologizing that our students do not measure up to their peers with high standardized test scores and the best high school grades, we always affirm that all students are distinct individuals, they develop at different rates, and they may not have had the same privileges and opportunities. In the age of "no child left behind" federal policies, the work of higher educators continues to focus on the transitions and educational development of students who did not have equal experiences in K-12. Because the achievement gap still exists, programs like GC remain essential to closing this gap.

Our faculty in General College, as noted in this book's chapters, work with students who are struggling to overcome the barriers in their lives while affirming their intellectual strengths. Despite terminology that continues to evolve to describe the work we do, this is what GC is about. The college affirms all individuals and their potential to achieve, be retained, and graduate through curricula, teaching, research, and service to the wider community.

A Developmental Education Curriculum

The curriculum of the General College goes far beyond the traditional developmental education courses in writing and mathematics and embraces multicultural approaches and discipline-based learning skills into the core of sciences, social sciences, arts, and humanities courses. Later chapters in this book reveal the many ways that General College courses foster educational development. General College faculty are researchers as well as teachers, so they are also studying the educational and multicultural development of underrepresented students. General College classrooms are sites for pedagogical and curricular experimentation as well as places where students figure out how best to succeed.

Future research opportunities for General College faculty and staff will focus on how to link courses, pedagogies, faculty, and students into communities of learning that go beyond content, bits of information, and discipline-based ways of knowing. Learning community models, which have been developed and examined across the country as a way to strengthen the first-year experience, have caught the attention of General College faculty and staff. We are now beginning to think more holistically about our course offerings and how they might be able to generate more synergy within the context of learning communities.

The importance of synergy between courses and pedagogies, the linking of intellectual content with social goals, and the creating of an atmosphere where a sense of community is developed seem critical if we are to take the next steps forward to work with students who are underrepresented in higher education. Students attending the University of Minnesota, a large urban university, do not always feel a sense of community. The challenge will be to create that sense of community not only in specially designed courses, and in a series of linked courses, but in every course taught by every member of the General College teaching staff and faculty.

Student Services: The Co-Curriculum

In many respects the co-curricular field of student development was pioneered nationally by faculty in the General College during the 1930s, 1940s, and 1950s. From the early work of Cornelia "Queeno" McCune (Johnson, 2003), who conducted extensive research on students for the enhancement of student counseling in the mid-1930s, to today's General College counselor advocates, the goal remains the same—to anticipate, assess, and respond to students' needs in ways that produce engagement and commitment to academic success.

As we look to the future, the commitment to student development must begin with precollegiate student outreach programs. Students must be academically prepared and motivated to attend postsecondary institutions. We must make better use of institutional data on student academic success in admissions decisions. We must assess student strengths and weaknesses to better identify skill development needs and opportunities. Finally, we must collaborate more effectively with other instructional and counseling units throughout the University of Minnesota. Such collaboration will enable effective student collegiate planning, matriculation, assessment, advisement, skill development, retention, and graduation.

The increasingly diverse cultural, economic, and educational backgrounds of Minnesota's K-12 students require proactive communication and contact within schools and communities that historically serve students with low college attendance rates. Assessment and the utilization of assessment results are needed to assist General College students as they are admitted and to ensure their continued development in other key areas affecting student success, such as study skills, time management, and test preparation. Skillful use of assessment information can enhance retention, transfer, and graduation rates and can be used to inform both early awareness messaging and collegiate admissions.

Finally, as General College students transfer into other academic programs at the University of Minnesota to complete their baccalaureate degrees, further communication and collaboration with the transfer colleges will be a core feature of learning more about the academic performance and preparation of our students. The optimal goal is the creation of a supportive web of academic and counseling services that is essentially seamless from elementary school through baccalaureate degree.

General College and the Future

The composition of the General College student body suggests that we are on the frontlines of a demographic change in higher education. Almost 50% of the General College student body currently is comprised of students of color. These students represent historically underrepresented populations in the United States as well as growing immigrant populations.

The changing classroom demography suggests the need for more research on how these students learn best. The lessons that we have learned, and the past research that we have conducted, will be important to developing workable strategies for engaging with and teaching these students.

It is clear that we do not have all the answers because we are only now beginning to ask the right questions. This book is a step in that direction, but the distance to be traveled remains far. General College's vision is to continue to develop learners and transform institutions to make learning accessible and successful for all those who wish to participate in higher education. We are hopeful that the insights in this book will assist our colleagues in higher education across the world with this endeavor.

References

General College. (2005). *Our mission*. Minneapolis, MN: Author. Retrieved May 10, 2005, from http://www.gen.umn.edu/gc/Mission.htm

Johnson, A. (2003, Spring). Cornelia "Queeno" McCune. *Access News, 2* (3), 4, 10. Minneapolis, MN: General College, University of Minnesota. Available: http://www.gen.umn.edu/programs/communications/access/access_v2-n3.pdf

Introduction

The Vision and Purpose
of the GC Book

Dana Britt Lundell and Jeanne L. Higbee

The chapters in this book reflect a situated analysis of the General College (GC), which is a flexible set of models that co-exist programmatically to support learners from diverse backgrounds who enter college with a variety of academic achievements, social skills, and workforce talents. This book essentially provides a historical look at the college's foundation with a more contemporary "snapshot" of the college's theoretical and curricular frameworks from the vantage point of faculty and staff members who write directly about their own classrooms and experiences. The goal of the chapters and ultimately the book collectively is to demonstrate how, as a group, the individual members of the GC professional community work together to provide an educational model that supports the widest range of students possible.

This is a highly developed, sophisticated, and somewhat complex approach to undergraduate education as the end goal of all individuals in the college is to move students successfully from GC to their desired major at the University of Minnesota. This includes not only providing success in academic skill development but also success in the social and economic purposes of education, such as developing engaged citizens, socially and culturally aware people, and skilled workforce employees. The notion of the General College presented at this time demonstrates a set of activities and ideas that support student learning in higher education, with an emphasis on drawing upon the expertise of recent theoretical and curricular approaches that provide the best means for transitioning undergraduates, specifically including those who were formerly underserved by their social contexts and educational institutions.

The General College includes curricular approaches and theoretical frameworks that reflect a type of programmatic coexistence, a "loosely coupled" system, where various disciplines of the college interact and design

3

approaches for their academic content area to embed skill development into their core areas. The educators all share concepts, such as supporting transitions, providing skill development, and preparing student learners for future academic courses and social activities such as work or civic engagement. GC educators address student motivation, skills, cultural awareness, social and academic literacies, and mastery of content areas. They may vary in their theoretical frameworks in terms of how their own courses, outcomes, and assignments are implemented and conceived. As the frameworks are diverse across the GC program, they may overlap or present divergent models for engaging students in the day-to-day activities of GC courses. However, in this diversity, they also complement each other to provide the widest range of supports for students who take the sequence of courses to prepare for their transition to a future major at the university. In other words, the GC model as presented in the examples in this book presents a variety of activities and approaches that, when operating together across the disciplines toward a central mission, complement each other as students move through the program. This is the most innovative approach possible, and the GC program has a historic legacy of providing flexibility and a comprehensive set of courses that best fulfill this mission and GC's role within the greater university community.

An important and central concept in the GC model is the notion of the "GC community," a phrase commonly used by faculty, staff, students, and alumni to describe their sense of location and role within this college. This phrase, while existing partially as college lore and popular vocabulary, certainly reflects a strongly held belief by many members of the college constituencies that GC is more than just an educational concept and curricular approach. There is a kind of cohesiveness and progressive coexistence at the core of this concept. This feeling of being within a community as an educator is more than a fuzzy notion of feel-good educational practices. GC has strength and cohesiveness as a comprehensive educational program, and the fact that the faculty, staff, students, and alumni refer to this college as a community of sorts by using the phrase "GC Community" is an affirmation of a central sense of identity, ownership, and agency that people hold related to its central mission, function, and day-to-day practices and outcomes. This book's chapters collectively attempt to identify some of the components of this educational community, both as it plays out in practice and as it is exemplified in the spirit of the purpose and goals of the college in higher education.

GC is also a unique program in the nation; it is a leader in research for issues of access and student success, such as transfer, retention, and graduation. The goal of this writing project is to finally capture this model at a point in time that reflects its historic origins and also its future innovations. The General College, like any forward-thinking educational program, is always evolving to serve its students and meet the needs of the greater context within which it exists. Thus, the model remains diverse, complementary, and flexible in its parts. Higher education programs serving undergraduates in this century must be highly adaptable and responsive to their student populations. Members of GC have always understood this, and the chapters in this book will demonstrate a shared awareness of the diversity of its staff, students, and the most appropriate and contemporary approaches in higher education that can serve the needs of all students in this society.

The section introductions throughout this book will explain how each set of chapters by GC faculty and staff authors collectively define the work of GC in several areas, such as history, multiculturalism, skill development and course content, student services, theory and research, and assessment. This book's publication, dedication of its authors, work of its editors, and support of GC's administrators centrally reflect the concept of how the GC community works together toward common goals and educational change for the broadest group of students.

CHAPTER 1

An Introduction
to the General College

Jeanne L. Higbee and Dana Britt Lundell

ABSTRACT

The purpose of this chapter is to introduce the General College and provide a brief overview of its programs and services as well as a profile of its students, faculty, and staff.

The General College (GC) is a freshman-admitting college of the University of Minnesota (UMN). Founded more than 150 years ago, the University of Minnesota is both a selective research institution and a public land-grant university with a strong tradition of teaching, research, and public service. The University is dedicated to the advancement of learning and the search for truth; to the sharing of this knowledge through education for a diverse community; and to the application of this knowledge to benefit the people of the state, nation, and world. The UMN Twin Cities campus, situated in the state's major urban site, enrolls more than 45,000 students each fall.

The General College houses one of the oldest developmental education units in America. As defined by the National Association for Developmental Education (NADE; 1995),

> Developmental Education is a field of practice and research within higher education with a theoretical foundation in developmental psychology and learning theory. It promotes cognitive and affective growth of all postsecondary learners, at all levels of the learning continuum.
>
> Developmental Education is sensitive and responsive to the individual differences and special needs among learners.
>
> Developmental Education programs and services commonly address preparedness, diagnostic assessment and placement, affective barriers to learning, and development of general and discipline-specific learning strategies.

The General College was founded in 1932 to provide a more general education than previously offered by the University of Minnesota to a broader range of students in terms of both academic and demographic profiles. Students enrolled in GC could earn an associate of arts degree or a certificate to enhance employability, and later a baccalaureate degree. Historically GC has served many student populations that traditionally have been underrepresented in American higher education, including adults returning to school, students who are parents, students of color, students who are recent immigrants to the U.S., students with disabilities, and students who are considered by regular admissions standards to be underprepared for university course work. In 1986, following the advent of Minnesota's network of community colleges, the Regents of the University of Minnesota decided that the mission and focus of the General College should change. Degree and certificate programs were phased out. Since 1991 GC's role has been to prepare students who do not meet regular admissions requirements.

In 1996 members of the University's central administration proposed the closing of the General College, so that resources could be diverted to other initiatives. GC was required to defend its mission within a selective research university. As indicated in Chapter 6, a ground swell of local support prevented the closing of GC. A new president, Mark Yudof, took over the helm of the University of Minnesota, and a team of external evaluators lauded GC's many accomplishments in providing access to the University of Minnesota. Several years later Governor Jesse Ventura once again proposed eliminating GC, not realizing that GC generated revenues equal to more than six times what it cost the state (Facts and Figures, 2004). More important, however, is the role that GC has played in providing access to the University of Minnesota to students from populations that traditionally have been underrepresented in institutions of higher education in Minnesota and the rest of the nation. Further information regarding GC's history and mission is provided in Chapters 3, 4, 5, 6, 19, and 22.

As we are completing the final editing and revisions of this book as a whole, the General College is once again in a state of transition. A University task force recommended to President Robert Bruininks that the college be closed and that some of its functions be relocated as a department in a reenvisioned College of Education and Human Development. These recommendations were forwarded by the President to the Board of Regents in May 2005, and the Board of Regents voted to accept the recommendations on June 10, 2005 (*Transforming the University of Minnesota*, 2005).

Goals

The General College's goals are closely linked to its primary mission (see Foreword) of providing access, as follow:

1. Promote multiculturalism. GC facilitates the understanding and celebration of individual and cultural differences at every level of the educational experience. The GC Multicultural Concerns Committee (MCC; Ghere, 2003) actively engages in numerous projects that are both educational and transformative. Through initiatives like the MCC Multicultural Scenarios Project (Jehangir, Yamasaki, Ghere, Hugg, Williams, & Higbee, 2002) and the Multicultural Awareness Project for Institutional Transformation (MAP IT; Higbee, Miksch, Jehangir, Lundell, Bruch, & Jiang, 2004; Miksch, Bruch, Higbee, Jehangir, & Lundell, 2003; Miksch, Higbee, et al., 2003), which is discussed further in Chapter 7, GC faculty and staff members have endeavored to explore multicultural issues and assess GC's commitment to providing an equitable and welcoming multicultural learning and working environment.

2. Foster skill development. The GC model embeds skill development in credit-bearing core curriculum courses without the loss of content and without compromising quality. Students are able to progress toward graduation rather than being required to enroll in courses that are considered precollege level. The only GC courses that do not bear credit toward graduation are in mathematics, as discussed in Chapters 10, 14, 15, and 23.

3. Expect excellence in teaching. General College faculty and instructional staff members put teaching first. This emphasis is apparent in faculty members' teaching portfolios, which include a reflective statement of teaching philosophy and how it is implemented in the classroom. In addition to tenure-track and tenured faculty, GC is highly selective in its employment of professional teaching specialists and graduate student teaching assistants. Student evaluations further support the high caliber of teaching in GC.

4. Provide academic support. The Student Information Center, Academic Resource Center, Supplemental Instruction, learning communities, and professional and peer tutors provide services to complement the classroom experience. These services will be described further in Chapters 19 and 20.

5. Enhance student development. Counselor advocates and the Transfer and Career Center provide advising and counseling to assist students with academic and career decision making.

6. Encourage civic engagement. Students, faculty, and staff are involved in community service through individual and classroom activities and college-wide efforts like the African-American Read-In.

7. Conduct research to guide teaching. Faculty and staff conduct extensive research that is directly linked to improving instruction. In addition, through the Center for Research on Developmental Education and Urban Literacy (CRDEUL), the college has been influential in leading national discussions and disseminating information about theoretical perspectives and current research to developmental educators and learning assistance professionals throughout the U.S.

8. Promote student involvement and leadership. Through its academic pro-grams and extracurricular activities, such as the GC Student Board and posi-tions for student representatives on GC standing committees, the General Col-lege encourages student participation in planning and decision making.

These goals are integrally linked to GC's efforts to retain students and enhance opportunities for their success. The General College endeavors to develop the skills, build the confidence, and provide the educational experi-ences across the curriculum that enable all students to maximize achieve-ment. Access without retention is an empty promise. GC seeks to prepare stu-dents for successful transfer to degree-granting colleges of the University of Minnesota, and ultimately to graduate.

Admissions

An integral aspect of the mission of the General College is to serve the higher education needs of the State of Minnesota. In particular, GC provides a means of access to the state's flagship research university for students who would otherwise be denied entry. Rather than relying only on high school rank and standardized test scores, the admissions process for GC also includes consideration of essays and letters of recommendation that provide insights into such intangibles as motivation and other factors that cannot readily be measured by more traditional admissions criteria, especially among students from traditionally underrepresented groups. The student body of the General College should reflect the population of the major met-ropolitan area in which it is located. For example, the Twin Cities are home to significant populations of Native Americans and recent Hmong and Somali immigrants, as well as other people of color, in proportions not as yet reflected in the University of Minnesota's general student population.

One policy that differentiates the General College from many other devel-opmental education units at other universities in the U.S. is the decision not to limit admission to a group of students whose standardized test scores, high school rank or grade point average (GPA), or other admissions criteria place them immediately below the standard cut-off. GC does not focus its selection process on the "narrow misses." Instead, GC welcomes a wide range of stu-dents from diverse backgrounds. It would be a relatively easy task to improve GC's retention statistics by changing the college's admissions policies, but GC recognizes that graduation rates are not the only way to measure student suc-cess. The entire university community benefits from the contributions of a diverse student body.

Each fall GC admits more than 800 new first-year students and typically serves between 1400 and 1800 first- and second-year students each semester.

GC accepts students whose Academic Aptitude Ratings (AAR; i.e., two times ACT composite score plus high school percentile rank) do not meet the admissions standards of the University of Minnesota's other freshman-admitting colleges. For fall 2004, 4,838 prospective students applied for admission to the General College, and GC made admissions offers to 1,815 to meet a target enrollment of 875. GC also served 939 continuing students and 15 transfer or new students with advanced standing (i.e., having college credits previously earned through Advanced Placement [AP] testing and other programs). GC's first-semester students accounted for approximately 16% of the University of Minnesota's incoming freshman class. First-year students enrolling in GC in fall 2004 had a mean high school percentile rank of 54.35, with a range from 2 to 99, and a mean ACT composite score of 19.70, with a range of 11 to 31. The mean age was 19.38, with a range of 17 to 52. Of the 875 new freshmen in GC, 89% were from Minnesota, and 74% were from the greater Twin Cities metropolitan area; 8% were student athletes. Of all students enrolled in GC during fall semester 2004, 48.2% were students of color, including approximately 22% African American, 2% American Indian, 20% Asian American, 5% Chicano or Latino, 49% Caucasian, and 3% for which data was missing.

Curriculum

The General College is unique among postsecondary developmental education units in its focus on providing developmental education within the framework of an entire core curriculum of credit-bearing courses. The GC curriculum includes courses in the physical and biological sciences, logic, statistics, art, film, drama, literature, speech communication, history, sociology, anthropology, psychology, and law and society, in addition to the mathematics and composition courses traditionally offered in developmental education programs. GC offers 13 courses that meet the University's cultural diversity graduation requirement, and 14 that count toward the writing intensive requirement. All students at the University of Minnesota are required to complete four courses that bear the writing-intensive designation beyond freshman composition.

The only "precollege" courses that fit the more traditional model for developmental education that are offered within GC are prerequisites in mathematics, which are described further in Chapter 14. Throughout the curriculum, skill development is embedded within content, rather than being provided through "stand-alone" reading and study strategy courses. Curriculum Transformation and Disability (CTAD; Higbee, 2003), funded through a U.S. Department of Education grant, has trained GC faculty and staff to provide a universally accessible learning environment that does not isolate students with disabilities. Thus, GC students are earning credits toward graduation while developing the skills necessary for (a) transfer to one of the degree-granting colleges of the University, (b) retention at the institution, and (c) success beyond college. GC offers challenging course work, a supportive environment, and small classes in which students have access to their teachers. More specific information about some of the courses in the GC curriculum is provided in other sections of this book.

Personnel

As of fall 2004, the staff of the General College consisted of 35 tenured and tenure-track faculty members; 54 professional and administrative (P&A) staff members, some of whom are teaching specialists; 48 civil service and bargaining unit staff members; and 34 graduate teaching and research assistants. Of the faculty, 12 are female, and 23 are male. With the addition of three new faculty hires for fall 2005, the faculty will be 26% people of color, including four African Americans, four Asian Americans, one American Indian, and one Latina. The P&A staff of 38 females and 16 males is approximately 15% people of color; the civil service and bargaining unit staff of 33 females and 15 males includes 23% people of color; and of the 23 female and 11 male graduate assistants, 50% are people of color.

Faculty and Instructional Staff

The General College is known for its exemplary teaching. The mean response on student evaluations to items related to the overall teaching ability of faculty members, professional teaching specialists, and graduate teaching assistants is typically around 6.0 on a 7.0 scale. The General College's full-time faculty members are hired as developmental education specialists within their disciplines. Since 1967, 32 GC faculty members (more than any other college of the University) have received the H. T. Morse Award for Outstanding Contributions to Undergraduate Education, the University's most prestigious teaching award. In addition, members of the faculty and instructional staff are among the most productive researchers in the field of developmental education, as demonstrated by the bibliography provided at the end of this book.

Professional and Administrative Staff

The General College has an active professional and administrative (P&A) staff who also contribute to the college's scholarship, teaching, and administration. They also receive a variety of awards for their service, teaching, and research contributions to GC's mission. P&A staff publish, disseminate research and best practices at professional meetings, provide leadership at the regional and national levels, and pursue professional development opportunities to enhance student learning, access, and retention.

Civil Service and Bargaining Unit Staff

Additionally, the college has strong leadership and professionalism in its extensive Civil Service and Bargaining Unit Staff, who provide a variety of clerical, administrative, financial, technical, and managerial supports within the college. Civil Service staff are also a diverse group of individuals within GC who contribute centrally to the research, teaching, and service missions of the college, including community outreach support, leadership within the greater UMN community, and leading the daily activities of the college in support of student life and academics. They receive many performance awards for their professionalism and contributions to GC.

Student Services and Community Outreach

In addition to its curriculum and faculty, GC has been widely recognized for its outstanding student services personnel and the vast array of programs it makes available to its students, as well as its commitment to civic engagement and community partnerships. The General College offers comprehensive student services. GC's three federally-funded TRIO programs, which have earned national exemplary status, include Student Support Services (SSS), through which GC offers Supplemental Instruction (SI) and learning communities, Upward Bound, and the Ronald McNair Scholarship Program. The Academic Resource Center (ARC) houses both mathematics and writing centers, as described in Chapter 20. The Commanding English (CE) Program, which will be described further in Chapter 9, serves about 50 students per year, providing linked courses and other forms of assistance for English language learners. The college hosts the Student Parent HELP Program, an educational, social, and economic support program for students who are parents. The Transfer and Career Center assists students in preparing to transfer to other colleges within the University and also guides them through career exploration. For those who must "stop out" for a variety of reasons, many nonacademic, the center provides help in making the adjustment to the world of work.

GC offers an extensive counseling, advising, and student advocacy program that has received repeated national recognition from the National Academic Advising Association (NACADA). Six GC counselor advocates have received the University's most prestigious advising award. Teachers and counselor advocates work together to provide an effective early warning system to ensure that students receive assistance before it is too late. In addition, all GC students receive progress reports in each of their GC courses during the sixth and tenth weeks of each semester. Programs within the General College, such as TRIO and CE, assist in promoting the retention of GC's diverse group of students. GC student services are described further in Chapter 19.

Over the years the General College has hosted myriad community outreach programs. GC currently sponsors an American Indian math and science summer camp and numerous other programs that serve area high school students. GC is also home of the national African American Read-In.

Retention and Transfer Rates

Of students who began their postsecondary education in the General College in fall 2003, 75% were still enrolled in fall 2004, as opposed to 86% of all UMN students who entered the University system in fall 2003. Of students who entered GC in fall 2002, 63% were still enrolled in fall 2004, as compared to a retention rate of 76% for the University system as a whole.

Transfer rates from GC to other colleges of the University remained stable at approximately 39% at the end of 2 years for students who were admitted to GC in 2001 and 2002. (Transfer admissions requirements make it very difficult to transfer after the first year.) Within 3 years approximately 54% of students admitted in fall 2000 and 58% of students who entered GC in fall 1999 had transferred to other colleges of the University of Minnesota, and within 4 years 62% of students who began in GC in fall 1999 had successfully transferred to a degree-granting college of the University.

Notable Success Stories

Perhaps one of the best yardsticks for measuring GC's effectiveness is the loyalty of its alumni. Norman Borlaug, recipient of the 1970 Nobel Peace Prize for his agricultural research, has reflected,

> I often think what would have happened to me if I had not had the chance to enter General College. I was declined entrance to the College of Liberal Arts or to Agriculture. I was thought to be unworthy, incapable of doing University work. My work in advancing the 'Green Revolution'—helping developing countries produce more food—as far as I'm concerned, this work couldn't have happened had I not been given that chance. (*Access and Excellence*, 2001, p. 17)

Other notable alumni of GC include examples of success such as a CEO of a local broadcasting company and an individual who started an independent technical support company. Numerous accounts by graduates of GC or former attendees of its transfer and preparation programs have reported back that their experiences in GC prepared them for jobs, future educational opportunities, and civic engagement within their communities.

Notably even in the current public controversy surrounding the May 2005 recommendations by President Bruininks to close GC, many more GC alumni have written in and shared their personal stories of success, access, and achievement to lifelong learning through the GC programs. Since 1932 GC has served as a starting point for higher education for thousands of students.

References

Access and excellence. (2001). Minneapolis, MN: Campaign Minnesota, General College, University of Minnesota.

Fact and figures. (2004). Minneapolis, MN: General College, University of Minnesota. Retrieved October 31, 2004, from http://www.gen.umn.edu

Ghere, D. L. (2003). The triumphs and tribulations of a multicultural concerns committee. In J. L. Higbee, D. B. Lundell, & I. M. Duranczyk (Eds.), *Multiculturalism in developmental education* (pp. 51–57). Minneapolis, MN: Center for Research on Developmental Education and Urban Literacy, General College, University of Minnesota.

Higbee, J. L. (Ed.). (2003). *Curriculum transformation and disability: Implementing Universal Design in higher education.* Minneapolis, MN: Center for Research on Developmental Education and Urban Literacy, General College, University of Minnesota.

Higbee, J. H., Miksch, K. L., Jehangir, R. R., Lundell. D. B., Bruch, P. L., & Jiang, F. (2004). Assessing our commitment to providing a multicultural learning experience. *Journal of College Reading and Learning, 34*(2), 61–74.

Jehangir, R., Yamasaki, M., Ghere, D., Hugg, N., Williams, L.A., Higbee, J. (2002). Creating welcoming spaces. *Symposium proceedings: Keeping our faculties: Addressing the recruitment and retention of faculty of color,* 99–101.

Miksch, K. L., Bruch, P. L., Higbee, J. L., Jehangir, R. R., & Lundell, D. B. (2003). The centrality of multiculturalism in developmental education: Piloting the Multicultural Awareness Project for Institutional Transformation (MAP IT). In J. L. Higbee, D. B. Lundell, & I. M. Duranczyk (Eds.), *Multiculturalism in developmental education* (pp. 5–13). Minneapolis, MN: Center for Research on Developmental Education and Urban Literacy, General College, University of Minnesota.

Miksch, K. L., Higbee, J. L., Jehangir, R. R., Lundell, D. B., Bruch, P. L., Siaka, K., & Dotson, M.V. (2003). *Multicultural awareness project for institutional transformation: MAP IT.* Minneapolis, MN: Multicultural Concerns Committee and Center for Research on Developmental Education and Urban Literacy, General College, University of Minnesota.

National Association for Developmental Education. (1995). *Definition and goals statement.* Carol Stream, IL: Author.

Transforming the University of Minnesota: President's Recommendations. (2005). Minneapolis, MN: University of Minnesota. Retrieved May 11, 2005, at http://www1.umn.edu/systemwide/strategic_positioning/pdf/umn_pres_rec.pdf

Sharing Our Experiences: General College Students Give Voice to Their Perceptions of GC

Joshua G. Schmitt, Mark A. Bellcourt, Khong Meng Xiong,
Amanda M. Wigfield, Inge L. B. Peterson,
Sedrick D. Halbert, Leah A. Woodstrom,
Elizabeth Mai Tong Vang, and Jeanne L. Higbee

ABSTRACT

No book about the General College would be complete without student stories. Rather than sharing anecdotes passed along by faculty and staff, we have asked students to write about their experiences in the General College. These first-person accounts have been subjected to the same level of editing as the chapters written by staff and faculty, but otherwise appear as written by the students.

N o description of the General College (GC) would be complete if it does not include students' stories. Faculty and staff members enjoy providing anecdotal evidence of our students' successes. However, for this book we decided that it is important to hear from the students directly, to give them a voice in describing the GC experience.

Within the following pages, we will hear from the student co-authors of this chapter. Our first four student authors, Elizabeth Vang, Inge Peterson, Amanda Wigfield, and Sedrick Halbert, entered GC as freshmen in fall 2004 and participated in Jeanne's freshman seminar course. They wrote their reflections following their first semester at the University of Minnesota (UMN). All four addressed their initial misgivings about being admitted to GC rather than the University's College of Liberal Arts (CLA), but each eventually recognized the advantages that GC has to offer. For Elizabeth, GC assisted with the transition to college and encouraged her to make use of the academic support services important to her success. For Inge, a highly capable student who did not make good use of her time in high school, GC has provided a second chance, and Inge has risen to the challenge. For Amanda, a student with Attention Deficit Hyperactivity Disorder (ADHD), GC's faculty, many of whom have participated in training in Universal Instructional

Design (Higbee, 2003), provided a more welcoming and inclusive classroom environment than she had experienced in the past. For Sedrick, who was working to overcome his habit of procrastination, the smaller class size and high level of structure within GC has enabled him to excel. Both Sedrick and Inge also wrote about the benefits of being part of a diverse community of learners in the General College.

Our last three student authors have all held positions of leadership within the General College. Khong Xiong served as co-chair of the General College Student Board (GCSB) during the 2004–2005 academic year. Leah Woodstrom was elected as a freshman to represent GC students in the Minnesota Student Association (MSA). During her tenure as senator and member of GCSB, she became very active in correcting student misconceptions about GC. Leah reflected on an incident in an MSA meeting regarding the perceptions of a student not in GC.

Our final student author wrote from a very personal level about what General College means to him. Josh's family and educational history, although not so unusual for a student in the General College, certainly are not typical of students in general at the University of Minnesota. Josh's ambitions and hopes are anything but typical, and his motivation and drive to be successful are extraordinary. Josh's story exemplifies the critical role that the General College plays in providing unique opportunities for students who might otherwise never have had the opportunity to attend the University of Minnesota.

Elizabeth's Story

The idea of college made me freeze within the shadow of fear because I could only see myself piled with feverishly working to finish my homework until early dawn. I was told many things about college, like the professors are merciless and their expectations are high. In spite of my fears, I applied for University of Minnesota, Twin Cities' College of Liberal Arts, but as result I got into General College. At first, I felt like a failure because I couldn't get into CLA. When I read brochures about General College, I realized that General College was right for me because I needed help with the transition from high school to college.

I found General College's staff and professors to be friendly, and, as a result, my college experience to be easier than I originally thought. They encouraged me to receive help from services that will improve me academically. I really love the support I receive from General College. Since the class size is significantly smaller than for many college classes, I was able to get the help I need to get through an assignment. It seemed like high school because these classes were diverse, which made me feel at ease. General College has truly become my second home because I feel relaxed and comfortable there.

Inge's Impressions of GC as Contrasted to Stereotypes of the College

Initially when I got my letter from the University of Minnesota I was really excited about being admitted. I was a little disappointed about not being admitted through the College of Liberal Arts, but it was after I thought about it that I decided I was simply excited about going to the University of Minnesota. I figured I should be excited that I even got in. It felt like a second chance from high school. I didn't do much studying in high school, and this was my opportunity to show that I could do it and could do a far better job. When I applied to the U I truly didn't expect to get accepted, but I definitely feel like General College is giving me that second chance.

GC Provides Opportunity

Over the first semester I have come to the conclusion that I deserve to be at the University of Minnesota. I am using the opportunity that General College gave me. People say that college can be a cold place, but it was the General College that showed heart and is where I am receiving higher grades than I have ever received before. It wasn't that I wasn't intelligent in high school; I simply never did my homework. By being accepted through GC I feel I have something to prove.

What I like most about GC is the opportunity that it offers. During my first semester I participated in a learning community. There were several connections that could be made through the three classes involved in the community. I am not sure that the connection would have been so pronounced were there different circumstances. I also took a logic class, which I found most interesting.

What I dislike about GC has nothing to do with GC. More so it has to do with the people around GC who do not attend. The view of GC to others is so false. Somehow the great opportunity that GC offers is not appreciated by people outside of the college. It is viewed from what I have experienced from others as a lesser college, which it is not at all. It just goes all out and offers its students more than it would appear other colleges do. There are smaller class sizes, the teachers are very friendly, and there is more diversity. I truly appreciate GC. Maybe other students are just jealous.

I feel that the diverse learning environment is one of the things that really makes GC great. Coming from a small town with very little diversity, I feel I learned more about the world and society through GC. Having friends from diverse backgrounds has been enlightening and also helped my political correctness.

I love meeting the other students and faculty. I stop by some of my former professors' offices just because of the friendships I made with them. My feelings about GC are that people underestimate GC and judge it so wrongly. Also I really do appreciate all of the people I have met through GC.

Amanda's General College Experience

I opened the envelope from the University of Minnesota with a mixture of anxiety and anticipation. After preparing all the application paperwork, transcripts, writing samples, personal statement, and letters of recommendation, the subsequent months of waiting had been difficult. The University of Minnesota was my first choice in colleges. This was important to me; I really wanted to attend the U. I nervously opened the letter and read, "Dear Amanda, Congratulations! It gives me great pleasure to inform you that you have been admitted to the University of Minnesota-Twin Cities. Welcome to the Class of 2008!" (W. Sigler, personal communication, February 2, 2004). As I read these opening words I felt a rush of pride and excitement. I had been accepted! I had made it! But, as I read on, something in the fourth paragraph of the letter made my heart sink. "We are very pleased to offer you admission to the University's General College" (W. Sigler, personal communication, February 2, 2004). What? I had applied to the College of Liberal Arts, not General College. I felt confused and disappointed.

I didn't know much about General College. I asked around and got the impression that General College was for students who had academic issues or needed some kind of remedial help to be successful in college. At this point I felt angry. I felt so angry I did not want to attend the U. To me it seemed as if no one could see past my disability, Attention Deficit Hyperactivity Disorder, and its effects on my grades, to see that I am intelligent, hard working, and would do well in college.

I struggled with the decision regarding whether to attend a community college or General College. To help make that decision I came to General College, toured the facility, and met with one of the Admissions Advisors. I learned more about the General College program. I was told class sizes were smaller in GC than in most University colleges. I learned that the professors and instructors employed more hands-on and interactive teaching methods. I was told these professors and instructors are experts in their fields, and many had also received national awards for their effective and innovative teaching methods. However, at this point none of this mattered to me; I was still angry.

Ultimately I was, however, able to put aside my negative feelings and make the decision that was in my best interest. I knew that many of my friends had applied to the U and had been denied admission. I learned how difficult it was to get into the U, even with impeccable credentials. I also understood that if I spent a year or two in GC and maintained a 2.0 average, I could transfer out of GC and into another college at the U where I could complete my degree. GC would give me a foot in the door. I decided that a foot in the door at the U was a better choice for me than a community college. Thus, I accepted the offered admission to General College and became part of the Class of 2008.

Orientation

I attended a 2-day orientation during the summer in advance of starting at the U and GC. This orientation was a turning point for me in terms of my attitude toward General College. We received an overall orientation to the U in a large group. I was there with students from the College of Liberal Arts, Carlson School of Management, the College of Human Ecology, Ag College, and all the other University Colleges. Even though I would be attending General College, this orientation made me feel like I was part of the University student body. After the general orientation, students were divided into groups according to their college. I was grouped with other students who would be attending GC. We received an orientation to General College, and we spent the rest of the night together. Through that experience I came to realize that the other GC students were just like me. I hadn't expected that. I didn't expect them to appear well educated or to be so disciplined and dedicated. As I said, this was a turning point for me. Prior to orientation I had felt like GC was not part of the U. It had seemed to me that GC was the place where the U hid away its inadequate students. I equated it with the small building behind the main high school that educated pregnant or delinquent students. After orientation I felt like GC was just another college, another building at the U.

Remedial Versus Developmental

Because of its focus on "high potential students . . . (who) may not meet the competitive standards of other freshman admitting colleges" (University of Minnesota, 2003), I was concerned the GC program would feel remedial. Also, with its small class sizes and with most of the classes meeting in one building, I had feared that GC would feel like glorified high school. I found neither of these to be the case.

Overall, my General College experience has been good. The coursework is challenging. I feel my work and my classroom contributions are respected by my instructors and peers. I feel I am learning. Not having attended classes outside of General College, I cannot fairly compare my GC experience to what I would have experienced in classes outside GC. However, I suspect my GC classes have been a better fit with my learning style than what I would have experienced elsewhere. The classes have been engaging, interactive, and hands-on. For example, rather than simply studying art from a textbook, my General Art class made several trips to the Weisman Museum to view and discuss actual works. We also toured the campus to view and discuss various pieces of sculpture. In writing class, student groups were formed to critique each others' drafts. Through this, we became engaged in understanding the writing process. In General Psychology, my class was part of a research study on teaching methods. My section took multiple tests on each chapter to determine if this strengthened learning over the group who took one test per chapter. I found that the multiple test approach reinforced my learning, gave me a better understanding of areas where I was weak, provided an opportunity to learn what I had missed, and gave me the chance to demonstrate and be graded on what I had learned. I believe my GC classes brought out the best in me as a student and enabled me to demonstrate effectively what I had learned.

I am impressed with the General College instructors. Each is well versed in his or her field and is adept at using multiple modes of teaching in order to reach all students. I found the instructors approachable when I needed additional help understanding course material or when I had another problem or concern. It is clear the instructors care about me as a person and want to do what they can to help me succeed. They focused on what I did well, not what I did poorly, but still gave constructive feedback to enable me to grow.

I found the most difficult and frustrating part of General College to be class work involving groups. Two of my classes involved groups, and in both cases the other group members failed to do their share of the work, failed to do quality work, and failed to meet agreed-upon deadlines. Group members also often failed to attend group meetings and were difficult to contact. I was frustrated that my grade was dependent on the group's work product, which I could not control. Instructors seemed to have inadequate structure to ensure effective group functioning or equity in grading. However, it may be that group work outside of General College would present the same issues.

I have just completed my first semester in General College at the U. I took courses totaling 13 credits and earned a GPA of 3.79. This is the highest GPA I have had in my entire academic career. And I am enjoying school for the first time in my life. Clearly, the decision to attend General College was the right one for me. I feel confident that the remainder of my time at GC will go well and that I will successfully transfer to the College of Liberal Arts and complete my bachelor's degree.

Sedrick on "Being a GC Student"

My first semester in college attending the General College of the University of Minnesota has gone a lot better than I ever expected. While growing up and being in high school, I always heard that college is extremely difficult. I do not doubt that college is difficult, and I am not saying that it is not difficult for me because the truth is that it is. Things have just gone better than I ever imagined.

When I first received the letter that I was accepted into the General College, I was very excited just to be accepted into any college. But at the same time, I was also disappointed that I didn't get into the College of Liberal Arts, the college that I had applied for. At the time, I didn't really know all of the facts or difference between the College of Liberal Arts and General College— all I knew was the College of Liberal Arts was the college that I should be a part of in order to pursue my educational goals of becoming a writer. When I learned that I wasn't going to be in that college, I felt that I would be unable to reach my goals, and that made me sad.

But I soon learned that I was wrong. Just because I was in the General College didn't mean that I would never get into the College of Liberal Arts at all; it simply meant that I wouldn't be entering that college right away. In fact, I soon learned that anyone who was in General College had to transfer out of that college and into another one. So, knowing and learning that information comforted me.

As the semester progressed and I learned more and more information about the University and the General College, I began to feel better about being there. One of my professors for a freshman seminar urged all of us to take advantage of the resources and things that the General College offers. I learned that the General College had a computer lab where any General College student could print for free. Also, just because I was in General College didn't mean that I couldn't take other classes outside of GC. So I applied for a writing class from the College of Liberal Arts and was accepted into it. I learned that it was extremely rare for a non-GC student to take classes in GC, but I felt good knowing that I could take GC classes as well as some classes offered from other colleges.

There are more advantages in being in the General College: (a) class sizes are smaller than those of classes outside of GC so that teachers can focus more on students' individual needs, (b) counselors have fewer students to deal with so that they can offer more one-on-one help to their students, and (c) students receive two progress reports mid-semester so that we can see our progress in each class. (The University as a whole has recently implemented a mid-semester progress report also, based on the GC model.) All of these things have helped me a lot. I have never liked classes that are too big, so I feel more comfortable in classes with fewer students. I know that every time I go to see my counselor, I never have to wait. Unless she is out to lunch or on her way to a meeting or something, she always finds time to talk to me. Furthermore, the progress reports help me to plan ahead to improve my grades if necessary.

Diversity in GC

In college diversity is inevitable. There is no way that I am only going to have classes and be associated only with people with the same nationality as my own. For me, it feels good being a part of a diverse learning place, especially the General College, which has fewer students. I would like to think that I can learn something from someone else from a different background. Their insights on a subject may help me somehow, and even if they do not, it has never hurt me to listen, just to hear something different for a change.

Changing Habits

During the first semester in the General College, I have learned a lot of different things about myself. One of my main problems is that I procrastinate more than I previously realized. I am not one of those students who does not turn in assignments on time. It just means that I spent the previous night, all night, doing it, and this is something that I am diligently trying to break. During this semester I have learned different ways to manage my time better so that I can finish my assignments and do things that I like to do. I keep an assignment planner that keeps me organized and reminds me of the upcoming assignments that I have to do.

Khong's Insights From a Position of Leadership

As a freshman, I believe General College has made an immense impact on my life. General College is a place where I believe many wonderful academic resources lie. I have utilized these resources, such as the Academic Resource Center and the Transfer and Career Center, to develop my strong academic skills so I can become successful in life. I have perceived that the GC staff and faculty work hard and closely together to provide the emotional, academic, and leadership support system to enhance my educational learning experience. I have developed a close relationship with the teaching specialists, professors, academic advisors, and many other people I know who work in GC. They are compassionate, devoted, caring, and they work extremely hard to satisfy my needs. They have shown me how to be the best student that I can be by helping me to accomplish my academic, leadership, and personal life goals.

Opportunities for Leadership

As the Co-Chairman of the General College Student Board, I have emerged to become an outstanding leader to my peers and to the rest of the GC community. People have looked at me as a role model. I have established many leadership skills that will help me through my future career. I have attended leadership conferences through GC, including the National Conference for Student Leaders, and Student Activities Office Leadership Conference, to learn what it is like to become an excellent leader to the community. I have acted as the representative from the General College Student Board serving on various GC committees, such as the Multicultural Concerns Committee and Alumni Society Advisory Committee. I have amplified my professional skills and advanced in my communication skills by being involved with GC committees and engaging with the professional GC staff and faculty. I am pleased to thank GC for its leadership opportunity and to enable me to serve as a student leader of the college.

Unique Multicultural Environment

I have witnessed that GC is not like any of the other colleges at the University of Minnesota; I honestly believe it is a distinctive institution unto itself, and I am proud to be a part of it. The moment I came to General College, I knew that I had found myself a home. The one thing I found incredibly appealing was the amount of diversity GC has in its community! It is such a remarkable and welcoming feeling to see students, staff, and faculty from all cultural backgrounds engaging with one another and making an effort to accomplish academic and life goals. I feel my heart is set with GC; it is a warm-hearted and friendly multicultural environment that makes me feel elated, delighted, and motivated to learn in college.

I have discovered, while being in GC, that by surrounding oneself with, understanding, and celebrating individual differences associated with race, ethnicity, gender, disability, language, sexual orientation, and socioeconomic class, I have learned to become more open-minded and appreciate people more. When one acknowledges and appreciates a group of people from a certain group identity, he begins to see what he wants the world to be, and I want people to become more educated about and accepting of others.

I perform well academically in my classes when I am surrounded by a group of people in GC who come from similar backgrounds as mine, such as being a bilingual with English as my second language, first-generation born and to attend higher education in the United States, or low to middle economic class student. I find GC a place where I have these similar traits with many of my GC peers; I feel more comfortable and at ease to socialize with them without having the feeling to withdraw because of thinking that they do not understand where I come from or what my background is. I believe I am more easily connected in GC than in any other place on campus. I found that GC is the center of my network, my community, and where many of my incredible relationships with my peers began. I figure that my peers and I all share at least one similar trait through which we can relate to one and another. We understand the hardships that we had to go through in life—whether that was struggling with our education because we have an English language barrier, financial issues, or personal and family issues. With these struggles, I have learned to appreciate and help my peers. There is a peaceful, relaxing, incredible bond between them and me.

I believe that the one thing that will always stand out the most in my mind about GC is the way its staff and faculty prioritize their work by putting their students first. I have recognized this as a phenomenal and an exquisite act of a true and loyal group of people who have worked to change college students' lives positively, and they have done so for me as well. The staff and faculty have provided me with magnificent ideas on how to achieve my goals in life, and I am proud to thank all of them for their extraordinarily hard work. It is my pleasure to remain a proud supporter of GC staff and faculty and of the General College's mission at the University of Minnesota.

Leah's Role in Changing Misconceptions About GC

General College is a place where doors are opened for students to enter the University of Minnesota and become educationally set with the tools they need to succeed at a University level. However, this mission or idea gets lost among students outside of General College. My first year at the University of Minnesota, I served on the General College Student Board and as a General College Senator on the Minnesota Student Association (i.e., undergraduate student government).

I can distinctly recall a meeting of the Minnesota Student Association where a College of Liberal Arts student argued that the University of Minnesota, as a whole, would have better retention of students and save tuition dollars if General College did not exist. First, the General College retention rate was not falling, and students' tuition is sent to the college in which they are enrolled. College of Liberal Arts students' tuition is sent to CLA, and GC students' tuition is sent to GC. Clearly this student had no idea what he was talking about, and I felt offended being the only GC student in a room of 60 students. It seemed to me like students in other colleges did not really care to find out what this college is all about. In my eyes, criticizing the college in which I was enrolled felt like a personal attack on me.

Out of my frustration, I went and found out the retention rates and how tuition dollars are allotted. I did not dwell on this disappointment for very long, but corrected this student's understanding of General College.

Joshua's Story

I was born into a very poor, but loving family in southern Illinois. My family relocated to more than six different states during my youth. As you can imagine, this created a tremendous academic challenge for my parents. In addition, I had severe Attention Deficit Hyperactivity Disorder. My parents decided to start schooling me at home.

Being schooled at home certainly had both its advantages and disadvantages. One of the major disadvantages occurred when my mother tried to teach me subjects that she was weak in (i.e., math, chemistry, biology, etc.). These difficult subjects proved to be overwhelming for my mother, and I needed to take responsibility to teach myself until I finally graduated at the age of 18.

"Shelving" Dreams of Further Education

My father is a third-generation carpenter, and he strongly encouraged me to learn a trade rather than attend college. His advice was sincere and came from his heart. My mother also felt the same way. But I wanted to have a great career, and I knew that I needed to go to college. Lacking family support and knowledge on how to go about obtaining a college education, I finally shelved my dreams and tried to accept the reality of my situation.

I soon began to pursue various avenues of employment, ranging from ski instructor to assistant manager at a local bike shop. Disenchanted with my situation, income, and also lacking the foresight to make personal change in myself, I soon became very depressed and overwhelmed with feelings of insecurity and helplessness. For a couple of years I foolishly squandered my money, time, and health by living an irresponsible lifestyle. Upon realization that the consequences of my actions today would impact my future, I sought to fulfill my dream of having a career that would make a positive impact upon society.

Soon after my resolution, opportunity knocked in the form of an insurance direct-sales franchise. While marketing insurance to individuals, families, small businesses, and major corporations, I began to smooth my approach and found myself presenting and selling my product to groups of employees. In addition to selling the product, I also became responsible for recruiting other salespersons, their training, and the management of newly acquired accounts. After recruiting over 80 sales people and sometimes earning double and sometimes triple my father's weekly income in one day, I felt

I had finally reached the pinnacle of life. The business I had established created the respect from my parents that I had always longed for.

This feeling made me happy to a certain point, but still I had an unfilled desire in my heart to obtain a college education and to pursue a career that would have meaning. Unlike some of my wealth-driven peers working in my field, I realized that money wasn't making me happy. I often sought the things I had always desired but never could afford. This self-destructive habit started to have a negative impact on my lifestyle. I often found myself driven to work more than 100 hours a week in order to purchase the vanities that appeared so attractive to those who can not have them. This allowed me to achieve great success within my industry. But I was again feeling a desire for something more. I wanted an education and purposeful career of substance.

September 11th, 2001, brought these dreams to the forefront of my mind. At work in my office, where I was listening to the radio, the classical music was soon interrupted with some news that at first seemed unreal. Quickly finding a television, I watch the tragedy unfold. Flooded with concern for the useless slaughter of innocent people and gripped with the realities of the frailty of humanity, I wept and said a prayer for the victims' safety. 9/11 triggered my thoughts of my own life's purpose. Why should I continue to be unhappy with my career, when I longed for something more? It was something that I realize is a reflection of my compassion for humanity in need. Service to humanity, in some way, became my blossoming dream.

Pursuing Academic Goals

The tenacity within myself drove me to pursue my academic goals. After much research, the University of Minnesota-Twin Cities became my first choice. I resolved that, no matter what, I was going to attend the University of Minnesota. I was so confident in my academic goal that I moved to Minnesota, prior to knowing the status of my application. I was surprised when my application was quickly rejected. Bewildered, I pursued an explanation of the rejection. Explanations, like many things at the University of Minnesota, were hard to come by. Finally, I learned that my home-schooled background created a hurdle.

Distraught, I sought advice from professors, advisors, and the university Web site. I finally discovered General College. Wanting to find out more about what I had to do to gain admission to their "special" program, I sought out the persons in charge of admissions. My search led me to Rudy Hernandez. He humored me, while I spilled my story to him. I also presented him with a résumé, hoping the significance of my entrepreneurial achievements would prove worthy of admittance and also reveal that I was indeed smart enough to succeed in school.

Thankfully, this time spent with Rudy was indeed time well spent. I was accepted into General College. My realization of what is probably obvious to most high school students left me astonished. Why had I not pursued college sooner? Why did I not find this out a long time ago? Regardless, I was excited to begin pursuing my academic goal. I became enthralled with each class. Under the advisement of Susan Warfield, my General College advisor and now my trusted friend, I had selected numerous classes that would enable me to fill in the gaps left in my high school education.

In the midst of my happiness in finally attending the University of Minnesota-Twin Cities, I was perplexed by the distinct separation between GC and the other University student populations. It soon became apparent to me that we were the "outcasts." GC is a conglomeration of students of various underrepresented races, first-generation college students, products of very poor educational institutions, and students from families of low socioeconomic status. We stood out to the rest of the collegiate population as sore thumbs.

Soon I made many new friends with my General College peers. These relationships dispelled any significance in what the outside world thought of us. In fact, it confirmed my theories that General College's population is made up of wonderful people, who are very smart and also wise to the traits necessary to survive in the "real" world. Our ability to overcome tremendous obstacles while striving to obtain an education is exemplary and should truly be recognized.

Many of my GC peers, I have found, have a much greater intellectual capacity than many of the professionals I have met in the business world. Each student at General College is given the opportunity for a career and a way out. They are rejecting the bonds of mediocrity and are striving for a change that will finally break the unfortunate bonds that many generations of repetitive, self-destructive behavior have created. Somehow, we as General College students were supposed to be swept through the cracks, out of sight of the world, and demanded to adhere to the law of our various socioeconomic statuses.

Exploring Opportunities in the Medical Professions

With a passion to assist humanity, I naturally contemplated pursuing a career in medicine. I had researched earlier the admission requirements of medical schools and learned that research and research-related experiences were highly recommended by most medical schools. Inspired by this, and wishing to find an opportunity to gain research experience, I found an advertisement requesting help for cardiovascular research. Without having ever completed any formal high school chemistry, biology, or even algebra, I very humbly approached two very kind physicians, and asked to help out in their lab any way that I could. I even offered to wash the counters for free. They gladly accepted my offer and taught me the terminology of a lab.

The lab team was in need of a perfusion device for bio-artificial vessels. In an attempt to harness my ingenuity, the researchers gave me a box with various items and instructed me to build such a device. In 2 weeks, the final creation was being put to the test. Everything worked out perfectly on the device. Fully operational, it did indeed replicate the human cardiovascular system and allowed for adjustments and monitoring of perfusion.

New to the research environment, and urged by my mentors, I quickly agreed that we should submit an Intellectual Property application to the University of Minnesota. Prior to our submission, we sought out all the patent information available regarding any similar products. It was great to see that no other patented devices like it existed in either Europe or the United States. Impressive as this discovery was, I was more impressed when our representative at the University Intellectual Property Office became interested in pursuing a full patent. Soon I found myself meeting with the University Intellectual Property Office, the two physicians who took me under their collective wings, and also two patent attorneys. This moment I humbly hoped would certainly help to define General College as an impressive academic institution, worthy of equality by our peers.

Prior to building the device, I followed the advice of my mentors and pursued a Lillehei Scholars Award, offered by the renowned Lillehei Heart Institute, through the University's Undergraduate Research Opportunity Program. This, while making a nice addition to my curriculum vita, would also give me $1,300.00 to pursue the building of the project. Thankfully, I did indeed receive this award. This proved to be an even more spectacular event than I had previously anticipated. I received a request to attend an awards dinner, which is given to congratulate the current Lillehei Scholars, at a very posh local country club. With excitement my wife and I attended the dinner and were met there by one of my physician mentors and his wife. As we sat down at a table, which was off to the side, my mentor tapped me on the shoulder. He quickly pointed out that the Dean of the University of Minnesota Medical School and her husband were joining us at our table. What a fortunate event this was turning out to be. Soon following a nice dinner filled with wonderful conversation, they presented the awards. I watched as each recipient's academic backgrounds were announced. I was the only undergraduate amongst the M.D.s, Ph.D.s, and master's degrees. I almost laughed inside when I humbly realized that there wasn't much that they could say about me. I was only a freshman and had few academic achievements as yet. I was thrilled when I was announced as a "... motivated General College student who was pursuing medical school and who would become a cardiovascular surgeon someday." I truly was proud of my college; General College had created this opportunity for me. It had given me the support, enthusiasm, and the faith in myself.

Spurred by my success thus far, I continued to conduct various research projects with my mentors. One of the more significant projects led me to take on a four-credit, 4xxx-level Neuroscience Directed Research project to be conducted at the University of Minnesota Medical School Neurosurgery and Neuroscience Department. The bulk of the project required sensitive, highly invasive microsurgery on small laboratory animals. After assisting with numerous operations, I was allowed to incise, suture, and assume various other "surgeon" responsibilities. Again, I was sure that this beneficial experience would help to offset the level of skepticism by the majority of the collegiate community regarding General College students. Each of these events was a product of every faculty member with whom I had contact inside of General College. Few of these faculty members will probably ever fully realize how influential they have been in the academic successes that have occurred in my life.

As wonderful as the unity and support of the General College are for its student body, I must further emphasize the outside skepticism that I have experienced by students from different college communities. Even one of my own physician mentors laughingly poked fun at the fact that I was not really attending a "real" college yet. He had graduated from the University's College of Liberal Arts prior to receiving his M.D. from the University's Medical School. This, however infuriating, illustrates what we, as students, are faced with on a daily basis. Many of the students who are possibly more sensitive to such harassment, might decide that, after all, maybe it's just not worth going to school here anymore.

Unwilling to become another statistic, I began driving even more aggressively forward toward the attainment of my academic goals. Wanting to make a positive difference within my student community, I ran and was elected for an Alternate Co-Chair position on the General College Student Board. I was also elected to the General College Admissions and Advancement Committee, the University's Student Health Advocacy Committee, and the Institutional Review Board Medical IV Committee. Also, I accepted a position on the University's Finance Committee with Boynton Health Service's $14,000,000 request for funding for the 2005–2006 academic year.

As I continue to gain momentum in my pursuit of my degree, I wish to discredit the presumption that I have less academic potential than my peers in other colleges of the University. Every success that I have had has been a direct reflection of God's blessing on my efforts, General College's support

and encouragement, and lastly my own application of hard work and persistence. As a General College student, I seek to follow in the precedent set by the
successful General College alumni who have traveled before us, one of whom
has won the Nobel Peace Prize, and numerous others who are successful even
beyond most people's imagination. Each student within the General College
student body has it in him or her to succeed. By abstaining from the quick-
sand of mediocrity and pressing on towards our academic goals, we will har-
vest tomorrow's leaders from those society was content to let slip down society's proverbial cracks.

Conclusion

These stories from current and former General College students have several
themes in common. First, these students had apprehensions about attending
college and about their ability to be successful. Each had the intelligence and
motivation to achieve academically, but for a variety of reasons related to circumstances like home language, atypical educational history, or a hidden disability, there were reasons why the small classes and more personalized
instruction offered within the General College would be advantageous for
them.

Second, these students have been successful, in several cases earning higher
grades in college than ever before. Some have or currently hold positions of
leadership at the University. Although not all GC students achieve their goals,
these students' stories demonstrate the importance of the educational opportunities provided by the General College. Just as Norman Borlaug's (*Access
and Excellence*, 2001) contributions to humankind were made possible
through his educational attainment, so may GC's students of today, like
Joshua Schmitt, make revolutionary contributions in the future.

Finally, each of these students has become an ambassador for the General
College. They volunteered to write their stories for this chapter. They are concerned about general misconceptions about GC and its students, and they
wanted to contribute to overcoming stereotypes about the General College
experience.

As we noted in the introduction to this chapter, all of us who work in the
General College have many success stories to tell. We are very proud of our
students' accomplishments. But what is even more important is that our students have faith in themselves and are eager to share their own stories, and
that in doing so they become advocates for themselves as well as for GC.

References

Access and excellence. (2001). Minneapolis, MN: Campaign Minnesota, General College, University of Minnesota.

Higbee, J. L. (Ed.). (2003). *Curriculum transformation and disability: Implementing Universal Design in higher education.* Minneapolis, MN: Center for Research on Developmental Education and Urban Literacy, General College, University of Minnesota.

University of Minnesota. (2003). *General College.* Minneapolis, MN: Office of University Relations, Communication Services.

Honoring Our History

Honoring Our History
Introduction

Allen Johnson provides the historical context for the founding of the General College, including the influence of John Dewey's ideals. Johnson states, "The origin of the [General College] idea can be traced directly to the earlier efforts of political and educational leaders to build a democratic society by designing and offering effective general education programs in American colleges and universities." It was Lotus Delta Coffman, fifth president of the University of Minnesota and "an advocate of educational equality" who acted upon the democratic ideals of Dewey and others in founding GC "to serve an increasingly heterogeneous student body."

Cathy Wambach and Tom Brothen continue to inform us about the history of the General College through their chapter on the Minnesota Point of View, which demonstrates the significant impact of a group of University of Minnesota psychologists not just on the founding, mission, and counseling emphasis of GC, but also on the student personnel movement throughout the U.S. Wambach and Brothen also address the role of assessment in the early years of GC.

Katy Gray Brown builds upon this historical context by focusing more explicitly upon the multicultural mission of developmental education as practiced in the General College. She asserts, "The pedagogical approach of developmental education, designed to engage a broad spectrum of learners, becomes a fundamental aspect of the social mission of the University." Like Johnson, Brown reminds us of "the importance of access to the fulfillment of the land-grant vision of community service."

David Taylor, Dean of General College for the past 15 years, also contributes his historical perspective on the politics of GC's transformation over the years in response to external political forces and internal initiatives of the administration, faculty, and staff. Since 1985 GC has shifted its focus toward becoming a nationally recognized program for teaching, learning, and research in the field of developmental education. Taylor notes how over the years GC has undergone several periods of change in response to external constituencies and popular rhetoric about the role of access programs in higher education. In the University's future vision of becoming a world-class leader in research, GC's history as presented by Taylor illuminates how identities are changed and transformed over time and specifically how students are impacted.

CHAPTER 3

From the Beginning:
This History of Developmental Education
and the Pre-1932 General College Idea

Allen B. Johnson

ABSTRACT

This chapter traces the evolution of ideas that led to the planning and implementation, in 1932, of the general education program at the General College at the University of Minnesota. The first of these ideas embodies its basis and rationale in the nation's effort to build a democratic society. The second idea embraces the pioneering efforts to understand how learning occurs and how developmental strategies can enable individuals to achieve both academic and life goals. These ideas were shaped into a program that would serve those students deemed as nontraditional, underserved, and discards of higher education.

One day in 2002 while I was examining documentation concerning the beginnings of the General College, a colleague asked me what I was doing. I said "I am researching and planning to write about the origin of the General College." "Well," he said, "that shouldn't be too difficult; the college began in 1932."

That comment reinforced the importance of the idea that most things do not originate out of the clear blue and suddenly emerge with a physical presence. Instead, they begin in the human mind as an idea. I am reminded of H. G. Wells' quote that "Human history is in essence a history of ideas" (*American Heritage College Dictionary*, 2000, p. 673). The origin of the General College resulted from an assemblage of ideas that developed in the minds of educators several years before it first opened its doors on October 3, 1932. In fact, the concepts upon which the college was built began in the minds of political leaders and educators, many of whom would never know the physical General College. In addition to ideas, the politics and circumstances of the times played major roles in determining which ideas would be carried forward to realization and which would not.

It should also be noted here that reference is made to the origin of the General College, but the title "General College" actually did not come into existence until June 1933. I will, therefore, for lack of a more appropriate phrase, be referring to what I call the "General College Idea" as I discuss the pre-1932 college planning. The word "Idea" embodies the concepts, principles, thoughts, and convictions of many educational and political leaders that culminated in the building of a collegiate unit that would provide meaningful and realistic educational opportunities for all who sought them. This culmination is a combination of ideas over time, or more specifically, historical events, the combination of which eventually resulted in a historical event, namely the creation of the General College.

It is the aim of this chapter to trace and clarify the role of developmental education in enabling the nation to establish a truly democratic society. As the country looked to general education, which Boyer and Levine (1981, p. 35) defined as those interests and connections we all share with each other, as a means of mediating social and political disagreements and periodic unrest that happened throughout its history, it was implicit that to establish a stable government, each citizen must have an opportunity to contribute to the building of, and at the same time, benefit from a democracy. Developmental education encompassed an important component of general education because it enabled the individual student, who lacked adequate preparation, the opportunity to develop needed skills or knowledge allowing him or her to advance further in academic career and life goals than would have been possible without them (National Association for Developmental Education [NADE], 1995).

In order for a democracy to work, an educational system must produce an educated and enlightened citizenry. To accomplish this task the education system must reach and serve each individual learner. This is where the enabling processes we call developmental education must be applied to help the learner realize his or her academic and life goals. Developmental education, therefore, embodies how a college experience should address the needs of those students whose skills, knowledge, attitudes, and preparedness are not yet adequate to help them to be academically competitive and successful. Obviously, this is a smaller but very significant part of the original General College Idea. A more comprehensive history encompassing and linking the pre-1932 General College Idea to the post-1932 college operational history is being planned and composed as part of the much more extensive written history of General College.

Building a Democratic Society

In order to lay the foundation for the discussion on developmental education, it is necessary to identify and highlight the ideas, along with the people who expressed the ideas, and selected events in U.S. history that played significant roles in advancing the concept of general education, which eventually served as the basis for the General College Idea. The foundation of this idea was based on the national need to build and strengthen a democratic society through the establishment of meaningful and effective general education programs.

It should be noted that general education programs were not automatically put into place in colleges and universities because of an altruistic desire on the part of educators to democratize society, but instead were seen as a way to avert crises that, in a cyclical fashion, arose, especially at the lower-division level. Colleges periodically initiated general education programs in an effort to mediate student unhappiness, improve retention, stabilize financial income, counter the force of overspecialization, and establish a student-centered curriculum that made sense to the lower-division students. Miller (1988, pp. 29–31), however, reminded us that there were times during the history of higher education when colleges and universities did not adequately serve the educational needs of a significant number of students, especially freshmen and sophomores. Often during those times the highly specialized degree programs that focused on the preparation of professionals were emphasized and received the most attention and resources. At the same time, the general education that was intended to broaden the student's intellectual background was neglected due to indifference and the unwillingness of educational leaders to put sufficient resources into it.

As the pendulum swung toward greater specialization, some education leaders saw the need to restore general education as the solution to their problems. Many colleges and universities proceeded to design what they thought would meet the student needs and at the same time alleviate administrative problems cited earlier. It should be noted with caution that many colleges and universities independently designed and implemented their own particular version of a general education program, meaning that there were many different versions describing what general education was and still is. Most of them, however, do conform to the notion that general education highlights the commonality of interests and concerns that all persons share.

As introduced before, the most significant thinking that eventually led to the General College Idea addressed higher education's national role in nurturing and building a democratic society that considers the common people as the primary source of political power and is based on the principles of social equality and individual rights. Miller (1988) credited two major events in American history for challenging and forever changing the classical European emphasis that had dominated American college curricula since the 1600s when Harvard College was established. One event was the encompassing effect of the aftershocks of the American Revolution (1775–1783), followed by the beginning of the American Industrial Revolution. Both forces would reform American higher education as they gave ever-increasing power to the common people. Miller continued that the profound influence of the Industrial Revolution began just "as the wave of democracy, spirited by Thomas Jefferson and brought to a crest during the Jacksonian period, swept over the nation" (p. 10).

Jeffersonian and Jacksonian Influences

Thomas Jefferson (U.S. President, 1801–1809) focused his energies on establishing or applying his meritocratic view of democracy to higher education by urging free primary education followed by government support for those students deemed as having exceptional merit. Miller (1988, p. 10) highlighted Jefferson's belief that a natural aristocracy existed among men and that higher education should be selective and prepare this group for professional, civic, and governmental leadership. Even though Jefferson advocated for the education of the privileged, he succeeded in designing a curriculum that broke away from the traditional classical European curriculum by being much more student-centered and utilitarian. His creation of the University of Virginia, therefore, provided meritorious students an opportunity to prepare themselves for civic and professional leadership. As a part of the utilitarian curriculum, he believed that the students should have the opportunity to choose courses from eight different programs of study. In addition, he also believed that to prepare an educated populace necessary for the success of the republic, these students also must include the study of law and politics. Miller also noted that Jefferson's beliefs about a student-centered and utilitarian curriculum should be credited as being central to the general education movement later in the 20th century.

The views of Andrew Jackson (U.S. President, 1829–1837), differing greatly from Jefferson's elitist beliefs, significantly expanded and further defined education's role in building a stronger democratic society. He emphasized that the educational needs of the common person were paramount. Miller (1988) gave special importance to this belief by saying that the "Jacksonians talked about democracy in terms of 'real people,' i.e., the planters, farmers, and mechanics on whom the Industrial Revolution and the settling of the frontier depended and who were fast becoming a force in national politics" (p. 11).

The Jacksonian view gave rise to the land-grant college movement and stimulated the Industrial Revolution's demand for trained and educated workers, which resulted in the growth of vocationalism in higher education (Miller, p. 11). Another reason for increasing the educational opportunities for everyone arose as the nation extended the right to vote to a larger percentage of the male population, causing public officials and educators to become alarmed as they realized that "illiterates" could now vote and have influence on the course of the country. The implication that Americans deserved an opportunity to advance their education as far as they could defined the need for developmental education during Jackson's time. This resulting need for compulsory education created a great demand for teachers at all levels and called upon colleges to prepare them. The Jacksonian view may very well have served as the catalyst for the establishment of ideas that eventually led to the creation of the open-door, student-centered General College 100 years later.

The utilitarian views of Jefferson and Jackson began to show themselves in major ways during and right after the Civil War (1861–1865). Miller (1988, p. 14) introduced Charles Eliot, President of Harvard beginning in 1869, as a key figure in carrying forward the notion of utilitarian education. He strongly advocated for the free elective system, the goal of which was to allow individual students the opportunity to define their own courses of study, with some faculty input, in an effort to prepare themselves for a place of their own choosing in life. This free choice, general education system not only satisfied the students' interests, but as Eliot believed, was to insure "an intelligent public opinion," that was the "indispensable condition of social progress" (Miller, p. 15). The reemergence of this belief will appear later as University of Minnesota President Coffman and other leaders justify the establishing of the General College.

The expansion of the idea of social utility as a rationale for a university curriculum grew out of Eliot's leadership. A great impetus for this notion was the Morrill Land-Grant Act of 1862, which provided a funding mechanism by which each state could create at least one college designed to "promote the liberal and practical education of the industrialized classes in the several pursuits in life" (Levine, 1978, p. 558). The Morrill Act resulted in the expansion of public education, increased access to higher education by the nonelite, including ready access to the practical utilitarian studies of agriculture and engineering, and stimulated the growth of Western higher education. Cornell University, a land-grant institution in New York, pursued a mission, quoted by Miller (1988) from Ezra Cornell's Charter address, which was "to fit the youth of the country for the professions, the farms, the mines, the manufacturies, for the investigation of science, and for mastering all the practical questions of life with success and honor" (p. 16).

During the late 19th century, however, the zeal and enthusiasm of the utilitarian movement gradually resulted in increased specialization and fragmentation. The resulting reemphasis on research pushed free-elective, open-door general education onto the back burner in most universities until after World War I. After the war, however, in reaction to the overemphasis on research and specialization, a general education renaissance dominated the post-war period during which the General College was created.

Focus on Developmental Education

To begin a discussion of developmental education, Levine (1978) and Cross (1976) defined terms that have been used historically. Levine stated "that basic skills are the abilities and basic knowledge is the information a student needs to embark upon college study" (p. 54). He went on to differentiate the term remedial from compensatory and developmental. "Remedial education implies improvement of student skills and knowledge for the purpose of entering a program for which the student was previously ineligible with an emphasis on correcting weaknesses" (p. 55). Cross (1976) stated that "developmental or compensatory education emphasizes the building of new strengths or the enhancement of skills, knowledge, and attitudes that may not necessarily be needed to qualify students for more advanced academic programs" (p. 30). She continued that "compensatory education seeks to overcome deprivations associated with the home, family, and earlier study through increasing educational enrichment" (p. 31).

Levine (1978) noted that skill and knowledge requirements in American higher education can be traced back to 1640 when Harvard required that entering students must be able to speak and read Latin and know Greek grammar (p. 55). One hundred years later, Yale was the first college to require arithmetic. By the late 19th century, the admission standards at several colleges required entering students to have taken additional subjects in response to the classical curriculum that still prevailed. In the 1700s and 1800s, many of those colleges developed relationships with preparatory schools that provided the students with the necessary skills and knowledge and served as feeder schools. These opportunities were mainly available only to the privileged, however, which caused the majority of 19th century nonelitist colleges, in an effort to be financially solvent, to lower entrance requirements. In some cases these institutions became open-door colleges (actually revolving-door) or established their own form of preparatory divisions. By the early 1900s a proliferation of high schools resulted in less need for preparatory units. However, most colleges still admitted students who could not meet entrance standards, due to intense competition for students, wide variation of school requirements, and an effort to fulfill institutional financial needs. In fact, in 1907 more than half of the students entering Harvard and Yale had not satisfied the colleges' entrance requirements. As a result, Levine said that to solve their problems, colleges began creating remedial courses in order to bring students up to grade level in deficient areas (p. 57).

Cross (1976), in her study of compensatory education, found that the remedial courses in the early 1900s were voluntary how-to-study courses that dealt with note taking, good study habits, and health, based on the belief that the student's deficiencies were mainly due to immaturity and lack of discipline rather than to lack of ability or poor training. Levine (1978) and Cross made it clear that colleges struggled with providing for the developmental needs of students from the very early years of the nation's history.

The Contributions of John Dewey

One of the most respected and prolific writers on educational philosophy in American history was John Dewey (1859–1952). He grew up in Vermont and received degrees from the University of Vermont and Johns Hopkins University (Levine, 1978, p. 256). In the earliest years of his professional experience, he was an instructor of philosophy for 1 year at the University of Minnesota. He subsequently served 5 years as chairman of the Philosophy Department at the University of Michigan. From 1894 to 1904 his career blossomed at the University of Chicago, where he was professor of philosophy and pedagogy and director of the School of Education. He developed its Laboratory School, where he had the opportunity to try out many of his more progressive ideas where the students lived and learned in a highly social context. He began a writing career on educational philosophy that eventually spanned a period of more than 70 years, resulting in a bibliography that required 153 pages for a complete listing (Bernstein, 1966, p. 187). From 1904 to 1931 Dewey was a professor in the Philosophy Department at Columbia University, during which time he continued to achieve national and international acclaim for his efforts to define a philosophy of education for a modern industrial society by capturing the voice, accent, and temperament of the American tradition and the nature of the special uncertainties that would lie ahead (Levine, p. 257).

Dewey's Democratic Ideal
John Dewey (1916, p. 100) stressed that the democratic ideal is based on two criteria. One criterion addresses the numerous and varied points of common interest between individuals and between societies with the reliance on the collective recognition of mutual interests as a major factor in successful social interaction and control. As a result of these common interests, the second cri-

terion emphasizes that interactions between individuals or social groups result in easier exchanges and readjustments when confronting new situations, challenges, or problems. Boyer and Levine (1981, p. 35) later highlighted this sharing of common interests and connections as the prevailing definition of General Education.

Dewey's Aim of Education

Dewey (1916) believed and stated that the "aim of education is to enable individuals to continue their education and that the object and reward of learning is the continued capacity for growth" (p. 117). The quote, "enable individuals to continue their education" (p. 117), is also an appropriate statement of the overriding goal of developmental education. In a paraphrasing of its current statement of goals of developmental education, the National Association for Developmental Education (1995) further delineated Dewey's stated aim that education preserves and makes learning opportunities possible for each student by enabling the individual to develop the skills and attitudes necessary to attain academic, career, and life goals through the acquisition of needed competencies based on appropriate assessment of the learner's needs.

Mason (1975, p. 115) expanded on this notion as he addressed Dewey's liberal and progressive thinking. He stressed that any process that enhances learning has two sides—one psychological and the other sociological. The learner's emotional and behavioral changes and development must take place in the context of the individual's surroundings and social environment. Dewey also struggled with the relation or balance between the cultural, emotional, and behavioral influences. Levine (1978), in reference to Dewey's statement of the aim of education "that the object and reward of learning is the continued capacity for growth," expanded the meaning of the phrase to "set free and to develop the capacities of human individuals without respect to race, sex, class, or economic status" (p. 257). He went on to say that Dewey's method of accomplishing these changes was by "a constant reorganizing and reconstructing of experiences" (p. 257). This notion will reemerge later in this discussion concerning the views of President Coffman and Malcolm MacLean, the first director of General College, on how the University of Minnesota must adjust and reorganize to meet the needs of its students.

Alfred North Whitehead, a mathematician who, according to Levine (1978, p. 261), became one of the major thinkers in education, was a contemporary of Dewey. Even though his approach to education differed from Dewey's, both agreed that education was a thing of the present and that the mission of education was life; in fact, it was life now! They believed that education should not be thought of as preparation for some future time. They argued that if the learner's life is well served by education now, the future will take care of itself. Dewey (1916, p. 55) elaborated that the future lacks urgency and substance. To get ready for something in the distant future is to throw away any leverage and diminish any enthusiasm to learn now. This assertion has implications for developmental education programs in which the students may well believe that they are preparing for their life sometime in the future. Their resulting thought process and attitude is that there is little relevance or connection, and they will tend to procrastinate, potentially resulting in failure. This disconnect speaks to the benefit of embedding developmental skills and knowledge into existing degree-credit courses so that students realize their usefulness and impact concurrently with studying the course content.

One of the educational concepts that Dewey (1916, p. 65) advanced may be helpful when trying to understand the learning processes involved in developmental education. He said that education can be based upon the idea of development. In this case, development was conceived not as continuous growing, but as an "unfolding" of latent or undeveloped powers or talents from within the learner that lead toward a definite goal. In Dewey's mind, this ultimate goal was completion or perfection, which he said is unattainable. He said that life at any stage short of this goal is simply unfolding toward it. In this context, a developmental education program could very well be thought of as a program that enables the learner to "unfold from within" and proceed or grow toward greater academic and life accomplishments. Dewey also implied that learning proceeded from the known to the "unfolding into the unknown" (p. 79). The processes of inquiry discussed elsewhere also involve the unfolding toward the solution to a problem or the unfolding toward new knowledge. The science-in-context series of courses that began in the mid-1960s and the more recent inquiry-based courses in science are based on this idea.

The student-centered viewpoint of John Dewey's philosophy of education has been labeled as "progressive" and "instrumentalist" (Miller, 1988, p. 64). Levine (1978, p. 8) stated that progressivism is based on life experience in which the student's needs, readiness, abilities, knowledge, and interests determine the direction of the educational enterprise. This view will reemerge later in the discussion concerning the commitment of the founders of General College "to know the student," which laid the foundation for building a first-of-a-kind counseling program.

According to Miller (1988, pp. 57–61), Dewey's thinking built upon the earlier contributions of Charles Sanders Peirce, considered the father of pragmatism, and William James, who further interpreted Peirce's basic concepts of pragmatism in terms of individual behavior and the pursuit of religious and moral beliefs. Dewey gave pragmatism a new dimension by using the instrumentalist approach of inquiry and problem-solving methods to achieve individual and social change. He thereby defined pragmatism in operational terms in the instructional process. The instrumentalist principles define the processes of finding out information or learning, which today is often called "hands-on" learning, learning by doing, active learning, critical thinking, the scientific method, or processes of inquiry. According to Levine (1978, p. 258), the process builds on a real experience, in which students are interested for its own sake, and that contains a genuine or real problem that serves as a stimulus to thought. The students proceed to obtain information and make observations needed to define the problem. They then suggest possible solutions and test their validity. Dewey (1916) argued that these are the same processes that one must practice in "real" life, and furthermore, this is how knowledge is acquired and developed. There have been numerous efforts to use such inquiry methods of instruction in General College courses.

The student-centered progressive and instrumentalist views are in contrast with "traditionalism," which is curriculum-centered or subject-matter centered. As Berger (1975, pp. 126–127) pointed out, that type of learning is focused on the heritage, knowledge and information of the past. Berger continued to clarify Dewey's role in educational thinking by saying that he was not the originator of progressive thinking in education; rather, he tried to reconcile the apparent split between progressivism and traditionalism by showing that both philosophies were vital and essential to the future development of educational thought. We should be cautioned that even today Dewey is billed as the champion of the progressive movement, but in reality he vigorously argued against an "either-or" philosophy, stressing that one cannot exist without the other.

Student Personnel Movement

So far, this chapter has focused on the ways in which the concept behind developmental education was a vital part of the pre-1932 educational effort aimed at democratizing society. Most of the discussion has centered on the rationale for and development of the student-centered views of progressive, utilitarian, and instrumentalist education and how they focused on serving the practical needs of the individual learner. At the same time, a second educational paradigm emerged before World War I and flourished through the war that caused educators to look at progressive education from a different angle.

While John Dewey looked upon the scientific method of inquiry as a way of approaching life's problems and enabling the individual to continue learning, Edward Thorndike looked to science to provide "laws" by which to measure educational effectiveness and readiness. He believed that they were based upon the laws of psychology that were recognized and defined through psychological observations. Miller (1988, pp. 69–74) traced Thorndike's science of education back to its origin in France, where Alfred Benet and Theodore Simon, in 1905 through 1908, conceived the idea of an intelligence scale. This idea was put into use when Robert Yerkes, of the American Psychological Association, provided procedures and resources for aptitude and intelligence testing of new recruits in World War I. This new thrust concerned with measuring intelligence and behavior was greeted with both excitement and trepidation. It fit well into the American university's research environment with its insatiable appetite to measure anything and everything with high precision and accuracy.

One of the outcomes of this newfound research agenda was achievement and intelligence testing of the individual student with the intention of establishing appropriate programs that would suit the specific needs and talents of that student. Cremin (1961, p. 190) cited Dewey's reservations that although such test results might help the student achieve his or her potential, they also might reduce the student to nothing more than a set of statistics. Dewey also warned that IQ and achievement test results could serve as a tool for discrimination and antidemocratic forces. Such antidemocratic activities did, in fact, occur when statistics from the Army tests were used in the post-war selection and rejection of European immigrants, especially discriminating against Blacks. This partly contributed to causing the U.S. to close immigration in 1924.

The academic use of intelligence and achievement testing flourished in the 1920s as what Miller (1988, p. 71) called educational scientism and the child-centered approach of progressive education rapidly advanced. Cremin (1961) heralded William Kilpatrick as the chief advocate of this approach. He was not only a contemporary but also a colleague of Dewey and Thorndike at Columbia University. He was influenced by Dewey's inquiry approach or method and also by Thorndike's laws of learning. Kilpatrick established the "project method" (p. 72) in which he monitored and measured the student's involvement in direct, purposeful experience, which he believed was the best way to stimulate individual growth. He believed that the purposeful nature of the learner-centered approach was more important than the content studied, and he was very much opposed to content-centered instruction in which the learning activity was fixed on specific subject matter. Although Kilpatrick shared Dewey's concern with the relationships between the individual and society and the role of the inquiry method, he viewed it from a social context. He believed that the purpose of democracy was mainly for the growth of the individual with institutions as the means to that growth and that the growth of the whole learner was the only acceptable aim of the democratic school.

Kilpatrick was able to put his learner-centered convictions of education into operation later when he was involved in the planning and then the presidency of Bennington College.

A final note about student assessment and counseling is found in Gray's (1951, p. 348) appraisal of the views and activities of the first two University of Minnesota presidents, Folwell and Northrop. Both were viewed by Gray as paternalistic and student centered. He credited their efforts for laying the foundation for a state-of-the-art counseling system that may have "had its start in the brief period of John Dewey's association with the university in the 1890s" (p. 348). Gray continued by saying that "at least those who guided the evolution of educational ideas at Minnesota were disciples of Dewey and echoers of his belief that education is a process of living and not a preparation for future living" (p. 348).

Post-World War I Impact

Boyer and Levine (1981, p. 11) noted that by the end of WWI many Americans had grown tired of the progressive reform impulse featuring President Theodore Roosevelts' (1901–1909) "Square Deal" and President Woodrow Wilson's (1913–1921) "New Freedom." The disillusioned and war-weary Americans became callous to political idealism and sought a time of quiet and healing. In an effort to restore normalcy in their lives, they turned to President Warren Harding (1921–1923) and a conservative, nonintrusive government. This became a time of personal and national isolation.

Another social impact that affected higher education concerned the sudden and enormous number of soldiers who returned home from the war. Wecter (1944, pp. 265–269) provided many accounts of servicemen wanting to continue their education. Some had their curiosity piqued after seeing the world or observing the lives and plights of others. Some needed to adjust to physical or emotional wounds that prevented them from continuing in the job that they held before the War. Others developed a taste for books and knowledge in the several post-war schools that were established by the U.S. on the European continent. Still others needed to improve their skills and expertise because their earlier jobs were either obsolete or their salaries were inadequate. In essence, according to Wecter (pp. 269, 401), a significant number of returning servicemen had the will to remake their lives and saw higher education as a way to meet this need.

Boyer and Levine (1981, p. 11) stated that the effects of the WWI upheaval actually caused a revival of general education, which was looked to as a solution to many of the problems the nation faced. They enumerated the problems that general education could solve, such as responding to overspecialization and vocationalism, machine politics and corruption in government, social intolerance, and cynicism and disillusionment of the younger generation.

Miller (1988, p. 73) highlighted the influence of the conditions and politics of the times as affecting how learner-centered education was viewed after the war. The new general education movement grew along two lines during the 1920s and 1930s: the humanist approach that emphasizes the classical approach, and the instrumentalist or more practical approach. The instrumentalist approach will be pursued here because it encompasses the processes of developmental education and because Miller presented three case histories of this approach, of which General College was one.

Case Histories in General Education

In an effort to define the instrumentalist student-centered philosophy of education and illustrate how it worked in practice, Miller (1988, pp. 79–105) highlighted three case histories of general education programs in an effort to show how this philosophy could be interpreted. Two of the programs were in private women's colleges, namely Bennington College (founded in 1932) in Vermont and Sarah Lawrence College (founded in 1928) in the state of New York. The third example is explained in more detail below. This program, built upon an instrumentalist philosophy in a state-supported public university, was in the General College at the University of Minnesota.

The General College
This chapter has outlined some of the major ideas and events that eventually led to the creation of the General College Idea. The origin of the Idea can be traced directly to the earlier efforts of political and educational leaders to build a democratic society by designing and offering effective general education programs in American colleges and universities. There were a number of significant events in this effort to democratize society that ultimately had a direct impact on making the General College a reality. Among these events were early attempts, politically and educationally, to give all citizens the opportunity to improve their lives and realize better and more responsible lives, such as the efforts of leaders like Jefferson and Jackson and the creation of the land-grant legislation. A second major event was the impact of the great minds of Dewey, Thorndike, Kilpatrick, and other progressive thinkers toward understanding how individuals learn and how learners grow and contribute to improving society. A third event was the existence of political and educational leaders who were able to gather the ideas and wisdom from the first two events and translate them into operational entities or units that effectively resulted in improving democracy.

The Genius of Lotus Delta Coffman

The third event happened at many colleges and universities in the post-World War I period. The University of Minnesota was one of those institutions. It was especially fortunate because of the commitment of a man who possessed a deep understanding and profound belief in the first two events cited previously. He was Lotus Delta Coffman (1875–1938), who served as the fifth president of the University from 1920 to 1938. As we try to understand why Coffman championed the development of the General College, it is necessary to understand the man himself. What caused the fire in his belly that made him fight for a college that would serve a student body that did not belong at a major research university? The College would never have been created had it not been for the power of his wisdom and leadership at the University.

Coffman's strong democratic ideals were developed and strengthened while growing up in Indiana and during his professional development as an educator. William C. Bagley (1939), former professor of Education at the University of Illinois, recounted in a professional biography of Coffman how the early years of college preparation followed by teaching English in the public schools whetted Coffman's appetite for greater understanding of how one learns and develops as an effective citizen. Bagley cited comments from other teachers and students saying that Coffman had an exceptional ability to communicate and teach.

One of the events that had a remarkable impact on Coffman's understanding of needs in education was the period (1909–1911) during which he worked on and completed his doctorate at the Teachers College of Columbia University. According to Bagley (1939), this was a time when the Teachers College was considered the leading center in the world for the study of educational problems, especially those affecting elementary and secondary levels. Bagley also noted that Coffman's dissertation (1911), *The Social Composition of the Teaching Population*, opened the eyes of many people to the sorry state of teacher preparation in the U.S. (pp. 154–155). His findings and recommendations resulted in promoting significant improvements in the preparation of teachers. As importantly, it convinced him that higher education needed drastic attention, which directly impacted the subsequent development of the General College. During Coffman's brief stay at Columbia, he was introduced to, interacted with, and learned from such notables as John Dewey in the Philosophy Department, Edward Thorndike in educational psychology, William Kilpatrick, and other leading thinkers (Bagley, pp. 155–156). The progressive and instrumentalist philosophies were strong at Columbia at that time, and it can be assumed that they sharpened and deepened Coffman's conviction to provide educational leadership in the strengthening of democracy.

In 1913, L. D. Coffman, as Bagley (1939) accounted, became a professor of education at the University of Illinois, Champaign-Urbana. The University of Illinois did not yet have a college of education with its own dean; instead it was a department in the College of Liberal Arts. The University was definitely trying to build a college of education, so in an effort to build a stronger program, it offered a job to John Dewey at an unheard of salary of $10,000. This offer was twice as high as what the highest-paid professor received in any state university in the country. Illinois relied on Coffman and others who knew Dewey to try and convince him to come, but Dewey turned it down.

Meanwhile, a certain history professor at Illinois was offered a position of dean of the Graduate School at the University of Minnesota. The man was Guy Stanton Ford, later to become the sixth president of the University, who had a high respect for Coffman. When a position opened for the deanship of the College of Education at the University of Minnesota, Ford recommended Coffman. After five years as education dean, Coffman became president in 1920.

Malcolm Willey (1939), a colleague of Coffman, a professor of sociology at the University of Minnesota, and university administrator, in a tribute to the late-president Coffman, asserted that his strength and wisdom could be gleaned from his many writings and speeches. Coffman's energy, Willey said, came from deep faith that education is the only means of achieving the democratic way of life. Willey said that "men do live by faith, and through faith achieve great works" (p. 11). He continued that:

> the life of Lotus Delta Coffman is a shining example of this truth. It was characterized by a singleness of purpose, founded on his faith in democracy, and all that he thought and did had reference to his profound conviction that a good life was possible for all people if they would but achieve it. The school at all its levels was merely society's agent for helping them achieve it. (p. 11)

Willey quoted an encounter between Coffman and an attorney who said to him: "Mr. Coffman, civilization has been ruined by education. Do you suppose you can make people competent to vote on public questions by giving them an education?" Coffman's answer was: "I know of no other way" (p. 12).

Bagley (1939) concluded his biography of Coffman by stressing that, unlike other prominent leaders in education, he came from the rank and file of the "teaching population." His firsthand experience with the problems of teaching and learning prepared him, better than most people, to adjust the instruction and curriculum at the University of Minnesota, through the organization of the General College, to serve an increasingly heterogeneous student body. To quote Bagley, Coffman "was apparently the first to see realistically the intricate problems involved in unselective mass-education as it affects the higher institutions" (p. 158).

Gray (1951) discussed Coffman's concerns, early in his presidency, to remake the university to better serve all students. He stressed the need to "reorganize the materials of education" (p. 309), à la Dewey, in an effort to serve both the students who showed the capacity for leadership and those who must be trained for "followership" (p. 309). Miller (1988, p. 98) argued that the University of Minnesota was committed to the land-grant ideal of a university in service to society and stressed that the developers of the General College Idea shared many of the assumptions about general education that had been drawn from Dewey and others. Coffman, an advocate of educational equality, applied and began to blend these assumptions with the unique situation of a land-grant institution, the research ethos of a large state university, and the diverse characteristics of the students who the university was expected to serve.

Miller (1988, pp. 98–99) explained that in an effort to mediate the problem of filling the need of a nonvocational general education within a utilitarian university, Coffman formed the Committee on Administrative Reorganization, commonly referred to as "The Committee of Seven." It was composed of six deans and the assistant to the president, and it was responsible for reviewing and recommending changes in the undergraduate program for the whole university. A part of the committee's responsibility was to make recommendations on how to best, in Coffman's words, "adjust the institution to the individual" (Gray, 1951, p. 313), especially for that population that had been traditionally unserved, which eventually resulted in the establishment of the University College and the General College. As implied by Gray (pp. 309–311), the establishment of the two colleges was seen as a way of mediating the different views between President Coffman and his very good friend John Black Johnston, then Dean of Science, Literature, and the Arts (SLA). Johnston was viewed by some as elitist and argued with Coffman about bringing underprepared and uninterested students to the University.

One outcome of the Committee's work, as Gray (1951) cited, was to provide the student with an "honorable exit" (p. 313) after 2 years of general education, which became the Associate in Arts degree. It should be clarified that the Committee of Seven first proposed that a new unit be called the "Institute of Social Intelligence" (p. 315), but that title was never accepted. In 1932 the Board of Regents approved the new unit, calling it the "Junior College of the University of Minnesota." With this action, the General College Idea became a reality.

The Vision of Malcolm Shaw MacLean

As this new academic unit began to materialize, President Coffman brought in a young energetic educator to be its first director. He was Malcolm S. MacLean, and he strongly believed in the instrumentalist's role in providing meaningful education for all. In the spring of 1933 the Regents changed the name to the "General College" because its most important product was, after all, general education. MacLean (1934) argued for the name change explaining that it was important to reduce possible confusion because those unfamiliar with what junior colleges do would think the "new unit was a 'prep school,' a hybrid, or an illegitimate rival of the long-established University High School" (p. 442). Others might see it as "duplicating the first two years of the lower division of the College of Science, Literature, and Arts and want to know why this should be" (p. 442). MacLean concluded that "some equinimity had now been achieved by renaming the new unit General College of the University and reassigning Junior College to the Lower Division of the Arts College" (p. 442).

In somewhat colorful language, MacLean (1941) characterized the large unserved group of students as having been previously thrown out the back door and dumped into the "great slag heap of academic discards" (p. ix). This statement reflects the major concerns both he and Coffman shared over the high attrition rates during the 1920s when as many as 60% of the freshmen did not return for the second year (Gray, 1951, p. 282). They both believed that these "discards" had as much right to be served by the state-supported university as any group of students. MacLean (1934) argued that we should not look at these discards "as the waste products of higher education" but more importantly as "the raw materials of valuable by-products" (p. 443).

MacLean (1934) cited that certain changes in society during the past 100 years had resulted in a serious dilemma for the nation, forcing society to reconsider how it addresses academic discards. He said that the consequences of advances in birth control along with medical sciences' successful assault on disease had resulted in increased longevity and a population shift of three times as many adults as children and youth (p. 441). With the combination of these changes along with the impact of technological advances and automation in cutting jobs, it was MacLean's (p. 441) worry that there would soon result an adult-youth conflict. He feared that this conflict would become so great that adults would have to refuse all employment to those younger than 25 years of age and that the adults would "have to retire at 40 years to make room" (p. 441).

MacLean (1934) believed that there could only be three consequences to this conflict. One solution was that another world war could eliminate a quarter of the population. The economy would be stimulated for a short time but soon be followed "with the surety of deeper depression and disaster in the end" (p. 441–442). A second grim effect could be the development of sinister youth movements such as those that were leading to "intolerable phases of Nazism in Germany and the more recent rioting in Paris" (p. 442). The third alternative would be to greatly expand education at higher levels for a much larger portion of youth than had ever been believed possible. This would be coupled with programs that provided those youth who had insufficient interest, ability, or training with jobs in government-sponsored conservation corps and civil and public works projects (p. 442).

MacLean (1934) realized the opportunities that lay before him to mold an academic unit from scratch could address the third alternative stated in the previous paragraph. The General College provided a basis for addressing the university's high student graduation mortality rate by providing an educational experience that was tailored "in most cases to the individual student" (p. 445). MacLean realized that students are not "all ready for the same things at the same time as, I fear, we have too often assumed them to be." Instead, he continued, they vary from each other and "within themselves from one time to another" (p. 444).

A further reason for organizing the college was to develop a curriculum that overcame the impact of specialization, which drew resources away from the lower division general education experience. MacLean (1934), in an effort to counter the criticisms of the specialists, cited a statement made by Professor Munro of the California Institute of Technology that "there is or should be only one standard for all courses, general and special, of primary, secondary, or college grade" (p. 444). The one test is that a course must "awaken interest and stimulate the students." Furthermore, if a course does this, "there is no limit to its boundaries for the best of students and there is rich value in it for the humblest" (p. 444).

MacLean immediately set out to develop a curriculum for this college in which he advocated realistic and current overview courses that were designed, as Gray (1951) quoted Coffman saying, "to get at the heart of those problems upon which students must exercise judgment later on" (pp. 315–316). Faculty from all over the University were involved in the planning of the College and its curriculum. MacLean (1933) said that "taking an entirely fresh viewpoint, we were given *carte blanche* to pick out any teacher from any department or college on either campus and set up the kind of courses that seemed best" (p. 304). Gray listed some of the courses, including human biology, overview of physics and chemistry, basic wealth, conservation, mathematics as applied to business and consumerism, developmental psychology, formation of public opinion, background of modern world, and fine arts. Some of these course titles can be found in today's class schedule.

All the courses were to be taught from the standpoint of the students' needs, direct interests, and from the students' skill and knowledge level, thereby giving them a developmental component. To achieve this outcome, MacLean (1934) urged faculty to depart from the traditional approach to course planning where a chronological, classical approach was followed in which the students begin with the roots of the past and then work their way to the present. Instead, he stated that "ours reverses this process. We are experimenting to see if opening each course on the present will not so increase desire, strengthen motivation to learn, that a student will, in his self-propulsion, work his way back to the past" (p. 445). At the beginning almost all of the courses were taught by borrowed faculty, but in subsequent years the College developed its own faculty.

Conclusion

The story of the evolution of the General College paralleled, in many ways, the building of the nation. The nation's founding fathers had the strong desire and opportunity to build a democracy from scratch by employing the best ideas and ideals. Likewise, the founders of General College had an equally strong desire and opportunity to build a collegiate unit from scratch whose primary function was to democratize society by drawing from many of the same ideas and ideals. From the beginning, the evolution of the General College Idea centered on the democratic ideal of providing all people an opportunity to improve their lives and their abilities to carry out their civic responsibilities.

It might be said that the General College was a product of the times. During the earlier years of the republic, the leaders established the basis and rationale for building a democratic society. They looked to education to make this possible. During the 19th and early 20th centuries great advances were made in the understanding of how learning happens. Immediately after WWI the nation had to adjust to rapidly changing social and post-war employment conditions which, by the late 1920s, led to mass unemployment and a disastrous Depression. During these troubling times a national movement that defined higher education's role in democratizing society grew out of the ashes.

With two events that focused on the establishment of a democracy and the increased research and understanding of human behavior and learning, a third event was needed to pull the two together into a real, physical collegiate entity. That third event was the emergence of an individual who understood and believed in the first two events and who had the ability, conviction, power, and energy to bring together and fuse all the parts into a single physical unit. At the University of Minnesota that person was Lotus Delta

Coffman. He engaged the best minds in the University to plan and organize the administrative structure to create the physical unit. Coffman enlisted a like-minded man, Malcolm S. MacLean, to spearhead the operational planning and serve as the unit's first director. The General College became the University of Minnesota's answer to its role in democratizing society.

In a final note, it is necessary to bring attention to MacLean's concerns about academic discards and his worries about what problems society might be facing as their numbers increased. His effort to lead and provide rationale for curricular planning for the new college was greatly influenced by these worries and fears of what seemed to be emerging nationally. In this sense, the earliest curriculum was a product of the times. As one reviews the General College curriculum over the past 73 years, the emphasis and, in most cases, the kinds of courses have departed little from the earliest plan. The ideas and concerns have remained appropriate throughout the history of the college. What is important is that, because there continue to be discards, the college should continually take a deep and serious look at issues and problems in society and ask the following: what are the issues that continue to prevent people from participating in and benefiting fully in a democratic society, and what should higher education do about it? More importantly, what can General College do about it?

References

American heritage college dictionary (3rd ed.). (2000). Boston: Houghton Mifflin.

Bagley, W. C. (1939, *January*). Lotus D. Coffman as I knew him. *The Educational Forum,* 151–159.

Berger, M. I. (1975). John Dewey and progressive education today. In W. W. Brickman & S. Lehrer (Eds.), *John Dewey: Master educator* (pp. 126–131). Westport, CT: Greenwood Press.

Bernstein, R. J. (1966). *John Dewey.* New York: Washington Square Press.

Boyer, E. L., & Levine, A. (1981). *Quest for common learning.* Washington, DC: The Carnegie Foundation for the Advancement of Teaching.

Cremin, L. A. (1961). *The transformation of the school: Progressivism in American education 1876–1957.* New York: Vintage Books.

Cross, K. P. (1976). *Accent on learning: Improving instruction and reshaping the curriculum,* San Francisco: Jossey-Bass.

Dewey, J. (1916). *Democracy and education: An introduction to the philosophy of education.* New York: Macmillan.

Gray, J. (1951). *The University of Minnesota: 1851–1951.* Minneapolis, MN: University of Minnesota Press.

Levine, A. (1978). *Handbook on undergraduate curriculum.* A report for the Carnegie Council on Policy Studies in Higher Education, The Carnegie Foundation for the Advancement of Teaching. San Francisco: Jossey-Bass.

MacLean, M. (1933, *July*). The Minnesota Junior College. *The Educational Record,* 301–309.

MacLean, M. (1934). Reorganization at the University of Minnesota. *The Junior College Journal, 4,* 441–449.

MacLean, M. (1941). Editor's foreword. In C. R. Pace (Ed.), *They went to college* (p. ix). Minneapolis, MN: University of Minnesota Press.

Mason, R. E. (1975). Dewey's culture, theory and pedagogy. In W. W. Brickman & S. Lehrer (Eds.), *John Dewey: Master educator* (pp. 115–125). Westport, CT: Greenwood Press.

Miller, G. E. (1988). *The meaning of general education: The emergence of a curriculum paradigm.* New York: Teachers College Press, Columbia University.

National Association for Developmental Education. (1995). *Definition and goals statement.* Carol Stream, IL: Author.

Wecter, D. (1944). *When Johnny comes marching home.* Cambridge, MA: Riverside Press.

Willey, M. M. (1939, January). Lotus Delta Coffman: Educational statesman, 1875–1938. *The Educational Record,* 10–27.

CHAPTER 4

Counseling Psychology and the General College: An Implementation of the Minnesota Point of View

Cathrine Wambach and Thomas Brothen

ABSTRACT

The Minnesota Point of View is a theory of counseling developed in the 1920s by University of Minnesota psychologists who used information from counseling practice and research on students to improve student retention. This chapter describes how General College administrators, counselors, researchers, and teachers used the Minnesota Point of View to design a college for students who were not considered to be good candidates for bachelor degrees. Research on GC students identified important characteristics that had implications for the college curriculum and student personnel services including the need for vocational counseling and the morale problem created by participating in a college identified with less well-qualified students.

I n the 1930s, the University of Minnesota Psychology Department emerged as a leader in the field of counseling psychology. Led by Donald G. Paterson and Edmund G. Williamson, Minnesota psychologists developed a counseling perspective that became known as the Minnesota Point of View (cf., Patterson, 1966). The Minnesota Point of View was based on the assumption that characteristics of people could be measured through psychological tests and that counseling that made use of test scores could guide people to success in education and work. Research at Minnesota led to the development of important tests such as the General Aptitude Test Battery (Dvorak, 1947), the Minnesota Multiphasic Personality Inventory (Hathaway & McKinley, 1942), and a variety of measures of specific vocational aptitudes, interests, and personality traits. Less well known is the story of how the Minnesota Point of View was implemented in an educational experiment, the General College (GC) of the University of Minnesota (UMN). This chapter will describe the Minnesota Point of View, how it guided the development of GC, and how it remained influential in the work of the college.

The Minnesota Point of View: A Counseling Theory

The Minnesota Point of View is associated with several psychologists who were on the faculty of the University or who did their doctoral work in the department. They were inspired by the leadership of Donald Paterson, who came to Minnesota in 1921. Paterson served in the army during World War I and was involved in the development of the army's intelligence testing program. After the war, he worked for the Scott Company, the nation's first industrial psychology consulting firm. Paterson established the Minnesota tradition of research in individual differences, industrial psychology, and vocational and career counseling. An incredibly productive scholar, he advised 88 Ph.D.s, over 200 M.A.s, and published, on average, one article per month for over 30 years. His courses in individual differences influenced the careers of numerous Minnesota students who made important contributions to the field of psychology including Edmund Williamson, John Darley, Thomas Magoon, Harold Pepinsky, James Jenkins, Lloyd Lofquist, René Dawis, Marvin Dunnette, John Holland, Leona Tyler, Harrison Gough, Paul Meehl, Jane Loevinger, and Starke Hathaway (Keyes, n.d.).

The Minnesota Point of View is closely tied to the Student Personnel Point of View, a movement within higher education that began in the 1920s (Higbee, 2001). The American Council on Education (ACE) promoted the movement by sponsoring conferences and publishing papers advocating for the student personnel perspective. According to Cowley (1932) the colleges most involved in developing the student personnel movement were Columbia University, the University of Minnesota, Ohio State University, the State University of Iowa, and the University of Chicago. Northwestern University should have been included on Cowley's list. Northwestern's president, Walter Dill Scott, started a student personnel department at Northwestern in 1919 (Lloyd-Jones, 1929), and was the founder of the Scott Company where Paterson was employed before coming to the University. It is likely that Scott influenced the development of Paterson's views about student personnel. In the 1920s, applied psychology was an emerging field and the pioneers had strong connections with each other.

In 1937, ACE published a paper called the *Student Personnel Point of View*. Among the group that contributed to the paper were Paterson and C. Gilbert Wrenn, the Assistant Director of GC from 1936 to 1938 (Higbee, 2001). We searched psycINFO for student personnel publications between 1937 and 1950 and found that 31 of 163 (19%) were by UMN authors, suggesting that the Minnesota Point of View had considerable influence on the student personnel movement.

The most complete early description of the Minnesota Point of View as a counseling theory was put forth by Edmund G. Williamson and John (Jack) Darley (1937). Williamson had a long and illustrious career at the UMN. He was the first director of the UMN Testing Bureau, later called the Counseling Bureau, and Dean of Students until the mid-1970s. He was the president of the National Association of Student Personnel Administrators (NASPA) from 1966 to 1967 (NASPA, 2004). His influence was so important that a UMN building designed to house student affairs functions was named in his honor.

Williamson viewed counseling and education as part of a whole. Both, he believed, should have students at the center. He observed that students differed in their abilities, motivations, and interests and that these attributes could be validly measured. He believed that students should be guided toward the courses and curricula that were consistent with their abilities and needs. In order to achieve this goal, he proposed that courses and pedagogy should reflect the needs of real students, not hypothetical ideals. The only way to find out what real students were like was to gather data; to do research on their abilities, motivations, and needs. The counselor, then, had to be involved in ongoing research in order to remain informed about real students. Williamson also observed that students often lacked insight into their abilities and interests or were not motivated to develop them. The job of the counselor was to assess the student objectively, tell the student the results of the assessment, persuade the student that the assessment was correct, and encourage the student to make plans accordingly (Williamson & Darley, 1937).

Williamson acknowledged that many factors prevented students from correctly appraising their abilities. These factors included the unrealistic aspirations of their parents, faith that attending college provided economic security, loss of self-confidence due to economic adversity, and harsh criticism of their past work. Through objective appraisal, the counselor could help students better understand their aptitudes and direct their efforts toward developing them. One of the problems that Williamson identified in the process of vocational guidance was the lack of information available to counselors about the attributes of people who were successful in various careers. Williamson believed that research in vocational psychology would provide this information, but until the information was available, counselors were encouraged to focus on the role of training as a gatekeeper into occupations. Students were encouraged to consider not "should I become a doctor?" but "can I succeed in medical school?" (Williamson & Darley, 1937, p. 67).

Williamson observed that even when students were enrolled in appropriate courses, distractions could prevent them from learning. The job of the counselor included finding out what prevented the student from learning. Williamson believed that "Optimum learning is possible only when the desire to learn is fostered by sympathetic relations with teachers, by the alleviation of emotional distractions, and by selection of students capable of profiting from college courses" (Williamson & Darley, 1937, p. 65). The model was holistic in its view that every aspect of students' lives needed to be considered in understanding how they could most benefit from their education.

Williamson's perspective has been described as a "rational" approach to counseling (Patterson, 1966). Rational theories take a logical, intellectual approach to the client's problem and the process of problem solving. They construct the counselor as a teacher who works individually with the client to find solutions to problems. Although the emotional side of counseling is not emphasized in rational theories, it is clear from Williamson's work that he valued exploration of the student's emotions when they interfered with the student's performance or problem-solving process. The rational approach was particularly appropriate for use with students because it could be taught to faculty members who were not psychologists, but were interested in advising students (Williamson, 1935).

In this chapter we will describe how GC administrators, counselors, researchers, and teachers used the Minnesota Point of View to design a college for students we would now describe as "at-risk" or "underprepared." We will start with the events leading up to the founding of the college. We will then describe how a student personnel perspective was implemented in the college and how research on students, an important component of the Minnesota Point of View, influenced decisions about the college's curriculum. Finally we will discuss two persistent problems for the college, student morale and transfer within the university to baccalaureate degree programs, which continue to guide research and practice today.

Individual Differences and Success in College

At the turn of the twentieth century, any Minnesota high school graduate could be admitted to the UMN. Faculty were concerned that growing numbers of students were not prepared for college work (Gray, 1958). Pioneering work on the use of tests to select students for admission was begun by John Black Johnston, Dean of the College of Science, Literature, and Arts (SLA) (Johnston, 1930). Johnston collected information about students' high school ranks, and with Paterson developed a college aptitude test that was found to be a valid predictor of success in SLA. In a 1930 speech, UMN president Lotus Coffman (1934) said that although the university, as a state school, did not have the right to refuse admission to high school graduates, it was a "well recognized fact that students occasionally are graduated from high school who are not capable of doing satisfactory college work" (p. 137). He reported that the testing of high school students for college ability had resulted in those with low ability having been counseled by their high schools not to attend college, which led to a decrease in the number of low ability students enrolling in UMN colleges. In this speech he also claimed that the UMN had done more than any other school in the nation to understand the individual student. He stated that:

> With the physical, intellectual and emotional examination of students, the information obtained from the vocational and educational advisers, the student counselors, the psychiatrist, the personnel committee and the deans . . . we actually know more about our students today than at any other time in the history of the university. (p. 140)

Coffman's commitment to serving all Minnesota high school graduates led to the proposal that a new college should be developed that would meet the needs of students who were not well served by SLA. Dean Johnston believed that students must be assisted to discover the type of education and work best suited to their aptitudes and interests (Williamson, 1947). MacLean (1949), the first director of GC, suggested that Paterson, Williamson, Darley, and their associates provided the evidence that the UMN elder statesmen used to create flexible structures at the UMN designed to meet students' needs. The new junior college would be based on research on students, and a curriculum called general education would be designed to be relevant to the characteristics and goals of the student body.

The Implementation of The Minnesota Point of View in General College

By early 1932 the decision had been made to establish a college suited to the needs of students with low college aptitude ratings who were not likely to achieve success in the other UMN colleges. A collegiate counseling unit had been successful in SLA, so there was support for making counseling integral to the new college. During the 1920s, the first director of GC, Malcolm MacLean, had been part of this unit, which he described as Paterson's first faculty committee on student counseling (MacLean, 1949). Although MacLean's academic background was in English, he became so inspired by his work in student personnel that when he was invited to direct the college he put student personnel at its center. Williamson helped MacLean plan the unit's structure and goals. The plan for the college was that two professional counselor-researchers would be permanent staff members. They would guide the development of the college by learning about students through the process of counseling and through research.

Based on his experiences with the students the College would serve, Williamson believed that GC students would need a great deal of help identifying their aptitudes and selecting appropriate educational goals. Faculty and staff were to be trained in student personnel perspectives, and the practice and research of guidance counselors would inform the development of the curriculum (MacLean, Williams, & Darley, 1937). According to MacLean et al., the goal of the college was to adjust the student to the environment, and to place the student on the road to a satisfying life and satisfying work. Because the college was built around understanding the student rather than faculty interests or the demands of professional training, student personnel and guidance were integrated into the curriculum. For example, Williamson (1937a) not only organized the student personnel effort but also, with MacLean, taught a course called Vocations. This course offered students an opportunity to learn more about their aptitudes and interests and the jobs that matched their traits.

Darley and Williams Build the GC Student Personnel Program

From 1932 until 1934, guidance functions were carried out by GC teachers and administrative staff under the leadership of MacLean and Williamson. In 1934 Darley became one of two counselor-researchers in GC. The other counselor-researcher was Kathleen McConnon, who soon became Kathleen McConnon Darley. Shortly after her marriage, Mrs. Darley left university employment, a practice dictated by the anti-nepotism rules of the time. The Darleys' responsibilities were to establish the GC counseling and student personnel program, conduct research on adolescent college students, and teach psychology. In 1936 Jack Darley became the Director of the UMN Testing Bureau, but remained involved in a major study of GC students (General College, 1938).

In 1935 another of Paterson's students, Cornelia Williams, joined the college as a counselor researcher. In 1937 MacLean, Williams, and Darley described the guidance process in GC. The first step was testing. All GC freshmen took a battery of tests including three general ability tests, two specific achievement tests, and 12 attitude or adjustment scales. The second step was to collect other information about the student, including questionnaires describing the student's family, social and economic background, high school records, and the results of the student's physical examination. All UMN students were required to have a physical examination at the health service at entrance. The third step was for a counselor to interview the student at least once, but more typically two to six times during the student's first term. The purpose of the interviews was to gather more information, and more importantly to help the student clarify goals, stay motivated, and vent emotions. The fourth step was to advocate for the student in the community or refer the student to others for specific help. For example, if the student needed a course in another college, the counselor would call the dean of the college to arrange it. If the student needed more support from home, the counselor would call the parents and encourage it. The counselors made referrals for health problems, emotional problems, speech defects, disability assessment, remediation of skill problems, study problems, extracurricular activities, financial problems, and inadequate housing. The fifth step was evaluating the success of the program based on the extent to which the student achieved an appropriate goal.

In 1940, Royal Embree, a GC counselor-researcher, described the development of the GC counseling service as part of an annual report to the UMN president on the progress of the college. In this report, Embree reiterated the Minnesota Point of View: that guidance is a vital function of education concerned with the total adjustment of the student, that it required the cooperation of the entire college staff, and that it must be sensitive to the results of program evaluation. He claimed that it was impossible to give any individual credit for the GC counseling program because "counseling is and has been from the beginning a planned function of the college as a whole and not of any person or department" (p. 47). Embree identified seven factors that contributed to the development of the counseling program: (a) recognition on the part of college administration and staff of the need for individualized counseling, (b) ongoing administrative support for the work, (c) ongoing substantial financial support, (d) involvement of trained guidance leaders, (e) sound research that provided direction to the program, (f) willingness and ability of the staff to participate in the guidance process, and (g) constant awareness of what the program was and was not accomplishing for students.

According to Embree (1940), GC teachers and administrators played an important role in the guidance process. Each GC student was assigned to a staff advisor who assisted the student with program planning. By the late 1930s, GC had some faculty members who worked exclusively for the College who were identified as available for advising. Advisors had access to the students' counseling files and made use of the information on test results in the files. Advisors referred students who needed more in-depth help to the counselors. The success of the counselor staff collaboration in the guidance process reflected both the personal characteristics of the staff and the counseling system. Embree described the GC staff as very interested in and accessible to students: "Apparently, the selection of people who are adequately equipped to work on the educational frontier also selects men and women who are keenly conscious of the necessity for individualized work with students" (p. 49). Because the curriculum was supposed to be responsive to the needs of students, staff relied on the counselors to provide the in-depth understanding of students necessary to make the system work. In the GC system, both the results of formal research and the insights of counselors informed the curriculum.

The University of Minnesota Student Personnel Programs

The General College student personnel program was situated in a context of a broad and diverse UMN program. In the same year that GC was established, Williamson became the director of the newly formed University Testing Bureau. The Bureau was established to collect the data necessary for counseling all UMN students concerning vocational and educational issues. In 1936 Williamson joined the UMN administration, and Darley became director of the Bureau, which was renamed the Counseling Bureau. Under Williamson and Darley, the three divisions of the bureau, counseling, testing, and research, provided important information to colleges about the problems students encountered. This information was used to guide students in making educational and vocational choices and to inform the curricula of the colleges and the pedagogy of the faculty (Williamson & Darley, 1937).

By the 1940s the student personnel perspective was embedded broadly and deeply into the university. Williamson (1947) described the Minnesota student personnel program as a "balanced" student service that included (a) the Counseling Bureau with its measurement experts, reading specialists, occupational specialists, women's counselors, and "emotional counselors" (p. 153); (b) specialized services including counseling in dormitories and fraternities, speech and hearing therapists, and counseling for veterans and foreign students; and (c) advising and counseling in the colleges. Williamson stated that

> counseling is most effective when it is an integral part of a total environmental and institutional personnel program, consisting of many types of services brought to focus on the individual student's learning-needs to aid him in finding and perfecting methods of working out his own solutions to his own problems. (p. 154)

GC counseling existed as part of a large, coordinated set of student personnel services that shared goals, methods, and in some cases personnel. GC students were not only served by the College's student personnel unit, but were regularly seen as clients by counselors in the Counseling Bureau and by specialists in reading and speech clinics. This connection among the units allowed sharing of information to ensure that service to students was coordinated and consistent. The coordinated system put a high priority on research to both better understand students and to evaluate the effectiveness of programs.

Research on General College Students

The decision that the college was to be guided by the results of research on students led to three major and many other smaller research projects. Jack Darley and Cornelia Williams (Williams, 1943) led a massive research project designed to describe older adolescents in the college environment. Robert Pace (1941), who went on to a distinguished career in educational research at the University of California-Los Angeles, led an equally complex study of the characteristics of former university students. In the third study, Ruth Eckert (1943), who later became a Professor of Education at the UMN and the first woman faculty member honored with the title of Regent's Professor (Gray, 1951), led an evaluation of GC outcomes. These studies were instrumental in defining the characteristics of GC students, stimulating a discussion of the desired outcomes of general education, and evaluating the success of the fledgling college. These three studies: the Adolescent Study, the Adult Study, and the Outcomes Study, provide examples of the way research was used to inform practice in the early years of GC.

The Adolescent Study

Williams (1943) described the results of the Adolescent Study in the book *These We Teach: A Study of General College Students*. The study was also described by Darley and Williams in annual reports that McLean made to the university president (Williams, 1940). The complex and ambitious study was made possible by a 1935 grant from the General Education Board of the Rockefeller Foundation. The head of the Rockefeller Foundation was John Vincent, former president of the UMN and mentor to Coffman (Gray, 1958, p. 117). Guidance for the study was provided by a prestigious Advisory Board that included Williamson, Paterson, psychologists John Anderson and Florence Goodenough from the University of Minnesota Institute of Child Welfare, UMN sociologists F. S. Chapin and A. L. Shea, and Ruth Boynton, Director of the UMN Health Service.

The goal of the Adolescent Study (Williams, 1943) was to understand the educational, social, and family characteristics of GC students. The information was to be used to identify issues to be dealt with in counseling and to design a curriculum focused on the needs and characteristics of the students. Data on 1312 students first enrolled between 1935 and 1937 were coded and analyzed. In addition, 100 students were selected for more intense study. This group was interviewed, and interviews were also conducted with their parents. Interviewers also made observations of the parents' homes.

A concise summary of the results of the study was made by Williams (1940) in a report on the discussion of the outcomes by a committee of General College faculty. The major findings of the study were:

1. GC students were primarily from middle and upper-middle class families in the Twin Cities area. They lived at home while attending college.

3. GC students had conservative political and economic attitudes consistent with their middle class origins. They were apathetic about social issues.

4. GC students were generally well adjusted and physically healthy. Their main problems were vocational and educational.

5. The parents of GC students had experienced large economic gains without a college education and expected their children would experience even greater gains with more education. The parents of GC students viewed a college education uncritically and put much pressure on their children to earn degrees.

6. GC students expected to begin their adult working lives at the same economic level their parents had reached after many years of work. GC students expected to gain job training and financial security from their education. Women were more likely to want a broad general education and education for home and family life.

7. Most male GC students, but not females, paid for their own education.

8. GC students' prior education did not prepare them for the large lecture classes at the University.

9. GC students were from the lowest third of their high school classes, scored low on tests of academic ability, and whatever factors led to those outcomes in high school were likely still operating in college.

10. Only about 20% of the students admitted to GC entered voluntarily. The resistance of GC students and their parents to anything unconventional led them to resist the college, its courses, and procedures because they were unconventional.

11. GC students dropped in and out of school, and most did not return for a second year.

12. GC students were more sociable than other students and preferred less organized activities such as dating and discussing to organized clubs and activities.

The most problematic characteristics of GC students were their low academic ability, their resistance to new ideas, their desire for high-status jobs with high incomes, and their lack of interest in personal and intellectual growth. The Williams' study supported Williamson's (1937a) belief that GC students needed vocational guidance to identify appropriate educational and career goals. Also, because both the students and their parents regarded vocational preparation as an important educational goal, Williams proposed that the college add occupational preparation programs.

The Adult Study

While the Adolescent Study (Williams, 1943) was taking place, a second study, which began in 1936, examined the outcomes of UMN graduates and UMN students who did not graduate. Led by C. Robert Pace (1941), the Adult Study as it was called, contacted 1600 students who first attended the University in 1924, 1925, 1928, and 1929, before GC was created. The purpose of the study was to learn more about the needs, interests, and wants of adults who had attended college in hopes of developing a curriculum that was ultimately more useful to students.

The students contacted included both those who fit the profile of students who would later be admitted to GC and students who would continue to be admitted to other colleges. Students were sent long questionnaires that included items on issues ranging from their attitudes toward home decorations to their beliefs about philosophy. In addition, 172 respondents were interviewed to check the validity of the survey responses. The questions were created by a committee of GC faculty members and designed to determine if college graduates seemed to have benefited from their college experience. The study provided an incredibly detailed snapshot of college-educated young adults. Although those who graduated had more prestigious occupations and earned more money than those who did not graduate, both groups were occupationally and financially advantaged compared to the general population. There were no differences between students who graduated and those who did not graduate on lifestyle variables, suggesting that the main impact of college graduation was vocational. Graduation and marital status were related in women, with more graduates among the single women group. The respondents were interested in national issues rather than local community problems and few participated in arts or music activities. The genders differed in their interests, with men expressing more interest in the world of business and sports, and women more in the areas of popular entertainment, church, and school. Pace's book included a very detailed description of the interests, activities, and attitudes of young adults of that time period, information that was used to support the development of the general education curriculum.

According to MacLean (1949), the response of the faculty to the Pace (1941) study was "Thank God! Now that we know what our students are really like, we can plan real courses for them" (p. 25). The curriculum was designed to increase students' self-understanding, to direct them to fulfilling occupations, to help them establish healthy families, and to make them more involved citizens. The process of operationalizing these goals in the curriculum was described by Spafford (1943) and the result has been described as "functional" general education (Koch, 1980).

The Study of GC Outcomes

As the first cohorts of students entered the college, plans were made to follow up on their outcomes. The goal of the study was to determine if GC was successful in meeting its objectives, which included increasing the students' insight and understanding of self and others; developing students' skills in communication, thinking, and social interaction; developing students traits such as open-mindedness, engagement in civic affairs, and social maturity; and developing a personal philosophy and realistic view of the world. Ruth Eckert, who is described in the 1938–1939 *GC Bulletin* as an Associate Professor and Research Evaluator, took charge of the project. Eckert's (1943) study included students who entered GC between 1932 and 1940. The study concluded that GC students made significant gains in the areas that were important to GC and present in the GC curriculum: however, social attitudes and recreational interests did not change. Over time, GC students' vocational choices became more realistic. In comparing GC students to SLA students, GC students differed primarily in their academic abilities. There were no differences between the GC and SLA students in personality, other than a tendency for more GC students to have conservative social and political attitudes. Like Williams, Eckert found that GC students' career aspirations were not consistent with their academic abilities because half of GC students identified careers that required advanced degrees (e.g., business executive, medicine, law), while most left college before completing bachelor degrees. The most frequently identified vocational goals for men were business, engineering, teaching, accounting, embalming, and law, while women preferred nursing, teaching, business, designing, and social work. Eckert was also struck by the high level of commitment students had to their career choice. She found that only one in five students had doubts about their original choice. Combined with William's (1943) adolescent study, the GC follow-up study lent support to the development of occupational programs in GC. In the 1943 supplemental *GC Bulletin*, occupational programs are listed for the first time. The programs included child care, prenursing and related medical arts, pre-embalming, commercial art, general clerical, and sales and business. The choice of programs was based on information from the Pace (1941) Adult Study and the Eckert Outcomes Study, both of which identified career interests and future careers of GC students, and the exigencies of World War II. From 1943 until the mid-1980s, occupational programs served as an important complement to the GC general education curriculum.

The Ten-Year Follow-up Study of the 1958 Cohort

The commitment to research on the GC student continued for several decades after the founding of the college. An example was a 10-year longitudinal study of a group of freshmen admitted in the fall of 1958 (Kingsley, 1968–1969). The study was led by Gordon Kingsley, a GC counselor and faculty member who was hired in the mid-1950s to lead GC student personnel services. Assisting with the project were Frank Benson, David Giese, Leslie King, George McCutcheon, and Thomas Scheller. King and Scheller were part of the student personnel services unit, while Benson, Giese, and McCutcheon taught in other units of the college.

The purposes of the Kingsley (1968–1969) study were familiar ones: to document the worth of providing postsecondary education to students in the bottom half of the high school class and to continue monitoring the needs of students in relation to the curriculum. A random sample of 300 students was selected from among GC students beginning in the fall of 1958. The students were interviewed during their first term, at the end of their first year, and at the end of their second year. Students who transferred or left college were sent questionnaires surveying their educational and vocational plans. In 1966 almost all of the original participants were contacted to fill out a questionnaire. Of the original 300 students, 194 completed it and also completed the *Strong Vocational Interest Blank* (Strong, 1943).

In 1958, men still outnumbered women in the college by about three to one. The smaller number of women in the study made it harder for Kingsley (1968–1969) to draw strong conclusions about this group. Eighty percent of the students lived in the Twin Cities area with their parents while attending GC, and 43% lived in the city of Minneapolis. It remained the case that most of the parents of GC students had not attended college. Eleven percent of the fathers and 8% of the mothers of GC students were college graduates.

Kingsley (1968–1969) found that 67% of the students said they enrolled in GC because they had failed to gain entrance to any other college. Although 32% expressed disappointment at having been admitted to GC, 40% said their initial response to being admitted to GC was relief at being admitted to the university at all. A report on Junior Colleges in Minnesota prepared by Keller, Lokken, and Meyer (1958) supported the students' perception that GC was the only postsecondary institution in the state serving less qualified students. By the middle of their first terms, 82% of GC students said their feelings about the college were positive. Eighty-four percent of the students said they planned to transfer to a 4-year college, and only 14% intended to earn only an associate degree. By the end of the first year, 75% of the students were still satisfied with their GC experience, and 91% planned to continue their education the next year, either by returning to GC or transferring to a 4-year college.

At the 1966 follow-up, Kingsley (1968–1969) found that 28% of the men and 8% of the women had earned bachelor degrees. An additional 9% of the men was still enrolled at an educational institution, and 23% completed the requirements for an A.A. degree. Students who completed bachelor degrees had an average grade point average (GPA) of 2.8 while those who did not earn any degree had an average of 1.5.

Kingsley (1968–1969) concluded that there was little evidence that the participants had changed much as a result of their education. There was no evident shift in their political, economic, or aesthetic values. The participants in the 1966 survey indicated that:

> their religious convictions remained the same after college as they had been prior to it, that their political ties were divided almost evenly between the two major parties before and after college, that their economic and vocational aspirations (despite some realistic modifications) continued basically unchanged, and that their cultural interests (the kinds of music they listened to, the television programs they watch, the movies and plays they attend, the literature they read) had not changed as a result of attending college. In fact, the evidence makes it clear that the participants in the study did not at any time regard the University or the College as an environment where they might examine and appraise values and perhaps recast some of them in the light of newly discovered information. Most of them saw higher education as a means to an end, an essential step on the way to a vocation. (p. 14)

The men who participated in the study eventually found employment in the occupational area they originally chose, but at a lower level, and 70% were employed in business detail, sales, and technical work. Fifty-seven percent had jobs at the professional, management, or skilled levels; 26% had jobs at the semi-skilled level; and 13% had jobs at the unskilled level. Of the men, 72% expressed satisfaction with their employment, with those who had earned better grades and degrees expressing more satisfaction. In 1966 so few of the women were in career positions that an analysis of their occupations was not included in the study.

In drawing conclusions from the study, Kingsley (1968–1969) reaffirmed the Minnesota Point of View. He pointed out that GC should continue to "individualize its instruction and counseling to an even greater degree" and gear the curriculum "to the realities of the social and economic milieu beyond the campus" (p. 19). Although the institution could not be expected to supply all of the motivation that appears to make a difference in determining student success, "teaching methods which spur students' active involvement in the processes of learning tend to personalize and motivate the further pursuit of learning" (p. 20).

Kingsley's (1968–1969) study demonstrated that GC students continued to seek bachelor degrees and did not see their GC experience as terminal. It is another example of how research on students was used to support changes in the curriculum. The desire expressed by GC students to complete degrees, combined with the continuing poor fit between their interests and the degree programs available at the UMN, provided the justification for the creation of the baccalaureate program in 1970.

Major Challenges for GC Students

Research on GC students provided information about two ongoing problems that were first identified by GC counselors that have implications for the college's future: the stigmatization students experienced by participating in a program for less qualified students, and the need to offer not just general education and occupational programs, but to offer courses that would transfer to other colleges within the UMN. The stigmatization of GC students, described by early writers as the morale problem, has been amply documented and has affected the relationships between students and staff in the college and the attitudes of the staff toward their work. The transfer problem was resolved in 1985 when students' insistence on transfer was officially recognized as the college's mission.

The Morale Problem

From the inception of the college, students who were admitted were identified as being less academically able than other UMN students. The stigma attached to admission to GC was first mentioned by Johnston and Williamson (1934) and continues to the present (Wambach, Hatfield, & Mirabella, 2001). MacLean (1936) reported that "Our students are not, as is popularly rumored, 'dumbbells' and 'morons'" (p. 3). In 1938 MacLean wrote that GC

> was looked upon as a sort of internement [*sic*] camp for low-grade non-students, wherein the immature, the non-academic, the socialite could be impounded away from those of true scholarship. Some of our colleagues thought of these youngsters not ruthlessly, but in the same terms as the gentle Southerner thinks of the Negro—as problem children, sometimes pleasant, more often irritating, who had, nevertheless to be taken care of and served as pleasantly and well as they could be so long as they were kept out from under foot. (pp. 1–2)

MacLean saw the attitude of those who advocated that the UMN admit only elite students as comparable to racism, and he decried it on moral grounds and because it made the work of the college less effective. Williams (1943) reported that less than one fifth of GC students entered the college voluntarily. The resentment students felt at being placed in a college they did not choose and did not understand created dissatisfaction with the college and problems in the classroom. Besides the negative perceptions of many members of the university community, GC students faced active discrimination in some areas of university life. For example, in 1949 UMN sororities would not allow GC women to join. In a letter to Mrs. Alvin Wyatt dated October 10, 1949, GC Dean Horace Morse said that "it would contribute to the betterment of our college situation and also of the state of mind of our girls if some steps were taken by those sororities now discriminating against them to remove such regulations" (p. 1). Shortly after this letter, official discrimination by sororities against GC women ended.

A survey of GC students by Magoon (1950) found that 91% of the students who responded to the survey believed they were looked down upon by students enrolled in other colleges of the university. They reported acquiring negative attitudes toward the college before they entered and also reported that their attitudes had improved as they experienced the college. Most students, 51%, rated themselves as satisfied, 27% were neutral, and 22% were dissatisfied. Males were significantly more likely to express dissatisfaction than were females. The GC stigma affected students' perceptions of the college curriculum. For example, Magoon's results suggested that about a third of the respondents believed their GC courses were too easy, and 40% believed there to be too much overlap between the content of GC courses and high school classes. The dissatisfied students were much more likely to rate the courses as too easy or repetitive. Magoon found that 90% of the students agreed that "The more GC courses are like SLA courses the better I like it" (p. 31).

In the conclusion of his report Magoon (1950) stated a need to address "the individual student's lack of acceptance of himself and his relatively limited academic abilities, (in the sense of what we might term abstract and/or verbal reasoning)" (p. 76). He went on to comment that although GC students aspire to professional occupations, these goals were unrealistic and presented a major challenge to counselors who needed to "readjust" student's vocational goals.

GC counselors were well aware of the dilemmas they faced in their work. Most of the students admitted to the college did not have the academic ability necessary for college work and had vocational aspirations that were not likely to be achieved. Rather than ignore this fact, the counselors chose to confront it by giving students information about their aptitudes and interests and informing the students about curricula and training programs in which the student was likely to be successful. In the 1940s some psychologists such as Carl Rogers (1948) began to question the value of providing information during counseling. This nondirective approach was criticized by Williamson (1947) as too limiting. Williamson stated that

I know of no counselor at Minnesota who has imposed a vocational choice or any other kind of choice upon a student. . . . Though we avoid compulsion, we at Minnesota don't hesitate to suggest, inform, contribute, participate, help and even advise(!) students. (p. 150)

Minnesota counselors, including those in GC, continued to view the counselor more as an educational resource and only occasionally as a therapist. From Magoon's (1950) report it is clear that counselors occasionally became frustrated when students resisted information and that students sometimes resented being confronted with the need to change. Also, GC counselors were well aware of the fact that the predictions that led students to GC were not always accurate, and that for some students, transfer to a 4-year degree program was an appropriate goal.

The Transfer Mission

One of the earliest problems for GC counselors and administrators was working out ways for students who were successful in GC to transfer to the baccalaureate degree programs of other UMN colleges. This was viewed as a problem because the mission of GC was to provide students a general education leading to an associate degree. Given their high school records and standardized test scores, GC students were not considered good candidates for baccalaureate degrees. The psychologists who practiced student personnel from the Minnesota Point of View viewed test scores as pieces of information that could be used in conjunction with other information to make predictions about the likelihood that a student would be successful in a degree program. However, they were open to the idea that predictions could be wrong and acknowledged that motivation and circumstances played an important role in student success. As Williamson and Darley (1937) explained, tests "vary in reliability or consistency, in validity or meaning, and in applicability, as even a cursory acquaintance with the measurement literature will show" (p. 33). Williamson and Darley argued that using one test score to pigeonhole a person is not a student personnel program. Student personnel work also involves "breaking down habits that prevent the use of existing aptitudes" (p. 35). When students demonstrated through persistent effort that they were capable of earning a college degree, it was the job of the counselor to make sure students had the opportunity to transfer.

From the 1930s until the present, the first step for GC students who are preparing to transfer has been taking courses in other UMN colleges. In the 1930s arrangements were made for students whose goals required that they take non-GC courses to do so. If a counselor thought this was appropriate, he or she contacted the administration of the college offering the course and arranged for the student to register. Students were allowed to transfer if they were in at least the 75th percentile or higher in class average on the GC comprehensive test (see Chapter 22 for a discussion of the course ranking system and comprehensive examinations). Eckert (1943) reported that despite the fact that preparing students for transfer was not a GC goal, a fourth of all GC students who entered between 1932 and 1940 transferred. Among those who transferred, Eckert reported that slightly less than half either had graduated or were still enrolled.

Transfer was studied again for GC cohorts in the 1950s (Finnberg, 1960). In the 1950s, students admitted to GC had aptitude test scores and high school ranks below the 40th percentile. The percentile rating on the GC comprehensive test required for transfer had moved down to 65%. Finnberg reported that 975 students, 855 males and 120 females, transferred between 1951 and 1956. She estimated the transfer rate to be about one-third of students who matriculated to GC. This transfer rate suggests that nearly all of the students who scored above the 65th percentile on the GC comprehensive chose to transfer. Of the 975 transferred students, 47% earned degrees. Students who transferred to the School of Business Administration were more likely to graduate (65%) than those who transferred to SLA (42%) or the Institute of Technology (14%). Finnberg's study found that precollege admissions test scores did not predict which students would successfully transfer. Performance in GC was a predictor of transfer, leading Finnberg to the following conclusion:

> In some students an awakening occurred apparently during their experience in the General College—obviously not in time to be reflected either in aptitude test scores or in high school performance, but after their enrolling in the college, where they seem to have found in themselves what President Morrill has called the "determination and capacity to succeed." (p. 98)

Besides offering students the opportunity to earn associate degrees, GC was serving as a secondary selection process for students who aimed for baccalaureate degrees but were initially rejected by the baccalaureate degree-granting colleges.

Even after GC added baccalaureate degree programs in the 1970s, part of the student body continued to transfer. In 1985, GC was asked by then President Kenneth Keller to change its mission to preparation for transfer (University of Minnesota, 2000). Keller mistakenly believed the preparation for transfer mission to be the original mission of the college. Senior GC faculty members at the time pointed out that preparation for transfer had never been the college's mission, but was a by-product of the college's willingness to do what was best for the individual student. The preparation for transfer mission was adopted by the Regents in 1986. It required a complete redesign of the curriculum (Wambach & Brothen, 2002) and of the student personnel functions.

The Legacy of the Minnesota Point of View

During the 1970s and 1980s new advising models replaced older counseling models at the UMN and many other universities. Counseling functions that were located in colleges were centralized. The colleges developed academic advising offices that focused on educational planning. In the process student personnel workers lost faculty status, and in many cases people who were not trained in student personnel methods were hired to advise students. As counseling became a centralized function, counseling professionals were no longer in a strong position to have a direct impact on the curriculum. The tasks of conducting research on students and evaluation of programs were assigned to institutional researchers who have no regular contact with students or faculty. Although these models are efficient, the student personnel models of the 1930s brought different sources of information about students together in a synergy that is difficult to achieve now when faculty, counselors, and researchers have nonoverlapping roles.

The Minnesota Point of View called for colleges to use research on students to create curricula and services that meet students' needs. Research conducted by GC counselor researchers and faculty members provided some of the earliest studies of what we would now describe as underprepared students. Perhaps the most important findings of these studies were that some students who seemed unlikely to succeed in college could succeed, and that participation in college had positive effects on occupational attainment and economic success, even for developmental students who did not complete degrees. These studies and similar ones at other institutions provided justification for the expansion of educational opportunities that are available to students today. The research-based functional general education curriculum developed by GC faculty and staff provided a model for the curricula of the Minnesota community colleges that were founded in the 1960s.

There are also lessons in the history of the GC student personnel program for current developmental educators. We believe that the most important lesson is that curricula and services need to be constantly modified based on information about real students. We need to continually challenge our assumptions about students and the effectiveness of our programs by doing research. The practitioners who teach courses and advise students are in a better position to pose research questions and gather data than are institutional researchers isolated in administrative offices. Collaborations that bring the research design, data management, and statistical expertise of institutional researchers together with the student contact experience of faculty and staff should be encouraged if we are to conduct research that can be used to guide practice. We believe that making resources available for these collaborations has the potential to improve the educational outcomes of students, and should be a priority for college administrators. As we go forward we should continue to ask: What are our students like? How are we doing? How can we improve? Challenging assumptions with data is the ultimate legacy of the Minnesota Point of View. As Williamson stated in 1947, "It has long been the fundamental strength of Minnesota to try out new ideas and techniques, regardless of the source" and to test their validity by asking "what results does it produce and under what conditions?" (p. 144).

References

Coffman, L. D. (1934). *The state university: Its work and problems*. Minneapolis, MN: University of Minnesota Press.

Cowley, W. H. (1932). Who produces student personnel literature? *School & Society, 35*, 638–640.

Dvorak, B. J. (1947). The new U.S.E.S. General Aptitude Test Battery. *Occupations, 26*, 42–44.

Eckert, R. E. (1943). *Outcomes of general education: An appraisal of the General College program*. Minneapolis, MN: University of Minnesota Press.

Embree, R. B., Jr. (1940). Counseling: A service to the General College. In M. S. MacLean, J. W. Thornton, & I. Spafford (Eds.), *Curriculum making in the General College: A report on problems and progress of the General College* (pp. 46–57). Minneapolis, MN: University of Minnesota, General College.

Finnberg, F. F. (1960). *Those who transfer: A study of the achievement of General College students who transferred to other colleges of the University of Minnesota*. Minneapolis, MN: University of Minnesota, General College.

General College. (1938). *Report on problems and progress of the General College University of Minnesota*. Minneapolis, MN: Author.

General College Bulletin. (1939). Minneapolis, MN: University of Minnesota.

General College Bulletin Supplement. (1943). Minneapolis, MN: University of Minnesota.

Gray, J. (1951). *The University of Minnesota: 1851–1951*. Minneapolis, MN: University of Minnesota Press.

Gray, J. (1958). *Open wide the door: The history of the University of Minnesota*. New York: G. P. Putnam's Sons.

Hathaway, S. R., & McKinley, J. C. A. (1942). A multiphasic personality schedule (Minnesota): III. The measurement of symptomatic depression. *Journal of Psychology, 14*, 73–84.

Higbee, J. L. (2001). The student personnel point of view. In D. B. Lundell & J. L. Higbee (Eds.), *Theoretical perspectives for developmental education* (pp. 27–35). Minneapolis, MN: The Center for Research on Developmental Education and Urban Literacy, General College, University of Minnesota.

Johnston, J. B. (1930). *Who should go to college?* Minneapolis, MN: University of Minnesota Press.

Johnston, J. B., & Williamson, E. G. (1934). A follow-up study of early scholastic predictions in the University of Minnesota. *School & Society, 40*, 730–738.

Keller, R. J., Lokken, H. M., & Meyer, R. F. (1958). *The junior college in Minnesota.* St. Paul, MN: Minnesota State Department of Education.

Keyes, M. (n.d.). *A synopsis of our history.* Retrieved April 20, 2004, from http://www.psych.umn.edu/courses/about/index.htm

Kingsley, G. (1968–1969). The General College five-to-ten-year follow-up study. *The General College Studies, 5*(2), 1–20. Minneapolis MN: General College Archives, University of Minnesota.

Koch, G. A. (1980). The general education movement in American higher education: An account and appraisal of its principles and practices and their relation to democratic thought in modern American society. (Doctoral dissertation, University of Minnesota, 1980). *Dissertation Abstracts International A, 40*(11), 5749.

Lloyd-Jones, E. M. (1929). *Student personnel work at Northwestern University.* Oxford, UK: Harper.

MacLean, M. S. (1936). *Report of progress: General College, University of Minnesota.* Minneapolis, MN: General College Archives, University of Minnesota.

MacLean, M. S. (1938). *Report on problems and progress of the General College, University of Minnesota.* Minneapolis, MN: General College Archives, University of Minnesota.

MacLean, M. S. (1949). Adolescent needs and building the curriculum. In E. G. Williamson (Ed.), *Trends in student personnel work* (pp. 27–39). Minneapolis, MN: University of Minnesota Press.

MacLean, M. S., Williams, C. T., & Darley, J. G. (1937). Personnel work and guidance in the General College, University of Minnesota. *Education, 57*, 588–594.

Magoon, T. (1950). *Attitudes of General College students toward related aspects of their college and college life.* Unpublished master's thesis, University of Minnesota, Minneapolis.

Morse, H. T. (1949). *Letter to Mrs. Alvin S. Wyatt.* Minneapolis, MN: University of Minnesota Archives.

National Association of Student Personnel Administrators. (2004). *Past presidents of NASPA.* Retrieved September 24, 2004, from http://www.naspa.org/about/index.cfm?show=3

Pace, C. R. (1941). *They went to college: A study of 951 former university students*. Minneapolis, MN: University of Minnesota Press.

Patterson, C. H. (1966). *Theories of counseling and psychotherapy*. New York: Harper & Row.

Rogers, C. R. (1948). Some implications of client-centered counseling for college personnel work. *Educational & Psychological Measurement, 8*, 540–549.

Spafford, I. (1943). *Building a curriculum for general education: A description of the General College curriculum*. Minneapolis, MN: University of Minnesota Press.

Strong, E. K., Jr. (1943). *Vocational interests of men and women*. Stanford CA: Stanford University Press.

University of Minnesota. (2000). *University of Minnesota sesquicentennial history*. Minneapolis, MN: University of Minnesota. Retrieved September 20, 2004, from http://www1.umn.edu/sesqui/history/features/recent/

Wambach, C., & Brothen, T. (2002). The GC base curriculum: Description, historical antecedents, theoretical structure and evaluation outcomes. In D. B. Lundell & J. L. Higbee (Eds.), *Histories of developmental education* (pp. 73–81). Minneapolis, MN: Center for Research on Developmental Education and Urban Literacy, General College, University of Minnesota.

Wambach, C., Hatfield, J., & Mirabella, M. (2001). *A survey of former GC students*. Minneapolis, MN: General College, University of Minnesota.

Williams, C. T. (1940). Implications for the General College of the known characteristics of students and their parents as revealed in the adolescent study. In M. S. MacLean, J. W. Thornton, & I. Spafford (Eds.), *A report of the problems and progress of the General College University of Minnesota*. Minneapolis, MN: University of Minnesota. General College Archives.

Williams, C. T. (1943). *These we teach: A study of General College students*. Minneapolis MN, University of Minnesota Press.

Williamson, E. G. (1935). Faculty counseling at Minnesota: An evaluation study by social-casework methods. *Occupations, 14*, 426–433.

Williamson, E. G. (1937a). A college class in occupational information. *The School Review, 45*(2), 123–129.

Williamson, E. G. (1937b). To avoid a waste. *The Journal of Higher Education, 8*(1), 64–70.

Williamson, E. G. (1947). Counseling and the Minnesota point of view. *Educational and Psychological Measurement, 7*(1), 141–155.

Williamson, E. G., & Darley, J. G. (1937). *Student personnel work: An outline of clinical procedures*. New York: McGraw-Hill.

CHAPTER 5

Fulfilling the University's Promise: The Social Mission of Developmental Education

Katy Gray Brown

ABSTRACT

In this chapter I consider the foundation and development of the General College within the broader context of educational reform and expanding societal needs. Since 1932 the General College has created a "community space" essential to the work of the University of Minnesota. The General College's commitment to developmental education is particularly important to the mission of a land-grant institution. Drawing upon an analogy with multicultural education, I argue that the evolution of postsecondary education in this country makes access programs such as the General College vital to the social mission of institutions committed to serving diverse communities.

W hether or not it was articulated in the language of the "American Dream," I heard the message in innumerable ways: education is the great equalizer. My family history reflects the changes of the last century. My grandparents, like most people who lived where the Ozarks tumble slowly into the plains of Oklahoma and Kansas, finished their formal schooling somewhere around the eighth grade. They carved out livelihoods and raised children in a society increasingly separated along class lines. My parents considered themselves fortunate to be able to attend college, recognizing the doors that were opened by obtaining a degree. From the small, rural community in which I was raised, advancing my education meant first and foremost one thing: a way out. We began absorbing the implications of this message as early as we were divided into separate reading groups in grade school. We eyed each other, wondering how we measured up, and staked our hopes on the myth of meritocracy.

This is not an uncommon story. For generations, education has embodied the promise of both increased personal freedom and financial security. We were told that with a college degree, job opportunities would lead to comfortable salaries, or at least more satisfying work. By attending college and doing well academically, we simply would have more and better choices.

83

Higher education holds out this same promise today, even as changing social and economic contexts have raised the stakes for those who do not obtain a postsecondary degree. Dual forces of rising tuition and increasing admission standards work to diminish educational opportunities for two groups who yearn most for this particular American Dream: people who are working class or poor, and those who are academically unprepared for post-secondary study. In these pages, I will consider one movement to address this latter exclusion, as manifested in the developmental education program at the General College of the University of Minnesota. I will offer a brief overview of the historical context into which General College was born, emphasizing in particular the social mission of land-grant institutions. This will lay the groundwork for my understanding of General College as "community space" at the University of Minnesota. Drawing upon an analogy with multicultural education, I will argue that the evolution of postsecondary education in this country makes access programs such as the General College vital to the social mission of institutions committed to serving diverse communities.

Social Mission of Higher Education

The notion that colleges and universities should address the needs of the citizenry can be traced back to the Morrill Act of 1862, establishing "land-grant" schools and expanding African American educational institutions. Until then, higher education was regarded as the domain of the privileged. Schools were generally affiliated with religious organizations, and designed to train clergy and produce a professional class. The vision of the land-grant university reflected the aspirations of a relatively new nation for a meritocracy: a "new class of public universities" (Calhoun, 1999, p. 10) that would enable social mobility independent of one's origin. Designed to allow working class people access to education that would be meaningful to practical lives, land-grant institutions were to include programs devoted to military training and agricultural studies in addition to courses in classical education. Extension offices would provide students with venues to apply their academic studies while providing important services to communities outside the university. Thus, the social mission of the land-grant schools became clear: "... [a] democratic mandate for openness, accessibility, and service to people" (National Association of State Universities and Land Grant Colleges [NASULGC], 2004). For the first time, educational institutions would be uniquely accountable to the citizens of the state.

The educational expansion of land-grant institutions occurred just as the prevalent educational model was changing. After the U.S. Civil War, a new emphasis on technology and science emerged. In the 1870s, schools began to adopt a German model of education, with a tiered system of increasing specialization (i.e., bachelor's, master's, and Ph.D. degrees). The spread of this system spurred a move away from the general study of a so-called "classical" education (Calhoun, 1999).

The specialized nature of postsecondary education served some students well. Other students were disadvantaged by this system. The General College was developed in response to a "mismatch" between students desiring a college education and institutional emphasis on early specialization. In the 1920s and early 1930s, social and economic conditions led to unprecedented enrollment at schools such as the University of Minnesota. People who in other times might have pursued a career that did not require a college degree turned to postsecondary education when employment opportunities were scarce. In the throes of an economic depression, when job prospects were bleak, people invested their hopes and resources in the promise of a college degree (MacLean, 1962). Although the influx of students was welcomed, colleges and universities failed to recognize any need to adapt to the changing character of their students. In fact, during this time period, curricula became if anything more specialized. Increasingly, students were required to enter a specific "track" determining their educational path soon after entering college. This practice posed little difficulty for those students who had flourished in high school and came to college mentally and academically prepared for professional training. But nontraditional students struggled, and in astounding numbers they left college before obtaining a degree. At the University of Minnesota, Malcolm Shaw MacLean (1962) noted that students

> of a widening range of abilities and interest clamored for admission, were admitted and early ran head on into the rigid, traditional standards of academia which sooner or later bucked more than half of them back out into a cold and jobless world. (p. 2)

Self-interest alone would motivate a school to address an attrition rate of nearly 50%, but as a land-grant institution, the University of Minnesota was compelled by a mission to serve its communities. The General College, founded in 1932, was created to address these needs. In contrast to the specialized study of the greater university, General College offered a curriculum of general education courses. This provided a safety net of sorts for those students who would not complete a degree. General College advocates argued that if students left the university after a year of general education courses, they would be better served than had they spent their time immersed in the initial phase of a more specialized study (MacLean, 1962).

In addition, the decision to base the curriculum on general education courses carved out General College's position as a point of access for nontraditional students, or students from communities traditionally underrepresented in institutions of higher education. In the 1930s this group was comprised of military veterans and students from working class and rural families. Such students rarely had expected to continue their studies past high school, and plunging into a specialized field of study upon their university enrollment would do little to improve the likelihood of their academic success. The instructors at General College coupled broad, classical education courses with experimental pedagogies designed to address the economic and social realities of the students who came through General College's doors (MacLean, 1962; Wambach & Brothen, 2002). MacLean wrote, "We assumed that we could not really know what, how or when to teach until we know both whom we were teaching and the emerging world in which they were being taught" (p. 7).

This responsiveness to the needs of students has continued to shape General College's curriculum and support services, as the other chapters in this book clearly attest. Throughout the 1960s and 1970s, the General College focused significant attention on the recruitment and retention of students from communities of color. The Commanding English Program established support services for students for whom English was a second or third language. Such initiatives furthered General College's position as a point of access—a place where nontraditional students might find opportunity within the university.

General College's move in the late 1980s and 1990s to its focus on developmental education continued a commitment to making the University of Minnesota more accessible to students from Minnesota's diverse communities. Drawing upon the research of developmental psychology, developmental educators seek to combine alternative pedagogies with creative syllabi to accommodate a broad range of learning styles (National Association for Developmental Education, 1995). By incorporating a variety of teaching tools such as learning communities, Supplemental Instruction, cooperative learning, and interdisciplinary analysis, developmental educators seek to create a positive and successful learning experience for students who fail to flourish in traditional academic settings. Developmental education, as exemplified by the General College, offers a variety of ways that students can realize themselves as successful learners.

By admitting students who, for a variety of reasons, fail to meet traditional admission standards, General College has opened educational doors for those who otherwise would have been denied entry to the University of Minnesota. Again, General College provides a point of access to higher education. However, contemporary social and economic contexts have increased the importance of educational opportunity. Calhoun (1999) commented on the changing demographics of today's university students, noting that

> they are not in any similar aggregate sense an elite. Neither is a college degree training them for membership in an elite. A college degree is increasingly *standard*–at least for the middle class–rather than a mark of distinction . . . (p. 13)

The stakes have been raised. Positions that previously required only a high school degree now demand postsecondary work. Employers view a college degree as evidence of general competency and self-discipline, aside from any specific technical training a job may require. With minimum pay rates at poverty-line levels, obtaining a college degree is increasingly necessary for any kind of financial security.

These are the societal conditions that lead to a discussion of the social mission of the university and how access programs grounded in developmental education may fulfill this mission. That land-grant institutions are based upon a social mission is clear, if these schools acknowledge their obligation to serve the needs of their communities, as intended by the Morrill Act (NASULGC, 2004; University of Minnesota Board of Regents Policy, 1994). However, as the "community" served by the University of Minnesota has become increasingly diverse, and as the call for higher education has increased, the university has had to evolve to meet the demands of its mission.

General College contributes uniquely to fulfilling the social mission of higher education. The structural function of the college is to provide access for underprepared students: the students admitted to General College fail to meet the entrance criteria for other colleges at the university. However, access alone would do little to ensure the success of such students. After all, these are students who have failed to flourish in traditional secondary-level classrooms. Most of these students require more than the mere opportunity to attend college. This is why the pedagogical approach of developmental education, designed to engage a broad spectrum of learners, becomes a fundamental aspect of the social mission of the University. By combining an access program with a developmental pedagogy, General College has created a distinctive community space at the University of Minnesota, an educational environment that is particularly responsive to the needs of a changing student demographic.

The frequent metaphor for academia is a tower, isolating its inhabitants from the concerns and common sense of ordinary folk. Seldom explicit but nonetheless implied by the metaphor is a moat: a barrier that separates institutions of higher education from the communities that surround them. We have an image of students going to college, leaving their communities behind them. However, there are points of access that allow for exchange in addition to entry, avenues where a more reciprocal relationship between institution and community is possible. I understand these points of access to be community space, in which the needs and resources of both institution and community may intersect.

General College has functioned as community space at the University of Minnesota in three interrelated ways. First, General College has provided access to higher education for traditionally-excluded communities. Whether it was the former farmers of the 1930s or Somali immigrants today, General College has brought a tremendous diversity to the greater university. Second, General College has served as a conduit for community access to university resources. As nontraditional students have found a place for themselves through General College, they have created positive connections between their communities and the University. Programs based at General College such as Upward Bound, Day Community, and Commanding English have taken university resources off campus and into the schools and neighborhoods of Minneapolis and St. Paul. Finally, General College has provided a guide for the University of Minnesota in fulfilling its social mission. As an institution of higher learning, the University seeks to create an environment that encourages individual academic success; as a land-grant institution, we must also be committed to the needs of the communities of Minnesota.

In debates about the future of the General College, the benefits to individual students are not questioned. Time and time again, success stories are shared that illustrate the crucial role that the General College has played in individual lives. General College graduates include a Pulitzer prize-nominated playwright, distinguished journalists, and a state attorney general. Norman Borlaug, Nobel Peace Prize winner in 1970 for his work in genetics, was granted admission to the University of Minnesota only through the access made available by General College (Collins, 2004). If the point were simply that developmental programs are needed to promote the advancement of underachieving students, one might argue that community and technical colleges should serve this role. After honing basic skills and acquiring the attitudes necessary for academic success, such students may then transfer to a school such as the University of Minnesota to complete their studies.

This argument is often used as a reason to drop any access program from the work of the University. Yet such critics overlook the importance of access to the fulfillment of the land-grant vision of community service. In addition, contributions made by General College's understanding of developmental education are vital to the aims of the University as a whole. To make this point, I will draw a comparison with multicultural education.

Multicultural Education

Once, multicultural education—understood for my purposes here as incorporating noncanonical texts into the curriculum and fostering an appreciation of cultural diversity in students—was the exclusive domain of certain fields of study. A few classes within some departments required students to examine materials beyond the "classics" and reflect upon the roles of race, class, and gender. Confronted with demands that education meaningfully address our life experiences, academia has adapted its scope to reflect the diverse nature of our society (Banks, 1996, 1997). Over the past decades, the role of multicultural education has evolved to occupy a central position in many graduation requirements. Advocates have successfully argued that multicultural education is important for mainstream education for three principle reasons. First, multicultural education betters students as individuals. Upon graduation, students will go forth as citizens in a diverse society; they will benefit from an understanding of how difference—be it of class, race, gender, ability, or so on—is a factor in power dynamics in contemporary society. An appreciation of the history of such differences and language to interpret students' own social location with respect to difference become fundamental tools for living in a diverse society. For these reasons, universities see the importance of multicultural education (Banks, 1997).

A second manner of justifying multicultural education centers on improving the nature of our institutions, making them more responsive to their communities. If we think of the University of Minnesota as dedicated to the people of Minnesota, we must consider how "the people" have changed. Although never a homogenous group, those with rightful claim to the University of Minnesota are increasingly people of color. The university must respond to a social context that includes not only the sons and daughters of German and Scandinavian immigrants, but also Native Americans, African Americans, and recently arrived Latinos, Southeast Asians, and East Africans. If schools take their responsibility to address the educational concerns of community members seriously, multicultural education becomes a necessity for fulfilling this mission. Multicultural education betters the institutions themselves, fostering classrooms and curricula that provide meaningful and effective instruction to an increasingly diverse student body.

Third, multicultural education improves the quality of theoretical work generated by institutions of higher education. The inclusion of diverse perspectives, a principle at the heart of multicultural education, encourages a more thorough critique, expands the possibilities of illustrations and applications, and ultimately produces better academic research. Feminist theory has been at the forefront of this movement, providing solid theoretical critiques based not only on gender perspectives, but also broader analyses of power and oppression (Code, 1991; hooks, 1984).

Developmental Education and Access Programs

The justification for multicultural education rests upon its benefits to the individual student, the educational institution, and the research agenda of academia. Similarly, an argument can be made for an institutional commitment to developmental education. Individual students can benefit from courses that incorporate a wide range of pedagogical styles, rely upon a variety of assessment measures, and encourage cooperative learning rather than competitive models alone. Clearly, developmental education programs lay the groundwork for academic success for students who struggled mightily elsewhere. But the more radical influence of developmental education programs is found in their effect upon the broader institution. Developmental education approaches demand creative flexibility in pedagogy, curriculum design, and assessment measures. The fruits of this work benefit not only students ill-served by traditional classrooms, but all students who cross through our classroom doors. Finally, the research generated by developmental educators contributes importantly to practices across many types of institutions. Knowledge gained from developmental education classrooms has powerful applications to improve access for people of various learning styles and abilities. As access increases and more diverse perspectives engage with theoretical work, the better our theoretical work will become.

The promise of education, seen so clearly in the aspirations of the Morrill Act (1862) founding the land-grant universities, requires us constantly to return to questions of access. Like historic movements to expand opportunities for women and people of color, developmental education programs strive to create institutions that are accessible and responsive to diverse needs (NADE, 1995). I am reminded of my childhood impressions of higher education: the naïve conception instilled by public school teachers that if we applied ourselves to our studies, any of us could attend college and attain the success promised by a postsecondary degree. Of course, as we approached the age of SAT exams and college admission forms, more and more of my classmates ran into realities that made continuing their education impossible. College simply was not accessible to everyone who tried hard. Access programs that incorporate the principles of developmental education are a step toward diminishing these disparities. As opposed to the mythical American dream of educational opportunity, access programs provide not a "way out," extracting selected individuals, but rather a "way forward": a means for the university to contribute to the well-being of our broader communities.

My grandparents would be astounded by today's colleges and universities. Higher education is no longer the exclusive realm of the elite, as the rise of credentialism necessitates a college degree for more careers than ever. An increasingly diverse society has led to an expansion of the curriculum to include elements of multicultural education, internationalism, and interdisciplinary study. With these curricular changes, pedagogy must adapt as well if we are to maintain the tradition of education as a mechanism for social transformation. The dreams of generations for financial security and work of their choosing depend upon preserving educational opportunities. The dual aspects of access and developmental education situate General College uniquely for the University's charge as a land-grant institution: to offer a way forward for the peoples of Minnesota.

References

Banks, J. A. (Ed.). (1996). *Multicultural education, transformative knowledge, and action.* New York: Teachers College Press.

Banks, J. A. (1997). *Educating citizens in a multicultural society.* New York: Teachers College Press.

Calhoun, C. (1999). The changing character of college: Institutional transformation in American higher education. In B. A. Pescosolido & R. Aminzade (Eds.), *The social worlds of higher education* (pp. xxxvii–xli). Thousand Oaks, CA: Pine Forge Press.

Code, L. (1991). *What can she know? Feminist theory and the construction of knowledge.* Ithaca, NY: Cornell University Press.

Collins, T. (2002). *Foreword.* In D. B. Lundell & J. L. Higbee (Eds.), *Histories of developmental education* (p. v). Minneapolis, MN: Center for Research on Developmental Education and Urban Literacy, General College, University of Minnesota.

hooks, b. (1984). *Feminist theory from margin to center.* Boston: South End Press.

MacLean, M. S. (1962). The exciting early years of the General College. *The General College Newsletter, 9* (3), 1–17.

Morrill Land Grant Act of 1862. (1862). Retrieved January 11, 2005, from http://www.pvamu.edu/gridold/gen_info/morrill.html

National Association for Developmental Education. (1995). *Definition and goals statement.* Carol Stream, IL: Author.

National Association of State Universities and Land-Grant Colleges. (n.d.). *The history of land-grant institutions.* Retrieved July 8, 2004, from http://www.nasulgc.org/publications/Land_Grant/land.htm

University of Minnesota Board of Regents Policy. (1994). *Mission statement.* Retrieved October 1, 2004, from http://www1.umn.edu/regents/policies/boardoperations/Mission_Statement.html

Wambach, C., & Brothen, T. (2002). The General College base curriculum: Description, historical antecedents, theoretical structure, and evaluation outcomes. In D. B. Lundell & J. L. Higbee (Eds.), *Histories of developmental education* (pp. 73–82). Minneapolis, MN: Center for Research on Developmental Education and Urban Literacy, General College, University of Minnesota.

CHAPTER 6

The Politics of Transformation: Developmental Education in a Postsecondary Research Institution

David V. Taylor

ABSTRACT

The extant curriculum of the University of Minnesota's General College was forged out of a political compromise. What has become known as the General College Model for Developmental Education was conceived under an expressed mandate to restrict enrollment, to recruit better academically prepared students, and to retain a greater percentage of the students through graduation. This required a reconceptualization of the college's mission, its philosophy concerning teaching and learning, the role of academic support programs, and the delivery of student support services. Equally important was the redirecting of the creative energy of the faculty from an exclusive focus on teaching to research that supported innovation in teaching and learning. Developmental education became a disciplinary focus. What follows is an interpretive account of that transformation which took place between 1985 and 2001.

During the economic recession of the mid-1980s the State of Minnesota experienced difficulty in sustaining level funding for public postsecondary institutions. Although support for the University of Minnesota remained a high priority, the governor and members of the legislature noted that requests for increased funding were never matched by intentional consideration of program elimination. Their perception was that the University was continuing to increase in size and complexity without a thoughtful reassessment of its core mission.

The entire state budget for higher education, including the newly developed community college system, was becoming costly. It was reasoned that a portion of the state's budget could be reduced significantly if program redundancies between the University of Minnesota and the Minnesota State College and University systems were eliminated. Then Governor Rudy Perpich appointed a commission to explore differentiating the two systems with the intent of identifying and eliminating redundant programs, thus containing escalating costs (Sheldon, 2004).

Commitment to Focus

In 1984, when the commission failed to deliver meaningful recommendations, Governor Perpich took his concerns directly to the University Board of Regents. He requested that they undertake the task of differentiating their mission from the community college system and other institutions of higher education in the state. Of specific concern to the governor and some state legislators was the University's offering of associate in arts degrees, many of which were conferred by the General College, the College of Biological Sciences, and the College of Liberal Arts. These degrees were also offered by area community colleges. If the University would clarify its mission, eliminate programmatic redundancies, and agree to internally reallocate funds, the governor promised the possibility of enhanced state support (Sheldon, 2004). Within the span of a few weeks, in November of 1984, then Vice President Kenneth Keller (1985) created a document that would become the basis for *A Commitment to Focus*, the strategic plan that boldly attempted to reorganize the University. In January of 1985 Kenneth Keller became Interim President of the University. According to Keller,

> [T]he University . . . should pursue the realistic goal of being among the top five public institutions of higher education in the country. To achieve that goal, it must maintain the quality of its best programs and improve the quality of those programs which most directly serve to enhance its role as a university. (Keller, 1985)

He proposed that the University improve financial support for graduate students in an effort to increase their numbers and to improve quality, recruit high-ability undergraduate students, and improve the quality of undergraduate programs. More important, he proposed that the University redirect the efforts of its faculty away from programmatic activities that were not central to its mission and commit the faculty to priorities that preserve and enhance quality. With respect to assessing the quality of academic programs, he employed five principles for program continuance: "quality of the program, centrality to the University's core mission, comparative advantage, program demand, and efficiency and effectiveness" (Advisory Task Force on Planning, 1987, p. 2).

Keller's plan, now identified as *A Commitment to Focus: Academic Priorities*, was submitted to the Board of Regents in 1985. In the fall of 1986, each academic unit was required to conduct an assessment of its programs consistent with President Keller's vision of propelling the University of Minnesota into the ranks of the top five research institutions. To assist the provost in reviewing academic unit plans, an Advisory Task Force on Planning was created, better known as the "Campbell Committee." The charge to the task force was "to provide recommendations for campus-wide priorities; recommendations may include reorganization of the priorities within colleges and service units, as well as the setting of relative priorities across units" (Advisory Task Force on Planning, 1987, p. 2). It was noted in the charge that it was not possible to improve program quality at the University while sustaining existing programs at current levels. Something had to be reduced in scope or eliminated entirely.

Where Did the General College Fit?

The General College was an open-admission academic program for students who had not initially met the University's preparation standards. Established in 1932, the college admitted traditional and nontraditional (i.e., returning adult and part-time) students. These students required intensive academic support services. As documented in previous chapters of this book, during the early years of its founding, the college pioneered what was to become a nationally known general education curriculum, leading to an associate in arts degree, and was also a national leader in the emerging field of student development. During its evolution the college developed two baccalaureate degree programs, an associate degree, and certificate programs. The projected enrollment for fall quarter 1986 was 2,988 students (The General College, 1987, p. 3).

On March 31, 1987, the General College submitted its planning report, *Strategy for Focus*. The report represented a radical departure from the college's past by offering to eliminate its degree programs, to reduce enrollment, to admit and transfer students to other degree-granting colleges of the University, to conduct research on effective pedagogies for enhancing the teaching and learning of postsecondary students, and to revitalize its curriculum and students services program (The General College, 1987). The termination of baccalaureate degree programs and the phasing out of associate in arts degrees was recommended in a resolution drafted by President Keller and sent by way of a memorandum to the Board of Regents on January 2, 1986.

In spite of the General College plan to redefine and revitalize itself, the Campbell Committee recommended in June of 1987 that the General College be eliminated and integrated into the College of Liberal Arts as a reorganized preparatory program. Its faculty would be transferred into the academic units of their disciplinary training. The college's budget would be transferred to the new preparatory program of a reorganized College of Liberal Arts, called the Academy of Literature, Sciences, and Arts (Advisory Task Force on Planning, 1987).

Reaction to the Plan for Focus

The report of the Campbell Committee, *A Plan for Focus*, was received with anger and disbelief by supporters of the General College. In addition to the General College, the School of Veterinary Medicine, the Department of Mortuary Science, the Dental School, programs in vocational and technical education, and the University Art Museum were recommended for elimination. Other academic programs were recommended to be enhanced or reduced in scope. With the exception of the General College, which increased tuition revenue for the University, the programs cited for elimination were small with declining enrollments. Those programs could not be enhanced without considerable resources. The money saved by closure could be redirected to more competitive programs.

In the case of the General College, detractors pointed to the open-admission policy that allowed for a significant portion of the incoming freshman class to be represented by "underprepared students." The college employed 42 tenured faculty, 12 tenure-track faculty, 28 academic professional personnel, and 70 graduate teaching assistants and civil service employees serving 2,705 students with an all-sources budget of $5.16 million (Advisory Task Force on Planning, 1987).

Although the General College baccalaureate degree programs were considered rigorous, they were viewed as competing with more established programs in other academic units. The associate in arts and certificate programs offered were similarly viewed as competing with less expensive programs offered by area community colleges. General College faculty, hired primarily for their teaching competency, were not research oriented and not as successful in securing sponsored research funding as their peers in other academic units. More important, the freshman-to-sophomore retention rates were low, and 4-year graduation rates for General College students lagged seriously behind those of other degree-granting units. The most outspoken critics reasoned that fewer state resources should be allocated for "remedial" education and suggested that underprepared students might be better accommodated in community colleges, and not the state's flagship institution. It was clear that to survive, the college and its relationship to the University would have to be reconceptualized.

Plan for Focus was not well received and was roundly criticized by constituent groups and ardent supporters of programs identified for elimination. The supporters of the General College were vociferous and organized. The administration relented under pressure, and the college was given a reprieve. It could be argued that it was not the intent of President Keller to close or eliminate the General College. However, to placate the governor and legislators, significant concessions had to be made. They were demanding that tough decisions be made in the interest of accountability.

It was eventually negotiated that the unit would retain college status without degree-granting authority. All bachelor's degrees, 2-year associate degrees, and certificate programs would be eliminated. The entering freshman class and overall enrollment would be significantly reduced. The outline for restructuring the General College as presented in the college's *Strategy for Focus* (The General College, 1987) was accepted, and the college retained its allocated resources long enough to accomplish changes in its mission (The General College). It was tacitly understood by those who were politically knowledgeable, but not verbally stated, that failure to meet the stipulated terms would result in another, more vigorous attempt to close the college.

The General College Model Takes Shape

The genesis of the General College model for developmental education came out of the General College's plan for reorganization called *Strategy for Focus* (1987). The new mission statement defined three broad areas for institutional focus: (a) to admit underprepared students and support their transfer to baccalaureate degree-granting programs at the University; (b) to conduct research on effective pedagogies for teaching and learning with this population; and (c) to provide a laboratory for training undergraduate, graduate, and postgraduate students in the delivery of instructional and student services for underprepared students (Advisory Task Force on Planning, 1987; The General College, 1987).

The college's plan for transformation would require 5 years, under which five goals were articulated. The first goal was a reorganization of the administrative and operational structure of the college to accommodate new mission imperatives (i.e., the new curriculum). The second goal involved establishing new admissions criteria, revising the curriculum and academic and student services support programs, and developing a system for transferring students to other academic units. The third goal required establishing a culture of research and evaluation. Areas of emphasis included institutional research and evaluation; research related to effective strategies for teaching, learning, and advising; and discipline-based scholarship. The fourth goal articulated the need for sustained faculty and staff professional development opportunities, including a comprehensive review of compensation, workload, leaves, and performance review standards. The last goal outlined an orderly transition from the former degree-granting status. No new students would be admitted to degree programs, and all programs would be phased out by summer session 1991 (The General College, 1987).

In spite of central administration's approval of plans to reconceptualize the college, many General College faculty and staff were not convinced of the administration's sincerity. The *Commitment to Focus* and *Strategy for Focus* processes had been demoralizing for both faculty and staff. The failure of the administration to engage college personnel in discussions about their future and the proposed changes alienated many. Expressing concern that this concession only bought time for a more concerted attack on the college and its programs and students, some faculty who were unwilling to change the course and direction of their professional development to accommodate the new mission opted to transfer their tenure home to other disciplinary departments. Others simply chose to retire. Many of the remaining faculty expressed skepticism about the new emphasis upon "developmental education," but reluctantly embraced new teaching strategies. Some academic counselors and civil service employees also bolted for higher ground. The net effect resulted in a reduction in staff and faculty, consistent with a planned reduction in student enrollment.

In an effort to reassure the General College's faculty, staff, students, friends, and alumni of the administration's support for the new mission, a national search was undertaken in 1988 for a new dean. My task as the new dean, when hired in February 1989, was to reenergize the faculty and reduce admissions while improving the quality of the applicant pool. More important, the college was under a specific mandate to improve retention and graduation rates for these academically at-risk students. Students were advised that the last degrees and certificates would be awarded in summer session 1991. The remaining core of faculty and staff were challenged by the dean to recommit themselves to the future of the college and engage in another planning process to implement the new mission statement and goals and to contemplate a possible administrative restructuring of the college.

A new strategic planning steering committee was established during spring quarter 1989. It worked over the summer months. Its task was to plan and organize a college retreat for the beginning of fall quarter 1989 that would engage the entire college in putting the new mission into operation. Almost simultaneously, the faculty was implementing a new and more structured curriculum based upon the most recent research and literature on effective pedagogies for enhancing learning (Curriculum Committee, 1990). Counselors were encouraged to explore new ways to deliver "intrusive" advising based upon emerging literature on student retention. Administrative and program support personnel were asked to identify new ways to provide services that were more cost effective to ostensibly free up and redirect financial resources to new initiatives. The retreat program was structured in such a way that it involved participants in small-group discussions by academic divisions and by employment categories. These groups were charged with creating a list of goals and outcomes that could be implemented over a 3-year period. We believed that any plan longer than 3 years without measurable outcomes would invite further scrutiny and possible intervention by the administration.

Changes to Curriculum and Advising in the General College
The most important outcome of the college-wide planning process in 1989 was the General College Curriculum Committee's recommendation for adoption of *A Guiding Document for Continuing the Revision and Development of the General College Curriculum*. An operational definition of curriculum was presented within a context that described the mission, philosophy, and goals of the college. The guiding document presented a structural model for the curriculum: four areas that comprised the curriculum (i.e., academic skills, content knowledge, multicultural perspectives, and academic acculturation) and four characteristics of courses that would be offered (general courses, base curriculum courses, transition curriculum courses, and skills courses.)

Central to the success of this model was the concept of the "base curriculum" first introduced in a document called *A Base Curriculum for Students Entering General College* approved by the General College Assembly in May 1988 (General College Assembly Meeting minutes, personal communication, May 9, 1988). The concept behind the base curriculum was an attempt to improve "the retention of students by developing a supportive but intensive learning environment during their first two quarters in the college" (Curriculum Committee, 1990, p. 13). This was accomplished by restricting course selection, implementing an intrusive advising system, and imbedding in each course academic skills development (e.g., reading, writing, oral communication, and computer literacy) as well as Supplemental Instruction with active learning and critical-thinking pedagogy.

A second set of courses, the transition curriculum, was intended to meet the needs of students engaged in the college beyond two quarters. These courses placed greater emphasis upon content objectives rather than skill building, and a higher degree of student autonomy was expected (Curriculum Committee, 1990). These two focal points of the new curriculum were designed to take students from the point of admission through to the point of transfer to a degree-granting college of the University. According to the curriculum planners,

> As students move through the curriculum they will go from an environment characterized by intensive, content-related skills development, a high level of institutional support and low student autonomy, to one characterized by more traditional coursework, lower institutional support and expectation of greater student autonomy. (Curriculum Committee, 1990, p. 14)

The proposed revision of the curriculum identified three other areas of probable concern. The first suggested that the General College recruit students who were better prepared to meet the rigors of the new curriculum. Second, the curriculum should be formally reviewed every 5 years, and third, an assessment of student learning outcomes should be undertaken periodically (Curriculum Committee, 1990).

Administrative Restructuring
With the last elements of the revised curriculum in place, I was able to report in a presentation to the Board of Regents in January 1991 that the college had achieved all of its goals articulated in the *Strategy for Focus* document. However, implementing the new curriculum proved to be a challenge. Between 1991 and 1993 the college was projected to lose approximately $1 million in recurring allocations. It became apparent that a reallocation within the college budget was necessary if planning objectives were to be realized. Although not identified as a planning goal under *Strategy for Focus,* a reorganization of the college's administration was necessary for two reasons: the organizational structure needed to be brought into line with the new curriculum, and the old structure appeared to be antithetical to achieving new mission-related student outcomes. A new administrative plan was proposed in April 1992 and completed by September of that year. During the academic years 1992–1993 and 1993–1994, the General College continued to refine goals and objectives consistent with student outcomes anticipated by the changes in curriculum (F. Amram, personal communication, January 31, 1992). Preliminary studies conducted by the General College Office of Research and Evaluation detected perceptible and positive changes in retention rates.

University 2000

In January of 1989 Nils Hasselmo became the 11th President of the University of Minnesota. Two years into his administration he proposed another strategic planning process. In a manner consistent with *Commitment to Focus,* the previous planning initiative, the intent was to articulate a clear vision for the University and to redirect resource allocation based upon goals and priorities. In January 1993, a "Plan for Planning" was presented to the Regents, and 1 year later on January 14, 1994, the Regents gave their approval to 5 out of 18 critical measures and benchmarks for measuring institutional, campus, and unit performance. The plan became known as *University 2000* (University of Minnesota, 1993).

Critical Measures
The first five critical measures related to students: (a) Characteristics of Entering Students by Campus, (b) Graduation Rate by Campus, (c) Underrepresented Groups/Diversity, (d) Sponsored Funding by Campus, and (e) Investment per Student by Campus. The Board of Regents' resolution was very specific with respect to the first three critical measures. Under "Characteristics of Entering Students," 80% of the entering class by 2000 would be from the upper 25% of their graduating class, with a mean high school rank for entering freshmen at the 77th percentile. Students in the General College were exempted. With respect to "Graduation Rate," the institutional performance goal was for 50% of freshmen who matriculated at the University in 1996 to graduate in 5 years. The General College was not exempted. As the plan related to "Underrepresented Groups/Diversity," 33% of students of color in the 1996 cohort of freshman students would be expected to graduate in 5 years by 1996. The General College students were included. The Regents affirmed a plan that would raise the number of students of color in the incoming freshman class of 2000 to 16% of that class. The General College was not exempted (The Board of Regents, 1994). It was plain to see that without the General College, the University could not reach its diversity goal. It was also obvious that all academic units, including the General College, were being challenged to improve graduation rates.

It was not lost upon the leadership of the General College that the well-intended resolution of the Board of Regents was an explicit challenge to the concept of "developmental education" at a premier research institution. Conventional wisdom and data supported the fact that better academically prepared students persisted longer, generally had better grades, and graduated in larger numbers. In other words, it was assumed that better input yielded better output. In an effort to boost the University's ranking with regard to the caliber of students who attended, the weak link was students admitted to the General College, and students of color in particular. The stage was set for another confrontation over the General College mission within the context of a research university, under the guise of controlled access.

The General College's Response
On February 15, 1994, the General College submitted its response to the University 2000 Strategic Plan. In that plan it described itself as an academic unit whose instructional model was predicated upon proven teaching methods to enhance learning mastery (i.e., developmental education) and academic advising based upon principles articulated by Vincent Tinto (1993) and popularized by Lee Noel and Randi Levitz (1995; Noel, Levitz, & Saluri, 1985). The

document reminded administrators that approximately 25% of the University's students of color entered through the General College and that

> The General College is one of a few resources that the University has to address the growing disparity between this class of underprivileged citizens and an educational elite in Minnesota. It is one of the few colleges that has genuinely embraced multi-cultural education and cultural diversity as integral parts of its pedagogy. It is one of the few places on campus where a wider array of student services is available for disadvantaged students. (General College, 1994, pp. 1, 5)

The document offered a definition of developmental education as an "intervention strategy designed to increase the likelihood of retention and graduation of students defined to be at risk." (p. 1) The documented concluded by stating:

> For purposes of planning, it is assumed that for the foreseeable future the General College will remain a college within the University, with the responsibility of providing a "developmental education" experience for a student population yet to be defined. However, the size, shape, function, and outcome of the program are subject to negotiation and adaptation consistent with the vision and strategic direction that the University wishes to take . . . . The college remains open to discussion about implementation of alternative interventions and pedagogies if they are based upon accepted research models. (The General College, 1994, p. 9)

The remainder of the document responded to other University 2000 strategic directions.

The General College plan was well received by Vice President Anne H. Hopkins and President Hasselmo. In his private correspondence with Dr. Hopkins, President Hasselmo, initially a strong supporter of the General College, expressed concerns about appropriate access for disadvantaged students, the quality of the General College experience, issues surrounding student transfer into the College of Liberal Arts, and whether the College could meet Regents' expectations constrained by current resources and perhaps diminished resources in the future (D. V. Taylor, personal communication, May 5, 1994; A. H. Hopkins, personal communication, May 9, 1994; N. Hasselmo, personal communication, May 16, 1994).

Another Threat to the General College's Existence
One of the most visible changes occasioned by University 2000 was the reorganization of central administration in the fall of 1994. A provost system was adopted as a more efficient means to manage deans who formerly reported to a number of vice presidents. Former vice presidents were told that their con-

tracts were not being renewed, but they could compete for three provost positions. Vice President for Arts, Sciences, and Engineering, Anne Hopkins, chose not to compete and vacated her position. After a lengthy search W. Phillip Shively, a former chair of the Political Science Department, was appointed Provost for Arts, Sciences, and Engineering in April 1995. According to Tim Sheldon (2004), who interviewed Shively for his dissertation,

> Shively was active and visible on campus as well as at the State Capitol. A political scientist by discipline, Shively had served as lobbyist, department chair and committee member on the Campbell Committee—the committee that created the report, Plan for Focus. Shively, along with Ellen Berscheid, also co-chaired the committee that produced Commitment to Focus: Academic Priorities. He was a consummate University insider familiar with both Commitment to Focus and the politics of the University. (p. 149)

Early in his administration, Provost Shively had determined that the continued existence of the General College was antithetical to the success of University 2000 as expressed in the January 14, 1994, resolution of the Board of Regents. Although ostensibly praising the General College for the symbolic role that it played in fostering student diversity at the University and its success in reorganizing its curriculum under Commitment to Focus, the provost, with the approval of President Hasselmo, began to plan the college's demise almost immediately after assuming office. He and President Hasselmo were determined to achieve what former President Keller had failed to do—close the college.

The pretext for closure was the presentation of data suggesting that the cost of instruction in the General College (i.e., "remedial education") was prohibitively expensive, student retention and graduation rates were uncharacteristically low, and underprepared students were better served by the state community college system. Additionally he contended that students of color were not being well served, contrary to the perspective of the General College (Sheldon, 2004). Without proper consultation with the Board of Regents, the leadership of the General College, or internal and external constituencies of the University, the provost and president called a press conference on March 26, 1996, to announce their intention to seek approval from the Regents to phase out the General College by 1999.

In the 3 weeks that followed, the manner in which this decision was reached created great division among University faculty, staff, and students. It was the subject of newspaper editorials and TV news commentaries. The entire metropolitan Twin Cities area was divided over the proposal. Sensing a public relations debacle and not wishing to further jeopardize the image of the University, the Board of Regents on April 12, 1996, by a vote of 11 to 1, instructed the president not to pursue a plan to close the college (Board of Regents, 1996).

They requested that a study be engaged that reviewed the status of "at-risk" students at the University and that, on an annual basis for the foreseeable future, the General College submit to the Regents an update of its strategic plan and measurable outcomes (Sheldon, 2004). Within 15 months after the Regents' decision, the president retired, and the provost returned to the ranks of the faculty when the new president, Mark Yudof, was appointed. In a twist of irony, during his interview with the presidential search committee, candidate Yudof expressed his interest in the General College and stated that one of the enticements for seeking the position of president was the student diversity at the University of Minnesota and a nationally recognized program like the General College, a fact that he also alluded to in his inaugural speech.

A Turning Point

The struggle to maintain the college was an important turning point in its long history. The college's carefully crafted curriculum and academic support and advising programs were beginning to yield improved results. The data that the administration used to justify closure reflected problems with the old mission, not the new. At the close of the 20th century, all indicators of program impact upon students were markedly improving: freshman-to-sophomore retention, transfer rates, and persistence to graduation.

Increased national recognition for the General College program occurred in the year 2000, when the American Productivity and Quality Center (APQC) and the Continuous Quality Improvement Network (CQIN) presented the college with its award for Innovative Performance in the area of Best Practice in Developmental Education. A team of several persons spent two days on campus reviewing the college and its programs. In March 2001, the National Association for Developmental Education (NADE) presented the college with the John Champaign Memorial Award for the Outstanding Developmental Education Program. Dean David V. Taylor received from the National Academic Advising Association (NACADA) a Certificate of Recognition for Outstanding Leadership in May 2001. In July 2001 Noel-Levitz presented the college with its annual Retention Excellence Award.

The Current Challenge to the Future of the General College

During the summer of 2005 Robert Bruininks, the 14th President of the University of Minnesota, launched a "strategic positioning" initiative. The intent was to position the University of Minnesota as one of the three best public research institutions in the world. To accomplish this, a structural reorganization of the University to enhance institutional effectiveness and efficiency was deemed necessary. Two task forces composed of administrators and faculty were created—one to explore reorganization of administrative services and the other to reorganize academic units. The task forces met during fall semester of 2004 and delivered their reports to the President in April of 2005.

The Academic Task Force proposed 31 changes. The most contentious of the proposed changes was the transformation of the General College from a free-standing college to departmental status under a new College of Education and Human Development. The new Department of General Developmental Education would not admit students. Although praising the college for nationally recognized research in the discipline of developmental education, the administration resurrected past arguments concerning the effectiveness and efficiency of the college's academic program and added a new concern about General College students being segregated from the mainstream of campus life. As in the past, the General College's administrative team was never invited to discuss these concerns during the task force deliberations, and the dean was apprised of the recommendations just 24 hours before a scheduled press release to announce the release of the Strategic Positioning Proposal.

The debate that ensued went to the heart of long-standing and troubling issues for the University community—access or excellence, diversity or elitism. It has been the position of the General College that issues of access, excellence, and diversity are compatible within the framework of a world-class research institution. An excellent academic institution should be accessible to first-generation, low-income, underprepared students. Often these students come from families of underrepresented groups, people of color, immigrant groups, and students from rural school districts. However, underprepared students can also come from families with incomes exceeding $100,000 per year. These students have and continue to be successful at the University of Minnesota.

The University of Minnesota administration contended that in order to appear competitive in the *U.S. News and World Report* listing of top research institutions, the profile of the University's student body as measured by SAT and ACT scores of incoming classes needed a boost. The administration would require that students normally admitted through the General College would instead be denied admission and encouraged to attend community colleges first and transfer to the University later. Annually the General College has admitted 825 to 875 students of an incoming freshman class that exceeds 5,000.

On June 10, 2005, the Board of Regents voted on the administration's proposal to close the college and make it a department. The outcome reflected a significant change to the college's future, one that would take the college into its next phase and lead the college's students, faculty, and staff into another, more uncertain period of transition. Dean David Taylor, who led the college's fight to remain open, also announced his acceptance of a new position as Provost and Vice President of Academic Affairs at Morehouse College.

References

Advisory Task Force on Planning. (1987). *Plan for focus*. Minneapolis: University of Minnesota.

The Board of Regents, University of Minnesota. (1994). *University of Minnesota Board of Regents resolution related to the establishment of critical measures to assess institutional performance*. Minneapolis, MN: Author. Retrieved April 5, 2005, from http://www1.umn.edu/regents/minutes/1994/january/cow14.html

The Board of Regents, University of Minnesota. (1996). *Report of the committee as a whole*. Minneapolis, MN: Author. Retrieved April 5, 2005, from http://www1.umn.edu/regents /minutes/1996/april/board.html

Curriculum Committee, General College, University of Minnesota. (1990, May). *A guiding document for continuing the revision and development of the General College curriculum*. Minneapolis, MN: Author.

The General College, University of Minnesota. (1987). *The General College strategy for focus: Planning report*. Minneapolis, MN: Author.

The General College. (1994). *General College response to University 2000 Strategic Planning*. Minneapolis: University of Minnesota.

Keller, K. H. (1985). *A commitment to focus*. Minneapolis: University of Minnesota.

Noel, L., & Levitz, R. (1995). New strategies for difficult times. *Recruitment & Retention in Higher Education, 9*(7), 4–7.

Noel, L., & Levitz, R., & Saluri, D. (Eds.). (1985). *Increasing student retention: New challenges and potential*. San Francisco: Jossey-Bass.

Sheldon, T. D. (2004). *Forces and impacts of organizational change at General College, 1985–2003*. Unpublished doctoral dissertation, University of Minnesota.

Tinto, V. (1993). *Leaving college: Rethinking the causes and cures for student attrition* (2nd ed.). Chicago: University of Chicago Press.

University of Minnesota. (1993). *University of Minnesota strategic planning status report*. Minneapolis, MN: Author.

Promoting Multiculturalism

Promoting Multiculturalism
Introduction

As is depicted within these chapters, diversity is at the heart of the General College vision. In the first chapter of this section, Jeanne Higbee and Kwabena Siaka note that within GC we define diversity inclusively to include social identities related to race, ethnicity, religion, gender, sexual orientation, age, home language, and disability. Higbee and Siaka report on the next phase of the Multicultural Awareness Project for Institutional Transformation (MAP IT), a project originally undertaken by the GC Multicultural Concerns Committee to explore multicultural issues within the college.

The next chapter in this section by Barajas reminds us that developmental education and multicultural education are inextricably intertwined. By embedding multiculturalism in our daily practice we can create "spheres of freedom" to enable the success of all students. Barajas illustrates why students of color are likely to identify educational institutions as White spaces and urges us to "acknowledge that students have a sociological imagination that helps them negotiate the educational process" within these spaces.

In the next chapter, Laurene Christensen, Renata Fitzpatrick, Robin Murie, and Xu Zhang describe one of the General College's most successful programs, Commanding English (CE). They propose that collegiate English as a Second Language (ESL) programs designed for international students fulfill a separate mission but do not necessarily serve refugee and immigrant students well. They demonstrate how combining academics and language literacy instruction in credit-bearing content courses allows CE students to earn 25 to 30 credits toward graduation in their freshman year while developing the skills to transfer to other colleges of the University of Minnesota and graduate. With the increasing influx of immigrant populations to the Twin Cities, Commanding English plays a critical role in making the University of Minnesota accessible to students from a wide array of cultural backgrounds.

In both local and national conversations, when we discuss embedding multiculturalism in our courses we often hear comments like, "Well, I can see how that might fit in the social sciences and humanities, but not in math and science courses." In her chapter Susan Staats illustrates strategies for teaching mathematics in a multicultural context. She asserts, "By focusing on social issues associated with mathematics applications rather than simply contextual description, students are able to find points of contact between their own experiences and those of people whose lives seem very different from their own." Staats demonstrates that inclusion of multicultural content need not reduce the time available for mastering mathematical concepts and meanwhile enables students to display their "mathematical imagination."

This section concludes with a chapter by Pat Bruch and Tom Reynolds, who articulate how composition courses in the General College have moved beyond earlier standardized and process approaches to the teaching of writing to embrace a dialogical pedagogy. "Dialogical writing instruction encourages students to treat writing as an opportunity to shape people's understanding of writing at the same time that the conventions of academic writing shape them." They also discuss how the dialogue approach to both teaching and professional development fosters multicultural perspectives and challenges traditional assumptions of power and privilege.

CHAPTER 7

Students' Assessment of Their Multicultural Experiences in the General College: A Pilot Study

Jeanne L. Higbee and Kwabena Siaka

ABSTRACT

This chapter presents findings of a pilot study conducted during spring semester 2003 to explore student perceptions of their multicultural experiences within the General College (GC). The results of this research indicate that GC students understand the multicultural mission of the General College and believe that the college provides access for a diverse group of students. Students thought that GC provides a supportive learning environment that values diverse viewpoints and that GC administrators, faculty, and staff are invested in students' success. Students' perceptions of GC's student services were also very positive overall.

Enrolling a diverse student body and providing a multicultural learning experience are central to the mission of the General College (GC). For purposes of the research reported in this chapter, diversity is defined broadly to include the social group identities that shape and define our individual identities: race, ethnicity, culture, home language, religion, gender, sexual orientation, social class, age, and disability. Multiculturalism is defined for purposes of this project as how we respond to these diverse identities, both as individuals and as institutions: "If diversity is an empirical condition—the existence of multiple group identities in a society—multiculturalism names a particular posture towards this reality" (Miksch, Bruch, Higbee, Jehangir, & Lundell, 2003).

Development of the Multicultural Awareness Project for Institutional Transformation

Previous research (Bruch & Higbee, 2002) conducted in the General College indicated that further attention needed to be devoted to addressing multicultural issues both within GC and as related to the profession of developmental education and learning assistance as a whole. In Spring 2001 the General College Multicultural Concerns Committee (MCC) began to explore the possibility of adapting for higher education James Banks and colleagues' (Banks et al., 2001) *Diversity Within Unity: Essential Principles for Teaching and Learning in a Multicultural Society.* In addition to its 12 essential principles, *Diversity Within Unity* included an instrument to assess faculty and administrators' perceptions of educational climate in elementary through secondary (K-12) institutions. MCC formed a subcommittee, named the Multicultural Awareness Project for Institutional Transformation (MAP IT), to create a comparable assessment tool for use with postsecondary faculty and staff, and piloted that instrument in GC in February 2002 (Bruch, Jehangir, Lundell, Higbee, & Miksch, 2005; Higbee, Miksch, Jehangir, Lundell, Bruch, & Jiang, 2004; Miksch, Bruch, Higbee, Jehangir, & Lundell, 2003). In May 2002 the Center for Research on Developmental Education and Urban Literacy (CRDEUL) invited James Banks to GC as a visiting scholar (Bruch, Higbee, & Lundell, 2003, 2004). Banks reviewed the summary statistics from the MAP IT pilot study and praised the subcommittee on its endeavors, urging the group to proceed with its plans to develop a parallel instrument to assess student perspectives.

One of the criticisms of the original MAP IT instrument was that there were a number of items that did not apply to all faculty and staff members, resulting in too many responses of "don't know" or "not applicable." During the summer of 2002, MAP IT subcommittee members toiled at resolving this difficulty by developing three separate assessment tools for administrators, faculty and instructional staff, and professionals who provide student support services such as academic advising (Miksch, Higbee, et al., 2003). During this process, the committee also realized that it would be necessary to adapt *Diversity Within Unity's* essential principles to a higher education setting. The subcommittee's "10 Guiding Principles" have since been widely disseminated at professional meetings (e.g., Higbee & Pettman, 2003) and through a column in *Research and Teaching in Developmental Education* titled "The Multicultural Mission of Developmental Education: A Starting Point" (Higbee, Bruch, Jehangir, Lundell, & Miksch, 2003).

In fall 2002 Michael Dotson, Dean of Counseling and Advising for Minneapolis Community and Technical College (MCTC), collaborated with the MAP IT subcommittee in creating the fourth questionnaire to be used with students (Miksch, Higbee, et al., 2003). In winter 2003 plans began for administering the MAP IT Student Questionnaire both in GC as a pilot and at MCTC in Spring 2003. This chapter will present the results of the GC Student MAP IT pilot.

Theoretical Framework and Guiding Principles

This research is founded on a growing body of theoretical work that emphasizes the importance of providing a social context for learning (American College Personnel Association [ACPA] and National Association of Student Personnel Administrators [NASPA], 2004; Dewey, 1910/1991, 1916/1997, 1938/1997; Gee, 1996; Lundell & Collins, 1999), and particularly a multicultural context (Freire, 1968/1990; hooks, 1994). James Banks (1994, 1997) suggested the following dimensions of multicultural education to guide educators in creating welcoming spaces: (a) integration of multicultural content in the curriculum; (b) recognition of how knowledge is socially constructed; (c) reduction of prejudice through intentional acts; (d) provision of equity pedagogy; and (e) empowerment of students through empowering school cultures and social structures. These dimensions provide the foundation for both *Diversity Within Unity* and MAP IT.

Founded upon this theoretical framework, MAP IT offers 10 guiding principles for higher education, as follow:

Institutional Governance, Organization, and Equity

1. The educational institution should articulate a commitment to supporting access to higher education for a diverse group of students, thus providing the opportunity for all students to benefit from a multicultural learning environment.

2. The educational institution's organizational structure should ensure that decision making is shared appropriately and that members of the educational community learn to collaborate in creating a supportive environment for students, staff, and faculty.

Faculty and Staff Development

3. Professional development programs should be made available to help staff and faculty understand the ways in which social group identifications such as race, ethnicity, home language, religion, gender, sexual orientation, social class, age, and disability influence all individuals and institutions.

Student Development

4. Educational institutions should equally enable all students to learn and excel.

5. Educational institutions should help students understand how knowledge and personal experiences are shaped by contexts (social, political, economic, historical, etc.) in which we live and work, and how their voices and ways of knowing can shape the academy.

6. Educational institutions should help students acquire the social skills needed to interact effectively within a multicultural educational community.

7. Educational institutions should enable all students to participate in extracurricular and co-curricular activities to develop knowledge, skills, and attitudes that enhance academic participation and foster positive relationships within a multicultural educational community.

8. Educational institutions should provide support services that promote all students' intellectual and interpersonal development.

Intergroup Relations

9. Educational institutions should teach all members of the educational community about the ways that ideas like justice, equality, freedom, peace, compassion, and charity are valued by many cultures.

Assessment

10. Educational institutions should encourage educators to use multiple culturally sensitive techniques to assess student learning.

The questionnaire items for this research were categorized according to their relevance to these guiding principles.

Method

The questionnaire used for this pilot research was designed to assess how students evaluate multicultural aspects of their collegiate experience. When responding to the survey items, students were asked to think broadly and inclusively about such terms as "multicultural" and "diverse groups" (i.e., to include race, religion, gender, ethnicity, culture, home language, social class, sexual orientation, age, and disability). The Likert-type response scale provided options of 1 to 4 for which 1 was defined as "never or almost never," 2 indicated "occasionally," 3 signified "often," and 4 represented "almost always or always." In addition, students could select "not applicable" (NA) if they thought that the item did not apply to them, or "don't know" (DK) if they thought that they had inadequate information to choose another response. At the end of each set of items, students also had the opportunity to provide comments or clarify their answers.

Because this was a pilot of a new survey instrument, the questionnaire was longer than normally would have been desired. The pilot data would later be used to determine which items to retain in the final version of the MAP IT Student Questionnaire (Miksch, Higbee, et al., 2003). Items from the instrument are included in the presentation of the results.

The population for this pilot study was made up of all students enrolled in GC 1281: General Psychology during spring semester 2003. This course meets a general social science requirement throughout the university, and was selected because its enrolls a representative sample of all GC students; enrollment in GC 1281 generally mirrors the demographics of the General College as a whole. No demographic information was sought during this pilot study because of the small sample size; we were concerned that students might become identifiable based on their answers to a series of demographic questions about gender, race and ethnicity, home language, and disability.

The course is taught in a computer classroom. During the final 3 weeks of the semester, the instructors introduced the MAP IT project and asked students to log on to a Web site and complete the questionnaire. The Web site provided additional information about MAP IT as well as notification of implied consent, meaning that when the student submitted the completed questionnaire online, he or she was consenting to participation in this research. An incentive of two extra-credit points was provided to encourage students to respond to the questionnaire. Thus, students were required to provide their university ID number to receive credit. However, the ID numbers were stripped from the data file, so the researchers could not trace answers back to individual students. The response rate for this research can be calculated in two different ways. Out of the 241 students who enrolled in the course, 82 responded to the survey, for a response rate of 34%. However, 20 students withdrew from the course, and an additional 30 students "disappeared" without completing this self-paced, computer-assisted course. So for the 191 students who completed the course and would still have been participating in the course at the point in the semester when the opportunity to participate in this research was made available, the response rate was 43%.

Results

The results of the pilot study are presented as they relate to each of MAP IT's 10 guiding principles. We have not corrected spelling and grammatical errors in students' comments.

Commitment to Access

Excluding the data for the 12% of the respondents who either did not know (six students) or considered the item "not applicable" (four students), the mean for the first item, "As you understand the mission of the University of Minnesota General College (GC), does that mission make a commitment to access for diverse students?" was 3.45 ($Mdn = 4$, $SD = 0.672$, $n = 71$). Students also believed that GC "support[s] higher education for students from all cultural groups" ($M = 3.63$, $Mdn = 4$, $SD = 0.538$, $n = 76$), "attempt[s] to recruit and retain a diverse student body" ($M = 3.55$, $Mdn = 4$, $SD = 0.580$, $n = 71$), and "operate[s] in a manner that values a multicultural learning environment in which all students will learn" ($M = 3.42$, $Mdn = 4$, $SD = 0.676$, $n = 77$). One student wrote, "I think that professors are equally helpful towards students of all cultures." Another said, "I enjoy seeing a multicultural college, where lots of cultures are under one roof, all here to learn and be successful." But one student commented, "GC is very diverse and it has not come together yet. Everyone is scattered around [and] there is no unity."

During the admissions process, GC students for the most part felt welcomed ($M = 3.27$, $Mdn = 3$, $SD = 0.812$, $n = 79$). One student replied, "[F]rom the moment I got here I felt welcome and not once did I feel isolated or singled out as better or worse than my fellow classmates." GC students generally believed that they are valued members of the GC educational community ($M = 3.19$, $Mdn = 3$, $SD = 0.783$, $n = 75$) and thought that it is beneficial to be part of a multicultural learning environment ($M = 3.49$, $Mdn = 4$, $SD = 0.681$, $n = 77$). Sample student comments included:

"GC looks to achieve diversity, and it does so in a way that is beneficial to everyone."

"I love the diversity of this school. Gives me a better understanding of the real world life experience."

"I think GC is very diverse. I see a lot of things going on in the student lounge such as the salsa day, when everyone brought a different salsa from their culture."

"There is no place like GC to explore different cultures and enjoy it all."

Organizational Structures and Decision Making

The second set of items addresses students' roles in decision making. Although the means for these items were not as high as those for questions related to access, that was to be expected. When asked, "Are students involved in the decisions made at GC that affect the learning environment?" 43 of the 63 students (68%) who provided a response on the 4-point scale responded "often" or "almost always or always" ($M = 2.86$, $Mdn = 3$, $SD = 0.780$). Sixteen students replied "don't know." One student commented on the "very good diverse cultures in the student boards and groups." Although students thought that they had "the opportunity to participate in planning and/or decision making at GC" ($M = 2.94$, $Mdn = 3$, $SD = 0.906$, $n = 69$), they did not necessarily take advantage of that opportunity. The mode for the item that queried, "Through student organizations, campus-wide committees, or other participation in college life, do you personally play a role in decision making?" was 1 ($M = 2.24$, $Mdn = 2$, $SD = 1.125$, $n = 75$). Despite this lack of participation, students generally believed that "GC promote[s] cooperation between students, faculty, and staff" (M = 3.13, Mdn = 3, SD = 0.723, n = 75) and "operate[s] in a manner that values diverse views and experiences" (M = 3.33, Mdn = 3, SD = 0.729, n = 79), and that "the educational community of GC is a supportive environment" (M = 3.30, Mdn = 3, SD = 0.701, n = 80). They thought that "administrators, faculty, and staff (e.g., advisors) [were] invested in [their] success as a student" (M = 3.27, Mdn = 3, SD = 0.775, n = 81; the mode for this item was 4). The following student comments are representative of the views expressed:

"The advisors seem to be more close-knit with the GC student body than in other colleges [of the University of Minnesota]. The teachers are also more understanding if circumstantial occurrences come up."

"This is my first year at GC and I can definitely see that I am able to express my diverse views and be taken seriously by the professors and fellow students in my class. This is a very positive atmosphere."

Interactions With Faculty and Staff

The mean was 3.33 (SD = 0.689, n = 80) for the first item in this set: "Through your interactions with administrators, faculty, and staff at GC, do you believe that they understand the ways in which factors (such as race, ethnicity, home language, religion, gender, sexual orientation, social class, age, and disability) influence all individuals and institutions?" However it should be noted that although the median for this item was 3, the mode was 4. One student wrote, "They know that people have different cultures and followings. They respect it and aren't bias[ed] on the situation." Another added, "Although they need to be more aware of it and know more of people's background and culture." In general, students thought that GC administrators, faculty, and staff "demonstrate a knowledge and understanding of diverse groups" (M = 3.35, Mdn = 3, SD = 0.658, n = 80) and "seem aware of their own personal attitudes toward people from diverse groups" (M = 3.22, Mdn = 3, SD = 0.793, n = 76; the mode for this item was 4). Of the students who responded on the 4-point scale, 71% replied that their GC "teachers seem interested in understanding [their] background as it relates to learning" (M = 2.95, Mdn = 3, SD = 0.861, n = 79), and 88% thought that "teachers know how to effectively teach students from diverse backgrounds" (M = 3.22, Mdn = 3, SD = 0.697, n = 72) "often" or "almost always or always." A student wrote, "My teachers have been really creative so far in involving students from all backgrounds and tying us all together." Another explained,

> Not everyone can tell I am an immigrant simply because I am white. Certain professors who find out this about me treat me with special respect or curiosity. This shows how people adjust accordingly to their perceptions of others.

Equal Educational Opportunity

Means for the following items ranged from 3.06 to 3.54:

1. Does GC equally enable all students to learn and excel?

2. Do you have the same opportunity to achieve your academic goals as any other student here at GC?

3. Do your teachers provide the help you need to be successful at GC?

4. Do the teaching strategies used by faculty at GC accommodate diverse student interests and learning styles?

5. Do you have opportunities to interact with appropriate role models on campus?

6. Are you treated with respect by staff and faculty?

The students' comments regarding equal opportunity were very consistent: "Everyone is treated equal in this school."

The other two items in this set dealt with issues of grave concern. The first asked, "At GC have you or any student you know been discriminated against on the basis of race, ethnicity, home language, religion, gender, sexual orientation, social class, age, disability, or any other group identification?" Unfortunately, this item did not easily lend itself to a 4-point scale; 56% responded "never or almost never," and both the median and mode for this item were 1, but the mean was 1.91 ($SD = 1.281$, $n = 78$). The other item asked, "Are you concerned about your safety on campus?" Although the mode for this item was 1, and 42% of the responding students answered "never or almost never," 11% responded "almost always or always" ($M = 2.01$, $Mdn = 2$, $SD = 1.055$, $n = 81$). Several students made comments about safety:

"GC seems really open to a lot of things. I feel safe there."

"Sometimes I wonder, but I mostly feel safe on and around campus."

Knowledge Construction

Responses to the following items were very consistent, with means ranging from 2.95 to 3.33, means and modes of 3 for all 10 items, and no more than three students responding "don't know" or "not applicable" to any item:

1. Have the courses you have taken at GC helped you understand historical, social, and/or political events from diverse perspectives?

2. Do your courses or teachers present the idea that how a person sees the world is influenced by her or his personal, political, and/or economic experience?

3. Have the instructional materials such as textbooks, supplementary readings, computer applications, or videos described historical, social, and/or political events from diverse perspectives?

4. Do your teachers present different theories or points of view about topics discussed in class?

5. When an idea or theory is presented, do you learn about the person or group from which it came?

6. Are the references or examples presented in your classes drawn from different cultural groups?

7. Has your cultural group been portrayed accurately and respectfully in the courses you have taken?

8. Have the courses you have taken provided opportunities for civic engagement (community involvement), such as service learning?

9. Have opportunities for multicultural learning experiences outside the classroom been made available to you?

10. Are opportunities available to you to study in diverse cultural environments, whether within or outside the U.S.?

The mean for the final item under this guiding principle, "Is a course that explores multicultural perspectives a degree requirement at the University of Minnesota?" was 3.45, with a median and mode of 4, but 5 of the 82 students (6%) responded "not applicable," and 22 (27%) did not know.

Acquisition of Social and Communication Skills

The responses to this data set were also very consistent, with means ranging from 2.77 to 3.27; means and modes for all 8 items were 3, and no more than five students responded "don't know" or "not applicable" to any item:

1. Have your courses at GC included learning that "normal" is defined differently for different groups of people?

2. Has developing an understanding between people of different cultures been a goal in the courses you have taken?

3. Has the importance of communication skills been presented in the courses you have taken?

4. In the courses you have taken, have safe ground rules been set for engaging in meaningful discussions about multicultural issues?

5. Have your experiences at GC increased your ability or comfort in interacting with people from different cultures or groups?

6. Do administrators, faculty, and staff such as counselors and advisors talk openly and constructively with you about multicultural issues?

7. Have they provided you with factual information that contradicts misconceptions and stereotypes?

8. Have you had the opportunity to participate in simulations, role playing, writing as though you experienced something from another person's perspective, or other activities that enable you to gain insights into the impact of stereotyping, prejudice, and discrimination?

9. Have your courses required you to discuss cultural differences?

One student summed up the GC experience, "I am getting several different perspectives here at GC that have given me a better understanding of different racial groups."

Co-Curricular and Extracurricular Activities

Overall, this set of items yielded the lowest means (2.42 to 3.26) across the entire pilot study. Of the responding students, 11% thought that they never or almost never had "the opportunity to participate in extracurricular activities that enable [them] to develop positive relationships with people from diverse backgrounds," and 23% responded "occasionally." Meanwhile, 32% responded "often" and 42% replied "almost always or always" to the question, "Are activities or organizations available that encourage students' expression of identity and cultural differences (e.g., African American Student Association, Gay and Lesbian Alliance)?" When asked if they personally had "participated in college or university activities outside of class that promote multicultural understanding," 34% of the students answered, "never or almost never." One student explained, "I like how they have all the different groups that you can join but because I don't live on campus I don't ever get a chance join any of the groups." Another student wrote that it is "hard to find more information about activities."

Research (Astin, 1985) has indicated that "Frequent interaction with faculty members is more strongly related to satisfaction with college than any other type of involvement or, indeed, any other student or institutional characteristic" (p. 149). Only 10% of the responding students said that they had never or almost never had the opportunity to interact with faculty members outside the classroom.

Student Services

For the following items, means ranged from 3.30 to 3.51, and 4 was both the mode and the median:

1. Are support services such as counseling, advising, career planning and placement, tutoring, and computer labs equally accessible to all students?

2. Are support services available at times that accommodate diverse student needs?

3. Are you able to get the help you need outside of class to be successful at GC?

4. Are you comfortable asking a faculty member or staff person for help when you need it?

Except for a few remarks about the availability of parking, "if parking is considered a student service," the majority of student comments about the services offered were very favorable: "I like how they have the math center, writing and computer lab. These things help me a lot. My advisor is a good person to talk to about class schedules." However, one student wrote, "GC advising needs some help, a lot of the advisors don't know what they are doing and they are not as motivating as they should be. They are to help students not to discourage them."

Intergroup Relations

To the question, "In the courses you have taken in GC, have you learned about the ways that ideas like justice, equality, freedom, peace, compassion, and charity are valued by many cultures?" 77% of the students who answered on the 4-point scale ($n = 78$) indicated either "often" or "almost always or always," and 71% ($n = 79$) responded likewise to "Have you interacted with people from different cultures who share these values?" To "Do faculty use teaching strategies, such as collaborative groups, to model these values?" only 4% indicated "never or almost never," 24% responded "occasionally," 38% answered "often," and 33% replied "almost always or always" ($n = 78$). Sixty-four percent of the students said that they almost always or always and another 23% said they often "find that [they] are less likely to stereotype people once [they] get to know them," ($n = 78$).

Classroom Assessments

The medians and modes for both "In the courses you have taken in GC, have you had the opportunity to demonstrate knowledge in multiple ways, such as through discussion, oral presentations, essays, creative projects, and portfolios, as well as quizzes and tests?" ($M = 3.45$, $SD = 0.756$, $n = 82$) and "... have a variety of types (e.g., multiple choice, essay) of tests and quizzes been offered?" ($M = 3.41$, $SD = 0.800$, $n = 82$) were 4. Meanwhile, the mode for "Have the tests that you have taken included culturally-specific references that were unfamiliar to you and were not taught as part of the course content?" was 1, but the median was 2, and the mean was 2.54 ($SD = 1.440$; $n = 80$).

General Comments From Students

A number of students wrote concluding comments about their experience in the General College. Several of the messages addressed the sense of stigma (Pedelty, 2001) that often accompanies participation in a developmental education program:

"Students in GC usually don't want to be there, because they feel the need that they are part of a lower class at the university and this sometimes affects their decision making and knowledge of everything."

"GC is good academically, although many students get discouraged like myself who come to GC, by seeing you are part of the group that everyone is looking down on."

Other students focused their parting comments on what they appreciated about the academic preparation they received in the General College. One student wrote,

> I am glad that I started my college career at GC because I felt welcomed. There were a lot of resources available for me to improve my chances of becoming successful. I have used them to become a better student.

Another stated,

> I believe that GC is a good starting foundation for many students. Ever since I've been here the knowledge that I've obtained has been more than I ever expected. Not only are the classes taught differently but in ways where it can somehow relate.

Finally, several specifically addressed multicultural aspects of GC, like this student: "I really enjoyed being a student in GC. The diverse atmosphere was really one that I had to get used to at first, but once I was comfortable with everyone around me, I really loved being a student here."

Discussion and Implications

The purpose of this study, beyond piloting a new assessment tool, was to assess the multicultural experiences of students in the General College at the University of Minnesota. The General College may best be characterized as a diverse developmental education learning community. There is significant research (Akey & Bobilya, 2003; Chickering & Reisser, 1993) that demonstrates that being part of this kind of learning situation is helpful in making the transition to college life. Thus, it is not too surprising that the results of this pilot study generally indicate that students have a positive attitude toward their GC experience. For example, the results suggest that GC students are very aware of GC's mission to provide access to diverse students, and students also indicate that they feel supported in GC. In addition, the results indicate that students are paying close attention to the college's efforts to recruit and retain a diverse student body and that GC students believe that the college operates in a manner that values a multicultural learning environment and shows a commitment to providing a place where all can learn (e.g., "everyone is treated equal in this school").

Interactions With Faculty and Staff

With regard to the quality of student multicultural interactions with faculty and staff, this research suggests that students for the most part consider it positive. Although the responding students indicated that the GC faculty and staff demonstrated knowledge and understanding of diverse groups, some students thought that more can be done to understand where they are coming from as it relates to learning (e.g., "although they need to be more aware of it and know more of people's background and culture"). The first step in creating a welcoming space according to Banks (1997) is the integration of multicultural content in the curriculum. Even though most students thought that efforts were being made to take their background and culture into the learning equation, these results suggest that some students thought that more could be done to include their diverse perspectives in the construction of the learning process.

Discrimination and Safety

Potentially the most disturbing part of the survey results addresses issues of discrimination and safety. Although most students consistently reported that they believed that they were being treated equally in GC, not all reported feeling that way. For example, although 56% of the students reported never or almost never witnessing acts of discrimination against themselves or others, 44% of the students' responses indicate that some instances of discriminatory behavior had been observed on the basis race, ethnicity, gender, age, home language, religion, sexual orientation, or disability. With a mean of 1.91 (where 2 = occasionally) and standard deviation of 1.281, the interpretation of the responses to this question could signal trouble and should be taken seriously. Although the median and mode are both 1 (i.e., never or almost never), the frequency of other responses merits attention. In this case, any negative response is unacceptable. The institution is not likely to retain students who have experienced discrimination. Furthermore, the potential consequences of discriminatory behavior could be very problematic to the GC mission of establishing and sustaining a healthy multicultural learning environment. Banks (1994, 1997) suggested that to encourage a viable multicultural learning environment, intentional action is needed to reduce prejudice.

Safety was the other big issue of concern for students. Although students commented that they felt safe in GC, that level of confidence did not extend to the campus as a whole. With 58% of the responding students expressing a varying degree of concern for their safety on campus and 11% reporting that they always or almost always were concerned about their safety on campus, some institutional measures to reduce the level of anxiety related to campus security seem warranted. Students' safety needs must be addressed before students can be expected to flourish in developing intellectually and making progress toward self-actualization (Maslow, 1968, 1970).

It might be hypothesized that because of the diversity that exists in GC students would feel less safe there, and yet students indicated that they felt more safe in the General College than elsewhere on campus (e.g., "GC seems really open to a lot of things. I feel safe there"). One of the benefits of the kind of intimate multicultural learning environment provided by GC is that students get to know one another on a personal level; this may increase student's sense of safety.

Because the pilot sample size was relatively small, we cannot make widespread generalizations about students' perceptions about discriminatory behaviors and safety on campus. Furthermore, it was because of the small sample size that we could not explore whether differences in perceptions existed among different demographic groups. Nevertheless, this study suggests that perceived prejudicial behavior and safety needs are problematic and warrant further attention.

Knowledge Construction and Content Integration

Showing how knowledge is socially constructed and offering diverse points of view are considered important components of a multicultural classroom (Banks, 1997). The pilot data suggest that GC students often are exposed to different points of view with regard to how knowledge is constructed. These results may indicate that the students felt included in the curriculum, thus stimulating social integration within and outside of the classroom. This finding agrees with much of the research that has argued that it is critical for academic institutions to consider ways to increase social adjustment (Fisher, 1985).

With regard to the university's course requirement on multicultural perspectives, there seems to be a problem in getting the word out, according to the results of this study. Instituting a multicultural course requirement and communicating that policy effectively can send a signal to all constituents within the University community that the institution is committed to multicultural education. The results of this study indicate that both the University and the General College need to do a better job of communicating the multicultural perspectives course requirement to students.

An integration of multicultural content into the curriculum invites students to be part of the learning community and provides bridges for interaction (Bruch, Jehangir, Jacobs, & Ghere, 2004). Responses to whether students' course work has broadened their perception and understanding of those who are different yielded a consistent positive response from the students. Students often believed that the course work supported their learning about others.

Extracurricular Activities

The findings related to extracurricular activities were not as positive as those for in-class experiences. For example, most students responded that it was difficult for them to participate in extracurricular or co-curricular activities. There were various reasons put forth, but the reality is that opportunities to develop positive relationships outside the classroom are being missed. Out-of-class interactions with peers and faculty have been shown to provide many benefits, including enhancing learning and academic performance, encouraging risk-taking in class, and increasing feelings of empowerment (Akey & Bobilya, 2003).

Testing

Students' lukewarm responses to the question regarding testing suggest that different cultural perspectives have not been represented. Currently there is much controversy in academia regarding cultural bias in testing (Miksch, 2003). The results of this study indicate that this is still perceived as a hot issue by many of the respondents in this study. If it is important that there be a social context for learning (Lundell & Collins, 1999), and particularly a multicultural context (hooks, 1994), it is certainly as important to have multiple perspectives appear in the assessment phase of the learning process. Failure to do so has the potential effect of undermining all other efforts to promote and sustain an atmosphere of acceptance and respect for differing points of view. A thorough examination of this issue as it pertains to multicultural education needs to take place in the future.

Response to the Instrument Itself

Lastly, this student pilot study seems to have overcome the primary criticism of its predecessor (i.e., the 2002 GC faculty and staff multicultural assessment pilot study mentioned earlier), which found that respondents thought that too many of the questions simply did not apply to all faculty and staff members' roles in GC (Higbee et al., 2004). In this revised study, the high student participation in answering the individual questions and the lack of comments regarding inapplicability seem to indicate that the applicability of the items was not an issue with this instrument. The length of the MAP IT student questionnaire continues to be an issue. However, one of the purposes of this pilot study was to test the validity of the questions and determine which items would be used in future research.

The use of both quantitative and qualitative methodologies in the questionnaire was very helpful. Students' comments in response to the questionnaire allowed for a fuller or more complete assessment of the data provided by the quantitative analysis. For example, comments such as "GC is very diverse and it has not come together yet. Everyone is scattered around [and] there is no unity" would not have been captured if only quantitative methods were used to collect data. In this case, it seems that the student is aware that GC is a diverse environment; however, the comment expands on this piece of data by indicating that students may find it more difficult to come together or find a common ground. The student may be asking the question, "So what does all this diversity mean?"

In summary, overall students in GC seemed to think that what they are learning in GC about other cultures is helping them understand their common values, such as justice, freedom, peace, and compassion for others. The data also suggest that association with others who are different can promote open-mindedness and acceptance of individual differences. It is particularly worth noting that 87% of the students stated that they were less likely to stereotype once they got to know people from other backgrounds. It will be interesting to see whether an expanded study with a larger sample size corroborates this pilots study's results.

Limitations

This pilot research had four primary limitations, all of which were related to the fact that one of the purposes of the study was to evaluate the usefulness of proposed MAP IT Student Questionnaire items. As a result, the questionnaire was longer than desired, which reduced the response rate. Several students commented on the number of items and the perceived repetition among some items. Second, the items were previously untested with students, and in some cases questions arose pertaining to how to interpret student responses, particularly for items that did not really fit the 1 to 4 response scale provided. Third, because this was a pilot, the sample for the study was intentionally small. And finally, because of the small sample size, no demographic information was collected. This research has since been replicated (Higbee, Siaka, & Bruch, 2005) within the General College using the revised student questionnaire (Miksch, Higbee, et al., 2003) with a larger sample.

Conclusion

The small number of participants in this study makes it difficult at best to make generalizations. However, from the analysis of this data set what we can say is that the consistent theme seems to be that students are attuned to and have a positive attitude, for the most part, toward being a member of the multicultural learning environment that GC provides. More research is needed to gain a clearer assessment of multicultural perspectives in GC. Even so, research has found that students who hold a positive attitude toward their college experience are more likely to have a high level of institutional commitment and therefore are more likely to continue in their college career (Napoli & Wortman, 1998; Tinto, 1993). Furthermore, other studies examining cross-cultural environments have also found that supportive learning environments improve cross-cultural understanding, create positive perceptions of the college learning environment, and encourage student retention (Dale & Zych, 1996; Turner & Berry, 2000). We believe that although there is certainly room for improvement, the General College should be commended both for its attention to multicultural education and for its willingness to do this type of assessment and report openly on the results.

References

Akey, L. D., & Bobilya, A. J. (2003). A qualitative investigation of student outcomes in a residential learning community. *Journal of The First-Year Experience & Students Transition, 15*(2), 35–60.

American College Personnel Association & National Association of Student Personnel Administrators. (2004). *Learning reconsidered: A campus-wide focus on the student experience.* Washington, DC: Authors.

Astin, A. W. (1985). *Achieving educational excellence.* San Francisco: Jossey-Bass.

Banks, J. A. (1994). *Multiethnic education: Theory and practice* (3rd ed.). Boston: Allyn and Bacon.

Banks, J. A. (1997). Transformative knowledge, curriculum reform, and action. In J. A. Banks (Ed.), *Multicultural education, transformative knowledge, and action: Historical and contemporary perspectives* (pp. 335–346). New York: Teachers College Press.

Banks, J. A., Cookson, P., Gay, G., Hawley, W. D., Jordan Irvine, J., Nieto, S., Ward Schofield, J., & Stephan, W. G. (2001). *Diversity within unity: Essential principles for teaching and learning in a multicultural society.* Seattle, WA: Center for Multicultural Education, School of Education, University of Washington. Retrieved July 6, 2004, from http://depts.washington.edu/centerme/home.htm

Bruch, P. L., & Higbee, J. L. (2002). Reflections on multiculturalism in developmental education. *Journal of College Reading and Learning, 33*(1), 77–90.

Bruch, P. L., Higbee, J. L., & Lundell, D. B. (2003). Multicultural legacies for the 21st century: A conversation with Dr. James A. Banks. In J. L. Higbee, D. B. Lundell, & I. M. Duranczyk (Eds.), *Multiculturalism in developmental education* (pp. 35–42). Minneapolis, MN: Center for Research on Developmental Education and Urban Literacy, General College, University of Minnesota. Retrieved July 6, 2004, from http://www.gen.umn.edu/research/crdeul

Bruch, P. L., Higbee, J. L., & Lundell, D. B. (2004). Multicultural education and developmental education: A conversation about principles and connections with Dr. James A. Banks. *Research & Teaching in Developmental Education, 20*(2), 77–90.

Bruch, P. L., Jehangir, R. R., Jacobs, W., & Ghere, D. (2004). Enabling access: Toward multicultural developmental curricula. *Journal of Developmental Education, 27*(3), 12–14, 16, 18–19, 41.

Bruch, P. L., Jehangir, R. R., Lundell, D. B., Higbee, J. L., & Miksch, K. L. (2005). Communication across differences: Toward a multicultural approach to institutional transformation. *Innovative Higher Education, 29,* 195–208.

Chickering, A., & Reisser, L. (1993). *Education and identity* (2nd ed.). San Francisco: Jossey-Bass.

Dale, P. M., & Zych, T. (1996). A successful college retention program. *College Student Journal, 30*(3), 354–360.

Dewey, J. (1916/1997). *Democracy and education.* In S. M. Cahn (Ed.), *Classic and contemporary readings in the philosophy of education* (pp. 288–325). New York: McGraw-Hill.

Dewey, J. (1938/1997). *Experience and education.* In S. M. Cahn (Ed.), *Classic and contemporary readings in the philosophy of education* (pp. 325–363). New York: McGraw-Hill.

Freire, P. (1990). *Pedagogy of the oppressed.* (M. B. Ramon, Trans.; original work published in 1968). New York: Continuum.

Gee, J. P. (1996). *Social linguistics and literacies: Ideology in discourses* (2nd ed.). Bristol, PA: Falmer.

Griffin, O. T (1992). The impacts of academic and social integration for Black students in higher education. In M. Lang & C. Ford (Eds.), *Strategies for retaining minority students in higher education.* Springfield, IL: Charles C. Thomas.

Higbee, J. L., Bruch, P. L., Jehangir, R. R., Lundell, D. B., & Miksch, K. L. (2003). The multicultural mission of developmental education: A starting point. *Research & Teaching in Developmental Education, 19*(2), 47–51.

Higbee, J. L., Miksch, K. L., Jehangir, R. R., Lundell. D. B., Bruch, P. L., & Jiang, F. (2004). Assessing our commitment to providing a multicultural learning experience. *Journal of College Reading and Learning, 34*(2), 61–74.

Higbee, J. L., & Pettman, H. C. H. (2003). Report of the Future Directions Meeting multicultural theme track. In J. L. Higbee, D. B. Lundell, & I. M. Duranczyk (Eds.), *Multiculturalism in developmental education* (pp. 69–74). Minneapolis, MN: Center for Research on Developmental Education and Urban Literacy, General College, University of Minnesota. Retrieved July 6, 2004, from http://www.gen.umn.edu/research/crdeul

Higbee, J. L., Siaka, K., & Bruch, P. L. (2005). *Assessing our commitment to multiculturalism: Student perspectives.* Unpublished manuscript. Minneapolis, MN: General College, University of Minnesota.

hooks, b. (1994). *Teaching to transgress: Education as the practice of freedom.* New York: Routledge.

Jay, G. M., & D'Augelli, A. R. (1991). Social support and adjustment to university life: A comparison of African-American and White freshman. *Journal of Community Psychology, 19,* 95–108.

Maslow, A. (1968). *Toward a psychology of being.* New York: Van Nostrand.

Maslow, A. (1970). *Motivation and personality.* New York: Harper & Row.

Miksch, K. L. (2003). Legal issues in developmental education: The impact of high-stakes testing. *Research & Teaching in Developmental Education, 19* (2), 53–59.

Miksch, K. L., Bruch, P. L., Higbee, J. L., Jehangir, R. R., & Lundell, D. B. (2003). The centrality of multiculturalism in developmental education: Piloting the Multicultural Awareness Project for Institutional Transformation (MAP IT). In J. L. Higbee, D. B. Lundell, & I. M. Duranczyk (Eds.), *Multiculturalism in developmental education* (pp. 5–13). Minneapolis, MN: Center for Research on Developmental Education and Urban Literacy, General College, University of Minnesota. Retrieved July 6, 2004, from http://www.gen.umn.edu/research/crdeul

Miksch, K. L., Higbee, J. L., Jehangir, R. R., Lundell, D. B., Bruch, P. L., Siaka, K., & Dotson, M. V. (2003). *Multicultural Awareness Project for Institutional Transformation: MAP IT.* Minneapolis, MN: Multicultural Concerns Committee and Center for Research on Developmental Education and Urban Literacy, General College, University of Minnesota. Retrieved July 6, 2004, from http://www.gen.umn.edu/research/crdeul

Napoli, A. R., & Wortman, P. M. (1998). Psychological factors related to retention and early departure of two-year community college students. *Research in Higher Education, 39,* 419–455.

Pedelty, M. (2001). Stigma. In J. L. Higbee (Ed.), *2001: A developmental odyssey* (pp. 53–70). Warrensburg, MO: National Association for Developmental Education.

Tinto, V. (1993). *Leaving college: Rethinking the causes and cures of student attrition* (2nd ed.). Chicago: University of Chicago Press.

Turner, A. L., & Berry, T. R. (2000). Counseling center contributions to student retention and graduation: A longitudinal assessment. *Journal of College Student Development, 41,* 627–636.

CHAPTER 8

Creating Spheres of Freedom: Connecting Developmental Education, Multicultural Education, and Student Experience

Heidi Lasley Barajas

ABSTRACT

This chapter argues that developmental educators must continually examine the historical context in which we make decisions and how external institutional forces influence our choices. Without this reflection, we may find ourselves handcuffed to ideals about supporting students that may not see students as partners in educational solutions for success. I propose that by integrating multicultural education and developmental education ideals, educators may assist students in creating safe spaces or "spheres of freedom" (Collins, 1990) in which students successfully negotiate their educational careers. Finally, I observe ways that General College is creating safe spaces to insure stronger student partnerships.

In the 2003 Seeking Educational Equality and Diversity (SEED) summit, Peggy McIntosh stated that the greatest stride in multicultural education in the last 20 years could be seen in students' and teachers' ability to link the individual and the social structure. There are two ways this statement captures the progress of our understanding about multicultural education as socially-just educational opportunities for all students, but especially for those who are constantly challenged by social forces. First, the statement centers on both teacher and student learning. Second, it captures a way in which to "grasp history and biography and the relations between the two within society" (Mills, 1959, p. 6). In this statement, C. Wright Mills defined what he termed the "sociological imagination," a way in which to notice the connection between the individual and the social structure. The crucial feature of the sociological imagination is what Mills discussed as a way in which the individual may look beyond "personal troubles" to see the "social issues" operating in the larger society (p. 8). Mills argued that we live in an age and environment in which understanding the world around us as well as what is happening within us as individuals is dominated by an overwhelming amount of information. The sociological imagination may help us deal with this information by enabling its possessor

> to understand the larger historical scene in terms of its meaning for the inner life and the external career of a variety of individuals . . .
>
> The first fruit of this imagination . . . is the idea that the individual can understand his [sic] own experience and gauge his own fate only by locating himself within his period, that he can know his own chances in life only by becoming aware of those of all individuals in his circumstances. (Mills, p. 5)

Although the use of masculine pronouns referenced in a historical time when scholars were not sensitive to gender inclusivity may indicate otherwise, this concept is very useful in our approach to developmental education. Mills' statements were based on his belief that people tend to attack all problems by looking to the individual. By looking to external or social forces, and at the experiences of other people who have similar historical and social circumstances, we open ourselves to new resources for problem solving. As developmental educators, we work to support the educational needs of the individual student. However, some educational issues that affect the experiences and fate of some students are external to the individual because they arise from institutional practices that privilege some and disadvantage others. The sociological imagination provides an innovative framework through which we may view the influences of institutional forces as well as individual participation. For example, successful students are often noted for their individual characteristics that indicate motivation. Observing a variety of behaviors such as attending class, being on time, and completing reading or assignments in a timely way are traditional measures of motivation. However, motivation to behave as previously described may be affected by larger institutional issues such as experiencing overt or subtle racism as the only African American living in a college dormitory, or as a first-generation college student who does not have the cultural capital to navigate the bureaucracy of a large institution and has to put in considerable amounts of time and emotional labor to contend with these issues.

In practical terms, one way we as educators can use our sociological imaginations to assuage some of these issues for students is to integrate multicultural education, the process of seeking socially-just educational opportunities for all students, and developmental education, a discipline that promotes cognitive and affective growth of all postsecondary learners at all levels of the learning continuum (National Association for Developmental Education, 1995). Such a framework considers who we educate, how we educate, and the larger social issues that affect how we practice. Ultimately, we need to acknowledge that at the same time, students negotiate their personal educational troubles along with larger institutional issues on a daily basis.

In this process, students often create safe spaces in which to construct and maintain positive images and self-understanding. Collins (1990) referred to these spaces as "spheres of freedom" (p. 103). My research (Barajas & Pierce, 2001; Barajas & Ronnkvist, 2004) found that student spheres of freedom are functional or practical in nature because they are concrete strategies for dealing with institutional issues in their educational careers. Strategies include and most often involve informal strategies such as informal study groups, taking classes together, or just talking to other students who have similar backgrounds about problems they face in school. Some strategies do take advantage of formal programs such as student cultural centers, mentor programs, and involvement in community service learning. The concrete nature of learning to connect personal troubles and social issues, particularly in informal situations, is often not taken as a serious strategy for carrying out successful educational careers. This may be because student spheres of freedom are also symbolic in that they represent students' understanding of the individual-institutional link, something that is not often identified as an important partnership with us, the "educators."

Developmental Education and the "Golden Handcuffs" of Dichotomous Paradigms

I have often heard colleagues from the business world talk about their jobs and the economic remuneration they receive as "golden handcuffs." The reference defines a situation in which the work situation or work itself is not what these individuals want to be doing, but the pay is such that they allow themselves to be prisoners of the job. Being developmental educators often presents us with a golden handcuffs situation, but of a very different sort. As developmental educators we work to support increased student learning opportunities in a variety of ways. Unlike our business colleagues, the golden part of our dichotomous equation is the job itself—we love what we do and are rewarded by the nature of the work more often than the paycheck. The handcuffs part of the dichotomy lies in the assumptions we make about notions of inclusion and support for diverse student populations. We handcuff ourselves in unintentional or even unnoticed ways in our theory, classroom methods, and research.

Observed through the sociological imagination, Mills (1959) might have concluded that we forget to consider the institutional forces external to the individual that influence our choices and the historical context in which we make decisions. In addition, we may be handcuffed to the notion that students do not themselves own a sociological imagination and therefore do not see a link between the individual and the institution. More specific to educational practices, these handcuffs exist because as hooks (1994) observed, "most of us were taught in classrooms where styles of teaching reflected the notion of a single norm of thought and experience" (p. 35). The effect of this experience may be seen most patently in professors who "remain unwilling to be involved with any pedagogical practices that emphasize mutual participation between teacher and student" (p. 204). hooks' discussion is about classroom practice that ignores student experience and the possibility that students understand their historical location in the institution. However, the idea is also valuable in reference to various kinds of educational practices.

I believe that observed through hooks' (1994) notion of mutual participation, we as developmental educators often tend to think and practice from a top-down organizational level. For example, we may be horrified at the prospect of actually using the banking model, defined by hooks as a system of education that is "based on the assumption that memorizing information and regurgitating it represented gaining knowledge that could be deposited, stored and used at a later date" (p. 5) to support student learning. However, we may tend to hang our developmental intentions on the same kind of organizational hat rack. That is to say, we may understand the impact of the institution on student success. We may even make considerable attempts to assuage the issue. But what we may actually be doing is imposing support in ways that may or may not be effective from the standpoint of how students are driving their own educational processes. By doing so, we may be increasing students' burdens simply because we do not work to make changes within the space of the classroom or institution, or create spaces that allow us to meet students in their process rather than imposing or assuming our process to be the most valuable. In other words, just like educational practices, student involvement in education is a dynamic process changed by exposure to and experience with our attempts to support student success in new and better ways.

Several developmental educators have noted how our best intentions in creating what many see as nontraditional practices often wield the same outcomes as traditional educational practices. Particularly for diverse students, we tend to be handcuffed to ideas that at one time showed promise in theory but may need to be reconsidered in practice. For example, Johnson (1998) stated that critical race theory, linguistic theory, and cognitive theory all promote the use of personal narrative, and developmental educators utilize personal narrative in writing classes as a rhetorical strategy that helps students find a "voice" (p. 30) in early college writing. The problem with using narrative as a rhetorical strategy and a way to encourage students to write is that narrative is "rarely treated as a serious rhetorical device" and is too soon replaced with the "academic voice" (p. 30). Even when developmental educators invoke new practices to engage students such as narrative writing, an engagement that meets them rather than imposes on them, we abandon narrative as soon as possible in favor of more traditional academic work. Johnson referred to this process as a "trick" that creates a "chasm across which student and instructor often encounter one another" (p. 30). Moreover, well-intentioned practices such as this are often not critiqued simply because they were originally constructed as a nontraditional approach to meet the needs of marginalized student groups. As Johnson indicated in her work, our intent is golden, but our outcome continues to create educational handcuffs for both students and instructors. The reason for this does not lie in the actual definition of what is considered developmental education. Rather, it is a construction of our taken-for-granted position as student-centered educators. The problem is forgetting to examine and critique what sociologists would call the unintended functions of such practices.

Mason (1994) provided another excellent example by examining taken-for-granted assumptions about power in the classroom. Mason pinned down a problem with the discussion of power in the classroom by identifying the dichotomous relationship assigned to teacher-centered power as bad and the absence of such power as good. She disrupted this notion by questioning how the absence of teacher authority actually works for developmental students and particularly for students "from backgrounds other than the dominant culture" (p. 38). The argument is that power has been critiqued as a part of what feminists define as a male-centered, hierarchical structure in mainstream classrooms. In other words, all the power in the classroom, and therefore all the knowledge, lies with the instructor. Feminists also believe this kind of power structure in the classroom should be eliminated so that multiple voices command the classroom, the teacher's voice numbered among many. Mason argued that this assumes the students in the classroom are part of the mainstream power structure and have the cultural and social capital to benefit from the total leveling of power in the classroom. Instead, she suggested that power may be imagined as persuasive rather than coercive. Furthermore, the total elimination of a persuasive power, that is the power with the "genuine intent . . . to push and goad her students to learn" (p. 39) is considered unproductive for many diverse student groups. In my experience, persuasive power is often about giving students permission to be seen as actively involved in learning. As other research has pointed out, economically disadvantaged students, students of color, and females have been treated with contempt for being actively engaged in the educational conversation. Although this may not be what students experience in our classrooms, it is likely what they have historically experienced, or what is occurring in other classrooms. It may be that before we can actually level teacher power, we need to utilize that power not as a punitive practice, but as an informed tool to support students.

This critique of leveling teacher power in favor of a multi-voiced, dialogic, and collaborative approach has something in common with other critiques of what is thought to be student-centered practice. That is, we sometimes forget to revisit who we teach and how we teach them. In order to meet students where they are in their educational process we need to consider if we are imposing our own ideas about what supports their learning experience. We tend to be handcuffed to nontraditional paradigms that may produce the effects of traditional paradigms; that is, paradigms that are sometimes measured without considering the needs of historically marginalized groups, or even paradigms that we think apply to all marginalized groups, as is the case with a total leveling of power in the classroom. Unless we are willing to critique these paradigms, we are not truly considering who we teach and how we teach them. I suggest performing such critiques and creating new paradigms for practice through a multicultural lens supported by a sociological imagination.

Promoting a Multicultural Milieu

Part of the problem in promoting a multiculturally alive paradigm lies in how we approach multicultural issues in developmental education. Previously, I briefly defined multiculturalism as seeking socially-just educational opportunities for all students. My approach to multiculturalism tends to center on issues of race because, as Sleeter (1994) argued, an anti-racist approach is a necessary component of the multicultural framework. In addition, my primary work as a sociologist focuses on race and education. Although I view multiculturalism as inclusive of multiple issues of access and support, my approach does focus on issues surrounding race. I find that one assumption that contributes to problems with our approach to developmental education as a multicultural venture is the dichotomous thinking we have about race, particularly the effects of race on privileged groups and disadvantaged ones. We need to apply the sociological imagination in order to critique our assumptions concerning how U.S. society tends to assign race to individuals and groups of color, meaning all skin pigmentation variations other than White. Tatum (1992) noted that race, in the context of U.S. society, is a system that

> like other forms of oppression, hurts members of the privileged group as well as those targeted by racism. While the impact of racism on Whites is clearly dif-

ferent from its impact on people of color, racism has negative ramifications for everyone. (p. 3)

Tatum's work counters the taken-for-granted assumption that race and racism are about groups of color. Mills (1959), Johnson (1998), and Mason (1994) have provided good examples of noticing how our intent, based in a common-sense notion of what works, does not necessarily get us to our desired outcome. Tatum's observation exposes a common-sense assumption about race, a notion that affects our intent versus our desired outcome and is connected to our thinking about who we teach and how we teach them. Developmental education is intimately involved in improving the educational opportunities for underrepresented groups, groups usually noted as educationally disadvantaged because of class, gender, race, disability, home language, and age. Yet, we need to consider whether or not we tend to use developmental as a label we pronounce on the heads of individuals or groups, such as "developmental students," rather than as an alternative to educational access (i.e. "developmental programs and practices"). Why? The answer is because we as developmental educators walk a fine line between being handcuffed to normative and often invisible assumptions, such as the assumptions pointed out by Johnson, Mason, and Tatum, or seeking a way to shift into multicultural educational practices.

Creating a Shift in the General College Model

A shift in support of developmental educational practices begins by noticing what aspects of the General College model center the experiences of marginalized students in the discussion and then working to apply what we learn from marginalized students' experiences to a more universal approach for mainstream students. In order to do this, I have been working from a theoretical framework that defines educational organizations as "White spaces," a theory emerging from the examination of marginalized student experience. The qualitative research data from my research (Barajas, 2000; Barajas & Pierce, 2001; Barajas & Ronnkvist, 2004) as well as other research (Feagin, Vera, & Imani, 1996) indicate that students of color consistently refer to secondary and postsecondary educational institutions as "White" or "White space." Sociologists have long studied the interplay between social structures such as educational institutions and social agents such as students (Bourdieu, 1990; Coleman, 1986; Giddens, 1979; Sewell, 1992). Rather than focus on the macro-level analyses that many of these studies take, I examine how individuals and organizations influence one another by focusing on the *space* that mediates the relationship between educational organizations and individuals participating in the organization. Furthermore, I concentrate on how that relationship constructs thinking and behavior about race that, unless examined, may be a way in which many of us are handcuffed to taken-for-granted ideas about these relationships.

To begin, we need to understand that all of us have "common-sense" understandings about race. Omi and Winant (1994) observed that when people think common sense is responsible for how we interpret ideas about race, we also connect our thinking and behavior to common sense, rather to historical and social facts concerning race. In addition, common-sense meanings connect the ways "social structures and everyday experiences are racially organized" (p. 55). Put another way, common-sense notions that organize how individuals categorize people, and organize behaviors between people, also organize social structures such as educational institutions (Barajas, 2000; Barajas & Pierce, 2001; Barajas & Ronnkvist, 2004; Doane, 1997). What is important for developmental educators is the critique these ideas extend to educational institutions. What may seem like race-neutral practices are actually constructed by common-sense interpretations of what is the "other" *and* what is White. That is, the space in school that is defined as race neutral or "color blind" is actually a White space. More specifically, when a space is considered a race-neutral or color-blind space, that is to say the space where practices or policy occurs, what is actually present is White space.

There are transparent examples of students identifying a space as a White space in my research, but also in my everyday experiences as an educator in General College, that may help explain these abstract ideas. One example of students negotiating the school as a White space is about physical space and accepted forms of behavior in that space. General College students often have the majority of their classes meet in one building, and often have some of the same students in more than one class. This situation provides an opportunity for students to network with one another in both socially and academically beneficial ways. Because they have the opportunity to create these networks, students tend to congregate on the front steps, around the outside of the building, as well as on benches in the hallways, rather than moving to public spaces in the larger university. Although students do often mix in diverse groups, they also gather in groups with others like themselves. This was the case with one group of African American students who congregated in one particular area of the building that happened to be in a hallway with a bench. A problem arose not from the fact that a group of African Americans were congregating in the building on a regular basis; General College personnel were accustomed to that. The tumult on the part of a group of primarily White faculty and staff arose over the language and volume of the group gathering. The issue presented by this group of faculty and staff was that the student group conversation was too loud. Students who gathered should do so in appropriate voices. In addition, the language was inappropriate for a college building—the faculty and staff certainly would never use language like that. The problem from a sociological imagination perspective is that a mainstream group was evaluating the volume and language of the African American students as inappropriate. This is not to say the mainstream group should not identify that they had a problem with the noise level. The issue was that this group defined "appropriate" as something they were entitled to define because they represented a neutral understanding of what is appropriate. The behavior of the group actually did the opposite of identifying the space as neutral. They made it quite clear that the hallway is a White space.

Another example of students identifying schools as White spaces that occurs frequently centers on the classroom. Multiple times each semester students of color, most often female students of color, come to my office trying to understand why their course curricula only address mainstream concerns. For example, one student taking a course on marriage and the family showed me a syllabus where the majority of the research articles only use or primarily use White, middle-class, and educated respondents. The research acknowledges this fact, but the student asked the obvious question, "If all the readings make the same disclaimer, and that somehow makes it OK, how is this course about me?" The student makes a point worth considering. Consider if the majority of the research in a given course is about African Americans, would the course be billed as one on "marriage and the family," or would the institution and our own common-sense view this as an African American studies course on marriage and the family? This by no means suggests that we should not have courses specific to racial and ethnic groups. The point is why do we see a course that addresses primarily White populations as a neutral representation of a given topic?

Key work on Whiteness has demonstrated how neutral or color-blind perceptions operate in institutional spaces. One explanation comes to us from the idea of an invisible or hidden ethnicity, that is a lack of awareness of an ethnic identity, an identity that is not normally asserted in intergroup interaction (Doane, 1997; Frankenberg, 1993; Gans, 1979; Waters, 1990). As the mainstream group, White ethnic groups generally own invisible or hidden ethnicity. Doane defined a hidden ethnicity as having three important aspects: (a) ethnicity does not generally intrude upon day-to-day experience, (b) the privileges of group membership are taken-for-granted, and (c) ethnic identity can be asserted when dominant group interests are threatened by challenges from subordinate groups. Hidden ethnicity is often made visible when employed by individuals within the organization space of educational institutions. The visibility is most prominent when observed as the neutralizing process of Whiteness and of the power and privilege in that space that exists by creating a neutral category. What is really employed is an asserted group identity that is defined as neutral but gives power and therefore privilege to what appears to be neutral—Whiteness.

The problem with appropriating a perspective of schools as racially-neutral spaces is that it tends to hide ways that race is involved in school practices. When this occurs, we consider the intended but not unintended consequences of our practices and are then likely to diminish how issues of race can inform us. This occurs because racializing educational spaces as neutral diminishes the impact of race on the organization itself and generally focuses race on abstract ideas or on individuals as a part of identity politics (Feagin, 2001). In turn, a focus on abstract ideas and individuals allows us to dismiss claims that White space exists and therefore dismiss rather than learn from the experiences of students of color. Alternatively, observing the following may identify how the organizational spaces of schools function as White spaces and how our practices are affected:

1. Question how relationships in educational spaces are shaped, who shapes them, and according to what taken-for-granted and symbolic meanings.

2. Consider that a relationship exists between what is defined as White and what is defined as non-White.

3. Consider that what often constructs the relationship between what is White and what is non-White is the connection between White, middle-class assumptions about what characteristics and values are highly regarded and valued in school spaces, but which are accepted as neutral, color-blind values.

4. Understand that all students negotiate White space, but diverse students are required to negotiate that space differently.

All of these points help us recognize and critique what we do as developmental educators through a multicultural lens. The lens is presented through examples specific to race but could be incorporated into various kinds of diverse issues. Thinking about the last point in particular helps educators understand the importance of meeting students in their own negotiating process.

From Handcuffs to Spheres of Freedom

From here, the theoretical impetus of Collins' (1990) work is useful because only one part of my argument is that we should be developing our own sociological imaginations. The equally important part of the argument requires educators to acknowledge that students have a sociological imagination that helps them negotiate the educational process. Collins not only recognized that race, class, and gender are interacting and intersecting aspects of social life, but she also recognized the possibilities for collective resistance. In our case, resistance is defined as a successful negotiation of White space. Collins' work regarded the assignment of a racialized identity—that is, an identity that is based in common-sense notions of race—as one that is structurally imposed. However, she assumed that social actors, in our case students, have more agency than some may consider. Her research suggested that through a self-valuing identity Black women might resist rather than conform to negative images or ideas. To resist such images and ideas, a self-valuing identity is created in what she called a sphere of freedom, a safe space where Black women learn ways to deconstruct assumptions that may intentionally or unintentionally emerge from common-sense notions of race, and create more positive identities and self-understandings. Other researchers have observed the agency of various marginalized student social actors as proactive in creating safe spaces as a response to educational organizational assumptions (de Anda, 1984; Pope, 2000).

I have also observed marginalized student actors being proactive in constructing as well as deconstructing self-images while participating in the educational organization (Barajas & Pierce, 2001; Barajas & Ronnkvist, 2004). In fact, I found this activity to be essential for many marginalized students. For example, the General College Multicultural Concerns Committee recently had the opportunity to talk informally with a group of Somali students, all who had successfully transferred from General College into other colleges in the University of Minnesota and some who were graduating that semester. When asked what is the one thing other students could do to insure that they would have a better chance of graduating, the students discussed the importance of connecting with other students who are like them, either through formal student organizations or through informal study groups. Students also commented that having faculty and staff who understood that not all Somali students have the same history, and therefore had different educational needs, was imperative to their success. Like Collins' (1990) work found in the case of Black women, these students also identified or created spheres of freedom that helped them negotiate their educational careers successfully. In addition, students noted understanding the connection between personal history and the institution as well as suggesting that we as educators need to recognize that students come with this knowledge rather than make assumptions about the group as a whole.

In developmental education, a successful negotiation of White space is about multiple kinds of identity discovery on the part of students who participate in our programs, classrooms, and institutions as a whole. Collins' (1990) work is beneficial if we acknowledge and build on the idea that students are in an active negotiation process as they interact in educational organizations.

Student creation of spheres of freedom is functional because it is a path through which they successfully negotiate multiple kinds of assumptions on the part of the organization. Moreover, student-created spheres of freedom are symbolic in that they represent student understanding of the individual-structural link in which they are often unidentified partners in various aspects of the educational process. In addition, the informal formation of spheres of freedom on the part of students represents an uncanny use of the sociological imagination. Considered through this frame, the place and use of student experience and student knowledge about developmental issues takes on a new and possibly concrete dimension developmental educators have not yet fully tapped. In order to do so, we need to consider giving up our golden handcuffs by seeking student spheres of freedom and meeting them in that negotiation. At the least, this gives us possible insight into better classroom practices, such as those suggested by Johnson (1998), Mason (1994), and Tatum (1992). Meeting students in the process may also make us better partners in creating institutional change. In particular, partnership with students acknowledges that a successful negotiation of White space is about multiple kinds of identity discovery on the part of students who participate in our programs, classrooms, and institutions as a whole.

Drawing a Mental Picture

Burawoy's (1991) work suggested that expanding our knowledge rather than attempting to toss out all aspects of a theory in order to explain what we observe better utilizes theory. Burawoy argued that we extend the case, beginning with what we observe is useful in a given theory and extending its usefulness with new ideas. I argue this is what we need to do as multicultural developmental educators. Along with student assessment, we should continually be assessing institutional processes, be willing to change, and begin by a making a shift in our thinking about how multicultural and developmental education inform us regarding how students are negotiating their educational careers. What would a shift like this look like? By using the research observations discussed this far, and particularly Collins'(1990) and de Anda's (1984) work, we can draw a picture that will help us visualize how student process and institutional support can meet.

Understanding process is often thought of as a picture that depicts steps or movement toward a goal. Observing the lived experience of social actors and institutions is dynamic and fluid in some respect. This is true of movement as replication of the status quo or of attempts to change that process. It is important to note that students, when presented with various circumstances in need of negotiation, do not necessarily move stepwise through stages. Each negotiation depends on the circumstance, the student's history, and relationship to the educational organization. Students may find that they enter the process in different places at different times and even skip back and forth among the different stages to accomplish what they need. The purpose of mentally visualizing the process is to establish cues for understanding and documenting the interactions of students, educators, and the organization. An exercise such as this works only if both the social actors and the educational organizations are taken into consideration when assessing whether organizational practices are meeting student negotiations or imposing supports on students. For that reason, we begin by centering on the student process. Clearly, developmental education has always been student centered because we utilize student assessment to measure academic preparedness. However, measuring acquired skills is one piece of a complex process of negotiation. Therefore, our mental visualization needs to begin with the student perspective.

Three Stages of Negotiation

We begin with the notion "negotiation," a recognition that students and sometimes groups overall are continually negotiating their educational process in order to be successful. Negotiation, then, is a process that is engaged when students are looking for a way to succeed because the assumption or problem placed before them is that they somehow do not fit the organizational norm. Enfolded within the negotiation process are three stages of negotiation: recognition, translation and mediation, and accommodation.

Recognition

Recognition indicates that for a negotiation to take place, the individual must first recognize that an issue exists that can be or is in need of negotiation. For example, recognizing the need for a self-valuing identity in order to resist negative images or ideas that are structurally imposed occurs at different times and in different circumstances for individuals. The key is in understanding that recognition on the part of the individual or group does not always occur simultaneously with images or ideas that are imposed on the individual by the institution. This is particularly true in view of mainstream belief in meritocracy that rewards are dispersed according to the amount of work or effort put forth. For example, a student who has successfully negotiated the educational process well enough to enter a postsecondary institution may first face the recognition stage when labeled a "developmental student" by the organization. Or, a male African American student may face the recognition stage when he must negotiate the assumption he is in a postsecondary institution because he is an athlete. Race, class, and gender, as well as other kinds of statuses such as "developmental student," affect when and how a student recognizes the need for negotiation.

Translation and Mediation

The second of the three stages, translation and mediation, is the stage in which individuals seek out others who act as key informants to assist in successful negotiation. De Anda's (1984) work is especially helpful in explaining this stage. Although her observations were specific to ethnic and cultural populations outside of the mainstream, they remain helpful in looking at a variety of diverse student processes, particularly if culture is broadly defined as including immigrant status, socioeconomic class, age, sexual orientation, and disability. De Anda argued that key informants from both the ethnic or cultural background of the student and individuals in the mainstream culture are necessary for students to successfully negotiate educational organizations. However, she identified the most successful kind of key informant as a "translator," an individual from the person's own ethnic or cultural group who has undergone the process with considerable success. A translator is

> able to share his or her own experiences, provide information that facilitates understanding of the values and perceptions of the majority culture, and convey ways to meet the behavioral demands made on the minority members . . . without compromising ethnic values and norms . . . increasing success of each successive generation in dealing with mainstream culture depends not so much on the degree of assimilation as on an increase in the number of translators available. (p. 104)

In my research (Barajas, 2000; Barajas & Pierce, 2001; Barajas & Ronnkvist, 2004) translators were often students who had more experience or specific experiences that informed their relationship with the educational organization. Sometimes translators are older siblings or friends, translators with whom students informally created spheres of freedom. Translators are also mentors, individuals who have successfully negotiated educational careers without compromising ethnic or cultural values and norms such as instructors, professors, and academic advisors.

In addition to translators, de Anda (1984) suggested that mainstream individuals, either by example or because of their access to or control over resources, help mediate the differences nonmainstream individuals face in their relationships with educational organizations. Her argument was that in order for nonmainstream individuals to negotiate the dissimilarities between their lived experiences and the mainstream assumptions of the educational organization mediation by mainstream individuals provides "valuable instructive information about areas that the minority individual might not have ready access to on his or her own, might misinterpret, or might have to learn about by painful trial and error" (p. 104). There is another difference between mediators and translators besides owning mainstream membership. Mediators, unlike translators, are not often directly involved in the construction of spheres of freedom, but may support the idea as one that helps nonmainstream students to negotiate more successfully. Mediators assist in what Thorne (1994) referred to as successful border crossing, which is gaining access to mainstream activities by negotiating the junctures of social interaction.

Accommodation

Translators and mediators help students function successfully in the educational organization. However, they also serve to legitimate students' interpretations of their experience in the organization. By doing so, students find ways to accommodate organizational expectations and behaviors. Accommodation, the next stage to place in our visualization, is most often thought of as a process through which the organization manages the nonmainstream individual or group. In our picture, however, the accommodation stage reflects the way in which nonmainstream individuals or groups manage the organization. The accommodation stage recognizes the legitimized student experience and often finds students informally creating spheres of freedom while participating in the educational organization. Students informally create these spaces by choices they make such as performing community service learning in sites that are like their original home community (Barajas, 2002), seeking out other students who are like them to form study groups or social ties, or highlighting their ethnic or cultural identity by maintaining or sometimes increasing the use of traditional language, dress, food, and music. Sometimes informal activities become formal attempts to create spheres of freedom, such as joining culturally-specific fraternities or sororities. In my research, students actually organized and institutionalized a Latino fraternity and Latina sorority as a formal outcome of informal behaviors (Barajas & Pierce, 2001). Accommodation is a stage in which students modify what is offered by the educational organization by finding spaces within the White space of the organization to gain educational success while maintaining ethnic or cultural values and beliefs.

Just as White space mediates the relationship between educational organizations and individuals participating in the organization by neutralizing race, space created by students through the accommodation stage mediates that relationship by acknowledging race. Rather than be handcuffed to taken-for-granted ideas about educational spaces, developmental educators can actively look for spheres of freedom that students accomplish in their negotiation process, highlight their accommodations, and allow their knowledge to provide us with crossroads for the organization to meet students. The purpose of meeting students is symbolic in that we further legitimate their experience, but also functional in that by meeting them, we support their existing accommodations and then may also contribute to creating spheres of freedom.

Finding the Fit: General College and Spheres of Freedom

General College is a unique educational organization. The mission of General College is specific and challenging in the expectations to provide access and education to a variety of student populations and conduct developmental education research in a multidisciplinary setting. The work of General College by instructors and student support services staff is informed by the established best practices for developmental students. However, like many educators, what we do is also intuitive. Indeed, because our concern is with students as well as dissemination of research, understanding and measuring the real outcomes of our work means purposely creating opportunities for documenting and discussing how what we do works and does not work. The visual shift discussed in the last section emerged from research, some conducted by observing students participating in developmental programs and some data gathered by observing mainstream experiences. How General College specifically meets students in spheres of freedom has not been documented. The following applications represent observations of a number of ways in which General College meets students in the accommodation stage of their negotiation process. These observations are not an exhaustive list nor are they complete descriptions. Many of the formal and informal examples are fully explained in various parts of this book and so will be cited rather than fully explained. The intent of this chapter is to document the actions of like-minded people who tend to work intuitively toward the common goal of multicultural developmental education. These examples also tend to recognize educational practices that consider the link between individual troubles and social issues (i. e., the sociological imagination), if not in those words with that intent. Finally, these examples consistently reconsider and attempt to measure where students are in the negotiation process and attempt to reconsider how to engage students in the process.

The institutionalized action that first speaks to meeting students in their negotiation process is the mission statement. General College consists of both formal and informal activities that are informed by and in turn cultivate the General College mission. The General College mission (2000) is to provide access to the University of Minnesota for highly motivated students from the broadest range of socio-economic, educational, and cultural backgrounds who evidence an ability to succeed in the University's rigorous baccalaureate programs. . . the General College acknowledges a special role in the University's realization of the egalitarian principles that sustain its vitality as an urban, land grant, research institution.

The existence of this mission statement clearly outlines the core importance serving a diverse student population has in a postsecondary research institution. The statement leaves no room to question if a research institution should serve a diverse population, but rather indicates the necessity to provide a means for that to happen. In other words, the mission statement reveals that the link between individuals and the social institution requires negotiation. What may be unique about the General College mission is the dynamic treatment of the mission statement as an institutionalized practice among General College faculty, staff, and administrators in other formal and informal activities. Formal activities include programs that have institutionalized meeting the needs of particular students. One transparent example includes the General College Commanding English Program (see Chapter 9). This program works with University students and in partnership with several high schools in the Twin Cities Metropolitan area. The goal of this program is to meet students in the process of negotiating a home language that is different from the academic literacy in English required by both elementary-secondary (K-12) schools and the University of Minnesota. Commanding English offers a sphere in which talented high school and college students have the same opportunity for the college preparation, information, mentoring, and support as other high achieving students but specific to second language issues. For University students, this means a two-semester sequence of credit-bearing courses open to other GC freshmen that allows all students to work on academic English skills. The Commanding English Program has a high retention rate in both the first and second year, I believe, in part because they meet students and work together to create many spheres of freedom in classroom activities, support activities, and advising.

Another institutionalized program that supports the mission of GC and meets students in their negotiation process is the TRIO (2004) program. Three TRIO programs are jointly funding by General College and the U.S. Department of Education: (a) the Ronald E. McNair Program, which prepares low-income, first-generation college students for graduate study; (b) the Student Support Services (SSS) program, which provides comprehensive academic support such as supplemental student groups, learning communities, and specific academic counseling; and (c) Upward Bound, a college preparatory program for low-income and otherwise disadvantaged high school students. Like the Commanding English program, the TRIO design provides safe spaces for students to be who they are while learning to engage in high school and university educational literacy demands. What TRIO and Commanding English also provide is access to both mediators and translators, something not often found in one opportunity.

In addition, formalized activities include less obvious but parallel levels of institutionalized support for student negotiation. An organization that supports the student voice in GC work is the General College Student Board (2004). An elected group of General College students, the Student Board represents all GC students both on GC committees and in the larger university student governing groups. The Student Parent HELP (high education for low-income people) Center (2004) offers programs designed for students who are parents. The HELP Center offers a literal sphere of freedom, which is a physical space where college student parents may have their children with them while they meet together as groups or individuals to receive assistance addressing multiple issues that affect academic success.

Some formalized activities that support student success are not directly for students. A unique but formalized activity is the Multicultural Concerns Committee (MCC), a group that has "achieved significant changes within the General College and the University of Minnesota" (Ghere, 2003b, p. 56). Although offered standing committee status by General College, MCC remains a volunteer committee. In recent discussions about the mission and purpose of MCC, pieces of the discussion indicated only a voluntary committee could retain its unique identity as a place where multiple issues and standpoints could be brought to the table for open discussion. In other words, the space created for direct conversation about difficult multicultural issues faced by an educational organization needed to be a safe space—a sphere of freedom for those dedicated to working through institutional barriers for students, faculty, and staff. Like MCC, the Curriculum Transformation and Disability initiative (CTAD, 2003) was designed to support students through faculty and staff training opportunities. CTAD provided workshops to postsecondary instructors in the use of Universal Instructional Design, a specific curriculum design that provides access to multiple groups of students while making coursework more accessible to students with disabilities (see Chapter 21). The whole idea behind Universal Instructional Design is to provide a sphere in which students may make the most of what they bring to the classroom. Finally, the Center for Research on Developmental Education and Urban Literacy (2004) embodies vital research and dissemination opportunities for General College as well as other developmental education faculty and staff to push the current thought about who and what is developmental.

Informal levels of activity also represent ways in which General College approaches developmental education as a multicultural venture meeting students in their negotiation process. Such activities are defined as informal because they are often person dependent rather than institutional. Falling in this category are pedagogies practiced in individual classrooms that may inform others, promote discussions and alterations in others' teaching practices, but remain specific to individual rather than institutional practice. For example, service learning, considered innovative classroom pedagogy, pushes the pedagogical envelope in two cases in General College. One English composition course (see Chapter 11) frames composition as social justice, recognizing the individual link to the larger social world through participating in the community and producing writing about that experience. My own sociology course (see Chapter 18) teaches students to observe their own social statuses and how those statuses are related to individual choices and larger social issues by having students volunteer as tutors and mentors in a community organization assisting disadvantaged children. Using sociological concepts, students learn to read, speak, and write according to the disciplinary demands of critical sociology. In addition, students often reflect on their own negotiation process. Students, regardless of mainstream or nonmainstream status, observe such a process.

Another example of pedagogy through which the organization meets student negotiation is the use of simulations in a history course (Ghere, 2003a). This course creates historical scenarios in which students must understand the goals and attitudes of particular groups in making policy decisions. Students, by taking on various roles and interacting in groups with other role players, are able to see themselves in relationship to larger social ideas and institutions. The last example is a general art course (see Chapter 13) where students learn how creative thinking, self-expression, and academic thinking work together through multiple kinds of creative expression. The pedagogy of this course creates a sphere in which students benefit from the best of both worlds in terms of coming to the curriculum from their own negotiation space while being supported by the knowledge and experience of the instructor. Activities help students work through an understanding of art as creative but also as a way to engage in critical thinking and action.

In all cases, students are presented with opportunities to create spheres of freedom, places where they have others to support the deconstruction and reconstruction of self-identity, and assistance in negotiation of the White spaces of the educational organization. Each of these courses also addresses Tatum's (1992) concern that the issue of race in the United States has consequences for both mainstream and nonmainstream individuals and groups. The approach to this occurs directly through course materials or indirectly through self-reflection but is in all cases supported by students working together in small groups. And, because of the General College mission to serve a diverse population, the groups or the class as a whole tend to be a diverse student population. As noted in Gurin, Dey, Hurtado, and Gurin (2002) in support of affirmative action in the Michigan Supreme Court case, all students benefit from having a diverse student population in the classroom. Each course also addresses Johnson's (1998) concern about the value of personal narrative because narrative is linked to rather than separated from developing discipline-specific skills. Finally, each of these courses offers students the opportunity to understand power in White spaces. Mason's (1994) concern that the students in the classroom are assumed to be part of the mainstream power structure and have the cultural and social capital to benefit from the total leveling of power in the classroom is disrupted. Allowing students to recognize and work with the link between the individual and the larger social world also permits persuasive power on the part of both the instructor and other students "to push and goad students to learn" (p. 39).

Considering the Argument: Shift, Don't Shrug

In an article about reconsidering the application of service learning in the classroom, I ended with the sentence, "Shift, don't shrug" (Barajas, 2002). There are two reasons why this comment is important to this chapter. First, understanding that General College is a particular model of developmental education requires looking at a wide variety of projects and approaches. This is a large undertaking for those participating in and documenting the development of General College as well as for those reading about it. Sometimes such a large undertaking is easy to shrug away as unnecessary. Second, in many cases, developmental educators and higher education professionals in general need to consider that the link between an educational institution's intent and the actual effectiveness for students may be two different things (Astin, 1989). A shift in thinking rather than a shrug of indifference requires more focus on what is actually happening in a student's educational process as opposed to assuming what is happening. Once again, we must push the education envelope by noticing how we as professionals in institutions tend to operate under the assumptions of deficit models and normative socialization by not engaging in multicultural theory and practice. This is the purpose of looking at practice through a theoretical lens and of creating mental models. Theory and models help us visually observe what we do and recognize what kinds of assumptions continually creep into our best intentions and handcuff us to comply rather than free us to act.

Gurin et al. (2002) found that developmental theorists emphasize that discontinuity and discrepancy spur cognitive growth in students. The same is true for educational professionals and organizations. We spur growth by emphasizing the discontinuity and discrepancy in our thinking and practice, placing what we do inside theory and models, and shifting when needed. We can shift by using our sociological imaginations. We can shift by valuing student awareness of education as a White space. We can shift by considering how all students negotiate White space regardless of majority or nonmajority status. We can shift by placing our institutions, our organizations, our practices, and ourselves in a multicultural, developmental education model and reflecting on, then acting on, and hopefully expanding on what we find.

References

Astin, A. W. (1989). Moral messages of the university. *Educational Record, 70* (2), 22–25.

Barajas, H. L. (2000). Is developmental education a racial project? Considering race relations in developmental education spaces. In D. B. Lundell & J. L. Higbee (Eds.), *Theoretical perspectives for developmental education* (pp. 29–37). Minneapolis, MN: Center for Research on Developmental Education and Urban Literacy, General College, University of Minnesota.

Barajas, H. L. (2002). Changing objects to subjects: Transgressing normative service learning approaches. In D. B. Lundell & J. L. Higbee (Eds.), *Exploring urban literacy and developmental education* (pp. 25–32). Minneapolis, MN: Center for Research on Developmental Education and Urban Literacy, General College, University of Minnesota.

Barajas, H. L., & Pierce, J. L. (2001). The significance of race and gender in school success for Latinos and Latinas in college. *Gender and Society, 15*, 859–878.

Barajas, H. L., & Ronnkvist, A. (2004). *Race and public schools: School organizations as a racialized White space.* Unpublished Manuscript, University of Minnesota.

Bourdieu, P. (1990). *The logic of practice.* Stanford, CA: Stanford University Press.

Burawoy, M. (1991). *Ethnography unbound: Power and resistance in the modern metropolis.* Berkeley, CA: University of California Press.

Center for Research on Developmental Education and Urban Literacy. (2004). Retrieved September 28, 2004, from http://www.gen.umn. edu/research/crdeul

Coleman, J. S. (1986). Social theory, social research, and a theory of action. *American Journal of Sociology, 91*, 1309–1335.

Collins, P. H. (1990). *Black feminist thought: Knowledge, consciousness, and the politics of empowerment.* New York: Routledge.

Curriculum Transformation and Disability. (2003). Retrieved September 28, 2004, from http://www.gen.umn.edu/research/ctad

de Anda, D. (1984). Bicultural socialization: Factors affecting minority experience. *Social Work, 29* (2), 101–107.

Doane, A. W., Jr. (1997). Dominant group ethnic identity in the United States: The role of "hidden" ethnicity in intergroup relations. In N. Yetman (Ed.), *Majority and minority: The dynamics of race and ethnicity in American life* (pp. 72–85). Boston: Allyn & Bacon.

Feagin, J. R. (2001). *Racist America: Roots, current realities, & future reparations.* New York: Routledge.

Feagin, J., Vera, H., & Imani, N. (1996). Confronting White students: The Whiteness of university spaces. In J. Feagin (Ed.), *The agony of education* (pp. 49–82). New York: Routledge.

Frankenberg, R. (1993). *White women, race matters: The social construction of Whiteness.* Minneapolis, MN: University of Minnesota Press.

Gans, H. (1979). Symbolic ethnicity: The future of ethnic groups and cultures in America. *Ethnic and Racial Studies, 2,* 1–18.

General College Mission Statement. (2000). Retrieved June 4, 2004, from http://www.gen.umn.edu

General College Student Board. (2004). Retrieved January 10, 2005, from http://www.gen.umn.edu

Ghere, D. L. (2003a). Best practices and students with disabilities: Experiences in a college history course. In J. L. Higbee (Ed.), *Curriculum transformation and disability: Implementing universal design in higher education* (pp. 149–163). Minneapolis, MN: Center for Research on Developmental Education and Urban Literacy, General College, University of Minnesota.

Ghere, D. L. (2003b). The triumphs and tribulations of a multicultural concerns committee. In D. B. Lundell, J. L. Higbee, & I. M. Duranczyk (Eds.), *Multiculturalism in developmental education* (pp. 51–58). Minneapolis, MN: Center for Research on Developmental Education and Urban Literacy, General College, University of Minnesota.

Giddens, A. (1979). *Central problems in social theory.* Berkeley, CA: University of California Press.

Gurin, P., Dey, E., Hurtado, S., & Gurin, G. (2002). Diversity and higher education: theory and impact on educational outcomes. *Harvard Educational Review,* 330–336.

hooks, b. (1994). *Teaching to transgress: Education as the practice of freedom.* New York: Routledge.

Johnson, B. J. (1998). Cognitive, linguistic and critical race theory in the classroom. *NADE Selected Conference Papers, 4,* 28–30.

Mason, N. (1994). Cultural pluralism, power, and authority in the developmental writing classroom: A feminist perspective. *Research & Teaching in Developmental Education, 11*(1), 37–47.

McIntosh, M. I. (2003, September). *Fireside conversation with James A. Banks & Peggy McIntosh.* Seeking Educational Equality and Diversity summit, Minneapolis, MN.

Mills, C. W. (1959). *The sociological imagination.* London: Oxford University Press.

National Association for Developmental Eduation. (1995). *Definition and goals statement.* Carol Stream, IL: Author.

Omi, M., & Winant, H. (1994). *Racial formation in the United States.* New York: Routledge.

Pope, R. L. (2000). The relationship between psychosocial development and racial identity of college students of color. *Journal of College Student Development, 41,* 302–312.

Sewell, W. (1992). A theory of structure: Duality, agency and transformation. *American Journal of Sociology, 98,* 1–29.

Sleeter, C. (1994). White racism. *Multicultural Education, 1* (2), 5–8.

Student Parent HELP Center. (2004). Retrieved September 28, 2004, from http://www.gen.umn.edu/programs/help_center

Tatum, B. D. (1992). Talking about race, learning about racism: The application of racial identity development theory in the classroom. *Harvard Educational Review, 1,* 1–24.

Thorne, B. (1994). *Gender play: Girls and boys in school.* New Brunswick, NJ: Routledge.

TRIO. (2004). Retrieved September 28, 2004, from http://www.gen.umn.edu/programs/trio

Waters, M. (1990). *Ethnic options: Choosing identities in America.* Berkeley, CA: University of California Press.

CHAPTER 9

Building Voice and Developing Academic Literacy for Multilingual Students: The Commanding English Model

Laurene Christensen, Renata Fitzpatrick,
Robin Murie, Xu Zhang

ABSTRACT

Commanding English (CE) is a model program for multilingual students who lack fluency in academic English but may not fit well into traditional ESL programs. CE situates language development within the academic content of first-year coursework, placing students into the college curriculum and allowing them to earn the credit of the freshman year. Faculty, staff, and advisors collaborate to support students as they build voice and competence within the context of a multicultural curriculum that acknowledges the strengths of these students. This chapter describes a comprehensive program for second-language students in the General College.

The fall term has begun, and among the crowd of nervous and excited first-year students is Ifrah. A young woman of Somali heritage, Ifrah came to the United States 4 years ago, after having spent the previous 5 years living in a refugee camp in Kenya. Ifrah recently graduated from a local high school, where she earned above-average grades. She enjoyed being involved in the school's Somali Student Association, and she also participated in the school's Education and Public Service small learning community. Through this program, she served as a volunteer tutor to younger Somali students. Although Ifrah is proud of her accomplishments, she continues to find the demands of academic English challenging. While she feels confident using English with customers at her cashiering job at the Mall of America, she had a hard time taking the ACT, which was required for her admission to the University. She struggled to read the questions within the time limit, and she was disappointed with her ACT test results. As Ifrah begins her freshman year, she wonders how she will get through the stack of textbooks in her backpack. She wonders how well she will understand and take notes on the lectures in her anthropology class and how she will write the seemingly endless number of essays her courses require. Yet Ifrah knows that she must persevere through all of these challenges in order to realize her goal of becoming a nurse.

The Commanding English (CE) Program at the University of Minnesota was designed for students like Ifrah. This program was founded in the late 1970s in response to increasing numbers of Southeast Asian immigrant students in the General College (GC) who were underprepared for full academic coursework, yet unable, with their limited financial aid, to afford the higher tuition rates of the noncredit English as a Second Language (ESL) courses for international students on campus. Now, a quarter of a century later, the program continues to serve Southeast Asians, as well as other immigrant and refugee communities, including students from various countries in West and East Africa, Eastern Europe, Tibet, and Central and South America. Unlike traditional stand-alone ESL programs for international students, which focus on precollege language skills, the Commanding English program builds language support and academic orientation into an entire freshman curriculum of courses so that students can acquire a richer, more contextualized academic literacy, find support and connections through the first year of college, and do the academic work of the freshman year. In the process of addressing the real academic needs of the freshman year, the Commanding English program fosters small learning communities, encourages collaboration among students and staff, promotes multiculturalism through the content of the curriculum, and supports students' development of voice.

Our goal in this chapter is to situate the Commanding English program within a theoretical framework of best practices in the intersections of developmental education, literacy and learning communities, and English Speakers of Other Languages (ESOL) pedagogy. We describe the practical application of these best practices in the Commanding English program through an overview of the CE curriculum. We share evaluation data from the program to demonstrate not only the successes of the program but also the challenges. Finally, we conclude with some thoughts on implementing a CE-type curriculum in other educational contexts.

"Generation 1.5" Students

The number of second language students graduating from U.S. high schools has been growing since immigration policy changed in the 1970s; in fact, second language students are the fastest growing student population (Short, 2000). For example, according to last year's statistics from the Minnesota Department of Education (2003), nine high schools in Minneapolis and St.

Paul designate over one third of their students as "Limited English Proficient." In New York, according to 1997 data collected in the City University of New York (CUNY) system, 48% of the first-year students had been born abroad (Bailey & Weininger, 2002, p. 363). This U.S. resident student coming from a home language other than English has been given a variety of labels: "Generation 1.5" (Harklau, Siegal, & Losey, 1999); multilingual (Zamel, 2004); Limited-English Proficient (LEP); English Language Learner (ELL); ESL; bilingual. Equally varied are the students' educational experiences and backgrounds, from a fully educated, multilingual Bosnian refugee to a Sudanese adolescent who has had no formal schooling before arriving in the United States.

ESL Language Programs Versus Academic Literacy

When Generation 1.5 students enter U.S. colleges, their scores on English language placement tests may cause them to be designated as ESL once again, even when they have been in the U.S. for years or possibly were even born here. The academic language that students are expected to deal with at the college level, the discourse patterns, terminology, and embedded sentence structures are not part of daily-life English (Swales, 1990). For students who have not done much academic reading in their own language because they switched over to schools in the U.S., this difficulty is compounded. Oral fluency in English can be developed relatively quickly in the high school setting, but academic English skills take much longer to build (Cummins, 1981; Thomas & Collier, 1997). The college placement creates tensions, particularly if the ESL designation places students into noncredit skills-based courses designed for international students.

How well prepared a student is likely to be for the rigors of college will depend on the student's previous education, the amount of mentoring and connections available, the kinds of support offered in college, how familiar the family is with higher education, or financial aid available; this list can go on and on. Research points to a number of important considerations:

1. Age of entry to the U.S. and U.S. schools impacts literacy in the native language as well as in English, and where there is a lack of literacy in the first language, second language skills take much longer to acquire (Thomas & Collier, 1997). A student who has graduated from high school in the native country will have a stronger literacy background than a student who switches countries in the middle of junior high.

2. Changing to a new language of instruction in and of itself can cause interrupted education if there are no solid bilingual programs in place. It can take 6 to 10 years to reach grade-level parity in a second language (Thomas & Collier, 1997).

3. Interruptions in education or simply having an educational background from outside of the U.S. can mean gaps in the cultural and academic knowledge expected of college students (Spack, 2004).

4. Students receiving ESL services in school are often tracked in ways that impede strong academic preparation for college (Roberge, 2002; Smoke, 2001).

5. Oral fluency may mask difficulties with academic English (Ruiz-de-Velasco & Fix, 2000).

6. Issues of identity are complicated; for some students, being "American" rather than "ESL" or "foreign" is important. There may also be cultural conflicts between the worlds of school or college and home or family (Blanton, 1999; Leki, 1999).

7. There may be heavy family or economic responsibilities and pressures, especially for students who are supporting family members in the home country or serving as the primary culture-brokers and interpreters for families in the U.S. (Detzner, Xiong, & Eliason, 1999).

This list predicts a number of difficulties that students may find as they transition into higher education. Balancing these difficulties are strong family values, motivation and investment in higher education, a maturity that comes from being bilingual and bicultural, community support, and a willingness to seek assistance from writing centers and other sources of tutorial help. Nevertheless, the need for a supportive academic climate is clear, and this need extends beyond "learning English" as a discrete set of skills.

Acquiring Academic Language and Literacy Skills

One problem with stand-alone skills classes is that they focus on language learning rather than the development of academic literacy. Gee (2004) claimed that reading outside of a discourse is empty decoding. "Literacy is mastered through acquisition, not learning; that is, it requires exposure to models in natural, meaningful, and functional settings" (p. 57). If academic literacy is something that is acquired through practice, not learned in discrete lessons, then it is important to design a program that incorporates real academic work. From a language acquisition point of view, language is best learned in authentic, naturalistic environments where it can be acquired together with content-area knowledge (Krashen, 1982; Zamel, 2004). Vygotsky (1978) and his proponents (Lantolf & Appel, 1994; Lantolf & Pavlenko, 1995; McCafferty, 1994) held that language ability develops together with the learner's understanding of the world, and that the development of language and the development of knowledge in a given subject matter are mutually facilitative. It is not enough to work on English because language proficiency is only part of what is needed; just as important are study skills, time management, critical thinking, and the acquisition of content-area knowledge. Students need to know how to shape an academic argument, how to synthesize opposing viewpoints in historical documents, and how to evaluate and cite sources, just to name a few of the academic skills that are necessary for success. Learning to do this takes time; the "process of acquisition is slow-paced and continues to evolve with exposure, immersion, and involvement . . . learning is responsive to situations in which students are invited to participate in the construction of meaning and knowledge" (Zamel, 2004, p. 13).

Content-based instruction in a curriculum that integrates language skills and content knowledge enables immigrants and refugees to acquire this college-level academic literacy in a way that engages students and supports retention (Adamson, 1993; Harklau et al., 1999; Kaspar, 2000; Murie & Thomson, 2001; Spack, 2004; Zamel, 1998). Situating the CE program within the content of the freshman year allows students to read and write extensively and with sustained content in ways that a stand-alone ESL curriculum would not. Figure 1 outlines some of the contrasts between a traditional ESL program for international students, with its focus on language, and a content-based integrated program like Commanding English.

Finding Place and Voice in College

As permanent residents and graduates of U.S. high schools, multilingual students are expected to face the same academic challenges as the mainstream college population. University students are expected to participate actively and often cooperatively in class; read articles and textbooks that are written in formal, academic language; synthesize information and form opinions; produce papers; and know how to communicate effectively and appropriately with professors. The various demands of the university setting can be difficult for any first-generation college student, particularly if the student's home language is not English. First-year students must acquire "insider knowledge of the rhetorical communities [they] wish to enter" (Soter, 1992, p. 31). This insider knowledge is inevitably less accessible to multilingual students than to native English speakers, because it is implicit and culturally based. Collins (2001) observed that immigrant and refugee students may feel like outsiders in the university setting. One of our goals in the CE program is to reduce this sense of alienation among students who must overcome both linguistic and cultural barriers in order to succeed. There are various aspects of the program that help to create a space in which multilingual students can find place and develop voice during the freshman year, including small class sizes, learning communities, our close collaboration with advisors and with the writing cen-

	TRADITIONAL ESL MODEL	COMMANDING ENGLISH MODEL
Program Goal	Acquiring language	Acquiring academic literacy
Level of Instruction	Pre-college	College level
College Credits	Primarily non-credit bearing	Credit bearing courses
Pedagogical Focus	*Skills-based courses in:* 1. Reading (shorter) reading passages reading skills, strategies); 2. Writing ("process approach," essay topics created by instructor); 3. Listening (strategies for comprehension of native speaker vernacular); 4. Grammar (mastery of grammar rules of English).	*Content-based courses in:* 1. Different content/discipline areas (e.g., biology, sociology, literature, writing anthropology, arts); 2. Sustained reading in a discipline area connected to college content courses; 3. Using language and study strategies for reading 2 chapters a week; 4. Studying for college course tests (e.g., anatomy, biology, etc.); 5. Writing college-level academic/research papers in discipline areas such as anthropology and literature; 6. Acquiring grammar competence that is connected to developing editing strategies for writing.
Advising Focus	Visa regulation, ESL requirements	Course selection, transfer planning, choosing majors
Target Population	International students who are fully literate, comfortable reading and writing in their first language	A complex composition of resident students who brings diverse language and literacy experiences to the first year of college

Figure 1. A comparison of traditional ESL models and the Commanding English model.

ter's undergraduate peer tutors, process-based composition pedagogy, and the multicultural content of the Commanding English curriculum.

The Specifics of the CE Curriculum

The Commanding English program is a mandatory program for U.S. resident students admitted to the University of Minnesota who have been in the U.S. for only part of their schooling (currently defined at 8 years or fewer), whose home language is not English, and whose test scores indicate a need for English support as they enter the University. An ACT reading or English part score below 18 triggers a request for a Michigan English Language Assessment Battery (MELAB) or Test of English as a Foreign Language (TOEFL) score, as a better measure of English language proficiency than the ACT for the UMN Admissions Office. Students who score between 145 and 207 on the TOEFL or between 65 and 79 on the MELAB are placed into Commanding English for their freshman year.

Students enroll in the program full time for the entire academic year, earning 12 to 15 credits per semester. In the fall, to build a strong learning community and for ease of registration, courses are grouped together in sets, so that the same students will take basic writing, the grammar workshop, oral communication, and sociology, for example, together with the accompanying adjunct reading course. In the spring students choose their own sections of courses, based on schedule preference or, for the second writing course, on their preference of research topic. Second semester course offerings include immigration literature, research writing, and a second content course with its paired reading course. Students in the sciences typically add a math course this semester as well. At the end of the year, then, a CE student has filled the following college requirements: first-year writing, speech, literature, and two courses that fulfill a requirement in social science, humanities, or a science with a lab (see Figure 2).

As discussed earlier, acknowledging this interdependency of content knowledge and language learning, the CE curriculum builds language support into typical first-year courses so that students study the content and earn the credit of the freshman year. The language support is constructed in several ways. Where communication is central (e.g., writing, speech, grammar workshop), there are separate CE-designated sections, allowing for attention to second-language concerns and creating an environment in which students are less likely to be silenced by others in the classroom who have the advantages of full fluency in English. Where content is central (e.g., biology, anthropology, sociology, arts), CE students enroll in sections with other students in the college but have the benefit of a two-credit adjunct reading class for CE students

COURSES IN THE COMMANDING ENGLISH PROGRAM

Fall Semester 2003

■ GC 1041 DEVELOPING COLLEGE READING   2 credits

Comprehension and study strategies necessary for college textbook reading. This course uses the textbook from one of the content courses below. Previewing the textbook for content and organization, underlining and making marginal notes, outlining, anticipating test questions, and technical vocabulary.

■ Content courses: Choose one (These all fill requirements at the U of M)

GC 1211   PEOPLE AND PROBLEMS (sociology)   4 credits
GC 1311   GENERAL ART   3 credits
GC 1131   PRINCIPLES OF BIOLOGICAL SCIENCE   4 credits

■ GC 1051 INTRO TO COLLEGE WRITING: WORKSHOP   2 credits

This is a grammar workshop that focuses on developing editing skills and accuracy in written English through practice with grammar trouble-spots, editing strategies, and sentence combining.

■ GC 1421 WRITING LABORATORY I   3 credits

This is the first of a two-semester writing sequence required at the University. Focus is on reading and writing expository/analytical texts centered on the topic of education.

■ GC 1461 ORAL COMMUNICATION IN THE PUBLIC SPHERE   3 credits

Through discussion, prepared speeches, and debates, students develop strategies for effective oral communication. Theories of communication, ethics, citizenship, persuasion, language use.

Spring Semester 2004

■ GC 1042 READING IN THE CONTENT AREAS   2 credits

Taken in conjunction with an academic content course; additional practice with reading and study strategies specific to reading in a particular content area.

■ Content courses: Choose one

GC 1285   CULTURAL ANTHROPOLOGY   4 credits
GC 1135   BIOLOGICAL SCIENCE: THE HUMAN BODY   4 credits
GC 1311   GENERAL ART   3 credits

■ GC 1422 WRITING LABORATORY II   3 credits

Academic, research-based writing. Readings, essay assignments explore a topic of contemporary interest. Summaries, analysis, and research writing. Fills 1st year writing requirement.

■ GC 1364 LITERATURE OF THE AMERICAN IMMIGRANT EXPERIENCE 3 credits

Exploration of American immigrant experiences, both historical and contemporary, through readings in fiction, expository prose, biography, and oral history. Course includes substantial reading, discussion, journal writing, essays, and a class project.

Some students add courses such as Math, Career Planning, Physical Education in the spring semester, based on program approval.

Figure 2. Courses in the Commanding English Program.

only that uses the textbooks from the linked content course. Figure 2 lists the courses currently offered through Commanding English. All of the courses are credit bearing, and most fulfill specific requirements at the University.

Developing Academic Writing

Like all first-year students in the college, Commanding English students have two semester-long writing classes that are held in networked computer classrooms, allowing for a workshop setting in the writing classes where students type or research while the instructor circulates and responds to writing in progress. The overarching goal of the two basic writing courses is to build writing proficiency and confidence with academic writing: having a point to make that communicates importance, backing that point up with discussion, taking a stance in writing, and using a variety of sources (e.g., self, others in class, articles, library research, interviews). The first writing course begins with a literacy narrative, in which the writer explores an aspect of his or her education, and then progresses to more source-based writing, building to a focused research paper of six to eight pages. The second writing course centers around a particular theme, and students work up to a 10 to 15 page research project. This includes tasks such as writing position statements, creating annotated bibliographies, summarizing articles, and critically analyzing citation sources. By the end of the year in Commanding English, students will have written at least eight papers in the CE writing classes alone, two involving fairly extensive research.

CE sections of the two writing courses adhere closely to the standards and underlying principles of all of the writing courses in the General College. Students work on remarkably similar writing problems: developing a stance toward a topic, being organized, supporting general statements with specific examples, citing sources in American Psychological Association (APA) or Modern Language Association (MLA) format, and approximating academic tone. Commanding English sections of the writing courses do acknowledge the constraints of writing in a second language and differ from the other writing sections in basically four ways:

1. There is less graded in-class writing where students are asked to produce a short paper during class time, acknowledging the time that students need to formulate and write in a second language.

2. Readings and assignments are chosen mindful of topics for which students may have limited background information or of readings where the vocabulary load or length is not justified in a course where the focus is on writing.

3. Major papers go through three drafts, with the second draft specifically for purposes of attending to language and style, because the constraints of

second-language writing make it more likely that writers will struggle more with word choice and grammar.

4. There is a writing consultant, an undergraduate peer tutor from the GC Writing Center, present in the classroom, increasing students' access to one-on-one consultation about writing as they work, and strengthening ties with the Writing Center so that students are more likely to use it as a resource outside of class.

In all other aspects, these CE sections are similar to the other sections of the course in terms of the number of papers, amount of reading, goals of the course, credits earned, and so on.

Developing Grammatical Accuracy

During fall semester, in addition to the writing class, CE students enroll in a linked grammar editing workshop, where the focus is on building language editing strategies, overviewing the kinds of language troublespots that English causes (e.g., verb tense, agreement, soft -ed endings, sentence boundaries), and examining the kinds of errors marked by the writing teacher in the editing drafts of the papers from the basic writing course. This combination of explicit language information, practice with editing strategies, and attention to one's individual grammar errors reaches a wide range of students, from those who have studied English formally as a language and are familiar with intricacies of grammar rules, to students who have learned English more informally and may have a strong sense of idiom without knowing grammar terminology in much detail.

As an example, a student writer who has difficulty with past tense versus present tense consistency in writing may need (a) strategies for slowing down the proofreading process to make it more deliberate, (b) some knowledge and guidelines about using the present tense to signal general truth in contrast to simple past tense for past time events, or (c) practice differentiating between past and present tense verb forms. By working on grammar within the context of the student's own writing from this three-pronged approach (strategies, knowledge, practice), there is a better chance of effective learning than a student would get from simply having errors circled on a paper or being told to "go to the writing lab." The focus on editing is also continued in all of the writing classes at the final draft stage of paper writing.

Developing Academic Voice

Although accuracy is a feature of academic writing, writing instruction that moves beyond error correction to the wider development of academic voice is critical for multilingual students. CE writing instructors are well aware of what Shaughnessy (1977) called the "damage that has been done to students in the name of correct writing" (p. 9) and the loss of confidence these learners have often experienced through aggressive error correction of their writing. The focus on grammar error in writing instruction for multilingual students, although obviously necessary for the full development of academic literacy, often tends to be disproportionate, and it becomes, in effect, a focus on deficit. Zamel (1998) recommended that we should look for evidence of students' intelligence, and if necessary reread students' attempts as coherent efforts once we have overcome the tendency to be distracted by sentence-level errors. In short, she said, "value—don't just evaluate" (p. 263). The multi-draft approach that we use in CE writing assignments gives us the opportunity to show students that we value what they write. Students receive extensive feedback on first drafts both from instructors and from each other, and the feedback at this stage is exclusively on ideas and content. In the writing classes, then, we offer what Zamel (2004) called "multiple opportunities to use language and write-to-learn . . . classroom exchanges and assignments that promote the acquisition of unfamiliar language, concepts and approaches to inquiry" (p. 14).

In the attempt to encourage voice by reading beyond our students' errors, we do not seek to nurture student personal voice at the expense of academic voice. As Johns (1999) pointed out, personal identity or expressivist approaches to teaching are inward looking and can fail to prepare students for success in the larger environment of the academy. Although we focus strongly on the development of voice, we certainly do not limit the focus of student writing to personal experience. On the contrary, only one graded assignment in the writing courses, which is the first one of the year, is based on students' own life experience; they then begin to incorporate textual sources and to practice the "experience of remembering others' work, referencing it, pulling it in at just the right place in one's own emerging text, transforming it to serve one's own ends, and giving it space without privileging it over one's own words" (Blanton, 1999, p. 137).

For those students who are struggling with pronunciation or who might otherwise feel inhibited by their English, being in basic writing classes and in the editing workshop, which are offered exclusively for multilingual students, can make participation in class discussions and peer review sessions more comfortable. These CE classes validate and support the needs of some for a place to ask questions and work on skills related to language without fear of judgment by native-speaker students who may not understand those needs. Although the importance of this "safe" place is paramount for some students, others are more eager to be in mainstream classes alongside U.S. American freshmen. In fact, most cohorts include a few students who, at least in the beginning of the academic year, resent what they see as their "segregation" from the mainstream. These students regard Commanding English as a synonym for ESL, a label with which they are understandably tired of being identified. Such students tend to "feel strongly that they should not be placed differently from other U.S. high school graduates" (Blanton, 1999, p. 123). We are sensitive to this issue, and in addition to having our students take mainstream content classes in General College, we have also begun to offer seats in one of our own courses, GC 1364 Literature of American Immigrant Experience, discussed in more detail later in this chapter, to students from outside the CE program. As Kutz, Groden, and Zamel (1993) asserted, validation of student voice and nurturing of student confidence should be a priority during the freshman year, but our experience shows that there is no "one size fits all" way to honor that priority.

Developing Oral Communication Skills

Because most CE students have been in the U.S. for 1 to 8 years and have graduated from U.S. high schools, there is less need for the listening and speaking components of a traditional ESL program designed for recently-arrived international students. CE students do not need to learn conversational English expression. Although speech may be accented and some students may still be uncomfortable speaking in class discussions on academic content, there is a general competence in conversational English. Rather than a traditional ESL speaking class, the CE program offers its own sections of college speech where students work on formal academic presentation skills and researching and organizing informative and persuasive speeches on a variety of current topics. Students discuss strategies for compensating for accented speech, such as using visual aids, paraphrasing, checking for comprehension, and slowing the rate of speech. On an individual basis, some accent reduction work is available, but this is not a formal component of the class. Students comment frequently that the speech course makes a difference in their confidence in speaking in front of a class. In the reading adjunct courses students also prepare small group presentations of course information, building on the strategies learned in the speech course.

Developing Academic Reading Proficiency

All of the courses in the CE curriculum demand significant amounts of reading. Students analyze articles assigned in the writing courses; they read and research for their speeches, and all of the classes use college-level textbooks. A typical third week of spring semester might include 37 pages of anatomy, two chapters covering the skeletal system and genetic engineering and cloning, 115 pages of literature from Anzia Yezierska's (1925/1975) immigrant novel *Bread Givers*, and 10 pages of reading in the human rights research writing course, including a *Newsweek* (Levin, 1982) article on building a case for torture as well as numerous Web sites that the class is evaluating. Where we deliberately focus on reading proficiency in the curriculum is in the reading adjunct courses and the three-credit college literature course, Literature of the American Immigrant Experience. In the literature course, students build fluency through extensive reading (50 to 70 pages per night), at the same time that they are studying literature. In the reading adjuncts the focus is on academic reading.

Following the TRIO model of providing small seminar-style support courses linked to discipline-specific content courses, we have developed reading adjunct courses that combine the supplemental support with focused reading instruction (see Chapter 19 for a discussion of the TRIO program and Supplemental Instruction). Current choices of linked content courses in Commanding English are Cultural Anthropology, People and Problems (sociology), General Art (humanities), and two biology courses: General Biology and Human Anatomy. Students register for both the "content" course and the paired reading adjunct course, using the same textbooks for both classes. The adjunct courses emphasize reading skills within the context of their particular content areas, offering students extra time to study course material, a safe place to ask questions, an opportunity to review notes together with peers, and so on.

All the reading adjuncts courses work with students on developing their academic vocabulary, reading and note-taking strategies, study skills, critical thinking, and metacognitive awareness. Reading instructors facilitate review of the content course material, provide students with time to share lecture notes, clarify content course assignments and concepts mentioned in the content class, and mediate discussion on how to process and analyze the content area knowledge and how to study for course exams and quizzes. The reading adjunct courses help the students build academic vocabulary in ways that allow them to participate actively in the learning process, for example, through predicting or choosing the vocabulary to study for tests, designing mock quizzes, and presenting review sessions for each other. By taking ownership of part of the course curriculum such as negotiating vocabulary learning standards and designing quizzes, the students not only become more autonomous and successful learners, but also build metacognitive awareness of the learning experience that can be applied to future academic work.

The reading courses all have different focuses, because reading in social science, for example, is different from reading in biology. The human anatomy reading course places emphasis on helping students understand and memorize discipline-specific terminology, including affixes commonly used in the health sciences. Unlike other reading adjunct courses that can focus more on global concepts and critical reading, the human anatomy reading course assists students with strategies for memorizing terms and concepts, reading anatomy charts, and studying for difficult multiple choice tests. In contrast, the adjunct courses for sociology and general art explicitly teach reading strategies, such as Survey, Question, Read, Recite, and Review (SQ3R; Robinson, 1961, described in Pauk, 1993) and reading skills such as highlighting important sentences of a paragraph, paraphrasing, paying attention to pronoun references (e.g., she, he, they, it, these, that) in the text, differentiating reader opinion and the author's point of view, and reading for implied meaning. One focus of the anthropology adjunct draws the students' attention to the rhetorical structure of academic articles in anthropology. This reading adjunct course also tries to establish a link between the textbook and the students' lives through accurate understanding of course material, critical thinking, and a four-step response process involving: (a) personal response to the reading; (b) literal response to the reading; (c) interpretation of the reading; and (d) application to self, life, or a given context through experiential learning such as role-play and short simulations. The general biology adjunct course not only focuses on discipline-specific terminology learning, but also leads the students to compare the rhetorical differences between academic scientific and popular science writings in terms of audience, sentence structure, essay organization, and accuracy of information and sources. Students choose specific topics from the biology class in order to carry out this comparison and then create poster presentations of their findings both on the topics and the differences between the sources they used. All these focuses on different aspects of the reading process by different adjunct courses work together to assist the students in becoming not only competent but also critical readers of particular academic genres.

A close connection between the content course and the reading adjunct course is essential. The CE instructor designs the reading course to follow the goals and schedule of the connected lecture course. In the sociology pair, for example, the sociology syllabus lists the following goals: (a) we will learn to read social science texts, including summarizing articles and analyzing the author's main point; (b) after practicing the skill to summarize theoretical arguments and critique them in class orally, we will learn to write a social science paper, including how to compare and contrast our own ideas from the articles read in class; and (c) ultimately, our goal is to be able to back up our own points of view on various issues after a thoughtful exploration of the topic.

The sociology reading adjunct syllabus responds directly to these goals through its own objectives. Objectives for academic reading skills include:

1. Preview a book and chapter for content and organization.

2. Form questions about previewed material and read to answer these questions.

3. Highlight or underline main ideas and key supporting details, take notes on reading, and summarize.

4. Organize information into maps, outlines, or study cards.

5. Identify possible test items for review.

Objectives for reading analysis include:

1. Determine the author's purpose and point of view.

2. Distinguish between fact and opinion.

3. Recognize two sides of an argument and the evidence given for each.

4. Make inferences.

These reading objectives not only echo the general goals of the sociology class but also lay out the specific reading strategies to achieve these general goals (Zhang, 2002).

Besides reading skills and strategies, the reading courses also teach students a wide range of language, academic, and study skills. These include self-regulatory strategies such as time management, procedural skills such as understanding the routine of college classes, and strategic skills in the institution such as how to seek help from professors and teaching assistants. All of this is situated within the context of an academic discipline.

This close connection between the content-area college course and the adjunct reading course has led to consistently higher performance by the CE students compared with their native English speaker peers in the same class. For example, the average final grades earned by CE students during the last three semesters in the GC 1135 Human Anatomy course were consistently a full letter grade higher than final grades for non-CE students. In GC 1131 Principles of Biological Science, the same pattern of grades has been observed. The final grades for CE students in the fall 2003 section of GC 1131 averaged an A-, at least one full letter grade higher than the average final grade for non-CE students (Moore & Christensen, 2005). These successful, measurable outcomes are a result of accountability and motivation on the part of instructors and students alike.

Collaborative Nature of the Program

One of the strengths of Commanding English is the collaboration that a small, integrated program allows among teachers, advisors, and students. The small class size of 15 to 17 students provides opportunities for individual attention from the instructor, closer relationships and bonds with fellow students, and an easier environment in which to ask questions and voice opinions. The connected courses in the curriculum and the close work with program advisors all contribute to the success of the program.

Creating Learning Communities

Mlynarczyk and Babbit (2002) described the strengths of learning communities in academic programs for academic progress and retention. By situating learning within a structure in which students take courses together and teachers and advisors collaborate to support student success, students have a place to belong on campus. For fall semester Commanding English students enroll in "sets" of classes together as a cohort, where they collaborate and lead class discussions and participate in small-group presentations and projects, all of which help build a sense of academic community. The diversity of students, the comfort level students gain in classes together, and high academic motivation all work to set a tone that encourages academic performance in the program.

Students develop relationships with each other and with the program that may last throughout their university experience. Students often report that they have developed study groups outside of class and maintained connections with each other long after their year in the Commanding English program. Later on, students return to Commanding English to share their struggles as well as their successes. At the end of the year, a handful of CE "alumni" are brought in as graduating seniors to talk to students in the program about their experiences at the University: how they chose a major, how they survived difficult courses, what internships or other programs they have found; and what advice they would pass on to the "graduating freshmen" as they move out of CE into the sophomore year. The importance of having a place to belong on campus cannot be underestimated.

A Connected Curriculum

In the curriculum itself there is close connection between courses, and this close connection fosters both collaboration among instructors and a coherence of instruction for students. The most obvious connection is found in the reading courses that are paired with content courses. The reading courses, in addition to providing students with the kinds of reading and language support described earlier in this chapter, also provide the content professors with an ESL colleague with whom to consult on questions of course material and pedagogy for the CE students in their classes. The reading instructors also collaborate with each other to ensure that a variety of reading skills and strategies is offered in the different reading courses, so that no two reading adjuncts are alike. A second clear link in the CE curriculum is between the grammar class and the first-semester writing course. Students apply editing strategies learned in the grammar class to the drafts they are working on in the writing course, forging an important link between grammar study and application. This also creates collaboration between the two instructors and the Writing Center consultant who are working with that group of students.

Specialized Advising

Commanding English advisors work closely and collaboratively with staff and students in the program. They answer questions about college policies, course and major selection, and respond to the special concerns of refugee and immigrant students, such as the strain of working to support family members while managing full-time education. When a student appears to be having academic or personal difficulty, the advisor is notified through an academic alert system. Here it is important that the program has advisors who are sensitive to cross-cultural communication and who know how to listen between the lines. The advisor also works intensively with the students on making connections beyond CE: planning transfer to a degree-granting college of the University, choosing a major, looking for student groups to join, participating in mentorship programs, and exploring job opportunities.

The very nature of the program, with small classes, paired courses, special advisors, and a small teaching staff, encourages connections and opportunities for students to collaborate and learn from each other. Some students may resent the closeness at times, but it provides an environment in which they can develop a confident voice. At the end of the academic year, students tend to leave CE in groups and continue to benefit from the mutually supportive community formed during their freshman year in the program. As Tinto (1998) pointed out, this kind of shared learning through connection to the learning community increases student motivation, and this subsequently contributes positively to student persistence, which will be discussed in further detail at the end of this chapter.

Multiculturalism in the Curriculum

In addition to developing a learning community within the safe space of the program, Commanding English offers a multicultural curriculum in keeping not only with its own program goals but also the mission of General College overall. Multicultural education is defined in the General College community as being far more than an attempt to acknowledge diversity. Indeed, according to Miksch, Bruch, Higbee, Jehangir, and Lundell (2003), who piloted a *Multicultural Awareness Project for Institutional Transformation* (MAP IT; Miksch, Higbee, et al., 2003) within GC, diversity itself "includes a wider variety of social groups than race and ethnicity alone . . . such as home language, religion, gender, sexual orientation, social class, age, and disability" (p. 5). Also, for education to be truly multicultural, it must do more than provide students with the opportunity to celebrate their own social groups and perspectives. Rather, it is an orientation within the college that goes beyond merely inserting units of multicultural study into the main curriculum, moving towards a "transformative agenda" that "better serves the interests of all groups, especially those groups who historically have been marginalized" (Miksch, Bruch, et al., 2003, p. 7). The multicultural content of the CE classes seeks to offset some of the marginalization and the sense of cultural isolation to which many minority students attest (Collins, 2001).

One example in the CE curriculum of a course that gives students the opportunity (but not the obligation) to position themselves as the bicultural, bilingual experts they are, is the Life Histories or Ethnographic Research class offered as one of the sections of the research writing course in the spring semester. In the class, students are trained to interview an elder (three interviews for a total of 5 to 6 hours), to research events in that elder's life, and to write a 20- to 25-page ethnographic life history of the interviewee. Students are free to choose whether to interview an elder from their own or another community, but the majority of students do choose someone from within their own immigrant group. The elders frequently tell their stories in their native languages, and in these cases, the students must not only collect but also translate the material, as well as organize it into chronological sections that also contain textual research of background events. It is a complex task, but it is one that is built on the foundations of the considerable cultural and linguistic expertise that students already have, an expertise that is seldom recognized or rewarded in mainstream classes (Murie, Collins, & Detzner, 2004). The process exemplifies what Johns (1999) called the development of "socioliteracy," through which students apply their knowledge to "analysis and critique of known and new texts" (p. 163). As they construct the life history papers, students are expected to combine textual research (new texts) with the material gathered from interviews, which, while not necessarily "known," is more likely to be familiar and accessible in terms of background knowledge and culture when students interview elders from their own community. By its very nature, the course validates the identities of the elders and of the students who interview them. Such validation of identity is extremely important for encouraging confidence and voice for some students. This course also creates a place in the curriculum for the students' own histories.

Again, we do not assume that all students need this particular kind of validation. As previously mentioned, they are not *required* to interview elders within their own communities; to do so would be exploitative. The class itself is just one offering among several sections of basic research writing from which students choose according to their own preference. Spring 2004 choices included a section that was designed to dovetail with the sociology course and lead to research on topics of race, class, and gender within the United States. One strength of this topic choice for students is that the readings and assignments of the writing course and those of the sociology course complement each other in such a way that students have the opportunity to focus on social problems in greater depth than they might otherwise do, and therefore they are able to discuss and write about certain topics with a greater sense of competence. For those with an interest in social problems beyond the U.S., a good choice frequently offered for the spring research writing course is the topic of international human rights. This subject matter acknowledges the experiences CE students themselves may have had and validates an international focus. Research topics chosen by students in recent years have included the connection between the caste system and poverty in India and the extent to which the United Nations (UN) *Convention on the Elimination of All Forms of Discrimination Against Women* (1981) has been effective in protecting women's rights in two of its signatory nations. Another topic choice for basic research writing focuses on issues of biomedical ethics and genetic engineering. This is a demanding but popular topic for many current CE students who have a high level of interest in health science careers.

Another example of multicultural content in the program curriculum is the three-credit course we designed: Literature of the American Immigrant Experience (GC 1364). This course is part of the spring curriculum in CE. As previously mentioned, it was originally offered exclusively to our own students, but over the past 2 years we have opened seats to any undergraduates at the University. This literature course explores the common themes of U.S. immigration history through literature written by and about immigrants. Texts for the course typically include four novels. In the year 2004, for example, the list included *Thousand Pieces of Gold* (McCunn, 1981), *Bread Givers* (Yezierska, 1925/1975), *No-No Boy* (Okada, 1976), and *Odyssey to the North* (Bencastro, 1998). As an alternative, the students can choose three novels and an anthology of short stories, including *Imagining America* edited by Brown and Ling (2002), or *Hungry Hearts* by Yezierska (1920/1996). Texts also include poetry and supplemental readings relating historical or current events or contexts to the literature being studied. Although students often find the reading load of approximately 50 to 100 pages per class period challenging at first, they tend to warm to the task as they begin to recognize that many of the themes discussed have relevance to their own lives or the lives of those around them. Collins (2001) reported that students "saw themselves as part of a larger group of people who had made their way from another country to make their home in the United States" (p. 16). Moreover, the study revealed that students' motivation to learn and succeed was positively connected to the relevance of the curriculum to their experiences.

It is important to reiterate at this point that the program fully acknowledges that some of our students may not wish to identify as immigrants or refugees, and in keeping with this, we are careful in designing discussions and assignments never to pressure them to self-disclose, although the opportunity is often there for students who wish to do so. In keeping with this effort not to position students in certain cultural identities, we have also attempted to avoid choosing texts for the course that reflect the specific nationalities of our student population. Given the diversity of students' origins, however—in spring 2004, for example, one section of 26 students identified themselves as having 13 different first languages and 16 different ethnicities—and the impossibility of predicting the cultural backgrounds of all, it is difficult to ensure that text choices are "culture neutral," so to speak. And, again, just as the safety of CE-only classes is as important to some as the integration of mixed classes is to others, so too the multicultural nature of the curriculum allows space both for students who wish to position themselves as immigrants and for those who do not.

Curriculum From the Student Perspective

Thus far, we have provided a general overview of the Commanding English curriculum, and we would like to consider how the various threads of the curriculum we have described might weave together into the students' experience over the freshman year. Between September and May, students have read five novels, three textbooks (e.g., speech, biology, and sociology), and numerous shorter academic articles. They have written a total of at least 10 papers, including two major research papers with annotated bibliographies. They have given four speeches, several of them based on research, and three to six class presentations. These students have earned 25 to 30 credits and are well positioned for the sophomore year.

Looking more closely at one individual student's experience, we return to the example of Ifrah, the young woman from East Africa introduced at the beginning of this chapter. Well into her freshman year, we see that during her fall semester writing class, she read *The Color of Water* (McBride, 1996), the autobiography of an African American man whose Jewish mother raised a large family in poverty during the 1960s, various articles on aspects of education including the "culture of power" (Delpit, 1988), multiculturalism, and how history is taught in U.S. schools (Levine, Lowe, Peterson, & Tenorio, 1995), reflecting on her own educational experiences in relation to these texts. For her research paper, she examined the ESL curriculum in high school and the extent to which it has proven effective in serving immigrant students. Ifrah used a combination of textual research and interviews to support her findings in this paper, and she went on to share some of it in a persuasive letter to the principal of her former high school, asking that he pay more attention to the needs of the increasing immigrant population of that district. In the editing workshop, Ifrah looked at several of the recurring grammar errors in her own writing, including singular-plural agreement, verb tense, and sentence structure problems, and she learned some rules and techniques for self-correction. In anthropology she read several studies in an anthology by Spradley and McCurdy (2003) about the hidden elements of culture and the difficulties anthropologists experience in truly understanding the cultures they study. Using her new knowledge of anthropology, Ifrah also created a design for an anthropological study of a real-life problem in her own community. In her speech class, Ifrah gave an informative speech on "Capital Punishment: The Death Penalty in the United States" and two persuasive speeches about the abuses of sweatshops and the effects of second-hand smoke on children.

During the second semester, Ifrah, who hopes to major in health sciences, took a human anatomy course in which she struggled with the terminology-laden textbook and the multiple-choice exam format. In the reading adjunct course, she learned how to memorize and study scientific material, and although she failed the first anatomy exam, by the end of the class she had earned a low B, a full grade above the average for the mainstream human anatomy students. In literature, Ifrah resonated with the struggles of Sarah, a young Jewish immigrant in the novel *Bread Givers* (Yezierska, 1925/1975), and while she enjoyed the contemporary relevance of *Odyssey to the North* (Bencastro, 1998), she found its literary style, with its multiple story and time lines, quite challenging. She took three exams and wrote three essays on literature, and for a final project in that class she collaborated with two classmates to write a fictional Somali immigrant story which, when previewed in class, prompted requests from several other students for copies of the final 25-page project. In her writing class, Ifrah continued to struggle with the frustrations of academic research, and she ended the semester with a nine-page paper on the way Africa is portrayed in U.S. media. She used textual research to show the tendency for biased and incomplete reporting of news about African countries by the Cable News Network (CNN) news Web site, as well as to explore some of the possible reasons for the problem. It was a difficult topic, and disappointed by her grade on that paper, she abandoned her plan to write and send out a persuasive letter to the news editor on the topic. Finally, Ifrah has met with her advisor and worked out a transfer plan for the end of the sophomore year.

Looking ahead, Ifrah has registered for her sophomore fall courses and will begin the chemistry and math sequences that she needs for her major. She has filled the requirements for nursing majors for freshman writing, speech, a literature course with a multicultural focus, one social science, and one science with a lab. She has made numerous friends in the program with whom she plans to keep in touch next year.

Evaluation

Anecdotally, we know that the Commanding English program works for students like Ifrah when we are able to watch their transformation over the freshman year, but we also have more than 25 years of evidence that the program works. The Commanding English Program evaluates itself in a number of ways. As a small program of approximately 60 students, 9 instructors, and one or two advisors, it is not difficult to keep track of how the year is progressing. Two meetings per semester are devoted to discussions of student progress; advisors meet with students around topics of registration and transfer planning, and when an issue appears in the program, we communicate with each other, consult with students, and if possible, make necessary changes. Twice a year students are asked to fill out program evaluations, anonymously, asking for numerical ratings of courses and other aspects of the program as well as narrative answers to such questions as "Did your feeling about the CE program change during the time you were in the program?" The final question asks students to offer suggestions for improving the CE program. On the basis of responses to this question, the program has changed. In the early 1990s, the curriculum had a noncredit reading course during the fall term that used an ESL reading textbook. Students frequently commented that the course lacked interest and that they resented the noncredit status. This course was transformed into the three-credit immigrant literature course now in the curriculum. When we later considered the move to open up seats in the literature course to non-CE students, we polled the current students in the program that year, getting their input, and continued to monitor the change for the next 2 years. Last year, in response to comments about wanting more choice in the curriculum, we added a second biology course, so that students have a science option both semesters.

Student Satisfaction

In addition, Commanding English uses these program evaluations to measure student satisfaction. In these semiannual surveys, we look to measure satisfaction in the responses to the following two questions:

1. Think about your experiences in the CE program during fall and spring

semester. Overall, what do you feel was most important, useful or successful about your experiences in the CE program this year?

2. Overall, what do you feel was least important, useful or successful about your experience in the CE program this year?

Positive comments consistently outweighed negative comments. In the spring of 2004, students wrote 34 positive comments and 12 negative comments. In the fall of 2003, students wrote 49 positive comments and 23 negative comments. In the spring of 2003, students wrote 48 positive comments and 34 negative comments. Positive comments are generally about specific courses, in particular the writing classes, the teachers, the preparation the program offered, the friendly staff, small classes, and opportunities for encouragement. To quote from a few students:

"The CE Program helped me prepare more and gives me a sense of how the life in the U. would be. Most important part is the diversity."

"Smaller class size helped more one on one contact between the instructors and students. Good support for freshman."

"Gave me the confidence to move on! Very helpful."

"I guess spring was more complex and a bit harder than the fall. But, after all I feel good and I gained a lot of knowledge."

Negative comments usually center around two issues: the lack of course choices and general dissatisfaction with the grammar and reading adjunct courses, in particular because they do not fulfill particular University requirements. A few students also express a desire to be more integrated with other UMN students. A sampling of typical comments follow:

"I did not need reading courses which were not helpful to me. It was extra work for me."

"Could not choose or take what I wanted."

"Not knowing other kids outside of CE."

Typically the spring ratings are higher than the fall, suggesting increased satisfaction with the program. In year-end evaluations, students reported feeling more positive about being in the program. In 2003, 28 students reported feeling more positive about being in the program, 11 students reported feeling neutral, and 6 reported feeling more negative. In 2004, 18 students said they felt more positive about being in the program, 3 reported neutral feelings, and 2 said they felt more negative.

A number of students wrote that they were unsure when they began the program but felt more satisfied at the end. To quote from one response to this question: "At first I thought it was basically like ESL or something, but now I know . . . it's not ESL, it's much like the same as a regular program." Three students commented in the spring 2003 evaluations that they felt more positive now because they believed the program was listening to what students want. This was the semester when we decided to explore adding another course into the curriculum, in part in response to negative comments in the fall evaluations about the lack of choice in the program. We involved students in choosing which courses to look at, examining textbooks, and ultimately it was a panel of students who made the choice to add the general biology course. Evaluations the following year were higher, perhaps in part because this additional course added another science option in the curriculum.

Retention and Graduation

The more formal way in which we evaluate program outcomes is through gathering retention and graduation data. Roughly every 2 years, the GC Office of Research and Evaluation compiles this data for us. "Commanding English students still show very high retention rates . . . indeed, they are higher than those for GC cohorts as a whole" (Hatfield, 2004). After 5 or 6 years, 49% to 65% of the students who began in Commanding English have either graduated or are in good standing at the University. These statistics are well above the average for the General College, in spite of the fact that CE students are studying in a second or third language, without many of the resources that native-born U.S. students have.

Need for Further Evaluation

We have not conducted systematic longitudinal studies of what students face after they exit Commanding English. Are they able to pursue the majors they had wanted? What is the climate of the university for language-minority students? What factors enable a student to persist? The students who succeed tend to be the ones who keep in touch with us, and so we hear the success stories: (a) the Vietnamese woman who became the commencement speaker at the University of Minnesota's Institute of Technology graduation; (b) the first Somali cohort of six students who entered the program in 1999, five of whom are now graduated or about to graduate with majors in criminal justice, global studies, public health, biology, and human ecology; (c) the students who went on to graduate school; (d) the students who are now working as computer scientists; (e) the students who have graduated from the business school; or (f) the student who just got accepted into the highly competitive school of nursing on campus. We are less likely to hear from those who did not persist or meet whatever expectations they had set for themselves here at the University. A focused study that looks at the lives of a cohort of students as they go through their 4 or 5 years at the University of Minnesota would be a valuable project.

MODELS OF CONTENT-BASED LANGUAGE PROGRAMS

Programs directly modeled after the GC Commanding English Program

University of Wisconsin–Eau Claire
COMMANDING ENGLISH
Serves primarily Hmong students with ACT reading or English part scores below 17. One-year program includes writing, intro to psychology, reading, library skills, critical thinking, academic reading and writing, and human geography. (http//www.uwec.edu/cep/overview.html)

Minnesota State University–Mankato
LANGUAGE LEARNING FOR ACADEMIC SUCCESS
Pilot program (2004) to improve academic support for and retention of first-year students whose home language is not English. ESL writing/reading course connected with a social science course (fall) chemistry (spring), two basic writing courses, and a first-year experience seminar. Students work as a cohort, or learning community, receiving special advising and mentoring from the program coordinator.

Other content-based first-year programs

Kingsborough Community College
INTENSIVE ENGLISH PROGRAM
Content-based ESL learning communities: students enroll in ESL courses paired with a social science or history course, speech, and two student development courses. The pass rate for students in this model surpassed the pass rate for students in the more traditional ESL courses 76% to 58%. For more information see Mlynarczyk and Babbit (2002).

Suffolk University
SHELTERED ESL PROGRAM
For students with minimum TOEFL score of 173. Students enroll in U.S. History, Integrated Studies, Rhetorical Communications, with linked ESL reading and ESL writing courses. Students have the advantage of being in a learning community and having their ESL instruction relate directly to the academic courses they are taking. (http://sls.suffolk.edu)

University of California–Berkeley
STUDENT LEARNING CENTER SUPPORT SERVICE
Wide range of academic support services to build academic support into the college curriculum: adjunct courses, workshops, study groups, small-group tutorials, as well as individual tutoring. Some of this adjunct support is targeted toward second-language students, although not labeled directly as such. The aim is to support students with the challenges of rigorous assignments and exams on campus. (Margi Wald, TESOL 2003 presentation: "Building Academic Literacy for College Success," http://slc.berkeley.edu/nns/nns.htm)

Figure 3. Models of Content-Based Language Programs.

Conclusion

What we do know is that Ifrah is now a sophomore. She has stronger writing skills, a sense of reading both in the social sciences and in the health sciences, she has articulated strong opinions on topics that are relevant to her own experiences, and made some lasting friends. Commanding English can point to 25 years of success with students like Ifrah. This model of integrated academic and language work offers a path for students to survive the first year of college; build the academic literacy needed for introductory courses in anthropology, sociology, biology, literature, and writing; and to do so in a way that allows students to have a voice and a place on campus. Because the program extends through the entire first year, students have time to develop their academic writing and reading proficiency in significant ways that allow them to gain confidence with the challenges of a college curriculum.

In describing the Commanding English model, we are mindful that a content-embedded, academic skills program is a specialized English language program, not a replacement for stand-alone ESL programs that may be useful in other contexts. (See Figure 3 for ways that the Commanding English model has been adapted in other settings.) However, we maintain that students like Ifrah do not need continued preparation for the freshman year; rather, Generation 1.5 students need to be engaged in the learning of the freshman year while also developing reading and writing proficiency. Through engagement during the freshman year in the small learning community of Commanding English, students are able to learn academic content, build academic skills, develop academic voice, and make lasting friendships—all leading to their persistence and graduation from the university. In looking back on the last 25 years, we are confident that the Commanding English program has been a successful model for the development of academic literacy for multilingual students. As we look to the future, we are hopeful that more students like Ifrah will have access to the opportunity for higher education through programs that address the real academic needs of the freshman year for Generation 1.5 students.

References

Adamson, H. D. (1993). *Academic competence: Theory and classroom practice: Preparing ESL students for content courses.* White Plains, NY: Longman.

Babbitt, M., & Mlynarczyk, R. W. (2000). Keys to successful content-based programs: Administrative perspectives. In L. Kaspar (Ed.), *Content-based college ESL instruction* (pp. 26–47). Mahwah, NJ: Lawrence Erlbaum Associates.

Bailey, T. & Weininger, E. B. (2002). Performance, graduation, and transfer of immigrants and natives in City University of New York Community Colleges. *Educational Evaluation and Policy Analysis, 24(4),* 359–377.

Bencastro, M. (1998). *Odyssey to the north.* Houston, TX: Arte Público Press.

Blanton, L. L. (1999). Classroom instruction and language minority students: On teaching to "smarter" readers and writers. In L. Harklau, M. Siegal, & K. M. Losey (Eds.), *Generation 1.5 meets college composition: Issues in the teaching of writing to U.S. educated learners of ESL* (pp. 119–142). Mahwah, NJ: Lawrence Erlbaum Associates.

Brown, W., & Ling, A. (Eds.). (2002). *Imagining America: Stories from the promised land.* New York: Persea Books.

Collins, M. (2001). The multicultural classroom: Immigrants reading the literature of the American immigrant experience. *MinneTESOL/WITESOL Journal, 18,* 13–21.

Cummins, J. (1981). Age on arrival and immigrant second language learning in Canada: A reassessment. *Applied Linguistics, 2,* 131–149.

Delpit, L. (1988). The silenced dialogue: Power and pedagogy in educating other people's children. *Harvard Educational Review, 58,* 280–297.

Detzner, D., Collins, M., Murie, R., & Hendrickson, Z. (2004). Teaching about families and elders to immigrant students using an in-depth biography assignment. *Journal of Teaching in Marriage and Family, 4(1),* 59–75.

Detzner, D., Xiong, B., & Eliason, P. (1999). *Helping youth succeed: Bicultural parenting education for Southeast Asian families.* St. Paul, MN: University of Minnesota Extension Service.

Gee, J. P. (2004). What is literacy? In V. Zamel & R. Spack (Eds.), *Crossing the curriculum: Multilingual learners in college classrooms* (pp. 51–59). Mahwah, NJ: Lawrence Erlbaum Associates.

Hatfield, J. (2004). *Commanding English tracking report.* Minneapolis, MN: Office of Research and Evaluation, General College, University of Minnesota.

Harklau, L., Siegal, M., & Losey, K. M. (Eds.). (1999). *Generation 1.5 meets college composition: Issues in the teaching of writing to U.S. educated learners of ESL.* Mahwah, NJ: Lawrence Erlbaum Associates.

Johns, A. (1999). Opening our doors: Applying socioliterate approaches (SA) to language minority classrooms. In L. Harklau, M. Siegal, & K. M. Losey, (Eds.), *Generation 1.5 meets college composition: Issues in the teaching of writing to U.S. educated learners of ESL* (pp. 159–171). Mahwah, NJ: Lawrence Erlbaum Associates.

Kaspar, L. F. (Ed.). (2000). *Content-based college ESL instruction.* Mahwah, NJ: Lawrence Erlbaum Associates.

Krashen, S. (1982). *Principles and practice in second language acquisition.* Oxford, UK: Pergamon Press.

Kutz, E., Groden, S., & Zamel, V. (1993). *The discovery of competence: Teaching and learning with diverse student writers.* Portsmouth, NH: Boynton/Cook.

Lantolf, J .P., & Appel, G. (Eds.). (1994). *Vygotskian approaches to second language research.* Norwood, NJ: Ablex.

Lantolf, J. P., & Pavlenko, A. (1995). Sociocultural theory and second language acquisition. *Annual Review of Applied Linguistics, 15,* 108–124.

Leki, I. (1999). "Pretty much I screwed up:" Ill-served needs of a permanent resident. In L. Harklau, M. Siegal, & K. M. Losey, (Eds.), *Generation 1.5 meets college composition: Issues in the teaching of writing to U.S. educated learners of ESL* (pp. 17–43). Mahwah, NJ: Lawrence Erlbaum Associates.

Levin, M. (1982, June 7). The case for torture. *Newsweek, 99,* 13.

Levine, D., Lowe, R., Peterson, B., & Tenorio, R. (1995). *Rethinking schools: An agenda for change.* New York: The New Press.

McBride, J. (1996). *The color of water: A Black man's tribute to his White mother.* New York: Riverhead.

McCafferty, S. G. (1994). Adult second language learners' use of private speech: A review of studies. *The Modern Language Journal, 78,* 421–436.

McCunn, R. L. (1981). *Thousand pieces of gold.* Boston: Beacon Press.

Miksch, K. L., Bruch, P. L., Higbee, J. L., Jehangir, R. R., & Lundell, D. B. (2003). The centrality of multiculturalism in developmental education: Piloting the Multicultural Awareness Project for Institutional Transformation (MAP IT). In J. L. Higbee, D. B. Lundell, & I. M. Duranczyk (Eds.), *Multiculturalism in developmental education* (pp. 5–13). Minneapolis, MN: Center for Research on Developmental Education and Urban Literacy, General College, University of Minnesota.

Miksch, K. L., Higbee, J. L., Jehangir, R. R., Lundell, D. B., Bruch, P. L., & Barajas, H. L. (2003). *Multicultural Awareness Project for Institutional Transformation (MAP IT) 10 guiding principles for institutions of higher education* (rev. ed.). Minneapolis, MN: Multicultural Concerns Committee and Center for Research on Developmental Education and Urban Literacy, General College, University of Minnesota.

Minnesota Department of Education Data Center. (2003). *School and district fall population files.* Retrieved December 14, 2003, from http://cfl.state.mn.us/datactr/

Mlynarczyk, R. W., & Babbitt, M. (2002). The power of academic learning communities. *Journal of Basic Writing, 21*(1), 71–89.

Moore, R. & Christensen, L. (2005). *Academic behaviors and performances of immigrants who succeed in college science courses.* Unpublished manuscript, University of Minnesota.

Murie, R., Collins, M., & Detzner, D. (in press). Building academic literacy from student strengths: An interdisciplinary life history project. *Journal of Basic Writing.*

Murie, R., & Thomson, R. (2001). When ESL is developmental: A model program for the freshman year. In J. L. Higbee (Ed.), *2001: A developmental odyssey* (pp. 15–28). Warrensburg, MO: National Association for Developmental Education.

Okada, J. (1976). *No-no boy.* Seattle, WA: University of Washington Press.

Pauk, W. (1993). *How to study in college.* Boston: Houghton Mifflin.

Roberge, M. (2002). California's generation 1.5 immigrants: What experiences, characteristics, and needs do they bring to our English classes? *CATESOL Journal, 14* (1), 107–130.

Robinson, F. P. (1961). *Effective study.* New York: Harper.

Ruiz-de-Velasco, J., & Fix, M. (2000). *Overlooked and underserved: Immigrant students in U.S. secondary schools.* Washington, DC: The Urban Institute Press.

Shaughnessey, M. (1977). *Errors and expectations: A guide for the teacher of basic writing.* Oxford, UK: Oxford University Press.

Short, D. J. (2000). What principals should know about sheltered English language instruction. *NASSP Bulletin, 84* (619), 17–27.

Smoke, T. (2001). Mainstreaming writing: What does this mean for ESL students? In G. McNenny & S. H. Fitzgerald (Eds.), *Mainstreaming basic writers: Politics and pedagogies of access* (pp. 193–214). Mahwah, NJ: Lawrence Erlbaum Associates.

Soter, A. (1992). Whose shared assumptions? Making the implicit explicit. In D. Murray (Ed.), *Diversity as resource: Redefining cultural literacy* (pp. 30–55). Alexandria, VA: Teachers of English to Speakers of Other Languages.

Spack, R. (2004). The acquisition of academic literacy via second language: A longitudinal case study, updated. In V. Zamel & R. Spack (Eds.), *Crossing the curriculum: Multilingual learners in college classrooms* (pp. 3–17). Mahwah, NJ: Lawrence Erlbaum Associates.

Spradley, J., & McCurdy, D. W. (2003). *Conformity and conflict: Readings in cultural anthropology* (11th ed.). Boston: Allyn & Bacon.

Swales, J. M. (1990). *Genre analysis: English in academic and research settings.* Cambridge, UK: Cambridge University Press.

Thomas, W. P., & Collier, V. (December, 1997). School effectiveness for language minority students. *National Clearinghouse for Bilingual Education Resource Collection Series, 9.* Washington, DC: National Clearinghouse for Bilingual Education.

Tinto, V. (1998). Colleges as communities: Taking research on student persistence seriously. *The Review of Higher Education, 21* (2), 167–177.

United Nations. (1981). *Convention on the elimination of all forms of discrimination against women.* Geneva, Switzerland: Office of the High Commissioner for Human Rights.

Vygotsky, L. S. (1978). *Mind in society: The development of higher psychological processes.* Cambridge, MA: Harvard University Press.

Wald, M. (2003, March). *Building academic literacy for college success.* Paper presented at the Teaching English to Speakers of Other Languages (TESOL) conference, Baltimore, MD.

Yezierska, A. (1920/1996). *Hungry hearts.* New York: Penguin Books.

Yezierska, A. (1025/1975). *Bread givers.* New York: Persea Books.

Zamel, V. (1998). Strangers in academia: The experiences of faculty and ESL students across the curriculum. In V. Zamel & R. Spack (Eds.), *Negotiating academic literacies: Teaching and learning across languages and cultures* (pp. 249–264). Mahwah, NJ: Lawrence Erlbaum Associates.

Zamel, V. (2004). Strangers in academia: The experiences of faculty and ESOL students across the curriculum. In V. Zamel & R. Spack (Eds.), *Crossing the curriculum: Multilingual learners in college classrooms* (pp. 3–17). Mahwah, NJ: Lawrence Erlbaum Associates.

Zhang, X. (2002). *Teaching content-based adjunct reading courses in a college transitional program: An interview study for professional self-development.* Unpublished manuscript, University of Minnesota.

CHAPTER 10

Multicultural Mathematics: A Social Issues Perspective in Lesson Planning

Susan K. Staats

ABSTRACT

This chapter outlines an approach to introducing the slope formula and rates of change in an introductory developmental algebra class through the context of the epidemiology of global infectious diseases. Although only 29 minutes out of 48 hours of class time were allocated to purely social discussions, students surveyed found this unit to be the single most memorable topic that they studied in the class. Furthermore, over 96% of the students found it to be relevant to their learning of mathematics. Contextualizing mathematics applications with discussions of social issues is an equity pedagogy that can transform students' experience of mathematics.

Successful researchers in applied mathematics and science often describe their work in terms of subjective purpose rather than technical process. McClintock, for example, asserted that her advances in genetics reflected "a feeling for the organism," as the title of Keller's 1983 biography put it. Undergraduate mathematics classes, however, offer little opportunity or support for students to develop subjective, value-based purposes for mathematical study. The radical objectivity of mathematics is a powerful mechanism of exclusion for both developmental and mainstream mathematics students.

The General College mathematics faculty has initiated a teaching experiment designed to help students link their full sense of social awareness to mathematics through discussions of social issues associated with algebra applications. The project is designed to make gains in student engagement by dedicating small phases of class time to the context of mathematics, material that lies just outside of algebraic procedures—geographical and demographic information, policy debates, and perspectives on substantial social issues—all topics that are associated with, but not fully defined by, math applications. In our current project, public health and economic issues associated with worldwide infectious diseases serve as the enriched context of standard algebra topics like the slope formula and exponential growth. As a cultural anthropologist with field experience in malaria-plagued, indigenous communities in Guyana, I developed the unit to draw attention to the long-term personal and economic devastation caused by malaria. When planned carefully, socially-contextualized mathematics discussions can make a strong, positive impression on students and offer opportunities to support basic skills and mathematical thinking.

This social issues approach to mathematics instruction is inspired by the ethnomathematics and mathematics for social justice movements. Ethnomathematics involves understanding the mathematical principles underlying a variety of non-Western and non-academic activities (Ascher, 1991, 2002; Eglash, 2002; Selin, 2000; Zaslavsky, 1973). Although much of the work in ethnomathematics, notably essays contributed by Ascher, does develop the social and cultural context of mathematical activities quite thoroughly, the context serves primarily as an orienting background for the mathematics rather than as a springboard for deeper discussion. Ethnomathematics treatments of the Andean accounting textiles known as quipus, for example, usually do not fully examine their use in Incan statecraft or as indigenous women's resistance to Spanish colonialism (Silverblatt, 1987). Quipus are of interest to mathematicians primarily as mathematical artifacts rather than tools of local social action. This example suggests that the social grounding of a mathematics application can be an opportunity for active intellectual exploration of issues of gender, race, and resistance even when these ideas are not the object of direct computation. In the mathematics for social justice approach (Frankenstein, 1997; Gutstein, 2003), students use mathematics as a tool to uncover evidence of differential privilege within society. Although the epidemiological data sets of the current project certainly raise student awareness of global disparities in health care and consequent economic underdevelopment, instructors need not stop at data analysis in our attempts to engage students in mathematics. Students' discussion of their subjective, humanistic reactions to the context of an application will enhance their experience of it. Embedding social issues efficiently in a mathematics class may well draw a much broader range of students into heightened engagement with mathematics.

Dedicating modest amounts of class time to discussions of the social relevance of mathematics applications contributes to the General College mission of providing access to higher education through transformative developmental studies. Success in algebra often means the removal of one's personality and subjective perspective in preference for an objective, abstract mode of thinking that is both unfamiliar and dehumanizing for many students. The General College pedagogical experiment seeks to support students' self-transformation by allowing them to draw upon a full sense of their selves as they negotiate a developmental algebra class. The multicultural perspectives that are embedded in most General College classes support this transformation as well, and this project unfolds along a particular pathway within the array of pedagogical opportunities offered by multicultural education. Developing mathematical sophistication based on life experience is a recognized and effective means of engaging students in mathematics (Gutstein, 2003; Moses & Cobb, 2001). However, by the time a person reaches young adulthood, personal experience is not only a history of lived habits or practical knowledge, but also social awareness and reflection on values and action within the world. At General College, students from many heritages and personal histories come together in our algebra classes so that the experiences and perspectives are rich and diverse. By focusing on social issues associated with mathematics applications rather than simply contextual description, students are able to find points of contact between their own experiences and those of people whose lives seem very different from their own. For example, a student who has some knowledge of Human Immunodeficiency Virus (HIV) in the United States may then develop an appreciation of the serious consequences of malaria for people in parts of Latin America, a connection drawn by using similar mathematics to investigate both situations.

This chapter describes a series of classroom discussions of the slope formula and rates of change that were presented through the social context of the epidemiology of infectious diseases in an introductory developmental algebra class. A general outline of the unit is presented along with assessments of the time allocated for primarily social and for primarily mathematical discussions. Survey results suggest that students found the treatment of social issues in algebra class to be both memorable and relevant. I argue that the relatively modest amount of time spent on purely social discussions compared to the favorable student response positions socially-contextualized mathematics as a potentially transformative pedagogy. Because the most successful applications of issues-oriented mathematics will occur when instructors develop curricula that are meaningful to themselves and their students (epidemiology, for example, might not be the most appropriate choice for all instructors), the chapter focuses on exemplifying the approach and outlining effective classroom methods for implementing the lessons, especially through recommendations for leading discussions on social issues and for embedding skill practice within those discussions.

Mathematics Engagement Through Social Science Perspectives

Undergraduate mathematics classes may well lose efficacy through extreme efficiency: their vertical organization sets them apart from nearly all other treatments of knowledge in the U.S. undergraduate curriculum. A literature class, for example, often moves well outside the covers of a book to discuss the historical context, the architecture and music, the mores of gender prevalent in a novel's time period—in short, any laterally-connected knowledge that enhances student understanding and engagement. In contrast, when mathematics deals with "real-world applications," students usually engage only those aspects of the context that allow them to model the situation mathematically without regard to the social purposes that inspire experts to devote their professional lives to the application.

Opening the door to social purpose in algebra addresses documented student interest in interdisciplinary knowledge. In the first place, many first-year students value and have a significant interest in both mathematics and social science. There is, however, little support in the undergraduate curriculum for students who enter college with this sort of intellectual openness, and many discard their idealism by terminating their studies of mathematics and science early in their undergraduate careers. This is the case for both developmental and mainstream mathematics students. A comprehensive study of decisions that students make about changing their majors found that high-ability freshmen of all ethnicities who declare mathematics, science, and engineering (SME) majors frequently switch to majors in the social sciences at consistent rates in public and private universities of various sizes (Seymour & Hewitt, 1997). Almost a quarter of the students switching out of the physical sciences chose majors in the social sciences, the humanities, and the arts; social sciences was the destination major for the greatest portion of this group at 14.4% (Seymour & Hewitt, p. 17). Indicators changing majors and graduation rates demonstrate the ethnic achievement gap in higher education. In 1992, by the third year of college, 65% of students of color studying math or science had switched majors compared to 37% of White students (Culotta, 1992, p. 1209; Seymour & Hewitt, p. 319).

The choices that General College students make reveal a similar trend, although there is evidence that some students discover an interest in SME majors after entering GC as well. Of the fall 2000 cohort, for example, only 25% of the first-year students who entered with SME interests transferred with a declared SME major to a degree-granting college within the University of Minnesota. On the other hand, students who entered GC with a non-SME pre-major or with an undeclared pre-major transferred with a declared SME major at a rate of 8.3% (Office of Research and Evaluation, 2004). Experimental interventions tested within General College may well be relevant for both developmental and mainstream students nationally.

Students in Seymour and Hewitt's (1997) study reported that their classroom experiences were especially important in the decision to switch majors; many noted that the social sciences offer more engaging curricula and pedagogies, as well as a way to develop a sense of one's purpose within the world. Loss of interest in SME subjects was cited by 59.6% of all switchers, and disappointment with math and science pedagogy was cited by 36.1% (Seymour & Hewitt, p. 177)—of particular concern was the "disappointment with the perceived narrowness of their SME majors as an educational experience" (Seymour & Hewitt, p. 180). Seymour and Hewitt's study demonstrated that even students who have strong abilities in mathematics and sciences have a deep curiosity about social science and humanities issues that is not satisfied in the undergraduate curriculum—a disappointment that is strong enough to influence their career decisions. These results suggest that widening the content and pedagogies available in mathematics classes can support student interest in the subject, particularly if models are drawn from the social sciences. An undergraduate mathematics curriculum that harnesses the transformational capacity of the social sciences will likely mprove access and equity within higher education.

The Slope Formula: International Perspectives Through Epidemiology

Many General College students take a two-semester sequence of zero-credit algebra classes—Introductory and Intermediate Algebra—in order to prepare for credit-bearing mathematics classes. Starting in the 2003–2004 academic year, the mathematics division of General College introduced epidemiological applications of the slope formula in introductory algebra to all lecture and discussion sections of Introductory Algebra. Intermediate Algebra students used exponential growth models to assess the economic burden of infectious diseases on household income in developing countries. These units are intended to bring international perspectives into the algebra classes to foster interest, engagement, and purpose in mathematics students. An important outcome of this teaching experiment thus far is that including discussions of social situations and social issues in a mathematics class can generate substantial student interest and engagement without displacing traditional mathematics topics. To illustrate this point, I will outline classroom discussions on epidemiology and rates of change in my introductory algebra classes in fall 2003 with attention to the time allocated to both social and mathematical discussions.

The unifying theme of the unit was the United Nations Global Fund, which organizes funding and intervention efforts against the three most damaging infectious diseases in the world today: HIV, malaria, and tuberculosis. The major goal for the mathematical experience was to use realistic data from online sources (e.g., World Health Organization and United Nations Web sites) to introduce the concepts of slope and rates of change and to extend students' use of slopes to nonlinear graphs. Because several of the six faculty members adopting the unit preferred to work with examples that were strictly linear, I modified published data accordingly in order to develop sample problems that were comfortable for all of the teaching styles represented in our department. In any case, all of the sample problems presented students with data of plausible magnitude for the places and scenarios discussed.

The unit was handled predominantly through constructivist pedagogy for both mathematics and social discussions using small group discussions and full-class guided, "Socratic" discussions (e.g., Brissenden, 1988, p. 181). To introduce the social context of infectious diseases in a constructivist manner, I prepared a series of questions to allow students to open the topic with recollections of their own international experience, their knowledge of geography, and global health issues. In this way I was able to provide the minimum necessary level of didactic presentation. For example, many students knew that malaria is transmitted by mosquito bites, but none was familiar with the fundamental cause, infection by the plasmodium parasite that has life cycle phases in both insect and human hosts. Similarly, no student was aware of the severity of malaria as a global health and economic problem. Overshadowed by the stunning devastation of the HIV crisis in Subsaharan Africa, malaria as a long-term cause of underdevelopment is poorly recognized in the United States. Still, prominent development economist Jeffrey Sachs called malaria "the single greatest shaper of wealth and poverty in the world" (Appell, 2003, p. 37). While I prepared this commentary before class, I interjected it as responses to student statements rather than presenting it in lecture format to preserve the interactive, constructivist organization of the class. The unit was handled in "spiral" fashion, so that we returned to the topic for portions of several classes rather than covering it in consecutive class meetings.

The agenda for mathematics content was to introduce material on slopes and rates of change using realistic data on HIV, malaria, and tuberculosis from Latin America, Africa, and Southeast Asia. Students' first opportunity to discover the concept of slope was based on their analysis of data on malaria incidence in Guyana. They used rates of change to develop an understanding of positive and negative slopes and to predict future values of disease incidence. Students also extended their knowledge of slopes to graph nonlinear trajectories of epidemics through Euler's method for approximating the solution of first-degree differential equations as in

$$\frac{\text{new infections}}{\text{year}} = 0.2002x(200-x), x_0 = 25.$$

Euler's method is typically presented in second-semester calculus text-books (e.g., Smith & Minton, 2002) even though the topic is accessible at less advanced levels. This means that in a community of 200 people, initially 25 are infected, and at any given time, a total of x people are infected. The result-ing graph is the S-shaped curve known as the logistic equation. The epidemi-ology unit supported student investigation of core introductory algebra top-ics along with mastery of an advanced method that is usually introduced in the second semester of calculus. This was a reorganization of traditional cur-ricula for developmental students to include material that is new to all stu-dents and both challenging and significant.

I selected a handful of social topics to introduce for class discussion: the difference between infectious and noninfectious diseases, the geographic dis-tribution of the three major infectious diseases, the association between dis-ease and poverty, and the debate over treatment or prevention for HIV in Africa. I wanted students to appreciate the magnitude of the HIV crisis in Subsaharan Africa without contributing to negative stereotypes of Africa—the commonplace beliefs that all dangerous diseases originate in Africa, that Africans lack reason, and are that they are motivated by unreflexive cultural beliefs.

As students moved into the final phase of the unit, working with Euler's method to predict the trajectory of an epidemic, they spent a class period in a computer lab researching an epidemiological issue of their choice and col-lecting relevant data. For their write-up, students analyzed their data using class methods. Many students calculated rates of changes in disease incidence based on tables and graphs that they found online, interpreting the results in terms of linearity and increasing and decreasing disease incidence. A few stu-dents developed differential equation models of the global HIV epidemic by substituting world population data and estimates of global HIV incidence into Euler's method homework problems.

Social Discussions on Infectious Diseases in Introductory Algebra

In the comments below, I summarize the flow of the major discussions on epidemiology paying special attention to time allocation during class days when students engaged in discussions of social issues. Several other class days included discussion of homework problems on epidemiological rates of change and small group work on Euler's method to generate a logistic equa-tion model of an epidemic, but those class days are not summarized here because they did not generate a great deal of social discussion. At the end of each discussion phase, I have indicated whether the discussion covered primarily social or mathematical topics, or both, and the time spent on the discussion in minutes:seconds format. Tape recordings, ethnographic notes, and other data were collected.

Day 1: September 25, 2003
I introduced the epidemiology unit just after students had learned to graph linear functions using tables of values; slopes had not been introduced yet. We began the discussion with a map of South America. Students shared their knowledge of South American countries and their international travel experiences. I described the mode of transmission and methods of diagnosis of malaria. I introduced a data set on positive malaria blood tests in Guyana for the years 1980 to 1995 and asked the students if the data was linear (social, 5:55). Students worked in small groups to determine whether the data was linear. Many groups graphed the data, and a few calculated differences in the dependent variable, a movement towards discovering the slope formula (math, 4:23). As a transition back into full class discussion, I drew three increasing functions on the board as possible shapes for the data set: one concave up, one concave down, and one linear. A strong majority of the students correctly identified the first function as the worst scenario for the malaria example and the second one as the best, although still undesirable, scenario. Members of the class volunteered "exponential" and "doubling" as possible descriptions of the data. The class developed an appropriate scale and graphed the data (math, 6:17). I transitioned out of the topic through a discussion of languages spoken in South America (social, 0:35).

Day 2: October 3, 2003
The next major phase of social discussion developed from a review of a test question for which students calculated a rate of change of women testing positive for HIV in a rural Kenyan neonatal clinic and used it to predict HIV incidence 12 years after the last data point. A student explained her correct prediction of 31.5% (math, 2:21). I asked the students whether they thought this percentage was possible. Several students commented affirmatively and offered supporting data (math and social, 2:59). I asked students if they believed more funding should be allocated for treatment or prevention of HIV in Africa; a lively debate followed. Most students, including several Somali women, spoke in favor of funding prevention over treatment. An African American Latina woman vigorously disagreed, calling upon her classmates' sense of compassion and fairness:

> I think it should be fairly equal because . . . I mean, you know, you aren't going to sit here—help the people that is [sic] already sick! It wasn't their fault. Most

of the time, 9 times out of 10 it probably wasn't their fault that they got sick in the first place. You know they could have just been born with AIDS because their parents were not knowledgeable of it and then conceived a child with AIDS. You know half the time it is not their fault.

She related a news report that she had heard of a cultural belief that intercourse with a young girl would cure an HIV infection. A Somali woman, speaking for the first time since the class began, countered that the news story represented an incorrect stereotype and that she believed HIV infections were lower in Somalia than elsewhere. The first speaker responded that she did not believe that this practice happened everywhere (social, 4:30).

Day 3: October 21, 2003
I asked students to comment on the use of rates of change in analyzing health crises. We discussed what units characterize a rate of change and the interpretation of positive and negative slopes. Students had a short group discussion on the relationship between poverty and disease with the aim of understanding that poverty is the result as well as a cause of disease. Students identified this as an example of direct variation (a topic from their textbook); one offered the term "positive correlation." Students continued their discussion of treatment and prevention policy for infectious diseases (primarily social; some math discussion. Due to a tape recording error, times for this day are based on ethnographic notes, 15:00). Students discussed solutions for homework problems on epidemiological rates of change and began to work on Euler's method for solving differential equations in small groups (math, 20:00).

Day 4: October 23, 2003
Students spent the class period in a computer lab locating data on HIV, malaria, or tuberculosis for a writing assignment in which they were required to analyze the data using class methods. They consulted with the instructor on social topics and approaches to math analysis as needed (social and math, 50:00).

Summary of Unit

Overall, the unit covered a lot of ground. In the first place, it was the initial or primary means of developing understanding on several introductory algebra topics: (a) calculating slopes, (b) rates of change, (c) positive and negative slopes, (d) increasing and decreasing functions, and (e) nonlinear functions. The unit also supported student involvement in mathematics topics that are usually not included in introductory developmental algebra, specifically (a) concavity, (b) the logistic equation, and (c) approximate solutions of differential equations. In addition, several topics were reviewed, supported, or linked to the discussion based on mathematical perspectives that students volunteered independently: (a) ratios, (b) percents, (c) positive correlation, (d) exponential graphs, (e) direct variation, and (f) carrying capacity. Social topics that students discussed were (a) major infectious diseases, modes of transmission, diagnosis and treatment; (b) uneven geographic distribution of infectious diseases; (c) poverty exacerbates the effects of disease; (d) disease creates poverty; (e) allocation of funding for treatment and prevention programs; (f) stereotypes of Africa; and (g) social diversity in Africa.

As exit interviews showed, a majority of students found this unit to be both memorable and relevant. Students were asked which math discussions were most memorable for them. Of students (N = 25) interviewed in three introductory algebra classes during the 2003–2004 academic year, 48% thought that the epidemiology unit was the most memorable topic in the class, and 60% believed that one of the socially-contextualized math topics presented (epidemiology, global differences in resource use, and population growth units combined) was most memorable. Over 96% (N = 28) found socially-based discussions to be relevant to their study of mathematics. Even the single "dissenting" student had a somewhat positive view of the topic: "I think it's good, but sometimes not math, just material we talked about."

Not counting small group activities or online research, the class spent about the same amount of time on social and mathematical discussions during these particular days. Leaving out the online research day, classroom discussions that were listed as primarily social or social and mathematical required 28 minutes and 59 seconds. Discussions of mathematical topics during these days lasted 28 minutes and 38 seconds. It can be appreciated, then, that these 29 minutes of social discussion, out of just over 48 hours of classroom instruction during the semester, did not displace any topics that are typically offered in the course. A very modest reallocation of class time resulted in a strong, positive impact on students' impression of the class.

Supporting Discussions in Mathematics Classes

During the second day of discussion (i.e., 10/2/03), just under 3 minutes was spent in discussion that was strongly balanced between social and mathematical topics. This interaction between social thinking and mathematical thinking is likely the best target for this sort of curriculum and offers strong opportunities to develop math skills. The discussion also illustrates the major obstacle for teachers who may wish to develop socially-contextualized math lessons. As mathematics teachers, we are accustomed to knowing the answer to essentially all the questions that students ask us, but when we open the discussion to social topics, it is easy for students to bring out data and ideas that we cannot evaluate fully.

This dilemma can be addressed easily by attention to discussion techniques along with a reevaluation of traditional ideas of what constitutes a successful classroom exchange. When I asked students if they believed it was possible that 31.5% of women visiting a neonatal clinic could test positive for HIV, responses included:

"It is possible."

"Well, it is way higher in Africa. It is higher. I don't know how much it is but it is higher."

"Isn't it like 25 children die every day?"

"In China . . . for people who have AIDS or related things."

"Here actually, that is the number of Black women. 30% of the people who have AIDS in this country are African American women."

"I heard somewhere that in Mozambique, like 5 to 1 ratio."

Although the question, "is 35.1% possible?" contains numerical data, answering it calls for factual, geographical information and evaluative thinking as much as algebraic understanding. It is notable, then, that most students responded by offering data as evidence of their opinion, even though this was not specifically requested. Socially-contextualized mathematics discussions do not sacrifice opportunities to build math knowledge. On the contrary, speakers in this phase of the conversation displayed their mathematical imagination and opened the door for skill-building questions. Readers will no doubt find it easy to create questions that can clarify student thinking in developmental mathematics, along the lines of:

1. Which of these figures is a rate of change?

2. Can we use this figure to make a prediction?

3. Why do you believe that China is at risk for HIV?

4. What data would be necessary to evaluate your idea?

5. Can we compare our 30% figure from the U.S. with our 31.5% figure from Kenya?

6. What does your 5 to 1 ratio mean? In how many different forms can you write it? Is it the same as a rate of change?

Data-rich statements (e.g., the incidence of HIV in Mozambique) that an instructor may not be able to evaluate factually are nonetheless teaching opportunities to link student knowledge, indeed, student experience as intellectual beings, to skills review and to math questions that are novel for the student. Mathematics instructors who do not spend much, if any, time in social science and humanities classrooms may not realize that discussions can productively terminate in a list of questions or perspectives on issues, not only in a completed procedural problem. Those who desire a strong sense of topic closure or more precise mathematical expression may wish to offer individualized follow-up assignments like the online research assignment that these students completed. In any case, developing a set of focused questions and perspectives is a sound achievement for socially-contextualized mathematics discussions.

Besides inserting clarifying mathematics questions and summarizing discussion perspectives, several other approaches to planning and leading discussions may prove useful to instructors who wish to experiment with socially-contextualized mathematics lessons. In the first place, social issues discussions can be planned just as one prepares a math presentation: determining the order of topics, developing the format for engaging students, and predicting the types of misconceptions students may have. The social issues approach may be most effective when the instructor chooses a small number of social questions of unquestionable importance to introduce during the course. This will help students maintain a sense of relevance, and it helps the teacher work as a constructivist with student social understanding. Preparing for and moderating a discussion is easier if the instructor has in mind a small set of key social ideas to be connected to unpredictable student comments.

Instructors can create more engaging and powerful classroom discussions by controlling the organization of classroom discourse. The instructor's style of speaking is a controllable teaching resource fully as powerful as any mediation of learning through technology. In full class discussions, the "default" format for conversation is the pattern of teacher initiation, student response and teacher evaluation, known variously as the IRE sequence (Cazden, 1988, p. 29), the IRF sequence (i.e. teacher initiation, student response, and teacher follow-up and feedback [Wells, 1993]), and the Triadic Dialogue (Lemke, 1990). This discursive organization centers the teacher as the authority, and therefore the person responsible for doing most of the intellectual work. To displace more responsibility for mathematical imagining and evaluating onto students, Brissenden (1988, pp. 191–193) recommended deflecting the evaluation segment onto other students, introducing comparisons between different students, and offering positive but nonevaluative responses, among other well-recognized techniques. Cazden suggested that pauses of at least three seconds are rarely used but powerful methods of encouraging student-to-student talk (p. 60). Suggestions from educational psychologist Judith Puncochar (2003) are particularly useful to mathematics instructors who may have little experience leading social issues discussions that are very open ended: do not insist on agreement, and support the minority viewpoint. This approach fosters the broadest degree of participation and helps students encounter and respond to the broadest set of perspectives.

Conclusion

Broader attention to social meaning within the context of mathematics applications is a relatively untested means of connecting mathematics to other curriculum areas (Coxford, 1995). In fact, infusing mathematics classes with discussion of significant social issues is a timely experiment in a movement toward broad curricular diversification in higher education. In a survey by the Association of American Colleges and Universities, over 67% of the respondents were trying to improve and increase cultural diversity experiences in general education courses: "(m)any campus leaders now believe . . . that diversity needs to be addressed in more sophisticated and increasingly interdisciplinary ways and in more places throughout a student's college career" (Humphreys, 2002, p. 127). Interdisciplinary approaches to mathematics have usually attempted to inject quantitative reasoning into other subject areas, as in "Math Across the Curriculum" projects, but it is conversely possible to infuse the engaging content and pedagogies of other subject areas, particularly the social sciences, into developmental and mainstream mathematics classes without displacing traditional topics. Socially-contextualized mathematics lessons can make powerful contributions to the transformative multicultural educational experience that General College offers. During an exit interview, I asked a Somali woman to reflect on why she believed that discussions of epidemiological issues were relevant to mathematics: "Would it be just as good if we did those applications but we didn't talk about any issues . . . if we just did the math?" She answered:

> I don't think so. I think the issues [*sic*] is what makes it more real, what makes a person more interested or what makes them want to learn more about math or to achieve more, not in just math but in life . . . because when you solve a problem in your math class about a real life issue, then you feel like you've solved more, other things in your personal life or in other people's lives or you might want to make a change. So I think that's very important.

This student has expressed eloquently the goal of transformative developmental education: "you might want to make a change . . . " if classes, even mathematics classes, permit the voice of social awareness to be heard.

References

Appell, D. (2003). Science to save the world. *Scientific American, 288*(1), 36–37.

Ascher, M. (1991). *Ethnomathematics: A multicultural view of mathematical ideas.* Pacific Grove, CA: Brooks/Cole.

Ascher, M. (2002.) *Mathematics elsewhere: An exploration of ideas across cultures.* Princeton, NJ: Princeton University Press.

Brissenden, T. (1988). *Talking about mathematics.* Oxford, UK: Basil Blackwell.

Cazden, C. (1988). *Classroom discourse: The language of teaching and learning.* Portsmouth, NH: Heineman.

Coxford, A. (1995). The case for connections. In P. House & A. Coxford (Eds.), *Connecting mathematics across the curriculum* (pp.3–12). Reston, VA: National Council of Teachers of Mathematics.

Culotta, E. (1992). Scientists of the future: Jumping high hurdles. *Science, 258* (5085), 1209–1210, 1213.

Eglash, R. (2002). *African fractals: Modern computing and indigenous design.* New Brunswick, N J: Rutgers University Press.

Frankenstein, M. (1997). In addition to the mathematics: Including equity issues in the curriculum. In J. Trentacosta & M. Kenney (Eds.), *Multicultural and gender equity in the mathematics classroom* (pp. 10–22). Reston, VA: National Council of Teachers of Mathematics.

Gutstein, E. (2003). Teaching and learning mathematics for social justice in an urban, Latino school. *Journal for Research in Mathematics Education, 34*(1), 37–73.

Humphreys, D. (2002). Interdisciplinarity, diversity, and the future of liberal education. In C. Haynes (Ed.), *Innovations in interdisciplinary thinking* (pp. 122–138). Westport, CT: Oryx Press.

Keller, E. (1983). *A feeling for the organism: The life and work of Barbara McClintock.* New York: W. H. Freeman.

Lemke, J. (1990). *Talking science: Language, learning, and values.* Norwood, NJ: Ablex.

Moses, R., & Cobb, C. (2001). *Math literacy and civil rights.* Boston: Beacon Press.

Office of Research and Evaluation. (2004). *Rates of intra-university transfer for General College students.* Minneapolis, MN: General College, University of Minnesota. Retrieved January 10, 2005, from www.gen.umn.edu/research/ore/reports/transfer_report-S04/default.htm.

Puncochar, J. (2003). *Discussions that work.* Unpublished manuscript, Minneapolis, MN: University of Minnesota.

Selin, H. (Ed.). (2000). *Mathematics across cultures: The history of non-western mathematics.* Dordrecht, The Netherlands: Kluwer Academic.

Seymour, E., & Hewitt, N. (1997). *Talking about leaving: Why undergraduates leave the sciences.* Boulder, CO: Westview Press.

Silverblatt, I. (1987). *Moon, sun and witches: Gender ideologies and class in Inca and colonial Peru.* Princeton, NJ: Princeton University Press.

Smith R., & Minton, R. (2002). *Calculus.* Boston: McGraw Hill.

Wells, G. (1993). Reevaluating the IRF sequence: A proposal for the articulation of theories of activity and discourse for the analysis of teaching and learning in the classroom. *Linguistics and Education, 5,* 1–37.

Zaslavsky, C. (1973). *Africa counts: Number and pattern in African culture.* Brooklyn: Lawrence Hill.

CHAPTER 11

Multicultural Writing Instruction at the General College: A Dialogical Approach

Patrick L. Bruch and Thomas J. Reynolds

ABSTRACT

Theoretical discourses of multicultural education have a great deal to offer developmental educators. In this chapter we clarify specific theoretical insights from multicultural education theory that inform our program design and approach to developmental writing instruction. After that, we explore the implications of these insights for our practices. Specifically, we discuss the ways in which a dialogical understanding of writing grounded in multicultural education theory informs the General College writing program's work with its teachers and students.

Writing programs within institutions of higher education have long faced the challenge of working with students who are labeled as "developmental" or "remedial" writers in the admissions process (Boylan, 1988). Although many have assumed that this group of students has always been defined by the number of errors they make in writing, research in the field of basic writing has demonstrated the impact of cultural politics, social group power, and privilege as decisive forces in distinguishing students marked as basic, developmental, or remedial, from students left unmarked (Adler-Kassner & Harrington, 2002; Fox, 1999; Gallego & Hollingsworth, 2000; Horner & Lu, 1999; Shor, 1997). Accordingly, current approaches to basic writing instruction now deemphasize the old view of learning writing as learning to accommodate and use an unchanging standard, instead viewing writing as a process and emphasizing practice, drafting, increasing familiarity, and developing fluency (Curtis & Herrington, 2003; Sternglass, 1997). Concentrating on process has enabled teachers to provide meaningful support to students undertaking the difficult task of learning an unfamiliar and often threatening academic discourse. On the other hand, process approaches too often remain silent regarding the individual- and group-level dynamics of power and privilege that student writers are navigating as they write.

This chapter describes how the writing program in the General College moves beyond the limitations of a strictly process approach through what can be called a dialogical approach to writing instruction. Dialogical writing instruction encourages students to treat writing as an opportunity to shape people's understandings of writing at the same time that the conventions of academic writing shape them. Such an approach foregrounds the give and take of literacy—that people's actions can and do inform, as they are informed by, rules, conventions, and institutionalized expectations (Bartholomae, 1985; Farmer, 1998; Soliday, 2002). Writing, in this view, is an activity through which students can "take on" conventions in two senses—both adopting and challenging the forms of writing valued in the academy. Rose's (1989) book *Lives on the Boundary* described such an encounter with literacy as he succeeded by both critically examining and, in the act of writing his book, actively transforming how literacy is understood. In what follows, we will discuss how such a view of writing instruction operationalizes key insights from multicultural education theory in ways that help our students succeed. We then describe how a dialogical understanding of writing is implemented in our developmental writing program's curriculum and administration.

Theoretical Foundations

The General College writing program provides instruction to approximately 800 students each semester. All of these students are marked by the university as underprepared and developmental. But, of course, these univocal labels actually mask enormous diversity within our student group. Responding to this diversity, our work with and for these students is necessarily multilayered and complex, but can be understood as implementing a dialogical approach to knowledge making that translates insights from multicultural education theory into practice. Multicultural education theory invites a dialogical approach to developmental writing instruction through its emphasis on the relationship between knowledge and power, the importance of critical participation, and the transformative character of educational and social progress (Giroux, 1988; Rhoads & Valadez, 1996). In this section of this chapter we begin to clarify the meaning of the term "dialogical approach" by explaining how these emphases in multicultural education theory support a dialogical understanding of and approach to the teaching of writing.

Knowledge and Power

The dominant, common-sense approach to education views schooling as a gateway that provides each individual access to a better life. In this view "knowledge" grants individuals power in a straightforward way. Drawing on the experiences of social groups that have persistently been less able to realize this democratic promise of education, multicultural education theory has complicated the traditional understanding of the knowledge-power relationship. First, multicultural education theorists have emphasized the partiality of institutionally-valued knowledge. Berlin (1987) phrased this insight in terms of its implications for writing instruction when he pointed out that "the ability to read, write, and speak in accordance with the code sanctioned by a culture's ruling class is the main work of education, and this is true whether we are discussing ancient Athens or modern Detroit" (p. 52). As Berlin highlighted, in addition to being partial in the sense of being incomplete, the knowledge valued in schools has historically been partial to those in power. In other words, valued knowledge about history, or good writing, or even science, presents a version of the truth sanctioned by a "ruling class." Here, in addition to possibly providing some access to power, knowledge *exercises* power, teaching people to see a particular version of knowledge as "real" or "true," and thus teaching people to see the social relations of a culture as "natural" and not alterable results of struggles over the truth. In contrast to providing neutral, universally enabling equipment for democratic social life, this view recognizes that institutionally-sanctioned knowledge tends to reproduce social inequalities that schooling tries to help people overcome. As a result, multicultural education theory leads many practitioners to think of knowledge dialogically—as a social construction properly involving participation as members of the knowledge-making community.

Critical Participation

Of course, the versions of truth sanctioned by a culture's ruling class never completely dominate people's views and perspectives to the point where we robotronically reproduce our own domination. Instead, real life involves constant official and unofficial struggles over what versions of the truth will receive what sorts of institutional recognition. For this reason, multicultural education theory has highlighted the importance of *critical* participation (Giroux, 1988; Goldberg, 1994; Kanpol & McLaren, 1995). To cite just one example, as long as most people accepted dominant versions of the truth about women's natural disinclination towards traditionally male-dominated activities like sports or politics (to name only two), the history of male domination in these fields perpetuated itself as if it were really natural. Institutionally sanctioned knowledge about history, politics, biology, psychology, and others reflected this bias (Young, 1990). In more recent times, more and more people have questioned older versions of the truth, and more and more women and girls have demonstrated aptitude and interest in traditionally male-dominated areas of life. The accepted truths about male domination have changed, and that domination itself has become problematic in ways it previously was not. This type of situation has led multicultural education theorists to an appreciation of the importance of participation. In both the old days and in present days, the versions of the truth that exercise power do so through the actions of people that validate those truths by giving them recognition and withholding recognition from others. Accordingly multicultural education theorists have concentrated on the significance of participation that is critical, that involves reflection, and that seeks intentionally to improve social life by participating in creating truths that sustain and enrich democratic life.

Transformation
Drawing from the related insights into knowledge, power, and participation, multicultural education theory envisions educational progress in terms of the democratic transformation of individuals and society. Just as dialogue is never one sided, educational progress is not a matter of thoughtlessly endorsing established truths, nor is it a matter of wholesale resistance. Instead, progress involves interpreting where truths come from, whose interests and perspectives they reflect, and whose interests, perspectives, and experiences they leave unrecognized or misrecognized. Applying in the classroom this emphasis on investigating the consequences of the versions of the truth that are currently valued leads us to emphasize dialogue for two reasons. First, if we assume that the power relations implicit in knowledge are most often not the result of diabolical intentions on the part of privileged people to justify their unearned advantages, but instead are unintended blindspots, then dialogue understood in its most literal sense provides an important potential antidote to misperception and lack of perception. Hearing from those who feel themselves to be devalued or misrecognized by valued knowledge provides an obvious potential first step toward creating more democratically enabling truths (Young, 1997). Secondly, dialogue is important because multicultural education is a project of improving the society, and that project requires deliberation concerning what aspects of current social life should be changed and in what ways.

Practicing Multicultural Theory Through Dialogical Writing Instruction
As it puts these theoretical emphases into practice, the General College writing program can be described as "dialogical" on several levels. As we have discussed previously (Reynolds & Bruch, 2002), our curriculum combines a practical focus on process with attention to the social contexts in which processes are inhabited by real people living in relationships of power. In this

sense our program places process theory in dialogue with critical theories of education. Translating this theoretical dialogue into pedagogy means helping students see and write about the ways that they are, in effect, dialoguing with conventions and expectations and thereby navigating power relations through their writing. Pointing towards the need for teachers to pay attention to social contexts, Lundell and Collins (1999) have theorized developmental education as a process in which students transform the "primary discourses" or ways of being that are learned before college in home cultures. As they become participants in the academy, developmental education students assume new discourses and come to inhabit new identities. As highlighted by the critical theories of multicultural education discussed above, this transformation takes place within a context of power relations and struggles. By formulating the content of writing courses as studying the back and forth, or dialogical, work of shaping and being shaped by academic and other discourses, writing courses can help universities and students themselves recognize students' primary discourses and home cultures as valid foundations for acquiring, and also contributing to and transforming, the secondary discourses of their academic studies.

In this, our approach extends Lundell and Collins' important insight explicitly to students. Because students marked as developmental are often made to feel ashamed of the language skills and knowledge they bring to school, it is especially valuable for students themselves, in addition to their teachers, to reflect on the ways that their work enacts a dialogue between home and institutional cultures. As we will describe further in the next section of this chapter, by thinking with students about how writing always works to locate one in a discourse and also provides opportunities for influencing that discourse, the General College writing courses give students the opportunity to navigate and discuss their college transition in a way that is reciprocally respectful.

Through its emphasis on knowledge and power, the importance of participation, and the transformative purpose of education, multicultural education theory provides useful foundations for theorizing writing as a dialogue. Just as our theory recognizes the significance of student involvement, it is useful to remind ourselves of the importance of practitioner involvement. Our theory inflects our interpretation of, rather than answers, the difficult questions that come up as we go about the complicated task of teaching writing. It thus positions teachers and students as intellectuals who meaningfully contribute to determining their own actions. We think that this is desirable, even though it can be frustrating to work without knowing ahead of time all the answers. As Smitherman (1977) has pointed out, "the material conditions of educational practice are so infinite and varied that a theory of pedagogy cannot lay out a day-to-day how-to, what-to, and why" (p. 206). Instead, the best route from theory to practice is always best mapped by local practitioners. In what follows, then, we offer examples of classroom practices and then program administration as one set of local negotiations that may be suggestive for others.

Classroom Practices

In our classrooms we strive to implement a dialogical approach that central-izes the key insights described in the previous section. Specifically, course materials, assignments, and assessments can be designed to involve students in using their writing dialogically. Here, critical dialogue becomes a metaphor for how we hope students will consider past experiences with writing and for how they will complete current writing. Past experiences that have positioned writing as a matter of correctness have often been expe-rienced by students as stifling their creativity, true feelings, and authentic voice. But at the same time, many of our students come into our classes wanting to master the "rules" and conventions of correctness that have been used against them in the past. In our classroom practices we seek to strike a delicate balance with such pressures, a balance that affirms the desire to be heard through being correct while also affirming the impulse to resist the power of conventions to stifle creativity and voice. As writers enacting a dia-logue between correctness and individuality, students are neither naïvely overconfident that writing provides a sphere of pure freedom and authen-tic individual expression nor cynically paralyzed by a belief that writing is a tool of oppression that completely dominates and homogenizes. Instead, dialogue is a middle road recognizing that "literacy simultaneously works on people by encouraging writers to conform to an accepted set of parameters and is put to work by people to influence peers and society and to shape expectations of language" (Reynolds & Bruch, 2002, p. 12). We pursue this teaching agenda through all aspects of classroom practice including course materials, assignments, and assessments.

Course Materials

The syllabus is a key aspect of classroom practice through which a dialogical understanding of writing can be established. Terence Collins (1997), a General College colleague, has written about the importance of a syllabus that invites and encourages students to see themselves as capable and informed partici-pants who bring strengths to class that they can build on. Syllabi can establish a productive dialogical framework for the class by describing the project of learning college-level writing as a matter of reflectively practicing and extending skills we all use with some proficiency on a daily basis. For example, the following passage from the syllabus of one section of first-semester writing in GC models this approach:

> In this class we will be doing two things. We will write, and we will think about writing and the consequences of writing in the ways we are expected to and in the ways we do. This approach seeks to build on what we already know and do—we already interpret texts and make decisions about the consequences of different ways of communicating.
>
> To put this another way, we already know how to interpret and create (read and write) texts that set us in relations with others, as, say, students-teachers, bosses-employees, experts-novices, customers-suppliers, women-men, adults-children. To use language is to be a person, to use language in *certain* ways is to be a *certain* kind of person, a person who sees the world and inhabits it in *certain* ways. In our class we will work towards using the language that marks and shapes those in the academy, and at the same time we will be thinking about what the language of the academy wants from us—who it wants us to be, what it wants us to see or not see, and how we might try to change what it means to use school writing as we use it.

This description of the course lays a foundation for classroom work that builds on the theoretical foundations described previously. Accepted truths about what constitutes good writing are not denied or ignored, nor uncritically celebrated, but engaged as an invitation to participate with the goal of constructive dialogue concerning truth-making and power relations. The passage explicitly recognizes that students already have some expertise as communicators navigating a dialogical relationship with conventions and expectations—responding to others' expectations and at the same time, in other ways, perhaps resisting those expectations. The description thus pursues a dialogical understanding of writing by inviting students to see their writing as a way that they can help shape the meaning of writing in our classes and more generally. As one student phrased this insight in a paper for class: "By me writing this paper in this way, I'm communicating my thoughts about communication to you, but yet a lot of people may not see it this way at first." Through a syllabus that encourages students to recognize their proficiency as communicators and the significance of the communicating they do, a dialogical understanding of writing is set in motion. Students are encouraged to become aware of their writing as an opportunity to actively dialogue with accepted conventions and the relations of knowledge and power those conventions embody.

Writing Assignments

This dialogical approach can infuse writing assignments as well. One common initial assignment asks students to construct a literacy autobiography that attempts to use their own experiences with learning writing to help readers appreciate something about writing that they may not have appreciated or understood before (see Figure 1). As the first assignment of the semester, students typically respond in one of two ways: either they focus on correctness and marginalize their own experiences, feelings, and interpretations, or they focus on their experiences and marginalize any effort to fulfill the academic convention of helping readers see the point of examples used in writing. Exemplary of the first tendency, one student wrote a paper that assumed a universal voice reminiscent of an encyclopedia entry:

> Literacy is more than just reading and writing, it's a means to gain access—to the people, places and knowledge we all want to know, visit, and have. Literacy can also restrict access to people based on the kind of literacy they possess. We're going to explore three particular kinds of literacy, academic, ebonic, and slang. Benefits and restrictive qualities more desirable, less desirable.
>
> Academic literacy is the standard that a society sets as the control, for all variations to be compared against. Having adeptness in this literacy makes one a more desirable member of society, as one can now teach others literary correctness. Also, by learning academic literacy, one will possess the language of the business and professional world which leads one to greater economic success.
>
> On the opposite end of the spectrum is ebonics. Depending on who you ask, ebonics or African American Vernacular English is either a language all its own, or a variation of common English, either way, it is loosely modeled after academic English. . . The establishment of ebonics seeks to cater to those that read and write it, rather than to teach them to obey the literacy rules of academia, the proven key to success in the literate world. Furthermore, the support of ebonic literacy, marginalizes African Americans, further separating them from traditional society.

In many ways, this piece of student writing is a success. It shows that the student has developed a certain command of conventions of paragraphs, thesis statements, and organization. But despite its strengths it is not dialogical. Instead of providing a means of active participation in which the author works to shape conventional academic discourse as it gives shape to him or her, this passage demonstrates writing as a ritual of conformity to conventions.

Another student from the same class went equally as far in the opposite direction. Writing in response to the same assignment, this student concentrated exclusively on his experience, refusing the academic convention of using examples only to substantiate an explicitly stated general point. Instead

ESSAY 1

In the first part of the term, we'll be thinking and writing about something we all have extensive experience with—learning to read and write. Your first formal essay will look critically at literacy using your own experiences as examples that show something or some things about literacy in general. Your paper should try to use your experiences to give others new ways to think about their own.

The question behind this paper might be: When we learn literacy, what are we really learning? What have your literacy experiences been? What specific experiences, people, and environments shaped the ways that you've encountered writing? What ways of using language have been most important to you and why? What are literacy's promises, and what are its perils? What does your language want from you?

Frederick Douglass, as we'll see, valued literacy as a way to overcome his condition of slavery. Meanwhile, the ruling class of the slave-holding society he lived in used literacy to maintain its position of domination over slaves. I'd like you to think about how literacy in school and/or out of school, has helped you to be free or has been used by others against you, or both.

As you get a draft of this piece going, you'll start looking for a main idea to hold it together. You might be able to state, for example, that "Literacy has freed me to consider other people's viewpoints fairly" or "literacy has freed me to develop myself in a number of directions." Then, the writing in the paper—the examples and experiences—can flesh out of this main idea, complete with specific details and explanation of how your examples show what you mean by your main idea. Your teachers, families, friends, backgrounds and interests are all fair game for discussion. Obviously, part of doing this paper well will be drawing especially important details and trends from the many at your disposal.

Figure 1. Assignment for Essay 1.

of setting up the example with general statements and context, his paper oriented readers to the following paragraph with the line "Example: Write about a meal your [*sic*] having, describe it to the best of your ability." The paper went on:

> A sandwich, with fresh moist oat bran bread. The roast beef is plentiful and piled almost as a reward or apology. The meat however is unevenly wadded so that the sandwich bulges in the middle. There is a very thin layer of crisp lettuce and some slices of red tomato. The sandwich is cut in a very neat diagonal line; none of the contents of the sandwich jut out. Next to the sandwich are old looking corn chips, you can smell the salt, feel it on your fingers as you touch it, the texture is falliable. A tall glass of milk lies to the left of the plate, the glass is cold and it feels smooth, stable; a glass you could trust, not like all those other bastard glasses. The milk is white like a pearl; it doesn't look like it would talk about you behind your back. Not like the chips, the chips appear questionable, for they bend both ways carrying an edge of good and evil. Did that sandwich move? You swore it did. Did the milk come from a cow that fed from the grass of a desecrated Indian burial ground? You think to yourself a glass of milk like that could kill your brother; best go out and find another. The milk could be haunted, perhaps working in league with the sandwich. The deceptive sandwich, so plump, so juicy, but when you least expect it bam! A shiv in the back, you think to yourself a glass of milk like that could kill your brother; best go out and find another. There is also a mother near the meal, at the table, staring at you, wondering . . . Why hasn't he-she eaten this meal? she's pausing, eating her salad with a fork, you wouldn't want to anger her for she has a fork and you have a whole lot of cursed finger food.
>
> I remember writing this and reading it, thinking to myself, yes, it's that "Moxy" that makes my writing and feeling quite good about it too.

Like the previous example, this student writing exhibits some important strengths. It is original and compelling. At the same time, its success as a piece of school writing is compromised by its categorical distance from conventions of presenting and developing ideas. Rather than seeing his writing as a means of dialogue between himself and conventions such as paragraphing, incorporation of examples, and explicit articulation of ideas, the writer simply ignores the power of convention to shape his writing. In such a case, conventions exercise power from outside of the text, marking the text as a radical departure that, while possibly interesting, fails to fulfill the assignment.

This early assignment attempts to ground students' introduction to a dialogical understanding of writing in a reexamination of their own experiences. Building on this foundation, later assignments for the class invite students to read and respond to historical and contemporary writers who model self-conscious dialogue with conventions and conventionalized knowledge through their writing. Students read and write about Blight's (1993) edition of

ESSAY 2

The assignment:

In this paper, I'd like you to do a careful analysis of Frederick Douglass's story of education. Specifically, discuss three or four especially important experiences of his in light of a thesis that you form about the power of education. Your main idea or thesis will be your answer to the question, "what does Douglass's book show about the power of education?" and the body of your essay will be a discussion of the ways that the book shows what you say it does about education.

In forming your thesis, you'll have to think about the ways that Douglass's book shows education to be powerful. Does his education liberate him from beliefs that would hold him down? Does it enable him to overcome some kinds of (personal, physical, psychological) obstacles? Does his book show the power of education to change others? What does Douglass seem to think education is for (individual success? social change?) and how does his book show that. Lots of possibilities present themselves through the story he tells.

How to go about writing the assignment:

I'd suggest that you spend some time skimming through the book, looking for exact sections that you may want to treat in the paper. Make marks in the book about what you might want to use in your paper, and what different sections seem to you to say about education. It might be helpful to type out or write out some quotes from different parts of the book, with page numbers, so you can see them all in one place and think about how they can be related to each other.

Then write a draft of the paper. As you are drafting your discussions of different parts of the book, concentrate on doing two things—describing to readers what happens and explaining what the example or experience shows about education.

After you have a draft that has examples and discussions of what the example show about the power of education, you can concentrate on your thesis statement or main idea—when you put all of the examples together, what do they show about the power of education?

Figure 2. Assignment for Essay 2.

Frederick Douglass's *Narrative of the Life of Frederick Douglass: An American Slave* (see Figure 2), as well as essays by recent critics of power dynamics in education.

In the final assignments for the class, students take on the role of more independent knowledge makers, finding and critically dialoguing with texts, and addressing issues they find significant (see Figure 3). Of course, assignments do not, in and of themselves, teach students to see writing dialogically. Instead, they invite students to write and create opportunities for teachers and peers to respond in ways that count toward meaningful revision and that also count as graded writing for the class.

Assessment

As is indicated by the examples of student writing quoted previously, a dialogical approach to developmental writing instruction requires individualized feedback and attention. A dialogical understanding of writing is so foreign to most students that course materials and assignments will not be enough. Instead writing dialogically is a learning process that can be facili-

---

ESSAY 5

Background:

Over the course of the term you have read and written about education from a variety of perspectives. You have reflected on your experiences in school, examined education historically, read current critics of education, and looked at the ways that people are "educated" outside of school. Your last paper gives you an opportunity to explore through research and writing your sense of good educational work in our society.

Your assignment:

In your fifth paper, I will ask that you describe, analyze, and evaluate an educator at work today or in the past. An educator can be a person, place, or thing—a text, an organization, or a genre (like hip hop music). The questions that your paper should answer is what is this "educator" teaching people and how? in what ways is this good and/or bad education? I expect that you will do some background research to gather materials for your paper.

Figure 3. Assignment for final essay.

tated through assessments that help students build on strengths to address shortcomings in their writing. In this sphere, a dialogical approach reminds students that the goal in writing is both to hear and be heard, to listen to the expectations of the audience, and to share with the audience in ways it might not have expected. For each of these students, one important kind of assessment came from their teacher's recognition of strengths in their papers and encouragement to pay more attention to that side of the balance that they are currently ignoring. As Gay (1998) has pointed out, the dialogue between teacher and student need not end with the teacher's comment. She has drawn attention to the potential value of having students formally respond to feedback they receive from teachers. In addition, the notion of dialogue provides a useful framework for peer responses to this kind of writing. One need not be an expert to find the first example well organized but too impersonal or cold sounding and the second interesting and fun but too hard to relate to the point. It is important to point out, in addition, the value of multiple types of assessment, so that all of a student's grade does not depend on performance on only one aspect of the work of the class, in this case the construction of finished writing. In writing classes, points can be awarded for all aspects and activities of the writing process including obvious parts like drafting, providing peer review, and revising, but also less obvious efforts like developing skills in finding useful constructive feedback, reflecting on process, and experimenting with new techniques.

Classroom practices such as these oriented towards a dialogical understanding of writing can be supported by a conversational approach to teaching, but conversation can be a part of many different ways of thinking about writing. Instead, the hallmark of a dialogical approach to classroom practices is that they invite students to see and practice writing as an opportunity to join the broad public conversations that shape the conditions of their lives and put pressure on institutional expectations of what and how they will write. They translate into the classroom a dialogical understanding that writing is not a single stable practice, but is, instead, an interaction between institutionalized conventions and peoples' real uses of language to accomplish goals in particular circumstances. Dialogical classroom practices help students learn writing by learning to reflectively participate in these interactions.

Administrative Practices

Because teaching takes place within institutional boundaries, we direct our writing program with an eye to institutional practices and traditions that have defined how that teaching gets understood and carried out. We encourage teachers to question and place under scrutiny the seemingly natural way of working within the University of Minnesota and General College in order to work toward more effective instruction of students and just working conditions for themselves. Here, we discuss the areas of teacher training, teacher performance, and our own roles as administrators of a writing program within a large research university by highlighting in each case some of the recent projects that attempt to bring a dialogic approach to administration.

Professional Development

Teachers in our program are a collection of tenured and tenure-track faculty, teaching specialists hired full time with renewable contracts, and one or two graduate assistants. We recognize and value the particular perspectives that each group brings to the project of teaching our students by holding regular training sessions that review what we know about our best practices for teaching the particular group of writing students in General College while at the same time questioning those practices so that new perspectives find their way into the mix (Reynolds, 2001). Efforts to include the voices and perspectives of all teachers apply multicultural education theory to our program's administration. Here, rather than conceptualizing professional development as "training" in which those without knowledge or skills are taught, we understand professional development as a continuous, recursive, dialogical process.

One of the challenges of holding formal professional development sessions is to get teachers of different ranks to work together in ways that recognize but do not reinforce power and privilege markers set by the institution. Getting wide input into the meetings' agendas, making sure that everyone gets a chance to speak and be heard, and including our common concern, the students, in the meetings has helped to make such meetings more democratic than if they were run strictly from above by the tenured experts in composition. Honoring the expertise of the teaching specialists, whose full-time job is to teach our classes, as well as the apprentice status of the graduate students, who also have fresh perspectives, has become a way to give the program even, highly invested instruction. We have also invited to our meetings experts from other institutions to gain new approaches and help understand what we already do in a new light. Through these approaches we have worked to focus our formal program development sessions around a dialogical understanding of writing that is informed by the multiple views and perspectives of stakeholders who work in the program.

In addition to formal meetings, we hold smaller ongoing informal group meetings convened around teachers' particular teaching interests. Recent groups have organized around reading, technology uses, multicultural theory, and the teaching of particular writing forms in our classes. Such groups typically discuss their topics from the ground up, noting what was thought to have been possible in the past, what is currently the case now, and what might be in the future. In the case of technology use, for example, an effort at making good use of computer technology and online writing opportunities available to students in our classrooms stemmed from a workshop put on by basic writing expert Tom Fox (1999), followed by summer meetings among a subgroup of teachers to work out how Fox's approach might be adapted to our particular computer resources and course demands, and discussed more informally during the implementation in small groups. Such practices implement a dialogical approach to writing instruction by recognizing the significance of our practices for what writing instruction means on our campus and more generally. In addition, they centralize a dialogical approach by recognizing through ongoing meetings and conversations that outcomes and understandings evolve over time as students and teachers interact and cannot be predetermined.

Of course, opening up the writing program to new ideas and instructional approaches does not guarantee that teacher input and commitment will be strengthened. In fact differences in working conditions and power held within the institution can play a decisive factor in making a collaborative effort one that merely replicates past inequities (Aschauer, 1989; Horner, 2000). In the preceding example, implementing newer uses of technology entails new learning on the part of teachers, a commitment that is quite different depending on one's institutional rank. Teaching specialists teach twice as many students during the semester as do tenure-track teachers with research obligations. Committing time and effort to learning new technology may not be as possible for some teaching specialists whose teaching time falls during available technology training hours. Working with students once the technology is implemented presents another challenge; anyone who has worked with such technology knows it can be time-consuming when working out the bugs with students. Devoting time and energy in one direction involves, at times, taking it away from another activity, a serious work issue for any teacher, but all the more so for those with large numbers of students. Recognizing the realities of different groups of instructors, arguing for what is just and fair, and acting on what is discussed puts into practice the very difficult notion of directing a writing program with a dialogical approach at its core.

Program Assessment

Setting common goals and expectations for the writing classes has helped us to act as a group with common interests. Making process as relevant as the final end goals, an inclusive group of tenured and tenure-track faculty members, teaching specialists, and administrators recently formed a committee to review and revise the goals of our courses (Reynolds & Fillipi, 2003). Our discussion helped to remind us all that student learning was the goal of all of our jobs, and that our work can be guided by, if not defined in the context of, what is stated in the document. The document itself details the curricular approach that we are describing here as dialogical.

The statement of goals has also provided us a tool in effectively assessing teaching in our writing program. Teachers understand that their work should be understood within the discussion of the program's goals and expectations. Newer ideas such as the online magazine project inspired by Fox are discussed within the parameters set out in the goals document. We agree to develop our teaching practices within an understanding that we will, for example, "affirm each student's basic linguistic competence" (Reynolds & Fillipi, 2003, p. 21). It is not so much a sacred text to be followed line by line; however, the ideas expressed in it provide a way for teachers with new ideas to participate in what is an ongoing dialogue about what the program should be. If individual teachers want to try something new, and it does not seem to fit exactly with what is in the document, then we get together and discuss its implications and how the program needs to change or the individual effort might be made to fit more neatly within the already stated goals.

Putting the Program in Dialogue With the University

We operate our program within a large institution, and the writing program administrators advocate for the program within the larger institution. At the college level, we hold voting membership on standing committees and councils, and at the level of the university, we work on task forces organized to maintain quality of writing instruction on campus and in programs aimed at improving quality of teaching more generally. Maintaining visibility and letting people know that we are doing good work are goals we carry to this kind of work. Here too we make arguments for smaller classes, well-trained teachers, and other resources necessary to the work of our program. We also find opportunity to discuss with people in various power positions some of the dominant cultural and societal assumptions about writing that stigmatize our students and ourselves as teachers. In a recent review of University-wide goals for first-year writing instruction, for example, we were able to discuss with central administrators the need for students to understand, in addition to features of academic writing, some of the cultural functions of literacy.

Conclusion

Multicultural education theory challenges practitioners in all disciplines to rethink the educational enterprise. In terms of writing instruction, theories of multicultural education challenge the credibility of traditional approaches that seek only to distribute and not to question and change the forms of writing that are valued in schools. But these theories do not tell practitioners how to implement the necessary critical transformations of practice. In this chapter, we have described our program's efforts to operationalize the critical insights of multiculturalism through an approach to classroom practice and program administration that seeks to make writing a means for engaging and transforming relations of power. Although practitioners must design approaches that fit the contexts of their practice, we hope that the descriptions of classroom and administrative practice we have offered will be suggestive of the rich potential that lies in the application of multicultural theories to the field of developmental writing.

References

Adler-Kassner L., & Harrington, S. (2002). *Basic writing as a political act.* Cresskill, NJ: Hampton.

Aschauer, M.A. (1989). Reinforcing successive gains: Collaborative projects for writing faculty. *Writing Program Administrators, 12,* 57–61.

Bartholomae, D. (1985). Inventing the university. In M. Rose (Ed.), *When a writer can't write: Studies in writer's block and other composing process problems* (pp. 134–165). New York: Guilford Press.

Berlin, J. A. (1987). Revisionary history: The dialectical method. *PRE/TEXT, 8* (1–2), 47–61.

Blight, D. (Ed.). (1993). *Narrative of the life of Frederick Douglass: An American slave.* Boston: Bedford/St. Martin's.

Boylan, H. R. (1988). The historical roots of developmental education. *Research in Developmental Education, 5*(3), 1–4.

Collins, T. (1997). For openers . . . An inclusive course syllabus. In W. E. Campbell & K. A. Smith (Eds.), *New paradigms for college teaching* (pp. 65–87). Edina, MN: Interaction.

Curtis, M., & Herrington, A. (2003). Writing development in the college years: By whose definition? *College Composition and Communication, 55*(1), 69–90.

Farmer, F. (1998). Dialogue and critique: Bakhtin and the cultural studies writing classroom. *College Composition and Communication, 49*(1), 186–207.

Fox, T. (1999). *Defending access: A critique of standards in higher education.* Portsmouth, NH: Boynton/Cook Heinemann.

Gallego, M., & Hollingsworth, S. (Eds.). (2000). *What counts as literacy: Challenging the school standard.* New York: Teachers College Press.

Gay, P. (1998). Dialogizing response in the writing classroom: Students answer back. *Journal of Basic Writing, 17*(1), 3–17.

Giroux, H. A. (1988). *Schooling and the struggle for public life: Critical pedagogy in the modern age.* Minneapolis, MN: University of Minnesota Press.

Goldberg, D. T. (1994). *Multiculturalism: A critical reader.* Cambridge, MA: Blackwell.

Horner, B. (2000). *Terms of work for composition: A materialist critique.* Albany, NY: State University of New York Press.

Horner, B., & Lu, M. (1999). *Representing the other: Basic writers and the teaching of basic writing.* Urbana, IL: National Council of Teachers of English.

Kanpol, B., & McLaren, P. (Eds.). (1995). *Critical multiculturalism: Uncommon voices in common struggle.* Westport, CT: Bergin & Garvey.

Lundell, D., & Collins, T. (1999). Toward a theory of developmental education: The centrality of discourse. In J. L. Higbee & P. L. Dwinell (Eds.), *The expanding role of developmental education* (pp. 3–20). Morrow, GA: National Association for Developmental Education.

Reynolds, T. (2001). Training basic writing teachers: Institutional considerations. *Journal of Basic Writing, 20*(2), 38–52.

Reynolds, T., & Bruch, P. (2002). Curriculum and affect: A participatory developmental writing approach. *Journal of Developmental Education, 26* (2), 12–14, 16, 18, 20.

Reynolds, T., & Fillipi, P. (2003). Re-focus through involvement: (Re)writing the mission documents of the University of Minnesota General College basic writing program. *Journal of Basic Writing, 22*(1), 13–21.

Rhoads, R. A., & Valadez, J. R. (1996). *Democracy, multiculturalism, and the community college: A critical perspective.* New York: Garland.

Rose, M. (1989). *Lives on the boundary.* New York: Free Press.

Shor, I. (1997). Our apartheid: Writing instruction and inequality. *Journal of Basic Writing, 16*(1), 91–104.

Smitherman, G. (1977). Toward educational linguistics for the First World. *College English, 41* (1), 202–211.

Soliday, M. (2002). *The politics of remediation.* Pittsburgh, PA: University of Pittsburgh Press.

Sternglass, M. (1997). *Time to know them: A longitudinal study of writing and learning at the college level.* Mahwah, NJ: Lawrence Erlbaum Associates.

Young, I. M. (1990). *Justice and the politics of difference.* Princeton, NJ: Princeton University Press.

Young, I. M. (1997). *Intersecting voices: Dilemmas of gender, political philosophy, and policy.* Princeton, NJ: Princeton University Press.

Embedding Skill Development
in Content Courses

Embedding Skill Development in Content Courses

Introduction

This section begins with a chapter by history professors David Arendale and David Ghere. They focus on the teaching of an introductory history course that embeds skill development and learning directly within the content of their classes. Traditionally, disciplines like history, art, social science, and philosophy, for some examples, are not typically taught with an overt emphasis on student development the way that the subjects of math, reading, and writing have been discussed in the fields of higher education, learning assistance, and developmental education. By identifying how to incorporate learning strategies and student support more directly within the framework of a course like American History, Arendale and Ghere note how developmental education is effective in all the content areas for increasing student achievement and engagement.

The next chapter in this section is by Pat James, who chronicles the rich history of the arts as part of the GC curriculum and the role that art can have in the development of skills that are easily transferable to other college courses and to life in general. James describes how the arts are incorporated into GC courses in myriad forms. She then goes into greater depth in illustrating her own teaching methods and how they are perceived through the reflective writing of "Risa," a former student.

The GC math program is another part of the curriculum that serves a diverse range of students each year. Kinney, Robertson, and Kinney discuss the multiple models for math courses that are offered to GC students, depending on their preference. This includes lecture, computer-mediated instruction, group-guided discovery, active learning with a mastery approach, and cooperative learning. This array of approaches that are available to GC students acknowledges the range of learning styles and student needs to engage with real-world concepts and mathematical equations.

Kinney, Kinney, and Robertson follow up with another chapter specifically on the computer-mediated instructional model in General College. This type of approach to math instruction includes assessment of students, student feedback, use of the latest software available for instruction, and analysis of learning outcomes that can be tracked with the software itself. Students who self-select into the computer-mediated courses may prefer using technology as a tool for engagement and improvement of their math skills.

Carl Chung is very successful in making symbolic logic accessible and meaningful to General College students by integrating course content and basic skill development. Chung insists that "creating a learning environment that enables skill acquisition and development is as important as teaching the skills themselves." He also articulates the importance of offering symbolic logic as an alternative to traditional developmental mathematics courses because it allows students who have had negative experiences with math to start with a "clean slate" while also enabling students to "ground the symbols and symbolic manipulations" in their knowledge of language, "which is familiar to them, . . . [while] logic is not."

In his chapter, Leon Hsu presents a detailed description of his implementation of a "Physics by Inquiry" course that focuses on the development of critical and metacognitive thinking skills. Students learn in small groups by developing, testing, and evaluating scientific theories to predict real-world phenomena. Hsu notes that the course "cannot address as many different topics as a 'mile-wide, inch deep' survey course for non-science majors" but instead fosters scientific thinking that will be transferable to other settings.

Heidi Barajas and Walt Jacobs apply the concepts of Universal Design of Learning (UDL) to teaching sociology, with an emphasis on the sociological imagination. They begin their chapter by identifying similarities between the concepts and principles of UDL and the definition and goals of developmental education. They discuss "understanding the theoretical implications of treating all students as developing sociologists, able to identify their own social location in a historical as well as biographical context." Barajas and Jacobs also remind us that social status, like educational achievement, is not merely the result of hard work, but may also be "either constrained or facilitated by social group membership." They illustrate their points through the description of service learning and storytelling as powerful pedagogy.

CHAPTER 12

Integrating Best Practices of Developmental Education in Introductory History Courses

David R. Arendale and David L. Ghere

ABSTRACT

This chapter provides a practical model for social science teachers to integrate the best practices of developmental education within a course. The approach requires systemic changes in the learning environment that facilitate both higher educational outcomes and concurrent development of lifelong learning skills among all students. This new model stands in contrast with the traditional developmental education approach that identifies individual students within a class based on predictive measures and prescribes specific activities for them alone. This chapter's narrative identifies practices used by the authors successfully with their college students in introductory courses in American history and world history.

Higher education at a major research university and best teaching practices are not mutually exclusive. The mission of the General College (GC) at the University of Minnesota requires instructors to be innovative and varied in their teaching methodology while systematically embedding academic skill development into freshman-level courses. GC courses retain the rigorous content standards and high performance expectations of college-level courses while integrating activities and assignments that enhance the student's ability to perform college-level work. The accomplishment of this goal requires a thoughtful and creative approach to course design, including the revision of course procedures, classroom activities, written assignments, evaluation methods, and feedback to students. This chapter explores the experience and practice of the authors in teaching history at GC and provides a practical model as well as specific methods for incorporating the best practices of developmental education into other social science courses.

Statement of the Problem and Challenge

History teachers operate with multiple learning goals for their courses due to the complexity of the subject material, their own expectations for the course, and the standards of the education community. The following goals are just a few of the more traditional ones found in college history courses: (a) identification of the themes, concepts, and influences central to the time period studied; (b) formation of connections between historical events and personal interests; (c) development of intellectual skills of analysis, synthesis, critical evaluation, and application; and (d) development of an informed historical perspective and greater awareness of and respect for individual, cultural, ethnic, and religious differences. However, changes in the educational environment may require an expansion of these learning objectives for diverse student populations, particularly in introductory core curriculum courses.

Access to postsecondary education has increased due to a variety of factors including the increase in local postsecondary institutions and the availability of financial aid. As access has widened, more students are pursuing postsecondary education, including students who are first-generation to college and from historically-underrepresented groups (Kipp, Price, & Wohlford, 2002). History teachers and their institutions are faced with both maintaining high academic standards and increasing student success regarding outcomes such as mastery of course content material, reenrollment rates, persistence in the academic major, scores on junior- and senior-level examinations, and graduation rates. Nearly all entering students at GC are academically underprepared and share common traits with students who have developmental needs. Many of these students need a different educational experience to meet their learning needs than has been traditionally offered in the past by other institutions following the traditional approach to developmental education. GC provides an enriched learning environment for all students enrolled in the class rather than expecting individual students to seek help elsewhere. We believe that the classroom must be a seamless integration of both teaching and learning mastery with the professor as a catalyst for both.

With the growing diversity of college applicants, radical changes are required in postsecondary education to help it adapt to the needs of students rather than continuing the common practice of demanding students to conform to an arbitrary standard established by the institution. Despite the wide variety of academic interventions designed and implemented in the past 20 years, persistence and graduation rates have not changed significantly based on a national survey of institutions of various types in the U.S. (American

College Testing Program, 2003a). In a recent national study of 2,419 postsecondary institutions of various types, the mean graduation rate was 45% (American College Testing Program, 2003b). Tinto (1993) reported that the average national dropout rate from college has remained at 50% for the past 100 years in American higher education.

This mismatch between institutional expectations and initial student capabilities and preferences is further challenged by changes in the availability of traditional developmental education activities such as study skills courses, reading courses, workshops, and the like. Nationwide studies suggest that these traditional forms of academic enrichment and development for students are becoming less available and have even been eliminated at some institutional types depending on the state (Bastedo & Gumport, 2003; Boylan, Saxon, & Boylan, 2002; Martinez, Snider, & Day, 2003; Shaw, 1997; Stratton, 1998). This elimination of developmental education support has been noted at public 4-year institutions, especially at research institutions (Barefoot, 2003; Jehangir, 2002; Moore, Jensen, & Hatch, 2002; Yaffe, 1998). Rather than decrying the reduced availability of previous forms of developmental education, American postsecondary education has the opportunity to reinvent the learning environment through mainstreaming of academic assistance and enrichment within all classrooms. GC has been an ongoing experiment toward this goal since its creation in 1932.

Concurrent development of learning strategies while enrolled in an introductory core curriculum course such as history is a viable alternative to requiring students to enroll in separate developmental education courses. This requires a reengineering of the course to permit an expansion of purpose. In addition to the traditional content-specific learning objectives, a new one is added: acquisition of strategic learning strategies to master the course material. Other authors have presented models for such integration (Cruthird, 1986; Francisco, Trautmann, & Nicoll, 1998; Luvaas-Briggs, 1984). Building on previous scholarship concerning integration of strategies within a history course (Ghere, 2000; 2001; 2003; Wilcox, delMas, Stewart, Johnson, & Ghere, 1997), this chapter offers practical suggestions that instructors could implement in a wide variety of courses.

Regardless of their academic need, few GC students are interested in separate instruction in study skills, reading strategies, and so on. With the institution's recent emphasis on students completing their undergraduate degrees within 4 years, there is even less perceived flexibility for students to enroll in additional courses outside of their obligations of core requirements and prescribed degree programs. From our perspective, acquisition of lifelong learning skills must be within the context of the history course content material. Research suggests that the learning strategy must be directly applicable to learning the academic content material so students perceive that they will earn higher grades on the major examinations (Bohr, 1994; Kerr, 1993; Stahl, Simpson, & Hayes, 1992). Although we take a much longer view of the utility of learning strategies for lifelong learning, that view must be balanced by immediate application to learning demands perceived by students and short-term potential gratification through higher exam scores. This balancing of needs by both instructors and students is a constantly negotiated relationship concerning the choice of classroom activities and academic content material.

Educational Theory Supporting Embedded Developmental Education

Current studies report that nearly one third of all entering first-year students enroll in one or more developmental courses. This rate has not varied for many decades (Parsad & Lewis, 2003). This enrollment rate severely underreports the number of students with academic development needs. This occurs because it does not include students who enroll in developmental courses later in their college career nor does it indicate which students participate in noncredit academic enrichment activities such as individual or group tutoring like the Emerging Scholars Program (Treisman, 1985), Supplemental Instruction (Arendale, 1998), attendance at study skills workshops, and other activities and programs designed to increase student academic achievement.

The literature has frequently cited the use of linked courses (Gabelnick, MacGregor, Matthews, & Smith, 1990; Malnarich with Others, 2003; Tinto, 1997) as an effective means for accomplishing this goal. An example would be a study skills course linked with an introductory sociology course. In this model, student motivation to acquire academic skills and develop learning strategies is enhanced by its immediate application to the course and its positive effect on the course grade. While some institutions report success with this model, other institutions do not have the option since such study skills courses have been eliminated from the curriculum. In addition, this method still targets a specified subpopulation of students and does not place the institution in the leadership role of systemically changing the learning environment for all students.

The integrated and embedded approach to developmental education is based upon the following premises:

1. The development of mastery of core curriculum knowledge or skills and lifelong learning skills is most effective when accomplished concurrently.

2. The institution must adapt itself to the entering student population rather than expecting students to adopt the behaviors of the dominant culture.

3. Students with a disability are best served when mainstreamed with all students within the classroom.

4. Activities and services originally designed to meet the needs of developmental education and those with a disability often have high utility for all students within the class.

The educational practices contained within this chapter were selected first because of their grounding in educational theory and second for their utility within the classroom. Research studies suggest that most college students have extreme difficulty in applying principles learned from isolated study skills instruction, reading courses, and similar kinds of approaches with their core curriculum courses (Stahl, Simpson, & Hayes, 1992). This research suggested that students acquire and incorporate learning and study strategies most effectively when they concurrently apply them in the context of a content course. The concept of "situated cognition" states that more effective learning takes place within a context that is both personally meaningful and requires the student to make direct application of a new cognitive skill that has been recently taught (Wilson, 1993). New abstract ideas and skills are immediately grounded in concrete use with a learning task and an educational outcome measure. Immediate application and positive feedback concerning successful use of the skill increase the likelihood of further use.

In addition to the need to embed practice with learning strategies within the content classroom, students must gain more awareness of their own learning process. Their learning effectiveness is increased through development of metacognitive processes that allow them to self-monitor their comprehension level and then make changes in their study strategies to meet the learning task need. In addition to understanding the cognitive needs of the tasks, it is also essential for both students and classroom instructors to discover, understand, and deal with the impact of various facets of student motivation (Pintrich, 2000).

Associated with this concept of concurrent development of learning strategies is the concept of Universal Instructional Design (UID; Higbee, 2003). Although originally conceptualized as a transformation of the classroom environment for mainstreaming of students with disabilities (Silver, Bourke, & Strehorn, 1998), the approach has been extended for the transformation of the classroom experience to increase learning and outcomes for all students. This includes students who are academically underprepared and are mainstreamed into traditional, first-year college courses that present rigorous academic content and skills (Higbee). Practices that are helpful to developmental or disability needs have proven to be helpful for the entire student body because they contribute to an enriched environment. This paradigm requires the institution to present a transformed learning environment that capitalizes on existing student strengths and builds upon them throughout the course.

Finally, it is recognized that most students learn best as a member of a cohort of peers. The unique traits of students—demographic, cultural, intellectual—are important ingredients and resources for their learning experiences. In this sociocultural perspective, the education enterprise is viewed as a learning community dependent upon the active participation of all members (Vygotsky, 1978). Various educational activities associated with the course encourage extensive student dialogue, various ways to express mastery of academic content and demonstration of acquired skills, and small peer-group cooperative learning activities.

Teaching in a developmental context requires strategies that promote the student's success in GC. Because of the predominant background of GC students as first-generation college attenders, it is incumbent upon us as course professors throughout the academic term to model our thinking process concerning the academic content material and the various learning strategies that students can employ for more deeply mastering the material. We "make explicit the implicit" demands of the course and model ways to more deeply understand and appreciate the academic content.

Teaching in a developmental context also requires strategies that promote the student's successful transition to the greater university. Professors employ use of psychological "fading" strategies (Dembo, 1994, p. 56; Renkl, Atkinson, & Maier, 2000, pp. 1–6) to gradually withdraw the structural elements of the course (e.g., providing detailed advance organizers, PowerPoint slides, reminders of course requirements) to allow students to assume more responsibility for such matters by the end of the course. This practice facilitates the time of transition to new courses the following academic term that may not have the same type of embedded developmental education strategies.

Overview of the General College Introductory History Courses

GC has implemented this integrated and embedded approach to developmental education. In addition to seeking to meet individual course and content objectives, all courses offered in General College contain the following four objectives: (a) to develop student academic skills in writing and creative thinking; (b) to assist students in developing good academic habits; (c) to use innovative teaching methods and relate class topics to current issues; and (d) to increase the frequency and vary the method of assessment and feedback. These goals have been successfully implemented in Survey of U.S. History (GC 1231), a one-semester survey of American History, and World Civilization Since 1500 (GC 1251), through utilization of a variety of developmental course activities. Both classes enroll from 35 to 45 students per section to facilitate active learning methods, enhance student-instructor interaction, and promote fruitful class discussions. However, the basic concepts and teaching methods could be adapted to a wide variety of social science courses.

GC 1231 has been designated as a writing-intensive course by the University. These courses are designed to develop the students' writing ability, particularly in research papers, beyond the level provided by the required freshman-level composition courses. Students must successfully pass four writing-intensive courses in order to graduate. In GC 1231 students need to complete three different types of writing assignments: (a) short five- to seven-sentence essays in the form of 11 in-class writings and six questions on each of three exams, (b) a long essay question on each of three major exams, and (c) a 10- to 12-page formal paper. Because the course is writing intensive, a graduate teaching assistant (GTA) is available to critique and grade the homework assignments and provide a detailed critique of the first draft of the formal paper. The instructor grades all the long essays and the final draft of the paper.

GC 1251 meets two of the liberal education requirements for graduation from the University: Historical Perspectives and International Perspectives. A variety of writing venues are provided throughout the course, although not to the same intensity as in the American history course that has been designated as writing intensive. The first of the writing components is completing three essay questions on each of the four major exams. Six potential essay questions are identified for each exam on a study guide distributed at the beginning of each new unit. Four questions are provided on each exam, with students given the choice of completing three of them. A short paper of one to two pages is required concerning a "field trip" to a historically-related event or film from a list provided by the course instructor. Finally, eight short in-class writing assignments occur during class sessions to allow students to summarize major components of course material or to reflect on historical topics and their relationship to contemporary events. Because of the class size and course expectations, an undergraduate teaching assistant (UGTA) facilitates optional study review sessions outside of class 3 days per week. These sessions are called Excel Learning Groups (ELGs) and follow similar procedures as other peer cooperative learning programs such as the Emerging Scholars Program (Treisman, 1985), Peer-Led Team Learning (Dreyfus, 2004), Structured Learning Assistance (Doyle & Kowalczyk, 1999), and Supplemental Instruction (Arendale, 1998).

Modifications of the Classroom Learning Environment

Following is a sample of the activities and modifications to the classroom learning environment for either or both the American history and world history courses. To permit time for mastery of lifelong learning skills in addition to the traditional curriculum expectations and requirements, the course has been expanded from three to four semester credit hours.

Concurrent Development and Content Mastery

In the American history course students are expected each week to answer one homework question by composing a paragraph of six or seven sentences. These questions are constructed so that the answer cannot simply be copied from the text and are of two basic types. The first type requires students to identify key points or summarize events from a two- to three-page section of the text. This ability to recognize the key points in a piece of text and condense the information into a short concise paragraph will be invaluable to students throughout their lives. The second type of question asks students to assume a particular role given the background information from the assigned reading and reflect on what their actions or decisions would be in that situation. For example,

1. Why did the 13th, 14th, and 15th Amendments to the U.S. Constitution fail to secure equality for the ex-slaves? (examples: court decisions, state legislation, and violence)

2. Would you prefer to be a woman in colonial New England or colonial Virginia? Why? (examples: health concerns, property rights, social issues)

These writing exercises gradually enhance the students' organization and analysis skills, as well as their critical thinking and creativity.

American history students take three major exams during the academic term, each including a question to be answered in a lengthy essay encompassing four to eight pages in a test booklet (i.e., "blue book"). Essay questions focus on broad themes that require students to consolidate and compare information and ideas over the span of a historical period. Essay questions are announced one week in advance of the exam so students can organize their thoughts and look for evidence to support their arguments. This practice not only develops the students' writing skills, but it also enables the instructor to have much higher expectations about the preparation for the essay and the quality of the arguments. Poor performance can be dealt with appropriately because the problem, whether the students' lack of understanding or lack of motivation to study, can be more easily determined. Essays are written in class without notes, and the bluebooks are marked to prevent students from bringing a previously written essay into class.

Implementation of Universal Instructional Design

Universal Instructional Design is an approach to education in which systemic changes are made to the learning environment to accommodate the needs of students with a disability (Higbee, 2003). There has been considerable debate within education at the elementary, secondary, and postsecondary levels about the mainstreaming of these students. Through this spirited dialogue and review of educational outcomes, it has been clearly demonstrated that all students within the classroom benefit from these changes, which increase the accessibility of knowledge and the environment in which learning activities occur. These changes in environment can be especially useful for students who have issues related to academic underpreparedness. Following are a number of activities and modifications to the classroom directly related to UID for use in both the American history and world history courses. Throughout the rest of this chapter are other activities and modifications that could also be considered UID adaptations, but they have been placed under other categories for the sake of clarity for the reader.

Web-based access to knowledge. Accessing course-related materials, whether created by the instructor or provided by the textbook publisher, provides an opportunity for the student to study and practice with the material in privacy and to decide how much time to invest in the activity. Syllabi, course calendars, assignment guidelines, review sheets, topic outlines, and discussion questions can all be placed on the Web site as well as links to documents, maps, charts, images, resource sites, and PowerPoint lecture slides. Students with a disability can more easily use the material through text readers, enlarged print, and other adaptive technology. All students have an opportunity to be better prepared for class sessions and to be more confident in participating in small group and class-wide discussions.

Assessment of knowledge. Our purpose is to assess the student's knowledge and understanding of the course material, not the speed with which the students can compose their thoughts in written essays. Tests with time limits advantage the free-flowing writer and disadvantage the meticulous writer while imposing unnecessary limits on the student's demonstration of course content mastery. In both the American and world history courses, tests are designed to require 60 to 75 minutes, but at the end of the 2-hour class session students are allowed to finish their work in the professor's office. A few students request this provision each term. Generally accommodation for students with learning disabilities (usually time-and-a-half on tests) is not needed because all students have the time necessary to fully convey their comprehension of the course material. However, one or two students each term are approved by the institution's Disability Services—a unit of the Office of Multicultural & Academic Affairs—to take their exams in their office to provide an isolated environment for those who may become distracted by others in the room.

The provision of additional time benefits all students. It helps alleviate one source of test anxiety by eliminating time pressure. It helps students in being more reflective about taking the exam, more careful in reading exam questions, more practiced in writing short outlines for essay questions, and more proficient in gathering information from the vocabulary and multiple-choice sections of the exam that could be useful for supporting the essay question responses. Expectations can be raised by the instructor because students will have the time needed to create more reflective and analytical responses to essay questions. When quality work is not produced, the reason for the failure, whether lack of ability or lack of effort, is more apparent and the appropriate solutions more obvious to both instructor and student.

Preparation for lectures and learning. A challenge for some students is the difficulty of navigating a rich, fast-moving, and sometimes complicated college classroom learning environment. This pace contrasts with the more common public high school experience that is much slower, structured, teacher-directed, and that assigns time during class for silent reading of the textbook because there are insufficient copies for checkout to all students. In this case, students do not acquire the habit of advance reading of upcoming textbook chapters because the books are unavailable for home checkout.

Providing lecture outlines ahead of time or hiring a fellow student to provide copies of notes is not an uncommon practice for some students with a disability because of their challenge with the expectations of the college learning environment. The introduction of PowerPoint slide presentations to accompany class lectures has accentuated this problem for more students within the class because the amount of content information presented is often larger and moves at a faster pace.

In the world history course the instructor provides an incomplete copy of the upcoming PowerPoint lecture slides ahead of time for each student. The slides are sent via the course e-mail list in the PowerPoint handout format, which includes three slides on the left side of the page with the right side of the page blank for the addition of student notes. Students do not need the PowerPoint software installed on the computer because the document is sent in Acrobat PDF format. Each email message also provides a Web link to information for downloading a free software copy of the PDF reader. Several other academic units on campus, including the business and law schools, also send similar handouts via e-mail to students. However, the difference with the world history slides is that they are abridged. Common elements that are deleted include secondary or tertiary points on the text slides and all maps, art work, or slides that prompt students within the class session for small group activities, reading activities, class announcements, and so forth. For students with a documented disability, the complete set of PowerPoint slides with all secondary or tertiary points is provided ahead of time. Last academic term a student with a severe sight impairment was able to use this complete set of slides on his computer in advance of the class lecture. Using the Power-Point software program, he first converted the slides into the outline view and then used the adaptive software installed on his computer to convert the written outline into an audio narration of the complete slides.

One purpose of providing the incomplete slides in advance is to encourage students to focus on conceptual understanding and application rather than rote lecture note-taking. The incomplete notes relieve students from spending time during lecture segments rapidly taking notes. Rather, students listen, reflect, question, and then annotate their notes on the basis of the class discussion and the secondary and tertiary information on the PowerPoint slides presented by the course instructor that did not appear on the slides sent to the students earlier.

Another benefit of use of PowerPoint slides with the students is that it also prepares them for a pedagogy and a technology that, good or bad, is widely implemented throughout the University. As the term progresses, the instructor begins to fade the detail level of the PowerPoint slides. The goal is to enable the students to acquire more information through the oral comments of the instructor and fellow students and not to be completely dependent upon the PowerPoint slides to determine what content is most important and to master the course topics.

A cautionary note with providing the slides ahead of time, either by e-mail attachment or by placement on a Web site, revolves around the maturity level of some first-year students. In the first semester that the world history teacher provided the PowerPoint slides to the students, he provided the complete set of notes. Class attendance fell quickly. The instructor postulated that some of these students made the assumption that all that occurred within the lecture was contained in the PowerPoint slides displayed in class. It appeared that this same phenomenon did not occur to the same extent in the upper division and graduate courses on campus. When the instructor changed the format of the advance slides and made them incomplete, attendance rose in the class.

Valuing Course Materials

Students sometimes act on the maxim that the amount of time that an instructor spends on an issue in class is related to its overall relative importance. Students are not easily convinced when the instructor states something is important and then fails to mention it again in the course. This mismatch of expectations is especially profound regarding the use of the course syllabus, textbook, ancillary course materials, and associated Web-based resources. Although the first day of class is often uplifting for the course professor, it can be very intimidating for college students, regardless of their academic preparation level. In psychology a term that relates to this circumstance is "felt necessity" (Boekaertis & Niemivirta, 2000, pp. 419–421). People are more likely to remember information when it is immediately applicable, necessary, and needed by the individual. Reminding students about course tutors, course assignments, and textbook features before they have engaged the material has important, though limited, value. Instructors need to value such materials and procedures throughout the course term so that students emotionally understand that the material is important, relevant, and meets their learning needs (Martin, Blanc, & Arendale, 1994).

The course syllabus. Instructors often spend large amounts of time carefully crafting course syllabus documents and then quickly rushing through them on the first day of class so that the first lecture can be delivered. From an instructor's point of view it might seem reasonable to instruct students by telling them to read the syllabus on their own. The message received by students is that they have received another official university document, nearly incomprehensible as well as irrelevant to an anxious first-year student. Rather than seeing it as a tool to use continually throughout the term, it is dutifully filed or recycled. In both the American and world history classes the instructors bring the syllabus daily to class and frequently consult it in front of class when questions arise about assignments, due dates, grading criteria, or all the other issues that have been carefully addressed.

The required course textbook. The same comments also apply to the textbook. In the world history course on the first day of class the instructor takes an extended tour of the textbook and notes the important components that are sometimes overlooked: (a) table of contents that provides outlines of each chapter, (b) study questions and key vocabulary words at the beginning or end of the chapter, (c) glossary in the back of the book useful for defining key vocabulary terms in the exam study guides, and (d) an index in the back of the book useful for looking up topics or key vocabulary terms in the exam study guide. Parts of these pages have been scanned into the computer and then incorporated into a PowerPoint presentation to make it easier for students to note the features, especially for those students who have delayed purchasing their textbook due to the perception that such expenditures may be unnecessary.

In both the American and world history courses, textbooks are valued continually throughout the academic term by the course instructor in a variety of ways. First, the instructor always brings the textbook with him to class each day and finds ways to refer to material on specific pages. Examples for use of the textbook include drawing attention to specific questions listed in the chapter overview designed to guide the reading; moderating discussion concerning the meaning of maps, charts, illustrations, or brief historical primary documents in the book that are sometimes overlooked by the reader; illustrating the utility of the glossary or index in the back of the book to quickly locate information; or other activities. At least once each week students are required during class to work in groups of two or three to read a short passage or study an image, answer a question posed by the instructor in their small group, and then share during a large group session. The purpose of this activity is to learn from each other how to break down textbook material, develop confidence that they can effectively understand new material, and notice features that the textbook provides to deepen understanding of the material (e.g., chapter summaries, questions, coordinated images, key terms, bolded print, glossary, index, subheadings). To assist students in seeing how the teacher reads and interprets the material, one page from each chapter is provided to the students during class. On this textbook page, selected for being especially rich in content material that may appear on the exam, the instructor underlines key phrases and writes short comments in the margin area. To provide more space for the notes, the photocopy of the original textbook page is reduced to 75%. This process reveals the valuing system that the instructor employs when reading the textbook. It also provides a model for students for how to mark up textbooks, which is seldom done in high school because the books must be used by other students in succeeding terms or even by other students during the same class day.

Web-based resources. For teachers who seek to include Web-based resources, especially those provided by the textbook publisher, it is critical to practice extensively with accessing the materials from a computer and exploring all components of the package. Sometimes the test banks are heavily focused on knowledge-level questions of material that is obscure, even for course instructors. Encouraging students to test themselves with this type of material can be demoralizing and counterproductive. Secondly, the difficulty in accessing Web-based materials can be challenging, even for experienced computer users. It is best to demonstrate the use of such Internet resources in class. It would be a mistake to assume that today's students are equally savvy concerning use of computing resources. A cautionary note about relying upon Web resources is that not all Web sites have been modified to allow their use by students with vision or hearing disabilities. In such cases the material needs to be made available in an accessible format or it should be eliminated so as not to provide an unfair advantage for some students.

Alternative Formal Assessment Measures

Although the diversity of entering students has continued to rise, the use of diverse measures for student mastery often has not changed significantly. Too often, for instance, students are expected to navigate multiple-choice examinations expertly. In addition to providing some multiple-choice questions on exams, the two history courses have employed a mix of short and long essay questions, matching exercises, short answer, and identity questions. Other formal assessment methods have included journals, short in-class or homework writing assignments, reaction papers, short and long research papers, written reviews of history Web sites, historically-related films, guest speakers, and museum exhibitions. In-class activities and student presentations can be evaluated by the instructor or assessed through peer review and self-review.

Use of Classroom Assessment Techniques

In both history courses, nongraded classroom assessment techniques (Angelo & Cross, 1993) are frequently used to build metacognitive awareness and motivation for academic behavior changes. Helping students to see the link between their behavior and grades is a difficult task. Some students, because of previous unsuccessful educational experiences, already perceive that there is no relationship between their examination preparation behaviors and the grades received. Students are provided a safe environment to discover what they do and do not know through frequent use of ungraded quiz questions, small group discussions, in-class textbook or current newspaper short reading assignments, or other means. The goal is for students not to be surprised with results from their major examinations. Sometimes this is still a surprise, so in the world history course an activity is used in class on the day that the exams are returned to students.

After the first exam in the world history course is returned to students, the instructor hands out a detailed 30-item survey for students to complete before they depart class on that day. The survey asks them to recount the exam preparation behaviors they engaged before the exam and techniques used during the exam. Students are instructed not to identify themselves on the survey except by indicating whether they scored in one of the following grade categories: AB or CDF. This activity provides an opportunity for students to reflect on their test preparation and test-taking behaviors and discover potential relationships between the behaviors and grades received on the exam. At the following class session, the instructor returns a summary of this class survey that groups responses for each of the 30 items between those who earned an A or B versus those who earned a C or lower on the exam. The summary provides feedback to the students from their peers on which behaviors were associated with those who did well and those who did not perform well on the exam. Rather than relying on the instructor to deliver an exhortation on particular behaviors, students observe their peers and hopefully will be more likely to adopt new positive behaviors. This same process is repeated after the third of the four examinations administered during the academic term.

Fostering Critical Thinking Through Simulations

A challenge for students who are academically underprepared is their preoc-cupation with locating "correct" information and seeking the "one" answer to questions. This narrow focus can be a barrier to the development of critical thinking skills that will be necessary in upper-division courses both to under-stand material and to complete course examinations successfully. Fostering the development of critical thinking skills is essential for students who are academically underprepared (Adams & Hamm, 1990; Chaffee, 1992; Higbee & Dwinell, 1998; Paul & Elder, 1999; Stone, 1990).

One way to help stimulate critical thinking skills is through the use of his-torical decision-making simulations. An additional benefit of this strategy is that it provides more engagement for the students because most report that they find it interesting and relevant, and they have the opportunity to work in small groups. These are just some of the many educational benefits for stu-dents from simulations (Bennett, Leibman, & Fetter, 1997; Bredemeier & Greenblat, 1981; Druckman, 1995; Randell, Morris, Welzel, & Whitehall, 1992).

All simulations involve the students in active learning situations requir-ing some level of role playing. These roles can be very specific as a historical individual; more general as a representative of a country, region, or state; or very generic as a decision maker assessing the historical options that might have been available. Simulations provide the background material necessary for each student to evaluate the various decision options in the historical sit-uation and to play the role assigned. Sometimes a reward system is utilized to create a situation, which fosters competition between groups and cooper-ation within each group. In these "game" simulations, students articulate their position, negotiate with other students, and compromise when neces-sary to reach a consensus decision or political bargain that achieves their goals. Other simulations employ maps to convey information to the students, to designate various territorial options, and to ultimately display student decisions. Following are several examples of simulation activities:

1. What principles would you employ to govern a large empire that was extremely culturally diverse and geographically dispersed? This simulation is based on common experiences from the three great Muslim Empires from 1500 to 1700 that enabled them to successfully govern and expand their influence.

2. What factors would you consider as you reorganized the borders of

European countries to prevent future aggressions? This question asks students to compare and contrast the same historical scenarios experienced after three world wars: the Napoleonic Wars, World War I, and World War II.

3. As a United Nations commission, what political organization and degree of autonomy would you recommend for a specific region based on data concerning its ethnic and religious composition? Students must analyze the question based on historical events in different geographic locations of the world that encompass different cultures and traditions: West Bank, Northern Ireland, Kosovo, and Bosnia.

4. As U.S. Senators representing specific states or regions, negotiate and compromise on important legislative issues. Students must draw conclusions at different historical time periods in United States history: first session of Congress, Jacksonian Period, Compromise of 1850, and the Gilded Age.

In each case, natural interests of role playing, competitive play, and intellectual curiosity are channeled into an educational activity that helps to foster students' critical thinking skills.

Examination Preparation Strategies

Many GC students experience major problems with formal course examinations for a variety of reasons already discussed earlier in this chapter. Too many see a disassociated relationship between their behaviors and the grades received on exams. To counter this student assumption, practice with good test-taking strategies is integrated into both history classes.

Valuing material to study for the exam. Some students find it difficult to study for exams because they are unable to sort out the course content and decide what material to study more intensely. Some of these students take lecture notes much like a court stenographer, taking down everything spoken during class, but they are unable to sort, reorganize, and value the material differently. In both the American and world history courses, study guides are provided in advance to identify key vocabulary terms, potential essay questions, and topic areas for the multiple-choice questions.

Communicating what is required for the exam. Many first-year students report difficulty with the shift from secondary school test formats that emphasized multiple-choice questions to the use of essay questions more prevalent in the postsecondary environment. To help students develop in this area both history courses incorporate frequent opportunities for practice in writing essay questions during class with feedback provided by the instructor, GTA, or fellow students through peer review. Because of its writing-intensive nature described earlier in this chapter, the American history course includes more practice in this area.

Additional opportunities to practice for the exam occur through class time devoted to practice with mock examinations that emulate the style and format of the exams. Instructors help students identify key language in directions, common terms used with essay questions and their specific meanings, and methods for using one part of the exam (i.e., vocabulary matching and multiple choice) to help answer the essay and short answer questions. A handout details the recommended strategies for answering different question types: true or false, multiple choice, and essay. Other instruction regarding test-taking strategies occurs by using the frequent classroom assessment techniques as an opportunity also to analyze the strategies used for completing them.

Metacognitive learning strategies. To maximize the learning experience from the exam, the instructors return the exams to students within two class periods after the exam. The exams are debriefed with the students. During the process, the course instructor shares whether the question is based on the textbook or lecture and the key elements of the question that helped to identify the reason for selection of the correct response. Previously described in this chapter was the use of the exam survey in the world history course for students to consider their test preparation and test-taking strategies and how they might be related to the grade received on the exam.

Peer Cooperative Learning Strategies

Interactive student activities increase student engagement, build learning networks, encourage students to see one another as learning resources, and increase content mastery of challenging material (Astin, 1993; Bruffee, 1993; Cooper, Prescott, Cook, Smith, & Mueck, 1990; Light, 2001). Opportunities for peer learning are often especially important for students who may be underprepared and need to seek out peers to assist them in succeeding in academically challenging courses. Helping them to become comfortable with one another in class, even when acknowledging their ignorance of course material, is a vital step to enabling them to form their own study groups outside of class for this or other courses in their degree program. Students may be more likely to engage in dialogues with one another without the course instructor who is responsible for evaluation and assignment of final course grades.

Peer cooperative learning groups are frequently formed for short-term tasks in each of the history classes. One example already discussed in this chapter is the use of small groups to engage in historical simulations. Another is using a variety of peer cooperative learning strategies to process a difficult short reading assignment of several paragraphs from the text, a newspaper article, or a historical documentary shown during class. Students are more likely to engage in the material and have increased confidence to participate in class discussion through use of carefully assigned and monitored peer cooperative learning activities (Johnson, Johnson, & Smith, 1991). Students who are academically underprepared often battle deficits in content knowledge as well as self-confidence and self-esteem that erect powerful barriers to learning. It is important for class instructors to follow protocols carefully for implementing peer cooperative learning activities to create safe environments for students to work in small teams where they can feel comfortable to self-disclose what they know and do not know about the content. Success and confidence built in ungraded small-group activities can spur higher confidence and self-esteem.

For example, "Think-Pair-Share" is a common strategy used in the world history class. Students are assigned during class to read a short textbook selection of a historical source document (e.g., account of a woman's perspective of the French Revolution). This activity comprises the "Think" part of the process because students silently read the selection after viewing a question guiding their reading previously posted by the instructor on the blackboard. The next part of the process, "Pair," requires students to turn to fellow students next to them, jointly discuss what they just read, and then discuss the thought question posed by the instructor. The class often quickly becomes an energized collection of small group discussions in which nearly all class members participate. The instructor circulates around the room to monitor the discussion but generally does not participate other than to respond to questions or prompt the occasional group to move forward with the activity. The activity concludes with "Share" when the instructor calls the class back together once again and solicits volunteers to discuss what their small group discovered about the subject and to share a response to the thought question. Gradually throughout the academic term more students volunteer to discuss their ideas in front of the entire class. Students begin to engage more frequently with one another rather than always directing their responses to the instructor.

Summary and Recommendations for Further Investigation

The educational practices contained within this chapter can be used in whole or in part by classroom instructors, learning assistance personnel, or student paraprofessionals in a variety of ways. Instructors of history or other academic content courses could select activities from this chapter that are appropriate to the academic preparation level of the students and the academic expectations for the particular institution. Another variable that comes into play is the resources made available to the instructor by the campus. Is there a campus faculty development center, academic learning center, or developmental education department that the faculty member can consult and that can provide additional suggestions for embedding effective practices? Most of the recommended practices in this chapter do not require extensive preparation or formal coursework in developmental education, as helpful as those would be.

Another potential user of these recommendations is a person who teaches reading or study skills or perhaps administers a learning assistance center that employs peer tutors. A short unit of a history period or topic could provide the academic content material for practice and mastery of academic study strategies. Providing practice with real-world academic tasks is helpful for student paraprofessionals such as peer mentors or academic tutors. As previously noted, research suggests that students learn study strategies best when they make immediate application to real academic content material that they will encounter in their general education and degree completion courses. Using short textbook sections, guest lectures by college instructors, and historical documentaries can provide the real-world learning environment that enables students to learn more from their study skills classes, reading courses, learning strategy workshops, and peer tutoring sessions. These sorts of collaborative activities provide another opportunity for partnership among the academic community of advisors, counselors, faculty members, learning assistance personnel, staff, and others at the institution.

Embedding the best practices of developmental education within core curriculum subjects in General College has shown some elements of success over the past several decades. However, not all students who could benefit from the General College experience are successful. Although the activities and pedagogies described in this chapter have enabled many to succeed, the question remains concerning why some students opt out of availing themselves of these resources and opportunities. Additional research and investigation concerning deeper issues of student motivation are needed. Cognitive psychologists have begun these investigations, especially with elementary and secondary students. These studies need to be more fully extended to postsecondary education. Research partnerships among cognitive psychologists and content-area classroom instructors can illuminate the complicated nature of student motivation and guide institutions and all members of the learning community to adapt themselves to the needs of their students regarding the optimum learning environment. This represents the next wave of innovation that demands our immediate attention to meet the needs of our diverse student population and requirements for living in an increasingly complex and interrelated world.

References

Adams, D., & Hamm, M. (1990). *Cooperative learning: Critical thinking and collaboration across the curriculum.* Springfield, IL: Charles C. Thomas.

American College Testing Program. (2003a). *ACT institutional data file for 2003.* Iowa City, IA: Author. Retrieved July 1, 2004, from http://www.act.org/oeep/droptables.html

American College Testing Program. (2003b). *National collegiate dropout and retention rates.* Iowa City, IA: Author. Retrieved January 11, 2005, from http://www.act.org/path/postsec/droptables/pdf/2003.pdf3

Angelo, T. A., & Cross, K. P. (1993). *Classroom assessment techniques: A handbook for college teachers.* San Francisco: Jossey-Bass.

Arendale, D. (1998). Increasing the efficiency and effectiveness of learning for first year students through Supplemental Instruction. In J. L. Higbee & P. L. Dwinell (Eds.), *Developmental education: Preparing successful college students* (pp. 185–197). Columbia, SC: The National Association for Developmental Education and the National Resource Center for the First-Year Experience and Students in Transition, University of South Carolina.

Astin, A. W. (1993). *What matters in college: Four critical years revisited.* San Francisco: Jossey-Bass.

Barefoot, B. O. (2003). *Findings from the Second National Survey of First-Year Academic Practices, 2002.* Brevard, NC: Policy Center for the First Year of College. Retrieved March 5, 2004, from http://www.brevard.edu/fyc/survey2002/ findings.htm

Bastedo, M. N., & Gumport, P. J. (2003). Access to what? Mission differentiation and academic stratification in U.S. public higher education. *Higher Education: The International Journal of Higher Education and Educational Planning, 46,* 341–359.

Bennett, R. B., Jr., Leibman, J. H., & Fetter, R. E. (1997). Using a jury simulation as a classroom exercise. *Journal of Legal Studies Education, 15*(2), 191–210.

Boekaertis, M., & Niemivirta, M. (2000). Self-regulated learning: Finding a balance between learning goals and ego-protective goals. In M. Boekaertis, P. R. Pintrich, & M. Zeidner (Eds.), *Handbook of self-regulation* (pp. 417–450). San Diego, CA: Academic Press.

Bohr, L. (1994). Courses associated with freshman learning. *Journal of The Freshman Year Experience, 6*(1), 69–90.

Boylan, H. R., Saxon, D. P., & Boylan, H. M. (2002). *State policies on remediation at public colleges and universities.* Unpublished manuscript, National Center for Developmental Education, Appalachian State University, Boone, NC. Retrieved March 5, 2004, from http://www.ced.appstate.edu/centers/ncde/reserve%20reading/state%20Policies.htm

Bredemeier, M. E., & Greenblat, C. S. (1981). The educational effectiveness of simulation games: A synthesis of findings. *Simulation & Gaming: An International Journal, 12,* 307–332.

Bruffee, K. A. (1993). *Collaborative learning: Higher education, interdependence, and the authority of knowledge.* Baltimore, MD: The Johns Hopkins University Press.

Chaffee, J. (1992). Critical thinking skills: The cornerstone of developmental education. *Journal of Developmental Education, 15*(3), 2–4, 6, 8, 39.

Cooper, J., Prescott, S., Cook, L., Smith, L., & Mueck, L. (1990). *Cooperative learning and college instruction: Effective use of student learning teams.* Long Beach, CA: The California State University Foundation.

Cruthird, J. R. L. (1986). *Remedial/developmental instruction in an actual classroom situation: Interfacing social science, English, and writing.* Unpublished manuscript, Kennedy-King College, Chicago, IL. (ERIC Document Reproduction Service No. ED286978)

Dembo, M. H. (1994). *Applying educational psychology* (5th ed.). New York: Longman.

Doyle, T., & Kowalczyk, J. (1999). The Structured Learning Assistance Program model. In M. Hay & N. Ludman (Eds.), *Selected Conference Papers of the National Association for Developmental Education, Volume 5* (pp. 4–7). Warrensburg, MO: National Association for Developmental Education. Retrieved June 22, 2004, from http://www.umkc.edu/cad/nade/nadedocs/99conpap/tdcpap99.htm

Dreyfus, A. E. (Ed.). (2004). *Internet homepage of the Peer-Led Team Learning Program* [On-line]. Retrieved June 22, 2004, from http://www.pltl.org

Druckman, D. (1995). The educational effectiveness of interactive games. In D. Crookall & K. Arai (Eds.), *Simulation and gaming across discipline and culture* (pp. 178–187). London: Sage.

Francisco, J. S., Trautmann, M., & Nicoll, G. (1998). Integrating a study skills workshop and pre-examination to improve students' chemistry performance. *Journal of College Science Teaching, 60,* 273–278.

Gabelnick, F., MacGregor, J., Matthews, R. S., & Smith, B. L. (1990). *Learning communities: Creating connections among students, faculty, and disciplines.* San Francisco: Jossey-Bass.

Ghere, D. L. (2000). Teaching American history in a developmental education context. In J. L. Higbee & P. L. Dwinell (Eds.), *The many faces of developmental education* (pp. 39–46). Warrensburg, MO: National Association for Developmental Education.

Ghere, D. L. (2001). Constructivist perspectives and classroom simulations in developmental education. In D. B. Lundell & J. L. Higbee (Eds.), *Theo-*

retical perspectives for developmental education (pp. 101–108). Minneapolis, MN: Center for Research on Developmental Education and Urban Literacy, General College, University of Minnesota.

Ghere, D. L. (2003). Best practices with students in a college history course. In J. L. Higbee (Ed.), *Curriculum transformation and disability: Implementing universal design in higher education* (pp. 149–161). Minneapolis, MN: Center for Research on Developmental Education and Urban Literacy, General College, University of Minnesota.

Higbee, J. L. (Ed.). (2003). *Curriculum transformation and disability: Implementing universal design in higher education.* Minneapolis, MN: Center for Research on Developmental Education and Urban Literacy, General College, University of Minnesota.

Higbee, J. L., & Dwinell, P. L. (1998). Thinking critically: The relationship between student development and the ability to think critically. *Research & Teaching in Developmental Education, 14*(2), 93–97.

Jehangir, R. R. (2002). Higher education for whom? The battle to include developmental education at the four-year university. In J. L. Higbee, D. B. Lundell, & I. M. Duranzyk (Eds.), *Developmental education: Policy and practice* (pp. 17–34). Auburn, CA: National Association for Developmental Education.

Johnson, D., Johnson, R., & Smith, K. (1991). *Active learning: Cooperation in the college classroom.* Edina, MN: Interaction Book.

Kerr, L. (1993). Content specific study strategies: A repertoire of approaches. *Journal of College Reading and Learning, 25*(1), 36–43.

Kipp, S. M., Price, D. D., & Wohlford, J. K. (2002). *Unequal opportunity: Disparities in college access among the 50 states.* Indianapolis, IN: Lumina Foundation for Education. Retrieved September 27, 2004, from http://www.luminafoundation.org

Light, R. J. (2001). *Making the most of college: Students speak their minds.* Cambridge, MA: Harvard University Press.

Luvaas-Briggs, L. (1984). Integrating basic skills with college content instruction. *Journal of Developmental Education, 7*(2), 6–9, 31.

Malnarich, G., with Others. (2003). *The pedagogy of possibilities: Developmental education, college-level studies, and learning communities.* National Learning Communities Project Monograph Series. Olympia, WA: The Evergreen State College, Washington Center for Improving the Quality of Undergraduate Education, in cooperation with the American Association for Higher Education.

Martin, D. C., Blanc, R., & Arendale, D. (1994). Mentoring in the classroom: Making the implicit explicit. *Teaching Excellence Newsletter, 6*(1), 1–2.

Martinez, S., Snider, L. A., & Day, E. (2003). *Remediation in higher education: A review of the literature.* Topeka, KS: Kansas State Board of Education.

Retrieved March 5, 2004, from http://www.ksde.org/pre/postsecondary_
remediation.doc

Moore, R., Jensen, M., & Hatch, J. (2002). The retention of developmental
education students at four-year and two-year institutions. *Research &
Teaching in Developmental Education, 19*(1), 5–13.

Parsad, B., & Lewis, L. (2003). *Remedial education at degree-granting postsecondary institutions in fall 2000, statistical analysis report.* Washington,
DC: U.S. Department of Education, National Center for Education Statistics. Retrieved March 5, 2004, from http://nces.ed.gov/pubs2004/
2004010.pdf

Paul, R., & Elder, L. (1999). Critical thinking: Teaching students to seek the
logic of things. *Journal of Developmental Education, 23*(1), 34–35.

Pintrich, P. R. (2000). The role of goal orientation in self-regulated learning.
In M. Boekaerts, P. R. Pintrich, & M. Zeldner (Eds.), *Handbook on self-
regulation* (pp. 451–502). San Diego, CA: Academic Press.

Randell, J. M., Morris, B. A., Welzel, C. D., & Whitehall, B. V. (1992). The effectiveness of games for educational purposes: A review of recent research.
Simulation & Gaming: An International Journal, 23, 261–276.

Renkl, A., Atkinson, R. K., & Maier, U. H. (2000). From studying examples to
solving problems: Fading worked-out solution steps help learning. *Pro-
ceedings of the 22nd Annual Conference of the Cognitive Science Society.*
Philadelphia, PA: Institute for Research in Cognitive Science. Retrieved
January 14, 2004, from: http://www.ircs.upenn.edu/cogsci2000/PRCD-
NGS/SPRCDNGS/PAPERS/RENAT-MA.PDF

Shaw, K. M. (1997). Remedial education as ideological battleground: Emerging remedial education policies in the community college. *Educational
Evaluation and Policy Analysis, 19*, 284–296.

Silver, D., Bourke, A., & Strehorn, K. C. (1998). Universal Instructional Design
in higher education: An approach for inclusion. *Equity and Excellence in
Education, 31*(2), 47–51.

Stahl, N. A., Simpson, M. L., & Hayes, C. G. (1992). Ten recommendations
from research for teaching high-risk college students. *Journal of Developmental Education, 16*(1), 2–4, 6, 8, 10.

Stone, N. R. (1990). Ideas in practice: Developing critical thinkers: Content
and process. *Journal of Developmental Education, 13*(3), 20–26.

Stratton, C. B. (1998). Transitions in developmental education: Interviews
with Hunter Boylan and David Arendale. In J. L. Higbee & P. L. Dwinell
(Eds.), *Developmental education: Preparing successful college students* (pp.
25–36). Columbia, SC: National Association for Developmental Education
and the National Resource Center for the First-Year Experience and Students in Transition, University of South Carolina.

Tinto, V. (1993). *Leaving college: Rethinking the causes and cures of student attrition* (2nd ed.). Chicago: The University of Chicago Press.

Tinto, V. (1997). Classrooms as communities: Exploring the educational character of student persistence. *Journal of Higher Education, 68,* 599–623.

Treisman, U. (1985). A study of mathematics performance of Black students at the University of California, Berkeley. *Dissertation Abstracts International, 47*(05), 1641A.

Vygotsky, L. S. (1978). *Mind in society.* Cambridge, MA: Harvard University Press.

Wilcox, K. J., delMas, R. C., Stewart, B., Johnson, A. B., & Ghere, D. (1997). The "package course" experience and developmental education. *Journal of Developmental Education, 20*(3), 18–20, 22, 24, 26.

Wilson, A. L. (1993). *The promise of situated cognition.* (New Directions for Adults and Continuing Education, No. 57). San Francisco: Jossey-Bass.

Yaffe, D. (1998, May 27–June 2). Ivy League remediation? Yes. *The Village Voice,* Issue 22. Retrieved March 5, 2004, from http://www.villagevoice.com/ink/news/22yaffe.shtml

Aesthetic, Metaphoric, Creative, and Critical Thinking: The Arts in General College

Patricia A. James

ABSTRACT

This chapter describes ways that the arts have been used in General College. First, I outline contributions of the arts to education, including aesthetic, metaphoric, creative, and critical thinking and a deeper understanding of other people and cultures. Second, I sketch the history of the arts in General College and describe a few of the many ways that General College faculty have used the arts in arts-focused classes and other subjects. Next, I paint a portrait of one student's learning in a hands-on art course. Finally, I offer suggestions for teaching the arts in developmental education.

A s you walk through Appleby Hall, the home of the General College (GC), you encounter five colorful murals designed and painted by students. The mural near the entrance of the ground floor features portraits of students painted by their classmates (see book jacket), and in the Writing Center there is a vibrant, puzzle-like mural about learning and creativity. A third mural features a "tree of learning," and the fourth mural, a landscape of the Mississippi River and downtown Minneapolis as seen from the art lab window, is framed by students' writings about the river. The newest mural, "Face to Face," is a visual symbol of students' sense of unity as a learning community. A first-floor display case promotes the "Horatio Project," an ongoing musical collaboration among students, staff, and faculty; two second-floor display cases often are filled with students' photomontages and expressive writing; and on the third floor there are exhibits of students' artwork about biological concepts.

In addition to the visual art in the halls, you might hear an insistent rap beat emanating from a basic writing class doing a critical study of hip-hop culture, the rhythmic sounds of anthropology students playing traditional indigenous instruments in a drum circle, or Teaching Specialist Jeff Chapman playing an Ojibway flute for his students (Opitz, 2004). If you go into some of the classrooms, you might observe basic writing students performing dramatic monologues of Sapphire's (1997) novel *Push* or students in the course Film and Society enthusiastically discussing Erroll Morris's (1988) documentary film, *The Thin Blue Line*. In the art lab, you might see students moving together in paper masks to explore metaphors of identity and anonymity, or students in General Arts watching a video about Pacific Rim dancers (*Dancing in One World*, 1993) to learn about relationships between art forms and cultural beliefs. Students' involvement in the arts does not stop at the doors of Appleby Hall, however. On campus, you might encounter a class of General Arts students discussing a work of public art, heading over to the Weisman Art Museum, which is less than two blocks from Appleby Hall, or going to a concert put on by the School of Music.

Each of the above examples illustrates ways that GC students learn about, through, and with the arts (Goldberg, 1997) in art content courses as well as in other subjects. Despite rich possibilities for learning, however, the arts are not often part of developmental education. This omission may be a consequence of beliefs that the arts have little relevance to the verbal and mathematical skills needed to succeed in higher education, that they are merely subjective expressions of personal emotions that cannot be evaluated, or that they require skills only a talented few can achieve. The arts, however, can be accessible at any level of ability and experience when they are taught in ways that help students make sense of them, and they offer alternative ways for students to develop knowledge and thinking processes needed in higher education. Artistic content and processes can be a valuable part of developmental education for all students, including those who have little previous interest or experience in the arts, who have actively participated in the arts, who learn best in nontraditional ways, or who plan to major in subjects such as graphic design, performing arts, or architecture.

The arts have been part of GC since the 1930s, and they continue to play an important role in courses dedicated to the arts as well as in other disciplines such as anthropology, basic writing, and biology. In this chapter, I discuss contributions of the arts to learning and various ways that artistic content and processes have been incorporated in the GC curriculum. To show learning from students' perspectives, I include samples of their writing and a case study of one student as she created art in a first-year learning community. Students' names have been changed to protect their anonymity. I use the term "art" to signify the aesthetic, metaphoric, and creative processes and products that symbolically express human experience throughout history and across all cultures. I take a broad approach that includes fine arts found in museums, galleries, and theaters; traditional arts from cultures around the world; and popular art forms such as movies, music, and commercial design.

The Arts and Learning

The Arts as a Bridge

Students in developmental education have to navigate and negotiate the traditions, discourse, and values of higher education, which may be very different from their home world of family, work place, and peers (Beach, Lundell, & Jung, 2002). The arts offer students ways to construct bridges between their personal and cultural knowledge and that of the academic world. Many students have been actively involved with the arts through high school experiences, church, private lessons, community groups, or self-instruction. Some of these students participate in artistic communities, such as a Hmong student who performs traditional dances at cultural gatherings, an African American student who sings with a gospel group, a Caucasian student who plays drums in a rock band, or a Native American woman who practices traditional dancing and beading. Other students engage in the arts as a form of personal expression, including the young woman who practices modern dance 40 hours per week or the football player who loves to draw. Victor, a Vietnamese American who writes and records his own rap songs, described what making art means to him:

> I open up my audio recording tools and breath tough as the instrumental I created starts up. Words jolt out of my mouth in a rhythmic tune and I must concentrate on lyrics and pronunciation. The chorus is up, and this is when I get a chance to do a little singing. I don't make songs for money or for fame, I just make them for myself. With the experience of producing and recording tracks since 1998, I've made about 20 tracks ranging from Rap and R & B, and they're only getting better!

Students who practice the arts in their own lives learn valuable skills such as collaborating with others, discerning patterns and nuances in what they see and hear, trusting their own judgment, and managing their time. These abilities can be a foundation for learning new concepts and skills in school (Ball & Heath, 1993). Victor sees his learning in music as an evolutionary process, and he has learned to critique his own work. Equally importantly, Victor has learned to place himself within larger artistic traditions and to care passionately about his music for its own sake, not for external rewards like grades. Victor's experiences making music give him confidence and skills that he can use in his academic courses.

Even if they do not actively create art themselves, most students are immersed in the images, sounds, and ideas of the popular arts, including music, television, movies, and computer games. Because it relates to students' own experiences, interests, and peer culture, popular culture is a valuable resource for teaching many kinds of concepts (Pedelty, 2001). For example, hip hop can provide a bridge between students' own knowledge and academic discourse. Professor Geoff Sirc, who uses hip hop culture as a springboard for teaching academic writing, suggested that "rap provides more of a common ground for my students than mainstream literary sources. Using it in the classroom lets students use their own language" (Weber, 2001, p. 7).

Multiple Paths to Learning
Researchers are finding that it is important that students develop a repertoire of ways to construct knowledge:

> The ways in which we conceive of learning and alternative ways of knowing are expanding our notions about what it means to be literate in today's society. A heightened awareness of multiple paths to learning and knowledge construction has begun to emerge. (Sweet, 1997, p. 272)

The polymodal nature of the arts offers students opportunities to build on their intellectual strengths and improve in weaker areas. By engaging in artistic processes or studying works of art, students experience new kinds of academic success and ways of being engaged in learning. The arts help students develop a multiliterate approach to learning. As Bleedorn (1998) put it, "the question becomes not so much 'how smart are you?' but 'how are YOU smart?'" (p. 19).

In a synthesis of research about creative people in all fields, Root-Bernstein and Root-Bernstein (1999) identified transdisciplinary "thinking tools" (p. 25) that shape the theories and practices of all disciplines, including observing, imagining, abstracting, analogizing, empathizing, transforming, and synthesizing. The authors suggested that college students must become adept with these thinking processes if they are to understand disciplinary concepts and construct new knowledge:

> Creative thinking—the kind of thinking in every discipline that generates and conceptualizes new insights—relies on what the philosopher Michael Polyani has called "personal knowledge": images, patterns, sensual and muscular feelings, play acting, empathizing, emotions, and intuitions. Those forms of knowledge have almost no place in our universities, where thinking is almost universally presented as if formal logic were its basis, and words and mathematics its languages of choice. New ideas, however, originate in nonlogical and nonverbal modes that are translated only later into symbolic languages. By slighting those preverbal forms of thinking, we stifle the inventive capacities of many students. . . . The most successful people in every field share an ability to think in ways that we seldom teach in the classroom. We owe it to our students, and to the world that can benefit from their creativity, to teach them how to recognize and use those mental tools. (Root-Bernstein & Root-Bernstein, 2000, p. A54)

The Root-Bernsteins (1999) believed that the arts are an important means for developing these thinking tools:

> To think is to feel and to feel is to think. . . . In some cases, sensing and feeling are most naturally communicated as visual, literary, or musical expressions. Indeed, the arts in a liberal arts education are important because they provide the *best* and in some cases the *only* exercise of many thinking tools, both in imagination and in expression. . . . The arts are not merely for self-expression or entertainment. (p. 317)

The open-ended, complex nature of the arts can help students become "self-authoring" people who understand themselves not as mere receivers of preauthorized knowledge, but as independent thinkers who are comfortable with the uncertainty of knowledge and capable of contributing to new knowledge (Baxter Magolda, 1992). For example, Mark, a freshman in the Creativity Art Lab, reflected about how the arts affected his thinking when he struggled to make two photomontages:

> The most profound insight [that] came to me while doing the photomontages involved the pictorial nature of the human mind. How we assimilate pictorial images and put them together to form some sort of a whole. [Making photomontages] asked me to ponder the idea of the universe being quarks all fitting together though some not as well as others. I really enjoyed working with this idea and have taken it outside the classroom. I think that this type of assignment may stimulate some part of the brain or internal process that helps us to see this is how we construct our reality.

Thinking in the Arts

The arts engage students in complex, open-ended interactions with media, ideas, cultural beliefs and values, symbolic systems, and personal knowledge. Four closely related processes are involved: aesthetic, metaphoric, creative, and critical thinking.

Aesthetic thinking. Parker Palmer (1999) suggested that the educational system of this country forces students "to live out of the top inch and a half of the human self; to live exclusively through cognitive rationality and the powers of the intellect; to live out of touch with anything that lays below that top inch and a half—body, intuition, feeling, emotion, relationship" (p. 17). The integrative nature of the arts helps students go beyond traditional dichotomies, such the separation of body and mind or feeling and thinking, to learn in more embodied, holistic ways that increase insight and retention of learning. Making art and experiencing the arts are aesthetic experiences that demand thoughtful, wholehearted, and embodied participation.

One quality of aesthetic thinking is paying close attention to sensory information. Although this seems like a natural process, aesthetic perception needs to be learned, especially in our fast-paced society in which experience is too often mediated by the highly produced images, sounds, and messages of popular culture. To practice aesthetic perception in the General Arts class, students find a place inside or outside the nearby Weisman Art Museum (2004) and take notes for 20 minutes on everything they see, hear, smell, or touch; they then use their notes to write a descriptive paper. Although this strange metal-clad building, which some have likened to a crushed tin can, often elicits dislike when students see it for the first time, writing about their perceptions helps them put aside premature judgments and be more open to learning about it. Students often describe the overlapping steel panels, reflections of the sky on the intersecting curved planes, the way air smells, shadows, and the sounds of traffic. This kind of perceptual experience engages students' minds, senses, and emotions—they will never again see the building in quite the same way. Aesthetic perception of the environment, objects, and other people can serve as a rich foundation for writing, reading, and discussion and as a catalyst for further study of historical, environmental, and sociological contexts.

Metaphoric thinking. Metaphors shape everyday discourse and our understanding of the world (Lakoff & Johnson, 1999). To understand and express abstract concepts, it is important that students know how to think metaphorically (James, 2000a, 2002; Pugh, Hicks, & Davis, 1997; Sanders & Sanders, 1984). Metaphoric thinking is an imaginative and empathic process that is at the heart of artistic expression, but it also shapes theories in other disciplines, including the sciences and social sciences (Root-Bernstein & Root-Bernstein, 1999). Metaphors enable students to make abstract ideas more immediate and engaging and to experience the way the world looks, sounds, and feels from other points of view. Students can use metaphors to express and understand ideas that cannot be articulated in any other way (Feinstein, 1996; Greene, 2001). By making metaphoric associations between seemingly dissimilar entities, students think about one thing, such as "community," in terms of another, such as "circles," and develop greater insight by connecting these concepts with their memories, senses, and emotions.

When students make or interpret art, they construct metaphors that express their emotions, experiences, and ways of seeing the world. As dancer and choreographer Twyla Tharp (2003) pointed out, "metaphor is the lifeblood of all art, if it is not art itself" (p. 64). In the arts, all parts of a work can have metaphoric significance, not only the overt subject matter. Students learn that *how* something is expressed is as important as *what* is expressed. In a painting of a woman, for example, thick jagged black lines that harshly outline her face and body convey very different metaphoric meanings than if she were drawn in blended pastels that softly delineate her contours. The same woman painted as a tiny figure framed by a large space will evoke different thoughts and emotions than a painting in which her face boldly fills the entire picture plane.

Creative thinking. With the continually evolving nature of knowledge and society, it is important that students learn to be creative thinkers who can push beyond familiar boundaries and envision new ways of thinking and acting (Bleedorn, 1998; Caine & Caine, 1997; Root-Bernstein & Root-Bernstein, 1999). By engaging in the arts, students develop dispositions and skills that promote creative thinking, such as being adventurous and open-minded about unfamiliar ideas and experiences, exploring complexity, ambiguity, and paradox, and working with multiple perspectives (Eisner, 1998). The arts are an especially valuable way to help students develop imagination:

> [Imagination] makes possible the creation of "as-if" perspectives, perspectives that can be opened metaphorically and, oftentimes, through the exercise of empathy. Without the release of imagination, human beings may be trapped in literalism, in a blind factuality.... It is imagination that discloses possibilities—personal and social as well as aesthetic. (Greene, 2001, p. 65)

We sometimes think of artistic creativity as free-flowing and spontaneous, but it is actually a complex, evolutionary process shaped by a sense of purpose as well as by chance (Gruber, 1989). Students who are engaged in creative processes learn how to navigate between order and chaos, abstraction and concreteness, and spontaneity and logic. They have to solve problems, work with mistakes, and choose materials and methods that support their ideas. When students are creating, they learn to use diverse ways of knowing, including their emotions, senses, personal knowledge, and established cultural concepts, traditions, and practices.

Although many students declare, "I'm not a creative person," creative strategies and dispositions can be taught and learned (Cropley, 1992). When students know how to use specific strategies, such as juxtaposition, analogizing, elaborating, and substitution (Roukes, 1982), and when they understand the nonlinear stages of creativity, including researching, incubating, refining, and evaluating, they are better able to develop meaningful ideas and to find the resources with which to actualize them. Creative thinking is transferable to other situations: "Learning to think creatively in one discipline ... opens the door to understanding creative thinking in all disciplines. Educating this universal creative imagination is the key to producing lifelong learners capable of shaping the innovations of tomorrow" (Root-Bernstein & Root-Bernstein, 1999, p. viii).

Critical thinking. "Creative thinking can be critical even as critical thinking can be creative" (Bleedorn, 1998, p. 19). Making sense of art is an open-ended, exploratory process that uses diverse kinds of knowledge. Although images, music, and movement are pervasive in our culture, we cannot assume that students know how to really see and hear them and to construct meanings that go beyond obvious subject matter. Each work of art offers students a new world of ideas—a world that they have to take time to think about, both in its own aesthetic terms and in relation to other art, ideas, and experiences. One way for students to understand a work of art is to use a four-stage model of art criticism: description, formal analysis, interpretation, and evaluation (Cromer, 1990). In this model, students first perceive the obvious physical qualities of the work and the formal relationships. They use this information, along with personal beliefs and experiences and knowledge about larger social and cultural contexts, to construct meaningful interpretations and evaluations of the work.

The arts can serve as a focus for critical thinking about social and cultural issues. Contemporary art forms that explicitly comment on the norms and practices of society challenge students' beliefs and heighten their awareness of social inequities. In a cultural studies approach to the arts, students learn to think critically about the impact of the arts on people's lives and how society and culture inform artistic production, meaning, and worth (Freedman, 2003). Students also learn to distinguish different functions of art, including fine arts, the sacred and folk arts of traditional cultures, functional arts used in daily life, and popular media.

The arts as shared experience. What students bring to a work of art is as important as what they find in it. Experiences with art are "situated encounters," in which "the perceivers of a given work of art apprehend that work in the light of their backgrounds, biographies, and experiences. We have to presume a multiplicity of perspectives, a plurality of interpretations" (Greene, 2001, p. 175). When students study or make art together, they articulate and deepen their awareness of their own and others' experiences and worldviews. Students can understand diverse cultures in ways they might never have known if people had not translated their stories, traditions, values, and concerns into aesthetic forms. For example, *Wacipi-PowWow* (1995), a video about a national PowWow of the Mdewankanton Dakota Community, shows the particular colors, sounds, movements, and regalia of a culture that cannot be represented through any other means, and helps students understand ways that Native cultures have both adapted to and resisted dominant cultures.

The arts promote dialogue and collaboration among students. Students learn to understand culture not as a fixed body of knowledge, but as an open-ended, shared, negotiated process. When students make and study works of

art together, they articulate their own points of view and hear multiple interpretations and different life perspectives. For example, when students create
performances that express their own experiences, they teach their peers about
diverse cultures from a student perspective, such as what it is like to be an
immigrant in this country or how it feels to make choices between staying in
the 'hood or going to college.

Although making art is often thought to be a solitary process, it is made
richer through interactions with other people (Amabile, 1983; Hurwitz, 1993).
Students develop collaborative skills such as piggybacking on each other's
ideas and asking for and offering feedback and support. Making and thinking
about art with others encourages self-understanding and promotes empathy
with other people. Toya, a student in the Creativity Art Lab, wrote about how
other students influenced her learning:

> Risk taking plays a big role in art. I think that is what made me finally realize
> that putting myself out there, and opening myself up to comments and criti-
> cism is what turned this class into an artistic learning experience. . . . I never
> knew some of my classmates thought in the ways that they did. I like that we get
> to see some of the thoughts that are going through their minds because oth-
> ers may be thinking the same thing.

Historical Role of the Arts in General College

The arts have been a part of GC since its inception. In 1934, the Carnegie Corporation of New York gave a 2-year, $10,000 grant to GC, with which Dr. Ray
Faulkner and his staff developed a new arts curriculum and experimented
with innovative teaching methods. They hoped to shift from the traditional
academic model of arts appreciation courses, with an emphasis on works
from the past, to an approach that would be more responsive to contemporary students' lives (General College, 1938). To achieve their goals, the college
created a three-quarter long sequence of courses called General Arts Orientation to provide students with an overview of the arts that would be relevant
to their lives.

The main objective of the General Arts sequence was to promote understanding and enjoyment of the arts as "expressions of vital, human living"
(Hill, 1940, p. 204) that influence our everyday lives and environments. The
staff created an ambitious curriculum that included painting, sculpture,
architecture, music, literature, theater, movies, photography, crafts, and commercial art. The first course in the General Arts sequence focused on the arts
as an expression of universal human needs, the second course explored problems of formal organization in the arts and factors that contribute to good
design, and the third course studied materials and techniques in various art

forms. Students who completed this sequence could go on to take specialized courses such as Art Laboratory, Music Laboratory, and Film and Drama.

These traditions continued through the 1960s and 1970s, when a number of professional artists and musicians taught on the GC faculty. Among them were Louis Safer, a visual artist whose portrait of John Berryman is owned by the National Gallery in Washington, DC (T. Brothen, personal communication, September 24, 2004); Richard Byrne, who conducted the choir at the St. Paul Cathedral; and Jerry Gates, who made and exhibited paintings, jewelry, and later, computer graphics (General College, 1968; Weber, 2001). An increased emphasis on career development after World War II fostered a number of commercial arts courses that trained students in graphic design.

In the 1970s the GC's Humanities in Modern Living two-course sequence was taught by a rotating team of professors who organized the courses around themes related to students' lives, including community, mental health, and friendship. One of the themes that Professor Robert Yahnke worked with was "aging," in which he combined poetry, film, and readers' theater to help students construct a deeper understanding of concepts and experiences related to aging. Although this course ended after several years, the idea of working thematically was continued in several interdisciplinary "package courses" that integrated the arts and humanities with the sciences and social sciences, one of which was called "Toward the Good Life." Three courses were combined into one for a total of nine credits. The professors contributed their disciplinary knowledge to the exploration of themes such as family and leisure. The openness of the collaboration allowed for students and professors to use multiple approaches to explore some of the "big questions" in life (R. Yahnke, personal communication, March, 2004).

Another interesting package course involved a collaboration between art and mathematics. Professor Doug Robertson and art instructor Carol Nelson designed two linked courses to explore relationships between mathematics and the visual arts. Students learned mathematical concepts such as measurement, graphing, scaling, plane and solid geometry, and patterns, and then they drew, constructed models, and painted works of art based on these principles. The goal was for students to find greater real-world relevance in mathematics, to learn to solve mathematical problems, and to practice problem-solving tools in the arts. For their final project, students completed a work of art that expressed a mathematical concept (Robertson & Nelson, 1976).

Contemporary Role of the Arts in General College

The first issue of *Access*, the GC magazine, highlighted the college's ongoing commitment to the arts. General College Dean David Taylor (2001) suggested:

> Recent research has demonstrated the relationship between the arts and intellectual growth in other areas of development. For example, it is possible to teach the practical application of mathematics to music and the application of the visual arts to speech and language. The visual and performing arts have long been a part of the General College curriculum. We have always appreciated the connectivity between the arts and learning. (p. 2)

The following section is a sample of ways that students have learned about, through, and with the arts (Goldberg, 1997) in recent years. This is not a comprehensive survey of such courses, however; there are many more ways that GC instructors use the arts in their courses.

Learning About the Arts

Many students have little knowledge of the artistic traditions of their own or other cultures, whether it is Hmong needlework, Cubist paintings, the arts of the Harlem Renaissance, classical Greek sculpture, or American Indian powwows. Studying diverse forms of art helps undergraduates become "informed learners" who have a "deeper understanding of the world [they] inherit, as human beings and as contributing citizens" (Association of American Colleges and Universities, 2002, pp. 16–17). Two courses in General College teach the forms, methods, and traditions of the arts.

The Movies. Professor Robert Yahnke's film class introduces students to films that relate in some ways to their lives, but which also expand their knowledge of film, including Martin Scorsese's (1976) *Taxi Driver* and the Italian film, *Cinema Paridiso* (Tornatore, 1989). Students learn to do a close analysis of formal qualities, such as shots and angles, lighting, movement, editing, and sound. They also learn to read film as a form of literature with themes, character and plot development, dialogue, and conflict. By seeing repeated viewings of films, both in their entirety and in small segments, doing writing assignments, and engaging in class discussions, students develop a film vocabulary and learn to identify the aesthetic choices of various directors, which helps them dig deeper into the ideas and values in the film. Students learn to understand film as a medium for expressing and understanding complex personal and social issues.

General Arts. In this course, students study ways that various cultures use the arts to express ideas. Through prints, slides, readings, museum visits, music CDs, and videos, students learn how to think about a wide range of art forms, so that when they encounter works of art in their own lives, they will know how to begin to answer questions such as: How do materials and techniques affect the meaning of the arts? How are the formal aspects of art works organized? How do the arts reflect and shape culture? How do our own expectations, values, and experiences affect our interpretation and evaluation of art? How do the arts contribute to a meaningful life?

To prepare to write critical papers about works of art in local museums, students participate in activities that offer developmental practice in perceiving, analyzing, interpreting, and evaluating art. Students visit the Weisman Art Museum to write about works of art of their choice. The goal is to write as if they are teaching someone else how to look at and think about the work. In one paper, students write a complete description of what they perceive, including materials, size, subject matter, and setting. This is harder than it sounds, for students have to translate sensory information into words through which others can "see" the work. In another paper, they write a formal analysis about how the work is composed, including color and shape relationships, focal point, repetition, and balance. Doing a sketch of the work helps students recognize the underlying structure of the work. They also write a paper in which they do a personal interpretation of a work of art.

Students then go to the Minneapolis Institute of the Arts to write a longer paper about a work of 20th or 21st century art. This time, their interpretation includes contextual information, such as how society influenced the work. Many students have never been to a large art museum, so the paper assignment gives them an opportunity to see that museums are both accessible and enjoyable. They are thrilled to see such a wide range of arts from many cultures and historical periods in one building and to see work by artists that they have been reading about in their text (Yenawine, 1991), including Picasso, Matisse, and Warhol.

The objects and images found in museums, however, represent only a small part of artistic expression. Works of public art on local campuses and neighborhoods are accessible examples of art in our own communities. Teaching Specialist Jeff Chapman introduces General Arts students to public art in a number of ways, including a video titled *Public Sculpture: America's Legacy* (1994), a tour of public art on campus, and slides of local public art. Using everyday materials, students make connections between art and their own lives by creating models of imaginary works of public art and presenting them to the class.

Art is an integral part of students' daily lives, whether it is in the form of artifacts handed down from generation to generation or contemporary objects and clothing. To better understand the arts from a multicultural perspective, students see videos about artists from diverse cultures, including an American Indian potter (*Daughters of the Anasazi*, 1990), *Islamic Art* (1988), and modern Nigerian art (*Kindred Spirits*, 1991). These videos help students understand that art is an integration of cultural beliefs and values, symbol systems, and form and materials. Toward the end of the semester, students do poster presentations about a work of art in their own lives. Some of their choices have included a Somalian water jug, a Vietnamese song, a blown-glass vase from Hungary, an American wedding ring, Japanese cartoon books, and contemporary tattoos. Students' posters present information about form and technique, a brief history of the art form, relevance of the work to the culture in which it was made, and relevance of the work to the student. By seeing each other's posters, students learn about a wide range of art forms and deepen their awareness of the cultural diversity of their peers.

Learning With the Arts

Another way that the arts are used in GC is in courses such as basic writing, literature, anthropology, and biology. The arts offer content, symbol systems, and ways of knowing that can enrich other subjects and help students construct a deeper understanding of concepts. Theorists suggest that there is an interactive "dual coding" process through which people use images and other sensory information to think about words and words to think about images and other senses (Paivio & Walsh, 1993). By integrating visual or musical arts with writing, for example, students shape meanings that are richer and different from each of the modes of communication by themselves. Students also develop a greater awareness of aesthetic qualities in the world around them and build a sensory memory bank that can inform their reading and writing.

Composition. Many students share a love of rap music and hip hop culture. In GC 1422: Basic Writing, Professor Geoff Sirc draws on the powerful emotional, social, and physical impact of rap to help students construct bridges between their familiar worlds and the unfamiliar discourse of academic writing and research. Students in his course critically examine various texts about hip hop culture, including Internet sites, videos about dance and graffiti, and scholarly texts such as *Black Noise: Rap Music and Black Culture in Contemporary America* (Rose, 1994). They then write a research paper about an aspect of the hip hop culture that interests them. Sirc reported, "It becomes very compelling for students to examine something they know about. They see they have a knowledge pool to draw on, which allows for a transition from natural writing to scholarly writing" (Weber, 2001, p. 7).

Literature. Different forms of art have different kinds of meanings that enrich one another and contribute to a deeper understanding of a subject (Eisner, 2002). There are a number of ways that Teaching Specialist Barbara Hodne uses visual and musical art forms in her literature courses. For example, students see early 20th century Cubist paintings and listen to Stravinsky's

Rites of Spring symphony to grasp Modernist literary traditions. To help students better understand the creative impetus for poetry and how it drives people their own age to create poems, Hodne invites spoken word artists to perform in her class, including Frank Sentwali (*Edupoetic Enterbrainment*, n.d.). Students were touched by Sentwali's passion for using art to create social change, and his performance enabled students to make connections between a familiar rap format and more unfamiliar forms of poetry. Hearing live and recorded spoken word performances helps students learn to listen to poetry and to understand poetry as a vital form of communication. A student in Hodne's class told her that after hearing live spoken word, he now reads poetry differently.

Hodne uses visual arts to augment the readings in her American literature course. The photos both illustrate and contradict perspectives taken by the authors in the stories. For example, Jacob Riis's photos of workers in the Lower East Side (Alland, 1974) challenge the American ideal that hard work equals success, and photos of Americans from the 1930s (*Modern American Poetry*, 2002) are a contrast to Meridel LeSueur's (2002) autobiography, "Women on the Breadlines." Visual art also helps Hodne's students connect the readings to their own lives. When they read literature from the 1950s, students look at assemblages by Pop artist Robert Rauschenberg and answer the question: "How would *you* depict *your* times?"

Anthropology. Associate Professor Mark Pedelty uses music and performance to help students develop an awareness of their ethnocentric assumptions about other people and an understanding of other cultures from an insider's perspective. Students dramatically perform Mexican plays and poetry and write and perform fictional dialogues based on ethnographic readings. Pedelty noted that role playing discourages stereotypes and promotes empathy and identification with people from other cultures. In addition, students' learning is enhanced by using multiple senses (Weber, 2001, p. 9).

Pedelty's students enact rituals associated with myths, such as the Templor Mayor ritual once practiced by the Mexica as part of the Coyolxauhqui myth. Students use cross-cultural comparison to gain a critical understanding of their own cultural lives. Through these enactments, students learn the historical context of the ritual and begin to understand both ancient and contemporary use of ritual as a conduit between people and their gods. Using real and improvised instruments, small sections of students create percussive rhythms that underscore Pedelty's oration of the myth and ritual. In the process of doing this performance, abstract and esoteric knowledge becomes much more immediate and engaging to students, and they are better able to understand underlying anthropological concepts (Pedelty, 2004c).

Celebrating Diversity in Twentieth Century America Through Fiction and Film. In Professor Jeanne Higbee's freshman seminar, students read short stories and view films that explore cultural diversity. Higbee uses movies as a catalyst for a deeper understanding of cultural issues and experiences. For example, to help students better understand immigration and race issues, Higbee shows *Snow Falling on Cedars* (Hicks, 2000), a movie in which a Japanese-American man is falsely accused of killing a White man. Seeing and hearing the historical settings, clothing, facial expressions, tones of voice, atmosphere, sounds, and music helps students empathize with the characters and imagine themselves in the situation. At the end of the semester, students do expressive projects to demonstrate their learning in the course. In one such project, Hmong students adapted lyrics of "America" from *West Side Story* to create and perform a song titled "Because I'm Hmong."

Psychology of Personal Development. The primary focus of Jeanne Higbee's psychology course are the theories, vocabulary, and research methods related to individual growth and development. Students are tested on these topics through quizzes, essays, and exams, but Higbee also uses films, such as *The Breakfast Club* (Hughes, 1985), to help students learn psychological concepts and demonstrate their learning in alternative ways. At the end of the semester, students do an expressive project in which they work individually or in small groups to present course content. Some students have written poetry, created collages, skits, or videos about a theme they read about in their text. For example, one student created a half-hour video based on a TV talk show, including a live band and interviews with guests about various psychology topics, and another student created a comic book to illustrate psychological concepts.

Law and Society. At the end of the semester, students in Assistant Professor Karen Miksch's class, acting as lawyers, defendants, and judges, engage in a mock trial. To prepare for the trial, students do reading and writing assignments, but they also read Sophocles' classical play, *Antigone* (442 B.C.E.) and see part of an updated film interpretation of the play (Taylor, 1986). To help students understand and apply the concepts of natural law and positive law that underlie the play, Miksch asks: "How do the characters know the right way to act, and what do they look to for that information?" In small groups, students write scripts that update a scene from the play and perform it for the class. A number of groups creatively adapt the concepts to the current social scene; an imaginary conversation between Hillary Rodham Clinton and Bill Clinton, a Jerry Springer television show, action movies, and rap songs have served as taking-off points for thinking about the concepts of natural and positive law.

Multicultural Mathematics. In this Freshman Seminar, Assistant Professor Susan Staats uses visual arts from diverse cultures as a way for students to understand mathematical concepts and learn about ways that various cultures think mathematically. Students study textiles and crafts of other cultures to see how their patterns translate into mathematical terms and to learn about the cultural significance of shapes and colors in the designs. For example, students see ideals of beauty in Ghanian textiles, in which circles symbolize feminism, zigzags symbolize judicial authority, and blue connotes infinity (Antubam, 1963). Part of the course is based on *African Fractals, Modern Computing and Indigenous Design* (Eglash, 2002) and *Culturally Situated Design Tools* (Eglash, 2003), a Web site that shows how various cultures' designs can be thought about in terms of mathematical principles such as transformational geometry and Cartesian coordinates. Using computer simulations and graph paper, students create their own designs based on the principles.

Biology. Perhaps the sciences are the last subject in which we might expect to find the arts. Associate Professor Murray Jensen, however, has developed an assignment in which students represent biological concepts in nontraditional ways. In his "Do Something Cool" assignment toward the end of the semester, students in the human anatomy and physiology course show their learning by creating drawings, paintings, photographs, sculptures, or even live performances about topics such as muscle physiology, the consequences of crack cocaine on a human body, or the anatomy of a hand (Jensen, Moore, Hatch, & Hsu, 2003). Learning takes place not only when students plan and create these projects, but also when they present them to their class so that other students have the opportunity to think about biological concepts in new ways. Many of the projects are displayed on a course-related Web page (Jensen, 2004) as examples for future classes.

This arts-based biology assignment provides a "hook" that helps increase student retention in a science course that traditionally experiences attrition, especially among students who have difficulty learning through lectures, labs, and exams. Making visual representations of science concepts stimulates students' imaginations and gives them practice "thinking outside the box" when they are learning science. The "Do Something Cool" assignment also helps students understand that creative thinking is an important part of the sciences (Jensen et al., 2003).

Learning Through the Arts
Several courses in GC give students practice in actively creating art. Although students usually do not have sufficient expertise to work on a professional level, they are able to experience the kinds of thinking engaged in by accomplished artists and to create works of art that express their own worldviews and life experiences.

Film and Society. In Robert Yahnke's documentary class, students study a variety of documentary films and make videos about social issues that are relevant to them. To gain a visual and conceptual understanding of the documentary genre, students first study works by masters such as Werner Herzog, Errol Morris, and the Maysles brothers. Working in collaborative teams that include a director, videographer, and editor, students write a proposal that explains the rationale and methods of their potential work to an imaginary granting agency. After Yahnke approves the proposals, students take digital video cameras out to film in relevant locations. The real work, however, begins as students edit their raw footage into a coherent, 10-minute documentary. The digital editing process is like a puzzle; students know the general theme, but it is only when they struggle to connect the parts and add music that they are able to understand the relationships and meaning of their images. Recent student documentaries have included work about a local bike group, Karaoke in local bars, and a comic book artist.

Identity, Community, and Culture: Connections in the Arts and Humanities. In this interdisciplinary course, Mark Pedelty uses visual arts, dance, storytelling, and music to explore the political dimensions of the arts and ways that "the identities, ideologies, interests, and affiliations of those who create, support, or experience art inevitably influence artistic meanings" (Pedelty, 2004a, p. 1). To help students understand concepts in multiple ways and to provide practice with various song writing and performance processes, activities in every class session shift among a variety of media, including drum circles, films, discussions and peer reviews, socially-conscious music, poetry, and story-telling. In the "Horatio Project," which is based on Shakespeare's *Hamlet* (Edwards, 1985), students read the play and see scenes from various traditional and contemporized film versions of Hamlet (for example, Almereyda, 2000; Branagh, 1996) as they write, tell, or illustrate their own poems, songs, and stories of social injustice and corruption. Students record their work on a CD.

Music and Social Movements. This freshman seminar, taught by Mark Pedelty, uses music to focus on issues related to public education. Daily drum circles help students develop a sense of rhythm, deep listening skills, and responsiveness to music, and they provide opportunities for students to learn to collaborate and to try out their individual and ensemble musical projects. In addition to reading about and discuss opposing views on educational policy issues, students read a biography by or about a socially-engaged musician and give a presentation to the class about it. Students also write an autobiography about their own musical education and write music and song lyrics about education. There are several approaches: students compose their own music for their lyrics, write lyrics to music composed by Pedelty, and write lyrics for which Pedelty composes the music. A finished CD of the music and lyrics has been produced and sold to the local community to support projects related to public education (Pedelty, 2004b).

Creativity Art Lab: Experiments in the Media. In this course, students practice a variety of art forms. The approach of the course changes from semester to semester. One of the focuses is mural making, in which as many as 26 students collaborate with each other to design and produce a mural. Other semesters, the course focuses on multimedia performance, which I describe in the following section.

Art in Practice

When I teach the Creativity Art Lab, I emphasize creative and metaphoric process more than specific artistic techniques and finished products. Students learn to generate ideas and invent ways to translate them through ordinary materials, including their own bodies. The assignments are relatively open-ended problems with no set answers; although I establish some material, size, and thematic constraints, students develop content and methods that are meaningful to their own experiences and interests. Caine and Caine (1997) suggested that ill-formed, open-ended problems are a necessary part of meaningful learning: "Much more learning takes place when learners are constantly immersed in complex experience; when they process, analyze, and examine this experience for meaning and understanding; and when they constantly relate what they have learned to their own central purposes" (p. 19).

The design of the course is based on my belief that every student has artistic and creative potential. The unusual nature of the activities gives both artistically inexperienced and experienced students opportunities to think and act in new ways. We start with a photomontage assignment and shift to a focus on multimedia performance, including movement, spoken word, and music. Throughout the semester, students engage in reflective and expressive writing, hands-on activities, and discussion. Students contextualize their work within larger artistic traditions by seeing videos, slides, and a live performance. Small group and all-class exercises help students learn to trust and support one another and to feel confident taking creative risks.

To better understand how students learn aesthetic, metaphoric, creative, and critical thinking in the Creativity Art Lab, we can focus on one student, Risa. Risa was originally from South Asia, but she attended an American high school where she took a few art courses. Identifying herself as "somewhat" of an artist, Risa wrote that she was taking Art Lab "because I enjoy arts and it's something that gets better to my heart than my brain." She planned to major in retail merchandising when she transferred from General College.

Risa was part of a culturally-diverse cohort of 18 lower income, first-semester, first-generation, predominantly non-White TRIO students enrolled in a learning community of three linked courses. The goal of the learning community was to help students build social, cultural, and cognitive bridges between their nonacademic lives and higher education. We presented both academic and experiential ways for students to think about and express their personal and cultural identities, to practice actively being part of a community, and to become agents of their own learning instead of passive consumers. Multicultural Relations, taught by Counselor Advocate Rashné Jehangir, was a seminar in which students examined issues of class, race, gender, disability, and sexual orientation. Students read and discussed two texts: *Race, Class, and Gender in the United States: An Integrated Study* (Rothenberg, 1995) and *A Different Mirror: A History of Multi-cultural America* (Takaki, 1993). In the Writing Lab, taught by Assistant Professor Pat Bruch, students worked together to strengthen their ability to use writing to express ideas. Content from these courses served as resources for students' art work in Creativity Art Lab.

Learning Metaphoric Thinking: Getting the Inner Us Outside of Ourselves
As an introduction to metaphoric thinking, students' first assignment in the Art Lab is to write personal analogies (Gordon, 1973) about works of art. Students each choose a portrait from a collection of prints and free-write about it as if they are inside the work—first, as the person in the image, and then, as a smaller part of the image, such as an eye, hand, chair, or the sky (James, 2000a, 2002). Students begin each paragraph by writing "I am. . . ." After they finish writing, they read their paragraphs to a partner. Risa reflected about what it was like to do "I am" writing and share it with another person:

> Analyzing [the print] was like getting the inner us outside of ourselves . . . .
> I think it wasn't just analyzing a piece of art. Rather analyzing ourselves. I guess the way we view art could be a result of way how we view ourselves, I don't know. I felt connected to this activity. Also, hearing what someone else had for their art was interesting. My partner wanted to be air, which would mean she treasures freedom. Indeed, she did say that she fears her freedom is being taken away.

The "I am" writing requires students to spend extended time looking at the subtleties of one work of art and making metaphoric connections between the image and their own emotions and experiences. By taking an "as-if" perspective, students are encouraged to imagine and empathize with things outside of themselves and to reflect about their own thinking. Over the semester, students do "I am" writing about objects, music, dance, and their own photomontages.

Photomontages: Thinking "From Bottom to Top and West to East"
In the first major assignment of the semester, students cut and reassemble pictures from magazines and calendars to create two portrait photomontages. One photomontage has to feature a head or body, and another focuses on hands. I ask students to use substitution, juxtaposition, scale changes, and alteration to transform familiar images into abstract, visually unified, metaphoric works of art (James, 2000b). In addition to seeing slides of photomontages by established artists, students do several developmental exercises to practice creative thinking, develop visual perception, and gain a sense of themselves as creative people.

Hand exercises. In one set of exercises, we focus on multiple ways to think about hands. First, students do blind contour drawings by sketching one of their hands without looking down at their paper (Edwards, 1989). When students walk around the room to look at the jagged, disconnected lines of their peers' drawings, they learn that the process of *looking carefully* is important, not only the artistic product. Many students comment that when they draw in this way, it is as if they see their hand for the first time.

Next, students get into small groups and study one group member's hand. Students learn to pay close attention to sensory information by describing everything that they perceive in this person's hand, including wrinkles, scars, roughness, and color, as well as weight, thickness, smell, and even taste. In the next stage, the group interviews the group member about his or her hand: "What does the hand tell you about the person attached to it?" As students talk, a history of the hand emerges and students learn about the person's life. Each group then introduces "the hand" to the rest of the class. Students enjoy hearing stories about their classmates' hands, such as how they got their scars and what kind of work they do, and they begin to recognize relationships between form and content.

Finally, students write a list of movements they do with hands in their daily lives, such as eating or playing a musical instrument. Much to their surprise, I ask them to stand up and mime that movement in slow motion. After students practice for a while, they put on paper masks and, in small groups, repeat their movements for two minutes while the rest of the class observes. Students see that ordinary movements like putting on a shoe, eating, or brushing teeth become small, elegant dances when repeated in slow motion by a person wearing a mask. Risa reflected about what she learned by doing this series of hand exercises:

> I never thought about how much hands had to offer to our lives. How many memories it has, how unique our hands are—the palm, the lines, the knuckles, the nails, the fingers and everything else seemed unique and artistic. If just a hand was full of so many things, I couldn't imagine analyzing every other part

of our bodies. I am sure that the human body in itself is an art if you think about it. If you think as an artist there is art everywhere within us, like even in our hands.

Making photomontages. Before starting their two graded photomontages, students create an ungraded practice photomontage. They have about 40 minutes to cut out pictures and reassemble them into an image of a head. We hang the practice photomontages on the wall and discuss them in terms of visual composition, interpretation, and creative processes. By doing practice photomontages and seeing slides of successful student photomontages from previous semesters, students realize that that this assignment asks them to think in new ways. Although students often think that making a photomontage will be an easy assignment, they discover it can be an uncertain and often frustrating process.

Students spend several days in and outside of class working on their graded photomontages. They usually find that the appearance and meaning of their finished photomontages are very different from what they first planned. Some students start with a specific idea in mind, and they become frustrated when they cannot find the perfect picture for it. Others cut out random pictures but do not know how to put them together into something new. I encourage students to turn magazine pictures upside-down to see them in new ways. To make successful photomontages, students have to learn to choose images for their aesthetic qualities and metaphoric meanings, not only the literal subject matter.

When Risa started cutting random pictures from magazines, she did not know what she was going to do for her first photomontage, but she developed a sense of purpose as she worked. Her imagery started to make sense to her when she placed a column of flowers on each side of the paper. A sensuous arm reaches from the column on the right side across a central space of dark shapes and jagged edges to touch the other column, and the central area indicates ambiguity and tension between the two columns. Risa's finished photomontage (Figure 1) can be interpreted as an expression of the conflicts and pleasures of making a transition from childhood into adulthood. As part of the assignment, Risa wrote an "I am" paragraph interpreting her photomontage:

> I am coming out of innocence
> Entering through life,
> Passing by the mysteries,
> Full of certainty,
> Carrying along hope,
> Hiding the secret fear,
> I hope to make it through,

I hope to break it through,
Until I reach peace and love for eternity.

Risa knew that she wanted her second photomontage to be a visual statement about how adults force little girls to grow up too quickly, and she
started by cutting out a little girl's head and gluing it on a sexy adult female
body. Risa wrote about her artistic intentions:

> [The] photomontage of a baby face with a slim female body juxtaposed
> together looked like something I had wanted. Why, I didn't know at that time.
> It made sense to me because I felt that little kids have to grow up too quick
> these days. Whether it's in the case of Jon Bonnet Ramsey or many other little
> beauty pageant girls or even in my case. Children are expected to act as adults
> when they should enjoy their young days having fun, as your age is something
> that will never come back.

Risa went through various stages of problem-solving and discovery. When
I observed how her work was progressing, I noticed that the many pictures
of small dolls scattered in the background distracted from her central figure.
Risa was at a frustrating impasse and did not know how to proceed. When I
asked her to tell me what part of the image she cared about the most, she
replied that she liked the central figure. I encouraged her to emphasize that
area and to downplay other parts. Without further help, Risa made a number of artistic decisions and threw away many of the pictures she had already
spent time cutting out. She wrote:

> I was thinking about having dolls around my face and body photomontage to
> show that she was an innocent little girl. But then I found that was a mistake
> because it would have distracted viewers' attention from her to the dolls
> around her. I let her be all by herself.

Risa constructed a completely new background from articles on child
psychology:

> I picked up a few magazines to find articles because I am going to have a text
> background. As other backgrounds may hold back the focus of the girl. So the
> text would support my message indirectly as well as it'll stick out, making the
> girl a focal point.

Risa's finished photomontage was visually unified and meaningful (Figure
2). Risa framed the child's head with long hair, eliminated extraneous objects,
and replaced them with relevant fragments of printed articles and images of
childhood, including a headline, placed sideways, which read: "Our Forebears
Made Childhood Unbearable." The unobtrusive text added historical dimensions to her central image and created a visual texture that complemented the

Figure 1. Risa's first photomontage.

main figure. Risa's "I am" writing about the photomontage revealed some of the paradoxes of being female:

> I am a girl
> Pure and innocent,
> I am a girl
> Bold and beautiful,
> I am a girl
> Praised and pressured,
> I am a girl,
> Free and controlled,
> I am a girl
> Trying to fake it,
> I am a girl
> Trying to make it,
> I am a girl
> Dying and surviving,
> I am a girl
> Being judged and witnessed,
> I am a girl, simply live my life as a girl.

Students' finished photomontages can serve as visual texts that offer insights into their own lives. Although Risa originally intended to create a social statement about other people, her reflective paper at the end of the semester revealed that her photomontage could also be interpreted as an expression of her own experiences as a teenager going to school in the United States while her parents remained in her native country:

> I am trying to stand on my own feet without any help from my parents as they are out of this country. I am taking care of my food, shelter, clothing, school, job, everything by myself. From paying bills to cleaning my apartment. It is all on me. When I should just be having fun and not worry about these things except school like most of my friends. I don't regret my duties. I find myself a lot more mature and confident. But, sometimes I feel exhausted as I am a teenager and am living a life like a middle-aged woman. In a way I am still young with my brain but a grown up with my actions, like my photomontage. Which I didn't realize before making it. When I was making my photomontage it never occurred to me that my thinking process would create something like that.

As she made her photomontages, Risa went through many of the same thinking processes that are engaged in by experienced artists, including generating ideas, making visual decisions, solving problems, and interpreting her work as it evolved (John-Steiner, 1997). Each of Risa's decisions caused her

Figure 2. Risa's second photomontage.

photomontages to evolve in ways she could not have predicted when she began making them:

> [What was] pleasurable was the surprise that came out of my piece. It was totally different than what I had on my mind when I started it. So many pieces weren't even used. What surprised me is you can do so much with pieces of magazines. Art is a combination of so many tiny pieces. It's really fun, it makes you think in an unusual manner. From bottom to top and west to east, just awkwardly. It is surely fun but not easy. You really have to think!

Performance: Showing, Not Telling

During the second half of the semester, students in Creativity Art Lab practice creative and metaphoric thinking by creating live performances that express social issues through images, movement, music, and spoken word. At the end of the semester, students create their own small group performances that they present to the rest of the class. Several videos of performing artists, including an African American women's dance troupe called Urban Bushwomen (1996), give students a deeper understanding of the expressive purposes and strategies of performing artists. We also attend a professional theatrical performance.

Although some students have prior experience performing, most are apprehensive about speaking or moving in front of others. To gain confidence in their own abilities and to feel comfortable with their peers, students engage in a number of creativity exercises in which they learn to generate ideas, improvise, and critique their own work and others' work. At first, students feel silly and there is a lot of giggling, but with repeated practice, they start to take the exercises more seriously. When everyone does the same exercises, they learn to support each other and to value their peers' ideas. Risa wrote about the important role other people played in her creative process: "I didn't know what to do, what inspired me was that most people in the classroom weren't experts either but they kept on going so I kept on trying many weird things."

Paper masks. In one creativity exercise, students make and wear paper masks based on a pattern from *Mask Improvisation* (Eldredge, 1996). The whole class uses the same color paper—usually green or blue—to emphasize sameness. In an exercise loosely based on an activity titled "Exposure" (Spolin, 1994), half the class, the masked "actors," stand in a row for 3 minutes while the other half, the "audience," sit and observe them. It is both a comical and an uncomfortable experience; many students never realized that 3 minutes could be so long! Afterwards, a discussion about what it is like to stand in front of or watch people with masks on helps students interpret masks as visual metaphors for concepts such as anonymity, individuality, and conformity. Some students report that when they wear the mask, they feel like prisoners, but others say they feel they have more control. Students often say that wearing the mask makes them think about what it feels like to be completely anonymous, but as others talk they become more aware of the individuality of movements and postures. Risa reflected:

> I liked today's activity because it was different than what I have done in the past. It was weird how having a mask on made everything so confusing. Besides the fact that I felt strange breathing with it and not being able to itch anywhere on my face. I felt as if it was blocking my thoughts too. The mask made me feel isolated somehow. I felt distance to the world. While I was standing in front of the room I felt as if I was being judged. I felt as if I had done something wrong and people watching me will soon declare their verdict.

Spoken word. The next series of creativity exercises culminates in individual spoken word performances. To become more comfortable speaking in class and interpreting poetry, students do several group spoken word exercises, including a whole-class reading of Maya Angelou's "Alone" (Angelou, 1994). We sit in a circle, and each of us takes a turn reading a line of the poem. Throughout the reading, we hear the poem's refrain:

> Alone, all alone
> Nobody, but nobody
> Can make it out here alone. (p. 74)

Our shared reading brings the poem to life. After we complete the round of reading, we talk about how our different voices and ways of speaking affect the meaning of the poem. As we interpret metaphors in the poem, students become aware of the relationships between the poem, their learning community, and the social issues they are studying in the other courses. Next, students get into small groups to plan readings of "Alone." Each group has half an hour to plan and rehearse before they perform the poem for the rest of the class. The groups enact the poem in many different ways, such as moving in a circle as they speak, standing at the back of the audience to deliver the lines, repeating lines, speaking in unison, and singing.

Next, students bring in poems or songs that are important to each of them. The topics of students' poems or lyrics, which are treated as if they were poetry, include subjects like war, inner-city life, life choices, love relationships, and peace. Poets may include Langston Hughes, Sojourner Truth, or Robert Frost, and the song lyrics might be by performers such as Loryn Hill, Nas, Tupac Shakur, and even Johnny Cash. Some brave students bring in poetry they wrote themselves, and a few choose to read poetry in their native languages. To prepare for individual readings, students practice reading with a partner in class, and they also practice at home.

On the next class day, each student stands at the front of the room and reads his or her choice to the whole class. Many students incorporate movement with their reading, some use rap rhythms and gestures, and a few sing. Risa read a poem dedicated to her mother in her native country. Later, she reflected about what it was like to hear her classmates do spoken word:

> The class environment was quiet and focused which made me personally very comfortable. Everyone was respectful of each other. That was nice. We all listened to each other, which is unusual. It was weird how I could see people's personalities in their poems. Even the way they read or the topic of their poem matched a lot with how they are. It was almost like I could tell whose poems belonged to whom if all the poems were piled together. It was a unique activity, it was fun and required us to focus.

Mini-performances. During the last part of the semester, students go through a series of small group mini-performances to prepare for their final performances. Students have about 40 minutes to plan and rehearse before presenting their 3-minute performances to the rest of the class. I assign certain constraints, such as not using words, using only three words, or using particular props. Each group chooses a social theme that shapes its work. Risa joined a group with an African American male, a European American male, and another Asian American female who decided to focus on the theme of racism and sexism. Other groups chose gay-lesbian-transgender issues, education, and other aspects of racism.

Rather than being literal skits with plots, the mini-performances focus on metaphors, which means that lighting, movement, sound, space, and images are as important as words in expressing ideas. Although there is an element of childlike play, it is a difficult assignment, for students have to work together to generate divergent ideas, negotiate with each other, and evaluate their work. There are often moments of frustration as students look to me for external structure before they find their own. Students' work is most effective if they stand up and physically try out their ideas rather than sitting and talking about them.

In one mini-performance, I ask students to express their theme without speaking, and I give each group audio-visual equipment to incorporate in their performance. Risa's group received an overhead projector, blank transparency, and marker. Risa, Nate, Mai, and Jason lined up chairs as if they were at a bus stop. As they took turns sitting next to each other, they showed obvious fear or dislike directed toward the person of a different race sitting next to them. On the wall behind them, they projected overhead transparencies of the characters' thoughts about sitting next to people of a different race, such as: "He's Black. He might steal my purse." The group's methods were effective, for it was disturbing to see these bigoted thoughts projected large on the wall. Risa wrote about their silent mini-performance:

> It wasn't too hard for our group to do a presentation not talking! However, rather than using words like before, we had to use actions, which was interesting. The audience had to pay more attention that way b/c most people are used to getting messages through what they have been told rather than what they are shown. This time we had to show not tell which I think is more powerful to make our audience get our message.

Final performance. To prepare for the end-of-semester performance, each group writes a short paper about the ideas they intend to express in their final work. Risa's group planned to examine "issues of racism as well as sexism, specifically, internalized oppression and interpersonal discrimination." They described their goals:

> We will be dealing with and exposing stereotypes in an attempt to dissolve them. . . . Delving into our personal experiences, such as Nate being a Black athlete, Jason as a White male at the top of the food chain, so to speak, and Risa and Mai's experiences as minority women. The best way to get people to think about something is to throw it at them, to make them examine themselves and question what they have been taught. . . . We [hope to] get our audience to get the "aha" thought running through their heads, and feeling the same emotions inside themselves as we display on stage. Through passion and intensity, and music and poetry, we will open up eyes and minds to serious issues.

After many hours of difficult discussion and practice, Risa's group juxtaposed several situations and readings to create a performance about racism and sexism in private lives, which they titled "Behind Closed Doors." They started with a scene with the two men—one Black and one White—watching a basketball game and having a heated discussion about who was allowed to use the "n" word; then they shifted to a kitchen scene in which one woman encouraged another to leave her abusive marriage. The next scene featured Mai sitting on a couch quietly reciting the poem, "Alone." The performance segued into a frozen action pose of Jason hitting his "wife" while Risa stood to the side reciting facts about domestic abuse and reading Ntozake Shange's (1995) poem, "Every Three Minutes." To finish, Jason sat on a stool and gave a chilling spoken word performance of the lyrics of "Wolves" by a rap group named Dead Prez (2000), which uses poetic metaphor to suggest that oppressed people are lured into extinction by the riches of the dominant culture.

As she performed with her group and watched other performances, Risa was part of a community of students who were feeling, imagining, and discovering together. As performers and audience, all of the students in the class shared a common mission to create meaning. The other woman in Risa's group, Mai, reflected about the experience:

> I couldn't believe how much effort was put into this. I was so happy to see so many peoples [*sic*] talents and I almost cried because I was so touched. Today I saw everything we've learned put into the two hours and I couldn't believe what an amazing performance we did. At first, I was very nervous and found no way to release any stress. I forgot one important part & it all came back to me when I told Nate I was nervous. He replied just remember, we live this everyday, just act like you livin' a normal day. That was what pushed me to have so much courage and I will always remember our group to be strong that way.

Constructing a Philosophy of Art: "Am I an Artist?"

Although students often enter the class believing that art should be a realistic picture of something familiar and pleasant, like a Monet painting of a landscape, they broaden their definitions of art over the semester. Risa wrote:

> Learning about art, different kinds of art has taught me that everything is an art or can be an art. I have found even our thinking process is a process of art. Or rather art is the part of our thinking process. Whether it's a painting, a plain drawing, a poem or a movie. One can get some sense out of the art as to how the artist is.

Risa also rethought her ideas about who is an artist:

> Today's class made me think of a question that I didn't think before! Am I an artist? I figured that everyone is an artist in a way. Everyone has their own unique talents and attributes that make them artists. So, I guess I am an artist too. There are lots of artists in this world. Many are well known and many more are anonymous. They are hidden by their mask, which covers the artistic side. Meaning they are behind the mask. Many of the artists don't ever realize the true artist inside them.

In her writing, Risa showed that she had developed an understanding of the complex, sometimes ambiguous nature of the arts:

> Thus, I definitely see growth in my understanding of art. Now, I try to analyze most things I see. I try to think why would an artist create something like that. What was it he/she had on his/her mind? I try to get the abstract meaning of the piece rather than just what is visible such as the color combination, its features and its words. I also try to see the bigger picture of it, not a smaller portion of it. Art doesn't require any specific format like math or science. It doesn't require proper steps or reasons, it can be the smallest and quickest thing but can have the biggest and the most complicated meaning behind it. Or it can be something that takes the longest time to create but have a very simple meaning.

Teaching Artistic Content and Processes

Teachers in many kinds of courses often ask students to "do something creative," but they may find that students do a lackluster job, become frustrated, or are resistant. Part of the problem might be an overly broad use of the word "creative," so that students are leery of it or do not know what it means. Some students are self-conscious about creating work that is technically less sophisticated than the quality of their ideas. Other students experience cognitive, cultural, emotional, and social "blocks" that inhibit them from engaging fully in creative processes (Cropley, 1992; James, 1999–2000; Jones, 1993). A number of students fear embarrassment in front of their peers, especially if they perceive themselves to be "uncreative" or "not artistic." Students who look for absolute answers, or who are used to lectures and multiple choice tests, may not recognize open-ended, self-constructed, or collaborative learning as real education (Baxter Magolda, 1992).

Conditions for Creativity

In this section, I suggest conditions that help students at all levels of experience learn to make sense of and value the arts and creative processes. These conditions are relevant to art-specific courses, but they also apply to courses in which students are asked to construct meaningful connections between their own experiences and disciplinary concepts. Aesthetic, metaphoric, creative, critical, and social processes are foregrounded so that students develop skills and attitudes that will help them do meaningful work.

Personal meaningfulness. Students are more likely to take risks in their work and to create something in which they are invested if they think that what they are doing is authentic and self-expressive, that it is contributing to a greater good, and that the process itself is worth doing. Strategies for helping students develop personal meaning in their work include metaphoric ("I am") writing and experiential exercises that emphasize students' awareness of their own emotions, senses, and bodies. Ongoing reflection, whether through writing or discussion, helps students understand the relevance of the assignments to their own lives and academic goals and promotes transfer to other educational situations (Perkins, 1994).

Supportive social environment. It is important to think of the classroom as a place in which students and teachers are mutually engaged in a shared mission to give meaning to their lives. A sense of community in the classroom encourages confidence, risk-taking, feedback, and an understanding of the arts as shared forms of expression. When there are multiple opportunities for collaboration, students give voice to their own experiences and develop empathy with others. Strategies for establishing a creative community include discussing the value of shared learning and acknowledging students' knowledge and artwork as an important part of course content.

Open, well-structured assignments. Many students are more accustomed to working with presented problems than with problems they formulate themselves. It is valuable, therefore, to design a variety of exercises and assignments that give students developmental practice with ambiguous assignments. There should be multiple opportunities for students to receive feedback on various aspects of their work, to critique their own and others' work, and to experience success. Because students sometimes have difficulty managing time and following through on projects, meaningful constraints such as deadlines, materials, or themes help them focus their thinking. Assignments should be intellectually challenging but not technically difficult, and they should be open-ended enough so that students can develop their own ideas and methods of working.

Explicit teaching of creative processes. By modeling creative thinking and behavior, showing diverse examples of creative work, incorporating activities that ask students to reflect about their creative process, and building in accountability for all stages of creativity, teachers can help students understand that creativity is both orderly and unpredictable. Developmental practice with strategies such as brainstorming, doing thumbnail sketches, elaborating on a theme, generating multiple interpretations, and doing non-graded exercises before graded assignments helps students gain confidence in their own ability to go beyond their familiar boundaries. Exercises that promote play, spontaneity, and unpredictable ways of thinking help students develop their imaginations. Books such as *Fanning the Creative Spirit* (Girsch & Girsch, 1999) and *The Creative Spirit* (Goleman, Kaufman, & Ray, 1993) provide concrete suggestions for developing creative strategies and attitudes.

Teaching for Creativity

Teaching for creativity is an unpredictable process that requires imagination, flexibility, comfort with ambiguity, personal vulnerability, and an appreciation that students are creating something that has never before been seen or heard in quite that way. Students' work often brings up unexpected issues and presents information in challenging ways that can enrich course content if the teacher is able to make use of this emerging information (James, 2002–2003). Teaching itself becomes a creative process, complete with the joy of new discoveries, the satisfaction of making meaningful connections among seemingly disparate kinds of information, and the potential for understanding students—and oneself—in new ways.

There may be a number of difficulties in teaching for creativity, however. Although the openness and complexity of creative processes generate excitement about learning, these qualities bring unpredictability to teaching that can be problematic. If a teacher is not comfortable with creative thinking and has set outcomes in mind rather than allowing for open-ended, unpredictable products, students will work toward the teachers' expectations rather than exploring new territory. Another problem is the tension between course content and creative processes, especially in content-based courses like biology in which specific concepts need to be covered. This conflict may be alleviated by pairing content-based and arts-based courses in learning communities. A third problem is students' difficulty in thinking of the creative arts as "real" learning. Explicit discussions with students about constructivist theories of learning can help them value creative processes as an important part of their education.

Evaluation

Although assessing students' learning in art—especially student-made artwork—may seem to be difficult, there are numerous strategies that teachers can use to give students feedback and grade their work. In courses in which making art is the primary focus, grades can be based on artistic qualities, on specific aspects of creative process such as divergent thinking and elaboration, or on how well the work solves a particular conceptual or formal problem. In the photomontage assignment, for example, the assignment handout describes the qualities of a good photomontage, including unified composition, good craftsmanship, graphic interest, and evidence of a range of creative strategies. Grades are based on how well students accomplish these qualities in their work and on written reflections about their creative process.

In courses in which artistic expression demonstrates content learning, such as Mark Pedelty's anthropology class, teachers often ask for a written report about how the work relates to the course concepts. These papers may be process papers about how the work was created or expository papers explaining the relationship of the work to the concepts being studied (Pedelty, 2001). In Karen Miksch's class, students receive participation points for their adaptations of *Antigone*, but it is expected that their performances will lead to a greater understanding of concepts in their graded work. In the "Do Something Cool" biology assignment, students complete a form in which they describe their project, explain why they chose to do it, and indicate how many points they think they should receive. Jensen uses this information to help him assign points. He wrote that because the range of possible approaches to this kind of assignment is so broad, it is often easier to spot poor quality projects that "include little detail, thoughtful planning, or time investment" (Jensen et al., 2003, p. 32) than it is to identify specific criteria for excellence.

The Arts in Developmental Education

Over the years, GC has been a rich environment for experimentation with using the arts in developmental education. Students in courses that are specifically about the arts have learned to think critically about ways that the arts express the ideas, emotions, and experiences of people who are both alike and very different from them. Students taking courses as diverse as math, psychology, and anthropology have used the arts to better understand the disciplinary concepts of the course. Students in hands-on art courses have used the arts to express their own thoughts, emotions, and experiences. In each case, the arts have added dimensions of knowing that are not found in reading, writing, or test-taking by themselves. Through the arts, students have had opportunities to develop a repertoire of ways of knowing and representing knowledge. The arts also provide innovative teaching methods, multicultural content, and alternative ways to assess students' knowledge.

In addition to the various ways that the arts have been used in the GC curriculum, there are many possibilities for how the arts may be used in the future, both in the college and in other educational settings. One direction that merits continued exploration is combining art-making with other content courses in learning communities. Evolving technologies make it easier for students to create their own visual art, music, photographs, Web sites, and videos in many kinds of courses. In addition, community outreach programs can extend the arts beyond the classroom, such as when Mark Pedelty's freshman seminar visited a school in Minneapolis to give a performance about Aztec myths and music (Weber, 2001, p. 7).

Studying about, through, and with the arts promotes integrative, embodied thinking that goes beyond traditional divisions of mind, body, and emotions. The arts heighten a sense of belonging and help students express and understand their own identities. Students learn to perceive themselves as people who are capable of thinking creatively and expressing ideas and experiences in multiple ways. They develop an awareness of the significance of their own actions in relation to others and of their ability to shape their education meaningfully.

It seems fitting to end with a quote from Risa about how her new understanding of art interconnects with her search for meaning in her life:

> There is no rule with art and that is what makes it the most creative topic of all. You can turn sideways, upside down, reverse an art and still have a meaning to it. Art is the hidden meaning of life. Only if people learned to see things from other angles, from the other side things would be so much better. So, to me a person's understanding of art can help he/she understand life much better. Not that I am saying I understand life now. I have begun the process of understanding art as I am with life.

References

Alland, A., Sr. (1974). *Jacob A. Riis: Photographer & citizen*. Millerton, NY: Aperture.

Almereyda, M. (Director). (2000). *Hamlet* [video]. New York: Miramax.

Amabile, T. (1983). *The social psychology of creativity*. New York: Springer-Verlag.

Angelou, M. (1994). Alone. In *The complete collected poems of Maya Angelou* (pp. 74–75). New York: Random House.

Antubam, K. (1963). *Ghana's heritage of culture*. Leipzig,Germany: Koehler & Amelang.

Association of American Colleges and Universities. (2002). *Greater expectations: A new vision for learning as a nation goes to college*. Washington, DC: Author.

Ball, A., & Heath, S. B. (1993). Dances of identity: Finding an ethnic self in the arts. In S. B. Heath & M. W. McLaughlin (Eds.), *Identity and inner-city youth: Beyond ethnicity and gender* (pp. 13–35). New York: Teachers College Press.

Baxter Magolda, M. (1992). *Knowing and reasoning in college*. San Francisco: Jossey-Bass.

Beach, R., Lundell, D. B., & Jung, C. (2002). Developmental college students' negotiation of social practices between peer, family, workplace, and university worlds. In D. B. Lundell & J. L. Higbee (Eds.), *Exploring urban literacy & developmental education* (pp. 79–108). Minneapolis, MN: Center for Research on Developmental Education and Urban Literacy, General College, University of Minnesota.

Bleedorn, B. (1998). *The creativity force in education, business, and beyond*. Lakeville, MN: Galde Press.

Branagh, K. (Director). (1996). *Shakespeare's Hamlet* [video]. Beverly Hills, CA: Columbia Pictures, Castle Rock Entertainment, and Columbia TriStar Home Video.

Caine, R. N., & Caine, G. (1997). *Education on the edge of possibility*. Alexandria, VA: Association for Curriculum and Development.

Cromer, J. (1990). *Criticism: History, theory and practice of art criticism in art education*. Reston, VA: National Art Education Association.

Cropley, A. (1992). *More ways than one: Fostering creativity*. Norwood, NJ: Ablex.

Dancing in one world [video]. (1993). New York: Thirteen/WNET and RM Arts.

Daughters of the Anasazi [video]. (1990). Taos, NM: Film Project.

Dead Prez. (2000). Wolves. On *Let's get free* [CD]. New York: Loud Records.

Edupoetic Enterbrainment. (n.d.). Retrieved September 16, 2004, from http://www.edupoetic.com/ home.htm

Edwards, B. (1989). *Drawing on the right side of the brain: A course in enhancing creativity and artistic confidence* (rev. ed.). New York: J. P. Tarcher.

Eglash, R. (2002). *African fractals, modern computing, and indigenous design.* New Brunswick, NJ: Rutgers University.

Eglash, R. (2003). *Culturally situated design tools: Teaching math through culture.* Retrieved September 20, 2004, from http://www.rpi.edu/~eglash/csdt.html

Edwards, P. (Ed.). (1985). *Hamlet, Prince of Denmark.* New York: Cambridge University Press.

Eisner, E. W. (1998). Does experience in the arts boost academic achievement? *Art Education, 51* (1), 7–15.

Eisner, E. (2002). *The arts and the creation of mind.* New Haven, CT: Yale University Press.

Eldredge, S. (1996). *Mask improvisation for actor training and performance.* Evanston, IL: Northwestern University Press.

Feinstein, H. (1996). *Reading images: Meaning and metaphor.* Reston, VA: The National Art Education Association.

Freedman, K. (2003). *Teaching visual culture.* Reston, VA: National Art Education Association.

General College. (1938). *Report on problems and progress of the General College.* Unpublished manuscript, University of Minnesota, Minneapolis.

General College. (1968). *The General Education Sounding Board, V* (1). Minneapolis, MN: University of Minnesota.

Girsch, M., & Girsch, C. (1999). *Fanning the creative spirit: Two toy creators simplify creativity.* St. Paul, MN: Creativity Central.

Goldberg, M. (1997). *Arts and learning: An integrated approach to teaching and learning in multicultural and multilingual settings.* San Marcos, CA: California State University.

Goleman, D., Kaufman, P., & Ray, M. (1993). *The creative spirit.* New York: Plume.

Gordon, W. J. J. (1973). *The metaphorical way of knowing & learning* (2nd ed.). Cambridge, MA: Porpoise Books.

Greene, M. (2001). *Variations on a blue guitar: The Lincoln Center Institute lectures on aesthetic education.* New York: Teachers College Press.

Gruber, H. E. (1989). The evolving systems approach to creative work. In D. B. Wallace & H. Gruber, *Creative people at work: Twelve cognitive case studies* (pp. 3–24). New York: Oxford University.

Hicks, S. (2000). *Snow falling on cedars* [video]. Hollywood, CA: Universal Studios.

Hill, G. (1940). The general arts. In *Curriculum making in the General*

College (188–210). Unpublished manuscript, University of Minnesota, Minneapolis.

Hughes, J. (1985). *The breakfast club* [video]. Hollywood, CA: Universal Studios.

Hurwitz, A. (1993). *Collaboration in art education.* Reston, VA: National Art Education Association.

Islamic art [video]. (1988). Princeton, NJ: Films for the Humanities.

James, P. (1999). Ideas in practice: The arts as a path for developmental student learning. *Journal of Developmental Education, 22*(3), 22–28.

James, P. (1999–2000). Blocks and bridges: Learning artistic creativity. *Arts and Learning Research Journal, 16*(1), 110–133.

James, P. (2000a). "I am the dark forest": Personal analogy as a way to understand metaphor. *Art Education, 53*(5), 6–11.

James, P. (2000b). Working toward meaning: The evolution of an assignment. *Studies in Art Education, 41*(2), 146–163.

James, P. (2002). Ideas in practice: Fostering metaphoric thinking. *Journal of Developmental Education, 25*(3), 26–28, 30, 32–33.

James, P. (2002–2003). Between the ideal and the real: A reflective study of teaching art to young adults. *Arts & Learning Research Journal, 19* (1), 1–22.

James, P., & Haselbeck, B. (1998). The arts as a bridge to understanding identity and diversity. In P. L. Dwinell & J. L. Higbee (Eds.), *Developmental education: Meeting diverse student needs* (pp. 3–20). Morrow, GA: National Association for Developmental Education.

Jensen, M. (2004). *"Do Something Cool" projects for GC 1135.* Retrieved May 15, 2004, from http://www.gen.umn.edu/faculty_staff/jensen/1135/example_ student_projects/

Jensen, M., Moore, R., Hatch, J., & Hsu, L. (2003). Ideas in practice: A novel, "cool" assignment to engage science students. *Journal of Developmental Education, 27*(2), 28–33.

John-Steiner, V. (1997). *Notebooks of the mind: Explorations of thinking.* New York: Oxford University Press.

Jones, L. (1993). Barriers to creativity and their relationship to individual, group, and organizational behavior. In S. G. Isaksen, M. C. Murdock, R. L. Firestien, & D. J. Treffinger (Eds.), *Nurturing and developing creativity: The emergence of a discipline* (pp. 133–154). Norwood, NJ: Ablex.

Kindred spirits [video]. (1990). Washington, DC: Smithsonian.

Lakoff, G., & Johnson, M. (1999). *Philosophy in the flesh: The embodied mind and its challenge to Western thought.* New York: Basic Books.

LeSeur, M. (2002). Women on the breadlines. In P. Lauter (Ed.), *The Heath anthology of American literature,* Volume II (4th ed.; pp. 1807–1811). Boston: Houghton-Mifflin.

Morris, E. (Director). (1988). *The thin blue line* [video]. New York: Miramax.

Opitz, D. (2004). Story teller. *Access, 3*(3), 8–9.

Paivio, A., & Walsh, M. (1993). Psychological processes in metaphor comprehension and memory. In A. Ortony (Ed.), *Metaphor and thought* (pp. 307–328). Cambridge, UK: Cambridge University.

Palmer, P. (1999). The grace of great things: Reclaiming the sacred in knowing, teaching, and learning. In S. Glazer (Ed.), *The heart of learning: Spirituality in education* (p. 17). New York: Jeremy P. Tarcher.

Pedelty, M. (2001). Jenny's painting: Multiple forms of communication in the classroom. In B. L. Smith & J. McCann (Eds.), *Reinventing ourselves: Interdisciplinary education, collaborative learning, and experimentation in higher education* (pp. 230–249). Bolton, MA: Anker.

Pedelty, M. (2004a). *GC 1312 Syllabus.* Unpublished manuscript, University of Minnesota, Minneapolis.

Pedelty, M. (2004b). *GC 1903 Syllabus.* Unpublished manuscript, University of Minnesota, Minneapolis.

Pedelty, M. (2004c). Ritual and performance. In P. Rice & D. McCurdy (Eds.), *Strategies for teaching anthropology* (pp. 150–154). Upper Saddle River, NJ: Prentice Hall.

Perkins, D. (1994). *The intelligent eye: Learning to think by looking at art.* Santa Monica. CA: The Getty Center of Education in the Arts.

A photo essay on the Great Depression. (2002). In *Modern American poetry.* Retrieved on September 30, 2004, from http://www.english.uiuc.edu/maps/depression/photoessay.htm

Public sculpture: America's legacy [video]. (1994). Washington, DC: National Museum of American Art, Smithsonian Institution.

Pugh, S. L., Hicks, J. W., & Davis, M. (1997). *Metaphorical ways of knowing: The imaginative nature of thought and expression.* Urbana, IL: National Council for Teachers of English.

Robertson, D., & Nelson, C. (1976). *Mathematics and art.* Unpublished manuscript, University of Minnesota, Minneapolis.

Root-Bernstein, R., & Root-Bernstein, M. (1999). *Sparks of genius: The thirteen thinking tools of the world's most creative people.* Boston: Houghton-Mifflin.

Root-Bernstein, R., & Root-Bernstein, M. (2000). Learning to think with emotion. *Chronicle of Higher Education, 46*(19), A54.

Rose, T. (1994). *Black noise: Rap music and Black culture in contemporary America.* Middletown, CT: Wesleyan University Press.

Rothenberg, P. S. (Ed.). (1995). *Race, class, and gender in the United States: An integrated study* (3rd ed.). New York: St. Martin's Press.

Roukes, N. (1982). *Art synectics: Stimulating creativity in art.* Worcester, MA: Davis.

Sanders, D. A., & Sanders, J. A. (1984). *Teaching creativity through metaphor: An integrated brain approach.* New York: Longman.

Sapphire. (1997). *Push.* New York: Random House.

Scorsese, M. (Director). (1976). *Taxi driver* [video]. Hollywood, CA: Columbia Pictures.

Shange, N. (1995). Every three minutes. In P. S. Rothenberg (Ed.), *Race, class, and gender in the United States: An integrated study* (3rd ed.; pp. 236–238). New York: St. Martin's Press.

Sophocles (442 B.C.E.). *Antigone* (R. C. Jebb, Trans.). Retrieved October 2, 2004, from http://classics.mit.edu/Sophocles/antigone.html

Spolin, V. (1994). *Improvisation for the theater* (5th ed.). Evanston, IL: Northwestern University Press.

Sweet, A. P. (1997). A national policy perspective on research intersections between literacy and the visual/communicative arts. In J. Flood, S. B. Heath, & D. Lapp (Eds.), *Handbook of research on teaching literacy through the communicative and visual arts* (pp. 264–285). New York: Macmillan Library Reference USA.

Takaki, R. (1993). *A different mirror: A history of multi-cultural America.* New York: Little Brown.

Taylor, D. (2001). From the Dean. *Access, 1*(1), 2. Minneapolis, MN: General College, University of Minnesota.

Taylor, D. (1986). *Sophocles, the Theban plays* [video], translation by D. Taylor. Princeton, NJ: Films for the Humanities.

Tinto, V. (2002, February). *Taking student learning seriously.* Keynote address presented at the Southwest Regional Learning Communities Conference, Tempe, AZ. Retrieved June 4, 2004, http://www.mcli.dist.maricopa.edu/events/lcc02/presents/tinto.html

Tharp, T. (2003). *The creative habit: Learn it and use it for life.* New York: Simon & Schuster.

Tornatore, G. (Director). (1989). *Cinema paridiso* [video]. New York: Miramax.

Urban Bushwomen. (1996). *Women's work* [video]. Richmond, VA: Virginia Museum of Arts.

Wacipi-PowWow [video]. (1995). Saint Paul, MN: Twin Cities Public Television.

Weber, L. (2001). GC and the arts. *Access, 1*(1), 4–9. Minneapolis, MN: General College, University of Minnesota.

Weisman Art Museum. (2004). *Architecture and history.* Retrieved September 26, 2004, from http://www.weisman.umn.edu

Yenawine, P. (1991). *How to look at modern art.* New York: Harry Abrams.

CHAPTER 14

Overview of the
General College Mathematics Program

D. Patrick Kinney, Douglas F. Robertson, and Laura Smith Kinney

ABSTRACT

The General College developmental mathematics program teaches elementary algebra and intermediate algebra using several different instructional models. This chapter provides a rationale for offering students an array of instructional models, along with a description of each model. The instructional models used are lecture, computer-mediated instruction, guided group discovery, active learning with a mastery approach, and cooperative learning with real-world problems. Students are allowed to self-select into the instructional model that they prefer. A mathematics placement test is used to determine if students should enroll in Elementary Algebra, Intermediate Algebra, or a higher-level course.

The developmental mathematics program at the General College offers noncredit-bearing mathematics courses along with a credit-bearing introductory statistics course. Each year approximately 17 sections of Elementary Algebra and 19 sections of Intermediate Algebra are offered. Class sizes range from 15 to 35 students in each course, depending on enrollment patterns, time of day, and teacher preferences. To meet the needs of students who place into arithmetic, along with those who desire more time to learn elementary algebra, the program offers Elementary Algebra Part I and Elementary Algebra Part II. This sequence splits elementary algebra into a two-semester sequence and includes topics from arithmetic. It also includes information about developing effective study skills, overcoming math anxiety, and becoming a successful student. Once students successfully complete Elementary Algebra Part I and Elementary Algebra Part II, or Elementary Algebra, they enroll in Intermediate Algebra. After successfully completing Intermediate Algebra students typically enroll in College Algebra or Precalculus, which are taught by the faculty of the Mathematics Department in the

Institute of Technology in a separate building on campus. Also, some students enroll in the introductory statistics course offered by the General College in order to meet the all-university Mathematical Thinking requirement.

The General College developmental mathematics program offers classes using a variety of instructional models and takes the position that no single instructional model is best for all students. This view is based on research on students' learning styles, which is discussed in the next section, and on feedback from students. The methods used to deliver developmental mathematics instruction at the General College are (a) lecture, (b) computer-mediated instruction, (c) guided group discovery, (d) active learning with a mastery approach, and (e) cooperative learning with an emphasis on "real-world" applications.

Rationale for Offering a Variety of Instructional Models

There is evidence that students benefit when they are able to learn using their preferred learning styles (Higbee, Ginter, & Taylor, 1991; Lemire, 1998). A commonly used definition of learning styles is that given by Galbraith and James (1987, pp. 27–28), who identified seven perceptual modes related to learning: print, aural, interactive, visual, haptic, kinesthetic, and olfactory. However, as noted by Higbee, Ginter, and Taylor, "the connotations of the term 'learning style' are varied and in many instances divergent in nature" (p. 5).

We believe that the discussion of learning styles can be extended to include additional factors related to students' preferences for how they learn. Some students, for example, prefer a lecture class where the instruction is teacher-centered and the instructor "shows and explains everything" (Kinney, 2000). Other students, however, prefer instruction that is student-centered, such as when using software in a computer-mediated class. Students also vary in their preference for the pace of the instruction and the order in which material is presented. In a lecture class, the instructor exerts significant control over the pace of the instruction and the order in which the content is presented. In a computer-mediated class, however, students control the navigation path and the pace of instruction. These features are of particular interest to students who are able to learn significantly faster than the pace in a lecture class, to students who want more time to process the material, and to those who need a review after a lapse in their mathematics education.

The nature of the human interaction in a classroom is another important issue for many students (Kinney, 2000). Some students prefer that an instructor lead class discussions and activities, such as in a lecture class. This allows students to interact with the instructor as the mathematics is presented, and it allows students to "listen in on" the discussion between the instructor and other students. Further, students frequently enjoy working with classmates on in-class activities and benefit from the discussion with classmates. Not all students, however, prefer the type of interaction in a teacher-centered classroom. Students who do not like being called on in front of the whole class may be uncomfortable in a lecture class, especially if they think that the instructor does not interact with students in a caring and respectful manner. These students may opt for a computer-mediated class. We found that students in computer-mediated classes still value working with classmates, especially informally as they proceed through lessons on the software. Finally, students who believe that a typical mathematics instructor is able to explain the material well may opt for a traditional lecture class, while students who think that a typical mathematics instructor does not explain the material well may select a computer-mediated class or a class that involves a large amount of group work or student-to-student interaction.

An issue that is becoming increasingly important to many students is flexibility in how, where, and when they learn mathematics. In a traditional lecture class students have little flexibility. They are expected to learn the mathematics by following the instructor's presentation, asking questions, reading the textbook, and working with classmates. Further, they are expected to learn the mathematics at a specific location and at a specific time. That is, they are expected to learn the mathematics while in class during the hours that the class meets. For some developmental education students the structure of a typical lecture class works well. An effective alternative to a lecture class for some students is computer-mediated instruction. In a computer-mediated class, the primary source of instruction and feedback is interactive multimedia software. During class students are given access to the software, individual assistance from the instructor as needed, a textbook, and the flexibility to work with classmates as desired. Because the instructor does not lecture, he or she is available to work with students individually or in small groups throughout the entire class period. Thus, students in a computer-mediated class are frequently able to receive more individual assistance than students in a lecture class. We have found that in a computer-mediated class students with learning disabilities, who are often reluctant to ask questions in a lecture class for fear of being embarrassed or of "holding up the class" (Kinney, 2002), often value being able to work individually with the instructor for an extended period of time during class.

Methods of Instruction

We consider lecture instruction first because it is familiar to instructors and therefore provides a frame of reference for the remaining instructional models. Each year, approximately 14 of the 36 developmental mathematics sections taught in the General College use a traditional lecture approach.

Lecture

Direct instruction is typically used to deliver content in a lecture class. Rosenshine and Meister (1987) observed that direct instruction usually includes (a) presenting new material in small steps, (b) modeling of the procedure by the teacher, (c) thinking aloud by the teacher, (d) guiding initial student practice, (e) providing systematic corrections and feedback, and (f) providing expert models of the completed task. This type of instruction is teacher-centered, and the instructor is the primary source of new material. In addition to listening to the lecture, students may ask the instructor questions, work in pairs or groups, and take notes. The applications discussed in these classes are typically those found in mainstream textbooks.

Computer-Mediated Instruction

In a typical year, 14 of the 36 developmental mathematics sections offered in the General College are taught using computer-mediated instruction. We structured our computer-mediated courses in a manner that is consistent with the definition of computer-mediated instruction as stated by Gifford (1996). Gifford defined computer-mediated learning as a learner-centered model of technology-mediated instruction for which the software is the primary vehicle for delivering the instruction. The computer-mediated courses use interactive multimedia software from Academic Systems (2001) to deliver the instruction. The software (a) provides a thorough presentation of the concepts and skills using interactive multimedia, (b) imbeds items requiring student interaction within the instruction, (c) provides immediate feedback and detailed solutions, (d) includes provisions for the development of skills, (e) offers online quizzes, and (f) includes a course management system that tracks students' time on task and progress.

The instructor is a critical part of the students' learning experience even though he or she does not present the content. The instructor provides individual and small group assistance as needed, structures the course in a manner that promotes students' completing the lessons on time, and provides feedback to students about their understanding of the math and their progress in the course. A schedule is given to students at the beginning of the semester that indicates the lesson for each day, the homework problems that will be assigned and collected for grading, the due dates for all written assignments, and the dates of the quizzes and exams. Homework, quizzes, and exams are all completed using paper and pencil.

The software used in computer-mediated classes provides students with the flexibility to study mathematics "anywhere, anytime," provided they have a personal computer (PC), Internet access, and know how to use these resources to utilize the software. If a student in a regularly scheduled class misses a class, the student can study the day's lesson outside of class. Also, students who attended class can review the lesson outside of class or complete the lesson if they did not finish while in class. Kinney, Kinney, and Robertson provide further details about computer-mediated instruction in Chapter 15.

Guided Group Discovery

Dr. Susan Staats, Assistant Professor of developmental mathematics in the General College, uses a guided group discovery method in her classes. Her implementation of this method is motivated by authentic applications such as the spread and effects of human immunodeficiency virus (HIV) and malaria around the world. Although the focus in her classes is on conceptual learning, she also addresses the development of algebraic skills. Students work cooperatively in small groups and engage in whole-class discussions while the instructor acts as a moderator and coach using a Socratic method. In her classes, Dr. Staats poses problems, asks clarifying questions, and has students decide collaboratively when a math statement is true. In this method, the instructor does not act as the ultimate authority of right or wrong; rather, the mathematics is the authority.

In some class meetings Dr. Staats presents a specific situation or algebraic problem at the start of the class. Initially, students work on the problem in small groups while the instructor observes and interacts with the groups, asking questions but not evaluating responses or giving authoritative answers. Once the class members are brought together as a group to discuss their findings, the instructor acts as a moderator and facilitator, but never as the final authority. The instructor continues to ask questions, such as, "How did you come up with that result?" or "Do the data support that conjecture?" or "Can you elaborate a bit more along those lines?" Through these discussions, the students and instructor develop the general concepts, formulas, and procedures related to the situation or algebraic problem that was given. For the interested reader, Brissenden (1988) described this method in some detail in *Talking About Mathematics*. Dr. Staats provides further details in Chapter 10.

Active Learning With a Mastery Approach

Dr. Irene Duranczyk, General College Assistant Professor of developmental mathematics, teaches using a sociocultural theory model (Duranczyk, Staats, Moore, Hatch, Jensen, & Somdahl, 2004). Students take an experiential approach to new topics or ideas in beginning algebra, explore the topics in context in their own words, and then translate their experience to mathematical language and concepts. Authentic forms of assessment are built into the class through the use of student-centered projects.

As previously mentioned, the General College offers Introductory Algebra as a one-semester course but also offers it as a two-course sequence. In the two-course sequence, Dr. Duranczyk uses a mastery-based approach that incorporates active learning techniques, student projects, and multicultural contexts to help make the mathematics familiar and meaningful to students from diverse backgrounds. Also, information about math study skills, ways to reduce math anxiety, math as a social and cultural activity, and problem solving are infused throughout the class.

Active learning according to Meyers and Jones (1993) "involves providing opportunities for students to meaningfully talk and listen, write, read, and reflect on the content, ideas, issues, and concerns of an academic subject" (p. 6). The American Mathematical Association of Two-year Colleges (AMATYC) Standards (AMATYC, 1995, p. 9) promote active learning. These standards advocate that students (a) acquire the ability to read, write, listen to, and speak mathematics; (b) expand their mathematical reasoning skills as they develop convincing mathematical arguments; (c) engage in rich experiences that encourage independent, nontrivial exploration in mathematics; and (d) learn mathematics through modeling real-world situations.

A mastery-based approach consistent with Keller's (1968) instructional model called the personalized system of instruction (PSI) is incorporated into the courses taught by Dr. Duranczyk. The PSI model demands that students study material and take tests on the material until they are able to demonstrate mastery. When a student completes a test the instructor is often able to review the students' work and provide immediate feedback. The feedback, according to Kluger and DeNisi (1996), should be specific to the task, corrective, and done in a familiar context that shapes learning. The PSI instructional approach has been shown to be an effective method to achieve student success (Kulik, Kulik, & Bangert-Drowns, 1990).

Cooperative Learning With Real-World Problems

Dr. Donald Opitz, the General College Mathematics Center Coordinator, uses a cooperative-learning pedagogy in which the activities are based on "real-world" applications. The rationale for incorporating cooperative learning is that it can promote more positive relationships among students, higher math self-esteem, and more positive attitudes towards mathematics (Johnson & Johnson, 1989). The applications lead students through a series of questions that prompt them to consider what mathematical tools can be used to answer the questions. The algebra concepts and skills necessary to answer the questions are introduced, and students then use them to solve the problems embedded in the real-world applications.

Full class discussions, rather than traditional lectures, are used to clarify procedures and concepts. In addition, students spend one class period per week in a computer lab to work on skill development using computer software. Students engage in online discussion threads and complete online activities using WebCT outside of class. Course projects require students to work cooperatively outside of class to collect and analyze real data. Groups adopt a variety of presentation styles to communicate their findings within the class and demonstrate their mastery of algebra skills needed for their analyses. When groups present their findings in class, they demonstrate their understanding of which algebra concepts and skills are needed to analyze their real-world problem and how to apply them.

Placing Students Into Mathematics Courses

Information about the General College math program is sent to prospective students in late February along with other orientation materials and instructions on how to take the General College mathematics placement test, which is located on the University of Minnesota's Web site, (University of Minnesota math placement exam, n.d.). A user name and password is required to access the test. The placement test assists each student, along with the advisor and the mathematics faculty, in determining the appropriate level of mathematics for the student.

To help students prepare for the placement test, the General College sends students a set of practice questions, with answers, that are similar to the questions on the actual test. The placement test questions were derived from the mathematics courses offered by the General College. Students are encouraged to study before taking the test to refresh their memory so that they do not place into a course that is below the level for which they have sufficient preparation. However, not all prospective students review prior to taking the mathematics placement test or even understand the importance of doing their best when taking the placement test. Therefore, students are given the opportunity to take a second version of the placement test at a later date. Students may also talk to a mathematics professor about placement during summer orientation. The placement test provides a guide to the level of course in which students should enroll, but the final decision regarding course level is left to the individual student in consultation with his or her advisor.

After a student and his or her advisor have decided on the course level that is appropriate, the student selects an instructional format. Students are provided with information about the General College mathematics courses during their on-campus orientation and through the University Course Guide (University of Minnesota course guide, n.d.). To view the General College course descriptions, students select "General College" in the subject pull-down menu. Students discuss the instructional models and different learning styles with their advisor and then select the format that they prefer. No formal assessment of learning styles is given. Students may also talk one-on-one with a General College mathematics professor to obtain more information about the various instructional formats and levels. Ultimately, students must select the instructional format that they believe will best meet their preferences. This process gives students ownership of the decision about which instructional format they enroll in.

We are in the process of developing an inventory that may be used to assist students in deciding whether to enroll in a computer-mediated or non-computer-mediated class. The items in Figure 1 were developed based on written responses from students about their views of computer-mediated and lecture instruction. Figure 1 contains data on the responses from students who preferred the instructional format that they were enrolled in at both the start and end of the semester. Students selected one of the following responses for each item: 1 = disagree, 2 = more disagree than agree, 3 = more agree than disagree, or 4 = agree. A four-point scale, rather than a five-point scale, was used so that students could not select a neutral response. Therefore, mean scores ranged from 1 to 4 for each item. A mean less than 2.5 indicates that students tended to disagree more than agree with the item. A mean score greater than 2.5 indicates that students tended to agree more than disagree with the item.

The results of the inventory suggest that students in computer-mediated classes tend to prefer to learn independently using software, provided the software effectively incorporates interactive multimedia, allows students to control the pace and navigate flexibly, and provides step-by-step explanations. Students in computer-mediated sections value having an instructor available to answer individual questions, although they may have a hard time paying attention and feel bored if the instructor were to lecture. Students in lecture sections, on the other hand, think that the interaction in a lecture class holds their attention better than would the interactivity of software. They also tend to view software as a less effective way to learn mathematics than students in computer-mediated classes. The inventory results support the view that no single instructional format is best for all students.

	COURSE FORMAT	M	N	SD	SEM
1. It is important that I attend class if I want to do well in math.	computer	3.43	81	0.87	0.10
	lecture	3.54	183	0.75	0.06
2. The structure and organization of this class has helped me do well.	computer	3.43	81	0.61	0.07
	lecture	3.39	183	0.67	0.05
3. I prefer to learn by watching a teacher lecture and being able to ask questions during the lecture.	computer	3.73	79	0.52	0.06
	lecture	3.63	183	0.67	0.05
4.* I would prefer to take a computer-based math class if an instructor were available to answer my questions fairly quickly.	computer	3.73	81	0.50	0.06
	lecture	1.65	183	0.86	0.06
5.* I would take a computer-based math class if the computer provided detailed step-by-step explanations on how to do problems.	computer	3.37	81	0.73	0.08
	lecture	2.04	182	1.06	0.08
6.* I would learn much better if I could control the pace at which the mathematics is presented.	computer	3.85	81	0.36	0.04
	lecture	2.80	182	0.96	0.07
7.* It would be helpful if I could go back and see explanations given earlier.	computer	3.90	81	0.30	0.03
	lecture	3.23	182	0.72	0.05
8.* A multimedia program for teaching math provides more visual ways to learn than a teacher lecturing.	computer	3.80	81	0.49	0.05
	lecture	2.09	181	0.93	0.07
9.* I prefer to learn more on my own using software rather than having a teacher show me everything.	computer	3.72	81	0.48	0.05
	lecture	1.55	181	0.76	0.06
10.* A good interactive multimedia computer program holds my attention better than a math teacher.	computer	3.59	81	0.59	0.07
	lecture	1.48	182	0.69	0.05
11.* I have a hard time paying attention and feel bored when a teacher lectures about math.	computer	3.54	81	0.69	0.08
	lecture	1.82	181	0.84	0.06
12.* A lecture math class has more interaction that helps me learn than a computer class using interactive multimedia software.	computer	1.90	81	1.02	0.11
	lecture	3.48	182	0.77	0.06

Note. *$p < 0.05$.

Figure 1. Inventory related to computer-mediated and lecture instruction.

The Mathematics Center

The Mathematics Center is coordinated by Dr. Donald Opitz. It provides free walk-in mathematics tutoring 35 hours per week in the same building that classes are held. The Mathematics Center contains reference books and five computers that can be used for mathematics-related activities. Students with additional individual needs may sign up with a tutor to receive one-on-one assistance throughout the semester.

The Mathematics Center works closely with the mathematics instructors to provide effective support for students. The tutors are undergraduate students, many of whom have completed mathematics courses at the General College. Tutors receive training throughout the academic year regarding how to be an effective tutor. Further, information regarding the content covered in the General College mathematics courses and the instructional models used to teach the mathematics are included in the tutor training.

Dr. Opitz also coordinates a Supplemental Instruction program for General College mathematics courses that provides students with structured assistance from tutors in a classroom-like setting. Students may sign up for free Supplemental Instruction in their regularly-scheduled classes. Every effort is made to make the sessions available at times that are convenient for students, including evenings. Further information about the Mathematics Center is provided in Chapter 23.

Summary

The General College developmental mathematics courses are taught using a variety of instructional models. Our view is that no single instructional model is best for all students and that students should be allowed to self-select into the instructional model of their choice. Each of our classes incorporates a developmental education approach and strives to provide an environment that fosters students' learning the mathematics, prepares students for subsequent mathematics courses, improves students' attitudes towards learning mathematics, and enhances student retention. Looking forward, we anticipate that we will continue to experiment with new ways to deliver developmental mathematics instruction and that we will learn from our colleagues and our students in the process.

References

Academic Systems. (2001). *Interactive mathematics* [computer software]. Bloomington, MN: Plato Learning.

American Mathematical Association of Two-Year Colleges. (1995). *Crossroads in mathematics: Standards for introductory college mathematics before calculus*. Memphis, TN: Author.

Brissenden, T. (1988). *Talking about mathematics*. Oxford, UK: Basil Blackwell.

Duranczyk, I. M., Staats, S., Moore, R., Hatch, J., Jensen, M., & Somdahl, C. (2004). Introductory-level college mathematics explored through a sociocultural lens. In I. M. Duranczyk, J. L. Higbee, & D. B. Lundell (Eds.), *Best practices for access and retention in higher education* (pp. 43–53). Minneapolis, MN: Center for Research on Developmental Education and Urban Literacy, General College, University of Minnesota.

Galbraith, M. W., & James, W. B. (1987). The relationship of educational level and perceptual learning styles. *Journal of Adult Education, 15*(2), 27–35.

Gifford, B. R. (1996). *Mediated learning: A new model of technology-mediated instruction and learning*. Mountain View, CA: Academic Systems.

Higbee, J. L., Ginter E. J., & Taylor W. D. (1991). Enhancing academic performance: Seven perceptual styles of learning. *Research & Teaching in Developmental Education, 7*(2), 5–9.

Johnson, D. W., & Johnson, R. T. (1989). *Cooperation and competition: Theory and research*. Edina, MN: Interaction Book.

Keller, F. (1968). "Goodbye teacher . . ." *Journal of Applied Behavioral Analysis, 1*(1), 79–89.

Kinney, D. P. (2000). *Student responses to survey, questionnaire, and focus group questions identifying reasons for students' enrollment in computer-mediated and lecture courses*. Unpublished raw data. Minneapolis, MN: University of Minnesota.

Kinney, D. P. (2002). Students with disabilities in mathematics: Barriers and recommendations. *The AMATYC Review, 23*(2), 13–23.

Kluger, A., & DeNisi, A. (1996). The effects of feedback interventions on performance: A historical review, a meta-analysis, and a preliminary feedback intervention theory. *Psychological Bulletin, 119*, 254–284.

Kulik, C., Kulik, J., & Bangert-Drowns, R. (1990). Effectiveness of mastery learning programs: A meta-analysis. *Review of Educational Research, 60*, 265–299.

Lemire, D. S. (1998). Three learning styles models: Research and recommendations for developmental education. *The Learning Assistance Review, 3*(2), 26–40.

Meyers, C., & Jones, T. (1993). *Promoting active learning*. San Francisco: Jossey-Bass.

Rosenshine, B., & Meister, C. (1987). Direct instruction. In M. J. Dunkin (Ed.), *The international encyclopedia of teaching and teacher education* (pp. 359–364). Oxford, UK: Pergamon.

University of Minnesota course guide. (n.d.). Minneapolis, MN: University of Minnesota Retrieved January 4, 2005, from http://onestop2.umn.edu/courseinfo/courseguide_selectsubject.jsp?institution=UMNTC

University of Minnesota math placement exam. (n.d.). Minneapolis, MN: University of Minnesota Retrieved January 4, 2005, from http://www.onestop.umn.edu/placement

CHAPTER 15

Learning Mathematics Through Computer-Mediated Instruction

D. Patrick Kinney, Laura Smith Kinney,
and Douglas F. Robertson

ABSTRACT

Computer-mediated mathematics instruction provides students with an alternative to lecture instruction. The interactive multimedia software presents the concepts and skills, provides feedback, and includes a course management system. The instructor works with students individually or in small groups throughout each class period to address students' questions and to provide feedback. This chapter presents an overview of computer-mediated software, along with details about how our computer-mediated courses are structured. Research regarding student outcomes in computer-mediated courses is also provided. Finally, trends in computer-mediated instruction are discussed.

The structure of the computer-mediated courses at the General College is consistent with the definition of computer-mediated instruction stated by Gifford (1996). Gifford defined computer-mediated learning as a learner-centered model of technology-mediated instruction for which the software is the primary vehicle for delivering the instruction. Software that supports computer-mediated instruction makes use of interactive multimedia. Najjar (1996) defined multimedia as the use of text, graphics, animation, pictures, video, and sound to present information. Interactivity allows students to control both the pace of the learning and the navigation path. Najjar examined the research related to interactivity and stated, "Interactivity appears to have a strong positive effect on learning (Bosco, 1986; Fletcher, 1989, 1990; Verano, 1987)" (p. 131). Reviews of research on the impact of technology-mediated instruction on student learning have consistently found that technology-mediated instruction can have positive effects on student learning (Becker, 1992; Khalili & Shashaani, 1994; Kulik & Kulik, 1991; Niemiec, Samson, Weinstein, & Walberg, 1987).

Bagui (1998) examined how multimedia makes it easier for people to learn because of parallels between multimedia and the "natural" way people learn according to the information process theory. The information processing theory is defined by Bagui as a theory that shows how people learn. The reasons for increased learning with multimedia according to Bagui include (a) interactivity, (b) flexibility, (c) rich content, (d) motivational effects, (e) better structured instruction, (f) immediate feedback, and (g) material presented in a more stimulating fashion. The success of multimedia can be attributed mainly to dual coding according to Bagui. Dual coding theory asserts that information is processed through one of two generally independent channels, verbal or nonverbal (Clark & Paivio, 1991). Bagui stated that learning is better when information is processed through two channels, such as when learning through multimedia, rather than one, because the learner creates more cognitive paths that can be followed to retrieve the information (Mayer & Anderson, 1991; Paivio, 1967, 1991).

Overview of Computer-Mediated Software

A basic premise of computer-mediated instruction is that the student is at the center of the teaching-learning enterprise. The software must thoroughly present and explain the concepts and skills, pose items for students to solve to check their understanding, provide detailed feedback to guide students' learning, and allow students to control the navigation path and the pace of instruction. Further, the software should utilize the capabilities of interactive multimedia to the extent possible and not simply move material from the printed page to the computer screen. At the General College we have used *Interactive Mathematics* from Academic Systems Corporation (2001) since 2000.

Each lesson in the *Interactive Mathematics* software contains six sections, and each section is identified by an icon on the computer screen.

1. Overview: The Overview section provides a preview to the lesson and includes an optional pretest. Students who obtain a high score on the pretest may only need to review the content in the lesson rather than studying the lesson in its entirety. Based on the pretest score, the software makes a recommendation for what the student should study.

2. Explain: This section is the primary source of instruction. It uses text, animation, graphics, video, and voice to provide a thorough presentation of the concepts and skills for each lesson. Items are embedded in the instruction to check students' understanding as they progress through the software. Students who correctly answer a question on the first attempt are informed that they are correct, and the solution is displayed in detail with an explanation

of the steps. Students who do not answer correctly on the first attempt are given a hint and allowed to attempt the item a second time. After the second attempt students are informed if they are correct, and the complete solution is displayed.

3. Apply: The Apply section contains a set of problems representative of those introduced in the Explain section. Students who are uncertain how to answer an item can click on an icon that links back to the relevant part of the Explain section. Once they have reviewed the content from the Explain section, they can link back to the Apply section and proceed. Students are provided with the complete solution after answering each item.

4. Explore: This section contains activities that extend the concepts and skills beyond the level covered in the Explain section. Many of the Explore activities involve applications and problem-solving activities and can be used for group activities.

5. Evaluate: The Evaluate section provides online quizzes. Students receive detailed feedback once they finish an Evaluate. The instructor has the option to allow students one, two, or three attempts on each Evaluate quiz. The course management system records each attempt by a student and displays the student's highest score in a summary report.

6. Homework: This section provides a suggested list of Homework problems for students to work based on their performance in the Explain and Apply sections. Some institutions do not assign homework but recommend to students that they work the problems assigned by the software. At the General College we assign specific homework problems for each lesson to all students. A convenient feature of the software is that it contains the entire textbook on a pdf file. This allows students access to the homework problems in class without having to carry the book to school.

The management system provides two types of reports. An individual report for each student includes the time spent on each section of the software and performance outcomes on the items in each section. A section report provides a summary of the scores for each class on the Evaluates and the total time each student has used the software. The information in these reports is useful for monitoring students' progress so that the instructor can intervene in a timely manner to assist the student in improving outcomes. The intervention may consist of working more closely with the student while in class, discussing strategies for learning mathematics more effectively, arranging to work with a tutor, and involving the student's advisor when appropriate.

Structure of Computer-Mediated Courses

When we designed the computer-mediated courses, we decided to draw upon the features of the lecture courses that promote attendance, provide students with feedback, and facilitate keeping students on track. We designed our computer-mediated courses so that they have a high degree of structure, including the expectation that students attend each class meeting, as opposed to something much less structured, such as a self-paced course in an open lab. This was done even though the *Interactive Mathematics* software can be used by students in their residence hall rooms and at home provided they have Internet access.

In the computer-mediated and lecture classes all students are expected to attend every class meeting. Classes are scheduled for 50 minutes per meeting for 4 days a week, or 100 minutes per meeting for 2 days a week. All students are given a schedule at the beginning of the semester that lists the material to be covered each class meeting and the problems that are to be worked using paper and pencil and turned in for grading. All students take paper and pencil quizzes and exams according to a set schedule. Class size in both computer-mediated and lecture classes is typically limited to 35 students.

Next, we discuss the computer-mediated courses in greater detail. The course structure we developed was primarily for traditional students who were able to attend regularly scheduled classes. The course structure for a different group of learners, such as those in a distance education class, may include some of the components of our course structure but certainly not all of them.

Daily Schedule of Class Activities

Students are given a schedule at the beginning of the semester that outlines the events for each class period during the semester. The schedule includes: (a) the lessons students are to study each day, (b) assignments to be turned in for grading and their due dates, (c) daily checkpoint dates, (d) exam dates, and (e) quiz dates. A set schedule informs students of the pace that they must progress through the course to complete it by the end of the semester. It also establishes a guideline for students and instructors to determine if a student is on track or behind. If a student is behind schedule, the instructor may talk with the student about his or her progress and develop with the student a plan for getting back on schedule. If the instructor thinks that intervention by the student's advisor may be helpful, the instructor will send an academic alert to both the student and the advisor.

Homework Assignments

Students are assigned problems to be worked using paper and pencil for each lesson. These are turned in for grading on a set schedule and usually returned to students the following class period. The homework is graded and recorded by an undergraduate teaching assistant who is present with the instructor during each class period. Collecting homework provides a mechanism for instructors to identify students who are not on track and need assistance. Because a computer-mediated course instructor does not lecture, it is critical that instructors find mechanisms to monitor students' progress closely. Collecting homework is one such mechanism. In focus groups (Kinney, 2000), 31 out of 32 students recommended that we continue to collect and grade homework. Students explained this by saying that it kept them on track, helped them learn the math, and that if it was not required, they would work a lot fewer problems and not be as prepared for exams. When assigning homework we take the approach that the amount of homework we ask students to do should be reasonable; that the due dates should be given well in advance; that students can receive assistance from classmates, the instructor, or in the Mathematics Center; and that quiz and exam items should be closely aligned with the assigned homework.

Exams and Quizzes

The exams are given to students on paper rather than on the computer. Students may use a calculator on the exams and quizzes. Five exams are given per semester plus a comprehensive final exam. By giving a fairly large number of exams, students are able to study smaller chunks of the course for each exam. This is especially helpful for students who struggle with math. Six quizzes are also given during the semester according to a set schedule, and students are informed about the contents of the quizzes. Students complete the quizzes individually using paper and pencil.

Checkpoint Questions

Checkpoint questions consist of one or two questions over recently covered concepts or skills. They are given to students typically early in the class period and are due by the end of class. Students are encouraged to work together, compare strategies, and determine if their solutions make sense. Students may use any available resource. When students believe that they have answered the question correctly and have provided a sufficient written explanation of how they arrived at the answer, the instructor checks their work. If it is correct and complete, the instructor informs the student of this and collects it so that the score can be recorded. If a student is having difficulty, the instructor provides feedback to point the student in the right direction. The checkpoint questions count for a small part of students' grades, and because they can only be taken during the scheduled class meeting, they promote good attendance.

Checkpoint questions also promote student-student interaction, which makes a computer-mediated course feel more like a regular class rather than an open lab. In addition, checkpoint questions help instructional staff identify students who do not yet understand recently covered concepts or skills, which opens the door for the instructor to work with students in need of assistance. This can be important because students do not always ask questions when they should, in part because they are not always aware of things that they do not yet know. The checkpoint questions also promote student-instructor contact. This is important to establish early in the semester so that students and instructors establish good communication. In the focus groups, when students were asked if we should use checkpoint questions again, 30 students indicated "yes," and 2 marked "no."

Evaluates

The Evaluates are online quizzes. The software provides three parallel forms for each lesson. Students' scores are recorded in the management system. In our initial implementation of computer-mediated learning we included the Evaluates, but later we discontinued them and now use the checkpoint questions instead. Many of the students still complete the Evaluates because they provide students with feedback about their understanding of the mathematics. Although many colleges use the Evaluates, we discontinued using them in part to save time and in part because the checkpoint questions generate more student-teacher interaction.

Role of the Instructor in a Computer-Mediated Class

In a computer-mediated class the student is at the center of the teaching and learning enterprise, not the instructor. The role of the instructor, therefore, does not include presenting the material. Instructors may be responsible for selecting the software, ensuring that the computer lab is functional, developing a course structure that is effective for their students, and completing other duties that instructors typically incur when teaching a lecture course.

During the computer-mediated classes the instructor continually moves about the classroom, stopping to assist students as requested and when the instructor senses that a student can use assistance. We found that it is important that the instructor be available to students throughout the class period. Being available to our students in a meaningful way means that the instructors move about the room so that they are within an arm's reach of each student on a regular basis. This means that instructors do not engage in any administrative tasks that can be completed outside of class, conversations not related to teaching the class, or other activities that communicate to students that the instructor is not available to work with students. When an instructor appears to be disengaged from working with students, students are less likely to attempt to engage the instructor. In computer-mediated classes instructors sometimes take the view that they are not "teaching" because they do not present the content. Students, however, still tend to view the instructor as the "teacher" and therefore believe the instructor should be focused on students' learning and should always be available to assist them.

The instructor typically views or prints the data from the course management system just prior to the start of class to be aware of which students are behind schedule or are having difficulty in certain areas. This information better enables the instructor to intervene early when a student is having difficulty. We have found that students often do not ask questions as soon as they should or that they do not ask a question until the instructor initiates the discussion.

Student Performance in Computer-Mediated and Lecture Classes

We compared the performance of students in the computer-mediated and lecture courses using both quantitative and qualitative measures (Kinney, 2001). Data were gathered on a total of 668 students, most of whom were incoming freshmen while the rest were predominantly sophomores. An inventory was administered on the first day of class that included items related to students' past experiences learning mathematics, learning styles, and attitudes towards mathematics and computers. A second inventory was administered just prior to the final exam that contained items related to course satisfaction in addition to the same items that were administered at the start of the semester. Student focus groups were conducted with computer-mediated courses during the last week of class to gather information related to their learning experiences using interactive multimedia software and their attitudes toward computer-mediated instruction.

The Mathematics Placement Exam

The mathematics placement exam scores were obtained from the university database for the 462 incoming freshman participants to examine potential differences in the mathematics background of students at the start of the semester. The math placement exam contained 41 items that were representative of the items covered in the courses. In the Introductory Algebra classes, the math placement test data revealed no significant differences for students enrolled in the computer-mediated (M = 12.3, SD = 3.1) and lecture classes (M = 11.4, SD = 3.5), $t(219)$ = 1.76, p = .08. Also, in the Intermediate Algebra classes there was no significant difference in the computer-mediated (M = 20.4, SD = 4.9) and lecture classes (M = 20.4, SD = 5.2), $t(246)$ = .150, p = .88 on the math placement exam (Kinney, 2001).

Common Final Exams

Students in the computer-mediated and lecture sections of each course were administered the same final exam. Because different instructional materials and midterm exams were used in the computer-mediated and lecture classes, instructors who taught in each format reviewed the items on the final exam to ensure they were thoroughly covered. There was no significant difference (Kinney, 2001) on the final exams in Introductory Algebra computer-mediated (M = 70.12, SD = 14.57) and lecture classes (M = 70.82, SD = 16.61), $t(233)$ = .30, p = .76, or in the Intermediate Algebra computer-mediated (M = 67.19, SD = 12.26) and lecture classes (M = 68.47, SD = 11.61), $t(336)$ = 1.02, p = .31.

Pass Rates

The pass rates revealed no significant differences (Kinney, 2001). In Introductory Algebra, 81% of the computer-mediated and 78% of the lecture students passed with a grade of D or higher, χ^2 (1, N = 235) = .24, p = .63. In Intermediate Algebra, 88% of the computer-mediated and 90% of the lecture students passed the course with a grade of D or higher, χ^2 (1, N = 338) = .58, p = .45. The pass rate data excluded students who had officially withdrawn or received incompletes.

The lack of a significant difference on the final exams was not surprising. Students, whether in a computer-mediated or lecture class, must learn essentially the same content. In general, this process involves viewing a presentation of the material, asking questions as needed, and working a sufficient number of problems to develop the necessary mathematical understanding. The purpose in offering both computer-mediated and lecture classes was to provide students with a choice about how they learned mathematics. Therefore, the lack of a significant difference on the final exam scores supports the view that students can learn effectively in both instructional formats. It is worth noting that nearly all students were able to self-select into the instructional format of their choice.

Proportion of Withdrawals

In Introductory Algebra, we (Kinney, 2001) found the proportion of withdrawals from computer-mediated classes was .04 (N = 76) while the proportion of withdrawals from lecture classes was .09 (N = 206). In Intermediate

Algebra, the proportion of withdrawals from computer-mediated classes was .01 (N = 134) while the proportion of withdrawals from lecture classes was .07 (N = 252). The values of N represent the number of students enrolled at the end of the second week of classes because students can withdraw from a class during the first two weeks of the semester with no record on their transcript (Kinney). Students in lecture courses were significantly more likely to withdraw than students in computer-mediated courses according to a chi-square test, χ^2 (1, N = 210) = 7.5, $p < .01$. Data from the previous year found that an almost identical proportion (.07) of students withdrew from both computer-mediated and lecture classes. Two possible explanations for the lower proportion of students withdrawing from computer-mediated classes in the second year are improved procedures for informing students of the nature of computer-mediated instruction and changes in the computer-mediated course structure that promoted better attendance and timely completion of assignments.

Attendance

There was no significant difference (Kinney, 2001) according to t-tests in the attendance patterns between students in computer-mediated and lecture classes for each course when excluding students who had withdrawn. In Introductory Algebra, computer-mediated students attended 75.4% of classes while lecture students attended 76.4%, $t(258) = .395, p = .693$. In Intermediate Algebra, computer-mediated students attended 78.9% of classes while lecture students attended 81.2%, $t(361) = 1.29, p = .199$.

Survey Items

We obtained feedback from students through an end-of-the-semester survey and through focus groups (Kinney, 2001). The end-of-the-semester survey included the following six items related to course satisfaction, with students responding: 1 = Disagree, 2 = More disagree than agree, 3 = More agree than disagree, and 4 = Agree.

1. Overall, I enjoyed this math class.

2. This course was designed in a way that helped me learn mathematics.

3. This course has prepared me for future math courses.

4. Most of the math that I learned this semester I learned while in class.

5. The materials for this class, book and/or software, were helpful in learning the math.

6. I was satisfied with the instruction in this class.

The results, shown in Table 1, indicate that the Introductory Algebra students in computer-mediated classes were significantly more satisfied than students in lecture classes, $t(229) = 3.29, p = .001$. Similarly, Intermediate

TABLE 1

Course Satisfaction

Course	N	Mean	SD	SEM
Introductory Algebra				
Computer-mediated	65	3.52	.48	.06
Lecture	166	3.23	.63	.05
Intermediate Algebra				
Computer-mediated	120	3.51	.46	.04
Lecture	216	3.33	.48	.03

TABLE 2

Activities that Contributed to Learning Mathematics

	Computer-mediated		Lecture	
Activity	N	%	N	%
Software/lecture	101	69.7	158	36.3
Doing homework	39	26.9	227	52.2
Using the math center	1	0.7	31	7.1
Reviewing for exams	4	4.4	19	4.4

Note. Software/lecture refers to "using software" for computer-mediated classes and "listening to lectures" for lecture classes.

Algebra students in computer-mediated classes were significantly more satisfied than students in lecture classes, $t(334) = 3.39, p = .001$.

The end-of-the-semester survey also asked students about their perceptions of the activities that contributed most to their learning. Computer-mediated students were asked the following question: Which of the following activities resulted in your learning the most mathematics? Students selected from the following choices: (a) using software, (b) doing homework, (c) using the math center, and (d) reviewing for exams. For students in lecture classes, the first choice was changed to "listening to lectures."

The choices "using software" and "listening to lecture" are the primary methods of delivering the instruction in the computer-mediated and lecture formats, respectively. The results, shown in Table 2, indicated significant differences in the activities that contributed most to student learning according to a chi-square test, $\chi^2 (3, N = 580) = 51.1, p < .001$. Computer-mediated students indicated that using the software was the primary activity that resulted in learning mathematics, whereas lecture students learned mathematics primarily by doing homework.

It is interesting to note that 69.7% of the students in the computer-mediated classes indicated that they learned the most mathematics through their primary mode of instruction, which is the software. In contrast, only 36.3% of the students in lecture classes indicated that they learned the most mathematics through their primary mode of instruction, lecture. One explanation for this difference is that the software, through its use of multimedia, interactivity, and feedback, was simply more effective than lecture. Another explanation is that the software provided more opportunities for students to work problems actively in class than were provided to students in lecture classes. Thus, the computer-mediated instruction may have provided students with an opportunity to learn the content but also to work a substantial number of problems like those that are in the homework.

Next, we asked students about their confidence to succeed in math with the following item. During this semester my confidence to succeed in mathematics has: 1 = Decreased a lot, 2 = Decreased slightly, 3 = Not changed, 4 = Increased slightly, and 5 = Increased a lot. The responses from computer-mediated students ($M = 3.89$, $SD = .97$) were significantly higher, but just slightly, than those of students in the lecture classes ($M = 3.72$, $SD = .89$), $t(595) = 1.996$, $p = .046$. What was important, in our view, is that students in both formats tended to report an increase in their confidence to succeed in mathematics.

Finally, we examined students' attitudes toward mathematics with this item. During this semester my attitude towards mathematics has gotten: 1 = Much worse, 2 = slightly worse, 3 = not changed, 4 = slightly better, and 5 = much better. Students in both the computer-mediated and lecture classes reported an improved attitude towards mathematics. The responses from computer-mediated ($M = 3.71$, $SD = .95$) and lecture classes ($M = 3.72$, $SD = .88$), $t(598) = .12$, $p = .90$, showed no significant difference.

Focus Groups

Five focus groups were conducted during the last week of class with a total of 30 students from the computer-mediated classes (Kinney, 2001). Students completed a written set of questions prior to attending the focus groups. These questions served as a basis for discussion during the focus groups. Among the items discussed were the Explain and Apply sections of the software.

The Explain section introduces and explains the concepts and skills using interactive multimedia. When students were asked, "Overall, how good was the software at explaining the mathematics?" all but one student responded positively. Features that students valued were multimedia explanations that helped them understand the concepts and skills, control the pace as they navigated through the software, and get opportunities for practice and feedback within the instruction. Students who wanted more time to process the material or to take notes found being able to control the pace and being able to go back to previous instruction particularly valuable.

The Apply section contains a set of practice items that are typical of the skills and concepts covered in the Explain section. Students receive detailed feedback as they complete each item. When students were asked, "Overall, how helpful was working the Apply problems in learning how to do problems for each section?" all but two students responded positively. Several students said that they understood the material fairly well before attempting the Apply section, and therefore they did not benefit very much from working the Apply problems. Students had the option of not working the Apply problems, but most students worked them because they found the practice and feedback helpful. Also, students liked being able to practice a set of problems immediately after completing the Explain section.

Students were also asked if they thought they understood the mathematics better in a computer-mediated class than they would have in a lecture class. All 30 students who responded indicated "yes." This result was due in part to satisfaction with the software and how the computer-mediated classes were structured, but it was also due in part to considerable dissatisfaction with their experiences in high school mathematics classes. Students indicated that they enrolled in the computer-mediated classes primarily to avoid enrolling in a lecture class because of negative experiences in high school lecture classes and because they wanted more control over their learning. All participants indicated that they thought they had more control over their learning in a computer-mediated class than they would have had in a lecture class. Students also strongly recommended that we continue to assign, collect, and grade homework according to a set schedule, and give daily checkpoint questions because these encourage students to stay on task and provide feedback.

Trends in Computer-Mediated Mathematics Instruction

Technology has led to the development of new models for delivering developmental mathematics instruction. Students today have more choices in terms of where, when, and how they study mathematics. Although software is an important part of these new models, the instructor remains a vital component. The instructor must still organize the course, provide feedback to students, assess their learning, answer individual questions, and often handle technical issues.

Before examining details about various models for delivering developmental mathematics instruction using software, we will discuss two basic types of software that are used in these courses, "bolt-on" software and mediated learning software. Bolt-on software is software that was developed by publishers by combining resources that were originally designed to support students in a traditional lecture class. These resources include: (a) software for generating problems algorithmically, (b) videotapes of a teacher presenting each lesson, and (3) the textbook. These resources are typically "bolted on to" a traditional course, but do not fundamentally change how the instructor teaches or how students learn. That is, the instructor still lectures, and students take notes and ask a few clarifying questions.

The process of combining existing resources does not necessarily result in software that effectively incorporates interactive multimedia to provide complete and detailed presentations of concepts and skills or other attributes that support computer-mediated learning. This is because these resources were designed to support traditional lecture classes rather than to support mediated learning as described by Gifford (1996). Software developed from bolt-on resources is often best suited for an instructional model that includes the instructor presenting or reviewing the content during at least part of the instructional class.

Computer-mediated software, in contrast to bolt-on software, is designed from the ground up to support mediated learning as defined by Gifford (1996). In mediated learning, the student is at the center of the teaching and learning enterprise rather than the instructor. The implication for software selection is that the software must be capable of replacing the instructor as the primary vehicle for delivering the instruction. That is, the software must provide a thorough presentation of the concepts and skills, pose items for students to solve to check their understanding, and provide detailed feedback to guide students' learning. Further, the components of the lessons should be organized in a logical manner so that the navigation path is easy for students to follow. To perform these functions effectively, the software should utilize the capabilities of interactive multimedia to the extent possible and not simply move material from the printed page to the computer screen.

Instructional Models

When developing an instructional model that involves technology, it is worth considering two suggestions made by Johnstone (2002). First, the thinking and planning must start from the student's perspective. Second, plan a project that solves a problem, not one that just brings more resources into the institution. Many developmental mathematics classes taught using a form of alternative delivery, such as distance education, now use interactive multimedia software such as *Interactive Mathematics* from Academic Systems Corporation (2001) as the primary source of instruction.

There are two primary reasons for incorporating software in a course taught using an alternative delivery such as an online course. First, it is difficult for an instructor to present the content online in a manner that is effective and efficient. Because the software is capable of providing a comprehensive presentation of the content through interactive multimedia, the instructor is able to focus on answering students' questions rather than on presenting the content. The second reason for incorporating software is that it allows the students to study anywhere, anytime. This is particularly important for students whose work and family obligations make it difficult to attend regularly scheduled class meetings. It is also interesting to note that students studying mathematics perform significantly better when they are able to learn at the time of day that best suits their preferences (Callan, 1999). Callan found that the scores of students who took math tests in the morning were significantly higher than those of students who took tests in the afternoon. The most commonly used instructional models that involve technology in developmental mathematics are shown in Figure 1.

Direct instruction. We briefly consider direct instruction because it provides a frame of reference for the other instructional models. In this model the teacher and students are in the same location, and students receive instruction at the same time during the day. The instruction is synchronous because students study the same mathematics at the same moment in time because the instruction is teacher-centered. The presentation of the content is linear because in a teacher-centered classroom the instructor determines the order of the presentation of the content. Technology, other than calculators, is typically not used. Most publishers, however, include a technology component with the textbook such as a CD or a Web site. These resources may include a review of concepts and unlimited practice with skills using algorithmically-generated questions, digital videos of each lesson, and online tutorial help from a tutoring center.

Hybrid instruction. There are two basic implementations of this model. Both implementations include teacher-directed instruction for part of the class and students using software during the remaining part of class.

1. Software presents the content. In this model software that supports computer-mediated instruction presents the content through interactive multimedia during part of the in-class instructional time. For example, students may use the software 2 days per week while a third day involves teacher-directed instruction. When students use the software, they typically learn asynchronously. That is, they are learning the same content at different moments in time even though they are using the software during the same class period. The presentation of the content may be nonlinear because students are able to navigate through the software along the path of their choice.

Instruction Model	Characteristics of Each Model A. Location of teacher and student. B. Time of day when learning occurs for students in a class. C. Synchronous or asynchronous learning for students in a class. D. Teacher-centered or student-centered instruction. E. Linear or nonlinear instructional materials				
	A	B	C	D	E
1. Direct instruction	Same	Same	Synchronous	Teacher-centered	Linear
2. Hybrid instruction i. part using direct instruction	Same	Same	Synchronous	Teacher-centered	Linear
ii. part using software	Same	Same	Asynchronous	Student-centered	Nonlinear
3. Open labs supported by instructional staff	Same	Different	Asynchronous	Student-centered	Nonlinear
4. Mediated learning	Same	Same	Asynchronous	Student-centered	Nonlinear
5. Interactive television	Different	Same	Synchronous	Teacher-centered	Linear
6. Distance learning incorporating software	Different	Different	Asynchronous	Student-centered	Nonlinear

Figure 1. Instructional models in developmental mathematics.

One student, for example, may take a pretest first, while a second student may begin by studying the content in the lesson. During the time that students are using the software, the instructor is available to assist students individually or in small groups. The second component of this implementation involves teacher-directed instruction. Here the instructor may lead a whole-class discussion to address any questions that students have on the concepts or skills in the lesson. This time may also be used to have students work in groups, supplement the content in the software, or administer quizzes and exams.

2. Instructor presents the content. In this implementation the instructor presents the content. After the instructor provides an overview of the content, students use the software to develop skills and review the main concepts. This implementation provides students with the benefits of direct instruction for the presentation of the content, yet allows students greater flexibility in the

development of skills than may be possible in a traditional classroom. The software used in this model should allow students to quickly identify the skills or concepts that they are interested in studying and to access them easily.

Open labs supported by instructional staff. In this model students make use of an open lab supported by instructional staff at the times that fit their schedules. Software that supports mediated learning is appropriate for this model because students learn independently most of the time. The lab may also be used for administering quizzes and exams. Even though students have a great deal of flexibility in when and where they learn in this model, it is important that students understand the course expectations and that they are able to receive frequent feedback about their progress. Students who study mathematics through an open lab should have good study and time management skills. The open lab model is a convenient model to structure with a mastery-based approach consistent with Keller's (1968) instructional model called the personalized system of instruction.

Computer-mediated learning. Because computer-mediated instruction was discussed in depth earlier, we briefly mention several points here. First, computer-mediated instruction and lecture instruction differ on several important characteristics. The instruction in a lecture class is teacher-centered, synchronous, and linear, whereas instruction in a computer-mediated class is student-centered, asynchronous, and nonlinear. Clearly, a computer-mediated class requires that students take control of their own learning.

Second, in both computer-mediated classes and in open labs the instruction is student-centered, asynchronous, and nonlinear. Students in a computer-mediated class meet at the same time and with the same instructor, whereas students in an open lab typically meet at different times and may work with several different instructors. For developmental education students, the benefit of computer-mediated instruction is that they are able to work closely with a single instructor and with classmates during each class meeting. Further, computer-mediated classes are typically more highly structured than open labs. This can contribute to students remaining on schedule and to instructors providing more timely feedback regarding progress in the course.

Interactive television (ITV). In this model students are located either in the same classroom as the instructor or at a remote location connected through interactive television (ITV). Television cameras and microphones at each site allow the instructor and students to communicate in real time. Instruction may be supported by a projection unit that projects what the instructor writes on paper to each site, a mimeo whiteboard that captures the images the instructor writes on a whiteboard, or a computer connected to the ITV system. Hodge-Hardin (1997) conducted a study to determine if there were differences in the math achievement of students taught in an ITV class setting with the instructor present (i.e., host site), students receiving instruction via television at an off-campus location (remote site), and students taught in a traditional classroom setting. The results showed no significant differences in math achievement among the three groups, and students in both television settings had positive attitudes toward future ITV course participation.

ITV allows students to learn from various locations, yet interact with their instructor and classmates in real time. The ITV sessions may be recorded and broadcast again at a later time or reviewed by students after class. Software may effectively support an ITV class by providing students with additional instruction and practice outside of class, which may be important in part because students at a remote site may not be able to attend the instructor's office hours.

Distance learning incorporating software. Distance education courses that incorporate appropriate software can effectively meet the needs of students who desire flexibility in where and when they study mathematics. Software that supports computer-mediated learning such as *Interactive Mathematics* from Academic Systems (2001) is often incorporated because it provides a thorough presentation of the concepts and skills using interactive multimedia, detailed feedback for students' responses, and online quizzes. Also, distance education instructors often develop their own Web site to support their courses or include a Web platform such as Blackboard or WebCT to facilitate communication between students and the instructor. Many of the students who enroll in distance education courses are full-time students at the same institution that offers the distance education course. This is due in part to the flexibility that distance education offers in terms of time and location.

When designing a distance education course for developmental education students we believe it is important that the instructor: (a) selects software that supports students learning independently, (b) develops a course structure that provides flexibility yet promotes students completing the course on schedule, and (c) provides students with individual feedback and assistance as necessary. The instructor's role typically does not include presenting the content because the software is the primary vehicle for delivering the content. Not all students, however, are good candidates for distance education courses. Carr (2000) found that distance education courses often have lower completion and retention rates than classes that meet face-to-face. To assist students in determining if they are likely to have a successful experience studying through distance education, many institutions have developed questionnaires that students can complete before enrolling in a distance education course. For example, the Western Governor's University, an online institution that offers online degrees, developed an online questionnaire that provides students with immediate feedback regarding their fit for a distance education course (Western Governors University, n.d.). The questionnaire is available at http://www.wgu.edu/admissions/requirements.asp and can be accessed through the link, "Is online study for you?"

Future Directions in Computer-Mediated Learning

In the previous section we discussed a variety of instructional models that are currently used to offer developmental mathematics courses. However, software is increasingly being used in other areas too, such as: (a) technical mathematics courses; (b) preparation for the General Education Diploma (GED); (c) support for courses such as chemistry, physics, and business; and (d) workforce training.

In a technical mathematics course students study the concepts and skills of arithmetic and algebra, but they also are required to apply the mathematics to technical applications. Software such as *Academic.com* from Academic Systems (2000), which provides a brief review of the skills and concepts using interactive multimedia, can be used to support the instruction of the concepts and skills. The instructor can then focus on teaching the technical applications. Preparation for the GED, which often involves students studying independently much of the time, can be supported by software to provide a review of the relevant concepts and skills. Students who study independently often find that the interactivity of software, unlike print materials alone, helps to keep them engaged when studying.

Another area where software is increasingly being used is for support in courses that use mathematics, such as chemistry, physics, and business. Because many students enter these courses with inadequate backgrounds in mathematics, instructors are increasingly looking for ways to address this issue. In the past most instructors of these courses devoted at least some time to teaching or reviewing the necessary mathematics as it was needed. Today, however, departments or even entire colleges are providing students with access to software such as *Academic.com*, which is Web-based, so that students can review the necessary mathematics outside of class prior to the time that it is used in class. This frees up the instructor from having to cover the mathematics, but it also makes it possible for students to acquire the necessary mathematics background without having to enroll in a developmental mathematics course.

Finally, institutions or companies that provide workforce training make extensive use of software because it is a cost-effective and flexible solution. In many cases software is used to provide the fundamentals of the concepts and skills, and applications are added that are tailored to the company's specific needs.

Summary

Through our research on computer-mediated instruction we sought to understand students' learning experiences in computer-mediated classes designed for developmental education students. Our research provides evidence that for some students, computer-mediated instruction is a viable alternative to lecture, both in terms of supporting students' preferred learning styles and in effectively learning the mathematics. As technology continues to evolve, developmental educators will continue to be given both the opportunity and the challenge of developing more effective developmental education courses.

References

Academic Systems. (2000). *Academic.com* [computer software]. Bloomington, MN: Plato Learning.

Academic Systems. (2001). *Interactive mathematics* [computer software]. Bloomington, MN: Plato Learning.

Bagui, S. (1998). Reasons for increased learning using multimedia. *Journal of Educational Multimedia and Hypermedia, 7*(1), 3–18.

Becker, H. J. (1992). Computer-based integrated learning systems in the elementary and middle schools: A critical review and synthesis of evaluation reports. *Journal of Educational Computing Research, 8,* 1–41.

Bosco, J. (1986). An analysis of evaluations of interactive video. *Educational Technology, 25,* 7–16.

Callan, R. (1999). Effects of matching and mismatching students' time-of-day preferences. *The Journal of Educational Research, 92,* 295–299.

Carr, S. (2000). As distance education comes of age, the challenge is keeping the students. *Chronicle of Higher Education, 46*(23), A39–A41.

Clark, J. M., & Paivio, A. (1991). Dual coding theory and education. *Educational Psychology Review, 37,* 250–263.

Fletcher, D. (1989). The effectiveness and cost of interactive videodisc instruction. *Machine-Mediated Learning, 3,* 361–385.

Fletcher, D. (1990). *The effectiveness and cost of interactive videodisc instruction in defense training and education* (IDA Paper P-2372). Alexandria, VA: Institute for Defense Analyses.

Gifford, B. R. (1996). *Mediated learning: A new model of technology-mediated instruction and learning.* Mountain View, CA: Academic Systems.

Hodge-Hardin, S. (1997). *Interactive television versus a traditional classroom setting: A comparison of student math achievement.* Retrieved January 11, 2005, from http://www.mtsu.edu/~itconf/proceed97/hardin.html

Johnstone, S. M. (2002). Can distance-learning planners share? *Syllabus, 16*(5), 27.

Khalili, A., & Shashaani, L. (1994). The effectiveness of computer applications: A meta-analysis. *Journal of Research on Computing in Education, 27,* 48–61.

Kinney, D. P. (2001). A comparison of computer-mediated and lecture classes in developmental mathematics. *Research & Teaching in Developmental Education, 18*(1), 32–40.

Kulik, C., & Kulik, J. (1991). Effectiveness of computer-based instruction: An updated analysis. *Computers in Human Behavior, 7,* 75–94.

Mayer, R. E., & Anderson, R. B. (1991). Animations need narrations: An experimental test of a dual-coding hypothesis. *Journal of Educational Psychology, 83,* 484–490.

Najjar, L. J. (1996). Multimedia information and learning. *Journal of Educational Multimedia and Hypermedia, 5*(2), 129–150.

Niemiec, R., Samson, G., Weinstein, T., & Walberg, H. (1987). The effects of computer-based instruction in elementary schools: A qualitative synthesis. *Journal of Research on Computing in Education, 20,* 85–103.

Paivio, A. (1967). Paired-associate learning and free recall of nouns as a function of concreteness, specificity, imagery, and meaningfulness. *Psychological Reports, 20,* 239–245.

Paivio, A. (1991). *Imagery and verbal processes.* New York: Holt, Rinehart, & Winston.

Verano, M. (1987). *Achievement and retention of Spanish presented via videodisc in linear, segmented and interactive modes.* Unpublished doctoral dissertation, University of Texas, Austin, TX.

Western Governors University survey. (n.d.). Retrieved January 15, 2005, from http://www.wgu.edu/admissions/requirements.asp

CHAPTER 16

Integrating and Enabling Skill Development in a Symbolic Logic Class

Carl J. Chung

ABSTRACT

This chapter illustrates an approach to teaching students considered at risk that integrates skill acquisition and development along with regular college-level course content. Using an introductory symbolic logic course as the focal point, I distinguish three different layers of skills: content skills, general academic skills, and affective skills. By detailing specific teaching techniques from the logic course, I show how an integrated skills and content approach avoids shortcomings and questionable assumptions associated with a more traditional approach, which offers stand-alone courses in basic reading, writing, and mathematics.

A compelling case can be made that developmental education is, essentially, about helping students acquire and hone basic academic skills. For example, this includes being able to read college-level material and demonstrate understanding; being able to take notes from text or lecture; being able to write prose that is clear, effective, and meets the requirements of a given assignment; being able to engage the world of mathematics through symbol manipulation, quantitative reasoning, and translation from English to mathematical expressions and back again; and, finally, being able to manage one's time in the face of multiple commitments, including school, family, work, and friends. These examples are "skills" in the sense that they require an individual to be able to *do* something. They are "academic" in the sense that college success requires proficiency in such skills, though not exclusively so. They are also "basic" in the sense that most mainstream college students have skill sets that encompass them, while students considered at risk, for a variety of different reasons, do not.

Traditionally, developmental educators and learning assistance professionals have met the needs of students considered at risk by offering stand-alone courses in study skills, basic reading, basic writing, and basic mathematics

(Casazza & Silverman, 1996; Maxwell, 1997). More recently, stand-alone "learning-to-learn" courses have been implemented that attempt to teach higher-order thinking and self-regulation to students considered at risk (Simpson, Hynd, Nist, & Burrell, 1997). Alternatives to stand-alone course offerings have also been developed, including Supplemental Instruction, paired courses, summer bridge programs, self-paced learning labs, and learning assistance centers (Simpson et al.). Yet the growing list of alternative options for delivering help to students considered at risk has not rendered the stand-alone course model obsolete. For example, Perin (2002) summarized 1996 National Center for Education Statistics data documenting that more than 50% of community colleges offer stand-alone developmental education courses in reading, writing, and mathematics through regular academic departments. As Perin observed, "developmental education courses are the most visible form of remediation in community colleges" (p. 27).

When such stand-alone courses are required and carry no graduation credit, critics have argued that the à la carte approach is neither successful nor cost effective (Maxwell, 1997). Although particular historical contexts, institutional climates, and financial support for such programs need to be borne in mind, two main problems stand out. First, students often feel stigmatized when required to take such courses (Pedelty, 2001), which in turn leads to lower motivation and self-esteem. Second, those students needing the most help are often relegated to a whole series of such courses, thereby making little or no progress toward their long-term educational goals (Boylan & Saxon, 1998).

Another way to express the shortcomings of the stand-alone course model is to consider how it is consistent with a set of questionable assumptions, or at least assumptions that we, as developmental educators and learning assistance professionals, are moving beyond. First, the stand-alone model is consistent with a stage or hierarchical conception of skills. In other words, there are basic, regular, and advanced skills required to succeed in college, and students need the basic skills in order to acquire the regular and advanced skills. Therefore, students considered at risk cannot even attempt mainstream college coursework until they have demonstrated that they have mastered the basic skills that are prerequisites for the more advanced skills. Intuitively this seems to make good sense, but as I illustrate later, skill acquisition and skill development are more dynamic processes that turn on student motivation and the meaningfulness of the context in which they are taught.

Second, the stand-alone model assumes that basic skills transfer readily to new contexts, so that once students have acquired basic reading, writing, and mathematical skills in their developmental courses, they carry these skills with them and successfully apply them when they move on to regular college coursework. But based on my own experience as an instructor, students considered at risk, especially those with learning disabilities, often start from scratch when they find themselves in a new learning environment. It may be that students know how to do X, and even believe that they ought to do X, but nonetheless they do not do X or are unable to do X in a new context.

Third, the stand-alone model appears to subscribe to a "one size fits all" approach to helping students acquire basic academic skills. In other words, it assumes that the same course in basic reading, writing, or math will be suitable for any at-risk student. But one of the defining changes facing developmental education continues to be the influx of new students with diverse backgrounds, such as immigrants, refugees, adults, and students with a whole range of learning, psychological, and other disabilities. Offering a set of standardized, stand-alone basic skills courses might work if the target population were reasonably homogeneous, but given the increasing diversity of students considered at risk and shortcomings of the stand-alone model, exploring more holistic alternatives seems worthwhile (Roueche & Roueche, 1999).

Whatever the perceived merits or shortcomings of stand-alone courses, alternatives to this traditional approach are being explored. As Martha Maxwell put it in her 1997 revision of the classic text, *Improving Student Learning Skills*,

> As students have become more diverse, courses have become more integrated. Now paired courses such as math/physics, math/chemistry, freshman English and biology, and developmental courses combining reading, writing, and sometimes mathematics skills are offered more frequently. Basic reading, writing, and mathematics are viewed as processes, not as separate courses. (p. iii)

In this quote, Maxwell pointed to the integration of traditionally isolated learning activities. My purpose in this chapter is to illustrate another sort of integration, the integration of basic skill development with regular freshman-level course content. In particular, I describe how I have integrated and enabled basic skill development in an Introductory Symbolic Logic class that is credit bearing and fulfills the University's "mathematical thinking" requirement. My main goals are to illustrate (a) how a developmental course can address basic skill development while at the same time teaching content and more advanced skills and (b) how creating a learning environment that enables skill acquisition and development is as important as teaching the skills themselves. In addition, I explore how such an integrated skills and content model is a step in the right direction as far as the shortcomings and problematic assumptions associated with the stand-alone model.

Given that few developmental education programs offer logic courses, however, I will begin with a brief discussion of the role and value of such a course in a developmental curriculum. Although it is not appropriate for every student, a symbolic logic course offers a number of advantages over more traditional developmental mathematics offerings.

The Role of a Logic Course in a Developmental Education Curriculum

Along with a course in statistics, introductory symbolic logic is offered in the General College (GC) curriculum as an alternative way for students to fulfill their mathematical thinking requirement. The course is particularly appealing to students who have not succeeded in other math courses such as algebra. Some students have had such negative experiences in high school math that they have come to believe they are "too stupid" to understand the material, while others have failed one or more university math courses and are desperate to get this requirement out of the way to complete their coursework and graduate. Based on my experience teaching the course, I believe there are two reasons why a logic course is a useful supplement to a more traditional set of developmental math courses. First, because the vast majority of students have not had any prior experience doing symbolic logic, it is easier for them to begin with a "clean slate." Second, symbolic logic sits at the intersection of language and mathematics, and thus I can appeal to students' knowledge of language to help ground the symbols and symbolic manipulations they need to learn. This helps students feel more comfortable with the material by providing an intuitive link between language, which is familiar to them, and logic, which is not.

Basic Skill Development in an Introductory Symbolic Logic Course

In this section, I begin with a brief overview of the logic course, including course structure, learning objectives, and why I think the course has been successful with "math phobic" (Tobias, 1978) students. Next, I delineate three different skill "layers" and connect different elements of the course overview to them. Finally, I present specific teaching techniques from the course and describe how each technique contributes to the acquisition of one or more of these skill types.

Overview of the Logic Course

The main goal of any introductory symbolic logic course is to teach students formal or symbolic techniques for evaluating the underlying logical form of arguments. Focusing on the underlying form is important because it is the form that may or may not be "valid." Valid forms are truth preserving, which means that any time true statements are entered into the form, that form

ARGUMENT	SYMBOLIZATION	PROOF	
Socrates is human.	Hs	(1) Hs	A
All humans are mortal.	(x)(Hx?Mx)	(2) (x)(Hx?Mx)	A
Therefore, Socrates is mortal.	|- Ms	(3) Hs?Ms	2 UO
		(4) Ms	3,1 ?Out

Figure 1. Sample argument

guarantees a new, true conclusion. To isolate an argument's form, students learn a variety of translation conventions that result in symbolic representations of the original language. To determine whether a form is valid, a number of different formal methods are employed. Figure 1 provides an example of an argument, its symbolization, and a proof of the form's validity.

The bulk of student time is spent learning terminology, translation conventions, and proof techniques. By the end of the semester, students learn to use approximately 10 logical symbols, 15 translation conventions, and 28 or so rules of inference to use in proof construction. In addition to reading the text, working through course packet handouts, and taking notes in class, students submit weekly homework assignments, complete five in-class mini quizzes, and take three in-class examinations.

As with other mathematics courses, students often communicate their skepticism about the usefulness of learning any of this material. To motivate students to understand the usefulness and value of learning logic, I tell students that the long-term benefits go beyond the specific details of what they learn in one semester. First, just by engaging in this sort of rigorous, deductive, and analytic thinking they will stretch their brains' abilities a bit further (i.e., logic as "aerobics for the brain"). As such, they will have concrete experiences to fall back on when they encounter other formal, symbolic systems. Second, being exposed to logical translation conventions and valid patterns of reasoning can help them to evaluate arguments they encounter in other contexts more carefully, detect fallacious reasoning, and evaluate and follow complex chains of reasoning. Finally, I tell them that after I made it through my logic course in graduate school I was subsequently able to pull out the logical structure of whatever I read more easily, which helped me to identify an author's main points and arguments for those points, and I was able to structure my own thinking and writing more logically, which helped me to write better papers and earn higher grades on essay exams. In this way, I try to convince students that there are *indirect* benefits to completing the course (Chung, 2004b).

Overall, the course works well for the majority of my students, in terms of the number of students who successfully complete the course and student feedback and perceptions in the form of student evaluations and comments. I attribute a large part of this success to broader affective issues. That is, the overarching goal of the course is to give students a positive math-type experience. I want them to experience success early and build up gradually to harder material so that they gain confidence in their abilities to translate and construct proofs. I also want them to use this positive experience to broaden their conception of what it is possible for them to accomplish, whatever their educational or vocational goals.

Three Skill Layers

Three distinct skill layers lie embedded in my course overview and are worth distinguishing. I will call them content skills, general academic skills, and affective skills.

1. Content skills are the nitty-gritty, discipline-specific abilities students need to master in order to do well in a given course. In the logic course, this includes being able to translate sentences from English into symbolic notation, construct proofs, and apply definitions of rules to new or tricky situations. Content skills are what students spend the bulk of their time learning and being evaluated on in their regular college coursework.

2. General academic skills cut across disciplines and tend to be less concrete than content skills. This skill layer is best thought of as a continuum running from basic to more advanced generalizable skills. In the logic course, I consider the following to be more advanced general academic skills: being able to evaluate arguments in a range of contexts, detect fallacious reasoning and follow complex chains of reasoning with the aid of symbolic representations, read more critically, and write more cogently. I consider these more advanced because not all students will make significant progress on them; they have their hands full learning content skills. Skills such as these also require more than a semester's worth of study to master; that is, they are lifelong skills or desirable "habits of mind" (Standards for Success, 2003). What about basic general academic skills? Here we need to distinguish between, on the one hand, more generic skills such as reading texts, writing coherently, note taking, test taking, study strategies, and time management; and, on the other hand, basic mathematical skills such as symbol manipulation, quantitative reasoning, and moving between English expressions and their mathematical representations. In the logic course, students experience and are exposed to all of these except for quantitative reasoning.

3. Affective skills sound odd at first, but here I have in mind students' willingness to become more confident in their mathematical abilities, to adopt a more positive concept of self, and to be open to broadening their conception of what it is possible for them to accomplish. By calling these "skills" I

mean to highlight the fact that students need to exert what is sometimes considerable, conscious effort to overcome low confidence, negative self-concept, and a diminished sense of possibility. Although instructors cannot do this for any given student, they can, nonetheless, create a learning environment in which affective skill development is more likely to occur.

This schema of skill layers is useful in several ways. First, it helps to clarify the difference between the stand-alone and integrated skills and content approaches further. Stand-alone courses focus on the basic end of the general academic skills continuum, and would thus usually tend to downplay content skills and affective skills, the latter being handled by another course or counseling staff, for example. The integrated approach, on the other hand, acknowledges that the classroom encompasses all three skill layers simultaneously and that learning one type of skill may promote the learning of the others.

Second, the schema is useful for thinking about what students get out of our classes and what constitutes a successful learning experience. For example, some students may come to class with strong affective skills but weak basic skills. Using their affective skills as a foundation, these students could focus their energies on learning content skills and use this as a springboard for improving basic general academic skills. Other students may come to class with weak affective skills but strong basic skills. In this case, students could rely on their basic skills as a foundation, and focus their energies on learning content skills and more advanced general academic skills. Success in these latter two areas would then help them to improve their affective skills. For those students with weak affective and general academic skills, successfully acquiring content skills could also come to serve as a foundation for improving other skill areas. Success will be different for different students. For example, I have had students who have barely passed my course with a D that, because of the growth they experienced in their affective skills, I would consider successful.

Third, the schema encourages instructors to expand their repertoires to include teaching general academic and affective skills as well as content. How can instructors possibly teach such different skill types and help all students progress, regardless of their initial skill sets? One promising way is to try teaching to more than one skill layer at the same time, or creating an overall learning experience that regularly cycles through teaching content, general academic, and affective skills.

Teaching Techniques and Their Target Skills
To provide one far-from-perfected example, I now turn to some of the specific teaching techniques from my own course and explain how each one connects to one or more of the skill types.

Rapport and atmosphere. From the first day of class I try to establish a positive rapport with students and create an atmosphere in class that is welcoming, respectful, and comfortable. Although it is easy to list these desirable attributes, it is notoriously difficult to spell out how to accomplish them, because it will vary from instructor to instructor and from class to class. This may include passing out a complete syllabus that reflects time and effort, offering ample office hours, coming to class a little early and lingering a few minutes for questions, never putting down a student for asking a question, including questions you have already answered, being available for one-on-one help, and being flexible with deadlines whenever possible.

A more course-centered example is what I call the hand-switch exercise. Toward the end of my syllabus I include specific advice to help students to succeed, such as forming study groups, asking questions, and so on. I preface this list by acknowledging that students often feel anxious about doing well in a course like this, but that this is due in large part to the unfamiliarity of the material and not necessarily due to lack of "logical ability." To drive this point home, I ask each of them to take out a piece of paper, copy down a definition I put up, and imagine that their entire course grade will be determined by how quickly and how neatly they can write. The hitch is that they have to write with their opposite hand. As they copy down the definition I ask them: What does your definition look like? How does it feel to write? How do you feel about your whole grade riding on this? Students laugh, grunt, and have some choice things to say in answer. But the main point is usually also taken: students' brains may feel just as uncomfortable doing logic as their opposite hand does writing under pressure, but if they stick with it, it will get more doable. The exercise also acknowledges student anxieties, communicates that everyone is in the same boat, and presents students with the idea that if they work hard they will learn the material.

Rapport and atmosphere clearly target affective skills, but the goal is not to help students acquire or develop them at this point. Rather the goal is to convince students that affective skills are significant and that they are connected to learning, especially if students come to class with performance anxieties from previous negative experiences. In this way, rapport and atmosphere are critical because they enable and encourage students to reflect on their affective skill set and to think of affective skills as part of the learning experience.

Learning and evaluation cycles. These cycles define the overall structure of my course and serve to highlight how content and affective skill acquisition can be used to reinforce one another. Learning cycles proceed as follows: (a) instructor lectures briefly on a new concept or technique, (b) students ask questions, (c) instructor provides examples, (d) students ask questions, (e) students work another example individually or in small groups, (f) whole class discusses the example, and (g) instructor moves to another concept, and the cycle repeats. In this way, content is broken down into smaller units, and students more actively engage each new concept as it comes along. The ongoing student-instructor and student-student interactions also help students feel more confident with material because if they can work and discuss an example, then they are more likely to "know that they know."

The evaluation cycle has students read the text, come to class and participate in the learning cycle described in the last paragraph, do homework outside of class, ask questions on the homework, take an in-class mini quiz on the homework, work through a mock examination, review, and finally take an in-class examination. Again, the evaluation cycle focuses on content skills. But early on in the cycle, students are given lots of support such as instructor feedback and working with peers on homework both in and out of class, which gradually diminishes as they approach the in-class examination. The idea is that the level of offered support is inversely proportional to student understanding. By structuring the evaluation cycle in this way, students learn material in manageable steps and gradually become more confident and comfortable as they progress in the cycle (Higbee, Chung, & Hsu, 2004).

Logic "labs." Unfortunately, excellent rapport and carefully crafted learning cycles do not guarantee student understanding. Because students do not always come and get help when they need it, I also began offering logic labs to encourage more students to seek help regularly. The labs are 2-hour blocks of time scheduled away from my office. Instead of having to make an appointment, students can drop by anytime during the lab and ask questions on homework, catch up on missed material, go over material again, or just sit and work on their assignments. Often students meet peers and work together; if they get stuck, then I am there to help out. Research done by a colleague and me found that students like the informal atmosphere of the labs, benefit from meeting and working with peers, and are actually more likely to seek help because a lab was available (Chung & Hsu, in press).

Because the logic labs are informal and what happens during the lab is initiated by the needs of attending students, I have helped students with all three skill types. Most often, the focus is on content skills. But students who find themselves struggling in the course have come to lab and talked through what is not working, and then we usually end up focusing on basic skills or affective skills. Finally, some students just come by the lab to chat and check their homework answers. In some instances, these conversations naturally flow into more advanced skill development such as applying logical analysis to a puzzling quote found on a Web site or discussing arguments for or against the existence of God.

"Something different" activities. After 10 weeks of learning logic, students need a break from the routine. So for three class periods all I ask them to do is come to class and participate in small-group projects that try to demonstrate the wider value of what they have learned in class. For example, the first project requires students to form groups and read through a provocative philosophy article together. Then they work through a guided discussion project that helps them identify the author's premises, conclusion, and overall pattern of reasoning. As it turns out, the pattern is one of the first rules of inference taught in the course (If A, then B; A; therefore B). The goals of the project are (a) to give students first-hand experience applying what they have learned to a real-world example, (b) to convince them that anything they read has underlying logical structure, and (c) to show them that identifying logical structure can help clarify an author's main point and how the author goes about defending it (Chung, 2004a).

Such projects explicitly attempt to foster development of general academic skills. That is, students experience what it is like to think like a logician in a different context, they move between a philosophy text and symbolic representations of its main argument, and they can see how logical concepts and analysis can help them read more carefully and critically. Ideally, experiences like this one will also help students be more disposed to apply what they have learned in their other courses.

Sneaking in basic skill development. I have already touched on basic skill development in the discussion of the logic lab and the something-different activities, but a final word is in order given the centrality of this skill set for students considered at risk. Some readers might be surprised that more explicit attention is not given to helping students read a logic text, take notes, study, or write coherent answers on exams. Even if such help is available in logic lab, this seems insufficient. Part of the challenge here is that the majority of students firmly believe they *already* know how to do all of these things, and, in my experience, their initial reaction to explicit basic skills instruction is to be insulted. Additionally, students do not all need the same levels of help. If students end up failing the first major exam, then they are usually more open to talking about such skills, and it can be easier to initiate a conversation, but at that point they are also usually focused on their grade and what to do about it to the exclusion of anything else.

In the face of these challenges, my strategy is to "sneak in" basic skills instruction. For example, even while focusing on content skills, I occasionally have students read selected passages from the text and try to model how to pull out salient points. During lecture I pause and explain how to take good notes, how to structure and organize a notebook, and how to use it to study. As exam dates approach, I provide handouts with samples of short answers, a mock examination for practice, and I offer specific test preparation tips, such as using flash cards to help in learning translation conventions.

In addition I provide "grade trackers," in both print and electronic versions, that allow students to record their scores and calculate their current cumulative grade as work is returned. At weeks 5 and 10 I distribute updated grade trackers based on my records, and I encourage students to compare their version with mine. In this way, students know exactly how they are doing in the course, and it encourages them to monitor their progress regularly.

By describing my approach to basic skill instruction as "sneaking in," I do not mean to belittle these skills or their importance to developmental education students. In fact, I deliberately do not cover as much content as my colleagues in the philosophy department so I have the time to weave in basic skills instruction. But, based on my own experience, I have found that students do not completely lack these skills so much as they lack the disposition and knowledge of how and when to use what skills they have effectively. Students need to be reminded of the benefits of being mindful of such basic skills, and peppering them with concrete examples and tips seems to be an effective way of accomplishing this goal.

Some Evidence in Support of the Integrated Skills and Content Approach

Even though the main goals of this chapter are to characterize and exemplify the integrated skills and content approach to developmental education, readers may be wondering whether there is any empirical evidence in support of such an approach. For example, are students satisfied with the logic course as described here, and is there any evidence of metacognitive development? I have not had the opportunity to gather data that explicitly address these questions. However, the results of one end-of-semester survey and aggregate data from 4 years of student evaluations of the course offer positive, if indirect, support.

At the end of the fall 2001 semester, I administered a short five-item survey to students. The results indicated that 92% of students thought that the pace of the course was about right, and 90% thought that the amount of material covered was about right for an introductory course (N = 65). Student evaluations of the logic course between fall 2000 and spring 2004 (13 sections, N = 476) provide a range of data on student perceptions of the course. For present purposes, two items are worth highlighting. First, students were asked to rate how much they learned in the course on a seven-point Likert-type scale where 1 represented "almost nothing," 4 represented "amount expected," and 7 represented "an exceptional amount." For this item, the average student response was 6.2, with 79% of respondents choosing either 6 or 7. Second, students were asked to respond to the following statement: "Instructor stimulated me to think critically about course materials (yes/no)." For this item, 98% of students enrolled in the logic course answered "yes."

Clearly this data needs to be complemented by more rigorous studies that are comparative, longitudinal, and go beyond student perceptions. Nonetheless, the value of student perceptions should not be discounted. Overall, the data presented indicate that students are generally very satisfied with the logic course, that they are learning quite a bit, and that they believe they are being challenged to think critically.

Conclusion

In this chapter, I have provided one example of an integrated skills and content approach to working with students considered at risk. As exemplified by my logic course, such an approach attempts to integrate the instruction of content skills, general academic skills, and affective skills, thereby expanding the traditional focus of stand-alone courses on basic general academic skills. The success of my particular course hinges on two key elements: teaching techniques designed to provide meaningful learning experiences at multiple skill layers and an ongoing awareness of and attention to affective issues that foster student motivation and confidence.

The integrated approach avoids shortcomings that plague the stand-alone model. First, because students are enrolled in regular college-level classes, they are less likely to feel the same stigma associated with "pre-college" or "remedial" courses. Second, because integrated courses can earn full college credit, students are more likely to make timely progress toward their long-term educational goals.

In addition, an integrated skills and content approach embraces a more dynamic conception of skills compared to the stand-alone model. Instead of a stage conception of skills that are hierarchically related, the integrated approach views skills as interdependent, mutually enabling, and as potentially providing meaningful context for each other. For example, learning specific content skills can provide a meaningful context for the acquisition and development of general or affective skills, while for some students making progress in their affective skill set may be the key to overcoming content skill difficulties.

Also, by embedding basic skill development within the learning of regular course content, the integrated approach avoids tacitly assuming that basic skills readily transfer to new contexts. Instead, by explicitly reintroducing basic skills in each new content area, it can be argued that the integrated approach actually reinforces these skills and increases the likelihood that students will acquire and develop them.

Finally, an integrated skills and content approach does not attempt to place all students considered at risk into a standardized set of basic skills courses. Instead, this approach acknowledges that different students come to the classroom with a variety of skill sets, and it tries to construct learning experiences that will teach to multiple skill levels simultaneously. In this way, the integrated approach acknowledges and accommodates student diversity more readily.

All in all, an integrated skills and content approach does not solve all the challenges faced by developmental education professionals and, as exemplified by the logic course, it certainly does not guarantee success for every student. As part of a comprehensive developmental education curriculum, however, I believe I have shown that it is definitely a move in the right direction.

References

Boylan, H. R., & Saxon, D. P. (1998). The origin, scope, and outcomes of developmental education in the 20th century. In J. L. Higbee & P. L. Dwinell (Eds.), *Developmental education: Preparing successful college students* (pp. 5–13). Columbia, SC: National Resource Center for the First-Year Experience and Students in Transition, University of South Carolina.

Casazza, M. E., & Silverman, S. L. (1996). *Learning assistance and developmental education*. San Francisco: Jossey–Bass.

Chung, C. J. (2004a). Enhancing introductory symbolic logic with student-centered discussion projects. *Teaching Philosophy, 27*(1), 45–59.

Chung, C. J. (2004b). The impact of attendance, instructor contact, and homework completion on achievement in a developmental logic course. *Research & Teaching in Developmental Education, 20*(2), 48–57.

Chung, C. J., & Hsu, L. (in press). Encouraging students to seek help: Supplementing office hours with a course center. *College Teaching*.

Higbee, J. L., Chung, C. J., & Hsu, L. (2004). Enhancing the inclusiveness of postsecondary courses through Universal Instructional Design. In I. M. Duranczyk, J. L. Higbee, & D. B. Lundell (Eds.), *Best practices for access and retention in higher education* (pp. 13–25). Minneapolis, MN: Center for Research on Developmental Education and Urban Literacy, General College, University of Minnesota.

Maxwell, M. (1997). *Improving student learning skills: A new edition*. Clearwater, FL: H & H.

Pedelty, M. (2001). Stigma. In J. L. Higbee (Ed.), *2001: A developmental odyssey* (pp. 53–70), Warrensburg, MO: National Association for Developmental Education.

Perin, D. (2002). The location of developmental education in community colleges: A discussion of the merits of mainstreaming vs. centralization. *Community College Review, 30*(1), 27–44.

Roueche, J. E., & Roueche, S. D. (1999). *High stakes, high performance: Making remedial education work.* Washington, DC: Community College Press.

Simpson, M. L., Hynd, C. R., Nist, S. L., & Burrell, K. L. (1997). College academic assistance programs and practices. *Educational Psychology Review, 9*(1), 39–87.

Standards for Success. (2003). *Understanding university success.* Eugene, OR: The Center for Educational Policy Research.

Tobias, S. (1978). *Overcoming math anxiety.* New York: Norton.

CHAPTER 17

Teaching Thinking and Reasoning Skills in a Science Course

Leon Hsu

ABSTRACT

In this chapter I discuss the features of a physics course for which the primary goals are to sharpen students' thinking and reasoning skills and to improve their metacognitive abilities. Although physics is not a traditional part of a developmental education curriculum, the aims of the course have much in common with those of traditional developmental reading, writing, and mathematics courses. The science content helps accomplish the goals by providing an ideal context in which students can practice critical thinking skills.

As with the other chapters in this section, this chapter focuses on how one can design a content course to help students develop the skills they need to succeed in higher education. In the following pages, I describe how I am attempting to develop students' skills in both critical thinking and metacognition in the context of a university physics course.

One goal of many developmental education curricula is to raise the level at which students are able to think and reason (Pogrow, 1992). Half a century ago, a group of educators led by Benjamin Bloom developed a classification of intellectual behavior in three domains related to learning—the cognitive, affective, and psychomotor. In the cognitive domain, they described a taxonomy of educational objectives consisting of six levels of abstraction into which questions commonly asked in educational settings could be categorized (Bloom, 1956). In order of increasing complexity and sophistication, the categories were knowledge, comprehension, application, analysis, synthesis, and evaluation. The last three of these objectives comprise what are commonly referred to as "critical thinking skills." The importance of improving students' critical thinking skills is reflected in the fact that the *Journal of Developmental Education* publishes a regular column on critical thinking (e.g., Paul & Elder, 2004).

Another important goal of many developmental education efforts is to help students develop metacognitive skills (Stahl, Simpson, & Hayes, 1992).

Metacognition, literally "thinking about thinking," refers to the ability of a learner to monitor his or her own learning of new knowledge through activities such as restating the new knowledge in the learner's own words, trying to explain the new knowledge to someone else, or comparing the new knowledge to previously learned knowledge. Successful students often possess well-developed metacognitive skills, which help them to recognize situations in which they need to adjust their learning strategies or obtain further help in order to succeed (Butler & Winne, 1995).

At the General College, I teach a physics course for which the primary goals are to help students develop both critical thinking and metacognitive skills. Although taught as part of a developmental education program, the science content of the course is not remedial or watered down in any way. In fact, the same curriculum is used in courses taught in physics departments at many postsecondary institutions around the country. In the following pages, I discuss the role of a science course in a developmental education program and why science is an ideal context in which to teach such skills. I also describe the structure of my course in detail, giving specific examples of how the curriculum and the assignments contribute to fulfilling those goals.

The Role of a Science Course in a Developmental Education Curriculum

The idea of teaching a physics course as part of a developmental education curriculum is not a traditional one and may strike many readers as unusual. After all, science, especially physics, is typically considered one of the more difficult subjects in college, requiring competency in reading, writing, and mathematics. Would it not make more sense for students to hone their skills in these areas first by taking more traditional developmental courses before attempting a science course? From my point of view and that of the General College, the answer is no.

One basic reason it can be beneficial for students to take a science course such as physics right away is that the demands on students in such courses are similar to those in many other college courses that students take to earn their degree. Students must work on assignments outside of class, study for exams, come to class prepared to discuss the subject material, and learn to work productively with other students. During the semester, some students find that they are unable to complete the assignments or to understand the material on their own and must seek help from either the instructor or their peers. In a typical college course, the instructor assumes that the students are all well prepared to handle these tasks without any support, making the courses difficult for many students. However, within a developmental education program, the class can be structured to meet students at their present level and help them improve their ability to fulfill these demands.

A second reason for including a science course is that such courses can provide students with the motivation for working hard and doing well if it is a subject in which they are or become interested. Furthermore, there is evidence that learning thinking skills in the context of a content course, rather than in a course dedicated to study skills, can make it easier for students to transfer those same skills to their future courses (Anderson, Greeno, Reder, & Simon, 2000; Cobb & Bowers, 1999).

Finally, as a practical matter, including content courses such as physics as part of the curriculum for students in a developmental education program can help them to graduate more quickly. Developmental reading, writing, and mathematics courses often do not count towards graduation, and in some places they have come under attack by state legislatures (Arenson, 1998; Irving, 1995; Wessel, 1998). However, virtually all postsecondary educational institutions require students to take at least a few courses from a wide variety of fields, including science, as part of a core curriculum. A strong argument can be made for allowing a physics course, even one taught as part of a developmental education program, to count towards fulfilling the core curriculum requirements, making it possible for students to complete graduation requirements at the same time that they are acquiring the skills necessary for coping with future college courses.

Science courses offer excellent opportunities to help students develop critical thinking skills, and there is a large body of research in the science education literature about effective ways to teach such thinking and reasoning skills (Adams, 1993; Eliason, 1996; Hogan, 1999; Lawson, 1985; Zimmerman, 2000). Science is about making sense of the world and figuring out how things work from observations of real-world phenomena. This process of deducing rules from observations and of designing systematic experiments requires extensive use of the skills that make up "critical thinking." In the context of Bloom's Taxonomy of Educational Objectives (Bloom, 1956), students must *analyze* the outcomes of experiments and decide what conclusions can be drawn, and they must *synthesize* several observations to devise general rules about whole classes of phenomena. Where multiple observations provide contradictory or seemingly contradictory conclusions, students must *evaluate* the validity and quality of the observations. These types of thinking skills are useful not only in science courses, but also in almost every other course, field of study, and profession.

Science courses also provide natural opportunities for students to collaborate. Virtually all science courses with a laboratory component have students working in small groups, providing opportunities for students to get to know each other and to form social bonds. These bonds, in turn, can provide students with support networks during their first years in college and improve retention (Fullilove & Treisman, 1990).

Finally, based on responses to a survey given at the beginning of the semester in my class, about one third of the students believe that physics is a demanding subject that they will have difficulty understanding. This attitude usually stems from negative experiences in previous science courses, whether in high school or college, or from conversations with peers. However, in modern society where science and technology play a major role in every aspect of life from medical procedures to consumer electronics to the newest diet fads, it is more important than ever that citizens feel comfortable discussing and thinking about science and see it as something they can understand and make decisions about. A science course geared to the needs of its students could make great strides in giving students the skills and confidence they need to deal with the science they will encounter in their lives.

The General College Physics Course

The majority of students enrolled in the course I teach, hereafter referred to as GC 1163, are taking it to fulfill the university's core curriculum requirement for a physical science course with a lab. Between 5% and 10% of the students plan to take further courses in physics at the University of Minnesota, but they do not feel ready to jump into the physics department's own introductory course and are using the class as a warm-up. Most students are in their first year of college, with a sprinkling of second-year students.

Goals

GC 1163 is somewhat different from most science courses in that the primary emphasis is on developing students' thinking and reasoning skills. Learning science facts is secondary. In order of importance, the four main goals of the course are for students to:

1. Develop scientific thinking and reasoning skills, including the ability to make careful observations, to develop coherent and consistent explanations of how things work based on those observations, to design and conduct controlled experiments to test the validity of their explanations, and to modify those explanations to fit new data, if necessary. I have made this the primary goal because not only are such thinking skills the foundation of doing science, they are also applicable to any field in which students may be interested, whether it is a head of a company developing a business strategy based on current market trends, a doctor prescribing a treatment regimen based on a patient's symptoms, or an engineer prototyping a structure to meet a client's

requirements. In addition to the general skills of analysis, synthesis, and evaluation described earlier, scientific thinking skills include the ability to interpret and generate graphs and charts and to use proportional reasoning.

2. Develop metacognitive skills. Students will develop an explicit awareness of the study strategies they use and of the relative effectiveness of their strategies. Such knowledge can help students succeed in future courses by making them more efficient learners who are better able to monitor their own learning and to adjust their learning strategies as necessary to cope with different courses.

3. Learn that science is a process of discovery and testing in which they themselves can participate. Students taking introductory science classes tend to think that science is a collection of facts and theories discovered by "smart" people doing complex experiments and that learning science means learning those facts and theories through listening to a lecture by a person of authority (Hammer, 1994; Roth & Roychoudhury, 1994; Ryan & Aikenhead, 1992). Although this is certainly one aspect of science, I would also like students to learn that doing science means developing the best possible theories for explaining and predicting real-world phenomena based on limited and possibly imperfect evidence. Sometimes, further investigations confirm the original theories. At other times, new evidence forces a revision or reconsideration of what were thought to be well-established theories. Students often have a great fear of being wrong, but in science, it is OK to be wrong as long as your proposed ideas fit the evidence available at the time.

4. Learn some basic physics concepts. In the process of conducting experiments and developing explanations for the results, students will learn about some of the laws that govern how the universe works. However, science knowledge merely provides the context for practicing critical thinking skills. Learning as many science facts and theories as possible is not the main goal of the course. In fact, if the rote learning of science facts were the only goal, it would be far faster, easier, and cheaper to read a good book than to take a one-semester college class.

My downplaying of the science content in favor of developing thinking skills might horrify some science teachers. However, I made this decision as a result of asking myself the question "What would you like these nonscience majors, for whom this is likely the only science course they will ever take, to get out of this class?" Although it is tempting to talk about topics that I personally find very interesting and that have captured the imagination of the public such as black holes, quantum mechanics, and special relativity, I decided in the end that I wanted my students to take away the kinds of knowledge and skills that would be difficult to gain from reading a book. These include critical thinking and metacognitive skills, a knowledge of what science is and what scientists do, and a sense that they themselves are capable of performing experiments to understand the universe and the technological devices they use every day.

Curriculum

The curriculum used in GC 1163 is known as "Physics by Inquiry" (PbI; McDermott & Physics Education Group, 1996) and was created by the Physics Education Group at the University of Washington. It had been noted that students from groups underrepresented in science had a higher rate of failures and withdrawals from the standard introductory physics course than other students (Rosenquist, 1982), and PbI was developed as a preintroductory physics course to help those students succeed. Although college students taking introductory physics are usually assumed to understand basic scientific concepts such as mass, volume, and density, and to be proficient in mathematical thinking skills such as proportional reasoning, research shows that a significant number of students do not and are not, and that this lack of understanding and proficiency impedes their learning (Arons, 1990). The PbI curriculum was developed to ensure that students have a thorough grounding in these skills before enrolling in introductory physics. Even though the vast majority of the students in my class do not intend to take any more science classes, the PbI curriculum is also appropriate for the goals outlined earlier.

During the more than 2 decades of development of PbI, the Physics Education Group at the University of Washington has used pre- and posttests, as well as interviews with individual students, to gauge the effectiveness of the curriculum and to guide revisions to the activities (McDermott & Shaffer, 1993; Shaffer & McDermott, 1993). Even now, this work continues.

The textbook for the PbI curriculum is divided into several units, each addressing a different type of physical phenomenon. Some of these units are Properties of Matter, Heat and Temperature, Light and Shadows, Astronomy by Sight, Electric Circuits, and Kinematics. The text differs substantially from traditional science textbooks in that it is not meant to be read and contains very little information. Instead, it is more like a laboratory manual with instructions about experiments to perform and questions to think about in considering the results of those experiments.

Some of the questions ask students to find a pattern in their experimental results and to develop a theory that explains them or to explain the results in terms of a theory they previously developed. Other questions ask students to use their theory to predict the outcome of an experiment before performing it. Yet another type of question presents a short discussion between two or three people and asks students to evaluate the correctness of each of the statements in the discussion, which are written to reflect the common difficulties and confusions that students have. All of the questions put a great deal of emphasis on students' ability to explain physical phenomena using a mental model of how things work. Very few ask only for a factual answer. Students perform the experiments and discuss the answers to the questions in small groups.

As an example, the unit on Electric Circuits begins by asking students to light a small bulb using only a battery and a single wire and to examine arrangements of these objects that do and do not make the bulb light. Students thus develop the concept of a circuit and how a closed path is necessary to light the bulb. Students then test materials such as iron, rubber, paper, and copper to see which ones are useful for making working circuits. They also examine in detail common circuit components such as bulbs, sockets, and switches to determine how they work.

Next, students begin to build a mental model, or theory, of how more complicated circuits work. They are first given two rules for circuits that are too difficult to infer by direct experimentation at this level: (a) that there is something flowing in the wires called electric current, and (b) that the brightness of a bulb is an indicator of how much current is flowing through it. Students then connect circuits with two bulbs in two different arrangements and use the rules to judge whether the amount of current coming from the battery is the same or different as in a circuit with only one bulb. Because the answers are different than what almost all students initially think, they are challenged to reason out the answer using the given rules and the experimental evidence, rather than their own incorrect intuitions.

Subsequently, students tackle even more complex circuits, and by the end of all the activities they are capable of predicting and explaining the behavior of complicated circuits with multiple batteries and bulbs and of making quantitative calculations of currents and voltages in such circuits. In the process, students use experimental evidence to invent their own rules for determining the behavior of more complex arrangements of circuit elements and revise those rules as they try new arrangements.

After every few experiments, there is a designated checkpoint. Each group calls over a member of the course staff who checks to make sure that the experiments have been performed properly and that the group discussions have led to explanations and theories that are consistent with the results. The checkpoints are very important for insuring that the students' thinking processes are well grounded. The instructor or a teaching assistant can point out any experimental evidence that the students may have overlooked or any gaps in the students' chain of reasoning.

In summary, the PbI curriculum provides students with laboratory experiences in which students must interpret and synthesize experimental results to develop theories that can explain and predict the physical phenomena they see. By working in small groups, students simulate the process by which professional scientific investigations are conducted, advancing their own theories and checking to see that other students' theories are consistent with the experimental evidence. These activities help them to hone their thinking and reasoning skills.

Students at the University of Washington taking the PbI course subsequently passed the standard introductory physics class at rates comparable to the students who were not deemed "at-risk" by the school (Rosenquist, 1982). Since then, the course has evolved into a two-quarter sequence serving both students from underrepresented groups interested in pursuing a science or technology major and preservice elementary and secondary teachers. For the preservice teachers, this class helps students develop their scientific thinking and reasoning skills and gives them experience with an interactive hands-on curriculum. This experience is crucial because modern elementary and middle school science curricula now have substantial hands-on components. Teachers must be proficient at scientific reasoning and at using evidence to develop scientific models of how things work in order to be effective in helping their students learn.

Implementation

Because the main goal of GC 1163 is to help students improve their thinking and reasoning skills by devising their own theories and explanations from experimental evidence, the class is conducted entirely in a laboratory setting, with two 165-minute sessions each week and a short break in the middle of each session. There are no lectures because lectures would only reinforce the idea that science is a body of knowledge that is handed down from an authority. Furthermore, students cannot be expected to improve their critical thinking skills through listening to a lecture any more than they could be expected to become expert tennis players merely through attending lectures (Carey, 1986; Cooper & Mueck, 1990; Farnham-Diggory, 1992). Active practice that includes individualized guidance and feedback is crucial, and any class that teaches critical thinking skills includes such practice.

In a nontraditional class such as this, it is critically important to get students to "buy-in" to the instructional methods as early as possible. On the first day of class, I describe in detail the types of activities students will be performing in class, such as the pre- and posttests, the lack of lectures, and the emphasis on student explanations of reasoning, along with the rationales for them. In this way, students who strongly believe that lectures are the only way to learn or who dislike working in a group can transfer to a more traditional class. The students who remain understand what will be expected of them and are willing to put their time and energy into the activities.

Based on research in forming effective cooperative groups (Johnson, Johnson, & Anderson, 1983; Johnson, Johnson, & Smith, 1998; Slavin, 1983), students work in groups of three. The groups are initially formed by random selection. Approximately 4 weeks into the semester, after the first exam, the groups are shuffled according to students' performance on the exams, each group consisting of three students who scored in the upper, middle, and lower third of the class. Naturally, students are not informed of the criteria on which the groups are based. They are told only that it is good for them to learn to work with different lab partners. By forming groups in this manner, there is almost always someone in each group who has an idea of how to proceed. The weaker students can benefit from the knowledge of the stronger students, and the stronger students benefit from having to articulate their thinking to the weaker students (Heller, Keith, & Anderson, 1992). To encourage students to work cooperatively and to reduce the incidence of students freeloading off of their partners or refusing to participate, 5% of each student's grade is based on a series of both self- and peer-evaluations of his or her contribution to the group's learning. In addition, if a group's average exam score is 80% or higher, then all group members earn a 5% bonus on their individual exam scores.

Another benefit of having students work in groups is the reduction in the need for assistance from the staff, as students can answer each other's questions. Also, forming long-term groups enables students to get to know each other better than they would in a traditional class and gives them a source of social and academic support, which has been shown to be important in the retention of college students and can help insure regular attendance from each of the group members (Astin, 1993).

There are typically about 45 students forming 15 groups in the class. Because the checkpoints are intended to be performed with individual groups and can take a significant amount of time, it would be difficult for me to run the class by myself. To assist me in answering students' questions and conducting the checkpoints, I have hired undergraduate teaching assistants (TAs). Such support is not absolutely necessary, however. Instructors without TAs have been able to implement this curriculum in classes of up to 70 students by conducting the checkpoints with the entire class rather than with individual groups (Scherr, 2003). In this case, the checkpoint questions are deliberated by all of the students in the class at the same time in a discussion led by the instructor.

The TAs are students who have taken GC 1163 previously and have both done well and shown an ability to interact productively with other students. Because the primary goal of the course is for the students to improve their thinking and reasoning skills, the TAs are trained not to give students answers. Instead, they ask questions that will lead the students to reason out the answers for themselves.

Because the ability to ask such questions requires a thorough knowledge of the material and an awareness of some of the common difficulties students have, extensive training of the TAs is required. Each week I conduct a 2-hour training session for the TAs. The TAs first work through the activities that the students will be doing that coming week. Although the TAs have already taken the course, it is necessary to refresh their memories and for them to be aware of potential pitfalls or difficulties. Next, the TAs and I discuss the checkpoint questions we will ask the students, along with common misconceptions and difficulties that students have. Such preparation helps the TAs to ask good questions.

Pedagogy

The pedagogy of the class is based on the cognitive apprenticeship model (Brown, Collins, & Duguid, 1989; Collins, Brown, & Holum, 1991). In this paradigm, students learn cognitive skills in the same way that apprentices learn a trade from a master. As will be described in the following paragraphs, the crucial elements of a cognitive apprenticeship are modeling, scaffolding, fading, and coaching.

In a traditional master-apprentice relationship, modeling occurs when the master demonstrates the work to be done to the apprentice. In GC 1163, one type of modeling occurs during the first and last 15 minutes of each class. During these times, a short "Question of the Day" (QoD) is presented for the students to answer. The QoD deals with material that students have previously encountered and functions either as a warm-up at the beginning of class to get students into a science frame of mind, or as a wrap-up at the end of class of what they have just learned. After the students' answers to the question are collected, I model the problem-solving process by demonstrating how one can solve the problem. The critical feature of this modeling is that I make the thought processes involved in answering the question explicit, showing students how to solve such problems in general, rather than simply getting the answer to one particular question.

As an example, a problem might ask students to predict the relative brightnesses of the bulbs in a complicated electric circuit. In demonstrating how to solve this problem, I would show the students how they can use the rules they developed in class to trace the path of the electric current through the circuit and determine which bulbs would receive the greatest amount of current. This would give students a way to determine bulb brightnesses not only in the circuit in question but also in any other circuit they may encounter.

A second type of modeling, peer-modeling, also takes place in GC 1163. In class, students observe the other members of their group presenting their explanations for the experiments or their answers to the questions in the textbook. Outside of class, students may observe each others' reasoning processes while working on homework problems.

Scaffolding is the help that an apprentice receives while practicing a task, and fading is the gradual withdrawal of that help, forcing the apprentice to work more independently. Coaching refers to the guidance and feedback the apprentice gets throughout the training process. During the class, all three of these functions are accomplished as the students work on the activities with their groups and receive help from peers and the course staff. As students perform the activities, they discuss the results of their experiments and the answers to the questions posed in the text with the other members of their group. Because the questions in the text almost always demand that students explain the reasoning behind their answers, the students are forced to make explicit the thinking processes by which they arrived at their answer. The other group members then evaluate the proposed answers and explanations. If a group is stuck, a staff member helps by asking questions that lead the students to discover the answer for themselves. The questions serve to bridge the gap between the group's current state of knowledge and the correct answer by reducing the size of the logical steps the students must take. In addition, during each checkpoint one of the course staff reviews the material with each group by asking the students to explain key results from that section and posing further questions about related hypothetical situations. The student-student and student-staff interactions constitute the scaffolding and coaching. As the course progresses, the students are expected to have improved their thinking abilities, and the staff may ask more difficult questions or give the students hints that require more thinking. This is the fading process. Ultimately, of course, students must be able to answer questions on an exam on their own.

Addressing Class Goals

All of the activities in which students engage during class are designed to help them meet the four class goals outlined previously. The connections between the assignments and the goals are made explicit to students in order to help them focus on the knowledge and skills they should be gaining from an assignment, rather than on simply completing it. The course assignments that support each of the four goals are described in the following paragraphs.

Learning scientific thinking and reasoning skills. Students accomplish this goal principally through performing the experiments and discussing the results and questions from the text with their lab partners and the course staff. The problems on homework assignments, tests, and QoDs reinforce the importance of critical thinking skills by constantly asking students to explain the reasoning by which they arrived at their answer. Furthermore, students keep careful notebooks of their class work, and they are always allowed to use these notebooks while doing homework and taking the exams. Doing so places the emphasis on being able to write logical and experimentally-justified explanations on essay-type exam questions, rather than on memorizing facts or outcomes to specific experiments. Finally, homework and exam questions often present situations that the students have never encountered before, but which they can analyze successfully if they apply the rules they have devised.

In the grading of exams, much weight is placed on the explanation that students give. A correct answer that is accompanied by a poor explanation will receive less credit than a wrong answer that is explained well and has only minor mistakes in the reasoning process.

Developing metacognitive skills. There are two mechanisms by which students learn to monitor and reflect on their learning. The first is through a series of journals. Each week, students are required to submit a journal entry in response to some specific questions. These questions ask students to reflect on the assignments in the class, the study strategies they are using, and the effectiveness of their study habits. To encourage students to generate well-considered responses, these journals are graded subjectively by me on the amount of thoughtfulness displayed. Responding to these questions can help students to become aware of how they learn and to realize what strategies are most and least effective for them.

For example, in a journal entry early in the semester, students reflect on how they are coming to learn the material in GC 1163:

1. Name an important concept you have learned in sections 1, 2, or 3. Why do you think this concept is important?

2. How did you learn the concept? Was it because the instructor told you about it, or did you learn it through performing a particular experiment? If so, what experiment was it?

3. Were discussions with your group partners useful in learning the concept?

A couple weeks later, I ask students to reflect on the class assignments:

The assignments in this class are homework, exams, exam revisions, pretests, posttests, Questions of the Day, and journals.

1. Which of these help you to understand physics concepts better?

2. Although the journal items have not been directly related to physics concepts, have they helped to get you thinking about how you learn the concepts and how best to approach this course?

3. Has having pre- and posttests for each section helped you to internal-

ize the concepts you are learning? Do you see any advantage in having pretests at the start of every section?

Near the end of the course, I ask students to synthesize what they have learned by reflecting on their study habits:

> Suppose that you were explaining to your friend Diana, a student just like you (with the same ability and intelligence) who is thinking of taking GC 1163, exactly what is expected and how to understand what is happening in class. She wants to know what she should do and how to study for the class in order to be able to learn best. Diana really wants to understand the material and does not care too much about her grade, as long as she can pass.

If students do not object, I post their submissions anonymously on the class Web site so interested students can see the wide range of points of view held by their peers. In addition, if a student's response piques my interest in some way, I will respond to a student by e-mail.

A second way in which students reflect on their learning is through an evaluation of their group and the roles they play in their group members' learning of the material. Approximately once per week, time is set aside for students to discuss their group's strengths and weaknesses and to evaluate each member's contributions to the group's learning. Some questions they discuss are:

1. Have you had any experience in working in groups in your other classes? Is the group work in this class any different from the group work in other classes?

2. What are some ways in which your group functions well?

3. What are some changes that could be made to improve how well the members of your group learn?

4. What are some things each group member could do to help the functioning of the group?

5. What do you like best about your group?

Affecting students' attitudes and epistemologies of science. The grading scheme and emphasis on thinking and reasoning in GC 1163 are designed to give students a more realistic sense of science. Because paramount importance is placed on the ability to draw conclusions and to develop explanations that are based on and consistent with experimental observations, students' theories that differ from the accepted ones, but that are consistent with observations, are considered correct and receive full credit.

Many students are initially uncomfortable with this way of learning science and dislike the fact that the instructor and TAs will not simply tell them the right answer. However, this policy has three advantages:

1. Because students are forced to develop their own explanations and theories, they are likely to remember them better and to use them more spon-

taneously. The mental processing students perform to devise a theory is much deeper than if they had simply read or been told about it.

2. Students see that they can do science and develop for themselves the same scientific principles and laws that they have read about in textbooks. The process by which those laws were discovered is no longer mysterious.

3. It becomes clear to the students that, as in real science, any testable theory that fits the experimental evidence must be taken seriously.

Situations in which an incorrect explanation is consistent with the experimental results are relatively rare, however. Over the more than 20 years of development of the PbI curriculum, the experiments have been carefully designed so that ordinarily, students cannot help but arrive at the commonly accepted theories. Although alternative explanations might work during the early sections of a unit, students soon gather additional experimental evidence that forces them to modify their theories to resemble the established ones. However, it is important to note that it is the students themselves who direct the development of their theories using experimental evidence and not the course staff or some other figure of authority.

Learning science content. When students first enroll in an introductory science course, they often have ideas that are very different from those of practicing scientists (Halloun & Hestenes, 1985; McCloskey, 1983). Much research has shown that these initially held ideas are highly resistant to change, making learning new concepts that conflict with them very difficult (Dykstra, Boyle, & Monarch, 1992). This is particularly true when trying to help students learn concepts in such a way that they can be applied flexibly to a wide variety of situations, and not just parroted back as a simple definition or law. Simply presenting students with new knowledge through a lecture or having them read a textbook has been found repeatedly to be an inefficient mode of learning for the vast majority of students (Hake, 1998).

The method by which students learn new concepts in GC 1163 is based on the conceptual change theory of Posner, Strike, Hewson, and Gertzog (1982), which stated that the replacement or modification of students' initial nonscientific conceptions can only occur when students (a) become dissatisfied with their initial ideas, (b) explore possible alternatives, and (c) choose an alternative that fits their needs.

Before starting each section within a unit, students take a pretest consisting of questions dealing with material from that new section. Naturally, the students are not expected to be able to answer the questions correctly. In fact, students usually answer them incorrectly because the questions are specifically chosen to address common misconceptions they have before learning the new material. However, the questions are always posed in such a way that they can be understood and answered by the students. The students then work through the new section. As mentioned previously, many of the questions in the textbook ask students to make predictions about situations that they have never encountered before setting up those situations and observing the actual result. Both of these mechanisms, pretests and predictions, are designed to elicit students' ideas about science and to make students articulate them explicitly. After performing the experiment, if the students find that their initial ideas lead them to an incorrect prediction, then they become dissatisfied with those ideas.

Next, students discuss alternative ideas with their peers, and these ideas can be evaluated based on how well they fit the observations. Finally, the group chooses an idea that it thinks works best. During this process, the role of the instructor and TAs is merely to facilitate the thinking process and to help the students brainstorm lines of thought. It is not to advocate one idea over another or to tell students which idea is "right." Further experiments might confirm a group's ideas or show the students that further modifications to their theories are necessary.

After each section, the students return to their pretest and revise their answers. This serves both to help solidify the students' new ideas in their minds and also to provide the students with evidence that they are learning.

Assessment

I have used several methods of assessment for GC 1163 to evaluate how well the course is meeting its goals and also to obtain guidance in improving the course. Because the course has been taught only for a few semesters using this curriculum, the data is still limited.

One type of assessment is to measure student satisfaction with the course. Although student satisfaction is not necessarily correlated with how effectively the course goals are being met, it is important in the sense that if the course is unpopular, only a few students will enroll, and it may not continue to be offered. I measure student satisfaction using three techniques. The first is by the Student Evaluation of Teaching forms. These evaluations, which are completed near the end of each semester and are similar to the student evaluations at hundreds of other universities and colleges, allow students to give anonymous individual feedback about the course by either writing comments or rating some standard items such as "Instructor's knowledge of the material" or "Instructor's respect and concern for students" on a seven-point Likert-type scale.

A second technique for getting feedback on student satisfaction is through the weekly journals. In addition to helping the students develop metacognitive skills, the weekly journals provide an avenue for students to give me feedback about how the course is going for them. For example, one of the journals asks the students if they think that the exam questions have been fair and if not, which one was the most unfair and why. As was mentioned previously, I respond to the students' submissions by e-mail if it seems appropriate.

The third technique used to obtain student feedback is called Small-Group Instructional Diagnosis (SGID; Coffman, 1991). In SGID, a staff member from the university's Center for Teaching and Learning comes to the class and conducts a 30-minute focus group with the students. The session is conducted without any of the course staff present so students feel comfortable voicing their opinions. The students first meet in small groups that are different from the ones they normally work in during the class to make lists of features that they like about the course and those they feel should be changed. A whole-class discussion is then held to find items of both types on which there is a consensus. This kind of evaluation allows the instructor to identify strengths and weaknesses of the course that a large proportion of the class agrees upon, rather than just the feelings of what might be a very vocal minority. SGID also gives students a chance to hear what other students think of the class.

Thus far, the vast majority of students who have taken the course are happy with it. Consistently, more than 95% of the students completing the anonymous university course evaluation forms respond positively to the statements, "Instructor stimulated me to think critically about the course material" and "I would take another course with this instructor." Often cited as strengths on the evaluations are the fact that students interact extensively with their peers and get to know them well, that they enjoy the hands-on learning, and that they appreciate and find helpful the individual attention they get from both the instructor and the TAs. The journals have also allowed me to see to some extent how student attitudes towards science have changed. Last semester, out of 43 responses to a question on how their attitudes towards science had changed from the beginning of the course to the end, 32 students reported having a better attitude, and 11 students reported no change. Some responses typical of the students who reported an improved attitude were:

> Before I took this class I was deathly afraid of physics. I had heard so many horror stories about how hard the material was and how the tests were so difficult. Now that I have experienced this course my attitude has changed. Sure it was difficult for me at times to understand the material, but it is all a part of learning. I am glad that I had the opportunity to take the course in the style it was presented in.
>
> I didn't take physics in high school because I was told it was really hard by everyone, which scared me away since I'm terrible at science. Now I know that physics isn't all about math, it's about learning the way things work. To me, that is much more interesting.

To assess whether students have improved their scientific thinking skills, I have used Lawson's (1978) Test of Scientific Reasoning. Each semester, I have given the test on both the first and last day of class. The difference between students' pre- and posttest scores has been statistically significant but small, going from an average of 12 to 14.5 questions answered correctly on the 24-question test. One confounding factor in using this test is that it was originally developed for use in a biology class, and many of the questions are posed in a biology context. Because some transfer of thinking skills from a physics to a biology context is required, the interpretation of the results of this test is not straightforward. Individual interviews with students will be necessary to obtain more detailed information about their reasoning abilities.

An instrument I have used to measure the affective impact of the curriculum is the Rotter (1966, 1990) Internal:External Locus of Control scale. This is a survey developed to assess to what extent students believe they have control over events in their lives. Students with an internal locus of control generally believe that their own actions play a large part in what happens to them (e.g., that their grade in a class depends on how much effort they put into the class), and this is considered desirable (Thomas, 1980). Thus far, no significant differences have been observed on this scale when giving the survey at the beginning and end of the semester. However, research has shown that students' attitudes are context-dependent, and the questions posed in an everyday nonscience context on the Rotter survey may not accurately reflect students' attitudes in a science class (Hofer & Pintrich, 1997). It may be necessary to use other surveys that pose similar questions in a science context such as the Epistemological Beliefs Assessment for Physical Science (Elby, n.d.).

Adaptability of the Course Model

Although the topic of this chapter has been a science course, there is no reason why many of its techniques and philosophies could not be implemented in other courses as well. Evidence-based reasoning, regardless of whether that evidence is a laboratory experiment, the events of history, market data, or the writings of an author, is the cornerstone of practice in all fields. With the increasing popularity of problem-based and case-based learning, resources abound to help instructors in all fields incorporate activities designed to help students practice thinking and reasoning skills into their classes (Rhem, 1998). Such activities can also give students a better understanding of what it means to work in a given field than simply reading about it from a textbook. Similarly, the activities designed to help students reflect on their learning and improve their metacognitive abilities through journal writing could be adapted to any class without much modification.

The most difficult part of the course to adapt, especially to large classes, is the interactive aspect in which students discuss ideas with their peers. However, such interaction is becoming increasingly valued in science classes of all types and techniques have been developed for fostering peer interaction in large lecture classes. For example, Mazur (1997) and Adams and Slater (2002) discussed how they implemented group activities in their 200-student classes.

Summary

Science courses can play an important role in a developmental education curriculum by providing a content course for developing students' reasoning and metacognitive skills. Although the emphasis I have chosen to place on such skills means that my course cannot address as many different topics as a "mile-wide, inch-deep" survey course for nonscience majors, I think that ultimately, my students are better served by practicing critical reasoning skills they can apply outside of science, experiencing the process of doing science by constructing theories based on experimental evidence to explain and predict real-world phenomena, and reflecting on the different activities in which they engage to learn new knowledge. These are skills that should serve them well not only in their future college courses, but in their life beyond their formal education.

References

Adams, D. L. (1993). Instructional techniques for critical thinking and lifelong learning in science courses. *Journal of College Science Teaching, 23,* 100–104.

Adams, J., & Slater, T. (2002). Learning through sharing: Supplementing the astronomy lecture with collaborative-learning group activities. *Journal of College Science Teaching, 31,* 384–387.

Anderson, J. R., Greeno, J. G., Reder, L. M., & Simon, H. A. (2000). Perspectives on learning, thinking, and activity. *Educational Researcher, 29*(4), 11–13.

Arenson, K. W. (1998, May 7). Pataki-Giuliani plan would curb CUNY colleges' remedial work. *New York Times,* p. A1.

Arons, A. B. (1990). *A guide to introductory physics teaching.* New York: Wiley.

Astin, A. W. (1993). *What matters in college: Four critical years revisited.* San Francisco: Jossey-Bass.

Bloom, B. S. (Ed.). (1956). *Taxonomy of educational objectives: The classification of educational goals.* New York: Longman, Green.

Brown, J. S., Collins, A., & Duguid, P. (1989). Situated cognition and the culture of learning. *Educational Researcher, 17*(1), 32–42.

Butler, D. L., & Winne, P. H. (1995). Feedback and self-regulated learning: A theoretical synthesis. *Review of Educational Research, 65,* 245–281.

Carey, S. (1986). Cognitive science and science education. *American Psychologist, 41,* 1123–1130.

Cobb, P., & Bowers, J. (1999). Cognitive and situated learning perspectives in theory and practice. *Educational Researcher, 28*(2), 4–15.

Coffman, S. (1991). Improving your teaching through small-group diagnosis. *College Teaching, 39,* 80–82.

Collins, A., Brown, J. S., & Holum, A. (1991). Cognitive apprenticeship: Making things visible. *American Educator, 15*(3), 6–11, 38–46.

Cooper, J. L., & Mueck, R. (1990). Student involvement in learning: Cooperative learning and college instruction. *Journal on Excellence in College Teaching, 1,* 68–76.

Dykstra, D. I., Boyle, C. F., & Monarch, I. A. (1992). Studying conceptual change in learning physics. *Science Education, 76,* 615–652.

Elby, A. (n.d.). The idea behind EBAPS. Retrieved June 7, 2004, from http://www2.physics.umd.edu/~elby/EBAPS/idea.htm

Eliason, J. L. (1996). Using paradoxes to teach critical thinking in science. *Journal of College Science Teaching, 15,* 341–344.

Farnham-Diggory, S. (1992). *Cognitive processes in education* (2nd ed.). New York: Harper Collins.

Fullilove, R. E., & Treisman, P. U. (1990). Mathematics achievement among African American undergraduates at the University of California, Berkeley: An evaluation of the mathematics workshop program. *Journal of Negro Education, 59,* 463–478.

Hake, R. R. (1998). Interactive-engagement versus traditional methods: A six-thousand-student survey of mechanics test data for introductory physics courses. *American Journal of Physics, 66,* 64–74.

Halloun, I. A, & Hestenes, D. (1985). Common sense concepts about motion. *American Journal of Physics, 53,* 1056–1065.

Hammer, D. (1994). Epistemological beliefs in introductory physics. *Cognition and Instruction, 12,* 151–183.

Heller, P., Keith, R., & Anderson, S. (1992). Teaching problem solving through cooperative grouping. Part 1: Groups versus individual problem solving. *American Journal of Physics, 60,* 627–636.

Hofer, B. K., & Pintrich, P. R. (1997). The development of epistemological theories: Beliefs about knowledge and knowing and their relation to learning. *Review of Educational Research, 67,* 88–140.

Hogan, K. (1999). Thinking aloud together: A test of an intervention to foster students' collaborative scientific reasoning. *Journal of Research in Science Teaching, 36,* 1085–1109.

Irving, C. (1995). A line in the sand. *Crosstalk, 3*(3), 20.

Johnson, D. W., Johnson, R., & Anderson, D. (1983). Social interdependence and classroom climate. *Journal of Psychology, 114,* 135–142.

Johnson, D. W., Johnson, R., & Smith, K. (1998). *Active learning: Cooperation in the college classroom.* Edina, MN: Interaction.

Lawson, A. E. (1978). The development and validation of a classroom test of formal reasoning. *Journal of Research in Science Teaching, 15,* 11–24.

Lawson, A. E. (1985). A review of research on formal reasoning and science teaching. *Journal of Research in Science Teaching, 22,* 569–618.

Mazur, E. (1997). *Peer instruction: A user's manual.* Upper Saddle River, NJ: Prentice-Hall.

McCloskey, M. (1983). Naïve theories of motion. In D. Gentner & A. Stevens (Eds.), *Mental models* (pp. 229–324). Hillsdale, NJ: Erlbaum.

McDermott, L. C., & Physics Education Group. (1996). *Physics by inquiry: An introduction to physics & the physical sciences.* New York: Wiley.

McDermott, L. C., & Shaffer, P. S. (1993). Research as a guide for curriculum development: An example from introductory electricity. Part I. Investigation of student understanding. *American Journal of Physics, 60,* 994–1003; erratum (1993), *61,* 81.

Paul, R., & Elder, L. (2004). Critical thinking . . . and the art of close reading (Part II). *Journal of Developmental Education, 27*(3), 36–37.

Pogrow, S. (1992). A validated approach to thinking development for at-risk populations. In C. Collins & J. N. Mangieri (Eds.), *Teaching thinking: An agenda for the 21st century* (pp. 87–101). Hillsdale, NJ: Erlbaum.

Posner, G. J., Strike, K. A., Hewson, P. W., & Gertzog, W. A. (1982). Accommodation of a scientific conception: Toward a theory of conceptual change. *Science Education, 66,* 211–227.

Rhem, J. (1998). Problem-based learning: An introduction. *National Teaching & Learning Forum, 8*(1), 1–4.

Rosenquist, M. L. (1982). *Improving preparation for college physics of minority students aspiring to science-related careers: Investigation of student difficulties and development of appropriate curriculum.* Unpublished doctoral dissertation, University of Washington, Seattle.

Roth, W. M., & Roychoudhury, A. (1994). Physics students' epistemologies and views about knowing and learning. *Journal of Research in Science Teaching, 31,* 5–30.

Rotter, J. B. (1966). Generalized expectancies for internal versus external control of reinforcement. *Psychological Monographs, 80* (Whole No. 609).

Rotter, J. B. (1990). Internal versus external control of reinforcement: A case history of a variable. *American Psychologist, 45,* 489–493.

Ryan, A. G., & Aikenhead, G. S. (1992). Students' preconceptions about the epistemology of science. *Science Education, 76,* 559–580.

Scherr, R. (2003). An implementation of Physics by Inquiry in a large-enrollment class. *Physics Teacher, 41,* 113–118.

Shaffer, P. S., & McDermott, L. C. (1993). Research as a guide for curriculum development: An example from introductory electricity. Part II. Design of an instructional strategy. *American Journal of Physics, 60,* 1003–1013.

Slavin, R. (1983). *Cooperative learning.* New York: Longman.

Stahl, N. A., Simpson, M. L., & Hayes, C. G. (1992). Ten recommendations from research for teaching high-risk college students. *Journal of Developmental Education, 16*(1), 2–4, 6, 8, 10.

Thomas, J. (1980). Agency and achievement: Self-management and self-regard. *Review of Educational Research, 50,* 213–241.

Wessel, D. (1998, November 9). Who will teach Johnny to read? *Wall Street Journal* (Eastern edition), p. A1.

Zimmerman, C. (2000). The development of scientific reasoning skills. *Developmental Review, 20*(1), 99–149.

CHAPTER 18

Reading, Writing, and Sociology? Developmental Education and the Sociological Imagination

Heidi Lasley Barajas and Walter R. Jacobs

ABSTRACT

Disciplines such as sociology have not traditionally participated in the developmental education field. Our experience as sociologists working with developmental education professional associations and educators found a particular focus on the three basic skill areas of reading, writing, and mathematics. Beyond identifying sociology as a discipline not manifestly concerned with developmental issues, we have noted that entering the developmental education field has been challenging because a limited focus on reading, writing, and math as skills rather than as disciplines has historically tied the field to a definition of *who* is developmental. However, developmental education is now also concerned with the generation of discipline-specific learning strategies that support the academic progress of all postsecondary learners, at all levels of the learning continuum. This chapter uses the sociology-specific learning strategies of "Universal Design for Learning" and "the sociological imagination" to provide general developmental opportunities and address a wide range of access issues.

Developmental educators have to make choices about teaching. In fact, we often spend research as well as teaching time making choices about teaching. No matter where we are teaching, in a large urban setting, in rural areas, or in suburbia, we often make choices that attempt to meet the needs of a variety of student learners as well as support the particular theoretical and philosophical approach we bring to the classroom. However, our experience as sociologists working with developmental education professional associations and educators found a particular focus on the three basic skill areas of reading, writing, and mathematics. In addition, we have experienced some surprise on the part of both developmental education associations and educators that disciplines other than reading, writing, and mathematics are developmental in nature. Why would this be?

There are three obvious answers to this question. First, developmental education historically is based in a theoretical foundation that promoted skill building by assessing individual students' skill deficiencies in reading, writing, and mathematics. Even with recent attempts by the National Association for Developmental Education (NADE; 1995) to reexamine the definition and guiding principles of developmental education, Lundell and Collins (1999) asserted that

> as a profession, we operate from an assumption that students or their home environments must be "fixed," that the students served in our programs or their families or their neighborhood are in some way pathological when seen against an imagined "healthy" norm. (p. 6)

In other words, we are tied to a historic definition of *who* is developmental. However, if we were to look seriously at the overall deficiency of students, regardless of their status as participants in developmental programs, our assessment might be a lack of critical thinking skills in all academic areas, something lacking in the majority of students in higher education. Such an observation seriously challenges a focus on the individual student, particularly when not limited to three academic areas.

Second, developmental educators may not think beyond the three basic skill areas because as an academic focus other disciplines such as sociology have not traditionally participated in or attempted to broaden the developmental field. Although sociologists may have assembled courses that are "developmental" in nature—that is to say, courses that develop thinking and learning skills—they may not think of it in those terms. Mainstream sociology is concerned more with explaining the abstract forces that structure students' lives rather than developing students' individual skills in negotiating these powerful forces.

Third, higher education tends to link the educational needs of diverse student groups to additive "remedies" that, in general, do little to assuage the needs of diverse students (Moore, 2002). Although relatively new in application to higher education classrooms, an alternative to additive remedies does exist. Some of the most dynamic ideas about the relationship of student learning and the curriculum appear in the research and application of Universal Instructional Design (Silver, Bourke, & Strehorn, 1998). Universal Instructional Design (UID) emerged from the architectural concept "universal design" that emphasizes meeting the accessibility needs of people with disabilities in both public and private spaces by developing "comprehensive plans that would be attractive to all the individuals who use that space" (p. 47). In like manner, Silver et al. stated that universal design strategies also apply to the development of postsecondary instructional design accommodations formally set aside for students with a variety of disabilities. Rather than focusing on modifying instructional approaches on a case-by-case basis, UID encourages instructors to concentrate on developing instructional strategies that "most students can use to gain knowledge and skills related to the specific content areas" (p. 48). In other words, UID suggests accessibility issues are an integral part of instructional development, and accessibility benefits multiple students in multiple ways.

The problem for diverse student groups is that an assumed element of educational spaces is neutrality (Barajas, 2000, 2002; Eliasoph, 1999; Feagin, Vera, & Imani, 1996; Moore, 2002). Therefore, the current "universal" design of the classroom is normalized in terms of race, class, gender, language, and physical ability to mean middle-class, White, male, English speaking, with no physical or psychological challenges. For this reason, the definition of UID, in most cases applied to students with disabilities, benefits from the expanded concept presented by the Center for Applied Special Technology (CAST) definition of universal design for learning (UDL):

> The central practical premise of UDL is that a curriculum should include alternatives to make it accessible and appropriate for individuals with different backgrounds, learning styles, abilities, and disabilities in widely varied learning contexts. The "universal" in universal design does not imply one optimal solution for everyone. Rather, it reflects an awareness of the unique nature of each learner and the need to accommodate differences, creating learning experiences that suit the learner and maximize his or her ability to progress.

This definition of universal design is more inclusive than previous definitions that focus on only those with disabilities. The accommodation of "differences" takes on an expanded meaning allowing us to consider other kinds of differences, such as race, class, and gender differences that have traditionally suffered in terms of access issues (Barajas & Higbee, 2003). How, then, can the premise of UDL facilitate expanding our understanding and application of developmental education?

As often happens in our attempts to expand our research and practices, we tend to look for the theoretical holes in existing definitions and practices. However, a review of the "Definition and Goals Statement" (1995) created by the National Association for Developmental Education also reveals similarities in the definition of UDL and the definition of developmental education. For example, principles within the NADE definition may also be useful to consider in the evolution of sociology as a developmental course.

> Developmental Education is a field of practice and research within higher education with a theoretical foundation in developmental psychology and learning theory. It promotes cognitive and affective growth of all post-secondary learn-

ers, at all levels of the learning continuum. Developmental Education is sensitive and responsive to the individual differences and special needs among learners. Developmental Education programs and services commonly address preparedness, diagnostic assessment and placement, affective barriers to learning, and development of general and discipline-specific learning strategies.

The similarities between UDL and developmental education principles are important. Both address postsecondary learning needs. Both promote responsibility to all postsecondary learners. Both advocate attention to discipline-specific learning as well as general learning. Some tensions also exist when considering the specifics of NADE principles and the more universal approach of UDL. For example, NADE grounds the practice and research of developmental education in developmental psychology, which could be perceived as a tension when integrating developmental concepts into disciplines such as sociology. Sociology was established as a discipline because it identified influences external to the individual as fundamental in understanding individual behavior. However, it is this very point that requires consideration in the integration of sociology, developmental education, universal learning design, and a diverse student population.

Sociology as Developmental, Universally-Designed Instruction

As instructors in the discipline of sociology, we know that we develop our courses through the curriculum we teach, the choice of materials, and the order and focus of the goals and objectives. We also develop our courses in terms of how we present the material and consider what kinds of experiences with the material will most significantly provoke student learning. Specifically, we strive to develop students' ability to connect abstract concepts with observable phenomena. We do this for a specific reason: our goal, as Bourdieu (1993) suggested, is to keep people from uttering all kinds of nonsense about the social world. To accomplish this goal, students must push through their taken-for-granted, common-sense ideas about the social world to reveal the history that makes the social world function in particular ways, and the processes that sustain or challenge those functions. However, connecting the abstract to the empirical is a skill that is developed, and one that can be developed simultaneously with reading and writing skills. We approach this developmental method through C. Wright Mills' (1967) concept of "the sociological imagination."

Mills framed the sociological imagination in the notion that people, when considering their personal troubles, seldom look to explanations outside of the individual. According to Mills, individual social actors rarely connect what is happening in an individual life to history, historical change, and institutions within society. As Mills (1967) stated:

> The sociological imagination enables its possessor to understand the larger historical scene in terms of its meaning for the inner life and the external career of a variety of individuals. It enables him [or her] to take into account how individuals, in the welter of their daily experience, often become falsely conscious of their social positions. Within that welter, the framework of modern society is sought, and within that framework the psychologies of a variety of men and women are formulated. By such means the personal uneasiness of individuals is focused upon explicit troubles and the indifference of publics is transformed into involvement with the public issues. . . . The sociological imagination enables us to grasp history and biography and the relations between the two within society. (pp. 5–6)

Constructing a course based in the sociological imagination is more than a "best practices" phenomenon. It requires understanding the theoretical implications of treating all students as developing sociologists, able to identify their own social location in a historical as well as biographical context. Two assumptions are readily apparent in grounding student learning in the framework of the sociological imagination. First is Mill's assumption that individual social actors rarely consider that to "grasp what is going on in the world, and to understand what is happening in themselves" (p. 7) is in large part the intersection of biography and the formative power of history. Second is that differences in student cultural capital become less hierarchical, leaving the impression of diversity rather than deficiency of a cultural norm. Cultural capital, according to Bourdieu (1993), referred to the specific skills and competencies, such as the ability to use language, that middle- and upper-class parents are able to pass on to their children. Combined with economic capital, the possession of cultural capital provides advantages to members of the middle and upper classes, increasing the probability that they will succeed in maintaining or increasing social status and rewards. When students gain a sociological imagination, they learn that the possession of social status and rewards is not "natural," or gained merely through individual hard work and effort, but it is either constrained or facilitated by social group membership.

Constructing a course based in the sociological imagination allows students to make more expansive and critical "articulations," which are discursive connections of personal troubles and societal issues that serve particular interests and powers (Slack, 1996). These connections are social constructions created through discourse, therefore they can be broken through discourse and replaced with different understandings:

> With and through articulation, we engage the concrete in order to change it....
> articulation, then, is not just a thing (not just a connection), but a process of
> creating connections, much in the same way that hegemony is not domination
> but the process of creating and maintaining consensus of co-ordinating inter-
> ests. (Slack, p. 114)

This process is especially important in classes with students from diverse backgrounds. Not only does this process place more articulations in the air, but the illustration of how some articulations are embraced while others are ignored can lead to powerful teaching moments in the development of the sociological imagination. Such a process also addresses the problematic practice of developmental education stressed by Lundell and Collins (1999). Articulations created in the development of the sociological imagination may generate a teacher-learner, learner-teacher format envisioned by Freire (1970), where all members of the learning community are receiving and providing valuable knowledge. Accordingly, instructors as well as students learn to question the historic definition of *who* is developmental and what process creates and maintains interests in attaching an individual deficit meaning to the developmental concept rather than understanding developmental as something that "promotes cognitive and affective growth of all post-secondary learners, at all levels of the learning continuum" (NADE, 1995). Creating a teaching space in terms of both curriculum and pedagogy that promotes multiple articulations necessitates expanding and integrating the use of developmental education principles and the principles of Universal Instructional Design. Developmental education is less about the deficiency of particular individuals and more about promoting the growth of all postsecondary learners and whatever "preparedness" issues students face. We also need to change our definition of universal, beginning with the idea that "centering our classroom activities and requirements around what we used to consider 'special needs' students in reality creates a classroom that simply promotes student centered learning for all students" (Barajas, 2002).

Service Learning and the Sociological Imagination

For Barajas, the most effective way of teaching college students the realities of the social world is to read classical and current interpretations of the social world, and to compare what they read to what they observe while performing community service. Combining these two approaches is beneficial, but may not have the developmental importance believed to exist if not performed within the framework of the sociological imagination. Current research in the area of service learning indicates that overall, service learning has a positive effect on student development (Astin & Sax, 1998; Driscoll, Holland, & Gelman, 1996; Dunlap, 1998). Overall, mostly survey research about service learning has been collected and analyzed, but little has directly addressed the possibility that diverse student groups experience service learning differently. Of the few qualitative studies conducted, a research method more likely to describe the *process* of student development involved in service learning, they tend to be about White, often middle-class students entering service sites where the population is considered disadvantaged and has a large racial and ethnic minority population (Dunlap). Although important research in itself, the research traces personal development of White student attitudes about larger social issues, interpretations of how these students regarded specific race-related, gendered, or classed incidents, and how the experience affected their view of the larger social world. What this literature does not do, however, is examine or at times even acknowledge the differences among students. Working class or poor students of color, for example, unlike their White, middle-class peers appearing in much of the literature, may experience the service learning site as an outsider, as a member of the community, or as a community site very much like their original community. In other words, although most often considered an alternative to conventional classroom routines, service learning often assumes a position of neutrality, a normative classroom practice through which students respond to the larger social world without considering how their own biography may affect their observations and analyses. If, on the other hand, service learning is approached through the framework of the sociological imagination, it may serve as a theoretical space for students to see connections between personal troubles and social issues, the biography of the individual, and history of the social world.

Two examples from student final paper projects in a sociology course taught by Barajas highlight how students come to understand social issues when perceived through the sociological imagination. Student names have been changed to maintain confidentiality. Both students are freshmen but differ in other social characteristics such as race, ethnicity, social class, and gender. As the course progressed, the students self-identified race, ethnicity, and social class, building their own biographies according to sociological definitions of these social characteristics.

Tom, an 18-year-old White, middle-class male, discussed gender inequity in education in his final paper. His conclusion stated:

> I have always felt that as a White male, I am blamed for any unequal treatment others received. It especially bugged me to hear that girls are treated unfairly in school because I always thought girls were treated better than boys. Because of my personal experience, I was not convinced when I read Sadker and Sadker's (2002) article that said daily classroom interactions showed girls don't receive their fair share of education. Two things changed my mind. After

spending a semester in an [elementary] after-school program, and observing like a sociologist, I watched girls get crowded out of gym space, told they couldn't play ball with the boys, talked over, and ignored in the classroom activities. And nobody did anything about it, because nobody noticed it. This is the second thing that changed my mind. The fact that no one notices gender bias when it is there is about institutional sexism. This means that it is not about individual people being prejudice, it is about how the institution reinforces social inequality by making girls think they are worth less. This is a social issue, not just a personal trouble.

Like many students in higher education, particularly mainstream students, Tom was reluctant to think of other life experiences as different from his own. Tom is a fairly typical example of a student who, in trying to understand the realities of the social world, such as the existence of gender inequality, does not necessarily learn to think critically from reading and analyzing scholarly research. Even adding personal experience such as service learning would not necessarily push Tom to change the discourse surrounding his understanding of gender issues. However, identifying and integrating his own history with that of the institution, combined with the opportunity to observe through the lens of personal trouble and social issue, allowed Tom to observe differently than he may have without the framework of the sociological imagination.

Gender issues looked different to Kim, a Hmong female who performed service learning in her own community. Kim participated in a national after-school reading program for third graders. Although performing duties defined as "tutoring," Kim also saw herself as a mentor to other young Hmong females. Her final paper stated:

I want to bring back to my Hmong community the fact that education is a step forward in our culture [for girls]. . . . I think it is important for me to do service in the Hmong community because these girls don't see a lot of older Hmong girls going on to higher education. I am glad I go to this school [to do service learning], and am pretty sure they are glad I go there too. This is because of my personal social location and an understanding of the larger social issues. . . . I feel that I am a role model because I have made it this far. Not only as a role model for my family, but for my Hmong community as well. Statistics show that many Hmong girls, when they marry drop out of school and never go to college. Many may view this as an individual trouble because Hmong girls choose to marry young. However, this is also a social issue having to do with cultural differences, and the lack of multicultural education in educational institutions. In my high school, the majority of Hmong girls were married. In our culture, it is normal to be married and even have children around the age of 15 and 16. What was sad and difficult was that people at school teased them and made fun of them. Hmong girls lived their original culture gender norms, and not the White, middle-class, gender norms of the institution. Consequently, they did not feel they belonged in school. This is ethno-centrism, and therefore a social issue affecting Hmong girls.

In both of these examples, the use of the sociological imagination creates the space for articulations. Moreover, these articulations highlight developmental issues for students, including some "preparedness" issues that are connected to critical thinking skills we may not have observed with a more narrow definition of developmental education, especially one that does not "advocate attention to discipline-specific learning" (NADE, 1995). However, the articulations are specific because they integrate each student's own history with that of the institution. Both students had the opportunity to observe through the perspectives of personal trouble and social issues. This process allowed Tom to observe the reality of gender stratification. Kim also observed gender stratification, but she observed it through the lens of cultural differences. In other words, the process allows different articulations specific to the development of sociological learning in each student despite very different social characteristics and learning needs.

Performing the Sociological Imagination

Sociology instructors also have a variety of non-service-learning-based pedagogical strategies they can use to encourage students to develop their sociological imaginations and produce more complex articulations. A centerpiece of Jacobs' classes, for instance, is "The Educational Storytelling Project" (ESP), in which students create and share stories about "ghosts" of a social versus paranormal kind, the strong but usually unconscious forces that shape our everyday lives. These stories are developed through "intertextual" dialogue: students are required to reference each others' stories and discuss their educational experiences throughout the story writing and telling process. Specifically, each student (a) writes a short ghost story, (b) reads it orally in a small group, and (c) writes a reflection on another student's story and performance. Students also have the option of presenting their ESP story to the entire class. Finally, the class collectively analyzes the project in an instructor-led discussion.

Some students tell autobiographical narratives, while others tell stories about other people, both factual and fictional. All, however, are involved in an investigation of the complex interplay between social privilege and disadvantage, and they explore the development of certain articulations and the implications of accepting these articulations and not others. Gordon (1997) argued:

> to write stories concerning exclusions and invisibilities is to write ghost stories. To write ghost stories implies that ghosts are real, that is to say, that they produce

material effects. To impute a kind of objectivity to ghosts implies that, from certain standpoints, the dialectics of visibility and invisibility involve a constant negotiation between what can be seen and what is in the shadows. (p. 17)

Many students, for example, do not understand the connection of language and power; that is, we often unconsciously use certain words or phrases to stigmatize groups to prevent them from obtaining full societal acceptance and participation. For instance, students will use the phrase "that's gay" to signal disapproval or dislike. One student, John, came out in one of Jacobs' classes as a gay man in his ESP performance to the entire class, centering on the pain he feels when reminded about marginalization. In his reflection John noted,

> When each of us is pulled apart for some factor that we have no control over, it makes us debate many things, including how valuable we are as people. From writing stories like these people have to think how deep they would like to go in their writing, and what may be too personal for the reader versus what might be too personal for the writer to talk about. In my ESP story, I thought a lot about what I've learned from being a homosexual male, and tried to talk about my schooling, and the many ways and things I learned throughout because of it.

John went on to talk about how he wanted his ESP story explicitly to raise awareness about issues of difference specifically related to sexual orientation. As discussed in the previous section on service learning, many students are reluctant to consider life experiences of those different from themselves. They will often grudgingly read assigned articles about various minority groups, and only a few will participate in class discussion; usually these students are members of the topic group. The ESP provides another framework in which students can get outside of themselves. In reflection papers several students commented on John's coming-out experience. One student wrote, "this ESP project allowed me to look into myself and find socializing agents that make me who I am today. And, it also caused me to gain a newfound respect for gays and lesbians." Another believed,

> Thinking about social ghosts makes me want to be more understanding. I have so many social ghosts that it makes me sure that everyone has at least a few that effect them all the time. I think it would be good for everyone to realize that everyone has these issues and to be aware of them and treat people accordingly.

In other words, students gain an understanding of stigma and its effects, which may be especially important for developmental education students. Pedelty (2001) argued that many students participating in developmental education feel stigmatized as learners and that their peers hold negative perceptions about them and their academic programs. Among other things, they are labeled as "slow" or "dumb" and "not real students." Using their own stigmas as springboards to connections with larger social forces can help students see themselves as valuable members of the academic community. As Fingerson and Culley (2001) stated,

> If students see another undergraduate participating in the responsibility of transmitting and communicating knowledge, this can demonstrate the capacity of undergraduates to actively participate in this process and break down the notion that only an "expert" faculty member has anything worthwhile to contribute to the class. (p. 311)

Indeed, the use of tools such as the ESP and service learning courses encourages all students to take more responsibility for their learning and help each other create powerful learning strategies.

Conclusion

There are many similarities between the guidelines for universally-designed sociology courses and developmental education: both address postsecondary learning needs, promote responsibility to all postsecondary learners, and advocate attention to discipline-specific learning as well as general learning. The task we have encountered as sociologists building on a developmental education framework required discipline-specific strategies that integrate and expand existing developmental principles. In addition, as critical sociologists, we wanted to emphasize the positive role the institution can play by recognizing the value of differing experiences, particularly differences that have been historically labeled as deficits by the institution. Learning and utilizing the sociological imagination allows both students and instructors to bring a wide variety of skills, knowledge, and experiences to the academy, above and beyond institutional mandates about students who have traditionally been placed in developmental education programs that are located on the periphery of postsecondary education. The sociological imagination as a theoretical concept teaches us that a UDL sociology course is one in which one size does *not* fit all; it should make room for flexible, customizable content, assignments, and activities that are accessible and applicable to students with a variety of backgrounds, learning styles, abilities, and disabilities. In addition, by viewing practices such as service learning and the ESP through a sociological imagination lens, we create an awareness and active engagement with what students bring to academic spaces. This not only facilitates their successful negotiation of academic careers, but it also enhances their ability to succeed in nonacademic endeavors.

In UDL sociology courses supported by the sociological imagination, students do not learn just one set of assumptions. They learn to negotiate multiple—and often conflicting—sets of experiences and behaviors, evaluating which set is the most fruitful in a given context. Students develop specific skills that help them construct and demonstrate learning processes such as making strategic plans, seeking and evaluating reasons, creating intellectual curiosity and wonder, and sharpening metacognition. Students and teachers alike engage in continual dialogue and action on a never-ending quest to develop themselves as individuals, members of social groups, and actors on a host of institutional stages. UDL sociology courses, then, may be as fundamental to developmental education as reading, writing, and mathematics.

There is no question that what we are presenting in this chapter represents a first step in approaching developmental education as a sociological endeavor. What we suggest in addressing multiple aspects of the developmental education picture at one time is that exploring what educators, institutions, and professional organizations do to increase the educational opportunities for students is more complex than addressing how "developmental students" need to be fixed. To invite a more complex approach, we suggest that further investigation and possible integration of these complex ideas into all developmental education curricula should be explored by a variety of discipline-specific developmental educators. We are by no means suggesting we throw out the proverbial "baby with the bathwater." We acknowledge the work of developmental education but hope to extend the educational support and access for diverse student groups by integrating sociological ideas.

References

Astin, A., & Sax, L. (1998). How undergraduates are affected by service participation. *Journal of College Student Development, 39* (1), 251–263.

Barajas, H. L. (2000). Is developmental education a racial project? Considering race relations in developmental education spaces. In D. B. Lundell & J. L. Higbee (Eds.), *Theoretical perspectives for developmental education* (pp. 29–37). Minneapolis, MN: Center for Research on Developmental Education and Urban Literacy, General College, University of Minnesota.

Barajas, H. L. (2002). Changing objects to subjects: Transgressing normative service learning approaches. In D. B. Lundell & J. L. Higbee (Eds.), *Exploring urban literacy and developmental education* (pp. 25–32). Minneapolis, MN: Center for Research on Developmental Education and Urban Literacy, General College, University of Minnesota.

Barajas, H. L., & Higbee, J. L. (2003). Where do we go from here? Universal Design as a model for multicultural education. In J. L. Higbee (Ed.), *Curriculum transformation and disability: Implementing Universal Design in higher education* (pp. 285–292). Minneapolis, MN: Center for Research on Developmental Education and Urban Literacy, General College, University of Minnesota.

Barajas, H. L., & Pierce, J. L. (2001). The significance of race and gender in school success for Latinos and Latinas in college. *Gender & Society, 15,* 859–878.

Bourdieu, P. (1993). *Sociology in question.* London: Sage.

Center for Applied Special Technology. (2001). *Summary of Universal Design for learning concepts.* Retrieved January 28, 2002, from http://www.cast.org

Driscoll, A., Holland, B., & Gelman, S. (1996). An assessment model for service learning: Comprehensive case studies of impact on faculty, students, community and institution. *Michigan Journal of Community Service Learning, 3,* 66–71.

Dunlap, M. (1998). Methods of supporting students' critical reflection in courses incorporating service learning. *Teaching of Psychology, 25,* 208–210.

Eliasoph, N. (1999). Everyday racism in a culture of political avoidance: Civic society, speech and taboos. *Social Problems, 46,* 479–502.

Feagin, J., Vera, H., & Imani, N. (1996). Confronting White students: The Whiteness of university spaces. In J. Feagin (Ed.), *The agony of education* (pp. 89–116). New York: Routledge.

Fingerson, L., & Culley, A. B. (2001). Collaborators in learning: Undergraduate teaching assistants in the classroom. *Teaching Sociology, 29,* 299–315.

Freire, P. (1970). *Pedagogy of the oppressed.* New York: Seabury.

Gordon, A. (1997). *Ghostly matters: Haunting and the sociological imagination.* Minneapolis, MN: University of Minnesota Press.

Lundell, D. B., & Collins, T. (1999). Toward a theory of developmental education: The centrality of "Discourse." In J. L. Higbee & P. L. Dwinell (Eds.), *The expanding role of developmental education* (pp. 3–20). Morrow, GA: National Association for Developmental Education.

Mills, C. W. (1967). *The sociological imagination.* London: Oxford University.

Moore, R. (2002). The lessons of history: Transforming science to include developmental education. In D. B. Lundell & J. L. Higbee (Eds.), *Histories of developmental education* (pp. 83–92). Minneapolis, MN: Center for Research on Developmental Education and Urban Literacy, General College, University of Minnesota.

National Association for Developmental Education. (1995). *Definition and goals statement.* Carol Stream, IL: Author

Pedelty, M. H. (2001). Stigma. In J. L. Higbee (Ed.), *2001: A developmental odyssey* (pp. 53–70). Warrensburg, MO: National Association for Developmental Education.

Sadker, M., & Sadker, D. (2002). Failing at fairness: Hidden lessons. In S. J. Ferguson (Ed.), *Mapping the social landscape: Readings in sociology* (pp. 583–596). Boston: McGraw-Hill.

Silver, P., Bourke, A., & Strehorn, C. (1998). Universal Instructional Design in higher education: An approach for inclusion. *Equity & Excellence in Education, 31* (2), 47–51.

Slack, J. (1996). The theory and method of articulation in cultural studies. In D. Morley & K. H. Chen (Eds.), *Stuart Hall: Critical dialogues in cultural studies* (pp. 112–127). New York: Routledge.

Facilitating Development Through Student Services

Facilitating Development
Through Student Services
Introduction

General College (GC) has nationally recognized services in the college available to students, including advising, bridge programs for high school students, career services, academic resource centers, and support for student parents, among other programs. Its strength is in its breadth and active forms of outreach through an intrusive and multicultural advising philosophy, which is outlined in the chapter by Shaw and Neiman. GC's support services are the outgrowth of the college's strong foundations in student development theory.

Another popular and engaging resource for students in GC, as described by Opitz and Hartley, is the Academic Resource Center, which houses computer, writing, and mathematics support for GC students. Peer tutoring is available, and a multicultural approach is also embedded within the philosophy of this center. This model for supporting student learning in all subject areas reflects the multidisciplinary nature of the college and how student services work directly with curricular initiatives in academic affairs to strengthen the educational continuum for students.

CHAPTER 19

General College Student Services: A Comprehensive Model and How It Developed

Mary Ellen Shaw and Patricia J. Neiman

ABSTRACT

Throughout the history of General College, the student services area in the college has played a key role in the development of our students. This overview provides a history of General College student services, framing this history with a look at the changing mission and structure of the college. The chapter provides a full description of the current services provided to students in the college, with particular attention to the integration of exploration of majors and careers provided by the leadership of the Transfer and Career Center. Finally, the chapter presents a brief discussion of directions for future research and assessment in the program.

An important component of the General College model of developmental education is the role played by student services in the college. Through its history, the college has invested a significant amount of resources into supporting students outside the classroom, and a distinctive model of student support has evolved over the years. Three contributing factors to the development of this model have been (a) the mission of the college itself, including the changes in the mission over time and the target student populations the college was designed to serve; (b) the key place that counseling psychology played in the early years of student services (for details on the model of psychological counseling used for the early decades in the college, see Chapter 4; and (c) the long-standing tradition of collaboration between academic and student affairs personnel in the college. In this chapter we present our understanding of the history of student services in the college and an overview of its current structure. This includes attention to special programs within the unit such as the Student Parent HELP Center and the TRIO programs.

Changes and Continuities in GC Student Services' History

Student support services have played a key role in the General College since its beginning in 1932. Though the services have evolved with changing institutional goals and student populations, there has been a consistently high level of support provided for students, as can be seen from a scan of college bulletins published over the past 40 years. The history presented in this chapter will be broken roughly into four periods, with the evidence for the first two periods taken primarily from the biannual *General College University of Minnesota Bulletin* dating from 1961 into the mid-1980s, and the evidence for the second two periods obtained from later editions of the *Bulletin* as well as from personal recollection and a review of historic memos, reports, and committee minutes.

1961–1971: A Period of Relative Stability

From the discussion of counseling psychology in General College's first few decades presented earlier in this book (see Chapter 4), it would be reasonable to assume that the student services described in *Bulletins* for the period of the 1960s would reflect a continuity from the decades earlier than 1960. The 1961–1963 *General College Bulletin* section on "Student Services and Activities" (p. 9) described a division of labor between the faculty, who did academic advising (i.e., giving guidance in "matters relating to program planning and academic progress" [p. 9]) and the counseling staff, who did personal and educational counseling. Faculty advisors referred students who needed additional support to the psychological counselors; the counselors also referred students to other University offices as needed. The counselors, though they were psychologists, did a fair amount of what appears to be academic support as well:

> The College maintains a staff of professionally trained counselors whose time is devoted to working with students on an individual basis. These counselors can assist the student in assessing his [*sic*] own interests, abilities, and aptitudes, thereby enabling him to establish realistic educational-vocational goals and to progress toward those goals. The counselor can also assist the student in the areas of study habits, social skills, and emotional adjustment. (1961–1963 *Bulletin*, p. 9)

Interestingly, the work of the counseling staff described in this passage resembles the work done by present-day General College counselor advocates doing academic advising, with the exception of the assistance with "social skills" and "emotional adjustment," at least at the level of support appropriately offered by trained psychologists.

The 1965–1967 *Bulletin* has language in the section on Student Personnel

Services and Activities (p. 8) identical to that of the earlier *Bulletin*, indicating no changes in the structure or nature of the services offered. Counseling was described as being handled by the Division of Student Personnel Services in the 1965–1967 and 1967–1969 *Bulletins*; the Division was listed alongside the other academic divisions, and the staff members (five in 1965–1967, eight in 1967–1969, and nine in 1969–1971) held a dual rank of Instructor or Assistant Professor and Counselor. This speaks to a long tradition in the General College of treating the counseling staff as part of the faculty, by seeing them as playing an important role, rather than viewing them as primarily supportive to the work of the teaching faculty. It is possible that this tradition of full collegiate participation of those student personnel staff members has contributed to the legacy of collaboration and mutual respect that is such an important part of the interrelationship between academic and student affairs in the college today.

Through the 1960s, the college mission that informed the work of both academic and student affairs remained consistent. The 1961–1963 *Bulletin*, in the section on "The Role and Function of the General College," cited the two primary purposes for the college given by President Lotus Delta Coffman, under whose administration General College was established.

> One, to provide an opportunity for the study of individual abilities, interests, and potentialities of a very considerable number of young people whose needs were not being met elsewhere in the University; and second, to experiment with a new program of instruction, a program which involves the revamping, reorganizing, and re-evaluation of materials of instruction with a view to familiarizing students more with the world in which they are to live and which uses new techniques of instruction. (p. 7)

The centrality of the counseling function in the college was highlighted in the next passage in this section of the 1961–1963 *Bulletin*. The students intended by this statement were further described as those who,

> in some instances . . . received poor marks in high school, or . . . have a low standing in college aptitude tests. . . . Many years of study show that a large number of these students have difficulty adjusting themselves to the fast pace and vigorous scholastic competition found in the 4-year colleges and professional schools. They are therefore given the option of entering the General College, one of the regular undergraduate colleges of the University, where they can take advantage of a well-developed and effective personnel and counseling service, and where they may adjust gradually to college level work. (p. 7)

Later 1960s bulletins softened the language about the "deficiencies" of the students but continued to highlight the importance of the counseling function to help students explore their educational needs. These bulletins stressed the value of the general education provided by the college as distinctly different from preprofessional and narrow disciplinary study and as providing both personal and intellectual growth for students, including the ability to "develop a sense of personal integrity, . . . think critically and constructively, . . . partic- ipate intelligently in civic affairs, . . . [and] discover an appropriate life work" (1969–1971 *Bulletin,* p. 7). This set of expectations reaches back to the founding of the college, and it suggests the impact of educational philosopher John Dewey, whose work was especially influential in the first decades of this past century, and included an emphasis on career or vocational exploration and involvement in civic life (Dewey, 1916/1997; Shaw, 2002).

The 1970s Through Mid-1980s: Expanding Mission and Service
The 1969–1971 *Bulletin* showed the beginning of a new development in the college mission in a section on "Community Programs in the General Col- lege" (p. 9). In this section the *Bulletin* described the college's role as an "agent of the University" (p .9) in housing the federally-funded Upward Bound pro- gram as well as the Project New Careers, which combined "University courses and supervised work experience in the Minneapolis Police Department, the Minneapolis Public Schools, and a number of Twin Cities social service agen- cies" (p. 9). The growth of these programs corresponded with academic inno- vations and a development of career-specific certificate programs also shown in the *Bulletins* of the later 1960s, and they also were connected with the development of the early Higher Education for Low-Income People (HELP) Center, which served those students brought in by the special programs and helped them overcome academic skills deficiencies and adjust to college life. Here is a description of the early HELP Center:

> By means of a staff composed of faculty, counselors, tutors, and a social worker, the center offers academic advising, scholarship assistance, group orientation, vocational guidance, training in effective study, and other services to students enrolled in all of the college's community programs. (1969–1971 *Bulletin,* p. 9)

At the point of the 1969–1971 *Bulletin's* publication, the Upward Bound pro- gram had been in place for 3 years, but there had been no mention of it in the prior *Bulletin.* The "community programs" seemed to have been marginal to the rest of the college at the point of the 1969–1971 *Bulletin* as well, as no further mention of the programs or the associated HELP Center services was made. The HELP Center staff was also not listed in the staff section, and the section on student services was unchanged from earlier 1960s bulletins, list- ing only the advising and counseling services discussed previously.

However, by the 1971–1973 *Bulletin,* the HELP Center had a much more visible role in the *Bulletin*, including a more detailed description of the community programs it served and of its services, and listing its staff members parallel to the faculty listings of the academic divisions, suggesting a shifting emphasis in the college toward a more explicit role in social amelioration and being an agency of the University in responding to issues of poverty and racism. Indeed, on the very first page of the 1971–1973 *Bulletin*, under "The Mission," an explicit statement was made referring to the University policy that "there shall be no discrimination in the treatment of persons because of race, creed, color, sex, or national origin" (p. 1). In more recent decades the HELP Center took on a pivotal role in working with women receiving Aid to Families with Dependent Children (AFDC) as part of its community outreach. However, the work of the early HELP Center and the personnel who came into the college to staff the center has also had a profound effect on the eventual development of a distinctive GC student services mission and approach.

Through the early 1970s, the HELP Center existed as an alternative advising and counseling home for students in the community programs and for other "by-passed" students, the term used first in the 1971–1973 *Bulletin* (p. 8), meaning specifically students from low-income backgrounds and students of color. The 1971–1973 *Bulletin* first mentioned the academic skills centers in association with the HELP Center population. The 1973–1975 *Bulletin* listed 10 staff members associated with the HELP Center and listed the academic skills centers as a resource for all students. The staff level remained at this number for the next two *Bulletins*, and, beginning with the 1977–1979 *Bulletin*, the HELP Center was listed in the Student Affairs section of the *Bulletin*, alongside the advising and counseling services. The counseling staff during the 1970s had diminished to 4 or 5, contrasted to 9 or 10 in the 1960s. This speaks as well to a shifting of resources away from the needs of the prior GC population of underperforming students, who needed assistance in exploring interests and possible vocations, toward the personal and academic needs of "by-passed" populations. One such population, that of immigrant and refugee students who needed English as a Second Language support to be ready for college success, was served by a program first showing up in the 1981–1983 *Bulletin*, the Commanding English program (for further information refer to Chapter 9). At that point the HELP Center was at an all-time high with 12 staff members.

In the 1983–1985 *Bulletin*, the Upward Bound and Day Community programs were included in the general Student Services section for the first time, and with the 1985–1987 *Bulletin*, they were joined by the newly-initiated TRIO Student Support Services (SSS), a federally-funded program serving eligible General College students, "first-year students who have been habitually underrepresented in higher education" (p. 15), meeting at least one of the eligibility requirements of being first generation, low income, or having a physical or learning disability. These changes all speak to the college's investment in a new direction, that of reaching out to serve previously underrepresented populations. As a result of this investment, the current population includes a fairly high proportion of students of color, first-generation, and low-income students, as the college continues to reach out to an urban population.

The Mid-1980s Through Mid-1990s:
Consolidation and Reconfiguration of Services
In January, 1986, the University of Minnesota discontinued the General College baccalaureate degree begun in 1977 and the associate in arts degree, prompting a refocus onto the mission of preparing students for transfer and completion of degrees in other colleges of the University. Major changes were underway in student services at this time, as the counseling unit was gradually disbanded and a professional advising staff was added to the advising being done by HELP Center personnel and the TRIO Student Support Services personnel. Additionally, a separate academic progress unit was established to monitor students' progress and intervene when students did not maintain the requisite grade point average of 1.6 for a year or two, then 2.0, as well as providing advising to students who went on academic probation or sought return from academic suspension.

For the next several years, advising services were splintered among these different program offices, with an ongoing group of students continuing to be advised by the faculty, especially those students still in the pipeline to earn General College degrees. However, the academic progress, professional advising, HELP Center, and TRIO Student Support Services personnel were all generally under the Student Services umbrella, all reporting to the Assistant Dean of Student Services and Development, Marjorie Cowmeadow. For this reason, there was a great deal of cross-training and shared provision of services. One of the long-term HELP Center staff members, Beverly Stewart, took on the role of coordinating advising services for some time in the later 1980s. It was during this period that the title "counselor advocate" came into play for advisors, including those in the HELP Center, the TRIO Student Support Services program, and the professional advising program, along with the development of a three-step ranking system (assistant, associate, and full) and criteria for hiring and promotion.

In the early 1990s, following the recommendations of a series of task groups made up of faculty and advising staff who examined the college's advising model, the college accepted a proposal to move completely away from faculty advising to a model in which all assigned advising would be done by professional advisors in one or another of the sectors of student services. In fact, not very many students were still being assigned to faculty advisors at that point: all first-year students had been assigned to student services advisors, all students on probation were moved to specialized advisors in the academic progress unit, and many other students qualified for specialized advising in the HELP Center and Student Support Services programs. An argument for this transition to have all advising done by professional advisors was that as the mission of the college moved away from offering degrees to preparing students for transfer, advisors needed to be well trained and have advising at the core of their job functions to guide students effectively through transferring successfully into the wide range of degree programs at the University. The transition to an all-professional advising model utilizing full-time professionals with the support of graduate student and undergraduate student peer advisors was finalized in the spring of 1994. During this same period of transition, the old HELP Center disappeared, with some of its staff moving to the growing ranks of the professional advising staff. The service to student parents continued, however, resurfacing in the 1991–1993 *Bulletin* under the name of the Student Parent Support Unit, and then under the name it continues to have today of the Student Parent HELP Center in the 1993–1995 *Bulletin*. This center, in its early years, was staffed in part by two long-term counselor advocates who had been involved with the original HELP Center.

Even when faculty members moved out of direct advising, they remained committed to the goals of student development that had long been in place in the college. Several faculty members have involved themselves, along with representatives from student services, on the GC Admissions and Advancement Committee, the committee charged with policies and procedures regarding student admissions, advising, and academic progress. It was out of this committee, as well as out of the college's Curriculum Committee, that measures were put into place that assisted faculty and student services staff in working closely together in supporting students.

The Base Curriculum, first showing up in the 1993–1995 *Bulletin*, was a core effort that supported this collaboration between faculty and student services staff. In this program, a broad array of selected introductory courses were required for incoming first-year students. Participating faculty were expected to enrich these courses with a variety of learning experiences and provide students with frequent feedback—all designed to assist students in their acculturation to college learning. Faculty within the Base Curriculum were also expected to provide a mid-quarter academic progress assessment to each student, copied to the student's advisor. In addition, all faculty members in the college were asked to send "Academic Alert" forms out to students and to the students' advisors whenever any student in the college showed evidence of academic difficulty (e.g., poor attendance, poor performance on papers or exams, etc.). This reporting cycle, first begun with only Base Curriculum courses, was expanded at the time the college transitioned into semesters in the fall of 1999 to include the entire college curriculum and a requirement of two reports each semester; it has remained a cornerstone of communication and collaboration between faculty and student services personnel. No other unit in the University of Minnesota has such an extensive communication cycle related to student progress, though the University has recently adopted a system providing a one-time warning for students in 1000-level classes who are not performing well. Within General College, the frequent communication through this password-protected, Web-based system leads to additional telephone and e-mail correspondence between the advisor and instructor as well as frequently resulting in meetings with the student in need of support.

The first half of the 1990s in student services saw a good deal of reorganization and experimentation in the structure of service delivery. For a short time, there was a completely separate unit within student services providing advising to first-year students, who were then transferred to new advisors for their subsequent year. An exception to this split advising model was made for students served by the TRIO Student Support Services program, which maintained a continuous advising assignment for their students.

Mid-1990s to Present: Responding to Challenge
General College experienced a crisis in 1995–1996 when the University administration of that time proposed to close the college. After weathering the storm through an outpouring of support by alumni, current students, GC allies from around the University of Minnesota, and community supporters, the college gathered energy together to improve programs in every area. Student services accelerated the process of reorganization, and by the spring of 1996 it brought all the pieces of student services effectively and productively together. Most of the services and programs now in place were strengthened or established in some form during that time. The next section of this chapter will give an overview of the key components of student services, highlighting the ways that current practice reflects long-time commitments and values in the college, and also highlighting the development over the past decade and a half of work on multicultural awareness.

Overview of Student Services Structure and Programs

The broad outline of the structure of current student services in General College is that all students are assigned to a full-time professional in the counselor advocate ranks or a trained graduate teaching assistant (GTA), usually from the University's Counseling and Student Personnel Psychology program. This advisor remains assigned to the student throughout his or her time in the college, which was the same model that was used during the early decades of the college when faculty members were the primary advisors and remained the advisors of record through the student's tenure in the college. Current advising is supported by the Student Information Center, which functions as both a college office and as a quick, stop-in advising service for students.

Multicultural Awareness and the Role of the Counselor Advocate

It is important to highlight the role of the counselor advocate in student services. The role of the counselor advocate, with earlier ranks of "assistant" and "associate" created to parallel faculty ranks, was developed initially in the transitional time when the old HELP Center was being disbanded in favor of an expanding professional advising program and specialized TRIO SSS program. The title, however, reflects much of the approach of the staff who worked in the HELP Center during its years of being challenged by and challenging the more mainstream academic culture of the University on behalf of underrepresented student populations. A primary attribute of this approach is advocacy on behalf of students' needs within the wider institution, requiring the successful counselor advocate to take a stand and take initiative to foster change within the wider institution on students' behalf. The legacy of the early HELP Center to the developing counselor advocate role included a holistic understanding of the student, one which has continued to expand as our staff has developed greater familiarity with and understanding of cultural differences among students as our student population has changed over the years. Several members of the student services staff have taken leadership in the increasing centrality of multicultural awareness within the college for more than a decade. This multicultural emphasis, too, has contributed to the everyday work of the counselor advocate, as staff members are challenged each year to reflect about ways their work with students has been informed by multicultural awareness, as well as about which new multicultural issues have arisen during that year in their work with students. Staff members receive ongoing staff development in multicultural issues and are supported in individual professional development or contributions in this area.

Professional Development of Advising Staff
General College expects and receives a high level of professionalism from its counselor advocate personnel. Advising staff members are supported in doing professional development activities and in contributing to the profession of advising, as well as providing leadership and service within the college and the wider University community. Several members of the advising staff have held offices in the National Academic Advising Association; more than one of our staff members have been on the board of the University of Minnesota Academic Advising Network; and several members have been on University Senate committees as well. Many staff members serve on General College committees such as Policy and Planning, Curriculum, Admissions and Advancement, Multicultural Concerns, and the Student Scholastic Standing Committee. Within the University, contacts made with other colleges' advising staff members have been beneficial in creating strong connections with those colleges to support our students' entry into majors across the campus. Nationally, involvement in professional organizations has paid off as advisors bring back information about best practices in programs around the country. Additionally, a number of staff members have been active graduate students, many pursuing Ph.D. programs in higher education fields, taking advantage of the University's tuition benefit for professional and academic staff. The research and course work done by colleagues in those programs helps inform best practices in our advising program.

Program Components of Student Services
There are several separate programs within the current student services unit, all working closely together. The federally-funded TRIO Student Support Services serves as the advising home for around 200 eligible students at any given time. There is an advising component of the Commanding English program, which is described in Chapter 9, involving two professional counselor advocates who work closely with the academic staff of this program. The current Student Parent HELP Center, which provides services to all undergraduate students who are parents at the University of Minnesota, also serves as the advising home for General College student parents who are not in the TRIO SSS program or in Commanding English. Finally, a programmatically separate but also very centrally connected student services program is the Transfer and Career Center, discussed later in this chapter.

It is important to stress that all these component segments of the student services unit are united in reporting to the same Assistant Dean and Director of Student Services, they all include staff who serve as advisors of record to General College students, and staff members of these programs are part of the close-knit cadre of counselor advocates and Graduate Teaching Assistant (GTA) staff who share in the same professional training, meet frequently, and function as members of the same team. As indicated in the previous description of the early history of General College student services, this unity of purpose and team membership was not always the case; we believe it is an important component of our successful provision of services to students. This model of an integrated team of staff members who also specialize in separate services, including career services, is unique in our experience of how other collegiate student services are organized.

The Student Information Center

The Student Information Center, located centrally on the lower level of the building that houses GC, is the office responsible for official correspondence with students (e.g., admissions letters, academic standing letters), being available for student questions of all kinds during business hours, and handling student requests for advising appointments. Staffed by an experienced student personnel worker and undergraduate advising assistants reporting to her, the center is responsible for maintaining student records, although active student files are located in advisor offices; managing the flow of materials and the processes associated with admissions and assignment to orientation dates; and providing support for the advising function in the college. The Center also handles the registration of prospective students whose first language is not English and who need to take the Michigan English Language Assessment Battery (MELAB) exam as part of their admissions process to the University.

New Student Orientation

During the months of June and early July, and for one catch-up session in August, all student services staff members in all positions join together in providing our new student orientation program. Incoming first-year students are on campus for a 2-day period, with the first day handled primarily by New Student Programs, a central University of Minnesota office. In the afternoon of the first day, General College staff members present a 1-hour, large-group information session called the College Meeting, introducing new students to General College and its services, as well as providing an overview of policies and expectations in the college. Subsequently, for a second hour, students are placed in advisor-run, small group sessions in broad vocational or programmatic groupings (i.e., sciences, liberal arts, professional studies, Commanding English, and potential TRIO SSS-eligible students). In these sessions, more detail is offered about registration and liberal education requirements, and students are invited to start the process of planning their fall class schedules.

In their second day of orientation, students come to Appleby Hall to continue their planning and to work with an individual counselor advocate or

GTA. Ideally, this individual will become the student's assigned advisor of record, although it does not always work out in terms of numbers attending any given orientation session. At this point, those students who are eligible and who are being invited to consider joining the TRIO SSS program are given more information about the special TRIO SSS course packages they are eligible for and application forms; most invited TRIO SSS students do choose to join the program. Commanding English students meet as a group and are introduced to the requirements and packaged curriculum of their special program. Other student groups with special needs, such as students jointly admitted to General College and the School of Music, student athletes, and students who are parents, meet with advisors who are specially trained to help these students balance school with their additional responsibilities.

First-Year Advising
Contacts between advising staff and students in the first year are designed to bring students into the college experience. During their first year, students in all advising areas are invited into a relationship with their assigned advisor and encouraged to use that relationship as a springboard to engage in the process of making academic and life choices, explore the opportunities and possibilities of the University, and reflect on their academic experience. Advisors do traditional academic advising as is done in higher education throughout the U.S., assisting students with course selection and communicating the expectations and policies of higher education to students. It is important to recognize that as the profession of academic advising has matured over the past 20 years, academic advising has come to include attention to a wide set of students' developmental needs, as promoted by the National Academic Advising Association especially in its Statement of Core Values of Academic Advising. However, many advising programs lack the resources and institutional support to provide the level of outreach to students, advocacy on their behalf, and attention to their development as students and as maturing individuals, as the General College counselor advocates and GTA advising staff have been able to provide over the years.

During their first year, attention in advising is placed on assisting the students to come to know more clearly their educational aspirations and capacities, to engage in the beginning stages of career and major decision making, or to confirm the direction already chosen. If the student experiences academic difficulty during any semester, faculty members in General College classes will be communicating this information to the student and the advisor, giving the student ample time during the semester to seek out resources for academic support, or to modify the course load. Continued lack of progress leads to placement on academic probation, when students are required to agree to academic interventions and to work closely with their advisor.

Students in their first semester are invited to register for GC 1086, "The First-Year Experience," a course designed to assist new students in making a successful transition into college. This course has been taught for a number of years by student services personnel and is similar to first-year success courses taught elsewhere. However, beginning with fall 2004, a new model was piloted in delivering this course, through which students attended a lecture taught by a senior General College faculty member once a week and met for a second session with a General College advising staff member, who also served as the student's assigned advisor. This new model was a development intended to allow for expansion of the course offering to include more students, and an enhancement of the course based on the experience of prior instructors, who discovered that students in the course formed a strong bond with the instructor. Emphasis within the course continues to include learning about resources and expectations of college life, engaging in self-exploration and reflection, and addressing affective issues as well as the development of skills in areas like time management.

Second Year in the College

Advising during the second year supports students through their transition into degree programs elsewhere in the University. During the second year and any subsequent registration, students are supported in continuing their academic development, as well as in making their decisions about majors and beginning to move toward entry into their new academic home. The timing for this transition depends on the goal the student has chosen; many students move within three semesters into bachelor of arts majors in the College of Liberal Arts, while students choosing a professional major such as education or engineering generally take 2 years of preparation before they can transfer. Advising for students in their second year or beyond focuses on the process of testing out options and making good decisions about majors and subsequent career possibilities. Because our students have the opportunity to go into any program at the University if they can meet the admissions requirements, General College advisors must become aware of all the undergraduate majors and requirements available to University of Minnesota students, whereas advisors in other colleges are specialists in their own college's offerings. This broad knowledge base about the degree options at the University that advisors have is of benefit to our students, as many college students change their major one or more times during their first 2 years. General College students have an advantage over students in the other colleges of being provided with information about the widest possible array of choices when they begin the decision-making process or find their first choice impractical or no longer of interest.

During their second year, many students are encouraged to take a career planning course provided through student services. For several years, student services advising staff members have been the instructors of GC 1076, "Career Planning," a two-credit course intended primarily for second-year students to help them explore interests or confirm degree choices and begin to make the link to the world of work. Instructors in the course have received career development training or have been trained to teach the course through mentoring by senior instructors. This course guides students through self-exploration and assessment instruments such as the Strong Interest Inventory (CPP, 2004b) and the Myers-Briggs Type Indicator (CPP, 2004a), facilitates student reflection and discussion of different major options, guides students in exploring career options and employment trends, and introduces students to some of the activities in which they will need to engage when they are ready to enter the world of work.

Role of TRIO Student Support Services

General College student services programs have been shaped, in part, by the presence within the college of programs targeted to low-income and underrepresented student populations. The history discussed earlier in this chapter includes mention of the HELP Center, originally titled "Higher Education for Low-Income People," which was an early program housed in General College charged with supporting underrepresented students. The HELP Center shifted its focus in the middle 1980s to serving students who are parents; it is now the Student Parent HELP Center and serves undergraduate students who are parents from throughout the University. At that time, the mission of providing targeted services to General College low-income and first-generation students was taken up by TRIO Student Support Services, one of three federally-funded TRIO programs hosted by General College. The other two are McNair Scholars Program, which prepares undergraduates from around the United States for graduate study through a summer program and faculty-sponsored research project, and Upward Bound, a program that works with high school students in several inner-city high schools and prepares them for college admission and successful college study.

TRIO Student Support Services (SSS) provides advising and academic support to qualified General College students, those who are first generation and meet federal income guidelines, or those who have a disability. In reality, many more General College students could qualify for TRIO SSS than the 120 who are admitted each year as first-year students; for that reason, TRIO SSS staff do careful screening of admitted students prior to General College orientation to invite those students who seem best suited to take advantage of the program. Students invited often include past participants of other TRIO programs oriented to helping high school students prepare to enter into college, such as Talent Search and Upward Bound.

TRIO Student Support Services is currently staffed with a director, two full-time advisors, and two part-time graduate student advisors. In addition, the program hires teaching staff for the one-credit Supplemental Instruction courses attached to several of General College's most challenging courses, especially the sciences. Given the additional needs of the students admitted into the TRIO SSS program, advising loads are kept lower than the advising loads of GC advisors not associated with the program.

Beyond the intrusive and accessible advising that is part of the TRIO SSS model, the core of the program involves offering students learning communities and supplementary skills-building courses. Learning communities involve two or even three General College courses that a group of students take in common, usually in their first or second college semester, and often including a freshman writing course. In these learning communities the participating faculty generally work together to make connections between the courses. The one-credit Supplemental Instruction courses attached to challenging courses replaced the earlier model used in TRIO SSS of Supplemental Instruction involving voluntary study groups led by a trained undergraduate tutor meeting outside of the target large class. However, when the program moved to having a credit-bearing course associated with the target course, student participation and success were greatly enhanced. These one-credit support courses carry graduation credit, as they present additional material not covered in the target course. They are taught by experienced graduate student instructors or by teaching specialists with advanced degrees.

The TRIO SSS program is fully integrated into General College student services. Advising staff in TRIO SSS are part of the larger GC advising staff, participating in all training and staff meetings of the larger student services unit. The TRIO SSS director is a member of the planning group advisory to the Assistant Dean and Director of Student Services and also reports to him. At the same time, TRIO SSS is actively connected to similar programs around the nation, which helps the program stay fresh and innovative. In addition, the program is required to provide documentation of its effectiveness as part of the periodic grant renewal and report cycles to maintain its federal funding, which contributes to the motivation for innovation. For these reasons, as well as because a high quality of staff is attracted to the mission of the TRIO SSS program, a variety of innovations have been initiated within TRIO SSS that have led to enhancements in the larger General College student services program. Examples include the use of mid-term academic reporting, which was done in TRIO SSS before it became an expectation that all GC course instructors provide reports during the semester for all GC students. TRIO SSS started tracking student contacts as part of its grant reporting, which led to the same student contact tracking system being incorporated into the larger student services, and eventually the creation of the current electronic student data base that keeps track of student contacts and also houses electronic file notes. TRIO SSS has also influenced the development of the intrusive approach to advising that is common practice in General College. In these and other ways, TRIO SSS has served as a laboratory for developing new approaches to helping students overcome barriers and experience success, and has provided leadership within General College.

Transfer and Career Center

A core resource for advisors and students in assisting students through their first 2 years of exploration and major decision making is the Transfer and Career Center (TCC). This center, originally called the Career Resource Room (CRR), was established in 1988 when General College moved from Nicholson Hall to Appleby Hall. The CRR was located in the basement of Appleby Hall and was open on a walk-in basis. A limited amount of career resource books, college catalogues, and the American College Testing (ACT; 2004) program's computerized career guidance program, *DISCOVER Career Guidance and Information System,* were the available resources. The CRR primarily functioned as a place for students to come to discuss their interests and educational options. The coordinator also tracked transfer applicants and when appropriate advocated for individuals whose transfers to other colleges of the University were rejected.

During the summer of 1996 the CRR moved and became the Transfer and Career Center (TCC). The new room is a sunny, centrally-located former classroom on the first floor of the building, close to the main entryway. This move provided the opportunity for an increase of resources, staff, and visibility within General College and the greater University of Minnesota.

The TCC now has two missions: one short-range, which is helping students prepare for transfer, and one longer-range, which is helping students begin their career planning. The need for this expanded service was underscored when, for 2 years after the TCC's move to its new location, incoming first-year students were asked to take the College Student Inventory (CSI), a Noel-Levitz (2004) instrument, to assess their needs. One striking finding in the CSI aggregate results was that many incoming General College students felt the need for career planning services, which gave the administration of the college reason to allocate even more resources to the newly-expanded TCC.

Currently the TCC offers a number of resources and programs. An important resource produced and maintained by the TCC is the set of transfer guides to all undergraduate programs at the University, available for both students and staff to use. It would be impossible for any single advisor to maintain this knowledge completely and always keep it up-to-date, as programs and requirements are constantly changing. The TCC staff has the responsibility of regularly revising and updating these guides.

The TCC coordinator is currently the key liaison person reaching out to transfer colleges, keeping staff updated on collegiate programs and requirements, but also facilitating the acceptance of the General College curriculum as fulfilling major prerequisites and college requirements where appropriate in other colleges. As part of this liaison role, the TCC coordinator invites representatives of other colleges to be part of the Visiting Advisor Program, through which advisors from other colleges make themselves available to General College students to discuss their programs and the students' particular interests and preparation. Each spring semester the TCC hosts a program for first-year students, who are all required to attend a session in the TCC as part of their early preparation for transfer. Many of these sessions are co-hosted by advisors from other colleges as a way of helping students get the most current information about collegiate and major requirements and also helping them make a connection with a person in their prospective college.

The TCC has long offered some important self-exploration resources for students: access to the Strong Interest Inventory through the Web as well as trained interpretations of the results; *Do What You Are* (Human eSources, 2000–2004); access to computers to do Web browsing for career information; the online Minnesota Career Information System (MCIS; Minnesota Department of Children, Family, and Learning, 2004); and, in previous years, the online *DISCOVER Career Guidance and Information System* program. The TCC also has its own Web site, http://www.gen.umn.edu/transfer_career_ctr/, which hosts online versions of all the current transfer guides, as well as many links to useful resources for students.

Current staffing of the TCC includes the coordinator, who also does advising; two undergraduate peer advisors, who provide a significant number of hours of staffing; and two or three graduate students from the Counseling and Student Personnel Psychology program at the University, who contribute a couple hours each week as part of their training and development as GTA advisors. Having these CSPP graduate students as advisors and contributors to the TCC allows for a fruitful connection between General College and the CSPP program and gives these students a good foundation in the profession of academic advising along with career counseling skills. Over the years a number of these graduate students have gone on to become professional advisors, several of them being hired in General College as full-time counselor advocate staff members.

In many, if not most, colleges and universities that have career centers, the career center is physically and administratively separate from the advising services. This is not the case in General College, where the transfer and career services are an integral part of advising and are staffed by individuals who are part of the advising staff as well. There are a number of ways that the TCC is integrated into the advising model in the college. Because having students successfully transfer within the University is central to the mission of the college, all advisors need to be aware of transfer requirements and college programs around the University. The TCC is the hub for maintaining that information.

The TCC has been utilized over recent years by instructional staff in General College in a variety of ways, with TCC staff offering group interpretations of student self-assessment instruments for several classes, including GC 1421: Basic Writing, which is the first-semester composition class; GC 1511: Business in Modern Society; GC 1086: The First-Year Experience; GC 1281: Psychology in Modern Society; and GC 1280: Psychology of Personal Development. Some instructors give students an assignment to visit the TCC and write a report about the information they find there about their prospective major or career. The GC 1076 Career Planning course uses TCC resources extensively.

In looking at future challenges, it will be important for the TCC and for the college advising staff in general to keep up with changes in the nature of our student population as well as changes in the world of work. An example is the growing student interest in health science careers, which often results in students entering the University with unrealistic expectations of entering these professions. It is challenging to serve these students who sometimes enter into the University quite unprepared for the rigorous academic challenges their vocational interests will pose for them.

In summary, the TCC continues a long tradition of providing General College students with support for career and major exploration, a continuation of the long tradition of career and vocational counseling that was offered for so many of its earlier years by the counseling unit in the college, as was discussed in the section of this chapter on the history of student services. With the current TCC model, however, functioning as it does as a hub coordinating and informing advisors in their work with students around these issues of career and major exploration, the TCC is integrated into and strengthens the academic advising in the college in many ways, rather than being separate from it, as was the case with the earlier counseling model and is still the case in many other higher education settings.

Monitoring Student Progress

Throughout their time in General College, students' progress is monitored closely, and advisors are proactive and "intrusive" in responding when students are not doing well. Being intrusive means that advisors reach out by making phone calls, sending e-mail messages, and catching students in the hall when Academic Alerts or poor mid-semester reports are received. Our electronic Student Data Base makes it easy for advisors to download electronic data on their advisees in a form that facilitates group e-mail correspondence and also makes it easy to maintain good electronic file notes that keep advisors on top of students' situations.

Each semester advisors review the grades of their own advisees as part of the probation review. Letters are sent out with the signature of the Assistant Dean and Director of Student Services, but individual advisors have the information about their students' progress within 2 to 3 days of grades being submitted at the end of each semester, and they do individual follow-up with students who are not doing well. Students on probation are required to come in to meet with their advisor in the first 2 weeks of the semester to do an academic contract, making explicit plans to pursue interventions or changes to improve their situation. During their probationary semester, students are expected to meet with their advisor on a regular basis. If students fail to meet their probation requirements, they will need their advisor's support in petitioning the General College Student Scholastic Standing Committee to be able to return to school.

Summary Remarks and Future Directions

This has been a necessarily broad overview of the activities, programs, and approaches utilized in the General College student services area. In doing the historical review of changes in student services programs over the decades, it has been striking to realize how much has remained constant in the college. This can be accounted for by reflecting on the sorts of individuals who have been attracted to working in the General College, many of whom remain here throughout their professional lives, and the institutional culture that has been handed down from one institutional generation to the next. There are also many ways, subtle and direct, that the program has benefited from research and dissemination of best practice information in the advising profession, but the legacy of the past and the inspiration of the college's mission and student populations have been especially strong determinants in our creation of a remarkably rich and responsive student services program.

In the future, however, we are aware of the need to do more formal research on our students, recognizing that we will serve students most ably when we understand more about their backgrounds, experiences, and capacities. In addition, we are committed to finding better ways of systematically collecting information about our students as they move through their first 2 years of adjustment to college and decision making about their future directions. Working with the General College Office of Research and Evaluation, we are redesigning our Student Data Base to provide both support for individual advisors in their work—involving such resources as a paper-free student file system and on-demand electronic reports of advisees—and also aggregate information about our students' academic progress and their progress toward transfer and graduation. In recent years, the paper files kept by advisors have been examined by college researchers to find patterns explaining student attrition; in the future, we hope to keep more complete electronic information about students who stop out or drop out that will help inform both advising and admission decisions in the college.

Another important area for ongoing research and assessment is the relationship between students' academic goals upon entry into the General College, their academic preparation from high school in preparing for their goals, and their success in transferring into and completing their goals. In particular as mentioned in the Transfer and Career Center section, we have grown concerned about the numbers of students entering as first-year students with a goal of moving into health science careers or engineering careers but who have inadequate preparation for these competitive programs.

Assessment of students' advising needs prior to entering into the advising system is currently limited to the brief self-assessment they do as part of their preparation for coming to orientation. Students fill out the General College Student Inventory (GCSI) online at the same time that they take a math test online. The GCSI asks students to self-report on their academic goals and also indicate special circumstances or needs that they have. Students who have children are asked to report this, and students are asked about their parents' educational attainments. From the GCSI, programs such as the TRIO Student Support Services and the Student Parent HELP Center choose the students they will invite into their programs during orientation. In the future, we may investigate the use of other assessments for all or some incoming students designed to evaluate their preparation to be successful in the tasks of college learning.

In assessing our student services program, we have done brief questionnaires following orientation sessions and other programs, as well as a more comprehensive yearly online questionnaire evaluating individual advisors and the advising program more broadly. This questionnaire is administered through our first-year writing courses, which are held in computer labs. The leadership of the student services area continues to explore other means of program-wide assessment to ascertain if the structures we have in place are the most effective in helping students become successful.

References

ACT, Inc. (2004). *DISCOVER Career Guidance and Information System*. Hunt Valley, MD: Author. Retrieved October 4, 2004, from http://www.act.org/discover/index.html

CPP, Inc. (2004a). *Myers-Briggs Type Indicator (MBTI)*. Mountain View, CA: Author. Retrieved October 4, 2004, from http://www.cpp.com/products/mbti/index.asp

CPP, Inc. (2004b). *Strong Interest Inventory*. Mountain View, CA: Author. Retrieved October 4, 2004, from http://www.cpp.com/products/strong/index.asp

Dewey, J. (1916/1997). *Democracy and education*. In S. M. Cahn (Ed.), *Classic and contemporary readings in the philosophy of education* (pp. 288–325). New York: McGraw-Hill.

General College University of Minnesota Bulletin. (1961–1963). Minneapolis, MN: General College, University of Minnesota.

General College University of Minnesota Bulletin. (1965–1967). Minneapolis, MN: General College, University of Minnesota.

General College University of Minnesota Bulletin. (1967–1969). Minneapolis, MN: General College, University of Minnesota.

General College University of Minnesota Bulletin. (1969–1971). Minneapolis, MN: General College, University of Minnesota.

General College University of Minnesota Bulletin. (1971–1973). Minneapolis, MN: General College, University of Minnesota.

General College University of Minnesota Bulletin. (1977–1979). Minneapolis, MN: General College, University of Minnesota.

General College University of Minnesota Bulletin. (1981–1983). Minneapolis, MN: General College, University of Minnesota.

General College University of Minnesota Bulletin. (1983–1985). Minneapolis, MN: General College, University of Minnesota.

General College University of Minnesota Bulletin. (1985–1987). Minneapolis, MN: General College, University of Minnesota.

General College University of Minnesota Bulletin. (1991–1993). Minneapolis, MN: General College, University of Minnesota.

General College University of Minnesota Bulletin. (1993–1995). Minneapolis, MN: General College, University of Minnesota.

Human eSources, LTD. (2000–2004). *Do what you are*. New London, CT: Author. Retrieved October 4, 2004, from http://www.humanesources.com/cgapp/exec/login?url=umn

Minnesota Department of Children, Families, and Learning. (2004). *Minnesota Career Information System (MCIS)*. St. Paul, MN: Author. Retrieved October 4, 2004, from http://cfl.state.mn.us/mcis/

NACADA. (1994). *NACADA statement of core values of academic advising.* Retrieved January 11, 2005, from http://www.nacada.ksu.edu/Clearing-house/Research_Related/corevalues.htm

Noel-Levitz. (1998–2004). *Retention Management System/College Student Inventory.* Iowa City, IA: Author. Retrieved October 4, 2004, from http://www.noellevitz.com/solutions/retention/rms_csi/index.asp

Shaw, M. E. (2002). Recovering the vision of John Dewey for developmental education. In D. B. Lundell & J. L. Higbee (Eds.), *Histories of developmental education* (pp. 29–34). Minneapolis, MN: Center for Research on Developmental Education and Urban Literacy, General College, University of Minnesota.

CHAPTER 20

Collaborative Learning Beyond the Classroom: The Academic Resource Center

Donald L. Opitz and Debra A. Hartley

ABSTRACT

In curricular reform in developmental education, learning spaces outside of classrooms are critical sites for student development. In curricular planning when collaborative learning strategies are emphasized, learning centers should have central roles. Peer tutoring philosophies embrace collaborative education ideals, and cooperative study groups often gather in tutoring centers. This chapter thus presents a theoretical rationale for learning centers within frameworks adopting the principles of collaborative learning and practical ways in which theoretical strategies may be implemented, using General College's Academic Resource Center as a model. We conclude by proposing measures for building and strengthening a "model" learning center.

O ver the past couple of decades, postsecondary developmental educators have embraced curricular reforms that emphasize the principles of constructivism and cooperative learning—a trend also reflected in General College courses (Jehangir, 2001; Koch, 1996). In developmental mathematics, the reform standards of the American Mathematical Association for Two-Year Colleges (AMATYC; 1995) have also impacted our curriculum (Kinney, 2001; see Chapters 14 and 15). Moreover, writing-across-the-curriculum, learning communities, and first-year experience initiatives like the freshman seminar have reflected pedagogical innovations designed to enhance student learning through collaborative approaches (Bridwell-Bowles, 2003; Bruch, 2002; Koch & Anderson, 2004). Yet students spend only part of their educational lives within the classroom, and learning often occurs *outside* of it in spaces like the lounge, corridor, residence hall room, or learning center (Chism & Bickford, 2002, p. 94). Therefore, if we are to impact student learning, we must also consider spaces *beyond* the classroom within our curricular reforms. In this chapter, we point to the collaborative nature of learning center work and consider the centrality of this work in curricular initiatives.

This chapter begins by considering a theoretical rationale for the institutional role and learning assistance work of learning centers within a framework adopting the principles of collaborative learning. We then focus on practical ways in which theoretical strategies may be implemented within learning centers devoted to writing and mathematics, as illustrated by General College's Academic Resource Center (ARC). A key point in our discussion is the importance of flexibility in responding to the changing needs of students and the institution (Arendale, 2004). We will thus conclude by describing future directions in which the ARC is moving and identify the kinds of measures that should be considered for building, strengthening, and maintaining a "model" learning center.

Connecting With the Curriculum: The Role of Collaboration

At the heart of recent developmental education reform, particularly in writing and mathematics, are principles of collaboration between instructors and students to achieve learning goals. The pedagogy of cooperative learning, while having deep historical roots, owes much to the work of the Cooperative Learning Center at the University of Minnesota in the 1980s (Johnson & Johnson, 1984). Since that time, educators have elaborated and expanded on essentially the same principles, summarized by Johnson and Johnson as (a) positive interdependence, that is, each individual depends on and is accountable to the others; (b) individual accountability, by which each person in the group is responsible for learning the material; (c) promotive interaction, by which group members help one another; (d) social skills, including leadership and communication; and (5) group processing to assess how effectively group members work with one another. Proponents of these and related principles have offered a variety of models under such rubrics as "active learning," "interactive learning" "small-group learning," "team learning," and "collaborative learning" (e.g., Bonwell & Eison, 1991; Goodsell, Maher, & Tinto, 1992; Lyman & Foyle, 1990; Michaelsen, 1992; Reid, Forrestal, & Cook, 1990). To implement cooperative learning principles, reform educators have generally focused on structuring classroom activities within small groups. By the early 1990s, learning communities offered a broader approach to collaborative learning by emphasizing links between disciplines and building greater coherence within students' academic lives (Gabelnick, MacGregor, Matthews, & Smith, 1990; MacGregor, Cooper, Smith, & Robinson, 2000). As a rule, learning community models do not explicitly include learning centers; the exceptions are Writing Across the Curriculum programs that partner with writing centers (Barnett & Blumner, 1999).

Collaboration is a key concept in peer tutoring (Gillam, 1994). Although writing and mathematics skills exhibit inherent disciplinary differences, the ideal peer interaction in either subject is guided by the same principles. Topping (1996) defined peer tutors as "people from similar social groupings who are not professional teachers helping each other to learn and learning themselves by teaching" (p. 6). Consistently, Ender and Newton (2000, pp. 1–21) emphasized the paraprofessional (as opposed to professional) role models that effective peer educators assume. Individual tutoring may promote different dynamics from cooperative learning groups (Kail, 1983), but when guided through training and approached as a collaboration, the tutoring interaction can positively impact students' academic success as well as benefit the academic development of tutors themselves (Boylan, Bliss, & Bonham, 1997; Maxwell, 1994).

As we have observed in General College's Math and Writing Centers, many students work with peer tutors in groupings that often return throughout the academic term, creating small learning communities that closely resemble base groups in cooperative-learning classrooms (Johnson & Johnson, 1984). It is important that we connect the work of learning centers to curricular reform. The emphasis on collaborative learning in teaching writing and mathematics, as well as in peer tutoring services, provides an opportune means for making the connection.

Writing

Writing center theory has paralleled developmental writing theory in stressing the student-centered, collaborative, and multicultural nature of writing as a process (Mullin & Wallace, 1994). Writing pedagogy has shifted from a focus on the final writing product to the writer who is learning and practicing the many stages of writing—from generating ideas, to conducting research, to obtaining feedback and, finally, to proofreading. In the mid-1980s, North (1984) observed in this pedagogical transition "the marriage of what are arguably the two most powerful contemporary perspectives on teaching writing: first, that writing is most usefully viewed as a process; and second, that writing curricula need to be student-centered" (p. 438).

Writing center practice embraced this paradigmatic shift. Directors have found that student writers benefit from peer tutors who are knowledgeable about the writing process but, unlike the instructor, do not evaluate students' papers. Being semi-autonomous from the classroom has allowed writing tutors to support the student rather than serve as extensions of the instructors. As North (1984) put it, the "new writing center . . . defines its province not in terms of some curriculum, but in terms of the writers it serves" (p. 438). In a parallel shift, writing center staff emphasized the need to move away from images of remedial grammar "fix-it shops" and "skills centers" to locations for student-centered, collaborative conferences based on talking about writing. North's ideas about the writing curriculum and writing centers provided important cues for their interrelationship. The semi-autonomy of writing centers allows them to focus on students' needs rather than instructors' agendas, but in doing so they also support and supplement the aims of the writing curriculum (North, 1994).

Although most writing center theorists agree on the importance of collaborative learning, they debate over how collaboration should proceed. Lunsford (1991), who promoted a constructivist view of learning, distinguished among three types of writing centers. The first is based on the notion that "knowledge [is] exterior to us and . . . directly accessible" (p. 4). This writing center is a storehouse of knowledge that is handed out to students, perhaps through learning "modules." The second, the "Garret Center," is a space in which tutors help writers express what is in themselves, acting as listeners and encouragers; this assumes that "knowledge [is] interiorized, solitary, individually derived, individually held" (p. 5). The third, the "Burkean Parlor Center," is based on the "notion of knowledge as always contextually bound, as always socially constructed" (p. 8). The collaborative Burkean model provides a useful focus, but at times it is important to adjust to students' individual needs for knowledge about form or grammar, without compromising their own ideas and rights to self-expression.

Adopting a tutoring philosophy that allows one to be both sensitive and flexible to the needs of students is especially important when working with non-native English writers, whose language challenges may also include inexperience with academic writing standards. DiPardo (1992) stressed the need for tutors to listen for clues that give insight into the students' concerns and experiences, and to be willing to learn themselves—in other words, to engage in collaborative, peer learning. But Powers (1993) questioned traditional views of collaborative tutoring by arguing that non-native English writers often benefit from tutors who act as informants about academic writing, addressing issues like paper formats, use of evidence, and audience expectations.

Where writing instruction is viewed as participatory "literacy work, grounded in a theoretical understanding of writing as a social practice" (Reynolds & Bruch, 2002, p. 12), it is important to allow students opportunities to reflect on the effects of writing on themselves and others. Within this model, writing center tutors can assume the position of an audience affected by students' writing and reacting openly when moved by an example, informed by an analysis, or confused by a sentence. Peer writing tutors can participate in literacy work by reacting to students' writing in ways that raise questions and offer feedback rather than "expert" advice, thereby promoting students' development as writers in a collaborative way.

In light of the debates, a collaborative tutoring model must allow for flexibility in how little or how much direction is given, particularly for students who may never have received formal instruction on academic styles. The model should readily adapt to the individual needs of students, in some cases liberally providing information on the formal elements of academic style and audience expectations. In those cases, even when assuming the role of informant, the tutor preserves a student-centered model by responding to the student's immediate needs.

Mathematics

Cooperative learning became a trend in mathematics education reform (Walmsley, 2003; Wilson, 2003), particularly after the Treisman (1985) study that showed the differential success of students working individually and in study groups. The National Council of Teachers of Mathematics (NCTM; 1989, 2000) has recommended small groups in conjunction with other instructional methods to accomplish curriculum standards: mathematics as problem-solving, mathematics as reasoning, mathematics as communication, and making mathematical connections. Programs developed at a variety of institutions using cooperative learning models at times include computer or calculator laboratory components (Davidson, Reynolds, & Rogers, 2001, pp. 3, 7–10). Supplemental Instruction (SI) models also connect peer learning assistance with curriculum by offering structured sessions led by trained, "model" students who also attend lectures; SI sessions emphasize collaborative learning and academic skill development for mastering course content (Kenney & Kallison, 1994). Although practitioners often implement formal and informal ties between mathematics tutoring centers and mathematics courses, few have disseminated theoretical rationales and descriptions of practice in publication (Abel, 1977; Opitz, 2004; Testone, 1999).

A very clear justification for mathematics learning centers within curricular paradigms embracing the principles of cooperative learning appears in the work of Treisman (1985, 1992). Collaborative study sessions (or "study gangs") require space and benefit from peer facilitators who can promote effective group dynamics. The increasing emphasis placed on using technology in curriculum also requires access to computers. To effectively support student learning in courses, the mathematics learning center must thus move beyond traditional, individual tutoring and offer access to computers with mathematics software and Web sites, graphing calculators, and peer facilitation of cooperative learning groups working on projects. Tutors who work with small groups in classrooms and provide tutoring in the mathematics learning center are bridges between these two learning sites. Directors are increasingly wearing hats as SI coordinators, extending the role of peer education beyond the spaces of learning centers (Wright, Wright, & Lamb, 2002).

As with writing, a collaborative approach is critical in the tutoring interaction. Particularly in mathematics, students often carry the burden of prior negative experiences in their exposure to mathematical concepts and skills, creating attitudes that are usually summarized as "math anxiety" in the mathematics education literature (Tobias, 1993). Moving students beyond misconceptions and negative attitudes requires a dialogue within the tutoring interaction that empowers students to explore actively, learn independently, and develop conceptual versus procedural understanding of mathematics. Gourgey (1992) identified this approach as a "collaborative process" that tutors can accomplish by "listening to students to understand their thinking and approaches to math and by asking questions that encourage students to think through the material to find their own solutions rather than to passively imitate procedures demonstrated by others" (p. 12). To avoid premature correction of students' errors, thereby aborting the discovery process, Gourgey advocated a questioning method:

> Often tutors can prompt students with questions that encourage them to consider the implications of a false idea, until its falsity becomes inescapable. This can help students to move beyond an external standard of "correctness" as determined by an outside authority to an internal standard determined by whether the strategy they are using makes sense. (p. 12)

Increasingly, teachers and tutoring coordinators are promoting mathematical understanding within the context of students' histories and social experiences, thus emphasizing the multicultural nature of mathematical knowledge and learning styles (Opitz, 2003; see Chapters 10 and 23). Here we see much synergy with writing center theory.

Theoretically, learning centers need strong relationships with developmental curricular programs and should play vital roles within reform initiatives emphasizing collaborative learning. Peer tutoring should be guided by the ideals of collaborative learning, as well as by flexible peer instructional strategies that respond to the diversity of students' backgrounds and needs. But these ideals are also the key challenges felt among learning center directors who strive to build and maintain strong relationships with academic departments and train tutors to adopt good practices. In our next section, we will describe strategies implemented at the General College's Academic Resource Center to close the gap between theory and practice.

Theory Into Practice: The Academic Resource Center

Consistent with General College's developmental education mission, which emphasizes the holistic academic development of its students, the ARC exists to support student learning within and beyond the classroom. A distinction of General College is the centralization of its faculty and staff offices, classrooms, and learning resources within a single building on an expansive urban campus, which is a feature of effective developmental education (Boylan, Bliss, & Bonham, 1997, p. 3). By providing learning space only a corridor-length or flight of stairs away from classrooms, learning resources are readily accessible to students and instructors (White, 2004, p. 19). It should be noted that other colleges and departments at the University of Minnesota also offer tutoring locally: the College of Liberal Arts' Center for Writing, the Taylor Undergraduate Academic Center of the Institute of Technology, the Learning and Tutorial Center of Intercollegiate Athletics, and the Instructional Center of the Office for Multicultural and Academic Affairs. These centers vary in their student audience; hired staff (i.e., professional, graduate, and undergraduate); range of subject areas, from a focus on writing to multiple disciplines including chemistry, physics, and business; and hours of service (e.g., daytime versus evening). What makes General College's ARC unique is its direct support of the college's developmental education mission through centralized resources, staff trained in developmental education principles, and close partnerships with the college's curricular programs.

A decision was made in the early 1990s to bring together the college's separate writing and mathematics learning centers into a single learning space (see Figure 1). Owing to the efforts of former coordinators Susan Anderson (mathematics) and Dave Healy (writing), the ARC opened in 1995 with three primary areas: the Computer Center, Writing Center, and Math Center. Students first enter the ARC through the Computer Center and enjoy easy access to the adjoining Writing and Math Centers. While the space occupies three distinct rooms, their interconnection promotes a single "one-stop shop" atmosphere for students seeking learning resources. The reception area serves as a check-in station as well as reserve desk for course readings.

The Computer Center

The Computer Center consists of 18 computer workstations, including scanning, typing-tutorial, and disability-accessible workstations. About 1,300 users visit the center per week, a statistic that includes returning users. Users print, on average, 12 pages per computer per hour each day. In addition, two workstations provide access to VCRs and video monitors. The undergraduate desk receptionists help students move through the sign-in system and queue

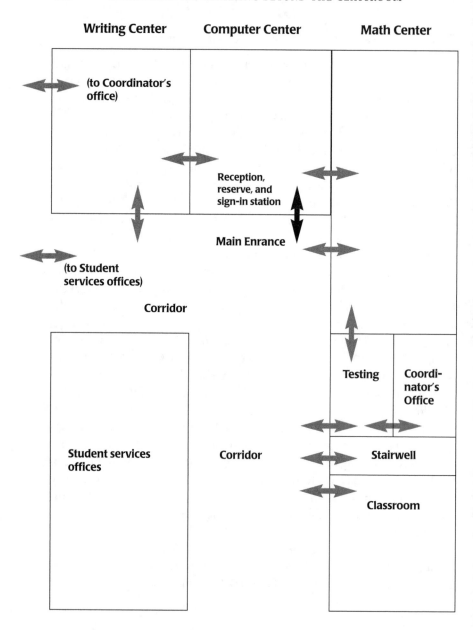

Figure 1. The General College Academic Resource Center occupies three adjoining rooms adjacent to a classroom and student services offices.

for available workstations. They also check out reserve items to students and provide computer users basic software and hardware support.

The Writing Center

The Writing Center has six tables that seat up to four students apiece. Lining the walls are bookshelves and document racks that hold writing reference books and handouts. Its mission statement stresses a commitment to student-centered peer consulting through collaboration:

> Our mission is to work collaboratively with students to build skills and confidence to improve their writing. Peer consultants facilitate the writing process by listening to writers, helping them clarify and articulate their ideas, and affirming the experiences and abilities students bring to writing. (Hartley, 2003, p. 2)

Peer consulting aids students' developmental learning by equalizing the balance of power in a writing conference. Peer tutors are called writing "consultants" to emphasize their training to approach writing as a collaborative process that makes the students' development central. The staff is comprised of up to 10 undergraduate writing consultants and two academic professionals, one of whom is a specialist in English as a Second Language. The staff participates in a 2-day training workshop in late summer and ongoing training meetings during the academic year.

The number of consultations per week varies with the semester cycle, from a few during the first week to over 200 later in the term. On average, a consultation with a student lasts 24 minutes. The students who visit the Writing Center are culturally and linguistically diverse; in fall 2002 and spring 2003, over 80% of students visiting the center self-identified as non-native English speakers. This high proportion reflects the close relationship the Writing Center enjoys with General College's Commanding English (CE) program, in which a few writing consultants also work within CE classes (Fitzpatrick & Hartley, 2002; see Chapter 9). In spring 2002, the Writing Center staff critically assessed their views of University of Minnesota writing standards and how they translate academic literacy within writing consultations. Our self-examination was motivated by an awareness of the nature of academic writing standards within a "culture of power" (Delpit, 1995, p. 25). From staff conversations and student interviews, we realized the need to make multicultural issues in writing a central part of our training, to ensure we are supporting the development of students' writing voices rather than simply promoting institutional expectations (Barron & Grimm, 2002; Fitzpatrick, Hartley, Linde, & Rusch, 2002). Again, the principles of collaboration guide our endeavors.

The Math Center

The Math Center occupies the largest room of the ARC, complete with nine tutoring tables that, combined, can seat 60 persons, and five computer workstations that support mathematics software and online resources. A quiet area for makeup testing exists in an adjoining office. Resources include a small library of mathematics texts and study guides, handouts, and calculators for temporary loan. Typically, two-dozen peer tutors are trained to promote a productive study environment in which both individuals and small groups may work. Consistent with the Writing Center's mission, we aim to work collaboratively with students to promote their independent learning.

Although individual peer tutoring has traditionally stood as our primary service, increasingly the Math Center staff has engaged in other forms of peer education that support curriculum and emphasize collaborative learning. For instance, peer tutors lead review sessions on evenings prior to examinations. In spring 2004, peer tutors served as leaders for SI sessions in intermediate algebra as part of a pilot program that continues in the 2004–2005 academic year. In the math center, peer tutors consistently work with small groups of students taking the same mathematics classes. The study groups are often student-formed, but some derive from cooperative-learning groups assigned in classes or, in the case of Multicultural Excellence Program scholars, arrangements made by program coordinators. Our interface with curriculum sometimes involves peer tutors serving as in-class teaching assistants or homework paper graders. These arrangements vary depending on the instructional modes used, reflecting the diversity of our curriculum.

Like the Writing Center, we have engaged in a process of self-analysis of our attitudes about mathematics learning and multiculturalism, and what multicultural issues might imply for our tutoring practices (Opitz, 2003). We emphasize in training that multiculturalism must infuse every aspect of our work with students. Taking a multicultural approach in mathematics education requires action beyond awareness; we must promote students' voices by listening and validating their needs, perspectives, and aspirations; and we must engage in ongoing self-assessment and growth.

Shared Practices

Both the Math Center and Writing Center enjoy strong relationships with academic departments and programs at the University of Minnesota. Building and maintaining these relationships requires active collaboration, however. Within General College, both coordinators teach courses in their respective subject areas of Basic Writing, Communicating in Society, Introductory and Intermediate Algebra, and Statistics. In Fall 2004, the coordinators team-taught a freshman seminar on urban literacy with a service-learning component (see next section). As instructors, we attend departmental meetings held by the writing and mathematics programs, participating in conversations on teaching and classroom management issues. In these meetings we also inform instructors of ARC initiatives and resources and invite colleagues to assign class activities that require use of ARC resources. Our collaboration with teaching faculty includes jointly-led tutor-training workshops, design of promotional literature and Web sites, coordination of supplementary learning opportunities (e.g., SI and review sessions), and provisions for in-class support (e.g., CE classroom assistance). Like many of our colleagues in academic support services, we collaborate in faculty and professional staff research, whether by offering collegial assistance in data collection or writing, or co-authoring research articles. Our service on college and campus committees has also nurtured partnerships.

Our commitment to multicultural education is reflected in our shared hiring strategies. When hiring, we employ the standard means for posting positions at the University's Job Center. However, many first-generation students from immigrant families are unfamiliar with job search protocols and learn about opportunities by word-of-mouth. To ensure we attract a strongly diverse pool of applicants, we actively invite referrals from General College instructors who often recommend highly-qualified students from their classes. We also seek referrals from our current ARC staff members and multicultural programs on campus, especially CE and the student programs of the Office of Multicultural and Academic Affairs. Our preferred qualifications state prior experience working with culturally-diverse populations.

As a tripartite unit, the ARC offers a full range of services in writing, mathematics, and computer technology assistance, summarized in Figure 2. A collaborative, peer-education philosophy, strong partnerships with academic departments and programs, and a centralized location are key ways in which we contribute to General College's developmental education mission.

Future Directions

The ARC, while possessing a rich historical background (ARC, 2003), is nevertheless only a decade old in its present configuration. Current and former staff have devoted much of this time to developing its infrastructure, practices, and policies, paralleling many of the growing pains experienced by new learning centers (Christ, Sheets, & Smith, 2000). We recognize that ours is a developing program. In this section we describe future directions of the ARC and identify criteria that guide us in our strategic planning and that also offer signposts for building a model program.

Computer Center

- Reception desk with Web-based sign-in
- Undergraduate student receptionists
- Serves students taking GC classes only
- 18 computer workstations
- Disability accommodation workstation
- Typing-tutorial computer station
- Image scanner
- Free printing (paid by GC student technology fees)
- 2 VCR/video monitors
- Windows Office software, online access
- Course reserve service
- Web site (linked to ARC home page)

Writing Center

- 6 tutoring tables, total seating capacity of 24
- 3 notebook computers
- Undergraduate student writing consultants
- Professional ESL consultant
- Peer, collaborative tutoring philosophy
- Serves GC students, other University of Minnesota undergraduate and graduate student writers
- Information sheets and handouts
- Small library of reference books
- Filing system for course syllabi and assignment sheets
- Consultant log sheets for data collection
- Commanding English classroom assistance
- Freshman Seminar on literacy (with Math)
- Web site (linked to ARC home page)

Math Center

- 9 tutoring tables, total seating capacity of 60
- 5 computers with math software, online access
- Undergraduate student math tutors
- Peer, collaborative tutoring philosophy
- Serves GC students, other University of Minnesota mathematics students
- Information sheets and handouts
- Small library of math textbooks and study skill references
- Filing system for course syllabi and assignment sheets
- Tutoring log sheets
- Makeup testing carrels
- SI instruction; math classroom assistance
- Freshman Seminar on literacy (with Writing)
- Web site (linked to ARC home page)

Figure 2. A summary of ARC resources in computing, writing, and mathematics assistance.

Assessment

Determining usage, assessing services, and monitoring students' needs are critical to maintaining quality academic support systems in a developmental education setting (Boylan, 1997). Over the years we have collected usage statistics in a variety of ways and have conducted surveys to assess our services (e.g., Lindoo, 1998). In Spring 2004 we implemented a Web-based sign-in system, created in-house, which will soon provide us with more details on who we serve in each center. The system, modeled on the standard sign-in system used at other computer labs at the University of Minnesota, is tailored to serve our multiple needs. It provides a queue for students waiting to use a computer workstation; it captures essential information about a student's visit such as date, time, and service selected; it supports input of additional details about peer-tutoring consultations; and it provides the ability to link to student demographic and academic records based on identifiers unique to each student who signed in. This last feature enables us to study characteristics of student users and, potentially, the impact of our services on academic progress, retention, and graduation.

An important source of information about our services comes from surveys administered to students in their General College classes. Many writing, literature, CE, and mathematics instructors include questions on surveys given in their classes to solicit students' feedback on various aspects to the services provided by the ARC.

Course Offering in Community Service Learning

To enrich the ARC's role within curriculum, we developed the idea of a credit-bearing course in tutor training. As we explored this option, we realized a need to move beyond strictly pedagogical issues and to embrace the social context of literacy, broadly defined to include reading, writing, and mathematics. We also desired to build community connections beyond campus while offering students opportunities that would promote their own career development. Making service-learning a central focus in the course seemed the natural solution. We wanted to attract undergraduates early in their academic careers and therefore chose the freshman seminar format. We offered the course, "Urban Literacy in Reading and Math," in fall 2004. The course requires weekly reading, volunteer tutoring in community centers, journal writing, seminar discussions, and a final course paper exploring a topic related to the course's themes. In addition to supporting the aims of the first-year experience, the course satisfies liberal education requirements in citizenship and public ethics and intensive writing. We find that in teaching the course, we embrace GC's social mission of building bridges between higher education and the broadest array of communities.

Strategic Planning

Over time, changes in student demographics, curriculum, and institutional priorities require our academic resources also to adapt (Stewart & Hartman, 2001). Budget realities prompting reassessment and retrenchment make research on the impact of tutoring services all the more critical (Boylan, Bonham, & Bliss, 1995). Variations in something as simple as the scheduling of classes may require concomitant adjustments in tutoring center staffing and hours. Students approaching the learning center with new requests, like arranged tutoring on a satellite campus, urge us to be continually open to innovation. Keeping up-to-date with the standards of Universal Design (UD) and ergonomics (Higbee & Eaton, 2003) requires periodic review, upgrades, and improvements. As General College entered strategic planning in the 2004–2005 academic year, the ARC's physical design and inventory of resources were areas for reconsideration.

Becoming a "Model" Program

In order to enhance the General College vision, we consider criteria defining a model program. For guiding our own strategic planning, we identify the following signposts. We believe these are appropriate for any learning center striving for excellence (Casazza & Silverman, 1996; White, 2004). This includes a clear mission reflecting both the interests of students and the institution; a philosophy of learning assistance, whether emphasizing cooperative education, multicultural education, or other pedagogical principles; accessible space, both in terms of its location on campus and its design, taking into consideration ergonomic and UD standards; and an environmental design that maximizes learning potential. It also requires a professional staff supported in teaching, research, and administrative roles; and peer tutors trained in the institution's missions and policies, good tutoring practice, and discipline-specific pedagogies. We also prioritize tutor accreditation; ongoing professional development of staff; good communications and publicity regarding the center within its immediate institutional context and in other strategic areas of the campus and community; Web site with links to resources; and annual reports. Also essential are computers with access to learning skills resources and disability accommodation software; supplementary curriculum or curriculum based in the center; and strong partnerships and collaborations with academic departments and programs. Finally, other signposts are ongoing assessment, strategic planning, and development; and membership in professional associations devoted to learning assistance, developmental education, or student development in particular disciplines. We find that the ARC meets most of these benchmarks; we are taking steps to ensure that we meet them all.

Conclusion

During an era marked by pedagogical reform and a growing recognition of the importance of multicultural approaches in developmental education, learning centers occupy central places in curricular innovations. A strong synergy exists between cooperative learning pedagogies in a variety of curricular models and the collaborative practice that is the hallmark of peer tutoring. As we have shown, mathematics and writing centers interface with academic departments in ways that build coherence within students' educational lives. On the other hand, their semi-autonomy from courses provide students spaces where *they* set the agendas, explore *their* learning potential, and create *their* learning communities. Our challenge is to embrace the principles of developmental education while achieving the flexibility required for serving our students and institutions effectively. Becoming a model program may involve reaching certain signposts, but ultimately we achieve excellence by making the difference in promoting students' academic successes.

References

Abel, J. P. (1977). *A survey of mathematics learning centers in the public two-year colleges of the United States.* Unpublished doctoral dissertation, University of Northern Colorado, Greeley.

Academic Resource Center. (2003). *Annual report, 2002–2003: Promoting academic success in writing, computer skills, and math.* Minneapolis, MN: Author. Retrieved June 7, 2004, from http://www.gen.umn.edu/resources/arc/images/annual_report_2003.pdf

American Mathematical Association of Two-Year Colleges. (1995). *Crossroads in mathematics: Standards for introductory college mathematics before calculus.* Memphis, TN: Author.

Arendale, D. (2004). Mainstreamed academic assistance and enrichment for all students: The historical origins of learning assistance centers. *Research for Educational Reform, 9*(4), 3–21.

Barnett, R. W., & Blummer, J. S. (1999). *Writing centers and writing across the curriculum programs: Building interdisciplinary partnerships.* Westport, CT: Greenwood Press.

Barron, N., & Grimm, N. (2002). Addressing racial diversity in a writing center: Stories and lessons from two beginners. *The Writing Center Journal, 22*(2), 55–83.

Bonwell, C. C., & Eison, J. A. (1991). *Active learning: Creating excitement in the classroom* (ASHE-ERIC Higher Education Report 1). Washington, DC: George Washington University.

Boylan, H. R. (1997). The case for program research in developmental education. *The Learning Assistance Review, 2*(2), 20–34.

Boylan, H. R., Bliss, L. R., & Bonham, B. S. (1997). Program components and their effectiveness to student performance. *Journal of Developmental Education, 20*(3), 2–8.

Boylan, H. R., Bonham, B. S., & Bliss, L. B. (1995). What we know about tutoring: Findings from the National Study of Developmental Education. *Research in Developmental Education, 12*(3), 1–4.

Bridwell-Bowles, L. (2003). *Literacy and Minnesota's academic culture: A case for institutional change. A report presented to the Committee on the Coordination of Writing on the Twin Cities Campus.* Minneapolis, MN: Center for Interdisciplinary Studies of Writing, College of Liberal Arts, University of Minnesota. Retrieved June 7, 2004, from http://cisw.cla.umn.edu/research_publications/publications/Bridwell-Bowles.pdf

Bruch, P. (2002, October). *A multicultural learning community for first year students: Developing identity, belonging, and agency.* Paper presented at the Focusing on the First Year Conference, Minneapolis, MN.

Casazza, M., & Silverman, S. (1996). *Learning assistance and developmental education: A guide for effective practice.* San Francisco: Jossey-Bass.

Chism, N. V. N., & Bickford, D. J. (2002). Improving the environment for learning: An expanded agenda. In D. V. N. Chism & D. J. Bickford (Eds.), *The importance of physical space in creating supportive learning environments* (pp. 91–97). (New Directions for Teaching and Learning, No. 92). San Francisco: Jossey-Bass.

Christ, F. L., Sheets, R., & Smith, K. (Eds.). (2000). *Starting a learning center: Conversations with CRLA members who have been there and done that!* Clearwater, FL: H & H.

Davidson, N. A., Reynolds, B. E., & Rogers, E. C. (2001). Introduction to cooperative learning in undergraduate mathematics. In E. C. Rogers, N. A. Davidson, B. E. Reynolds, & A. D. Thomas (Eds.), *Cooperative learning in undergraduate mathematics: Issues that matter and strategies that work* (pp. 1–11). Washington, DC: Mathematical Association of America.

Delpit, L. (1995). *Other people's children: Cultural conflict in the classroom.* New York: New Press.

DiPardo, A. (1992). "Whispers of coming and going": Lessons from Fannie. *The Writing Center Journal, 12*(2), 125–144.

Ender, S. C., & Newton, F. B. (2000). *Students helping students: A guide for peer educators on college campuses.* San Francisco: Jossey-Bass.

Fitzpatrick, R., & Hartley, D. (2002, November). *Making connections: Immigrant students and the writing center.* Paper presented at the annual conference of the College Reading and Learning Association, Minneapolis, MN.

Fitzpatrick, R., Hartley, D., Linde, A., & Rusch, A. (2002, October). *Academic literacies: Engaging writing consultants in the theoretical conversation.* Paper presented at the National Conference of Peer Tutoring in Writing/Midwest Writing Center Association, Lawrence, KS.

Gabelnick, F., MacGregor, J., Matthews, R. S., & Smith, B. L. (Eds). (1990). *Learning communities: Creating connections among students, faculty, and disciplines.* (New Directions for Teaching and Learning, No. 41). San Francisco: Jossey-Bass.

Gillam, A. M. (1994). Collaborative learning theory and peer tutoring practice. In J. A. Mullin & R. Wallace (Eds.), *Intersections: Theory-practice in the writing center* (pp. 39–53). Urbana, IL: National Council of Teachers of English.

Goodsell, A. S., Maher, M., & Tinto, V. (1992). *Collaborative learning: A sourcebook for higher education.* University Park, PA: National Center on Postsecondary Teaching, Learning, and Assessment.

Gourgey, A. E. (1992). Tutoring developmental mathematics: Overcoming anxiety and fostering independent learning. *Journal of Developmental Education, 15*(3), 10–14.

Hartley, D. (2003). *A manual for undergraduate teaching assistants in the writing center, 2003–2004.* Minneapolis, MN: General College, University of Minnesota.

Higbee, J. L., & Eaton, S. B. (2003). Implementing Universal Design in learning centers. In J. L. Higbee (Ed.), *Curriculum transformation and disability: Implementing Universal Design in higher education* (pp. 231–239). Minneapolis, MN: Center for Research on Developmental Education and Urban Literacy, General College, University of Minnesota.

Jehangir, R. R. (2001). Cooperative learning in the multicultural classroom. In D. B. Lundell & J. L. Higbee (Eds.), *Theoretical perspectives for developmental education* (pp. 91–99). Minneapolis, MN: Center for Research on Developmental Education and Urban Literacy, General College, University of Minnesota.

Johnson, D. W., & Johnson. R. (1984). *Cooperative learning.* Edina, MN: Interaction Book.

Kail, H. (1983). Collaborative learning in context: The problem with peer tutoring. *College English, 45,* 594–599.

Kenny, P. A., & Kallison, J. M., Jr. (1994). Research studies on the effectiveness of Supplemental Instruction in mathematics. In D. C. Martin & D. R. Arendale (Eds.), *Supplemental Instruction: Increasing achievement and retention* (pp. 75–82). (New Directions for Teaching and Learning, No. 60). San Francisco: Jossey-Bass.

Kinney, D. P. (2001). Developmental theory: Application in a developmental mathematics program. *Journal of Developmental Education, 25*(2), 10–18, 34.

Koch, L. (1996). The development of voice in the mathematics classroom. *Focus on Learning Problems in Mathematics, 18*, 164–175.

Koch, L., & Anderson, J. (2004). *Teaching freshman seminars: Faculty handbook*. Minneapolis, MN: University of Minnesota.

Lindoo, S. (1998). *Evaluation of the Academic Resource Center, General College, University of Minnesota*. Minneapolis, MN: Office of Research and Evaluation, General College, University of Minnesota. Retrieved June 7, 2004, from http://www.gen.umn.edu/research/ore/reports/arc_eval98_index.htm

Lunsford, A. (1991). Collaboration, control, and the idea of a writing center. *The Writing Center Journal, 12*(1), 3–10.

Lyman, L., & Foyle, H. (1990). *Cooperative grouping for interactive learning: Students, teachers and administrators*. Washington, DC: National Education Association.

MacGregor, J., Cooper, J. L., Smith, K. A., & Robinson, P. (2000). *Strategies for energizing large classes: From small groups to learning communities*. (New Directions for Teaching and Learning, No. 81). San Francisco: Jossey-Bass.

Maxwell, M. (Ed.). (1994). *When tutor meets student* (2nd ed.). Ann Arbor, MI: University of Michigan.

Michaelsen, L. K. (1992). Team learning: A comprehensive approach for harnessing the power of small groups in higher education. *To Improve the Academy, 11*, 107–122.

Mullin, J. A., & Wallace, R. (Eds.). (1994). *Intersections: Theory-practice in the writing center*. Urbana, IL: National Council of Teachers of English.

National Council of Teachers of Mathematics. (1989). *Curriculum and evaluation standards for school mathematics*. Reston, VA: Author.

National Council of Teachers of Mathematics. (2000). *Principles and standards for school mathematics*. Reston, VA: Author.

North, S. M. (1984). The idea of a writing center. *College English, 46*(5), 433–446.

North, S. M. (1994). Revisiting "The idea of a writing center." *The Writing Center Journal, 15*(1), 7–19.

Opitz, D. L. (2003, September). *Multicultural math tutoring? The role of training*. Paper presented at the Minnesota Association for Developmental Education Tenth Annual Conference, Grand Rapids, MN.

Opitz, D. L. (2004, Summer). Connecting with the curriculum: The General College Math Center at the University of Minnesota. *NCLCA Newsletter, 2*.

Powers, J. K. (1993). Rethinking writing center conferencing strategies for the ESL writer. *The Writing Center Journal, 13*(2), 39–47.

Reid, J., Forrestal, P., & Cook, J. (1990). *Small group learning in the classroom*. Portsmouth, NH: Heinemann.

Reynolds, T. J., & Bruch, P. L. (2002). Curriculum and affect: A participatory developmental writing approach. *Journal of Developmental Education, 26*(2), 12–20.

Rogers, E. C., Davidson, N., Reynolds, B. E., & Thomas, A. D. (2001). *Cooperative learning in undergraduate mathematics: Issues that matter and strategies that work.* Washington, DC: Mathematical Association of America.

Stewart, T. C., & Hartman, K. A. (2001). Finding out what the campus needs: The process of redefining a learning center. *The Learning Assistance Review, 6*(1), 39–49.

Testone, S. (1999). Mathematics support services—Tutoring and beyond. *Research & Teaching in Developmental Education, 15*(2), 93–97.

Tobias, S. (1993). *Overcoming math anxiety* (rev. ed.). New York: W. W. Norton.

Topping, K. (1996). *Effective peer tutoring in further and higher education.* (SEDA paper 95). Birmingham, UK: Staff and Educational Development Association.

Treisman, U. (1985). *A study of the mathematics performance of Black students at the University of California, Berkeley.* Unpublished doctoral dissertation, University of California, Berkeley.

Treisman, U. (1992). Studying students studying calculus: A look at the lives of minority mathematics students in college. *College Mathematics Journal, 23*(5), 362–372.

Walmsley, A. L. E. (2003). *A history of the "new mathematics" movement and its relationship with current mathematical reform.* Lanham, MD: University Press of America.

White, W. G. (2004). The physical environment of learning support centers. *The Learning Assistance Review, 9*(1), 19–27.

Wilson, S. M. (2003). *California dreaming: Reforming mathematics education.* New Haven, CT: Yale University Press.

Wright, G. L., Wright, R. R., & Lamb, C. E. (2002). Developmental mathematics education and Supplemental Instruction: Pondering the potential. *Journal of Developmental Education, 26*(1), 30–35.

Integrating Theory
and Research With Practice

Integrating Theory and Research With Practice

Introduction

Another strength of General College is its integration of research with the latest theory and best practices in higher education. Lundell, Chung, and Higbee outline some of the recent research trends and pedagogical accomplishments of the faculty and staff in the college. The college's strength lies in its multidisciplinary, collaborative approach to advancing the field of developmental education and access-related research on diversity in higher education. The college has historically offered a context for integrating theory and research with practice, which in turn has also influenced the development of assessment methods for diverse students with a range of academic skills.

Tom Brothen and Cathy Wambach's chapter provides the historical context and theoretical basis for an assessment model that was developed in GC. They point out how influential University of Minnesota faculty and administrators were in developing prediction models still used in college admissions throughout the U.S. today. Yet they also describe how the founding of the General College provided a means of access for students whose success might not have been anticipated on the basis of predictive formulae alone. Brothen and Wambach call our attention to the belief of such notable figures in UMN's history as President Lotus Delta Coffman that equal educational opportunity is a public good, a concept reasserted in a recent U.S. Supreme Court decision. They also delineate how an objective comprehensive examination was developed and implemented in GC, while the college's founders still asserted that no single test should determine a student's future.

This confluence of theories, research, and models for assessment have placed General College at the forefront of the nation's field of developmental education. This section will address two examples of this approach, past and present.

CHAPTER 21

Contributions of the General College to Theory and Research

Dana Britt Lundell,
Carl J. Chung, and Jeanne L. Higbee

ABSTRACT

General College (GC) has a visible national role in the field of access and developmental education research and theory. It is a leader in the field, and recent trends in research by faculty, staff, and graduate students in the college have created an enhanced view of the ways that theory, research, and practice intersect in the classroom to improve student learning. A variety of disciplinary areas are represented in this research, and engaging and progressive models for curricular revision and student-centered pedagogies are being developed and applied. The future of GC research reflects a continuation of its theory-grounded development of an integrated and inclusive model for access and advancement in higher education for a diverse range of learners.

The General College (GC) is a unique academic unit. It is a self-contained developmental education unit at a Carnegie I research university that integrates student support services with instruction, basic academic skill development with regular college course content, and the no-nonsense know-how of practitioners with the insights of a broad range of theoretical perspectives and active research agendas. As such, it is difficult to identify peer developmental education programs with respect to which GC might be compared or evaluated.

To get an overall picture of GC's contributions to student access, retention, and learning, then, requires a different tact. In this chapter, our approach will be to sketch the history of developmental education and learning assistance, with special attention to changing theoretical orientations and models. With this historical framework serving as a backdrop, we then turn to a discussion of GC's research mission, current research models, and the role of its two research centers, the Office of Research and Evaluation (ORE) and the Center for Research on Developmental Education and Urban Literacy (CRDEUL). In this way, we can situate and evaluate GC's contributions in the larger historical context of what has been tried, what has worked, and what has not worked.

A number of authors have begun reconstructing the history of remedial and developmental education, including Arendale (2002a, 2000b), Bullock, Madden, and Mallery (1990), Casazza & Silverman (1996), Clowes (1992), and Maxwell (1997). Although all of these sources provide useful perspectives, the work of Clowes stands out because it combines all of the following: it is more critical, it is written from more of an outsider's perspective, it addresses the low status of developmental education in higher education, and it explicitly points to research and theory as a means of improving that status.

Clowes (1992) loosely structured his account based upon historical periods presented in *Beyond the Open Door* by Cross (1971): the Period of Aristocracy (colonial time to Civil War), the Period of Meritocracy (Civil War to 1950s), and the Period of Egalitarianism (1960s and 1970s). Finally, Clowes added what he called the Period of Reconsideration or Retrenchment (1980s onward), in which all facets of public education came under increasingly critical scrutiny (p. 477). He noted in passing that this latter period may well signal a return to the more elitist ideological orientation of the Period of Meritocracy.

While remedial programs existed during both the Period of Aristocracy and the Period of Meritocracy, Clowes (1992) found no evidence of sustained study of such programs. One shift is worth noting, however. Remedial programs during both periods were dedicated to basic skill building. But whereas during the Period of Aristocracy such skill building occurred before students entered college in special preparatory departments and schools, the Period of Meritocracy saw the rise of specialized stand-alone college courses in reading, study skills, and mathematics.

It was not until the Period of Egalitarianism during the 1960s and 1970s that developmental education really came into its own (Clowes, 1992; Cross, 1971). During this period a key conceptual shift occurred away from the traditional emphasis upon academic skill building and its inherent deficit model, and towards an alternative approach that focused on enhancing student success, broadly conceived, to include not only academic skills, but social and personal needs as well (Clowes, 1992, p. 466; Dwinell & Higbee, 1991b; Higbee, 1988, 1993, 1996b). This shift marked the emergence of a distinction between "remedial education" as basic skill acquisition on the one hand, and "developmental education" as an integrated and pluralistic approach that considers the "whole person" on the other (Boylan, 1999; Clowes, 1992; Cross, 1971). What is not clear is just how far-reaching or successful this conceptual shift has been, a point to which we shall return later in our conclusion. Within the Period of Egalitarianism, Clowes identified several different strands in research and theory related to developmental education and offered negative assessments of each one.

The first strand involved attempts to identify and characterize effective developmental education program models and best practices. Researchers identified different ways of structuring programs: skills based versus more integrated, isolated courses based in traditional academic departments, specially designated courses not based in traditional departments but taught by disciplinary faculty, learning assistance centers, and separate instructional units dedicated to remedial or developmental education (Clowes, 1992). Attempts to determine the optimal structure were inconclusive, however. Some researchers concluded that a separate department was best, others stressed the importance of strong support services, and others advocated the learning assistance model. But as Clowes summarized, "It appears that the search for the ideal program is over. Acceptance that there is no 'one best way' to design remediation programs represents a tacit acknowledgment in the field that the delivery of remediation is a complex and multifaceted enterprise" (p. 469).

A second strand of research and theory goes beyond attempts simply to seek out exemplary developmental education programs. Instead, Clowes (1992) described three conceptual frameworks that were and perhaps continue to be explored in the hope of guiding the development of successful new programs. One framework focuses on characterizing different types of developmental education students and their different educational needs. Another framework stresses the need to consider affective as well as cognitive factors to enhance the success of at-risk students. A third framework emphasizes general organizational principles that call for different program tracks targeting pretransfer issues, basic skills acquisition, adult basic education, and students with disabilities. Attempts such as these can be viewed as trying to make sense of and get a handle on the complexity and multifaceted nature of developmental education. Unfortunately, Clowes contended that "No concept or theory has emerged to guide program design. Developmental education has emerged as a term frequently used, but developmental education is so broadly applied it is difficult to gain guidance from the multiple interpretations and practices with which it is associated" (p. 471).

Clowes (1992) characterized a third strand of research and theory that attempts to identify psychological traits of developmental students and to use these traits to clarify lack of satisfactory academic performance (p. 473). If such traits could be found, then educators would presumably know what to focus on in order to help developmental students improve their academic performance. Candidates for these general psychological characteristics or traits include "... intelligence, motivation ..., cognitive style ..., self-concept, locus of control, field dependence/independence, anxiety ..., coping behaviors, and . . . right and left brain dominance" (p. 473). Overall, though, Clowes argued that subsequent research has found ". . . no solid evidence to support a direct causal link between any one of these concepts and underachievement or poor achievement in higher education" (p. 474).

Finally, a fourth strand of research and theory centers on learning theory and using it to "provide a theoretical foundation for an instructional design that . . . allow[s] remediation to succeed" (Clowes, 1992, p. 475). Clowes considered three possibilities: behaviorism, cognitive psychology, and developmental psychology. Behaviorism is associated with such instructional approaches as "individualized instruction, programmed instruction, computer-assisted instruction, and mastery learning" (p. 475). Clowes associated cognitive psychology with teaching strategies that emphasize cognitive style. Developmental psychology is presented as the champion of the affective domain, especially as applied by student services professionals (Dwinell & Higbee, 1991b; Higbee, 1989; Higbee & Dwinell, 1990b, 1992, 1993, 1995). Although Clowes noted that developmental educators have tried hard to base sound practice on developmental psychology, nonetheless he concluded that "little evidence exists for the successful integration of developmental theory into the practice of remediation" (p. 475).

It might be objected that Clowes' (1992) discussion and conclusions are too negative and out of date. Is it not more accurate to say that, although no overarching theoretical framework has emerged to inform and strengthen developmental education, still progress has been made? Also, many of the research programs and theories that Clowes found wanting are still active areas of work. Is it not more fair to conclude that solid answers have not been found *yet*? And, finally, Clowes' overview was published in 1992. What about more recent developments such as constructivism, conceptual change theory, multicultural education, or Discourse theory? Have these newer approaches not made a difference?

We are sympathetic to such objections. However, the question remains, can we confidently assert that as a whole the field of developmental education is, in fact, currently grounded in research and theory? Or, as Clowes (1992) issued the challenge:

> No theoretical or conceptual basis has been established as an undergirding for program design in remediation. The field appears dominated by an eclectic approach in which promising ideas and practices are identified, modified, adopted, and occasionally assessed. Theory is used after the fact to justify practice as often as it is used to plan practice; there is no way to distinguish the two possibilities. It appears the field is driven by neither theory nor research; rather, it is grounded in practical experience . . . (p. 475)

For the field of developmental education taken as a whole, unfortunately, we believe that the answer is "no, we are not firmly grounded in good research and theory." But this is not to say that progress has been negligible or that there are no promising attempts to improve this state of affairs. Our basic contention is that in order for developmental education to meet Clowes' challenge, there must be sites at which developmental educators are actively researching and theorizing in addition to engaging in exemplary practice.

That brings us back to the General College. Because GC is one site at which faculty, staff, and students not only do developmental education but also have the opportunity to carefully and systematically study what they do, how they do it, and why they do it, we believe that considering GC's mission, theoretical models, and research centers is important. Doing so will provide a valuable glimpse at where the field of developmental education currently is, and, perhaps, where it needs to go.

Defining General College's Research Mission

As the historical chapters in this book have outlined, GC has focused its mission on theory, research, and practice that enhances student development for the widest range of learners possible. Situated in a land-grant, Carnegie I research university, this college has, as a central part of its focus, a strong mission of engaging in and contributing to research at the national level while also focusing on providing access for students and generating knowledge and insights that can enhance and work with the social community surrounding the university. Although the focus of the college has shifted over time and remained responsive to external political visions of its role, the central commitment of the college's faculty, staff, and graduate students has been to develop and strengthen the nation's canon of research addressing student development, learning, and diversity as it impacts and supports students' transitions into higher education and workforce settings. Specifically, this has included a focus on retention, transfer, and graduation issues, as well as discipline-specific and content-area emphases on improving curricula to address a range of students' talents, vocational goals, and their avocations in life.

Specifically, GC's mission centrally addresses theory, practice, and research on student learning and curriculum development. Its research emphasis is twofold, according to the current mission statement of the college:

1. To develop, through teaching, research, and service, the potential for baccalaureate education in students who are serious about fulfilling their previously undeveloped or unrecognized academic promise, and
2. To generate and apply knowledge concerning how best to understand,

broaden, and deepen academic achievement in our increasingly diverse, multi-cultural society. (General College, 2005)

This mission has historically placed GC's primary research activities in the related practice-driven fields of developmental education, student development, learning assistance, and higher education. As noted in Chapter 3 by Johnson and 22 by Brothen and Wambach, the areas of counseling and student personnel psychology were and continue to be largely influential in the work of the college's faculty and staff. As GC's educational mission shifted over the years, its research mission also reflects changes that have occurred both within the college locally and across the field at the national level. A unique feature of GC's curricular model is, and has always been, its multidisciplinary core curriculum that prepares students for future programs, jobs, and life work. This focus brings together a wide range of related research areas from fields such as mathematics education, composition studies, biological sciences, social sciences, arts, humanities, and literature. The interaction of professionals with expertise in their individual content areas with their colleagues working in different fields has always been key to GC's unique approach and contributions to progressive research trends in the field.

At the national level, GC is the oldest developmental, general education program in the nation. This anchors the college's work, research, and leadership in its innovative curriculum in the legacy of the progressive era of education and the work of John Dewey (Shaw, 2002). The relationship of research to the direct improvement of students' academic growth and the emphasis on its relevance to and impact on their worlds beyond the doors of the college has provided a type of pragmatic grounding for the college, from which it continues to shape challenging research questions and studies. Its ongoing focus on issues of providing access for nontraditional student populations is also an essential concept and driving force among its faculty and staff, to engage in meaningful, socially responsible research that results in illuminating the effectiveness and equity in its delivery of education and skill development. GC faculty and staff have been engaged in theory, research, and practice to enhance their programs since the inception of the college, a history that is described in other chapters of this book and is presently being documented further in the GC Archives Project. Although it is the primary scope of this chapter to address present trends in GC theory and practice, we acknowledge the foundations of the GC model and past research that has contributed to its present strengths and forms.

This past work in GC has resulted in the college's growing national reputation as a present leader in developmental education and learning assistance. While the quality of the work of the students and the college's faculty and staff has always been solid, recently the college has gained its national reputation through a series of awards, including the Noel-Levitz Award for Retention Excellence and the John Champaign Memorial Award for Outstanding Developmental Education Program from the National Association for Developmental Education (NADE). Beyond these awards, the college's focus on research that enhances access for students continues to attract national attention through work that is widely disseminated.

GC's mission will always and primarily be responsive to the needs of students, which change over time and are widely varied from student to student. As the college continues to be responsive to economic, political, and social forces beyond the doors of its programs, the research mission of the college will remain at the national forefront in predicting trends, providing for transformations, and interpreting and mapping out future directions in higher education. This can only occur in a college such as GC, which features a multidisciplinary offering of academically rigorous courses, attracts a truly multicultural student body, and recruits a diverse faculty and staff who are committed to creating a strong learning community for both its students and its professionals.

General College's Research in Postsecondary Developmental Education

Presently the college is focusing intensively on strengthening its research mission in postsecondary developmental education as a response to the 1997 external review of the college that was conducted to examine the effectiveness of GC's programs. This included the development of a research center, the Center for Research on Developmental Education and Urban Literacy (CRDEUL), and an increase in dissemination, publication, and grants and research development for access in higher education. This also included hiring a cohort of tenure-track faculty with an emphasis in scholarship and teaching that connects individual disciplines to the broader work of student development and learning innovations for diverse students. Teacher-scholars whose work focuses on areas such as critical pedagogy, multiculturalism, cooperative learning, qualitative research, statistics, anthropology, philosophy, sociology, and legal and policy issues joined the already productive GC faculty whose expertise includes psychology, art, film, writing, literature, history, science, counseling, and mathematics. Professional staff in the college, such as counselor advocates, administrative and teaching professionals, and support services staff also contribute their expertise in enhancing GC's research, publication, teaching, services, and grants development missions to highlight important research for the wider field of higher education. GC's role in shaping future trends, transforming present curricula, and supporting students from diverse backgrounds has continued since 1997 to focus more exclusively on making breakthroughs in the understanding of access and achievement issues.

Classroom-Based Interdisciplinary Research

GC's current core curriculum reflects its roots in providing general education to undergraduate students. This curriculum includes courses that have changed over the years to reflect both the college's mission and the changing social and economic landscape. Courses in workforce literacy have included business education, life skills development, and computer classes. The college has also provided courses to prepare students in content areas for academic transitions in areas such as math, writing, economics, sciences, and humanities. Current research trends in GC have followed a similar path, with most of the scholarly activities of the faculty, staff, and graduate students concentrating on improving learning and applying theories to enhance pedagogies for access and success. Because most of GC's courses have not historically been linked in an interdisciplinary way, much of the research has focused on scholars' applications of the most progressive research methods in their current fields to the work of providing solid general education courses to students.

Presently in 2005, the college still primarily functions with a diverse core curriculum that includes a variety of disciplinary-based subjects taught by faculty and staff with expertise in a specific content area. However, since 1997 the college's research and educational mission has focused more intensively on the work of a newer field called developmental education, which emerged in the 1970s from the work and knowledge of learning assistance professionals, community college educators, and those working to provide access for students entering 4-year institutions. Given the strong disciplinary-based expertise of most of GC's faculty and staff and the recent, decade-long focus on postsecondary developmental education, which emphasizes retention and transfer, the college has produced a rich body of theory, research, and practice that has contributed to improved curricular models and interventions that enhance social and academic access for diverse students (e.g., all students, including students of color, mainstream students, English Language Learners, first-generation college students, students with disabilities, and adults). Additionally, the priority of understanding the diverse ways that students learn, in a society that is increasingly global and multicultural, has also contributed to GC's increased work on academic literacy and sociocultural identity issues, K-16 outreach, and campus-community collaborations.

This transformation of GC's research focus has been a positive response to students themselves, whose needs as learners and citizens are at the heart of most of the research initiatives that are completed by these scholar-teachers. More recently, work on learning communities in the fields of learning assistance and developmental education (Malnarich with Others, 2003; Tinto, 1998) is beginning to shape the GC model toward a more multidisciplinary approach to its work. Perhaps a future trend of the college will be to become more interdisciplinary (Haynes, 2002), though the college is presently defined in part by its location in the University of Minnesota, which has a historically-based model of providing disciplinary-focused courses in a variety of subject areas.

Curricular and Pedagogical Models for Creating Educational Access

The General College continues to experiment with new ways of thinking about curricular transformation and engaging in student-centered teaching. As GC faculty, staff, and graduate assistants explore new models and rethink existing programs and strategies, it is important that they conduct related research and disseminate the results broadly.

Curricular innovation. One curricular innovation that has actually been in place in the General College for many years is the Commanding English (CE) program (see Chapter 9). Until the past decade, not many articles appeared in developmental education publications about programs for English language learners, but now this population is a central focus of developmental education programs in a number of geographic areas. CE director Robin Murie and her colleagues (Murie & Thomson, 2001) were among those who brought this facet of developmental education to the attention of the profession with their chapter in the NADE monograph.

One of the most recent curricular models adopted by a significant number of GC instructors to enhance access to higher education is Universal Instructional Design (UID; Bowe, 2000; Pliner & Johnson, 2004; Silver, Bourke, & Strehorn, 1998). UID is a relatively new pedagogical model originally conceived for providing access for students with disabilities by rethinking teaching practices to create curricula and classrooms that are inclusive for all students. An architectural concept, Universal Design (Center for Universal Design, n.d.), provides the foundation for Universal Instructional Design. When planning a space, the architect takes into consideration the needs of all potential users of that space. As a result, ramps, elevators, expanded doorways, door handles (as opposed to knobs), signs, bathrooms, and other features do not have to be added or modified at additional expense after the completion of a building. Some of the same architectural features that accommodate people with disabilities also benefit many others, including senior citizens, families with young children, and delivery people.

Universal Instructional Design applies this same concept, advance planning to meet the needs of all learners, to curriculum development and extracurricular programs. In the past, students with disabilities have been stigmatized by a medical model approach (Johnson & Fox, 2003), in which these students have been perceived as "deficient" rather than merely "different." Universal Instructional Design is an outgrowth of an interactional, social constructivist approach to disability issues. Instead of providing accommodations on a case-by-case, situation-by-situation basis, this model explores how individuals interact with the environment to construct knowledge (Aune, 2000; Johnson & Fox).

Although federal legislation assures access for postsecondary students with disabilities (Kalivoda & Higbee, 1989, 1994; Pliner & Johnson, 2004), legislation could not transform centuries-old academic practices overnight:

> Although higher education became more available to historically underrepresented groups, educational practices and culture did not shift significantly to address the experiences and learning needs of the students newly enrolled. So, although legislation opened the door to diverse student populations, the absence of efforts to change the culture or the educational practices in higher education (such as the curriculum, physical layout, and teaching and testing methods) have created significant barriers to access, retention, and graduation for many students, particularly students with disabilities. (Pliner & Johnson, p. 106)

Thus, despite significant increases in the number of students with disabilities pursuing postsecondary education (Henderson, 1999), students with disabilities are more likely to find access to 2-year institutions, and less likely to transfer and be retained and ultimately graduate from 4-year institutions (Pliner & Johnson).

Through the implementation of UID in the General College, faculty and staff strive to make the University of Minnesota more accessible to all students, but particularly to students with disabilities. In the film *Uncertain Welcome* (2002), created within the General College under the auspices of a U.S. Department of Education grant, Curriculum Transformation and Disability (CTAD), students with disabilities discuss why this work is so important.

Although UID was originally envisioned as a means for enhancing access to postsecondary education for students with disabilities, its benefits as a model for social justice and multicultural education as more broadly defined cannot be overlooked (Barajas & Higbee, 2003; Hackman & Rauscher, 2004; Pliner & Johnson, 2004). If student services and classroom and extracurricular experiences are designed to take into consideration the challenges faced not only by students with disabilities, but also by students who are not native speakers of English, students who come from families who have no previous experience with higher education or cannot afford all the latest technology, students whose religious beliefs prevent them from engaging in some activities, students who feel isolated because they are not of the "majority" race on a given campus, students who do not feel that they can comfortably share their sexual orientation with their classmates, and others who traditionally have felt excluded on college and university campuses, everyone will benefit.

The General College has made significant contributions to the literature surrounding Universal Instructional Design. GC authors (Barajas & Higbee, 2003) were among the first to suggest that UID serve as a model for multicultural higher education. They have also led the way in addressing how UID can be implemented in student services and their administration (Higbee, 2003) and in specific teaching disciplines (Higbee; Higbee, Chung, & Hsu, 2004). Unfortunately, it is easy for academic professionals to discount the material provided in professional development workshops and in-service training conducted by others (e.g., disability services personnel) whom they do not think can "really understand" the demands of their workload and the standards of their field. Only faculty, governed by the professional standards that guide their work, can determine the essential skills and knowledge that students should be able to demonstrate upon completion of their courses. Thus, it is imperative that faculty members write for publication about Universal Instructional Design in their own disciplines.

Pedagogical models. Faculty members and teaching specialists in the General College conduct research and write for publication regarding a wide range of pedagogical practices that enhance learning. For example, GC psychology faculty members Tom Brothen and Cathy Wambach, who will in fall 2005 add to their ranks Tabitha Grier and Na'im Madyun (Brothen & Wambach, 2000; Madyun, Grier, Brothen, & Wambach, 2004), have led the developmental education community in engaging in research and writing for publication regarding the use of the Personalized System of Instruction (PSI) and computer-assisted learning. Current GC faculty member Doug Robertson, former faculty member Pat Kinney, current teaching specialist Janet Stottlemyer, and former teaching specialist Laura Kinney have been influential in conducting research related to computer-assisted instruction and other teaching practices in mathematics (Kinney & Kinney, 2002; Kinney & Robertson, 2003; Kinney, Stottlemyer, Hatfield, & Robertson, 2004). Another significant contribution to the literature surrounding teaching developmental education mathematics courses has been the General College's emphasis on multicultural and ethnomathematics (Duranczyk, Staats, Moore, Hatch, Jensen, & Somdahl, 2004; also see Chapter 10).

The focus of the GC science faculty (Jensen & Rush, 2000; Johnson, 1993; Moore, 1991, 2002) has been pedagogical models for science that address the diverse learning styles of students taking developmental science courses, including the use of multimedia (Moore & Miller, 1996), cooperative learning techniques (Jensen, Moore, & Hatch, 2002a, 2002b), and inquiry-based instruction (Higbee, Chung, & Hsu, 2004). Science faculty members and others have participated in learning communities and "packaged courses" (Wilcox, delMas, Stewart, Johnson, & Ghere, 1997). Randy Moore (1993, 1997) has done significant work to demonstrate how writing enhances learning in the sciences.

Faculty members David Ghere and Karen Miksch (Ghere, 2001; Miksch & Ghere, 2004) have published about their use of simulations, mock trial, and other interactive strategies in the social sciences, while Mark Pedelty (2001a, 2004) has addressed his use of playwriting, performance, and other communication strategies. Walt Jacobs, Tom Reynolds, and former GC faculty member Greg Choy (Jacobs, Reynolds, & Choy, 2004) have shared their experiences using storytelling in the classroom. As demonstrated in Chapter 18, Jacobs (1998) and fellow sociologist Heidi Barajas have brought the sociological imagination to life in the General College, as well as teaming with other faculty members to develop interdisciplinary pedagogies (Barajas, Bruch, Choy, Chung, Hsu, Jacobs, et al., 2002).

General College art faculty member Pat James (1999, 2002; James & Haselbeck, 1998) has stirred the creativity of students and developmental educators alike with her work on teaching the arts and on metaphoric thinking, as clearly demonstrated in Chapter 13. GC basic writing faculty members (Bruch, 2004; Lee, 2000; Reynolds & Bruch, 2002) also strive to create assignments that require students to think in new and different ways.

Exploring Factors Related to Achievement
Another area in which General College authors have made significant contributions to knowledge is in research related to understanding why some students are more successful than others. A number of GC faculty members have been involved in studies that have explored the relationship between class attendance, for example, and course grades or grade point averages (Chung, 2004; Moore, Jensen, Hatch, Duranczyk, Staats, & Koch, 2003; Thomas & Higbee, 2000). Jeanne Higbee (Dwinell & Higbee, 1991a; Higbee, 1989; Higbee & Dwinell, 1990a, 1992, 1996; Higbee & Thomas, 1999; Thomas & Higbee) has spent much of her professional career researching affective variables that are related to student success, including test anxiety, mathematics anxiety, self-esteem and academic self-concept, and locus of control. Higbee (Higbee & Thomas, 2002) has also conducted research related to academic honesty issues and differences both between and among faculty and students in perceptions of behaviors that constitute cheating. Both Higbee (Higbee & Dwinell 1990a, 1992; Higbee & Thomas; Thomas & Higbee) and Cathy

Wambach (1993) have explored issues related to student motivation and academic autonomy, and Tom Brothen and Wambach (2001; Wambach & Brothen, 2001) have also conducted research on conscientiousness and procrastination. This research is important in then determining interventions to assist students in overcoming barriers to achievement.

Explorations of Theory and Its Role in Transforming Practice

One important role that GC has played in the field of developmental education is recent work that has been done on exploring the role of theory or theories in the teaching and research of developmental educators and learning assistance professionals. Lundell and Collins (1999), Wambach, Brothen, and Dikel (2000), and Bruch and Collins (2000) have noted a wide variety of theories that contribute to the work of developmental educators. Sometimes the work in the field is misunderstood in its broad scope and intersection of teaching theories and practices that shape it. These GC faculty and staff have urged others to explore further the role of theory and the development of more integrated theories in the teaching, research, and practice of developmental education and higher education.

Chung (2005) has more recently contributed an important perspective on the role theory plays in the daily work of practitioners in the field—those who teach without the formal charge of research as central in their work scope. This includes a majority of the field's professionals who work in 2-year community colleges or 4-year programs that do not emphasize direct research as an outcome for assessing student learning. Practice-based theories often shape the work of college educators and contribute widely to student success. Chung proposed that more formal explorations of the kinds of theories that contribute to work in these classrooms would help highlight the nature and foundations of the field. This would, in turn, also allow practitioners to play a larger role in articulating their own contributions to the field.

Multiculturalism, Discourses, Student Voice, and Literacy Theories

Many GC faculty, staff, and graduate students have also been committed to connecting their work in GC with the research, theories, and pedagogies that have been influential in the areas of multiculturalism, diversity, and literacy practices. GC scholar-teachers in the writing, history, and social science programs have been very active in contributing their ideas about the importance of access, diversity, and multiculturalism in developing courses that support the widest range of students. For example, GC faculty and staff in the field of basic writing, a subfield of college composition studies, have been nationally prominent as leaders in incorporating liberatory, democratic perspectives in their course design to engage students as active citizens and authors of their own ideas as writers and thinkers (e.g., Bruch, 2001; Reynolds, 2001). Also, GC's social science and history teacher-scholars have integrated their course subject matter and skill development with a constructivist, multicultural perspective (Barajas, 2002; Ghere, 2001; Jehangir, 2001; Pedelty & Jacobs, 2001), as well as further examinations and social critiques of how race and gender construct and constrict educational spaces (Barajas, 2001) for students from nonmainstream backgrounds. These scholar-teachers are also working across their disciplines to form cooperative, peer learning communities (Jehangir) that can provide students with more engaging environments from which to develop their talents, think critically, and gain workforce skills that are necessary to continue to develop skills beyond college.

Several GC faculty and staff have pointed out that the work of multiculturalism is key to the future of GC research and practice (Barajas, 2001; Bruch & Higbee, 2002). A more recent trend is to extend this work centrally within the field of developmental education (Higbee, Lundell, & Duranczyk, 2003), which already incorporates individually supportive programs and bases its work on supporting various learning styles and preferences of students. The work of the GC Multicultural Concerns Committee, a democratically and volunteer-run committee, has been instrumental since 1987 in focusing on academic, professional, and personal research activities that foreground conversations about students that recognize multiple meanings of diversity, such as race, ethnicity, social class, home language, sexual orientation, age and disability (Ghere, 2003).

This group recently formed a subcommittee to work on assessing faculty, student, and staff perceptions of multicultural issues in higher education settings. They adapted a survey from K-12 education (Banks, Cookson, Gay, Hawley, Irvine, Nieto, Schofield, & Stephan, 2001) that addressed institutional goals, curricular foundations, and culturally sensitive models for education. This resulted in the *Multicultural Awareness Project for Institutional Transformation* (MAP IT; Miksch, Higbee, Jehangir, Lundell, Bruch, Siaka, & Dotson, 2003), a set of survey tools for administrators, faculty, staff, and students in higher education. The project was piloted in GC (Higbee, Miksch, Jehangir, Lundell, Bruch, & Jiang, 2004) and is being disseminated nationally as a tool for colleges and universities to begin conversations about multiculturalism and inclusion in their own academic institutions. This work has also resulted in a variety of ongoing research publications from the group of MAP IT researchers (Bruch, Jehangir, Lundell, Higbee, & Miksch, 2005; Higbee et al.; Miksch, Bruch, Higbee, Jehangir, & Lundell, 2003).

In addition to GC research that examines issues of diversity and multiculturalism, a related strand of research in the college has considered the role of

"Discourses" (Gee, 1996) in the fields of developmental education and learn-ing assistance (Lundell & Collins, 1999). Social and academic identities, and students' ways of making meaning in their various intersecting "worlds" (Beach, Lundell, & Jung, 2002) in college, are featured in recent work of the college. College as a site of students' navigating their multiple roles as stu-dents, family members, sisters, brothers, peers, partners, and other social identities is an important contribution of GC's developmental education researchers in their consideration of how students can learn and develop within the spaces of higher education. Classes such as college composition in GC have based their own work on such theoretical perspectives, including a focus on the "dialogic" model for learning (Reynolds, 2001; see Chapter 11) that invites students to enter conversations about how they can change and impact their own futures and social worlds. This perspective gives agency to students as co-learners in the educational process and equalizes the space of the classroom as much as it can be possible in a traditional academic classroom.

Another area of growing research in GC is qualitative research that fea-tures the voices and standpoints of students (e.g., Beach, Lundell, & Jung, 2002; James, 2002; Pedelty, 2001a). Qualitative educational research looks at the rich details and nuances of students' experiences and perceptions of their college programs through interviews, longitudinal studies, narrative inquiry, writing analysis, ethnography, and short-response survey data. This kind of research has gained a national focus in graduate education and professional training programs in the past 2 decades (Merriam & Associates, 2002), and this trend has produced a variety of new scholars who incorporate either qualitative research or mixed-methods models for research combining qual-itative and quantitative data. GC scholars have added this type of data as a means of gathering information about student learning, and it is useful in addition to quantitative studies of GC students, such as institutional report-ing measures on GPA and academic progress, in providing individually-spe-cific information about students for whom the transition from high school to college is filled with more complexity. This type of research also can provide insights about why students experience "stigma" (Pedelty, 2001b) related to being in a program like the General College. Finding ways to learn more about this phenomenon is key to challenging public and personal stereotypes about students for whom access to higher education may traditionally have been viewed as not attainable.

Combined, these approaches to research that feature theoretical perspec-tives such as multiculturalism, democratic theory, and sociocultural literacy practices contribute a more socially-constructed perspective on learning to the field of developmental education, which has tended to feature more individualistic models of learning. These models, in fact, are complementary and not contradictory, and the legacy and present status of GC research acknowledges and demonstrates that this richness in approaches is a real strength of a college that strives to address the learning needs of all students.

K-16 Research and Community Collaborations
Another area of GC research has been to increase research relationships with partners in the region, such as community and county organizations, community colleges, and secondary schools. To study transitions from high school to college, particularly for disenfranchised and underserved student populations, it is a goal of GC researchers to work across academic institutions to examine the complex continuum of issues that concern teachers, students, legislators, and administrators. Because such a variety of constituencies is invested in the success and access of students in colleges and universities, it has become a priority of some GC researchers to explore their connections to other contexts in which students participate beyond the courses and services of the GC program. Viewed in a larger social context, research with students designed and conducted in a mutual partnership can provide better information about why students attend college, how they succeed, and how they view their skill development as relevant to future jobs and worlds outside of academia.

In this spirit, there have been several recent research initiatives that reflect GC's social and academic mission within the greater Twin Cities and statewide communities of Minnesota. First, a ground-breaking initiative led by the Hennepin County African American Men Project (Hennepin County Office of Planning and Development, 2002) led to a partnership with the University of Minnesota General College to examine college admissions and achievement of African American men, ages 18 to 24, from Hennepin County, which primarily includes the Minneapolis metropolitan area and surrounding suburbs. To learn more about what happens to men from a group that represents one of the most underrepresented and underserved populations in the nation's educational system, General College researchers led a localized project at the University to investigate the issues and learn more about what African American students themselves had to say about their transitions (Taylor, Schelske, Hatfield, & Lundell, 2002). This kind of community and college partnership is critical in answering complex questions and providing a better relationship between the research mission of the university and the concerns of the public.

Outreach programs also provide a site for research and inquiry in GC. The Commanding English program for English language learners, as well as the Upward Bound program for high school students from low-income, first-generation college, or other disadvantaged backgrounds, and students with disabilities are examples of sites that have provided places for GC's faculty and staff to develop and design research studies to learn about students' educational needs and implement curricular transformations that can improve learning (Murie & Thomson, 2001). Additionally, many faculty and staff incorporate methodologies such as service-learning into their courses and research projects (e.g., Barajas, 2002), thus providing a link with the community and engaging students in activities that continue to enhance their future skills for life and the workforce.

The college is also involved in national initiatives and has hosted "think tanks," such as the Future Directions Research Meetings for Developmental Education (Higbee & Pettman, 2003; Lundell & Higbee, 2000, 2002). An important aspect of these conversations has been the improvement and continuation of national research that includes collaborations with other developmental educators and learning assistance professionals. The focus of these meetings has been the expansion of national conversations to include a more centralized look at the role of theory, multiculturalism, and multidisciplinary models for research in the field as it applies to student learning. Most recently, an initiative of the General College's Dean David Taylor emphasized a research and service priority that examines issues of college preparation, readiness, and improvements in learning for underserved students in the Twin Cities metropolitan area. This is the Metropolitan Higher Education Consortium's Initiative on Developmental Education (Lundell, Higbee, & Hipp, in press), which is the outcome of a partnership of the University of Minnesota and the Minnesota State College and University system (MnSCU)—the two major delivery systems of higher education in the state. This also includes a goal of developing research and grants with secondary schools and community colleges, and it is stimulating projects in GC that examine high-school-to-college transitions from the perspectives of educators and students. These efforts, in the form of meetings, outreach programs, and national think tanks, are carving a future identity for GC as a site of engaged national research that invites collaborative models for theory, practice, and research in the work of making education accessible for all students.

General College Research Centers

Two research offices also exist in GC to address questions of access and student success. Assessing the effectiveness of GC's curricular models and student support programs is essential to the college's mission. It is also key to GC's mission to provide national leadership and dissemination of its theory, research, and practices to a wide variety of other professionals who can benefit from the kinds of projects that are undertaken and supported by these offices.

First, the Office of Research and Evaluation (ORE), named officially in the late 1980s, has tracked student progress, outcomes, and paths beyond the walls of the General College throughout the college's history. ORE's mission involves gathering and analyzing data, such as students' grades in various courses, the relationship of past academic achievements to their present successes, such as traditional college test-score predictors as they relate to their college GPAs, and feedback about the effectiveness of GC's programs in students' ongoing work in other UMN academic programs. This office collects and shares a variety of reports with collaboration opportunities for faculty and staff to work with the data sets to ask and answer specific questions related to academic interventions in their own courses, such as attendance and motivation predictors for student success in college classes. ORE's primary role is to provide internal support for the college as well as information for the UMN to assess the effectiveness of GC's programs.

Second, the Center for Research on Developmental Education and Urban Literacy (CRDEUL) was founded in 1996 to address a mission of promoting and developing multidisciplinary research and professional development for the fields of developmental education, access, and urban literacy (Lundell, 2002). The Center offers in-house resources, professional consultations, mentoring, publications, dissemination, and grants development for research in postsecondary developmental education. Its annual monographs and periodic books and reports (e.g., Higbee, 2003; Duranczyk, Higbee, & Lundell, 2004; Higbee, Lundell, & Duranczyk, 2003; Miksch et al., 2003) have gained national attention within the field's professional organizations, such as the National Association for Developmental Education, the College Reading and Learning Association (CRLA), the American College Personnel Association (ACPA), and the National College Learning Center Association (NCLCA). CRDEUL has provided a conduit for regional and national collaborations to expand the definition of developmental education to be more inclusive of a variety of theoretical perspectives.

The impact of the Center's work has just begun, as it has continued to expand in response to the professionals and communities that it serves both in the Twin Cities and in the nation. It also features an Advisory Board and two GC faculty advisors, Jeanne Higbee (Senior Advisor for Research) and David Arendale (Advisor for Outreach), in addition to an editorial team and its Program Director, Dana Lundell, who are all active in contributing to research and publications. A key insight of these professionals and the work of the Center has also been to challenge other developmental education programs to consider expanding their notions of student preparation to look more broadly at embedding skill development across content areas. This perspective is partially a unique feature of the GC program itself, but it is also a useful and progressive perspective for educators in all first-year, undergraduate courses to consider as a way to increase access for all students in their courses.

With the college's ORE and CRDEUL, GC has prioritized the highest caliber of professional research possible at the core of its mission. In a field that experiences constant external and public scrutiny, these offices ensure that the work of the field and the college is shared with professionals and that the contributions solidly address key questions that are most current and instrumental in creating sound educational programs.

The Future of Research and Theory at GC

The overview provided in this chapter demonstrates the range, depth, and scope of recent work by the GC community. In relation to Clowes' (1992) framework sketched at the outset, it is clear that the GC community is actively researching, theorizing, and exploring almost every facet of this complex phenomenon known as developmental education, as well as broader issues surrounding access, retention, and student learning. The ORE collects, analyzes, and disseminates data on GC program structure, organization, and student outcomes. CRDEUL and other GC faculty and staff members are engaged in a multipronged approach to generating and supporting innovative research and theorizing that spans all the conceptual frameworks and more specific research strands detailed by Clowes: investigating student characteristics and the needs of different students, taking seriously affective and social factors as well as cognitive ones, identifying and measuring particular psychological traits of our students, and utilizing and furthering newer theories of student learning. Indeed, with its exploration of learning communities, UID, multicultural education, critical literacy, sociocultural factors, Discourse theory, integrating basic skill development and regular college course content, and its commitment to a truly multidisciplinary approach to teaching and student learning, GC has clearly moved beyond what Clowes set out.

The impressive range of ongoing research and theorizing by the GC community also points to an implicit assumption in Clowes' (1992) evaluation of developmental education that may need rethinking. That is, Clowes implicitly assumes that a viable and mature field of developmental education will quite naturally identify or create a single, unitary theoretical framework to guide practice and research. The alternative assumption implicit in the GC approach, however, is that a plurality of theoretical frameworks is needed in order to make real progress and to grapple successfully with the underappreciated diversity of phenomena that comprise the developmental education enterprise. In fact, it may well be this need for a pluralistic approach that helps explain why more traditional unitary theories have not been embraced by all developmental educators, and why those looking for the emergence of such a singular theoretical framework have concluded that the theoretical state of developmental education is somehow inadequate or in disarray. But it appears to be the case that only by weaving together a number of complementary explanatory frameworks can we adequately understand diverse developmental education students and their variable needs.

Such a pluralistic, multidimensional approach does not mean that anything and everything goes, however. That is, in order to realize its potential, we believe that the GC community must take the next step and reflectively focus and coordinate its many strands of theory and research. This does not mean that a single approach must be agreed upon at the expense of others. But it does mean that core values, theoretical assumptions, shared goals, and concrete outcomes need to be articulated, discussed, and agreed upon. Focusing and coordinating the many different strands of GC research and theorizing are critical to enacting long-term change that is meaningful, transformative, and sustainable.

In this regard, multiculturalism, UID, and Discourse theory stand out as particularly important for the future of GC research and theory. This is so because each of these broader theoretical orientations can fulfill three critical functions: (a) serve as a guiding umbrella framework that embodies core shared values, goals, and outcomes; (b) help to organize and guide future research projects and theorizing; and (c) accommodate the defining aspects of GC practice, including multidisciplinary curriculum development, focus on student needs and perspectives, and the integration of affective considerations and basic skill development along with teaching regular course content. It may be that one of these approaches or a well-defined and developed hybrid of these approaches will need to be recognized and adopted as the inspiration and nexus for the next stage of GC research and theorizing.

Ultimately, though, it may be that the most important contribution GC will make to research and theory is a modest one: persistence. That is, in the current national climate of retrenchment, which has sometimes become hostile toward access and developmental education, the persistence of an egalitarian and progressive program such as GC is critical. The continuation of a program like GC is so important because both equitable access and developmental education have been afterthoughts in American higher education, and GC stands for the radical notion that nontraditional, nonmainstream students *belong* and ought to be valued as highly as other students. Therefore, if the community of GC scholars, teachers, and support staff can continue to exist in a meaningful form, then that community can continue to challenge both hegemonic ideas about nonmainstream students and the traditional structures of higher education that have become so efficient at discouraging and excluding them. Thought of in these terms, perhaps persistence is not such a modest goal after all.

References

Arendale, D. (2002a). A memory sometimes ignored: The history of developmental education. *The Learning Assistance Review, 7*(1), 5–13.

Arendale, D. (2002b). Then and now: The early history of developmental education: Past events and future trends. *Research & Teaching in Developmental Education, 18*(2), 3–26.

Aune, B. (2000). Career and academic advising. In H. Belch (Ed.), *Serving students with disabilities* (pp. 55–67). (New Directions in Student Services, No. 91). San Francisco: Jossey-Bass.

Banks, J. A., Cookson, P., Gay, G., Hawley, W. D., Irvine, J. J., Nieto, S., Schofield, J. W., & Stephan, W. G. (2001). *Diversity within unity: Essential principles for teaching and learning in a multicultural society.* Seattle, WA: Center for Multicultural Education, College of Education, University of Washington. Retrieved May 25, 2005, from http://www.depts.washington.edu/centerme/home.htm

Barajas, H. L. (2001). Is developmental education a racial project? Considering race relations in developmental education spaces. In D. B. Lundell & J. L. Higbee (Eds.), *Theoretical perspectives for developmental education* (pp. 65–74). Minneapolis, MN: Center for Research on Developmental Education and Urban Literacy, General College, University of Minnesota.

Barajas, H. L. (2002). Changing objects to subjects: Transgressing normative service learning approaches. In D. B. Lundell & J. L. Higbee (Eds.), *Exploring urban literacy & developmental education* (pp. 25–32). Minneapolis, MN: Center for Research on Developmental Education and Urban Literacy, General College, University of Minnesota.

Barajas, H. L., Bruch, P., Choy, G., Chung, C., Hsu, L., Jacobs, W., et al. (2002). Interdisciplining pedagogy: A roundtable. *Symploke, 10*(1–2), 118–132.

Barajas, H. L., & Higbee, J. L. (2003). Where do we go from here? Universal Design as a model for multicultural education. In J. L. Higbee (Ed.), *Curriculum transformation and disability: Implementing Universal Design in higher education* (pp. 285–290). Minneapolis, MN: Center for Research on Developmental Education and Urban Literacy, General College, University of Minnesota.

Beach, R., Lundell, D. B., & Jung, H-J. (2002). Developmental college students' negotiation of social practices between peer, family, workplace, and university worlds. In D. B. Lundell & J. L. Higbee (Eds.), *Exploring urban literacy & developmental education* (pp. 79–108). Minneapolis, MN: Center for Research on Developmental Education and Urban Literacy, General College, University of Minnesota.

Boylan, H. R. (1999). Exploring alternatives to remediation. *Journal of Developmental Education, 22*(3), 2–4.

Bowe, F. G. (2000). *Universal Design in education—Teaching nontraditional students.* Westport, CT: Bergin & Garvey.

Brothen, T., & Wambach, C. (2000). A research based approach to developing a computer-assisted course for developmental students. In J. L. Higbee & P. L. Dwinell (Eds.), *The many faces of developmental education* (pp. 59–72). Warrensburg, MO: National Association for Developmental Education.

Brothen, T., & Wambach, C. (2001). The relationship of conscientiousness to metacognitive study strategy use by developmental students. *Research & Teaching in Developmental Education, 18*(1), 25–31.

Bruch, P. (2001). Democratic theory and developmental education. In D. B. Lundell & J. L. Higbee (Eds.), *Theoretical perspectives for developmental education* (pp. 37–48). Minneapolis, MN: Center for Research on Developmental Education and Urban Literacy, General College, University of Minnesota.

Bruch, P. L. (2004). Universality in basic writing: Connecting multicultural justice, Universal Instructional Design, and classroom practices. *Basic Writing e-Journal, 5*(1).

Bruch, P. L., & Collins, T. (2000). Theoretical frameworks that span the disciplines. In D. B. Lundell & J. L. Higbee (Eds.), *Proceedings of the first intentional meeting on future directions in developmental education* (pp. 19–22). Minneapolis, MN: Center for Research on Developmental Education and Urban Literacy, General College, University of Minnesota.

Bruch, P. L., & Higbee, J. L. (2002). Reflections on multiculturalism in developmental education. *Journal of College Reading and Learning, 33*(1), 77–90.

Bruch, P. L., Jehangir, R., Lundell, D. B., Higbee, J. L., & Miksch, K. L. (2005). Communicating across differences: Toward a multicultural approach to institutional transformation. *Innovative Higher Education, 29* (3), 195–208.

Bullock, T. L., Madden, D. A., & Mallery, A. L. (1990). Developmental education in American Universities: Past, present and future. *Research & Teaching in Developmental Education, 6*(2), 5–73.

Casazza, M. E., & Silverman, S. L. (1996). *Learning assistance and developmental education.* San Francisco: Jossey-Bass.

Center for Universal Design. (n.d.). *What is Universal Design?* Retrieved March 6, 2002, from http://www.design.ncsu.edu:8120/cud/univ_design/udhistory.htm

Chung, C. J. (2004). The impact of attendance, instructor contact, and home-work completion on achievement in a developmental logic course. *Research & Teaching in Developmental Education, 20*(2), 48–57.

Chung, C. J. (2005). Theory, practice, and the future of developmental education. *Journal of Developmental Education, 28*(3), 2–4, 6, 8, 10, 32–33.

Clowes, D. A. (1992). Remediation in American higher education. In J. C. Smart (Ed.), *Higher education: Handbook of theory and research, vol. VIII* (pp. 460–493). New York: Agathon Press.

Cross, P. (1971). *Beyond the open door: New students in higher education.* San Francisco: Jossey-Bass.

Duranczyk, I. M., Higbee, J. L., & Lundell, D. B. (Eds.). (2004). *Best practices for access and retention in higher education.* Minneapolis, MN: Center for Research on Developmental Education and Urban Literacy, General College, University of Minnesota.

Duranczyk, I. M., Staats, S., Moore, R., Hatch, J., Jensen, M., & Somdahl, C. (2004). Developmental mathematics explored through a sociocultural lens. In I. M. Duranczyk, J. L. Higbee, & D. B. Lundell (Eds.), *Best practices for access and retention in higher education* (pp. 43–53). Minneapolis, MN: Center for Research on Developmental Education and Urban Literacy, General College, University of Minnesota.

Dwinell, P. L., & Higbee, J. L. (1991a). Affective variables related to mathematics achievement among high risk college freshmen. *Psychological Reports, 69,* 399–403.

Dwinell, P. L., & Higbee, J. L. (1991b). The relationship between developmental tasks and academic success among high risk freshmen. *College Student Affairs Journal, 11*(1), 37–44.

Gee, J. P. (1996). *Social linguistics and literacies: Ideology in discourses* (2nd ed.). Bristol, PA: Falmer.

General College. (2005). *Our mission.* Retrieved May 5, 2005, from http://www.gen.umn.edu/gc/Mission.htm

Ghere, D. L. (2001). Constructivist perspectives and classroom simulations in developmental education. In D. B. Lundell & J. L. Higbee (Eds.), *Theoretical perspectives for developmental education* (pp. 101–108). Minneapolis, MN: Center for Research on Developmental Education and Urban Literacy, General College, University of Minnesota.

Ghere, D. L. (2003). The triumphs and tribulations of a Multicultural Concerns Committee. In J. L. Higbee, D. B. Lundell, & I. M. Duranczyk (Eds.), *Multiculturalism in developmental education* (pp. 51–58). Minneapolis, MN: Center for Research on Developmental Education and Urban Literacy, General College, University of Minnesota.

Hackman, H. W., & Rauscher, L. (2004). A pathway to access for all: Exploring the connections between Universal Instructional Design and social justice education. *Equity & Excellence in Education, 37,* 114–123.

Haynes. C. (Ed.). (2002). *Innovations in interdisciplinary teaching.* Westport, CT: The Oryx Press.

Henderson, C. (1999). *College freshmen with disabilities.* Washington, DC: American Council on Education.

Hennepin County Office of Planning and Development. (2002). *African American Men Project—Crossroads: Choosing a new direction.* Minneapolis, MN: Hennepin County Office of Planning and Development. Retrieved May 25, 2005, from http://www.co.hennepin.mn.us/opd/opd.htm

Higbee, J. L. (1988). Student development theory: A foundation for the individualized instruction of high risk freshmen. *Journal of Educational Opportunity, 3,* 42–47.

Higbee, J. L. (1989). Affective variables and success in mathematics: The counselor's role. *College Student Affairs Journal, 9,* 44–50.

Higbee, J. L. (1993). Developmental versus remedial: More than semantics. *Research & Teaching in Developmental Education, 9*(2), 99–105.

Higbee, J. L. (Ed.). (2003). *Curriculum transformation and disability: Implementing Universal Design in higher education.* Minneapolis, MN: Center for Research on Developmental Education and Urban Literacy, General College, University of Minnesota.

Higbee, J. L., Chung, C. J., & Hsu, L. (2004). Enhancing the inclusiveness of first-year courses through Universal Instructional Design. In I. M. Duranczyk, J. L. Higbee, & D. B. Lundell (Eds.), *Best practices for access and retention in higher education* (pp. 13–25). Minneapolis, MN: Center for Research on Developmental Education and Urban Literacy, General College, University of Minnesota.

Higbee, J. L., & Dwinell, P. L. (1990a). Factors related to the academic success of high risk freshmen: Three case studies. *College Student Journal, 24,* 380–386.

Higbee, J. L., & Dwinell, P. L. (1990b). The high risk student profile. *Research & Teaching in Developmental Education, 7,* 55–64.

Higbee, J. L., & Dwinell, P. L. (1992). The development of underprepared freshmen enrolled in a self-awareness course. *Journal of College Student Development, 33,* 26–33.

Higbee, J. L., & Dwinell, P. L. (1993). A new role for counselors in academic affairs. *College Student Affairs Journal, 13*(1), 37–43.

Higbee, J. L., & Dwinell, P. L. (1995). Affect: How important is it? *Research & Teaching in Developmental Education, 12*(1), 71–74.

Higbee, J. L., & Dwinell, P. L. (1996). Correlates of self-esteem among high risk students. *Research & Teaching in Developmental Education, 12*(2), 41–50.

Higbee, J. L., Lundell, D. B., & Duranczyk, I. M. (Eds.). (2003). *Multicultur-alism in developmental education*. Minneapolis, MN: Center for Research on Developmental Education and Urban Literacy, General College, University of Minnesota.

Higbee, J. L., Miksch, K. L., Jehangir, R. R., Lundell. D. B., Bruch, P. L., & Jiang, F. (2004). Assessing our commitment to providing a multicultural learning experience. *Journal of College Reading and Learning, 34*(2), 61–74.

Higbee, J. L., & Pettman, H. C. H. (2003). Report of the Future Directions Meeting multicultural theme track. In J. L. Higbee, D. B. Lundell, & I. M. Duranczyk (Eds.), *Multiculturalism in developmental education* (pp. 69–74). Minneapolis, MN: Center for Research on Developmental Education and Urban Literacy, General College, University of Minnesota.

Higbee, J. L., & Thomas, P. V. (1999). Affective and cognitive factors related to mathematics achievement. *Journal of Developmental Education, 23*(1), 8–10, 12, 14, 16, 32.

Higbee, J. L., & Thomas, P. V. (2002). Student and faculty perceptions of behaviors that constitute cheating. *NASPA Journal, 40*(1), 39–52.

Jacobs, W. R. (1998). The teacher as text: Using personal experience to stim-ulate the sociological imagination. *Teaching Sociology, 26*(3), 222–228.

Jacobs, W. R., Reynolds, T. J., & Choy, G. P. (2004). The Educational Story-telling Project: Three approaches to cross-curricular learning. *Journal of College Reading and Learning, 35*(1), 50–66.

James, P. (1999). Ideas in practice: The arts as a path for developmental stu-dent learning. *Journal of Developmental Education, 22*(3), 22–28.

James, P. (2002). Ideas in practice: Fostering metaphoric thinking. *Journal of Developmental Education, 25*(3), 26–28, 30, 32–33.

James, P., & Haselbeck, B. (1998). The arts as a bridge to understanding iden-tity and diversity. In P. L. Dwinell & J. L. Higbee (Eds.), *Developmental edu-cation: Meeting diverse student needs* (pp. 3–20). Morrow, GA: National Association for Developmental Education.

Jehangir, R. (2001). Cooperative learning in the multicultural classroom. In D. B. Lundell & J. L. Higbee (Eds.), *Theoretical perspectives for developmental edu-cation* (pp. 91–99). Minneapolis, MN: Center for Research on Developmen-tal Education and Urban Literacy, General College, University of Minnesota.

Jensen, M., Moore, R., & Hatch, J. (2002a). Cooperative learning: Part I. Cooperative quizzes. *The American Biology Teacher, 64*(1), 29–34.

Jensen, M., Moore, R., & Hatch, J. (2002b). Cooperative learning: Part II. Set-ting the tone with group Web pages. *The American Biology Teacher, 64*(2), 118–120.

Jensen, M., & Rush, R. (2000). Teaching a human anatomy and physiology course within the context of developmental education. In J. L. Higbee &

P. L. Dwinell (Eds.), *The many faces of developmental education* (pp. 47–57). Warrensburg, MO: National Association for Developmental Education.

Johnson, A. B. (1993). Enhancing general education science courses. *College Teaching, 41*(2), 55–58.

Johnson, D. M., & Fox, J. A. (2003). Creating curb cuts in the classroom: Adapting Universal Design principles to education. In J. L. Higbee (Ed.), *Curriculum transformation and disability: Implementing Universal Design in higher education* (pp. 7–21). Minneapolis, MN: Center for Research on Developmental Education and Urban Literacy, General College, University of Minnesota.

Kalivoda, K. S., & Higbee, J. L. (1989). Students with disabilities in higher education: Redefining access. *Journal of Educational Opportunity, 4,* 14–21.

Kalivoda, K. S., & Higbee, J. L. (1994). Implementing the Americans with Disabilities Act. *Journal of Humanistic Education and Development, 32,* 133–137.

Kinney, D. P., & Kinney, L. S. (2002). Instructors' perspectives of instruction in computer-mediated and lecture developmental mathematics classes. In J. L. Higbee, I. M. Duranczyk, & D. B. Lundell (Eds.), *Developmental education: Policy and practice* (pp. 127–138). Warrensburg, MO: National Association for Developmental Education.

Kinney, D. P., & Robertson, D. F. (2003). Technology makes possible new models for delivering developmental mathematics instruction. *Mathematics and Computer Education, 37,* 315–328.

Kinney, D. P., Stottlemyer, J., Hatfield, J., & Robertson, D. F. (2004). Comparison of the characteristics of computer-mediated and lecture students in developmental mathematics. *Research & Teaching in Developmental Education, 21*(1), 14–28.

Lee, A. (2000). *Composing critical pedagogies: Teaching writing as revision.* Urbana, IL: National Council of Teachers of English.

Lundell, D. B. (2002). History of the Center for Research on Developmental Education and Urban Literacy: 1996–2002. In D. B. Lundell & J. L. Higbee (Eds.), *Exploring urban literacy & developmental education* (pp. 3–8). Minneapolis, MN: Center for Research on Developmental Education and Urban Literacy, General College, University of Minnesota.

Lundell, D. B., & Collins, T. C. (1999). Toward a theory of developmental education: The centrality of "Discourse." In J. L. Higbee & P. L. Dwinell (Eds.), *The expanding role of developmental education.* Morrow, GA: National Association for Developmental Education.

Lundell, D. B., & Higbee, J. L. (2000). *Proceedings of the first intentional meeting on future directions in developmental education.* Minneapolis, MN: Center for Research on Developmental Education and Urban Literacy, General College, University of Minnesota.

Lundell, D. B., & Higbee, J. L. (2001). *Proceedings of the second meeting on future directions in developmental education.* Minneapolis, MN: Center for Research on Developmental Education and Urban Literacy, General College, University of Minnesota.

Lundell, D. B., Higbee, J. L., & Hipp, S. (in press). *Proceedings of the Metropolitan Higher Education Consortium's developmental education initiative.* Minneapolis, MN: Center for Research on Developmental Education and Urban Literacy, General College, University of Minnesota.

Madyun, N., Grier, T., Brothen, T., & Wambach, C. (2004). Supplemental Instruction in a Personalized System of Instruction general psychology course. *The Learning Assistance Review, 9*(1), 7–16.

Malnarich, G., with Others. (Eds.). (2003). *The pedagogy of possibilities: Developmental education, college-level studies, and learning communities.* (National Learning Communities Project Monograph Series). Olympia, WA: The Evergreen State College, Washington Center for Improving the Quality of Undergraduate Education, in cooperation with the American Association for Higher Education.

Maxwell, M. (1997). *Improving student learning skills: A new edition.* Clearwater, FL: H&H.

Merriam, S. B., & Associates. (2002). *Qualitative research in practice: Examples for discussion and analysis.* San Francisco: Jossey-Bass.

Miksch, K. L., Bruch, P. L., Higbee, J. L., Jehangir, R. R., & Lundell, D. B. (2003). The centrality of multiculturalism in developmental education. In J. L. Higbee, D. B. Lundell, & I. M. Duranczyk (Eds.), *Multiculturalism in developmental education* (pp. 5–13). Minneapolis, MN: Center for Research on Developmental Education and Urban Literacy, General College, University of Minnesota.

Miksch, K. L., & Ghere, D. (2004). Teaching Japanese incarceration. *The History Teacher, 37* (2), 211–227.

Miksch, K. L., Higbee, J. L., Jehangir, R. R., Lundell, D. B., Bruch, P. L., Siaka, K., & Dotson, M. V. (2003). *Multicultural awareness project for institutional transformation: MAP IT.* Minneapolis, MN: Multicultural Concerns Committee and Center for Research on Developmental Education and Urban Literacy, General College, University of Minnesota.

Moore, R. (1991). Critical thinking in biology classes. *Strategies for Success in Anatomy & Physiology and Life Science, 5,* 1–3.

Moore, R. (1993). Does writing about science enhance learning about science? *Journal of College Science Teaching, 22,* 212–217.

Moore, R. (1997). *Writing to learn science.* Philadelphia, PA: Saunders.

Moore, R. (2002). The lessons of history: Transforming science to include developmental education. In D. B. Lundell & J. L. Higbee (Eds.), *Theoret-*

ical perspectives for developmental education (pp. 83–92). Minneapolis, MN: Center for Research on Developmental Education and Urban Literacy, General College, University of Minnesota.

Moore, R., Jensen, M., Hatch, J., Duranczyk, I., Staats, S., & Koch, L. (2003). Showing up: The importance of class attendance for academic success in introductory science courses. *The American Biology Teacher, 65,* 325–329.

Moore, R., & Miller, I. (1996). How the use of multimedia affects student retention and learning. *Journal of College Science Teaching, 26,* 289–293.

Murie, R., & Thomson, R. (2001). When ESL is developmental: A model program for the freshman year. In J. L. Higbee (Ed.), *2001: A developmental odyssey* (pp. 15–28). Warrensburg, MO: National Association for Developmental Education.

Pedelty, M. (2001a). Jenny's painting: Multiple forms of communication in the classroom. In B. L. Smith & J. McCann (Eds.), *Reinventing ourselves: Interdisciplinary education, collaborative learning and experimentation in higher education* (pp. 230–252). Boston: Anker.

Pedelty, M. H. (2001b). Stigma. In J. L. Higbee (Ed.), *2001: A developmental odyssey* (pp. 53–70). Warrensburg, MO: National Association for Developmental Education.

Pedelty, M. (2004). Ritual and performance. In P. Rice & D. McCurdy (Eds.), *Strategies for teaching anthropology: Vol. 2* (pp. 150–154). Upper Saddle River, NJ: Prentice Hall.

Pedelty, M. H., & Jacobs, W. R. (2001). The place of "culture" in developmental education's social sciences. In D. B. Lundell & J. L. Higbee (Eds.), *Theoretical perspectives for developmental education* (pp. 75–90). Minneapolis, MN: Center for Research on Developmental Education and Urban Literacy, General College, University of Minnesota.

Pliner, S. M., & Johnson, J. R. (2004). Historical, theoretical, and foundational principles of Universal Instructional Design in higher education. *Equity & Excellence in Education, 37,* 105–113.

Reynolds, T. (2001). Bakhtin's notion of dialogic communication and a Discourse theory of developmental education. In D. B. Lundell & J. L. Higbee (Eds.), *Theoretical perspectives for developmental education* (pp. 121–126). Minneapolis, MN: Center for Research on Developmental Education and Urban Literacy, General College, University of Minnesota.

Reynolds, T. J., & Bruch, P. L. (2002). Curriculum and affect: A participatory developmental writing approach. *Journal of Developmental Education, 26*(2), 12–14, 16, 18, 20.

Shaw, M. E. (2002). Recovering the vision of John Dewey for developmental education. In D. B. Lundell & J. L. Higbee (Eds.), *Histories of developmental education* (pp. 29–33). Minneapolis, MN: Center for Research on Developmental Education and Urban Literacy, General College, University of Minnesota.

Silver, P., Bourke, A., & Strehorn, K. C. (1998). Universal Instructional Design in higher education: An approach for inclusion. *Equity & Excellence in Education, 31*(2), 47–51.

Taylor, D., Schelske, B., Hatfield, J., & Lundell, D. B. (2002). African American Men from Hennepin County at the University of Minnesota, 1994–98: Who applies, who is accepted, who attends? In D. B. Lundell & J. L. Higbee (Eds.), *Exploring urban literacy & developmental education* (pp. 109–128). Minneapolis, MN: Center for Research on Developmental Education and Urban Literacy, General College, University of Minnesota.

Thomas, P. V., & Higbee, J. L. (2000). The relationship between involvement and success in developmental algebra. *Journal of College Reading and Learning, 30*(2), 222–232.

Tinto, V. (1998, January). *Learning communities and the reconstruction of remedial education in higher education.* Paper presented at the Conference on Replacing Remediation in Higher Education, Stanford University, CA. Retrieved October 22, 2004, from http://soeweb.syr.edu/faculty/Vtinto/Files/DevEdLC.pdf

Uncertain welcome [video]. (2002). Minneapolis, MN: Curriculum Transformation and Disability, General College, University of Minnesota. Retrieved May 25, 2005, from http://www.gen.umn.edu/research/ctad

Wambach, C. (1993). Motivational themes and academic success of at-risk freshmen. *Journal of Developmental Education, 16*(3), 8–10, 12, 37.

Wambach, C., & Brothen, T. (2001). A case study of procrastination in a computer assisted introductory psychology course. *Research & Teaching in Developmental Education, 17*(2), 41–52.

Wambach, C., Brothen, T., & Dikel, T. N. (2000). Toward a developmental theory for developmental educators. *Journal of Developmental Education, 24*(1), 2–4, 6, 8, 10, 29.

Wilcox, K., delMas, R., Stewart, B., Johnson, A., & Ghere, D. (1997). The "package course" experience and developmental education at the General College, University of Minnesota. *Journal of Developmental Education, 20*(3), 18–20, 22, 24, 26–27.

The Criterion Model of Developmental Education in General College

Thomas Brothen and Cathrine Wambach

ABSTRACT

This chapter traces the history of the criterion model of developmental education in the General College. This model is an alternative to using standardized tests to place students in educational interventions. Since the founding of General College in 1932, the curriculum has served as an alternative to a single-test procedure in making important judgments about students. We trace the development of the standard college predictors, the history of selection at the University of Minnesota, the development of the General College curriculum, and the use of tests to measure curricular objectives. We conclude that the criterion model is firmly rooted in the rationale for establishing and maintaining the General College for over 70 years.

I n this chapter, we explore the origins of the criterion model through a historical examination of prediction and placement at the University of Minnesota (UMN) and the subsequent founding of General College (GC) in 1932. This history, we believe, is instructive for developmental educators in understanding how the GC model of developmental education is based on the criterion model and how it might have generalizability to their own situations. We consider three issues in our historical assessment. First, we review the genesis of the current selection process in higher education and the concern among its creators about errors in prediction. Second, we examine the development of a curriculum designed to serve the broad range of students in their everyday lives as citizens. Finally, we review the development and use of tests that were in service to the curriculum rather than guardians of admission to it.

On several occasions, we have argued that developmental educators should adopt the criterion model of student advancement (Brothen & Wambach, 1988; Wambach & Brothen, 1990, 2000). The criterion model is based on the argument that single administrations of reading, writing, and mathematics skills tests in typical testing-placement programs are weak predictors of student behavior and are unlikely to classify all students correctly as to their need for skills interventions. Furthermore, because a broad curriculum consisting of a variety of disciplinary courses provides many possible avenues to assess student capabilities, we argue that it can provide a much more sensitive measure of student potential while simultaneously sorting for characteristics such as motivation and need for skill development.

We have supported our argument by pointing out that no test is perfectly valid or reliable and that students can change quickly to render out-of-date the snapshot provided by a test. We have further argued that developmental education students could be conceived of as falling into one of three groups: those likely to be successful without any interventions, those needing interventions, and those unlikely in any case to be successful in a college-level curriculum. We pointed out that no test is able to make such distinctions, but that a curriculum can do so. Although we agree that developmental education must be adaptable to a wide variety of situations and students (Brothen & Wambach, 2004), we remain convinced that using a single test to place students in educational interventions is inadequate in several respects.

Testing students and then placing them in a skills course, giving them restricted curricular choices, or completely denying them access to a college-level curriculum all operate on the same basic principle. This prediction-placement model of determining students' potential for academic success is ubiquitous in higher education. Students' scores on the SAT or ACT help determine which college they may attend, and their scores on reading, writing, and math placement tests determine if they must take skills courses after matriculation. Because colleges often cannot serve everyone who applies, they use admissions tests to help allocate their resources. This use of tests is typically not within the control of developmental educators, but using the criterion model to avoid some of the problems inherent in the prediction-placement model might well be.

Developmental educators using the criterion model respond much differently to students who score low on standardized tests of reading, writing, or mathematics skills. Instead of being restricted to basic skills courses, these students participate in a coordinated educational system that recognizes that skills sometimes develop in response to demands from courses that students see as important to their future. Introductory courses that count toward students' degree goals can develop students' academic skills at the same time if these courses also demand high skill levels and provide opportunities for skill improvement. This chapter examines the historical and theoretical basis for just such a model in the General College of the University of Minnesota.

Who Should Attend College?

In several important ways, the founding of GC has its roots in the work of J. B. Johnston, Dean of the UMN's Science, Literature, and Arts College (SLA) from 1914 to 1938. Johnston was concerned that universities were not adapting to a changing society and needed reorganizing (Gray, 1958). A comparative neurologist, his interests ranged widely and when he became dean in 1914, he set about determining why only about half the students enrolling in his college ultimately got degrees at the University. He suspected that the high school grading system was not distinguishing between those able and unable to be successful in college and was concerned that the huge enrollment increases at colleges and universities during the early years of the 20th century would overwhelm their resources if too many of these new students were inappropriate for college work. His quest led to his becoming a pioneer in the selection of students for college matriculation and set the stage for the experiment in postsecondary education now known as General College.

Johnston (1930a) summarized his work and his ideas in a book that dealt with problems in education that are with us yet today. He believed in relatively fixed intellectual traits, a conception much in favor about the time of World War I. This notion pervaded his writings and apparently guided him as he did the groundwork for his ultimate theories of whom to select for higher education and how to select them. Instead of grades alone, he believed that comparative ranking of students on their performance would provide a more accurate picture of student abilities. In 1914, upon assuming the deanship, he himself traveled to high schools to record the high school grade percentile ranks (HSRs) of students who had registered in his college. He ultimately showed that those students in the bottom three deciles of HSR were unlikely to be successful in college. In 1917, desiring to improve on the predictability of HSR alone, he adapted the approach of E. L. Thorndike, who was using early IQ tests with college students to predict their grades. Johnston secured copies of the newly developed Army Alpha IQ test from R. M. Yerkes, who had accepted a position in the UMN's Department of Psychology but was then working for the U. S. Army. Johnston tried these tests with students to determine if they would predict college success.

In 1921 D. G. Paterson, a psychologist who worked on developing the army intelligence tests, became a member of the UMN Psychology Department and began the rich history of research on testing that characterized psychology in that department for several decades. He took over the testing work, "revising and perfecting the tests from year to year" (Johnston, 1930a, p. 115). Paterson's and Johnston's work ultimately led to a college aptitude test given across the state of Minnesota to all college-bound students. By the early 1920s,

Johnston had put students' HSRs and aptitude test percentile ranks together into the combined aptitude rank (CAR) and showed that it predicted college success very well. This work on a measure that has become ubiquitous in higher education was apparently the first of its kind, and although Paterson made significant contributions to this work, Johnston should probably be considered the "inventor" of the CAR. Johnston's data showed that no student below the 30th percentile rank on CAR was successful in the liberal arts college. He began a campaign to ensure that these students would not attend the University.

Classification of Students and Traditional Conceptions of Education
The UMN is a land-grant institution, as defined by the U. S. Congress in 1862, which gave to the states federal lands for the establishment of colleges offering programs in agriculture, engineering, and home economics as well as in the traditional academic subjects to better the lives of their citizens (Moen, 1983). Johnston (1930a) worried that this justified admitting any high school graduate to the university, even though many who came were not suited for university study. He needed a way to convince people that higher education should not be universally applied and that open admissions was not a good policy. Undoubtedly drawing upon his discipline of comparative neurology, Johnston classified individuals into six classes respective to their educational prospects. Johnston's first two classes were mentally challenged and either not suited for any formal education (i.e., profoundly retarded) or suited only for rudimentary education (i.e., educably mentally retarded). The third class consisted of people with ordinary intelligence who were able to gain only the skills taught in primary education. The fourth class of individuals was able to finish high school, and a subgroup of them possessed characteristics indicating possible success in college. This subgroup was apparently deficient in the traditional indicators of college success such as preparatory courses explicitly required by some colleges, but was noticeably different from other fourth-class individuals in ways that suggested possible success. For example, Johnston pointed out that one avenue for college admission across the country in the 1920s was a procedure whereby high school principals certified such students as acceptable. However, this proved to be unworkable due to the intense pressure on principals from some parents. It was clear to him that higher education needed a more reliable and defensible procedure to allocate admission to these borderline individuals.

Johnston (1930a) deemed his top two classes suited for college, although the fifth class he termed "learners rather than scholars," reserving the top class for those with "unusual intellectual endowments" (p. 29). He allowed that these top two classes would likely be successful in life without college, but that a college education fit them best and that society should recognize this and reserve college admission for them. Although Johnston believed that the CAR would make the discriminations necessary to select the right students for college matriculation, it is significant that he also believed there was college potential undiscovered by conventional measures in the fourth class of individuals. This fact makes Johnston's theories more complex than they might seem at first.

Considering Johnston's positions on access to education, developmental educators today might be tempted to write him off as an elitist. However, he also took positions that made it more accurate to describe him as a meritocratist. He was very concerned that students from lower income families were underrepresented at the University because they could not afford it and advocated strongly that ways be found to help them fund a college education. Johnston (1930a) viewed ability as basically a stable trait and believed that the "object of modern universal education is to enable each child to enter that occupation for which his native endowments best fit" (p. 87). However, he was also cognizant that adolescents develop at different rates and espoused a major tenet of developmental education by advocating that they should not only be classified, but also reclassified as they develop and show their accomplishments.

Johnston (1930a) reflected the zeitgeist of an era in which many believed that talent was largely inborn, but he left open the possibility that classifications could be wrong. He wanted higher education to be done less by chance and to be more prescriptive, not admitting inappropriate students, serving those of the highest ability, and providing what he called general education for those of moderate ability. But he was justifiably skeptical about the validity of the means available to identify this moderate ability group as likely to be successful in baccalaureate study. He wrote that it would not be completely possible, "until we have had them under instruction for a considerable time" (p. 229). This recognition of the possibility of prediction error and his suggestion for a general education alternative both presage the GC criterion model.

Johnston did not wait for educational theories to be worked out but rather did several things to implement his ideas. He enlisted the help of Paterson to establish a comprehensive advising system in SLA and believed it would help students make good decisions about their future education. This system became a model for the GC advising and counseling program (see Chapter 4). He worked to get high schools to compute HSRs, have college-bound students take the college aptitude test, and provide that information to them so that they could make intelligent choices about attempting university study. He implemented an experiment that gave "non-degree candidate" admission to students with low CARs and showed that virtually none of them proved successful (Johnston & Williamson, 1934). He also developed a developmental writing course called "sub-freshman composition" for students with poor writing skills (Avery & Williamson, 1938). Finally, he wrote a pamphlet giving students information about their chances of success based on more than a decade of research (Johnston, 1930b). By 1930 he felt confident that things were moving in the right direction, pointing out that fewer low CAR students were coming to the University, that "the problem of the inferior student" was on the way to solution, and that the college could move on to creating a better environment for the superior student (Johnston, 1930a, p. 236).

L. D. Coffman and the Principle of Access

Lotus Delta Coffman served as president of the UMN from 1920 to 1938 and was probably the individual most responsible for founding the General College (Moen, 1983). Without his leadership, it simply would not have happened. Our purpose here is not to recount that entire history, but to show how Coffman's original ideas and their apparent change over a few years set the stage for both founding the college and allowing it to adapt in its early years. In a fiery, populist speech he gave in 1928, Coffman (1934) revealed about himself what Moen found so important to the founding of General College.

Coffman (1934) began by stating that public educational institutions "were founded on the assumption that society's welfare is best promoted by providing as nearly free and equal educational opportunities and privileges as possible" (p. 39). Speaking of attempts to select students for college admission, he said that the "student of few talents shall not be denied his opportunity while the student of many talents is given his" (p. 41). In a comment laced with the sarcasm he reserved for those he believed were championing privilege over democracy, he characterized attempts to select students:

> Among other things these authors have set up a new conception of social justice. They argue that fewer students should be admitted and more should be eliminated, because the mediocre students are trespassing upon the time and rights of a high-minded faculty who are giving generously and with high altruistic motives of their energy and ability for the advancement of society; because mediocre students are depriving the brilliant students of the opportunity for maximum achievement; and because the mediocre students are defrauding their parents, friends, and society in general of the greater returns and rewards which would accrue if society invested only in the gifted. (p. 53)

It is clear from Coffman's (1934) perspective that the president might not have been quite in agreement with what his SLA dean was up to. In fact, Gray (1958) pointed out that the two were often at odds about such matters. Nevertheless, in March of 1930 Coffman wrote the foreword to Johnston's (1930b) pamphlet, *Who Should Go To College?* His brief paragraph stated that the pamphlet will help students make an important decision about college and that they are entitled to all the information the University has on the matter. His rather lukewarm last sentence, however, does suggest Coffman may not have been totally convinced by Johnston's arguments: "It is believed that a careful reading of this pamphlet will help prospective students to make this decision more intelligently than otherwise" (p. i). Furthermore, Coffman was reinforcing the principle that a broad range of students had choices in their educational futures at the UMN and that it was important to provide adequate information for them to make these choices.

A speech Coffman (1934) gave just a month after the publication of Johnston's (1930b) pamphlet suggested that he was adapting to Johnston's approach. Saying the university "must change to conform with the spirit of the times" (p. 134), he pointed out that the university had taken the "forward" step of selecting "students competent to do university work" (p. 134), allowing in his inimitable way that it had been possible for unqualified students to graduate from high school and thus be eligible for a state university because high school teachers might desire "to cultivate the spirit of Christianity among college teachers; having suffered so many years themselves, they seek that companionship in humility by making it necessary for college teachers to suffer with them" (p. 137).

Coffman's (1934) speech was important to the establishment of GC in several ways. In it, Coffman recognized selection as desirable and pointed out that student quality was improving because the information that selection procedures gave to students and their parents helped them make more realistic choices. But he was not comfortable with an invariable system of selection, reminding his audience of the "great American principle—the right to try. . . that industry sometimes succeeds even when high intelligence is wanting" (p. 139). This assertion that students change and other qualities matter is a critique of the validity of selection procedures and became a foundation of the GC mission. Coffman also presaged the new college's curricular mission by pointing out that the University was reorganizing in response to the realization that students "who are sharpened to a point must have broad bases if the broader interests of human welfare are to be considered" (p. 143). Coffman held firm to his belief that the University should be open to all. The early staff of the college pointed to this often by citing his writings in GC bulletins for many years afterward.

An Experiment in General Education

President Coffman appointed the Committee on University Reorganization, commonly referred to as the "Committee of Seven," to suggest how the UMN should respond to a growing national concern that higher education was not relevant to the challenges of the Depression and did not give students the education they needed (Gray, 1951; MacLean, 1962). The committee he appointed recommended expanding counseling and testing, established the University Committee on Educational Research, formulated a plan for the University College where students could design their own baccalaureate degree programs, and created a new college to experiment with higher education curricula. Coffman envisioned the new GC as a solution to several problems, the most important being a potential solution to the national educational problem of disorganized and decreasingly useful curricula.

Coffman believed that the increased specialization of higher education made it difficult for students to receive a liberal education and that this trend was accelerating (Gray, 1951). As former dean of the College of Education, he was particularly concerned about how the University was educating its students. His primary goal was to remake college education, and he believed that establishing an experimental unit could be a first step towards that. The Committee of Seven recommended, and Coffman secured Board of Regents approval for, establishing the General College—for the first year called the University Junior College—and accepting students for fall 1932. By this time, the idea of creating the new college had attained wide acceptance even from the SLA dean. Apparently reconciling his differences with Coffman about admitting students not clearly predicted to succeed, Johnston (1932) wrote to Graduate School Dean Guy Stanton Ford suggesting for the new unit a basic structure that ultimately was implemented largely as he suggested.

For director of the college, Coffman and Dean Ford, who was serving as acting president while Coffman was consulting in Australia, selected Malcolm MacLean (1894–1977), at that time vice-director of the Milwaukee Center of the University of Wisconsin (Ford, 1932). MacLean had experience with the Minnesota Point of View in counseling, serving as a counselor in Johnston's and Paterson's faculty counseling program from 1924 to 1929 while he completed his doctoral work in English at the UMN (MacLean, 1949). MacLean began work in February 1932 with one secretary and later that spring, a graduate assistant (Fred Hovde, later to become president of Purdue University), to prepare for an incoming class of approximately 500 students that next fall in a building that had just been vacated by the School of Dentistry (MacLean, 1977).

Coffman's ideas about the problems of higher education and the solution to them are appropriately fitted into the rubric of general education (Gray, 1934). But just what this was to mean in practice was open to wide interpretation. Koch (1980) described general education as a movement that stretched back to 1800 but had never attained an agreed-upon definition. The founders of GC attempted to create one and put it in practice. As Malcolm MacLean (1977), wrote, "I found there were many conflicting theories about what general education was and should become. I accepted in full Coffman's own" (p. 38). MacLean went on to write that his task was to find ways to meet Coffman's concern that college education was getting too specialized while also preserving access to the University. It was clear that the overall task was to do this for people that today we call "developmental education students." MacLean reported that Coffman asked him "to find out what such people are like, where their talents lie, and to give them the kinds of education they needed and wanted" (p. 38). MacLean took that charge literally, as has the college staff for 7 decades since.

MacLean was a tireless advocate for the college and its mission to provide "education for living" (Wilson, n.d.). He accepted dozens of speaking and consulting engagements around the country from educational institutions during his tenure as director from 1932 to 1940. He and his staff also secured outside funding for educational experimentation from the General Education Board of the Rockefeller Foundation, the Carnegie Foundation, the American Council on Education, and the Federal Works Projects Administration. MacLean (1938) also presented his ideas for reshaping American education in the invited Inglis Lecture at Harvard University in 1938. The college was clearly a national leader in the general education movement.

However, nearly 2 decades after the founding of GC, the college's dean would conclude that there still was no agreed upon definition of general education (Morse, 1951). More pointedly, the Harvard report on general education (The Committee on the Objectives of a General Education in a Free Society, 1945) had specifically rejected the GC definition. The committee identified GC's courses as "functional" and stated that "a merely functional approach to teaching is inadequate" (p. 176). Koch (1980) asserted that the Harvard Report basically settled the issue as to what general education was to be, and it was not to be courses that gave students practical information they could use in their everyday lives. The committee decided that at the college level it should mean a broad sampling of disciplinary coursework—what we think of today as liberal or general education requirements. At the high school level it would include the practical information they referred to as education for living. The GC version of general education became a minority view while most of higher education accepted the liberal education meaning that is common today. The liberal education meaning, in the GC conceptualization, was too broad and did not solve the problem the college was founded to address. Instead, a broad general education curriculum remained the centerpiece of the GC model. While the counseling and advising system was important to help students adapt, they had to adapt to the curriculum.

What instructors did in their classrooms to give students knowledge they could use in their lives trumped everything.

The General College Curriculum

The Harvard committee notwithstanding, the GC curriculum was openly and proudly functional. MacLean described it that way in works he published for national audiences early in his career in the college and for the rest of his life (MacLean, 1934a, 1934b, 1949, 1951, 1962, 1977; McCune, 1951). His was a fiery reaction to what Morse and Cooper (1951) termed the rationalistic method of armchair theorizing about how curriculum development should proceed. The college curriculum was, in contrast, a result of what Morse and Cooper referred to as the empirical method of curricular development. In Chapter 4 we show how the college counseling methods were an implementation of the Minnesota Point of View in counseling. The same tradition of an empirical approach was central to both counseling and curriculum.

A dominant figure in Minnesota psychology embodied the empirical approach to a broad range of issues from 1921 until his retirement in 1961. D. G. Paterson's hard-nosed empiricism earned the UMN Department of Psychology the reputation as the center of "Dustbowl Empiricism" in the 1930s (Gray, 1958). MacLean's 5-year service in the faculty counselor program Paterson started in 1924 helped him learn how important gathering information about students was in running a successful educational program and gave him experience on how to obtain information about students and how to use it effectively (MacLean, 1949; 1977). Paterson's influence on psychology at Minnesota extended in many directions and set the stage for numerous advances in applied psychology including the classic, empirically-derived Minnesota Multiphasic Personality Inventory and the growth of the student personnel and vocational guidance fields. His influence also led to the establishment of the GC model.

President Coffman, through his graduate school dean Guy Stanton Ford, gave MacLean the task to develop a new curriculum and teach it with a barebones Depression-era budget. MacLean accomplished this at first by utilizing borrowed faculty from around the University. He recruited the best teachers in varied departments, and if there were none to spare, department heads or deans did the job. As an indication of how prominent in the UMN these people were, 16 University facilities carried their names in later years. Figure 1 lists the individuals, their relationship to GC in its first decade, and the facilities.

The first step in the process of building an empirically-derived curriculum was necessarily rationalistic. MacLean (1951) gathered expert opinions from deans, faculty, and students and "spun courses out of common sense blended

Individual	Position at University	Primary contribution to GC	Facility
John Ackerman	Professor of Aeronautical Eng.	Taught GC technology course	Ackerman Hall (Mpls. East Bank)
William Anderson	Chair of Political Science	Advisory Comm. on GC Curriculum	Anderson Hall (Mpls. West Bank)
Theodore Blegen	Professor of History	Taught GC Minnesota history course	Blegen Hall (Mpls. West Bank)
Ruth Boynton	Director of Health Service	GC Advisory Comm.; wrote items for GC Adolescent study	Boynton Health Service (Mpls. East Bank)
Walter C. Coffey	Dean of Agriculture (later, President)	Taught GC basic wealth course	Coffey Hall (St. Paul)
Lotus D. Coffman	President	Driving force behind founding of GC	Coffman Student Union (Mpls. East Bank)
Guy Stanton Ford	Dean of Graduate School (later, President)	Responsible for early staffing of GC	Ford Hall (Mpls. East Bank)
Harriet and Vetta Goldstein	Professors in Home Economics	Taught GC euthenics courses	Goldstein Gallery (St. Paul)
Elias P. Lyon	Dean of Medical School	Taught GC biology course	Lyon Laboratories (now demolished)
Wylle B. McNeal	Dean of Home Economics	GC Advisory Comm.; wrote items for Adult study	McNeal Hall (St. Paul)
William V. Middlebrook	University Comptroller	Established U Film Service, housed in GC	Middlebrook Hall (Mpls. East Bank)
J. Anna Norris	Director of Women's Phys Ed.	Consultant on GC curriculum	Norris Gymnasium (Mpls. East Bank)
Walter H. Peters	Professor of Agriculture	Taught GC basic wealth courses	Peters Hall (St. Paul)
Carlyle M. Scott	Professor of Music	Taught GC music courses	Scott Hall (Mpls. East Bank)
John T. Tate	Professor of Physics; Dean of Liberal Arts	GC Advisory Comm.	Tate Laboratory of Physics (Mpls. East Bank)
E. G. Williamson	Professor of Psychology	GC Counseling program	Williamson Hall (Mpls. East Bank)

Figure 1. Distinguished contributors to the early history of General College who were later recognized by University of Minnesota facility names.

with imagination" (p. 34). Prospective instructors were asked to build courses that were broad, not narrow as their disciplinary courses might be, and to focus on developing knowledge useful to a citizen in a modern democracy (Spafford, 1943). The first term in fall of 1932 found 47 such courses in the new *General College Bulletin*. These courses differed from the standard university freshman curriculum in that they were focused on practical matters that students were likely to encounter in life. Most were three-quarter sequences. For example, Basic Wealth consisted of one quarter each of the economic utilization of natural resources, plant life, and animal life. Human Biology was divided into basic human biology, anatomy and physiology, and personal and community health. Appreciation of the Fine Arts consisted of one quarter of motion pictures and the theater, one on the graphic arts, and one on music. Human Development and Personal Adjustment consisted of adolescent development, early childhood development, and the problems encountered by adults in raising children.

In addition to delivering a general education curriculum, student development became a paramount concern in the college. The bulletin listed a "How to Study" course first and encouraged students to take it to improve their chances of success. The GC writing program functioned in a laboratory setting and focused on grammar and reading development as well as writing. The writing lab also served to help students write papers for their other courses. In addition, faculty and advisors watched for students with communications problems and referred them to a speech clinic to work on listening and speaking effectively. Director MacLean and the head of the University Testing Bureau, E. G. Williamson, also taught a course in vocations to help students think realistically about their vocational options. In all these cases, the intent was to integrate academic skill and personal development with the courses' educational goals.

Over the next 2 decades, the curriculum changed often, and the faculty added and deleted courses based on research on student needs and performance. Generally speaking, after adding 24 new courses in the second year, the General College followed President Coffman's direction to avoid proliferation of courses, and the curriculum maintained a fairly constant size. The biggest changes were the three-quarter sequences coalescing or dividing into separate courses and occupational courses being added as the college adopted occupational programs after World War II. This changed greatly when the University administration allowed the college to develop a baccalaureate program (BP). This story is told elsewhere (Hansen, 1980; Hansen, Moen, & Brothen, 1983), but two aspects are relevant to this chapter. By 1983 to 1985 at the height of the BP, the *General College Bulletin* listed 418 courses including 180 junior- and senior-level courses developed primarily for baccalaureate students and 238 introductory and occupationally-oriented courses ranging from human services to legal assisting that served a student body of about 3,000 with a broad array of career interests. This curricular explosion occurred to accommodate students whose needs were not being met by the University and illustrates how the curriculum has always been responsive to student needs and not disciplines. However, a primary teaching faculty of 50 created and maintained this huge curriculum and was spread too thinly to do justice to all the college was charged with doing. The University administration's ultimate reaction to this untenable situation was to eliminate all degrees and certificates in the college in 1986. This action led directly to the current GC structure and mission. Wambach and Brothen (2002) described the significant changes that took place as the college was set on the mission that other chapters in this volume describe in detail. Our concern here is how the development of a general education curriculum through its history affects the college today.

Origins of the Criterion Model in GC

Koch (1980) described two approaches in American education that help us understand the general education for living curriculum developed for the college in 1932 and carried forward for nearly three quarters of a century. She distinguished between the Jeffersonian model of education that aims to identify and nurture talent and the Jacksonian model that aims to bring up the population average. The traditional, selective higher education model, by this distinction, selects good students and educates the best of them to become leaders in society. Johnston's (1930a) highest class of potential scholars typifies the clientele for this approach. The founders of GC, by contrast, recognized that they were getting average people as students and were concerned with improving their ability to be good citizens. The first clientele of the college was, and continued to be for several decades, students below the 30th and later 40th percentile on CAR. Given the concern with fixed traits at that time, the staff was interested in students' intellectual abilities and administered IQ tests on a regular basis. For example, Williams (1943) reported that GC students had an average IQ score of 107. Interestingly, unpublished classroom research (T. Brothen, personal communication, January 20, 2005) also revealed an estimated mean IQ of 107 for GC students in the early 1980s and 110 in 2004. To create a curriculum for these students, the founders set out in a systematic, empirical manner to understand students, determine their needs, develop a curriculum for them, and evaluate their progress.

General Education for Living

In Chapter 4 we describe how the college was founded on the Minnesota Point of View and how its focus was on the student. We will briefly recap some of that history here to show how it affected the college's approach to curriculum and still influences it today. As described above, the GC staff attracted foundation support to do the research necessary to develop and evaluate the curriculum. A series of articles and books reported this work.

The two initial large studies (Pace, 1941; Williams, 1943) aimed to determine what the students were like and what their needs were. MacLean (1949) advocated early and persistently that educational institutions should know as much as possible about the students they serve. As MacLean (1934b) stated, "Our focus is upon students individually and upon their needs, interests, and desires, present and future, rather than upon any traditional or preconceived notion of what we think may be good for them" (p. 241). Pace reported an extensive survey of 951 students who had matriculated at the University a decade earlier. This study aimed to determine whether the students' experiences had been useful to them. Williams reported an intensive study of 100 representative GC students conducted to understand them better on both academic and personal levels so that the staff might "better shape our courses from year to year" (MacLean, 1934b, p. 317).

Curriculum development in GC proceeded as a recursive process with courses developed, revised, or discarded given the staff's experience with how they were benefiting students. Spafford (1943) reported the extensive process of curriculum development during the college's early years. She described the basic approach as establishing "experimental courses in order to explore certain areas of student need, and to attempt by trial and error to find desirable, workable classroom methods for meeting these needs" (p. 310). Eckert (1943) examined the academic progress of GC students and reported a broad array of outcomes, including the fact that the approximately 12% ultimate baccalaureate graduation rate was an "unusually good salvage job" because of the students' inherent lack of interest in and ability to do extended university work (p. 88). This type of intensive study continued into the 1950s. Borow and Morse (1954) reported that the fundamental curriculum and aims of the college remained basically unchanged until then with the exception of added occupational courses, but that the increasing need to recognize a transfer mission was changing the college. However, the central principle, that student characteristics and needs must be understood and programs designed to serve them, has remained constant through all periods of change.

The Comprehensive Examination

The founders of GC not only were concerned with creating a new general education approach, they were also concerned with measuring the effectiveness of their curriculum. This led them to another national issue—testing. Haggerty (1934) pointed out that the use of tests to certify student achievement was proliferating around the country. He also anticipated today's concerns about what is now called high-stakes testing when he pointed out "too little concern about improving the quality of examinations has appeared among the apostles who clamor for their increased use" (p. 2). As dean of the College of Education, Haggerty optimistically predicted that the new GC with a new curriculum and a committed staff could be "a rich field for educational investigation" (p. 4) and that its work with examinations would inform other educational institutions.

MacLean (1934c) described courses in the new GC curriculum as "experimental and empirical, kept consciously malleable so that [they] may be changed to suit the need, interests, and drives *of students*" (p. 7; italics in original). Highlighting the comprehensive exam as well as the counseling focus of the college, MacLean wrote that student needs can be discovered by "adequate and revealing examinations on the one hand, and individual counseling and conferences on the other" (p. 7). He contrasted the new curriculum as different from traditional college courses that he described as "each an academic principality surrounded by high walls and moats and guarded by drawbridges to keep out the unwanted—to be explored only by the few who pass the barriers or manage a stealthy entrance through a postern gate" (p. 7). Reflecting this sentiment, the college for many years had no prerequisites for entry to its courses. These sentiments survive today in the GC criterion model that allows all students immediate entry into courses that count toward baccalaureate degrees.

The GC comprehensive examination was an ever-changing product of an extensive research and development project that began in the first year of GC (University Committee On Educational Research [UCER], 1934, 1937) and continued for 2 decades (Morse, Borow, & Williams, 1951). After 1950, the comprehensive examination continued in use, but its basic structure did not change except for the items, which were updated by faculty on a regular basis (A. Johnson, personal communication, April 5, 2004). The college abandoned the exam in the early 1980s when other tests and procedures replaced an aging test that had not had the work done that was necessary to keep it valid for new generations of students. First, nationally created tests replaced its entrance function in suggesting student placement in reading and writing courses (Brothen, Romano, Robertson, & Garfield, 1981). Second, the math faculty revised the math portion of the examination and used it as a stand-alone test to suggest appropriate math courses to students and their advisors (D. Robertson, personal communication, April 6, 2004). Finally, completion of 90 quarter credits replaced the comprehensive examination's function in determining whether students had met the requirement for the Associate in Arts degree. However, the tradition that single administrations of any test are never viewed as the only or final determinant of what students would be allowed to do continued to be central to the GC model.

Because the courses in the original GC curriculum were new, broad, and taught in large sections, the founders decided the comprehensive examination was necessary to determine whether students were meeting the overall curricular goals. The examination allowed the staff to deemphasize grades, especially fail grades, and take a developmental approach from the very start. As MacLean put it, "at no time before the student attains a passing grade is he regarded as a failure; he is merely on his way up" (UCER, 1937, pp. 13–14). This philosophy guided the comprehensive exam and has served as a major pillar of GC for over 70 years.

MacLean (1934b) described succinctly the construction of the comprehensive exam in the first year of the college:

> How, then, are these examinations constructed? Dean Haggerty, of the College of Education and Chairman of the Committee on Educational Research, acts with me as adviser. Four professors, members of the Committee, serve as examination counselors. They place in each [course] a research assistant who attends all class meetings, takes notes on them, and reads and notes all assigned and recommended reading. The research assistant then analyzes and separates all materials gathered into vocabulary essential to understanding the field, vital facts and information items, laws and principles stated. He then sets aside for the examination counselors all materials which may properly be included in examinations other than the one for which he is responsible. For example, if the lecturer in human biology comments on the cost of the common cold to American business, or the cost of free clinics, veterans' hospitals, public-health nursing, these go for inclusion in the economics examination. If he talks on the swing toward government supervision of medical care, questions are formulated from his remarks for the government test. If he describes a new surgical or diagnostic instrument, the description is carried over into the physical-science and technology examination. If he speaks of the mental reactions and behavior of patients, the material is referred to the assistants in charge of the psychology examinations. All the materials from the blanketing courses just described are thus distributed. Everywhere, at all times, there is watchfulness for interlocking elements, and thus is the concept of vital unity built up.
>
> The research assistant having passed on his interlocking elements and having received those of the other assistants sets out to construct his examinations. He gives quizzes sometimes as often as once each week. These are marked on a percentile basis. Item analyses are made, and the validity and efficiency of each question tested; the poor questions are discarded; the good are retained for probable inclusion in the comprehensive test . . . (pp. 316–317)

MacLean then enumerated the nine separate exams in euthenics (i.e., home life and personal development), psychology, English, history and government, current affairs, fine arts appreciation, physical sciences, biological sciences, and economics, from which students chose five to satisfy their Associate in Arts graduation requirement. He also described their form: vocabulary, facts and information, laws and principles, application questions using class material, and student attitudes toward the subject matter.

MacLean (1934c) went on to describe the comprehensive examinations' objectives in clearly developmental terms. The first objective was to counter the notion that education was about piling up courses and credits and then forgetting the material as soon as possible. The comprehensives were to stimulate regular study and learning because they covered so much material that students could not cram for them. Second, the comprehensives were to be guideposts in a process of learning that told students how much progress they had made and how much was yet to be made. MacLean wrote, "the comprehensive approach gives the slow-paced student a true sense of gradual achievement instead of a feeling of futility and failure" (p. 9). Third, they had a student development function in that "Under the benevolent pressure of comprehensive examinations, fear of examinations likewise tends to diminish" (p. 9). Fourth, as a standard apart from individual courses, they countered the stereotype "that the best way to 'get by' a course is to study not so much the subject as the instructor, to learn to feed him what he wants, play up to his prejudices and enthusiasms" (p. 9). Finally, because the comprehensive examination measured student attitudes towards subject matter, they revealed, "the questionings, the foci of interest, and the hitherto untapped mental and emotional needs of students" (p. 10).

The exam development process created a great number of examination forms. Eurich and Johnson (1937) reported that in the first 3 years of the college, the staff created 398 different examinations consisting of 22,000 different items—a database of separate test questions that grew to 50,000 within a couple of years. The tests changed as the curriculum developed, with items combined with others to form new examinations or rearranged in different ways to reflect a changing curriculum.

The basic structure of the GC comprehensive examination has its origins in the work of D. G. Paterson. As we noted previously, he took over development of the college aptitude tests in 1921 for Dean Johnston. He continued to work on test development throughout his career and had a great influence on testing at the UMN, including GC. Paterson's influence on the comprehensive examination is apparent in the way in which the test was created. Paterson opposed essay tests and championed complex or applied multiple-choice items (UCER, 1934). He pioneered this type of test development while developing introductory psychology examinations for the UMN Psychology Department. The procedure involved writing items, trying them on quizzes and examinations, doing item analyses, and writing them on note cards to develop a database to draw from for future examinations (Paterson, 1929). Interestingly, in this article reporting his foundational work on test development, he noted that Cornelia Williams, the future head of counseling in GC, was his undergraduate project assistant. He continued to use this technique through the 1950s in his teaching and research (J. J. Jenkins, personal communication, February 29, 2004). A similar empirical process also characterized development of the famous Minnesota Multiphasic Personality Inventory (Butcher, 2000; Hathaway & McKinley, 1940) and likely was influenced by Paterson's work. His was the technique used to create the comprehensive exams and to interpret their meaning for each student (Paterson, 1949; Williams, 1943). MacLean (1934c) characterized the use of Paterson's style of items for the comprehensive as a settled issue. He wrote, "It seems clear that the battle between essay and objective type examinations is over, and the field is held by the latter" (p. 13).

Early issues of the *General College Bulletin* reveal that in the first years of the college, the comprehensive certified that students had completed the requirements for the Associate in Arts degree. The college experimented with grading procedures—going from a "fail" (later "withheld"), "pass," and "honors" grading system based on percentile ranks achieved in each class, to reporting traditional A through F course grades along with percentile ranks, to traditional grades and a year-end percentile rank based on all students' performance, and finally to the standard college grading system used today. During this experimentation, the comprehensive served as a stable measure of student achievement. In the late 1930s it began use as an indication of whether students had met the standard for transferring to a baccalaureate program at the University. As grades were then only honors, pass, or withheld, the college worked out conversions for percentile ranks to GPA to help other colleges to make transfer acceptance decisions. For example, MacLean (1936) reported that the 42nd percentile was designated equivalent to a C grade. For several years after the college began giving traditional grades, students could waive individual course grades and have them determined by their scores on the comprehensive exam. Parenthetically, MacLean (1951) characterized the move toward giving traditional A–F grades in the late 1930s as the result of a battle the college lost because of the transfer issue—clearly a principle given up to ultimately benefit students who needed traditional qualifications to satisfy the educational traditionalists who were deciding on their transfer to baccalaureate programs.

The 1937–1938 *General College Bulletin* stated that students had to have passed three different comprehensive exams with scores above the 50th percentile to transfer. In the 1940s the comprehensive exam began use as a diagnostic test with students taking it at entry to guide course choice and at the end of their coursework to qualify for the Associate in Arts degree. In the late 1940s a major research and development effort created a single, 700-item comprehensive exam (Morse, Borow, & Williams, 1951) that students took at entry to guide course selection, at the end of the first year for evaluation purposes, and then when they were ready to apply for their degree. By the 1960s a score on the exam that was above the 75th percentile of entrance test scores qualified students for the Associate in Arts degree. The college bulletin encouraged students to take the comprehensive one quarter before planning to graduate so that if they scored low in an area they could take a course to remediate the deficiency.

The comprehensive examination had little to do with course placement in its original conception. Its primary purpose was to certify completion of the curriculum and the first use of it in pre- and posttesting was to measure students' improvement in their knowledge. The primary concern was always a developmental one—that students begin at different places and that the best outcome is one in which a student learns much from a course rather than coming into it with prior knowledge and getting course credit for learning little. As MacLean (1934c) writing about early experimentation in a physics course put it:

> A pre-comprehensive, administered on the first day of the first quarter of the [physics] course, reveals the fact that student A knows only 3 of the 250 items in the test. On a comparable form, given at the end of the quarter, A knows 122 items. He has made, for him, rapid progress in mastery of new and unfamiliar vocabulary, scientific facts of physics, concepts, laws, and principles and is able, in some measure, to apply these to new situations and problems. And yet, if we follow the standard grading system, he is given a grade of failure because he does not respond correctly to 125 of the given test items. Four more would have done it. This is patently absurd. Moreover, its effect upon A is vicious. He is stung by the mark of failure. He feels inferior. His growing desire to progress in physics, to learn more, to forge on into the field which is beginning to attract him, is clipped off, left sore and blunted. This strikes us as educationally inexcusable. (p. 12)

In the late 1940s the comprehensive began more explicit use as an advising tool modeled after Paterson's (1949) methods of vocational counseling. It gave students guidance on their strengths and weaknesses and helped them select courses to remediate deficiencies so they could pass the degree comprehensive or to transfer to a baccalaureate program. In the early 1980s this advising function became more intrusive as the number and variety of reading and writing skills courses in GC had increased greatly. However, research at that time showed convincingly that the comprehensive's successor tests did not place students accurately, and this approach was abandoned (Wambach & Brothen, 2002). Clearly, the comprehensive examination served throughout its history primarily as an indication of whether students achieved the objectives of the college curriculum, not as a placement device. It guided faculty thinking about curriculum and whether their courses were helping students advance in their general education.

Conclusion

Our thesis in this chapter is that the criterion model of developmental education is firmly rooted in the history of GC. We support this thesis in two ways. The first concerns the UMN's approach to selection and Johnston's (1930a, 1930b) work that led to development of the CAR. That statistic depends a great deal on single-test predictions, and we argue that single tests can easily misclassify students. Johnston's primary advisor on testing acknowledged the potential for testing error in judging students as inappropriate for regular college work but justified the risk as long as provision was made for "giving the 'poor college risks' a type of educational program better adapted to their lesser talents" (Paterson, 1937, p. xiii). The history of classification by tests at the UMN is tied to providing reasonable alternatives to those both correctly and incorrectly classified.

The UMN founded GC to provide an alternative educational experience for students correctly identified as not appropriate for baccalaureate work as well as for those who either later improved their academic potential for baccalaureate work or had been misclassified by the selection process. We stress that our argument against placement tests is not anti testing (Brothen & Wambach, 2003). The college would not exist without a selection procedure that categorizes students and sends some of them to us so we may determine how to serve them appropriately. Providing education that would be useful to correctly-classified students was the college's original general education mission while developing or "salvaging" academic potential was the original developmental one. At the same time, the curriculum had to be useful to those students who were misclassified by the traditional predictors and needed only to demonstrate they had high academic potential. Stavig (2004) pointed to an example of this type of student, Norman Borlaug, winner of the Nobel Peace Prize in 1970 for his work developing new strains of wheat that greatly improved world food production. He was assigned to GC as a freshman in 1933 because he lacked prerequisite courses for regular admission. He quickly demonstrated his potential, transferred, and eventually earned his Ph.D. from Minnesota in 1942. To this day, he has positive recollections of his placement in GC.

The second way in which the criterion model is embedded tightly in the history of GC is the tradition of providing a curriculum that is relevant to students. Because the curriculum delivered "education for living," it was about students' journeys through life rather than an endpoint defined by credits attained. This is fundamentally developmental and allows for starts and stops and changes that are difficult to capture with a single test or even a past history of educational attainment. For example, throughout the college's history it is a common finding that college aptitude tests predict our students' degree attainment least well, HSR predicts next best, and that first-term grade performance in the curriculum predicts best (Eckert, 1943; Wambach & Brothen, 2000). The college's developmental approach recognizes that students change for a variety of reasons from physical maturation to increased social consciousness and that the curriculum is the best way to evaluate their potential for academic success (Wambach, Brothen, & Dikel, 2000; Williamson & Darley, 1937).

Throughout its early years, GC served as a national model for curricular development in general education and spurred numerous curricular reforms (McCune, 1951; Wilson, n.d.). The GC curricular model did not go unnoticed when the state of Minnesota was considering converting its junior colleges to community colleges in the 1950s. Educational leaders at the time worried that the first 2 years of a traditional liberal arts curriculum then offered in the junior colleges might not be appropriate for a much broader body of students. Keller, Lokken, and Meyer (1958) pointed out that GC had a history of working with students at the lower CAR ranges and recommended that the junior colleges in Minnesota revise their curriculum based on the GC model. The model still has great utility, as the chapters in this book demonstrate.

In summary, testing has always been a large part of the GC model but has never been the single, high-stakes test approach that is so widespread today. The comprehensive exam focused on the curriculum and had developmental objectives. Many other achievement and aptitude tests provided a picture of students early in the college history (Williams, 1943). However, the primary purpose of testing has always been to describe students, to mark their achievement, and to determine how the curriculum could serve them better, not to screen them out. This is the basis of the criterion model in GC. It has served us well for over 7 decades while also serving as a model emulated elsewhere.

References

Avery, C. E., & Williamson, E. G. (1938). Achievement of students in subfreshman composition. *The Journal of Educational Psychology, 29*, 257–267.

Borow, H., & Morse, H. T. (1954). Postwar research in General College. In R. E. Eckert & R. J. Keller (Eds.), *A university looks at its program* (pp. 64–77). Minneapolis, MN: University of Minnesota Press.

Brothen, T., Romano, J., Robertson, D., & Garfield, J. (1981). *Norms for the General College placement program*. Minneapolis, MN: General College Research Reports.

Brothen, T., & Wambach, C. (1988, March). *The prediction model vs. the criterion model: Which serves developmental students best?* Paper presented at the annual conference of the National Association for Developmental Education, Orlando, FL.

Brothen, T., & Wambach, C. (2003). Is there a role for academic achievement tests in multicultural developmental education? In J. L. Higbee, D. B. Lundell, & I. M. Duranczyk (Eds.), *Multiculturalism in developmental education* (pp. 43–49). Minneapolis, MN: Center for Research on Developmental Education and Urban Literacy, General College, University of Minnesota.

Brothen, T., & Wambach, C. (2004). Refocusing developmental education. *Journal of Developmental Education, 28*(2), 16–18, 20, 22, 33.

Butcher, J. N. (Ed.). (2000). *Basic sources on the MMPI-2*. Minneapolis, MN: University of Minnesota Press.

Coffman, L. D. (1930). Foreword. In J. B. Johnston, *Who should go to college?* Minneapolis, MN: University of Minnesota Press.

Coffman, L. D. (1934). *The state university, its work and problems*. Minneapolis, MN: University of Minnesota Press.

Committee on the Objectives of a General Education in a Free Society. (1945). *General education in a free society*. Cambridge, MA: Harvard University Press.

Eckert, R. (1943). *Outcomes of general education*. Minneapolis, MN: University of Minnesota Press.

Eurich, A. C., & Johnson, P. O. (1937). The experimental examination program in General College. In University Committee on Educational Research (Ed.), *The effective General College curriculum as revealed by examinations* (pp. 31–44). Minneapolis, MN: University of Minnesota Press.

Ford, G. S. (1932). *The junior college of the University of Minnesota: A statement to the general faculty by the Committee on Administrative Reorganization*. Minneapolis, MN: University of Minnesota Archives.

Gray, W. S. (1934). *General education: Its nature, scope, and essential elements*. Chicago: The University of Chicago Press.

Gray, J. (1951). *The University of Minnesota: 1851–1951*. Minneapolis, MN: University of Minnesota Press.

Gray, J. (1958). *Open wide the door*. New York: G. P. Putnam's Sons.

Haggerty, M. E. (1934). Studies in examinations. In University Committee on Educational Research (Ed.), *Studies in college examinations* (pp. 1–14). Minneapolis, MN: University Committee on Educational Research.

Hansen, E. U. (1980). *General College individualized baccalaureate degree programs: The first decade of experience.* Minneapolis, MN: General College Monographs.

Hansen, E. U., Moen, N., & Brothen, T. (1983). *Planning a General College baccalaureate program.* Minneapolis, MN: General College Archives, University of Minnesota.

Hathaway, S. R., & McKinley, J. C. (1940). A multiphasic personality schedule (Minnesota): I. Construction of the schedule. *Journal of Psychology, 10,* 249–254.

Johnston, J. B. (1930a). *The liberal college in changing society.* New York: Century.

Johnston, J. B. (1930b). *Who should go to college?* Minneapolis, MN: University of Minnesota Press.

Johnston, J. B. (1932, January 5). *Letter to G. S. Ford.* Minneapolis, MN: University of Minnesota Archives.

Johnston, J. B., & Williamson, E. G. (1934). A follow-up study of early scholastic predictions in the University of Minnesota. *School and Society, 40,* 730–738.

Keller, R. J., Lokken, H. M., & Meyer, R. F. (1958). *The junior college in Minnesota.* St. Paul, MN: Minnesota State Department of Education.

Koch, G. A. (1980). The general education movement in American higher education: An account and appraisal of its principles and practices and their relation to democratic thought in modern American society. (Doctoral dissertation, University of Minnesota, 1980). *Dissertation Abstracts International A, 40*(11), 5749.

MacLean, M. S. (1934a). A college of 1934 (Part 1). *Journal of Higher Education, 5,* 240–246.

MacLean, M. S. (1934b). A college of 1934 (Part 2). *Journal of Higher Education, 5,* 314–322.

MacLean, M. S. (1934c). The problem in General College. In University Committee on Educational Research (Ed.), *Studies in college examinations* (pp. 7–14). Minneapolis, MN: University Committee on Educational Research.

MacLean, M. S. (1936). *Report on problems and progress of General College.* Minneapolis, MN: General College Archives, University of Minnesota.

MacLean, M. S. (1938). *Scholars, workers, and gentlemen.* Cambridge, MA: Harvard University Press.

MacLean, M. S. (1949). Adolescent needs and building the curriculum. In E. G. Williamson (Ed.), *Trends in student personnel work* (pp. 27–39). Minneapolis, MN: University of Minnesota Press.

MacLean, M. S. (1951). General College: Its origin and influence. In H. T. Morse (Ed.), *General education in transition: A look ahead* (pp. 29–44). Minneapolis, MN: University of Minnesota Press.

MacLean, M. S. (1962). The exciting early years of General College. *General College Newsletter, 9,* 1–17.

MacLean, M. S. (1977). *Never a dull moment.* Unpublished memoir. Minneapolis, MN: General College Archives, University of Minnesota.

McCune, G. (1951). *Transcript of interview with Malcolm S. MacLean.* Minneapolis, MN: University of Minnesota Archives.

Moen, N. (1983). General College: The open door through fifty years: 1932–1982. *General College Newsletter, 30*(4), whole issue.

Morse, H. T. (Ed.). (1951). *General education in transition: A look ahead.* Minneapolis, MN: University of Minnesota Press.

Morse, H. T., Borow, H., & Williams, C. D. (1951). General College develops its comprehensive examination. *Journal of Higher Education, 22,* 31–58.

Morse, H. T., & Cooper, R. M. (1951). Problems of implementing programs in general education. In H. T. Morse (Ed.), *General education in transition: A look ahead* (pp. 282–304). Minneapolis, MN: University of Minnesota Press.

Pace, R. (1941). *They went to college.* Minneapolis, MN: University of Minnesota Press.

Paterson, D. G. (1929). Use of new-type examination questions in psychology at the University of Minnesota. *School and Society, 28,* 369–371.

Paterson, D. G. (1937). Introduction. In E. G. Williamson & J. G. Darley, *Student personnel work: An outline of clinical procedures* (pp. vii–xvi). New York: McGraw-Hill.

Paterson, D. G. (1949). Developments in student counseling techniques. In E. G. Williamson (Ed.), *Trends in student personnel work* (pp. 80–96). Minneapolis, MN: University of Minnesota Press.

Spafford, I. (1943). *Building a curriculum for general education: A description of General College curriculum.* Minneapolis, MN: University of Minnesota Press.

Stavig, V. (2004). Bread and peace. *Minnesota: The Magazine of the University of Minnesota Alumni Association, 103*(3), 34–36, 38, 40, 42.

University Committee on Educational Research. (1934). *Studies in college examinations.* Minneapolis, MN: Author.

University Committee on Educational Research. (1937). *The effective General College curriculum as revealed by examinations.* Minneapolis, MN: University of Minnesota Press.

Wambach, C., & Brothen, T. (1990). An alternative to the prediction-placement model. *Journal of Developmental Education, 20*(3), 14–15, 24–26.

Wambach, C., & Brothen, T. (2000). Content area reading tests are not a solution to reading test validity problems. *Journal of Developmental Education, 24*(2), 42–43.

Wambach, C., & Brothen, T. (2002). General College Base Curriculum: Description, historical antecedents, theoretical structure, and evaluation outcomes. In J. L. Higbee & D. B. Lundell (Eds.), *Historical perspectives on developmental education* (pp. 73–81). Minneapolis, MN: Center for Research on Developmental Education and Urban Literacy, General College, University of Minnesota.

Wambach, C., Brothen, T., & Dikel, T. N. (2000). Toward a developmental theory for developmental educators. *Journal of Developmental Education, 24*(1), 2–4, 6, 8, 10, 29.

Williams, C. T. (1943). *These we teach.* Minneapolis, MN: University of Minnesota Press.

Williamson, E. G., & Darley, J. G. (1937). *Student personnel work: An outline of clinical procedures.* New York: McGraw-Hill.

Wilson, E. C. (n.d.). *A sketch of the professional biography of Malcolm Shaw MacLean, Ph.D., director of General College, University of Minnesota.* Minneapolis, MN: University of Minnesota Archives.

Using Assessment
to Guide Practice

Using Assessment to Guide Practice
Introduction

Direct assessment of General College students and course outcomes themselves are other major strengths of faculty and staff in GC. Irene Duranczyk and Don Opitz, who convey the results of an assessment of students' perceptions of the math courses, present an example of an intensive research study done with GC math students. This assessment project examines a range of factors, such as students' socioeconomic status and parents' levels of educational attainment, as it relates to student performance and perspectives.

Student perceptions of GC are also primary to ongoing assessments in the college. Mark Bellcourt, Ian Haberman, Joshua Schmitt, Jeanne Higbee, and Emily Goff offer a chapter that features student voices on the subject of GC and its impact on their learning experience at the University of Minnesota. It is important to include student voices in the evaluation process of curricula, teaching, and theoretical perspectives in higher education.

Randy Moore addresses similar issues in a contemporary context in his chapter on accurate predictors of success for GC students. He asserts that factors related to motivation, like class attendance, are more closely related to achievement than standard measures of aptitude.

CHAPTER 23

Reaching for the Standards, Embracing Diversity: Students' Perceptions of the Mathematics Program

Irene M. Duranczyk and Donald L. Opitz

ABSTRACT

Standards issued by the American Mathematical Association for Two-Year Colleges (AMATYC) for mathematics curricula preceding calculus guide General College's efforts to improve the academic achievement and retention of students who are underrepresented in science, technology, engineering, and mathematics (STEM) careers. Assessment of students' curricular experiences is critical in judging the effectiveness of our mathematics program in meeting AMATYC standards, embracing student diversity, and enabling STEM careers. We present the rationale, design, and results of a survey of students' perceptions of our mathematics program and conclude with a discussion of this survey as an instrument for strategic planning and curriculum development.

The American education system in mathematics and science is differentially effective for students depending on their social class, race, ethnicity, language background, gender, and other demographic characteristics (Mullis et al., 1994; National Council of Teachers of Mathematics [NCTM], 2000; Oaks, 1990; Reese, Jerry, & Ballator, 1997; Secada, 1992; U.S. Department of Education, 1998). Exacerbating the gap in students' success rates, certain groups of students, particularly female students, students who live in poverty, and non-Asian students, are more likely than others to believe that they cannot succeed in mathematics because they do not possess innate mathematical skills (Oaks; Secada; Singham, 1998). Researchers have shown that affective factors, like students' self-perceptions, significantly influence mathematics learning (McLeod, 1993; U.S. Department of Education). The authors of the Third International Mathematics and Science Study (TIMSS) observed, "There was a clear positive association between self-concept and mathematics achievement within every country and within every benchmarking jurisdiction" (Mullis et al., p.129).

General College (GC) provides access to the University of Minnesota's academic programs for students from the broadest range of backgrounds; it is a point of entry for many students marginalized within our differentially effective academic system. Many GC students who take our developmental mathematics courses arrive with the same "fear of math" common to students who had negative experiences in their previous mathematics courses, whether owing to poor teaching or lack of self-confidence (Maxwell, 1997). Among cohorts entering GC between 1999 and 2001, those students who stated an interest in the physical, biological, or computer sciences upon entering were also those students showing the lowest retention rates when compared to other fields of interest (Wambach, Mayer, Hatfield, & Franko, 2003). Further research is needed to understand fully the factors involved in the attrition of GC students pursuing science, technology, engineering, and mathematics (STEM) careers, but the trends are consistent with what is known about the attrition of "at risk" students in the STEM pipeline: among all other factors, students are most often changing career plans to minimize the impact of mathematics in their lives (National Research Council, 1996).

The National Council of Teachers of Mathematics (NCTM) published standards for elementary through secondary (K-12) mathematics education in 1989 that most states adopted between 1992 and 1996 (NCTM, 1991). To recommend guidelines beyond K-12, the American Mathematical Association for Two Year Colleges (AMATYC) published standards in 1995 "intended to revitalize the mathematics curriculum preceding calculus and to stimulate changes in instructional methods so that students will be engaged as active learners in worthwhile mathematical tasks" (Cohen, 1995, p. xii). These efforts were intended to reduce the mathematics achievement gap between students based on their socioeconomic status. However, about 38% of all students enrolled at 2- and 4-year institutions of higher education in the U.S. are still testing into developmental mathematics courses (Reese, Miller, Mazzeo, & Dossey, 1997), and the gap based on socioeconomic status has not diminished (Mullis et al., 1994). There is still a wide gap between the retention of traditional and underrepresented students pursuing STEM fields. General College is committed to incorporating the AMATYC standards for precalculus mathematics education and creating opportunities for underrepresented students to prepare for STEM careers. We propose to take a closer look at how our mathematics program can be more empowering for our socioeconomically diverse college population by exploring if individual demographic groups within our student population perceive our mathematics curriculum differently.

Over the past 8 years, an increasing number of students attending General College enrolled in a reform mathematics sequence in middle school and high school. We observe many students blaming their placement into developmental mathematics courses on the failure of the K-12 reform curriculum. Studies, however, indicate the enhancing effects of elementary, middle, and high school level reform mathematics programs on (a) mathematical achievement on standardized tests, college placement tests, subsequent course grades, and college-level courses; (b) students' attitudes toward mathematics; and (c) access and equity across economic, racial, cultural, gender, and social groups (Coxford & Hirsch, 1996; Hirsch & Coxford, 1997; Huntley, Rasmussen, Villarubi, Sangtong, & Fey, 2000; Schoen & Hirsch, 2003). As we continue to incorporate reform standards into our curriculum, will we meet new areas of resistance? We know that 75% of these same students—those whom GC retains—will succeed in developmental mathematics (Hatfield, 2004). But given the attrition in the STEM pipeline, we need to assess whether student activities in problem solving, modelling, mathematical reasoning, communicating mathematical ideas, connecting mathematics to other disciplines, using technology, and developing mathematical power, are engaging and of sufficient regularity to empower students' progress toward their career objectives, particularly in STEM fields. Do students' perceptions match AMATYC guidelines? Do students feel more competent in their skill development? Do students see the connections between the multiple ways in which mathematical concepts are represented? Do the pedagogical approaches we use meet students' preferences and learning styles and encourage them to think independently and explore mathematics?

In fall 2003 the mathematics teaching faculty designed and administered a new student survey in GC developmental mathematics courses. Through the survey we (a) gathered information on students' perceptions of our developmental mathematics program in relationship with the AMATYC standards for intellectual development, content, and pedagogy; and (b) analyzed whether there were significant relationships between students' perceptions and demographics like age, gender, income, environment, or parents' educational background. This chapter will describe and report on our research and how this model can be used for programmatic review by other institutions.

The Importance of Assessment

Developmental educators are encouraged to assess developmental education programs for tracking student progress, building programs, and justifying developmental education work (Boylan, 1997a, 1997b). Many studies have demonstrated the effectiveness of developmental education through quantitative research methods (Roueche & Roueche, 1993), especially in retaining students (Durant, 1992; England, 1993; Feingold, 1994; Hamilton, 1993; Lyons, 1994; Mireles; Simmons, 1994; Umoh, Eddy, & Spaulding, 1994). Some studies investigated students' attitudes and other success factors within developmental education programs (Berenson, Carter & Norwood, 1992; Duranczyk, 2004; Elliot, 1990; Jones, 1994; Mireles; Stage & Kloosterman, 1995; Wachtel, 1994). Other studies have sought to identify the elements of a successful developmental education program (Bonnett & Newsom, 1995; Durant; Ironsmith, Marva, Harju, & Eppler, 2003). Although only 14% of 2-year colleges and 25% of 4-year institutions engage in ongoing, systematic evaluation, their reports demonstrate a positive correlation between program evaluation and successful outcomes including student retention and academic achievement (Boylan, Bliss, & Bonham, 1997; Casazza & Silverman, 1996; Congos & Schoeps, 1997; Maxwell, 1997). A call for assessment is also embedded in the AMATYC standards (Cohen, 1995), which include principles for assessing mathematics programs. But program assessment is closely wedded to student assessment within the classroom. A premise of our research is that we must consider students' perceptions when evaluating the effectiveness of our programs. By charting how our students are responding to our teaching methods and the levels of confidence they feel after completing our courses, we obtain important sources of information on how well we are meeting our programs' objectives, college mission, and AMATYC standards. This information complements grades and STEM retention data.

We are also acutely aware that students' perceptions of classroom activities and pedagogy may differ from the perceptions of faculty members. This study provides us with the feedback necessary to reflect on our achievements in implementing the standards and highlights areas for improvement. How effectively are we integrating the AMATYC standards for intellectual development, course content, and teaching pedagogy? How effectively are we promoting access across socioeconomic groups?

Background to GC Mathematics Program Assessment

Since 1999, students taking GC mathematics courses have been asked to complete mathematics program questionnaires during the last 3 weeks of the fall term. These questionnaires collected information on student satisfaction and perceptions of the GC mathematics program in the areas of homework, examinations, texts, support materials, and academic resources like mathematics tutoring. Mathematics faculty discussed the survey results each spring and planned curricular changes for implementation in the following academic year. Until now, the survey administrators made no systematic analysis of trends across years, nor have they studied potential demographic differences in responses. A study by Kinney (2001) compared student achievement between classes using computerized instruction (Academic Systems Corporation's Interactive Mathematics®, 1999a, 1999b) and traditional lecture instruction, with an eye toward using technology as a means for implementing AMATYC standards. The results of Kinney's study confirmed the benefits of having alternative classroom formats appealing to students' different learning styles.

Beginning in fall 2003 additional approaches for developmental mathematics education were implemented. In addition to the computer-assisted and lecture-based mathematics courses, project-based and inquiry-based courses were also taught at GC. Faculty chose to use a variety of beginning and intermediate algebra texts to complement their diverse delivery styles (see Chapter 14).

Research Design

Previously the survey queried students' opinions of the quality of the mathematics program and their usage of the program resources, delimited in the previous section, to meet educational goals. Because we wanted to learn if we are differentially effective with our diverse student population, in fall 2003 we modified the questionnaire to collect the following new information: (a) students' self-reported socioeconomic status (SES), defined by demographics that include age, gender, parental income, college-generation status, neighborhood of upbringing; (b) students' perceptions of how effectively the mathematics program addresses GC's mission; and (c) students' perceptions of how effectively the GC mathematics program met AMATYC's major recommendations for introductory college mathematics before calculus. Twelve questions of the 2003 survey remained consistent with surveys given in 2001 and 2002. Six of these questions addressed the effectiveness of the Math Center, which provides drop-in tutoring, and six addressed pedagogical aspects of the GC mathematics courses.

Every year students participated on a voluntary and anonymous basis. Some instructors offered students extra credit as an incentive to participate. All submitted student questionnaires are analyzed in this chapter. We made case-by-case exclusions for missing data, so even though we had 178 completed surveys in 2003, most items have a sample size (n) of less than 178. Similarly, 2001 and 2002 data also have varying sample sizes.

In 2001 and 2002 students completed a paper, bubble-sheet version of the survey, and results were summarized using Microsoft Excel. In 2003 we invited students by announcements made in classes and by e-mail to complete online questionnaires accessible via a URL link. Data from 2003 questionnaires were analyzed using the *Statistical Package for the Social Sciences* (SPSS©) for Windows (Version 11.5.0).

We analyzed all of the sections and questions of the 2003 questionnaire first by noting frequencies of responses. We did not assume a normal distribution and we had categorical data, so we used nonparametric tests for the data analysis. First, we performed Pearson's chi-square (χ^2) tests to check for correlations between mathematics courses taken and SES demographic categories. Then we performed Pearson's χ^2 tests to determine whether significant differences existed among the responses categorized by course number or SES demographic groups. We used Cramér's phi $(F)_c$ to quantify strengths of association. We analyzed the frequencies of student responses to the 12 common questions from 2001 through 2003 using Pearson's χ^2 tests to see if there were statistically significant dependencies between the responses and the year of the survey.

Results

The findings are organized into the six sub-sections following the organization of the student survey: population SES demographics, GC mission, intellectual development, content, pedagogy, and the Math Center. This chapter focuses on questions in the survey that support the GC mission and our multicultural efforts. In each of these sub-sections, we report (a) summary frequency data; (b) Pearson's χ^2 tests, with Cramér's phi $(F)_c$ tests for strengths of association when there are significant differences among the groups based on population demographics or SES; and (c) Pearson's χ^2 tests when there are significant differences in students' responses between the years 2001 and 2003 on the 13 common questions asked in the survey.

Population Demographics

Our 2001, 2002, and 2003 populations consisted of all students registered for courses in introductory or intermediate algebra. The courses included GC712, the first of a two-semester sequence in introductory algebra; GC721, a one-semester, introductory algebra course; GC722, a one-semester, computer-mediated introductory algebra course; GC731, a one-semester, intermediate algebra course; and GC732, a one-semester, computer-mediated intermediate algebra course. In 2001, 492 out of 807 students (61%) participated in the survey; in 2002, 331 out of 520 students (64%) participated; and in 2003, 178 out of 490 students (36%) participated. Populations in GC721 and GC731—the lecture courses—had the lowest response rates (18% and 31% respectively). GC712, GC722, and GC732—classes held in computer classrooms—had the largest response rates (64%, 68%, and 54% respectively).

The 2003 survey was the only survey that collected background data beyond students' primary college of enrollment, so it is the only year for which we can describe and analyze the data based on SES demographics. Because 94% of the students reported GC as their college of enrollment, and 96% reported ages between 18 and 23 years old, we did not analyze responses by these two characteristics. By gender, the respondents were 57% female. This is higher than the general population of GC, which in 2003 was only 50% female. We used three categories to identify family income: (a) below $35,000 (poverty limit in Minnesota), (b) between $35,000 and $45,000 (average range of family income in Minnesota), and (c) above $45,000 (above average range of family income in Minnesota). Thirty-seven percent of the students did not answer this question, and 21% of the students indicated a family income below $35,000. Of the respondents, 35% identified that they were first-generation college students, while 43% indicated that at least one of their parents had a college degree. Of the responding students, 45% lived primarily in urban neighborhoods during their upbringing. Table 1 contains all the demographic counts and percentages.

We tested for possible dependencies between course numbers and SES data. This revealed a dependency between course number and (a) first-generation college students, $\chi^2(df = 4, n=159) = 15.288, p = .004$, and (b) students' neighborhoods of upbringing, $\chi^2(df = 8, n = 167) = 23.329, p = .003$. There were greater percentages of students from urban neighborhoods (75%) and of first-generation college students (59.5%) in GC712 than in other courses. Both intermediate algebra courses (GC731 and GC732) had lower percentages of first-generation college students.

GC Mission

To carry out GC's mission statement, the college strives to offer class sizes that are conducive to personalized attention. Of the responding students, 83% believed that GC accomplished this goal, perhaps unsurprising as far as mathematics courses are concerned. GC's developmental mathematics courses have maximum enrollments of 40 students as opposed to the University of Minnesota's credit-bearing survey courses in mathematics (e.g., precalculus and calculus) conducted in large lecture halls supporting more than double this number. Our survey measured three other areas guided by GC's mission: (a) courses teach strategies and study skills in addition to mathematics content (70% agreed); (b) courses enable students to learn more about how to succeed in a university setting (55% agreed); and (c) courses enabled students to reflect on their learning interests, skills, and weaknesses and set attainable academic and career goals (61% agreed; see Figure 1).

Two questions regarding the GC mission showed statistically significant differences in responses, one by parents' level of education and one by parents' income. When answering the question, "Class size at GC is conducive for

TABLE 1

Frequency and Percent Response for Population Demographics, Fall 2003

Category	Possible responses	*n*	Percent
Course number	GC712	39	22
	GC721	27	15
	GC722	25	14
	GC731	69	40
	GC732	14	8
	Missing	4	2
Gender	Female	101	57
	Male	74	42
	Missing	3	2
Parent's income	Below $35,000	37	21
	$35,000–45,000	23	13
	Above $45,000	53	30
	Missing	65	37
First-generation college student	Yes	62	35
	No	99	56
	Missing	17	10
Highest level of education either parent reached	College degree	77	43
	Voc/tech coursework	33	19
	High school diploma	36	20
	Less than high school diploma	30	17
	Missing	2	1
Neighborhood of upbringing	Urban	80	45
	Rural	25	14
	Suburban	65	37
	Missing	8	5

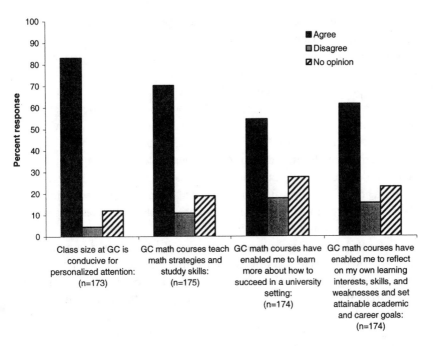

Figure 1. Student responses (*N*=178) to questions related to the GC mission.

personalized attention," χ^2(df = 8, *n* = 173) = 25.930, *p* = .001, 9% of the participants whose parents have college degrees disagreed with the statement compared to 0% in each of the other categories of students. One-hundred percent of the students whose parents had a vocational or technical degree agreed that the class size was conducive for personalized attention. For the question, "GC math courses have enabled me to reflect on my own learning interests, skills, and weaknesses and set attainable academic and career goals," χ^2(df = 4, *n* = 174) = 13.429, *p* = .009, more students than expected (a) had "no opinion" if their parents earned below \$35,000 annually (33%), (b) "disagreed" if their parents earned between \$35,000 and \$45,000 (39%), and (c) "agreed" if their parents earned above \$45,000 (71%).

Intellectual Development
We asked eight questions relating to the seven areas of intellectual development recommended by AMATYC standards: (a) mathematical problem solving; (b) modelling real-world situations; (c) developing mathematical arguments; (d) appreciating mathematics as a growing discipline, interrelated with other facets of human culture and other disciplines; (e) communicating with mathematics; (f) using appropriate technology as a means for

enhancing mathematical understanding and problem solving abilities; and (g) enriching experiences that encourage independent exploration of the power of mathematics. We posed each question in three ways. First, we asked students how often their classes involved activities encouraging their development of a particular skill identified by AMATYC (for example, mathematical problem solving): every class, weekly, occasionally, or never; students could also indicate that they did not understand the question. Next, we asked students to which degree they were engaged in those activities: highly engaged, moderately engaged, somewhat engaged, or not engaged at all; students could also indicate that the questions did not apply. Lastly, we asked students how often they would have preferred performing the activities: every class, weekly, occasionally, or never. Summaries of the eight questions and the frequency of responses provided in the following pages. We will report on the results for (a) modelling real-world situations; (b) appreciating mathematics as a growing discipline, interrelated with other facets of human culture and other disciplines; (c) communicating with mathematics; (d) using appropriate technology as a means for enhancing mathematical understanding and problem solving abilities; and (e) enriching experiences that encourage independent exploration of the power of mathematics.

Modelling real-world situations. Of the respondents, 48% reported at least weekly activities applying mathematics to real-world situations, 60% of the respondents were moderately or highly engaged in the activity, and 69% of them preferred activities that applied mathematics to real-world situations at least weekly. There were no statistically significant differences among the SES groupings or demographics for real-world activities.

Appreciating mathematics as a growing discipline. Thirty-seven percent of the students observed class activities connecting mathematics, culture, and other disciplines occurring at least weekly, 50% found these activities moderately or highly engaging, and 50% would prefer activities encouraging the use of class activities connecting mathematics, culture, and other disciplines at least weekly. There were statistically significant differences among students based on the course of enrollment, $\chi^2(df = 12, n = 164) = 28.394$, p = .005. The computer-mediated courses had more than 80% of their students reporting that activities connecting math, culture, and other disciplines occurred only occasionally or never. Students in GC721 reported the largest occurrence of activities interrelating mathematics with human culture and other disciplines.

Communicating with mathematics. Thirty-five percent of the students observed class activities encouraging them to read and write about mathematics at least weekly, 36% found these activities moderately or highly engaging, and only 35% would prefer activities encouraging reading and writing about mathematics. Class activities encouraging students to discuss mathematics were observed as occurring at least weekly by 35% of the students, 38% of the students found these activities moderately or highly engaging, and 42% of the students would prefer activities encouraging the discussion of mathematics. There were significant differences among the groups in response to this question.

The χ^2 analysis of student responses and course enrollment showed a dependency among courses and (a) level of engagement when activities encouraged students to read and write about mathematics, $\chi^2(df = 16, n = 173) = 31.936, p = .010$; (b) frequency of activities encouraging students to discuss math, $\chi^2(df = 12, n = 169) = 22.861, p = .029$; and (c) level of engagement when activities encouraged students to discuss mathematics, $\chi^2(df = 16, n = 172) = 30.767, p = .014$. The percentage of students in GC712 stating that activities encouraged them to discuss mathematics in every class was at least twice the percentage in each of the other courses. Only 8% of students in GC732 stated that activities encouraging them to discuss mathematics occurred in every class or weekly (see Table 2). Students in GC712 reported higher levels of engagement than students participating in any other GC developmental math course in discussing mathematics and higher levels of engagement when activities encouraged them to read and write about mathematics.

More surprising, the χ^2 analyses revealed significant differences in responses among urban, rural, and suburban students when asked about their (a) preference in the occurrence of activities encouraging discussion in mathematics, $\chi^2(df = 6, n = 165) = 17.470, p = .008$; and (b) level of engagement when activities encouraged mathematics discussions, $\chi^2(df = 8, n = 168) = 18.495, p = .018$. Of urban students, 21%, contrasted with 5% of suburban students, preferred daily class activities encouraging discussion in mathematics. Of urban students, 25% preferred only occasional mathematics discussions as opposed to 52% of suburban students (see Table 2).

Use of appropriate technology. Forty-five percent of the students reported class activities using technology at least weekly, 46% found these activities moderately or highly engaging, and 55% would prefer at least weekly activities using technology to enhance mathematical learning. The χ^2 analysis showed differences among the groups based on courses enrolled and responses to (a) the frequency of classes using technology to enhance mathematical learning, $\chi^2(df = 12, n = 171) = 103.976, p = .000$; (b) students' level of engagement in activities using technology, $\chi^2(df = 16, n = 172) = 49.921, p = .000$; and (c) students' preferences in how often technology use should occur, $\chi^2(df = 12, n = 171) = 52.073, p = .000$. The percentages of student responses for use of technology in every class were largest in computer-mediated courses (GC722 and GC732). GC712 had the largest percentage for weekly and occasional use of technology in class. Students reported higher levels of

TABLE 2

Percent Response for Questions on Communication of Mathematics
by Course or Childhood Environment, Fall 2003 ($N = 178$)

Course number	n	Level of engagement when activities encouraging reading and writing about mathematics				
		Highly engaged	Moderately engaged	Somewhat engaged	Not at all engaged	NA
712	39	12.8%	28.2%	28.2%	15.4%	15.4%
721	27	14.8%	18.5%	44.4%	7.4%	14.8%
722	24	12.5%	20.8%	25.0%	0.0%	41.7%
731	69	2.9%	37.7%	23.2%	15.9%	20.3%
732	14	0.0%	14.3%	14.3%	14.3%	57.1%

Course number	n	Occurrence of activities encouraging students to discuss mathematics			
		Every class	Weekly	Occasionally	Not at all
712	38	31.6%	18.4%	36.8%	13.2%
721	25	16.0%	16.0%	36.0%	32.0%
722	25	16.0%	8.0%	44.0%	32.0%
731	68	10.3%	27.9%	41.2%	20.6%
732	13	0.0%	7.7%	38.5%	53.8%

Course number	n	Level of engagement when activities encouraging students to discuss mathematics				
		Highly engaged	Moderately engaged	Somewhat engaged	Not at all engaged	NA
712	39	12.8%	38.5%	33.3%	7.7%	7.7%
721	25	12.0%	32.0%	12.0%	12.0%	32.0%
722	25	16.0%	8.0%	44.0%	12.0%	24.0%
731	69	8.7%	26.1%	40.0%	7.2%	15.9%
732	14	0.0%	21.4%	42.0%	0.0%	57.1%

Students' childhood environment	n	Level of engagement when activities encouraging students to discuss mathematics				
		Highly engaged	Moderately engaged	Somewhat engaged	Not at all engaged	NA
Urban	79	19.0%	22.8%	30.4%	10.1%	17.7%
Rural	25	0.0%	44.0%	44.0%	4.0%	8.0%
Suburban	64	6.3%	25.0%	31.3%	7.8%	29.7%

Students' childhood environment	n	Preference for activities encouraging students to discuss mathematics			
		Every class	Weekly	Occasionally	Never
Urban	79	20.3%	34.2%	25.3%	20.3%
Rural	25	12.0%	32.0%	44.0%	12.0%
Suburban	65	4.6%	20.0%	52.3%	23.1%

engagement in technology-based activities in the computer-mediated courses. Students' preferences for the use of technology varied, with computer-mediated courses having higher percentages of students preferring technology in every class (see Table 3).

When looking at students' preferences in the use of technology in class, we found significant differences between first-generation and non-first-generation students, $\chi^2(\text{df} = 3, n = 158) = 103.976, p = .034$. First-generation students had a higher percentage (32.2%) preferring the use of technology in every class.

Enriching experiences. Forty-six percent of the students observed class activities encouraging students to explore mathematics independently occurring at least weekly, 47% found these activities moderately or highly engaging, and 50% would prefer such activities at least weekly. We found significant differences between the groups by course of enrollment, $\chi^2(\text{df} = 16, n = 171) = 27.961, p = .032$, and generation in college, $\chi^2(\text{df} = 4, n = 158) = 10.267, p = .036$, among students' responses to questions on their level of engagement in class activities encouraging independent exploration of mathematics. A larger percentage of students in computer-mediated courses (33.3% and 28.6%) rated themselves highly engaged when class activities encouraged them to independently explore mathematics compared to 7.2% of GC731 students rating themselves highly engaged. While 25% of GC731 students responded that the question did not apply to their course, 3% of students in GC712 stated that this question did not apply to their course. First-generation college students rated themselves above the expected percentages for being highly engaged (18.6%) and moderately engaged (42.4%) in activities encouraging them to independently explore mathematics. Non-first-generation college students rated themselves slightly below the expected percentages in both categories. The reverse relationship existed for somewhat engaged, not engaged at all, and not applicable (see Table 4).

Content
Ten questions queried students' levels of confidence in content areas addressed by the AMATYC standards for mathematics. In only three areas did more than 20% of the students rate their courses as helping very little or not at all in increasing their confidence or competence. The three areas were: (a) translating situations into pictures and using measurement for solving mathematics problems, (b) using statistical and counting skills to solve problems and to make inferences about real-world situations, and (c) using mathematical logic to reason through situations.

When asked about the amount of new material presented in the introductory and intermediate algebra courses, 87% of the respondents said that their

TABLE 3

Percent Response for Questions on Appropriate Use
of Technology by Course and SES, Fall 2003 ($N = 178$)

Course number	n	Occurrence of technology used to enhancing mathematical understanding			
		Every class	Weekly	Occasionally	Not at all
712	39	12.8%	46.2%	35.9%	15.1%
721	25	4.0%	16.0%	52.0%	28.0%
722	25	60.0%	12.0%	24.0%	4.0%
731	68	0.0%	29.4%	30.9%	39.7%
732	14	78.6%	7.1%	14.3%	0.0%

Course number	n	Level of engagement using technology				
		Highly engaged	Moderately engaged	Somewhat engaged	Not at all engaged	NA
712	38	8.4%	28.9%	42.1%	7.9%	2.6%
721	26	11.5%	23.1%	30.8%	7.7%	26.9%
722	25	40.0%	36.0%	20.0%	0.0%	4.0%
731	69	7.2%	26.1%	24.6%	8.7%	33.3%
732	14	57.1%	21.4%	21.4%	0.0%	0.0%

Course number	n	Preference for using technology			
		Every class	Weekly	Occasionally	Never
712	39	25.6%	35.9%	33.3%	5.1%
721	26	7.7%	26.9%	12.0%	15.4%
722	25	48.0%	36.0%	44.0%	0.0%
731	67	7.5%	32.8%	40.0%	22.4%
732	14	71.4%	21.4%	42.0%	0.0%

First generation college student	n	Preference for using technology			
		Every class	Weekly	Occasionally	Never
Yes	59	25.6%	30.5%	32.2%	5.1%
No	99	7.7%	33.3%	33.3%	17.2%

Parents' income	n	Level of engagement using technology				
		Highly engaged	Moderately engaged	Somewhat engaged	Not at all engaged	NA
Below $35,000	36	19.4%	19.4%	47.2%	5.6%	8.3%
$35,000–$45,000	23	17.4%	43.5%	21.7%	4.3%	13.0%
Above $45,000	17.3	17.3%	25.0%	19.2%	7.7%	30.8%

TABLE 4

Percent Response for Questions on Enriching Experiences Encouraging
Independent Exploration by Course Number and SES, Fall 2003 ($N = 178$)

Course number	n	Occurrence of enriching experiences encouraged independent exploration			
		Every class	Weekly	Occasionally	Not at all
712	38	21.1%	21.1%	47.4%	10.5%
721	24	20.8%	25.0%	29.2%	25.0%
722	24	54.2%	8.3%	25.0%	12.5%
731	66	15.2%	25.8%	33.3%	25.8%
732	13	38.5%	23.1%	0.0%	38.5%

Course number	n	Level of engagement when enriching experiences encouraged independent exploration				
		Highly engaged	Moderately engaged	Somewhat engaged	Not at all engaged	NA
712	38	15.8%	26.3%	44.7%	10.5%	2.6%
721	26	15.8%	26.9%	30.8%	11.5%	15.4%
722	25	33.3%	37.5%	12.5%	8.3%	8.3%
731	69	7.2%	36.2%	24.6%	7.2%	24.6%
732	14	28.6%	14.3%	21.4%	14.3%	21.4%

First generation college student	n	Preference for using technology				
		Highly engaged	Moderately engaged	Somewhat engaged	Not at all engaged	NA
Yes	59	18.6%	42.4%	25.4%	3.4%	10.2%
No	99	14.1%	23.2%	32.3%	12.1%	18.2%

Gender	n	Preference for enriching experiences encouraged independent exploration			
		Every class	Weekly	Occasionally	Never
Female	98	27.6%	20.4%	33.7%	18.4%
Male	74	13.5%	37.8%	29.7%	18.9%

instructors presented new material at least weekly, while 63% of respondents reported that their instructors presented topics that they had before but did not remember well. Of the responding students, 84% thought that their placement was about right, and 85% believed that they were well prepared for their next mathematics class.

For three of the content questions there were significant differences between the groups by SES data (see Table 5). For the question, "Within the course topics, new material was presented: Every class, weekly, occasionally, not at all," there were statistically significant differences between responses by course number, $\chi^2(df = 12, n = 172) = 23.880, p = .021$, and parents' income levels, $\chi^2(df = 4, n = 167) = 10.224, p = .037$. The largest differences among the groups were in the percentages reported for new material being presented in every class or weekly. Of the students in GC721, 73% reported new material in every class while only 15% reported new material weekly. In GC722 only 28% reported new material in every class while 56% reported new material weekly. Looking at the same question by parental income, we found that 33.3% of the students who reported that their parents made less than $35,000 per year indicated that new material was presented in every class, and only 28% indicated occasionally encountering new material in class. Students reporting that their parents make more than $35,000 per year also indicated that new material was presented daily at higher percentages (52% and 54%) and that new material was occasionally presented at lower percentages (9% and 6%) than the students in the below $35,000 income group. All income groups had similar percentages when reporting that new material was presented weekly.

This question was also asked on the 2001 and 2002 surveys (see Table 6). Pearson χ^2 results indicated significant differences over the years, $\chi^2(df = 12, n = 976) = 160.506, p = .000$. The percentage of students reporting new material being covered in every class and at least weekly has greatly increased over the past 3 years. Likewise, the proportion of students who reported never seeing new material or only occasionally seeing new material has continued to decrease from 66% in 2001 to only 12% in 2003.

Two questions showed significant differences in responses by gender. When reporting on the question "This class helped me feel more competent using functions as an approach to problem solving," $\chi^2(df = 3, n = 167) = 13.703, p = .003$, women had lower percentages in the response to very much (30%), very little (3.2%), and not at all (5.3%), while men had higher percentages, 36%, 17%, and 8% respectively. Men's responses of "somewhat" (40%) were lower than women's (62%). The other question showing a gender dependency was, "Within the course topics, material that I have seen before but did not remember was presented: Every class, weekly occasionally or never," $\chi^2 (df = 3, n = 170) = 10.872, p = .012$. Of the women, 30% reported this

TABLE 5

Percent Response for Questions on Content
by Course Number or SES, Fall 2003 ($N = 178$)

Course number	n	Within the course topics, new material was presented:			
		Every class	Weekly	Occasionally	Not at all
712	38	28.9%	55.3%	13.2%	2.6%
721	26	73.1%	15.4%	11.5%	0.0%
722	25	28.0%	56.0%	16.0%	0.0%
731	69	58.0%	30.4%	11.6%	0.0%
732	14	42.9%	50.0%	7.1%	0.0%

Parents' income	n	Within the course topics, new material was presented:			
		Every class	Weekly	Occasionally	Not at all
Below $35,000	36	33.3%	38.9%	27.8%	0.0%
$35,000–$45,000	23	52.2%	39.1%	8.7%	0.0%
Above $45,000	52	53.8%	40.4%	5.8%	0.0%

Gender	n	This class helped me to feel more competent using functions as an approach to problem solving:			
		Very much	Somewhat	Very little	Not at all
Female	98	29.5%	62.1%	3.2%	5.3%
Male	72	36.1%	38.9%	16.7%	8.3%

Gender	n	Within course topics, material that I have seen before but did not remember was presented:			
		Every class	Weekly	Occasionally	Not at all
Female	98	29.6%	30.6%	36.7%	3.1%
Male	72	16.7%	50.0%	25.0%	8.3%

occurred in every class compared to 17% of the men. While 50% of the men reported this occurred weekly only 31% of the women reported this occurrence weekly. This question was also asked on each of the surveys over the past 3 years. Here too, over the 3-year period more students have recognized more material that they have seen before but did not remember. There is a significant difference over the years, $\chi^2(df = 12, n = 929) = 19.810, p = .000$. From 2001 to 2003 a decreasing proportion of students recognized material in every class that they have seen before but did not remember. Over the years, an increasing percentage of the students have reported recognizing material that they have seen before only occasionally or never.

Each student survey since 2001 asked students to judge the appropriateness of their placement. Here too, Pearson's chi-square tests indicated a significant

TABLE 6

Chi-Square Results and Percent Response to Questions on Texts, Computer
Software, and Placement from Fall 2001, Fall 2002, and Fall 2003

Question from survey	Response options	2001 N=492	2002 N=331	2003 N=178	χ^2
The text helped me to learn the content of the course:	Not at all	9.9	7.6	4.6	
	Very little	25.8	21.0	12.6	
	Somewhat	52.1	60.1	49.7	
	Very much	12.2	11.3	33.1	
					60.334
The computer software helps me to learn the content of the course	I did not use	50.4	53.8	39.3	
	Not at all	9.5	12.8	16.2	
	Somewhat	23.4	19.5	26.0	
	Very much	16.7	14.0	18.5	
					14.298
On average, I used computer software	Never	57.7	64.8	41.7	
	0–1 hrs/wk	12.4	8.3	18.3	
	2–3 hrs/wk	14.0	10.4	17.7	
	4–5 hrs/wk	13.0	14.4	15.4	
	6–8 hrs/wk	2.9	2.1	1.7	
	Over 9 hrs/wk	0	0	5.1	
					68.302
Within the course topics, new material was presented:	not at all	19.0	17.3	.6	
	Occasionally	46.9	39.2	11.3	
	Weekly	19.4	25.0	38.7	
	Every class	14.7	18.5	49.4	
					160.506
Within the course topics, material that I have seen before but did not remember was presented:	not at all	4.6	1.8	5.5	
	Occasionally	25.9	28.8	32.1	
	Weekly	28.0	30.2	37.6	
	Every class	41.5	39.3	24.9	
					19.810
My placement in this course was:	Too low	48.7	44.7	14.3	
	About right	46.0	50.3	57.1	
	Too high	.2	.7	2.4	
	Not sure	5.1	4.3	14.3	
					44.494

difference over the years, χ^2(df = 12, n = 948) = 44.494, p = .000. A smaller percentage of students are now reporting that their placements are too low. In 2001, 49% of the students indicated that their placement was too low, and in 2003 only 26% of the students made the same claim. In 2001 and 2002, 46% of the students indicated that their placement was about right, and in 2003 it increased to 57%.

Pedagogy

The survey posed 12 questions about pedagogy: activities promoting (a) collaboration, (b) speaking and presenting, (c) use of multiple approaches to problem solving, (d) independent thinking and exploration, (e) lecture-based teaching, and (f) computer-based teaching. In these areas, we asked students how often they did the particular activities in their class and how often they *preferred* that they *should* be done. In this chapter, we report on (a) collaboration, (b) speaking and presenting, (c) lecture-based teaching, and (d) computer-based teaching. Three additional questions were posed to explore the extent of students' use of computer software, the value of computer software to the course, and the value of the mathematics text (see Table 7). This area of the survey generated the largest number of significant differences between the groups. Only three questions about pedagogy revealed no significant differences between any groups, but there were significant differences between groups defined by course number for six of the questions and by SES data for five of the questions (see Tables 7, 8, and 9). We will now look at each of these areas for general trends, significant differences between the groups, and significant differences that occurred over the 3-year period of data collection.

Collaborative activities (group work). Only 21% of the respondents stated that their classes worked collaboratively in groups on activities at least weekly, whereas 63% said collaborative group activities never occurred. However, 30% stated that they would prefer their classes to work collaboratively in groups at least weekly. An even greater percentage, 35%, stated that they would prefer that collaborative group work never occur.

The response to this question was statistically significant when looking at the course number, χ^2(df = 12, n = 171) = 75.322, p = .0009, and neighborhood of upbringing, χ^2(df = 6, n = 167) = 16.375, p = .012. The area with the strongest measure of association was course number (Cramér's F_c = .664). The course that had the greatest percentage of students stating that collaborative group activities occurred in every class was GC712 (18.4%). The other courses had fewer than 6% of the students choosing that response. The course with the lowest percentage of students stating that collaborative group activities never occurred was also GC712, 10.5% compared to over 69% in each of the other courses. Urban students (9.1%) stated that collaborative group activities

TABLE 7

Frequency and Percent Response for Questions on Pedagogy, Fall 2003 ($N = 178$)

Question	Possible responses	Frequency	Percent
This class worked collaboratively in groups on activities	Every class	12	6.9
	Weekly	25	14.4
	Occasionally	25	14.4
	Never	112	64.4
I would prefer that the class work collaboratively in groups:	Every class	21	12.1
	Weekly	31	17.8
	Occasionally	59	33.9
	Never	63	36.2
This class encouraged us to speak/present:	Every class	30	17.3
	Weekly	15	8.7
	Occasionally	49	28.3
	Never	72	42.4
I would prefer that the class encourage us to speak/present:	Every class	21	12.4
	Weekly	24	14.1
	Occasionally	53	31.2
	Never	72	42.4
This class encouraged multiple approaches (numerical, graphical, symbolic,and verbal) to solving problems:	Every class	43	24.9
	Weekly	70	40.5
	Occasionally	48	27.7
	Never	12	6.9
I would prefer that the class use multiple approaches:	Every class	39	22.8
	Weekly	58	33.9
	Occasionally	65	38.0
	Never	9	5.3
This class involved activities that encouraged me to think independently and explore:	Every class	45	25.9
	Weekly	61	35.1
	Occasionally	49	28.2
	Never	19	10.9
I would prefer that the class involve activities that encouraged me to think independently and explore:	Every class	41	23.4
	Weekly	66	37.7
	Occasionally	52	29.7
	Never	16	9.1
The class had lectures:	Every class	83	47.4
	Weekly	26	14.9
	Occasionally	15	8.6
	Never	51	29.1
I would prefer that the class have lectures:	Every class	66	37.7
	Weekly	38	21.7
	Occasionally	31	17.7
	Never	40	22.9
This class used computer-based teaching:	Every class	42	24.1
	Weekly	43	24.7
	Occasionally	20	11.5
	Never	69	39.7
I would prefer that the class have computer-based teaching:	Every class	39	22.7
	Weekly	31	18
	Occasionally	39	22.7
	Never	63	36.6

occurred in every class whereas only 4% of the rural students and 3% of the suburban students chose that response. Of the urban students, 23% stated that collaborative group activities occurred weekly, but 0% of the rural and 11% of the suburban students chose that response.

There was also a significant difference in responses to the question of preference for collaborative group activities by course number, χ^2(df = 12, n = 171) = 30.691, p = .002. Of GC712 students, 24% preferred collaborative group activities in every class compared to less than 10% of the students in all other courses. Only 7.9% of the GC712 students preferred never having collaborative group activities compared to over 40% of the students in each of the other classes.

Speaking and presenting (by students). When asked whether their classes encouraged student presentations, only 26% of the students stated these occurred. A majority, 55%, stated that they would prefer that presentations never occur. Taking a look at student responses by course number there was a significant difference between classes identifying speaking and presenting as a part of the class, χ^2(df = 12, n = 170) = 66.199, p = .000, and preferring the activity occur, χ^2(df = 12, n = 167) = 40.662, p = .000 (see Tables 8 and 9). Students in beginning algebra (GC712 and GC721) had the largest percentages (34% and 23% respectively) in reporting speaking and presenting occurring in every class and the lowest percentages (13% and 35% respectively) in reporting that speaking and presenting never occurred in class. When reporting on preference for speaking and presenting in class, the computer-mediated courses (GC722 and GC732) had less than expected percentages in most categories except for preferring that speaking and presenting never occur in class (72% and 86% respectively). In this category they were over 30% higher than any of the other courses. Students in GC712 had the greatest preference for speaking and presenting in every class (21%). The preference for speaking and presenting was also statistically significant for students by parents' highest level of educational attainment, χ^2(df = 12, n = 159) = 33.338, p = .001. Here, students with parents having either a vocational or technical degree or a high school diploma as their highest level of education preferred never speaking and presenting in class (15% above the other groups, 49% and 69% respectively) and preferred speaking and presenting in every class below the other groups (by over 40%).

Lecture-based teaching. Sixty-one percent of the students reported that their classes had lectures at least weekly, and the same percentage stated that they preferred that lectures be given at least weekly. However, 47% reported that lectures occurred in every class, and only 38% preferred daily lectures. Only by course number was there a significant difference in students' reporting on lecture-based teaching , χ^2(df = 12, n = 172) = 125.457, p = .000. As

TABLE 8

Percent Response for Questions on Pedagogies by Course Number, Fall 2003 ($N = 178$)

Course number	n	Every class	Weekly	Occasionally	Never
		Occurrence of collaborative group activities			
712	38	23.7%	35.9%	28.9%	7.9%
721	26	7.7%	11.5%	34.6%	46.2%
722	25	8.3%	4.2%	41.7%	45.8%
731	68	10.1%	13.0%	34.8%	42.0%
732	14	7.1%	21.4%	28.6%	42.9%
		Preference for collaborative group activities			
712	38	34.2%	18.4%	34.2%	13.2%
721	26	23.1%	0.0%	42.3%	34.6%
722	24	0.0%	0.0%	8.0%	92.0%
731	69	16.4%	11.9%	34.3%	37.3%
732	14	0.0%	0.0%	0.0%	100.0%
		Preference for activities encouraging speaking or presenting			
712	38	21.1%	28.9%	31.6%	18.4%
721	26	15.4%	7.7%	50.0%	26.9%
722	25	0.0%	4.0%	24.0%	72.0%
731	67	14.4%	15.6%	29.7%	40.6%
732	14	0.0%	0.0%	14.3%	85.7%
		Activities encouraging multiple approaches to problem solving			
712	38	36.8%	42.1%	13.2%	7.9%
721	26	38.5%	34.6%	26.9%	0.0%
722	25	4.0%	28.0%	56.0%	12.0%
731	68	23.5%	45.6%	25.0%	5.9%
732	13	7.7%	38.5%	38.5%	15.4%
		Occurrence of lecture-based teaching			
712	38	39.5%	39.5%	10.5%	10.5%
721	26	76.9%	3.8%	11.5%	7.7%
722	25	0.0%	0.0%	4.0%	96.0%
731	69	65.2%	14.5%	8.7%	11.6%
732	14	0.0%	0.0%	7.1%	92.9%
		Preference for lecture-based teaching			
712	38	31.6%	34.2%	23.7%	10.5%
721	26	61.5%	11.5%	15.4%	11.5%
722	25	0.0%	8.0%	24.0%	68.0%
731	69	52.2%	27.5%	8.7%	11.6%
732	14	0.0%	0.0%	42.9%	57.1%

TABLE 9

Percent Response for Questions on Pedagogies by Course Number,
Fall 2003 ($N = 178$)

SES demographics	Occurrence of collaborative group activities				
Neighborhood of upbringing	n	Every class	Weekly	Occasionally	Never
Urban	77	9.1%	23.4%	16.9%	50.6%
Rural	25	4.0%	0.0%	12.0%	84.0%
Suburban	65	3.1%	10.8%	10.8%	75.4%
	Preference for activities encouraging speaking or presenting				
Parents' education level	n	Every class	Weekly	Occasionally	Never
College degree	75	13.3%	12.0%	41.3%	33.3%
Voc/tech course work	33	6.1%	9.1%	36.4%	48.5%
High school diploma	32	6.3%	9.4%	15.6%	68.8%
Less than high school diploma	8	50.0%	12.5%	12.5%	25.0%
	Preference for multiple approaches to problem solving				
Parents' education level	n	Every class	Weekly	Occasionally	Never
College degree	76	26.3%	22.4%	47.4%	3.9%
Voc/tech course work	33	24.2%	42.4%	24.2%	9.1%
High school diploma	33	9.1%	36.4%	48.5%	6.1%
Less than high school diploma	7	28.6%	71.4%	0.0%	0.0%
	Preference for lecture-based teaching				
Gender	n	Every class	Weekly	Occasionally	Never
Female	99	42.4%	25.3%	16.2%	16.2%
Male	74	31.1%	16.2%	20.3%	32.4%
Neighborhood					
Urban	78	30.8%	33.3%	17.9%	17.9%
Rural	25	44.0%	20.0%	4.0%	32.0%
Suburban	65	46.2%	10.8%	18.5%	24.6%
	Text help in learning course content				
First-generation college student	n	Every class	Weekly	Occasionally	Never
Yes	60	45%	31.7%	20.0%	3.3%
No	99	27.3%	57.6%	10.1%	5.1%

would be expected, the computer-mediated courses were the only courses having no counts for lecture-based teaching in every class or weekly, though sizeable proportions of students responded that they would prefer lectures occasionally. GC712 had the largest percentage of students preferring lectures weekly as opposed to every class, opposite the trend of responses by students in the other lecture-based courses.

When students reported on their preference for lectures in class, differences were statistically significant by course number, $\chi^2(df = 12, n = 172) = 79.518$, $p = .000$, gender, $\chi^2(df = 3, n = 173) = 8.315$, $p = .040$, and neighborhood of upbringing, $\chi^2(df = 6, n = 168) = 14.961$, $p = .021$. The greatest degree of association was by course number (Cramér's $F_c = .680$). Over 50% of the students in GC721 and GC731 preferred lectures in every class, more than 20% above the other courses. Students' preference for lectures by gender indicated women preferring lectures in every class (42%) and weekly (25%) and men preferring lectures in every class (31%) and weekly (16%). Thirty-two percent of the men preferred never having lectures compared to only 16% of the women. Suburban (46%) and rural (44%) students also preferred lectures in every class, as opposed to urban students (30%). Suburban (25%) and rural (32%) students also chose "never" as their response at a higher rate than urban students (18%).

Computer-based teaching. For computer-based teaching, 49% of the students stated that their classes used this method at least weekly, while only 41% preferred it at least weekly. There were significant differences in responses by course number, $\chi^2(df = 12, n = 171) = 197.625$, $p = .000$, and students' neighborhood of upbringing, $\chi^2(df = 6, n = 167) = 14.470$, $p = .025$ (see Table 10). As would be expected, the computer-mediated courses had the largest percentages of students indicating that computers were used in every class. GC712 had the largest percentage of students (34%) choosing weekly usage of the computer. Suburban students had the greatest variance from expected values (by a factor of 1.19) for computer usage in every class. Only urban students had higher than expected values for computer usage weekly and occasionally. There was a significant difference from expected values in preference for the use of computers only by course number, $\chi^2(df = 12, n = 169) = 88.497$, $p = .000$. Perhaps unsurprisingly, variance in actual values and expected values for each course follow the course's design. GC721 and GC731 are primarily designed to be computer-free, and student preferences are only higher than expected values in the "never" responses. GC721 is designed for at least weekly computer usage, and actual counts for "weekly" varied the most from the expected value (14 vs. 7). GC722 and GC732 are computer-mediated courses, and students' actual values for preferring computer usage daily were above the expected value.

TABLE 10
Percent Response for Questions on Computer-Based Teaching
by Course Number, SES, or Demographics, Fall 2003 ($N = 178$)

		Occurrence of computer-based teaching			
Course number	n	Every class	Weekly	Occasionally	Never
712	38	7.9%	71.1%	18.4%	2.6%
721	25	8.0%	4.0%	8.0%	80.0%
722	25	88.0%	12.0%	0.0%	0.0%
731	69	1.4%	17.4%	15.9%	65.2%
732	14	100.0%	0.0%	0.0%	0.0%
Neighborhood					
Urban	78	7.9%	71.1%	18.4%	2.6%
Rural	25	8.0%	4.0%	8.0%	80.0%
Suburban	65	88.0%	12.0%	0.0%	0.0%

		Average hours per week using computer software					
Course number	n	Never	0–1	2–3	4–5	6–8	9 or more
712	38	7.9%	26.3%	39.5%	18.4%	0.0%	7.9%
721	26	76.9%	3.8%	7.7%	7.7%	3.8%	0.0%
722	25	0.0%	12.0%	32.0%	44.0%	0.0%	12.0%
731	69	68.1%	18.8%	2.9%	7.2%	1.4%	1.4%
732	14	7.1%	35.7%	28.6%	14.3%	7.1%	7.1%

		Computer software helped with course content				
Course number	n	Very much	Some	Very little	Not at all	NA
712	37	29.7%	28.9%	16.21%	0.0%	5.4%
721	26	7.7%	23.1%	0.0%	7.7%	73.1%
722	25	52.0%	36.0%	8.0%	4.0%	0.0%
731	68	1.5%	26.1%	7.4%	11.8%	63.2%
732	14	35.7%	21.4%	28.6%	0.0%	7.1%
Parents' education level						
College degree	77	20.8%	22.4%	9.1%	6.5%	51.9%
Voc/tech course work	32	12.5%	42.4%	9.4%	0.0%	40.6%
High school diploma	35	25.7%	36.4%	11.4%	11.4%	25.7%
Less than high school diploma	7	0.0%	71.4%	0.0%	28.6%	14.3%

		Preference for computer-based teaching			
Course number	n	Every class	Weekly	Occasionally	Never
712	38	23.7%	36.8%	23.7%	15.8%
721	26	7.7%	7.7%	30.8%	53.8%
722	24	8.3%	16.7%	12.5%	4.2%
731	67	10.1%	13.4%	25.4%	58.2%
732	14	7.1%	14.3%	14.3%	0.0%

Forty-two percent of the students reported never having used computer software while 36% used software three or less hours per week. Computer usage per week was also significantly different from expected values by course numbers, $\chi^2(df = 20, n = 172) = 103.161, p = .000$. Only GC712 and the computer-mediated courses had higher than expected values for computer use nine or more hours per week. Only GC721 and GC731 had higher than expected values for never using computer software for their mathematics course. This question had been asked over the 3-year period of this study, so the test of significance for differences over the years was also conducted and proved statistically significant, $\chi^2(df = 18, n = 987) = 68.302, p = .000$. Computer software usage has been increasing over the years.

Of the students who used the computer software, 27% stated that the software helped them very little or not at all in learning course content. The value of the computer software to learning course content was statistical significant by course number, $\chi^2(df = 16, n = 170) = 103.667, p = .000$, and parents' education, $\chi^2(df = 16, n = 172) = 36.149, p = .003$. GC712 and the computer-mediated courses (GC722 and GC732) had higher than expected values choosing "very much" when responding to "the computer software helped me to learn the content of the course." Students (51.9%) whose parents had a college degree chose not to enroll in computer-based courses compared to students (14.3%) whose parents had less then a high school diploma. Students (32.5%) whose parents had a college degree found the computer software at least somewhat helpful compared to students (57.1%) whose parents had less then a high school diploma. χ^2 analysis also revealed a significant difference in students' responses to this question by year, $\chi^2(df = 12, n = 173) = 8.315, p = .040$, showing a positive trend between 2001 and 2003 (see Table 6).

Math Center

The surveys conducted in mathematics classes between 2001 and 2003 have included questions regarding students' usage of the Math Center and students' levels of satisfaction when working there. The new 2003 survey included seven questions consistent with questions posed in prior years as well as a new question asking if students thought that the Math Center encouraged them to explore mathematics and to be independent learners, consistent with a key AMATYC recommendation. These surveys have been important sources of feedback prior to the Math Center's implementation of a system for collecting daily usage statistics (see Chapter 20). It should be noted that the Math Center also serves current and former GC students taking other mathematics courses that are not represented in this survey (i.e., statistics, college algebra, pre-calculus, calculus, and a variety of other mathematics and mathematics-related courses).

For the 2003 survey, 71% of the responding students reported having used resources in the Math Center, 24% of the students used the center's computers once or more during the semester, 18% visited the center to make up quizzes or exams, and 48% worked in the center alone as opposed to 14% working in groups. Of those who reported having used the Math Center, 68% indicated that they were at least a little more confident in mathematics as a result of having used the center, 37% said "some," and 17% said "very much." Of the students using the center, 62% reported that they were encouraged to explore and to be independent learners at least a little, 35% said "some," and 13% said "very much."

Discussion

The discussion, too, is organized into six sub-sections. We analyze the data with emphasis on tems from the survey that bear on the GC mission, our quest to embrace the diversity of our student population, and our desire to advance the professional standards for undergraduate mathematics education set by AMATYC and NCTM. We cite research literature to support our interpretations. This discussion is intended to be a guide for self-reflection and program review.

Population Demographics
There was almost a 30% drop in student participation between 2002 and 2003 on the GC Mathematics Program Questionnaire. We attribute this drop in participation to the change in the survey format. We stopped using bubble sheets to collect data and moved to an online survey. Student participation in courses that had computers within their classrooms had response rates similar to the 2001 and 2002 questionnaire rates. Only courses that did not have at least weekly class sessions in a computer classroom had low response rates (18% and 31%). We will explore delivering the survey using both methods in the future to optimize participation.

The first time that we had sufficient data to determine that the introductory algebra courses have more first-generation college students and more urban students was in 2003. The intermediate algebra courses have more suburban and rural students. It is also evident that the developmental mathematics courses have more female students than the overall GC population. These are important factors to reflect on as we (a) prepare information for advisors, (b) review and revise mathematics placement criteria and tests, and (c) consider and prepare alternative formats for offering the developmental mathematics curriculum. First-generation, urban, and female students who begin their mathematics trajectories within the lowest-level developmental courses face a longer course sequence to satisfy college requirements for graduation than their male, suburban or rural, and non-first-generation peers who begin in the higher-level developmental mathematics courses. Is this creating another barrier to graduation for populations that have been traditionally underrepresented in STEM subject areas? Are we tracking certain students into GC712 or other introductory algebra courses rather than encouraging students to begin at the intermediate algebra level? Do our placement test items give an advantage to suburban, non-first-generation students? While we consider the possibility of hidden forms of discrimination embedded in our placement, counseling, and curricular practices, our teaching faculty are increasingly emphasizing multicultural pedagogies in our teaching and tutor-training (Duranczyk et al., 2004; Frisch, 2004; Opitz, 2003).

Thirty-seven percent of the students did not answer the question regarding family income. All other SES questions had less than 10% missing responses, and many had 2% or less missing responses. In subsequent studies we plan to gather student data on parental income, ethnic or racial identities, and performance or course outcome through the University's Office of Institutional Research and Reporting and correlate the information with students' responses by a coding system in order to ensure that demographic data will ultimately be anonymous.

Mission

The four questions on the survey geared toward evaluating the mathematics program's ability to meet the GC mission indicate that more than 55% of the respondents believe that we are successful. The two questions specifically addressing mathematics instruction are the strongest: 83.2% agree class sizes are appropriate for personalized attention, and 70.3% agree that mathematics strategies and study skills are taught. GC's mission is to provide access to the University of Minnesota for highly motivated students from a broad range of backgrounds. Beyond mathematics skills and mathematics study skills, students must also feel enabled to learn more about how to succeed in the university setting and set attainable academic and career goals while in GC. These two areas have the lowest proportion of students agreeing that they are enabled. More than 25% had no opinion on these two questions. Does this finding indicate that students are not seeing the connection between these two goals and their mathematics classes? Could we assume that we are doing no harm in these areas, but we are also not adequately addressing these concerns? This is an area for improvement. When we look at the statistically significant dependencies among questions regarding the class size and parents' highest level of educational attainment, there is a flag raised when we see that our first-generation college students (37.5%) have no opinion regarding appropriate class size. Could this indicate that the courses may not be conducive for personalized attention for many of these students, but that they are unsure if this is due to class size? These students do not have preconceptions or knowledge of helpful college class sizes derived from family experience; they are first-generation college students. We are also concerned that a higher percentage (39.9% versus 11.5%) of our lower income students (i.e., with less than $45,000 family income) indicated that they do not feel enabled by our classes in setting attainable academic and career goals, indicating another area for improvement in our program.

Intellectual Development
When evaluating the effectiveness of the GC mathematics program in meeting the intellectual development standards of AMATYC (i.e., modelling, reasoning, connecting, communicating, using technology, developing power), the percentage of students preferring at least weekly activities involving these developmental skills is greater than the percentage of students reporting at least weekly occurrence of these activities. This may indicate that students would appreciate it if we incorporate more of the other intellectual development skills at least weekly in our classes. In classes where more than 50% of the students were at most somewhat engaged in the intellectual development opportunities, more than 20% of the students requested that these activities never occur in class. Can we then say that when intellectual development activities occur and they are not highly or moderately engaging, students are more apt to suggest that the activity be eliminated from the curriculum? Interviews with students and faculty discussions may help further illuminate this issue. Amarasinghe (2000) had students complete a survey questionnaire on attitudes and beliefs and assessed responses against AMATYC standards for intellectual development. She followed up this survey by interviewing a few randomly selected students representing each class. For our study, adding individual interviews or a focus group from each class could help in the interpretation of our survey data.

A high percentage of students reported only occasional or no occurrence of activities that (a) made connections between mathematics, other areas of human culture and other disciplines (63%); (b) encouraged reading and writing about mathematics (65%); and (c) encouraged the discussion of mathematics (65%). The dearth of activities that made connections between math, other areas of human culture, and other disciplines was statistically dependent on course number. The computer-mediated courses had the lowest proportion of students reporting the occurrence of activities connecting mathematics with culture or other academic disciplines. If we are committed to increasing cross-disciplinary and cross-cultural activities, we may need to supplement the computer-mediated curriculum. Beyond significant dependence between the communication of mathematics and course numbers, there was a significant dependence between the level of engagement and preference for activities encouraging the discussion of mathematics and students' neighborhoods of upbringing. A larger percentage of urban students were more engaged and preferred activities encouraging the discussion of mathematics. Would increasing discussion activities in mathematics courses increase the retention and engagement of urban students and keep the STEM pipeline open for urban students?

In the areas of appropriate technology, in courses that used more technology, students were more engaged and preferred its use. In courses that only occasionally used technology, students reported being less engaged and had the lowest preference for its use. These results raise two questions. First, have students chosen courses to meet their preferred learning styles and preferences regarding the use of technology? Second, is the level of preference and the level of engagement related to the level of exposure within the classroom to the use of technology? First-generation college students and students from families with an income below $45,000 had a greater preference for the use of technology. Could one assume that first-generation students and lower-income students are less bombarded with technology in their daily lives and therefore have more engagement or preference for its use in the classroom? Could one assume that some groups of students just prefer the use of technology over other methods of instruction because (a) it allows them to learn the course material without having to rely on traditional communication techniques that may pose impediments for students who speak English as a second language or urban students who choose not or have not embraced "dominant" culture discourse or (b) nontraditional-age students coming back to school feel a social stigma in classrooms dominated by traditional-age students?

In summary, the survey results suggest that we can improve our curriculum to meet the AMATYC standards for intellectual development. Having this information about the occurrence, preference, and engagement of students in intellectual development activities within the mathematics classroom will help guide us in developing our program. Knowing that some of the SES groups that are most vulnerable in the mathematics pipeline (e.g., women, first-generation college students, low-income students, and urban students) and have an interest and high level of engagement in specific areas of intellectual development can help us to create more effective classroom environments to meet their needs and encourage their growth in mathematics and mathematics-based careers.

Content

During the 2002–2003 academic year, the GC mathematics faculty spent considerable time and effort evaluating and revamping course content in beginning and intermediate algebra. The impetus for this change began in fall 2002 as we negotiated teaching one section of college algebra within GC and as we identified areas within the GC developmental mathematics curriculum that could use improvement. Faculty were aware of the shortcomings of using a common text (Academic Systems Corporation, 1999a, 1999b) for introductory and intermediate algebra sections. As we studied the college algebra curriculum it became more apparent that we also needed to make changes in the course content and level of rigor of our developmental mathematics courses to promote retention beyond transfer to degree-granting colleges of the University. The results of our 3-year study indicate that students are responding more positively in 2003 than in previous years to changes in course content and delivery methods. We observed statistically significant results in three areas:

1. There have been significant increases in reporting the occurrence of new topics at least weekly in the courses. In 2003 over 62% of the students reported seeing new material at least weekly compared to fewer than 35% of the students reporting such in 2001. We attribute this to our adoption of new textbooks in 2003 and appropriate placement. But the variation in responses by income groups surprised us. More students from poverty-level families reported only occasionally seeing new material, whereas students from the highest income group reported seeing new material more often. Could it be that students from the highest income groups were exposed to less mathematics content in high school? To better understand students' precollegiate preparation, which we expect depends on their urban and suburban school systems, we will consider students' high school backgrounds in future studies.

2. There were larger proportions of students reporting appropriate placement and smaller percentages of students reporting a low placement. The greatest shift was between 2002 and 2003. Students reporting too low a placement moved from 49% (2001) and 45% (2002) to only 14% (2003). With the addition of rigor into the courses more students are recognizing an appropriate placement. It is important for students to recognize that they are being challenged and prepared for higher-level mathematics and mathematics-based course work. Armstrong (2000) reported, from a quantitative study of community college mathematics students examining the predictive validity of placement test scores, that student disposition and demographic variables had more explanatory power than did other variables, including test scores:

The interaction of student traits, instructional treatments, and instructor practices may have a greater effect on student performance than the skills measured by assessment tests. Poor prediction of performance or misclassification of students is thus exacerbated when the criterion for student success can vary depending on the class in which a student enrolls. A major finding of this study is that educational standards are maintained by the college, not determined by the entering ability of its students. (p. 691)

GC does have a mandatory mathematics placement test, but the results of the test are advisory. Armstrong's research supports this policy. GC advisors consider students' placement test results along with their mathematics history, academic habits of mind, and level of confidence.

3. In our survey, more than 69% of the students reported positively that their classes helped them to *feel more competent* in skills areas. This is an important step for continued growth and development in mathematics. Increased confidence begets increased achievement (Stage & Kloosterman, 1995). We need to move forward with adapting and refining this survey tool and complement it with students' achievement data in developmental and college-level mathematics course work to be able to add to the growing body of research linking affective factors and student achievement.

Pedagogy

The standards for pedagogy adopted by AMATYC (Cohen, 1995) and NCTM (2000) that we queried via the student questionnaires involve a range of approaches to stimulate student involvement with and understanding of mathematics concepts. This area of the questionnaire also had the most variability by course number, SES, and other demographic variables. There were no questions on the previous questionnaires soliciting information regarding students' experiences and preferences in pedagogy, so we are unable to evaluate whether the changes in teaching faculty, course content, or textbooks have impacted pedagogy. This will be an area in which we will continue to collect information to determine our progress toward AMATYC standards.

Preferred pedagogy is definitely impacted by students' SES and other demographic variables. The literature generally supports these findings (Secada, 1992, 1996; Stanic, 1991; Tate, 1995, 1997; Woodson, 1990). Secada, Stanic, and Woodson noted that the presentation of abstract and disconnected mathematical facts does not empower disenfranchised students. NCTM's (1991) *Professional Standards for Teaching Mathematics* called for mathematics pedagogy that builds on understanding of how students' linguistic, ethnic, racial, gender, and socioeconomic backgrounds influence their learning.

The greatest percentage of students preferred and experienced activities encouraging them to think independently and explore mathematics at least weekly (61%). Over 64% of the students indicated that their class never worked collaboratively in groups on activities, yet only 36% of the students indicated that they preferred no collaborative activities. There is a growing body of literature and research indicating that collaborative group work helps students learn and retain more content information than any other instructional format while increasing their satisfaction with their classes (Beckman, 1990; Chickering & Gamson, 1991: Cooper, 1990; Goodsell, Maher, & Tinto, 1992; Johnson, Johnson, & Smith, 1991; Leapard, 2001; Thomas & Higbee, 1996; Triesman, 1986).

The Math Center
In addition to academic classroom services, successful developmental programs provided learning support services that included tutoring, lab assistance, counseling, advising, and other services designed to eliminate barriers to learning identified by the students (Gibbs, 1994). Research by Boylan and Saxon (1998), Kulik, Kulik, and Schwalb (1983), McCabe and Day (1998), Roueche, Baker, and Roueche, (1984), and Starks (1989) indicated that comprehensive learning support systems are positively correlated with student success. Although our survey results in the area of GC Math Center usage show promising trends, we still need to look at how students' use of the Math Center correlates with their levels of competence and achievement.

Summary
The questionnaire could be enhanced by adding a modified version to collect faculty data. Faculty data would include: (a) personal goals, as they relate to the AMATYC standards and GC mission, for intellectual development, content, and pedagogy within developmental mathematics courses; (b) personal assessment of how effectively intellectual development, content, and pedagogy goals were implemented; and (c) personal assessment of students' engagement in course activities.

Recommendations for Further Research

As we look forward to annual data from our students on how they perceive our mathematics curriculum and how confident they feel after having taken our courses, we will obtain a better sense of the trends. From our 2003 analysis of student responses by course number and SES demographics, we have discovered that in some cases students resist precisely those approaches that emphasize interactive classroom methods while indicating a preference for traditional lecture methods. At the same time, in other cases students' use of computers has increased over prior years, and their preferences for computer-mediated instruction has not waned. Do the patterns in students' responses follow precisely those classroom environments with which they are most familiar? Do their responses beckon for keeping the status quo or moving our mathematics curriculum further in the direction of reform pedagogies? To what extent should we heed students' views on pedagogy?

Overall, students do express a desire to engage in problem-solving activities and to see the relevance of mathematical concepts to real-life situations. Moreover, the high proportion of women students in our developmental mathematics classes and the high proportion of first-generation, urban students taking our most elementary introductory algebra course suggest the further work we must do to promote the success of precisely those populations underrepresented in STEM careers.

Assessment of a mathematics program cannot rest solely on students' perceptions. This important source of information must be correlated with grades, retention statistics, faculty perceptions, and comparative data from comparable developmental mathematics programs at other institutions. Internal thermostats may help guide our program development, but external comparisons will help us judge our effectiveness in relation to peer institutions. National surveys such as Kull's (1999) point us toward this direction.

We encourage developmental mathematics educators at other institutions to engage in similar assessments of their programs comparing AMATYC standards and students' perceptions of mathematics content and pedagogy. We hope this chapter invites comparative studies between institutions that reflect the distinctiveness of individual programs, identify common challenges, and guide us toward increased retention, graduation, access, and equity for students' pursuing STEM careers regardless of race, gender, income, environment, or parents' educational background.

References

Academic Systems Corporation. (1999a). *Interactive mathematics–elementary algebra: Personal academic notebook*. San Diego, CA: Author.

Academic Systems Corporation. (1999b). *Interactive mathematic–intermediate algebra: Personal academic notebook*. San Diego, CA: Author.

Amarasinghe, R. (2000). A study of student attitudes and beliefs when learning introductory college mathematics in context (Doctoral dissertation, Indiana University, 2000). *Dissertation Abstracts International, 61*, 4314.

Armstrong, W. B. (2000). The association among student success in courses, placement test scores, student background data, and instructor grading practices. *Community College Journal of Research & Practice, 24*, 681–695.

Beckman, M. (1990). Collaborative learning: Preparation for the workplace and democracy. *College Teaching, 38*(4), 128–133.

Berenson, S. B., Carter, G., & Norwood, K. S. (1992). The at-risk student in college developmental algebra. *School Science and Mathematics, 92*(2), 55–58.

Bonnett, M., & Newsom, R. (1995). Education and empowerment: Confronting beliefs and attitudes to promote learning. *Adult Learning, 7*(1), 9–10, 27.

Boylan, H. R., Bliss, L. B., & Bonham, B. S. (1997). Program components and their relationship to student success. *Journal of Developmental Education, 20*(3), 2–8.

Boylan, H. R. (1997a). The case for program research in developmental education. *The Learning Assistance Review, 2*(2), 20–34.

Boylan, H. R. (1997b). Criteria for program evaluation in developmental education. *Research in Developmental Education, 14*(1), 1–4.

Boylan, H. R., & Saxon, D. P. (1998). *An evaluation of developmental education in Texas colleges and universities.* Austin, TX: Texas Higher Education Coordinating Board.

Casazza, M., & Silverman, S. (1996). *Learning assistance and developmental education: A guide for effective practice.* San Francisco: Jossey-Bass.

Chickering, A. W., & Gamson, A. F. (Eds.). (1991). *Applying the seven principles for good practice in undergraduate education.* (New Directions for Teaching and Learning No. 47). San Francisco: Josssey-Bass.

Cohen, D. (Ed.). (1995). Crossroads in mathematics: *Standards for introductory college mathematics before calculus.* Memphis, TN: American Mathematical Association of Two-Year Colleges.

Congos, D. H., & Schoeps, N. (1997). A model for evaluating retention programs. *Journal of Developmental Education, 21*(2), 2, 6.

Cooper, J. (1990). (Ed.). *Cooperative learning and college instruction.* Long Beach, CA: Institute for Teaching and Learning.

Coxford, A. R., & Hirsch, C. R. (1996). A common core of math for all. *Educational Leadership, 53*(8), 22–25.

Duranczyk, I. M. (2004). Voices of underprepared university students: Outcomes of developmental mathematics education. (Doctoral dissertation, Grambling State University, 2002). *Dissertation Abstracts International, 65*(06), 2111B. (UMI No. 3136045)

Duranczyk, I. M., Staats, S., Moore, R., Hatch, J., Jensen, M., & Somdahl, C. (2004). Introductory-level college mathematics explored through a sociocultural lens. In I. M. Duranczyk, J. L. Higbee, & D. B. Lundell (Eds.), *Best practices for access and retention in higher education* (pp.43–53). Minneapolis, MN: Center for Research on Developmental Education and Urban Literacy, General College, University of Minnesota.

Durant, L. A. (1992). A comparative study of the effects of self-concept and selected demographic variables on freshman college students' attitudes toward the effectiveness of developmental education programs. *Dissertation Abstracts International, 53* (12), 4145A. (UMI No. 9302873)

Elliot, J. C. (1990). Affect and mathematics achievement of nontraditional college students. *Journal for Research in Mathematics Education, 21,* 160–165.

England, D. C. (1993). The impact on the success of high-risk students of placement policies established by Texas higher education institutions in the implementation of the Texas academic skills program. *Dissertation Abstracts International, 54* (06), 2038A. (UMI No. 9329691)

Feingold, M. S. (1994). Occupational education and the effect of basic skill remediation on student retention in a community college. *Dissertation Abstracts International, 55* (06), 1457A. (UMI No. 942974)

Frisch, S. (2004). Ethnomathematics: Bringing the whole person into the math classroom. *Access: The General College Magazine, 3*(3), 6.

Gibbs, L. L. (1994). Analysis of developmental mathematics programs in Texas community colleges which are successful with Black and Hispanic students. *Dissertation Abstracts International, 55* (06), 1457A. (UMI No. 9428521)

Goodsell, A., Maher, M., & Tinto, V. (1992). (Eds.). *Collaborative learning: A sourcebook for higher education.* University Park, PA: National Center on Postsecondary Teaching, Learning, and Assessment.

Hamilton, J. M. (1993). Impact of Georgia's college preparatory curriculum on academic success at Gainesville College. *Dissertation Abstracts International, 53* (09), 3119A. (UMI No. 9301196)

Hatfield, J. (2004). *Rates of intra-university transfer for General College students.* Retrieved July 6, 2004, from http://www.gen.umn.edu/research/ore/reports/transfer_report-S04/default.htm

Hirsch, C. R., & Coxford, A. F. (1997). Mathematics for all: Perspectives and promising practices. *School Science and Mathematics, 97,* 232–241.

Huntley, M. A., Rasmussen, C. L., Villarubi, R. S., Sangtong, J., & Fey, J. T. (2000). Effects of standards-based mathematics education: A study of the Core-Plus Mathematics Project algebra and functions strand. *Journal for Research in Mathematics Education, 31,* 328–361.

Ironsmith, M., Marva, J., Harju, B., & Eppler, M. (2003). Motivation and performance in college students enrolled in self-paced versus lecture-format remedial mathematics courses. *Journal of Instructional Psychology, 30,* 276–284.

Johnson, D. W., Johnson, R. T., & Smith, K. A. (1991). *Cooperative learning: Increasing college faculty instructional productivity.* ASHE-ERIC Higher

Education Report No. 4. Washington, DC: School of Education and Human Development, George Washington University.

Jones, K. C. (1994). An educational application of Taguchi's quadratic loss function: Assessing the quality costs of the freshman assessment and placement program at a comprehensive state university. *Dissertation Abstracts International*, 55 (12), 3810A. (UMI No. 9514101)

Kinney, D. P. (2001). Developmental theory: Application in a developmental mathematics program. *Journal of Developmental Education*, 25(2), 10–18, 34.

Kulik, C. C., Kulik, J., & Schwalb, B. (1983). College programs for high-risk and disadvantaged students: A meta-analysis of findings. *Review of Educational Research*, 53, 397–414.

Kull, K. R. (1999). A developmental education survey: Results of a national survey of program design and mathematics instruction. *Research & Teaching in Developmental Education*, 16(1), 57–80.

Leapard, B. B. (2001). Affective, metacognitive, and conceptual effects of an Emerging Scholars program on elementary teacher preparation: An application of the Treisman workshop model. *Dissertation Abstracts International*, 61 (10), 3958.

Lyons, L. (1994, June). *The implementation of a local model to assess the basic skills program at a four-year public college*. Paper presented at the annual forum of the Association for Institutional Research, New Orleans, LA. (ERIC Document Reproduction Service No. ED 373 635)

Maxwell, M. (1997). *Improving student learning skills* (rev. ed). Clearwater, FL: H & H.

McCabe, R. H., & Day, P. R. (Eds.). *Developmental education: A twenty-first century social and economic imperative*. Mission Viejo, CA: League for Innovation in the Community College and The College Board.

McLeod, D. B. (1993). Connecting research to teaching. *Mathematics Teacher*, 86, 761–763.

Mireles, H. N. (1995). The cognitive and attitudinal effects of a precollege intervention program for enhancement in science, mathematics, and engineering. *Dissertation Abstracts International*, 56 (06), 2187A. (UMI No. 9534896)

Mullis, I. V. S., Dossey, J. A., Campbell, J. R., Gentile, C. A., O'Sullivan, C., & Latham, A. S. (1994). *Report in brief: NAEP 1992 trends in academic progress* (NCES 23-TR01). Washington, DC: U.S. Department of Education.

National Council of Teachers of Mathematics. (1991). *Professional standards for teaching mathematics*. Reston, VA: Author.

National Council of Teachers of Mathematics. (2000). *Principles and standards for school mathematics*. Reston, VA: Author.

National Research Council. (1996). *From analysis to action: Undergraduate education in science, math, engineering, and technology.* Washington, DC: National Academy Press. Retrieved March 27, 2004, from http://www.nap.edu/catalog/9128.html

Oaks, J. (1990). *Multiplying inequalities: The effects of races, social class, and tracking on opportunities to learn mathematics and science.* Santa Monica, CA: RAND.

Opitz, D. L. (2003, October). *Multicultural tutoring? The role of training.* Paper presented at the annual meeting of the Minnesota Chapter of the National Association for Developmental Education, Grand Rapids, MN.

Reese, C. M., Jerry, L., & Ballator, N. (1997). *NAEP 1996 mathematics state report for Minnesota.* Washington, DC: National Center for Education Statistics.

Reese, C. M., Miller, K. E., Mazzeo, J., & Dossey, J. A. (1997). *NAEP 1996 mathematics report card for the nation and the states: Findings from the National Assessment of Educational Progress.* Washington, DC: National Center for Education Statistics.

Roueche, J. E., Baker, G. A., & Roueche, S. D. (1984). *College responses to low-achieving students: A national study.* Orlando, FL: HBJ Media Systems.

Roueche, J. E., & Roueche, S. D. (1993). *Between a rock and a hard place: The at-risk student in the open-door college.* Washington, DC: Community College Press.

Schoen, H. L., & Hirsch, C. R. (2003). Responding to calls for change in high school mathematics: Implications for collegiate mathematics. *American Mathematical Monthly, 110*(2), 109–123.

Secada, W. G. (1992). Race, ethnicity, social class, language, and achievement in mathematics. In D. A. Grouws (Ed.), *Handbook of research on mathematics teaching and learning* (pp. 623–660). New York: Macmillan.

Secada, W. G. (1996). Urban students acquiring English and learning mathematics in the context of reform. *Urban Education, 30,* 422–448.

Simmons, R. (1994). Precollege programs: A contributing factor to university students' retention. *Journal of Developmental Education, 17*(3), 42–45.

Singham, M. (1998). The canary in the mine. *Phi Delta Kappan, 80*(1), 8–15.

Stage, F. K., & Kloosterman, P. (1995). Gender, beliefs, and achievement in remedial college-level mathematics. *Journal of Higher Education, 66,* 294–311.

Stanic, G. M. A. (1991). Social inequality, cultural discontinuity, and equity in school mathematics. *Peabody Journal of Education, 66,* 57–71.

Starks, G. (1989). Retention and developmental education: What the research has to say. *Research & Teaching in Developmental Education, 6*(1), 21–32.

Tate, W. F. (1995). School mathematics and African American students: Thinking seriously about opportunity-to-learn standards. *Educational Administration Quarterly, 31,* 424–448.

Tate, W. F. (1997). Race-ethnicity, SES, gender, and language proficiency trends in mathematics achievement: An update. *Journal for Research in Mathematics Education, 28,* 652–679.

Thomas, P. V., & Higbee, J. L. (1996). Enhancing mathematics achievement through collaborative problem solving. *The Learning Assistance Review, 1*(1), 38–46.

Treisman, P. U. (1986). A study of the mathematics performance of Black students at the University of California, Berkeley (Dissertation, University of California, Berkeley, 1985). *Dissertation Abstracts International, 47*(05), 1641.

Umoh, U. J., Eddy, J., & Spaulding, D. J. (1994). Factors related to student retention in community college developmental education mathematics. *Community College Review, 22*(2), 37–47.

U.S. Department of Education. (1998). *Pursuing excellence: A study of U.S. twelfth-grade mathematics and science achievement in international context.* (NCES Publication No. 98-049). Washington, DC: U.S. Government Printing Office.

Wachtel, H. K. (1994). A critique of existing practices for evaluating mathematics instruction. *Dissertation Abstracts International, 56*(01), 129A. (UMI No. 9632062).

Wambach, C., & Brothen, T. (1990). An alternative to the prediction-placement model. *Journal of Developmental Education, 13* (3), 14–15, 24–26.

Wambach, C., Mayer, A., Hatfield, J., & Franko, J. (2003). *Leaving General College: Interests and issues related to student departure.* Minneapolis, MN: Office of Research and Evaluation, General College, University of Minnesota. Retrieved July 26, 2004, from http://www.gen.umn.edu/research/ore/reports/leavers.htm

Whiteley, M. A., & Fenske, R. H. (1990). The college mathematics experience and changes in majors: A structural model analysis. *The Review of Higher Education, 13,* 357–385.

Woodson, C. G. (1990). *The mis-education of the Negro.* Trenton, NJ: Africa World Press. (Original work published in 1933).

CHAPTER 24

Student Perceptions of General College: A Student-Initiated Study

Mark A. Bellcourt, Ian S. Haberman,
Joshua G. Schmitt, Jeanne L. Higbee,
and Emily Goff

ABSTRACT

Within this chapter we report on the results of a survey constructed by former General College (GC) students Ian Haberman and Joshua Schmitt, in consultation with 2003–2004 GC Student Board Advisor Mark Bellcourt, to explore the perceptions of GC students regarding their satisfaction with their decision to attend the University of Minnesota, their admission to the General College, diversity within the University and GC, their level of preparation for college, and other factors. GC is the most racially, economically, socially, and academically diverse unit on campus, and the perceptions of GC's students are probably as individual as the students themselves. That hypothesis is supported by the findings of this research.

Within this chapter we will explore General College (GC) through the eyes of the students. We will examine the results of a survey by GC students regarding their perceptions of GC and the University. However, first it is important to recognize that GC does have the most racially, economically, socially, and academically diverse students on campus. High school rank for new students admitted to GC in 2004 ranged from the 2nd to the 99th percentile, ACT composite scores ranged from 11 to 31, and ages ranged from 17 to 52 years of age. Racially, about 49% identify as Anglo, just under 20% as Asian American, almost 22% as African American, more than 4% as Chicano/Latino, and just over 2% as American Indian, with information missing for 3% of GC students (*Facts and Figures*, 2004).

Before discussing the results of the survey on student perceptions, we need to establish the context of this discussion. Although General College has a long and rich history with the University of Minnesota, it has struggled with its identity, especially since Ken Keller's "Commitment to Focus" plan was unveiled in 1985 (Berman & Pflaum, 2001). The idea was to take away degree-granting status from GC and to focus the college's commitment on developmental courses. Keller's successor, Nils Hasselmo, took it one step further and in 1996 proposed to close GC completely. However, the Board of Regents rejected that proposal because of the University's commitment to providing access for students of color and other underrepresented groups (Berman & Pflaum). Berman and Pflaum further suggested that access and excellence have not always been considered compatible goals. Recently this debate arose again, and on June 10, 2005, the University of Minnesota Board of Regents voted to close the General College while retaining some of its functions as a department in the College of Education and Human Development.

The General College has endeavored to explore whether it is possible to achieve access and excellence at the same time. The concern of the authors of this chapter is that the student perception of GC is one of access, not excellence, and that this perception assists in forming a stereotype of the General College that is then shared by external constituencies and the public at large as well. This image of the General College is characterized by comments like:

"GC is for stupid people."

"GC is for the jocks."

"GC is for 'foreigners' who can't speak English."

"Only students who couldn't make it in other colleges of the University are admitted into GC."

Within the next few pages, we will report the results of a survey of student perceptions about GC and the University (Bellcourt, Haberman, & Schmitt, 2004).

Method

In the spring of 2004, the General College Student Board (GCSB) sponsored an online survey (Haberman, Schmitt, & Bellcourt, 2004) to explore the diverse social and academic perceptions that GC students had about themselves, GC, and the University. A team of students and staff reviewed potential survey items for face validity. The final survey consisted of 26 Likert-type scale items regarding student perceptions of GC and the University. Students responded on a five-point scale for which 1 represented strongly disagree and 5 indicated strongly agree (Haberman, Schmitt, & Bellcourt).

The General College Student Board extended invitations via e-mail and through classroom announcements to all GC students to participate in this voluntary online survey. More than 230 students, representing just over 15% of the GC student body, responded to the survey. The results cannot be widely generalized to the whole GC student body because of the low response rate and the factors that might have influenced the self-selection of participants.

Results

For all 26 items the responses ranged from 1 (i.e., strongly disagree) to 5 (strongly agree). Item means ranged from 1.96 for one of the negatively-stated items ("I feel that the U of MN Twin Cities Campus is too large for me") to 4.06 for the comparable positively-stated item ("I am comfortable with the size of the U of MN Twin Cities Campus"). Thus, none of the means were particularly high or low. Meanwhile, standard deviations for the 26 items ranged from 0.922 to 1.390, so there was quite a bit of variability among responses for each item.

A factor analysis of the data identified seven factors around which the variables tended to cluster, whether negatively or positively. The researchers (Bellcourt, Haberman, & Schmitt, 2004) explored the items within each cluster and identified their common characteristics and themes. The following paragraphs summarize the results of the survey by grouping items in those clusters.

As indicated in Table 1, the responding students were generally satisfied with their decision to attend the University of Minnesota ($M = 3.98$). They reported feeling comfortable with the size of the campus ($M = 4.06$) and somewhat agreed ($M = 3.53$) that they felt like a part of the University community.

Table 2 reports on other variables related to sense of satisfaction with the University. Participating students generally believed that the University of Minnesota's educational philosophy reflected their own ($M = 3.53$). They somewhat agreed that the University is interested in their well being ($M = 3.29$). Also included in this set of items was "I believe that only those who cannot get admitted to another college at the U of MN Twin Cities Campus are admitted to General College" ($M = 3.53$).

TABLE 1

Means, Standard Deviations, and Factor Loadings for Factor 1 Items:
Sense of Comfort With GC

Variable	N	M	SD	Loading
I feel that the U of MN Twin Cities Campus is too large for me.	225	1.96	.958	-.812
I am comfortable with the size of the U of MN Twin Cities Campus.	229	4.06	.923	.809
I am satisfied that I chose to attend the U of MN.	228	3.98	1.076	.602
I feel like a part of the U of MN Twin Cities Campus community.	229	3.53	1.049	.550

TABLE 2

Means, Standard Deviations, and Factor Loadings for Factor 2 Items:
Sense of Satisfaction With the University

Variable	N	M	SD	Loading
I believe that the overall educational philosophy of the U of MN reflects my own philosophy well.	231	3.53	.922	.639
I believe that only those who cannot get admitted to another college at the U of MN Twin Cities Campus are admitted to General College.	231	3.53	1.167	-.525
The U of MN is interested in my well-being.	231	3.29	1.012	.477

TABLE 3

Means, Standard Deviations, and Factor Loadings for Factor 3 Items:
Sense of Satisfaction With Diversity on Campus

Variable	N	M	SD	Loading
I believe there is more student diversity in the General College than in the entire U of MN Twin Cities Campus.	230	3.89	1.064	-.702
I believe the U of MN Twin Cities Campus has a diverse student population.	227	4.0	1.173	.652
I would have rather attended a different institution than the U of MN.	231	2.29	1.221	-.520

The next set of items is related to diversity within the General College and the University as a whole. As indicated in Table 3, the students responding to the survey agreed that the University of Minnesota's Twin Cities campus "has a diverse student population" ($M = 4.00$) and also thought "there is more student diversity in the General College than in the entire U of MN Twin Cities Campus" ($M = 3.89$).

Table 4 presents items regarding students' perceptions about the General College. With a range of responses from 1 to 5, standard deviations from 0.974 to 1.332, and means ranging from 2.57 to 3.52, none of the items for this factor were very conclusive. With means hovering near 3 on the five-point scale, on the average students neither agreed nor disagreed that they (a) "take pride in being in General College" ($M = 2.82$), (b) are "embarrassed to tell others" that they are in GC ($M = 3.05$), (c) "feel like a part of the General College community" (M = 2.99), or (d) "feel the student leadership of the General College is helpful and effective" (M = 2.95). Students did disagree somewhat with the statement that "I am uncomfortable or do not connect well to the other students in the General College" (M = 2.57) and agreed somewhat that they "would rather be in one of the other colleges" of the University (M = 3.50). They also agreed somewhat in their belief that GC's student body "is comprised mostly of students of color" (M = 3.52). In reality GC has a much larger proportion of students of color than any other college of the University of Minnesota, but Caucasian students still make up the majority.

The fifth factor identified by the factor analysis (Bellcourt, Haberman, & Schmitt, 2004) and reported in Table 5 is a sense of academic preparedness. On average, students agreed somewhat with the positively-stated items, "I felt very prepared for college" (M = 3.37) and "to take college-level courses" (M = 3.61) and somewhat disagreed or were noncommittal about the negatively-stated items, "I did not feel like my high school adequately prepared me for college" (M = 2.72) and "I was afraid that I would not do well in my college-level classes" (M = 2.98). Again, with standard deviations for these items ranging from 0.967 to 1.265, there is a fair amount of variation in student perspectives.

TABLE 4

Means, Standard Deviations, and Factor Loadings for Factor 4 Items:
Sense of Comfort With GC

Variable	N	M	SD	Loading
I take pride in being in General College.	231	2.82	1.179	-.820
I am embarrassed to tell others that I am in General College.	229	3.05	1.332	.785
I feel like a part of the General College community.	230	2.99	1.146	-.771
I would rather be in one of the other colleges at the U of MN	228	3.50	1.329	.762
I am uncomfortable or do not connect well to the other students in General College.	229	2.57	1.076	.693
I feel the student leadership of General College is helpful and effective.	230	2.95	.974	-.558
I believe the student body of General College is comprised mostly of students of color.	231	3.52	1.145	.420

TABLE 5
Means, Standard Deviations, and Factor Loadings for Factor 5 Items:
Sense of Academic Preparedness

Variable	N	M	SD	Loading
I felt very prepared for college.	231	3.37	.973	.816
I felt very prepared to take college-level courses.	228	3.61	.957	.782
I was afraid I would not do well in my college-level classes.	230	2.98	1.217	-.684
I did not feel like my high school adequately prepared me for college.	231	2.72	1.265	-.615

TABLE 6
Means, Standard Deviations, and Factor Loadings for Factor 6 Items:
Making use of Opportunities for Leadership

Variable	N	M	SD	Loading
I am aware of General College student leadership opportunities.	230	3.04	1.059	.755
If I chose to, I believe I could be involved in leadership positions.	231	3.63	.964	.719
I took college prep courses in high school.	231	3.05	1.390	.337

The sixth factor, consisting of only two items, dealt with other steps students might take to prepare themselves for college. The mean response to "I talked with college students about their experiences before choosing a college" was 2.94 ($SD = 1.093$). The other item asked whether students considered New Student Orientation to be helpful ($M = 3.30$, $SD = 1.132$).

The final factor, presented in Table 6, was related to students making use of leadership opportunities. At 3.05 the mean for "I took college prep courses in high school" fell almost exactly at the middle of the five-point range of answers. Students were as likely as not to be aware of General College student leadership opportunities ($M = 3.04$) and somewhat agreed that if they chose to they "could be involved in leadership positions" ($M = 3.63$).

Discussion

As previously noted by Berman and Pflaum (2001), the concepts of access and excellence seem to be perceived by many to be mutually exclusive. The results of this survey suggest that students have mixed views about gaining access to the University via admission to the General College, rather than having pride in GC as a college characterized by excellence in teaching and learning. Some students said they were embarrassed to be in GC, do not feel comfortable with other students in GC, and do not feel like a part of the GC community. Yet, the students were relatively positive on most of the questions related to their experience and perceptions of the University as a whole. Although we did not ask students any opened-ended questions about why they might feel embarrassed to be in GC, anecdotally during new student orientation and individual advising appointments and from student stories presented in Chapter 2, we have gleaned a widely-held perception that GC is somehow "less than" the rest of the University. For example, a number of students reported that their parents and friends were disappointed in them because they were not admitted to another college at the University.

The data, however, did present some perplexing contradictions, especially with questions surrounding diversity. Students who responded to the survey perceived that the University of Minnesota has a diverse student population. In reality, the overall undergraduate student body at the University is not particularly diverse, but it might be anticipated that students enrolled in General College courses would consider the University diverse because of their own classroom experiences. Meanwhile, participating students thought that GC "is comprised mostly of students of color," which is not true, but compared to the University as a whole it is not surprising that it might seem that way. Also, in the factor analysis questions regarding diversity did not tend to cluster as one might expect. For example, the question regarding students of color in GC was positively aligned with students not feeling comfortable in GC and the desire to be in other units at the University. Also, the item about students preferring to attend other institutions negatively aligned with the item regarding the diversity on the University campus. The researchers (Haberman, Schmitt, & Bellcourt, 2004) did not collect demographic information on the students who responded to the survey, so it is impossible to draw specific conclusions, but it appears that a number of the respondents either do not understand or simply do not appreciate diversity and its contributions to the undergraduate experience.

This research has only begun to scratch the surface regarding student perceptions of GC. Future research using qualitative methods is needed to gain a better understanding of the reasons why some students perceive GC as less than or inferior to the rest of the University. Also, this research, like the Multicultural Awareness Project for Institutional Transformation (MAP IT) pilot study presented in Chapter 7, raises some serious questions regarding student perceptions of diversity. Future research needs to explore the implications of diversity within GC.

Conclusion

This chapter should not be viewed as a negative reflection on GC, but rather a reality check of perceptions about GC. As noted in the introduction of this chapter, General College does have a long and rich history at the University of Minnesota. However, the achievements of faculty, staff, and students have been and continue to be overlooked by many administrators, government officials, and the general public. There does seem to be the perception by students and the general public that GC is more concerned with access for underrepresented groups and less concerned with academic excellence.

References

Bellcourt, M. A., Haberman, I. S., & Schmitt, J. G. (2004). *General College student survey results.* Unpublished manuscript. Minneapolis, MN: General College, University of Minnesota.

Berman, H., & Pflaum, A. M. (2001). *Historical legacies and recent events: Changes in state funding for the University of Minnesota 1981 to 2001.* Minneapolis, MN: University of Minnesota.

Facts and figures. (2004). Minneapolis, MN: General College, University of Minnesota. Retrieved October 12, 2004, from http://www.gen.umn.edu

Haberman, I. S., Schmitt, J. G., & Bellcourt, M. A. (2004). *General College student survey.* Unpublished manuscript. Minneapolis, MN: General College, University of Minnesota.

CHAPTER 25

Pre- and Post-Admission Predictors of the Academic Success of Developmental Education Students

Randy Moore

ABSTRACT

Traditional pre-admission criteria used to measure the academic aptitude of first-year college students (i.e., ACT scores, high school graduation percentile rank) are poor predictors of the academic success of developmental education students in General College. The behaviors that do accurately predict the academic success of students in General College (e.g., class attendance, engagement in course-related activities) are explicit expressions of students' academic motivation, and it is this motivation that is critical for students' success in GC. These results are discussed relative to recommendations for helping developmental education students succeed in college.

General College (GC) provides access for a diverse group of developmental education students to degree-granting colleges at the University of Minnesota. Students admitted to GC typically include disproportionate numbers of urban students, first-generation college students, students who are parents, students with disabilities, students of color, older students, and non-native speakers of English. To help these students succeed, GC provides a variety of centralized and accessible support services that are described in previous chapters, including a Transfer and Career Center, Academic Resource Center, Student Parent HELP Center, TRIO/Student Support Services, and the Commanding English Program. These resources are supplemented by an aggressive advising system and excellent teachers who are expected to offer rigorous, credit-bearing, up-to-date, and inclusive courses that include a variety of pedagogical approaches to accommodate our students' diverse learning styles. Together, these resources and individuals create a nurturing and challenging academic environment in which students can learn the academic skills and earn the course credits necessary to transfer to one of the university's many degree-granting colleges.

GC would like to give all underprepared students access to its programs, faculty, and support services. However, GC's limited resources allow it to enroll only about 20% of its applicants; for example, in the fall of 2003, GC enrolled 894 of its 4,953 applicants, which was approximately 17% of the University's incoming class (*About General College*, 2003). The fact that GC can enroll so few of its applicants magnifies the importance of its admissions decisions; GC must admit the students who are most likely to succeed. How can GC select students who have the best chances of eventually graduating from the university? That is, what traits predict the academic success of students in GC?

In this chapter I document the accuracy of various pre- and post-admission predictors of the academic success of developmental education students in GC. Students' academic performances are influenced by many factors (e.g., academic preparation, cultural background, academic and social maturity, and socioeconomic status), yet most studies of these factors have focused on characteristics that are not directly related to students' course-related behaviors, such as institutional commitment, personality traits, hours worked by students each week, and whether the student or others pay for the student's education (Cabrera, Nora, & Castañeda, 1993; Devadoss & Foltz, 1996; Friedman, Rodriguez, & McComb, 2001; Tinto, 1975). Here I focus on some measures and behaviors that can be accurately and objectively quantified, such as students' grades, attendance, test scores, and high school graduation percentiles. I have avoided self-reported data such as students' claims about time spent studying for exams and reading the course textbook; studies in GC (Moore, in press-a) and elsewhere (Sappington, Kinsey, & Munsayac, 2002) have shown that such data are often misleading.

A Brief Profile of GC Students

In the fall of 2003, GC's students had an average high school graduation percentile rank of 53 (range = 1–99), an average age of 19 (range = 16–50), and an average composite ACT score of 20 (range = 10–32). GC enrolls approximately equal percentages of men and women who are ethnically diverse: 20% African American, 2% American Indian, 51% Anglo, 20% Asian American, 4% Chicano/Latino, and 3% undeclared (*About General College*, 2003). These students earned an average first-semester grade point average (GPA) of 2.8, an average second-semester GPA of 2.6, and an average first-year GPA of 2.7. Approximately 18% of GC's first-year students end their first year of college with GPAs less than 2.0, 40% end their first year of college with GPAs between 2.0 and 3.0, and 42% end their first year of college with GPAs above 3.0 (Moore, in press-b).

The Academic Crystal Ball: What Criteria Predict Success?

To determine the factors that predict the success of developmental education students in GC, I measured a variety of pre-admission and post-admission criteria that could be measured easily and accurately.

Pre-Admission Criteria

The pre-admission criteria that I measured were students' academic aptitude ratings and their participation in a summer orientation program.

Academic aptitude rating (AAR). Many colleges and universities use students' academic performance in high school (e.g., their class rank or high school GPA), their scores on aptitude tests (e.g., ACT, SAT), or a combination of these factors as a basis for admission and placement in developmental education courses (Ray, Garavalia, & Murdock, 2003). Some studies have reported that students' high school grades and SAT or ACT scores accurately predict students' college grades (Neal, Schaer, Ley, & Wright, 1990; Petrie & Stoever, 1997), whereas others have reported low or no correlation between these scores and students' academic performance in college (Britton & Tesser, 1991; Côté & Levine, 2000; Meeker, Fox, & Whitley, 1994; Thomas & Higbee, 2000). However, virtually none of these studies have focused on developmental education students, who often have personal characteristics (e.g., test anxiety, fear of failure) that distinguish them from regular-admission students (Larose & Roy, 1991; Morrison, 1999).

The University of Minnesota combines a student's ACT score and high school graduation percentile rank to create the student's Academic Aptitude Rating, which equals the student's high school graduation percentile plus two-times the students' ACT composite score. Some colleges at the University of Minnesota use AAR scores as requirements for admission; for example, the College of Liberal Arts requires AAR scores of at least 110 for regular admission, and the Institute of Technology guarantees admission to students having an AAR score of at least 135 (*Advising Manual*, 2004; *Undergraduate Catalog*, 2004). Although GC bases its admissions decisions on individual reviews of a variety of factors (e.g., family history, diversity), it also tracks students' AAR scores. For example, students who entered GC in the fall of 2003 had an average AAR of 93 (*About General College*, 2003).

As Brothen and Wambach (2003) have noted, "the important question about standardized academic aptitude and achievement tests is whether or not they accurately predict college performance for all students who take them" (p. 45). To answer this question, I measured how the AAR scores of GC's first-year students relate to their first-semester GPAs. For the entire entering classes in the fall of 2002 and 2003, the correlation of AAR scores and students' first-semester GPAs was very weak (r [646] = 0.10 for fall, 2002; r [721] = 0.14 for fall, 2003; see Figure 1). Indeed, for each group of students, variability in students' AAR scores accounted for less than 2% of the variability in students' first-semester and first-year GPAs (Moore, in press-b). These results are consistent with those of others (Cloud, 2001; Langley, Wambach, Brothen, & Madyun, in press; Moore, Jensen, Hsu, & Hatch, 2002; Ray, Garavalia, & Murdock, 2003; Snyder, Hackett, Stewart, & Smith, 2003; Thomas & Higbee, 2000) and indicate that AAR scores (i.e., ACT composite scores and high school graduation percentiles) do not accurately predict the academic success of developmental education students in GC. These results are not consistent with the claim that standardized academic aptitude and achievement tests are effective for identifying the college potential of developmental education students (Brothen & Wambach, 2003).

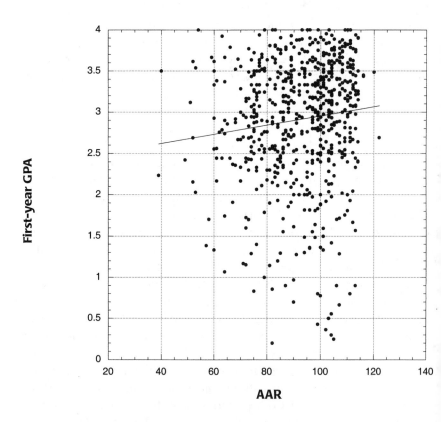

Figure 1. The association of AAR scores and first-year GPAs of GC students at the University of Minnesota. The equation for these data is $y = 2.40 + 0.006x$, and the correlation coefficient is 0.11.

Participation in a summer orientation program. GC requires all of its incoming students to attend a summer orientation program, at which they register for classes, learn about the university's academic policies, and meet their academic advisors. Although students select the dates and times of the orientation they would like to attend, in 2003 approximately 12% (N = 108) of the students neither attended nor made any effort to reschedule their orientation. These students were subsequently contacted by GC, after which many of them again did not attend or make any effort to reschedule the orientation that they had agreed to attend. These students finally attended an orientation only after being given an ultimatum to either attend a specially scheduled orientation or forfeit their admission into GC. Although these students knew that the orientation was important for their academic success at the university, they nevertheless were either not motivated enough to voluntarily attend the orientation, or faced other barriers to attending the orientation. Furthermore, they lacked the maturity or responsibility to contact GC if they were unable to attend the orientation. This lack of motivation or existence of other barriers was strongly associated with academic problems. For example, after their first year in college, these students (i.e., those who had to be forced to attend the summer orientation program) earned an average GPA of 2.1 and had a 32% chance of being placed on academic probation (i.e., having a GPA less than 2.0) after their first semester of college. For comparison, GC's other first-year students (i.e., those who voluntarily attended the summer orientation) earned an average first-year GPA of 2.8 and had only an 11% chance of being placed on academic probation after their first semester of college (Moore, in press-b). Although there were no significant differences in the AAR scores of students in these two groups, the differences in their subsequent GPAs and probabilities of being placed on academic probation were statistically significant ($p < 0.01$; Moore, in press-b).

Post-Admission Criteria

The post-admission criteria that I measured were students' class attendance, students' involvement in course-related activities, and students' first-semester and first-year GPAs.

Class attendance. Previous studies of the importance of class attendance for academic success have been inconclusive. Some studies have reported that class attendance correlates positively with high grades (Brocato, 1989; Grisé & Kenney, 2003; Jones, 1984; Launius, 1997; Thomas & Higbee, 2000), whereas other studies have reported that class attendance is unrelated to students' academic success (Berenson, Carter, & Norwood, 1992; Borland & Howsen, 1998). In light of this, it is not surprising that college instructors have a variety of attitudes and policies regarding class attendance. As Druger (2003) has noted,

"Some instructors don't care if students attend class at all . . . [whereas] other instructors feel strongly about the importance of class attendance. Some instructors check attendance at every class; others don't check it at all" (p. 350).

First-year students are often apathetic about academic behaviors such as class attendance. For example, several studies (McGuire, 2003; Moore, 2003a, 2003b) have reported that absenteeism in introductory classes often approaches 50%, and Friedman, Rodriguez, and McComb (2001) reported that "25 percent or more [of] students are absent from classes on any given day" (p. 124). Similarly, Romer (1993) reported that absenteeism is "rampant" and that "about one-third of [first-year] students are not in class" (p. 167), concluding that "A generation ago, both in principle and in practice, attendance at class was not optional. Today, often in principle and almost always in practice, it is" (p. 174). Students' apathy and high rates of absenteeism do not change the fact that it is difficult for instructors, advisors, or others to help students who do not attend class. As Thomas & Higbee (2000) have noted, "The best . . . teacher, no matter how intellectually stimulating, no matter how clear in providing explanations and examples, may not be able to reach the high risk freshman who has no real interest in learning . . . and will certainly not be successful with the student who fails to show up for class" (p. 231).

In GC, many students express their lack of academic motivation by skipping class, not attending help sessions, rarely if ever visiting with their instructors during office hours, missing deadlines, not studying, not complying with assignments, and refusing to attend summer orientation programs (Moore, 2003a, 2003b). These behaviors are associated with lowered levels of motivation, for which there are predictable consequences. Indeed, the strongest predictor of GC students' academic success is class attendance: Students who attend class regularly have a much greater chance of earning high grades than do students who miss lots of classes (Moore, 2003a, 2003b). This correlation is statistically significant (r [1,486] = 0.79, $p < 0.01$; see Figure 2) and occurs in a variety of courses in which students get no points for attending class (Moore, 2003a, 2003b; Moore, Jensen, Hatch, Duranczyk, Staats, & Koch, 2003). Variability in students' attendance rates, which are unrelated to students' gender or ethnicity, accounted for more than 60% of the variability in students' grades in some courses in GC (Moore, 2003a, 2003b; Moore et al., 2003). Similar correlations of class attendance and course performance have been reported previously by others (e.g., Street, 1975; Wiley, 1992).

Of course, high rates of class attendance do not guarantee high grades; some students do well despite the fact that they attend relatively few classes, and other students come to class regularly yet earn relatively low grades. Although students' GPAs are strongly correlated with their attendance rates, correlation does not imply causation. Causality might go either way; high

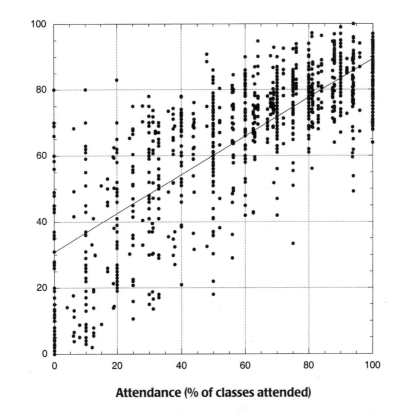

Figure 2. The association of attendance and grades in an introductory biology course taught in GC. The equation for these data is $y=30.9 + 0.58x$, and the correlation coefficient is 0.79.

rates of class attendance might help students earn better grades, or students' desires to make better grades might underlie their high rates of class attendance, or both. Nevertheless, the overall conclusion is unmistakable: the highest grades are usually earned by students who attend class regularly.

If class attendance is so important for academic success, why don't more developmental education students attend class? Students know that class attendance is important, and on the first day of classes they are confident that they will attend virtually all classes and earn an A or B in their courses (Moore, 2003a, 2003b). They also want and expect to receive academic credit for merely showing up at class (Launius, 1997; Moore, 2003a, 2003b). However, many instructors do not award academic credit for class attendance; these instructors agree with Davis (1993), who noted that "attendance should not be mandatory or a factor in your grading policy. Grades should be based on students' mastery of the course content and not on such nonacademic factors as attendance" (p. 138). However, this policy clashes with the fact that students' rates of class attendance are influenced by whether they receive academic credit for attending class; when they do not receive points for coming to class, they do not attend as many classes (Launius, 1997; Moore, 2003a, 2003b) and, as a result, do not meet their first-day-of-classes expectations about class attendance. These results are consistent with reports that developmental education students have a difficult time following through on their academic intentions (Pintrich & Garcia, 1994).

What about the lower grades that characterized students who had to be forced to attend the summer orientation? In GC's introductory biology course, these students attended 34% fewer classes and earned grades that were 33% lower than students who attended the orientation voluntarily (Moore & Jensen, in press). These differences were statistically significant ($p < 0.01$).

Students' involvement in other course-related activities. In light of the strong association of class attendance with high grades, I hypothesized that other motivation-based behaviors would also correlate positively with academic success. To test this, I measured how students' attendance at optional help sessions correlated with students' grades. Students received no points for attending any of these help sessions, and the sessions were conducted by teaching assistants who had no knowledge of upcoming exams (i.e., students did not get any "inside information" at the help sessions). Nevertheless, students who attended optional help sessions made significantly higher grades than did students who did not attend such sessions (Moore, in press-c). Similar results have been reported by Grisé and Kenney (2002), who noted that students who attended at least one session of Supplemental Instruction earned higher grades than students who did not. Students who attended help sessions also attended class more often than did students who missed help sessions (Moore, in press-c).

First-semester and first-year GPA. GC students' first-semester GPAs strongly predict their second-semester GPAs (r [831] = 0.59, $p < 0.01$) and their first-year GPAs (r [801] = 0.85, $p < 0.01$). Contrary to popular belief, there are relatively few students who "turn things around" after a bad start; most students in GC who earn GPAs less than 2.0 during their first semester also earn GPAs less than 2.0 during their second semester and are suspended from the university (Moore, in press-b). Similarly, most students who get off to a good start in college continue to do well in subsequent semesters. For example, only 9% of students who earn first-semester GPAs greater than 2.0 end their first year of college with GPAs less than 2.0 (Moore, in press-b).

Students who earn the highest first-year GPAs also have much higher probabilities of graduating from the university than do students who earn low first-year GPAs. For example, (a) 85% of the GC students who graduated from the university between 1995 and 2003 had first-year GPAs above 2.5, and (b) students having first-year GPAs less than 2.0 comprise only about 1% of the GC students who graduated from the university during the same period (*General College Graduate and Transfer Students*, 2003). To survive the "transfer shock" that occurs when developmental education students transfer to degree-granting colleges (Best & Gehring, 1993; Graham & Dallam, 1986; Graham & Hughes, 1994), most developmental education students need first-year GPAs above 3.0 if they are eventually to graduate from the University.

Academic Achievement Motivation

Because academic success results from a variety of factors, it is not surprising that GC's most successful students exhibit a variety of effective academic behaviors. For example, they are more likely to attend class, help sessions, and summer orientation sessions than are students who do not succeed in GC. These behaviors are a surrogate for, and a clear expression of, a student's academic achievement motivation, which is a student's motivation toward performance goals (e.g., high grades, praise, outperforming other students) or learning goals (e.g., improving oneself, learning for learning's sake; Cavallo, Rozman, Blickenstaff, & Walker, 2004). Although academic motivation can be expressed in many ways, one explicit expression of students' motivation is their class attendance and participation in other course-related activities. These behaviors require a consistent and ongoing effort that is related directly to a student's educational success.

Motivation is important because it affects students' willingness to approach academic tasks, invest the required time and energy, and maintain enough effort to complete academic tasks successfully (Ray, Garavalia, & Murdock, 2003). GC's most successful students invest in and excel at a variety of course-related activities that optimize their chance of academic success. For example, the students most likely to attend class regularly are also most likely to attend help sessions, study more, read the assigned chapters in the course textbook, and comply with course assignments (Moore, 2003a, 2003b). All of these behaviors are explicit expressions of students' academic motivation. Differences in academic motivation also help explain why many seemingly "smart" students do not do as well in college as "average" students. Motivation, which students express as persistence, hard work, and simply showing up, usually produces success; innate intelligence often does not. It is usually the most motivated students, and not necessarily those with the highest scores on standardized tests, who succeed in college. Developmental education students should heed Woody Allen's claim that "Eighty percent of success is showing up" (Moncur, 2004).

Although academic achievement motivation is especially important for the academic success of developmental education students (Allen, 1999; Prus, Hatcher, Hope, & Gabriel, 1995; Thomas & Higbee, 2000), there are alternate explanations for the data presented here. For example, students whose parents are unfamiliar with college may not be encouraged to attend summer orientation, classes, and help sessions. Alternately, students who do not come to class or other course-associated activities may be working and not have time to attend class. However, previous research indicated that students who support themselves financially while pursuing their education attend class more often and earn higher grades than students whose education is paid for by others (Devadoss & Foltz, 1996), and my interviews with students who seldom come to class indicate that their top non-illness reason for missing class is that they value socializing more than their academic coursework. These findings are consistent with the fact that students who drop out of GC cite a lack of motivation as the most frequent reason (e.g., far ahead of factors such as health and finances) for quitting school (Hatfield, 2003).

Discussion and Recommendations: Helping Students Succeed

My research is consistent with the following recommendations to help developmental education students succeed in college:

1. Emphasize the importance of motivation for academic achievement. Many high school students are poorly motivated and not involved with their education (Gehring, 2003). This lack of motivation clashes with the fact that academic motivation is the most important factor and accurate predictor of the academic success of developmental education students (Caballo, Rozman, Blickenstaff, & Walker, 2004; Ley & Young, 1998; Moore et al., 2003; Ray, Garavalia, & Murdock, 2003; VanZile-Tamsen & Livingston, 1999). Although traditional students usually have academic skills and experiences that enable them to cope with some absences from course-related activities, developmental education students often do not. This is why developmental education students wanting to succeed in college must be motivated enough to attend class regularly. The importance of class attendance was described this way by Thompson (2002): "If a student ever complains about a grade or how tough the course is, one of the first things I look at is class attendance. That usually says it all" (p. B5). Thomas and Higbee (2000) were more succinct when they concluded that "nothing replaces being present in class" (p. 229).

2. Emphasize the importance of class attendance throughout the semester. On the first day of classes, most instructors tell students that class attendance is important for academic success. However, such announcements seldom improve students' rates of class attendance (Moore, 2003a, 2003b).

Students are accustomed to hearing such proclamations and are not overly impressed. However, students' rates of class attendance and academic success do improve when students are shown quantitative data documenting the importance of attendance for academic success throughout the semester (Moore, 2003a). For example, in my classes I (a) include data such as those shown in Figure 2 in the course syllabus, (b) discuss these data on the first day of classes, (c) have students write and submit an essay interpreting Figure 2 on the first day of classes, and (d) show students Figure 2 every day in the minutes before class begins. This ongoing reinforcement of the importance of class attendance for academic success improves the attendance and grades of approximately 20% of students in the course (Moore, 2003a).

3. Use data to show students the importance of getting off to a good start in college. Developmental education students need to understand this harsh reality: If they earn low grades during their first semester, they will probably also earn low grades during their second semester and be dismissed from the university (Moore, in press-b). Although first-semester grades are not destiny, they do accurately predict students' academic success. Do not let students delude themselves into thinking that they merely had an "off" semester from which they will easily recover. They probably will not.

4. Emphasize the importance of hard work for academic success. Many developmental education students may not understand, or do not believe, that there is a causal relationship between academic preparation, effort, and performance, and may therefore believe that attending class, help sessions, and other course-related activities is not necessary for academic success. This belief may be well justified, for first-year students who entered college in the fall of 2002 nationwide spent "far less" time studying than any previous entering class of college students, yet had higher high school grades than any previous class (Marklein, 2003; Sax, Lindholm, Astin, Korn, & Mahoney, 2002; Young, 2002, p. A36). Indeed, (a) a record-high percentage (46%) of these students had an A average in high school despite the fact that a record-low percentage (33%) of these students studied less than 6 hours per week, and (b) in the past 15 years, the percentage of first-year students who study less than 1 hour per week has nearly doubled, from 8.5% to 15.9%. Although high school readies only about one in three 18-year-olds for college (Schouten, 2003), many first-year students believe that the same amount of effort that produced their high grades in high school will produce the same grades in college (Young, 2002). The worst study habits and lowest amount of effort on record have produced the highest grades on record, so we should not be surprised when students question or ignore advice about the amount of effort required for academic success in college. Even so, the fact remains: students who accept our claims that behaviors such as attending class are

beneficial and who follow through appropriately will incur a significant advantage. These students will probably learn more, make higher grades, out-compete their classmates, and have a greater chance of graduating from the university than poorly motivated students who ignore advice about the importance of course-related activities such as class attendance (Moore, in press-a, in press-b).

5. Tell students that they may not be ready for college. Although most students believe that graduation from high school ensures that they are well prepared for college, more than one-third of first-year college-students enroll in at least one remedial course, which is up from 28% in 1995 (Cavanagh, 2003a, 2003b). Even the best students are often underprepared for college; this is why 30% to 40% of students in many states who have earned academic scholarships for their high school grades have to take remedial courses when they start college (Schouten, 2003). Clearly, the tests used to measure high school students' academic skills are poor indicators of college readiness (Cavanagh, 2003a; Hebel, 2003), and graduation from high school is not synonymous with being prepared for college.

6. Emphasize that students are responsible for their education. Few circumstances will stop a motivated student who is determined to succeed academically. However, many developmental education students have behaviors that are inconsistent with academic success; for example, they often skip class, turn in assignments late, value socializing over studying, ignore valuable advice, and expend only enough energy to "just get by" (Grisé & Kenney, 2003; Yaworski, Weber, & Ibrahim, 2000). Although instructors should offer up-to-date, rigorous, and inclusive courses, a student's education is ultimately the student's responsibility. If students are to succeed academically, they must engage themselves in their education and be motivated to learn. This is especially true for developmental education students, who often lack some of the academic experiences and skills possessed by other students. If students are not motivated enough to engage themselves in their education, there is little that instructors, advisors, and others can do to help. Although we should continue to try to devise programs to help these students, we should not expect these programs to be overly successful. After all, the success of any such program depends on students' participation, and it is students' lack of participation in their education that correlates so strongly with their increased probabilities of academic failure.

7. Emphasize to students that they can succeed. Many developmental education students have become accustomed to below-average grades and test scores and often wonder whether they can succeed in college. Show students that motivated students, even those having relatively low high school graduation percentiles and low scores on standardized tests, can overcome many

obstacles with a strong work ethic that engages them with, and thereby enables them to take control of, their education. Scores on standardized tests, and the resulting "at risk" labels that often accompany students having such scores, are not destiny.

Developmental education programs continue to play critical roles in helping thousands of underprepared students become college graduates. Although these programs offer students many valuable resources, they cannot be overly effective if students do not understand what they must do to succeed. Students will be more successful if we provide explicit, research-based recommendations about what behaviors they will need to excel.

References

About General College-Fact Sheet. (2003). Minneapolis, MN: General College, University of Minnesota. Retrieved May 19, 2004, from http://www.gen.umn.edu/gc

Advising manual—College of Liberal Arts. (2004). Minneapolis, MN: General College, University of Minnesota. Retrieved June 1, 2004, from http://class.umn.edu:81/manual/3_3_m.html

Allen, D. (1999). Desire to finish college: An empirical link between motivation and persistence. *Research in Higher Education, 40,* 461–485.

Berenson, S. B., Carter, G., & Norwood, K. S. (1992). The at-risk student in college developmental algebra. *School Science and Mathematics, 92*(2), 55–58.

Best, G. A., & Gehring, D. D. (1993). The academic performance of community college transfer students at a major state university in Kentucky. *Community College Review, 21*(2), 32–41.

Borland, M. V., & Howsen, R. M. (1998). Effect of student attendance on performance: Comment on Lamdin. *The Journal of Educational Research, 91*(4), 195–197.

Britton, B. K., & Tesser, A. (1991). Effects of time management practices on college grades. *Journal of Educational Psychology, 83,* 405–410.

Brocato, J. (1989). How much does coming to class matter? Some evidence of class attendance and grade performance. *Educational Research Quarterly, 13*(3), 2–6.

Brothen, T., & Wambach, C. (2003). Is there a role for academic achievement tests in multicultural developmental education? In J. L. Higbee, D. B. Lundell, & I. M. Duranczyk (Eds.), *Multiculturalism in developmental education* (pp. 43–49). Minneapolis, MN: Center for Research on Developmental Education and Urban Literacy, General College, University of Minnesota.

Cabrera, A. F., Nora, A., & Castañeda, M. B. (1993). College persistence: Structural equations modeling test of an integrated lever retention. *Journal of Higher Education, 64*(2), 123–139.

Cavallo, A. M. L., Rozman, M., Blickenstaff, J., & Walker, N. (2004). Learning, reasoning, motivation, and epistemological beliefs: Differing approaches in college science courses. *Journal of College Science Teaching, 33*(3), 18–23.

Cavanagh, S. (2003a). Many state tests said to be poor indicators of college readiness. *Education Week, 23*(9), 13.

Cavanagh, S. (2003b). More in college taking remedial courses, NCES says. *Education Week, 23*(15), 9.

Cloud, J. (2001, March 12). Should SAT's matter? *Time*, pp. 62–70.

Côté, J. E., & Levine, C. G. (2000). Attitude versus aptitude: Is intelligence or motivation more important for positive higher-educational outcomes? *Journal of Adolescent Research, 15*(1), 58–80.

Davis, J. R. (1993). *Better teaching, more learning: Strategies for success in postsecondary settings.* Phoenix, AZ: Oryx.

Devadoss, S., & Foltz, J. (1996). Evaluation of factors influencing student class attendance and performance. *American Journal of Agricultural Economics, 78*, 499–508.

Druger, M. (2003). Being there: A perspective on class attendance. *Journal of College Science Teaching, 32*, 350–351.

Friedman, P., Rodriguez, F., & McComb, J. (2001). Why students do and do not attend classes. *College Teaching, 49*(4), 124–133.

Gehring, J. (2003). Report examines motivation among students. *Education Week, 23*(15), 17.

General College graduate and transfer students registered spring 2003-GPA at 30 Credits. (2003). Unpublished manuscript. Minneapolis, MN: Office of Research and Evaluation, General College, University of Minnesota.

Graham, S. W., & Dallam, J. (1986). Academic probation as a measure of performance: Contrasting transfer students to native students. *Community/Junior College Quarterly of Research and Practice, 10*, 23–24.

Graham, S. W., & Hughes, J. C. (1994). Moving down the road: Community college students' academic performance at the university. *Community College Journal of Research and Practice, 18*, 449–464.

Grisé, D. J., & Kenney, A. M. (2003). Nonmajors' performance in biology. *Journal of College Science Teaching, 33* (2), 18–21.

Hatfield, J. (2003). *Office of Research and Evaluation-Research 2002–2003.* Minneapolis, MN: General College, University of Minnesota.

Hebel, S. (2003). States' tests for high-school students are out of sync with college standards, report says. *The Chronicle of Higher Education, 50*(11), A26.

Jones, C. H. (1984). Interaction of absences and grades in a college course. *The Journal of Psychology, 116*, 133–136.

Langley, S., Wambach, C., Brothen, T., & Madyun, N. (in press). Academic achievement motivation: Differences among underprepared students taking a PSI general psychology course. *Research & Teaching in Developmental Education.*

Larose, S., & Roy, R. (1991). The role of prior academic performance and nonacademic attributes in the prediction of the success of high-risk college students. *Journal of College Student Development, 32*, 171–177.

Launius, M. H. (1997). College student attendance: Attitudes and academic performance. *College Student Journal, 31*, 86–92.

Ley, K., & Young, D. B. (1998). Self-regulation behaviors in underprepared (developmental) and regular admission college students. *Contemporary Educational Psychology, 23*, 42–64.

Marklein, M. B. (2003, January 27). A new sketch of college freshmen. *USA Today*, p. 8D.

McGuire, S. (2003). Teaching students how to learn chemistry. *Strategies for Success, 40*, 4–5.

Meeker, F., Fox, D., & Whitley, B. E. (1994). Predictors of academic success in the undergraduate psychology course. *Teaching of Psychology, 21*, 238–241.

Moncur, L. (2004). *Laura Moncur's motivational quotations.* Retrieved September 17, 2004, from http://www.quotationspage.com/quote/1903.html

Moore, R. (2003a). Does improving developmental education students' understanding of the importance of class attendance improve students' class attendance and academic performance? *Research & Teaching in Developmental Education, 20*(2), 24–39.

Moore, R. (2003b). Students' choices in developmental education: Is it really important to attend class? *Research & Teaching in Developmental Education, 20*(1), 42–52.

Moore, R. (in press-a). Advising students in developmental education: How accurate are developmental education students' self-assessments of their course-related behaviors? *Research & Teaching in Developmental Education.*

Moore, R. (in press-b). Pre-enrollment and post-enrollment predictors of the academic success of developmental education students. *Journal of College Student Retention: Research, Theory, & Practice.*

Moore, R. (in press-c). Who's helped by help-sessions in developmental education courses? *Research & Teaching in Developmental Education.*

Moore, R., & Jensen, M. (in press). What factors predict the academic success of developmental education students? *The Learning Assistance Review.*

Moore, R., Jensen, M., Hatch, J., Duranczyk, I., Staats, S., & Koch, L. (2003). Showing up: The importance of class attendance for academic success in introductory science courses. *The American Biology Teacher, 65,* 325–329.

Moore, R., Jensen, M., Hsu, L., & Hatch, J. (2002). Saving the "false negatives": Intelligence tests, the SAT, and developmental education. In D. B. Lundell & J. L. Higbee (Eds.), *Exploring urban literacy & developmental education* (pp. 47–57). Minneapolis, MN: Center for Research on Developmental Education and Urban Literacy, General College, University of Minnesota.

Morrison, B. (1999). Acknowledging student attributes associated with academic motivation. *Journal of Developmental Education, 23*(2), 10–16, 30–31.

Neal, K. S., Schaer, B. B., Ley, T. C., & Wright, J. P. (1990). Predicting achievement in a teacher preparatory course of reading methods from the ACT and Teale-Lewis Reading Attitude scores. *Reading Psychology, 11*(2), 131–139.

Petrie, T. A., & Stoever, S. (1997). Academic and nonacademic predictors of female student-athletes' academic performance. *Journal of College Student Development, 38,* 599–608.

Pintrich, P. R., & Garcia, T. (1994). Self-regulated learning in college students: Knowledge, strategies and motivation. In P. R. Pintrich & D. R. Brown (Eds.), *Student motivation, cognition and learning: Essays in honor of Wilbur J. McKeachie* (pp. 113–133). Hillsdale, NJ: Erlbaum.

Prus, J., Hatcher, L., Hope, M., & Gabriel, C. (1995). The learning and study strategies inventory (LASSI) as a predictor of first-year college academic success. *Journal of The Freshman Year Experience, 7,* 7–26.

Ray, M., Garavalia, L., & Murdock, T. (2003). Aptitude, motivation, and self-regulation as predictors of achievement among developmental college students. *Research & Teaching in Developmental Education, 20*(1), 21.

Romer, R. (1993). Do students go to class? Should they? *Journal of Economic Perspectives, 7*(3), 167–174.

Sappington, J., Kinsey, K., & Munsayac, K. (2002). Two studies of reading compliance among college students. *Teaching of Psychology, 29,* 272–274.

Sax, L. J., Lindholm, J. A., Astin, A. W., Korn, W. S., & Mahoney, K. M. (2002). *The American freshman: National norms for fall 2002.* Los Angeles: Higher Education Research Institute, University of California, Los Angeles.

Schouten, F. (2003, October 21). Grade inflation takes a toll on students. *USA Today,* p. 9D.

Snyder, V., Hackett, R. K., Stewart, M., & Smith, D. (2003). Predicting academic performance and retention of private university freshmen in need of developmental education. *Research & Teaching in Developmental Education, 23*(2), 171–180.

Street, D. R. (1975). Noncompulsory attendance: Can state-supported universities afford this luxury? *Journal of College Student Personnel, 16,* 124–127.

Thomas, P. V., & Higbee, J. L. (2000). The relationship between involvement and success in developmental algebra. *Journal of College Reading and Learning, 30*(2), 222–232.

Thompson, B. (2002). If I quiz them, they will come. *The Chronicle of Higher Education, 48*(41), B5.

Tinto, V. (1975). Dropout from higher education: A theoretical synthesis of recent research. *Review of Educational Research, 45*, 39–125.

Undergraduate Catalog—Institute of Technology. (2004). Minneapolis, MN: Institute of Technology, University of Minnesota. Retrieved June 1, 2004, from http://www.catalogs.umn.edu/ug/it/itinfo.html

VanZile-Tamsen, C., & Livingston, J. A. (1999). The differential impact of motivation on the self-regulated strategy use of high- and low-achieving college students. *Journal of College Student Development, 40*, 54–60.

Wiley, C. (1992). Predicting business course grades from class attendance and other objective student characteristics. *College Student Journal, 26*, 497–501.

Yaworski, J., Weber, R. M., & Ibrahim, N. (2000). What makes students succeed or fail?: The voices of developmental college students. *Journal of College Reading and Learning, 30*(2), 195–221.

Young, J. R. (2002). Homework? What homework? *The Chronicle of Higher Education, 49*(15), A35–A37.

Conclusion

Conclusion

David R. Arendale

It has been an amazing experience to document the scope and diversity of ideas of students, faculty, and staff members of the General College (GC) as they approach their work and service to students. In anticipation of GC's 75th anniversary in 2007, we undertook this book project 2 years ago. Our primary intent was to document the General College's current contributions, as well as those of GC administrators, faculty, and staff who have preceded us, and to share our ideas with colleagues at other institutions. We have learned much from our colleagues here in the U.S. and internationally, and we saw this book as an opportunity to inform the greater higher education community about how we have implemented what we have learned in the General College.

As we complete the editing of the book, the General College is again being challenged to transform itself to comply with new priorities presented by a University-wide strategic planning process initiated by the University's central administration. Change is nothing new for GC. As some of the chapters in this book have illustrated, GC has modified its mission and transformed its curriculum approximately every 10 to 20 years. Twice within the past 2 decades serious attempts have been made to close the college due to perceptions that its mission was unessential for a major public research university. The recently approved plan for strategic restructuring of the University includes significant reorganization of GC, and its loss of status as a freshman-admitting college also reflects that point of view.

The forces of change that are currently enveloping the University of Minnesota are not unique or new to American public postsecondary education. Crushing economic forces have been buffeting postsecondary education for over a decade. The proportion of state funds devoted to public higher education has been significantly and perhaps irrevocably diminishing for a long time, both here in Minnesota and around the nation. State legislative leaders are devoting more resources to health care, prison construction, and rebuilding of transportation infrastructure. Public elementary and secondary (K-12) education initiatives generally receive first preference for scarce infusions of state funding; however, K-12 school districts are fighting major battles as well.

The historic notion that substantial financial investments in education programs yield significant and long-term benefits for society has been too often forgotten. During a conference presentation recently given by one of this book's co-editors, a high-ranking college administrator exclaimed that her first priority each morning was to figure out how she could keep the doors open at her institution. Although her concern was perhaps exaggerated, many state and federal reports that increasingly document the dismal funding prospects for public postsecondary education confirm this anecdote. It appears that a lack of fiscal resources is driving much of the change within higher education, including the significant restructuring currently under way at the University of Minnesota. Fiscal exigencies combined with rapidly changing demographics, and particularly the projected decline in the number of students of traditional college age, are causing postsecondary administrators in the U.S. to rethink their budget priorities.

An increasing trend is a shift of access and developmental education programs from a shared responsibility by all postsecondary institutions to an obligation of only public community colleges. This reduction or elimination of this responsibility is appearing with increased frequency in urban public colleges and universities. This issue bears increased investigation regarding the scope of institutional mission changes and the consequences for the diversity of the student body and impact on student outcomes.

At the time of publication of this book, the ultimate future is uncertain for the General College. When draft recommendations were circulated in early spring 2005 that recommended significant campus reorganization including demotion of GC to departmental status, a spirited and vigorous campaign was waged by supporters of GC. They advocated for its continued status as a college with the authority to manage its mission, admissions, curriculum, and budget. Of particular concern was maintaining access to the University for students from populations that traditionally have been underserved in U.S. higher education, and especially at its most prestigious public research I institutions. These populations include students of color, students who represent the first of their families to attend college, students who are English language learners, students who have spent major portions of their lives living as refugees without a country, students with disabilities, and students from low-income families. For almost 75 years General College has provided the gateway to the University of Minnesota for these students. The recent debate involved many people throughout the campus, members of the community, and other policy makers. People of good will on both sides of the argument engaged in a dramatic battle related to the future vision of the University as a whole and the role of the General College in particular.

In June 2005 the UMN Board of Regents approved by a vote of 11 to 1 that GC be demoted to departmental status and be assigned to the College of Education and Human Development. Final details concerning the implementation of this change will be studied by campus task forces that will present their recommendations for action and approval by UMN central administration in December 2005. UMN President Robert Bruininks has announced that the transition process will take place over several years.

Change is coming to what is now the General College. That is not new for GC, which is probably the most flexible academic unit within the University community. As demonstrated in the history section of this book, it has often been called upon to modify its mission to meet the needs presented to it. If the old expression is correct that "form follows function," then also is the fact that function is dependent upon values and mission. The recognition of the importance of shared values is critical to understanding GC and the endeavors of its students, faculty, staff, and administrators to maintain GC's unique vision and sense of community.

At a spring 2005 GC faculty meeting the group reviewed GC's core values. Regardless of the administrative organization of our unit, our values are central to who we are and hopefully will always be reflected in our collective work. This discussion and others that have been occurring throughout the college have identified the following values that are held by the group: (a) the diversity of our student body as well as our faculty and staff, (b) the centrality of multiculturalism to all the activities of the college, (c) the necessity to address issues of social justice in our work, (d) our focus on student-centered teaching, and (e) the importance of classroom-based research.

This book is about "The General College Vision." Regardless of our future, we plan to continue to remain steadfast to our vision and values. We hope that readers of this book have learned new means for tangible expressions of these values at their home institutions. Perhaps in some small way this book can help nurture and spread the glow of the General College vision to other colleges and universities throughout the land. Regardless of our future, maybe the embers of the fire of our convictions can inspire others to experiment and implement strategies that work best for their institution. We hope that through the collective flames of a thousand fires the GC vision can spread to impact more students in the future.

About the Editors

Jeanne L. Higbee has a B.S. in sociology (1972) from Iowa State University and earned her M.S. in Counseling and Guidance (1976) and Ph.D. in educational administration (1981) from the University of Wisconsin-Madison (UW). She began her career in developmental education and learning assistance as a graduate student coordinating the Learning Skills Program for the UW Counseling Service. She worked full-time in student affairs at a variety of institutions from 1977 through 1985, and then taught in the Division of Academic Assistance at the University of Georgia from 1985 to 1999. She currently serves as professor and senior advisor to the Center for Research on Developmental Education and Urban Literacy (CRDEUL) at the University of Minnesota General College. She is the recipient of the American College Personnel Association (ACPA, 2005) Voice of Inclusion Medallion, the Henry Young Award for Outstanding Individual Contribution to the National Association for Developmental Education (NADE, 2002), the award for Outstanding Article in the *Journal of Developmental Education* (2000), and the Hunter R. Boylan Outstanding Research/Publication Award (NADE, 1999), as well as the General College's 2004 Multicultural Recognition Award. In addition to serving as co-editor of *The Learning Assistance Review* and on numerous other journal editorial boards, she has edited 12 monographs and published more than 75 articles related to access to higher education and success in the first year of college. She has also edited a book titled *Curriculum Transformation and Disability: Implementing Universal Design in Higher Education* and is currently working on a monograph addressing issues for professionals with disabilities.

Dana Britt Lundell received her Ph.D. in education, curriculum and instruction, at the University of Minnesota in 1999. Her emphasis was literacy in higher education, with a minor in composition, literacy, and rhetorical studies. Prior to this she received an M.A. in English from the University of Minnesota, and a Bachelor of Philosophy in interdisciplinary studies from the Western College Program at Miami University (OH). Since 1993 Dana has worked in General College. During that time she was an instructor in the writing program for 5 years. In 1996 she helped establish and implement the Center for Research on Developmental Education and Urban Literacy, and in

2000 she became its first full-time director. Dana's ongoing research emphasizes access in higher education, postsecondary developmental education, multicultural education, graduate education, and literacy issues. She is co-editor of the CRDEUL publication series and has published several articles, chapters, and reports. She was 2004 President of the Minnesota Association for Developmental Education (MNADE) and recently coordinated the planning committee for the developmental education initiative of the Twin Cities Metropolitan Higher Education Consortium. Most importantly, in her real life Dana plays guitar, owns a house, enjoys the outdoors, and loves cats.

David R. Arendale earned his B.S. in history and philosophy in 1977 and M.S. in history in 1985 from Emporia State University (KS), Certificate in developmental education in 1990 from Appalachian State University (NC), Ed.S. in higher education administration in 1991, and Ph.D. in educational administration and history in 2000 from the University of Missouri-Kansas City. In General College Arendale serves as assistant professor in social sciences and faculty advisor for outreach with the Center for Research on Developmental Education and Urban Literacy (CRDEUL). Previously he directed the National Center for Supplemental Instruction and the campus learning center located at the University of Missouri-Kansas City. He also directed learning centers at two Kansas community colleges during the 1980s: Highland Community College and Pratt Community College. Arendale has held a variety of leadership positions within the National Association for Developmental Education, including president. The American Council for Developmental Education Associations selected Arendale in 2000 as a Founding Fellow of Developmental Education

About the Authors

Heidi Lasley Barajas earned a B.A. in spanish and education, an M.S. in sociology from the University of Utah, and a Ph.D. in sociology from the University of Minnesota. She currently works in the General College as assistant professor in social sciences and focuses her research on the relationship of race and educational institutions, and on community service-learning as a pedagogy and key to educational access as well as individual and citizenship development.

Mark A. Bellcourt is currently a doctoral candidate in higher education policy and administration at the University of Minnesota. His undergraduate and master's degrees are in counseling and psychology. During his 13 years working in student services in the General College, Mark has coordinated its academic progress system, taught freshman experience courses, and advised the General College Student Board. His areas of interests are in student affairs, first-year students, and Native American education.

Thomas Brothen is currently Morse-Alumni Distinguished Teaching Professor of psychology and social sciences in the General College, where his primary teaching responsibility is general psychology. Brothen received his Ph.D. in social psychology from the University of Minnesota. His research interests include teaching psychology, computer-assisted instructional methods, and student academic progress.

Patrick Bruch received a B.A. in English from Western Michigan University in 1992 and a Ph.D. in English from Wayne State University (MI) in 1999. He is currently assistant professor of writing studies, co-director of the Writing Program, and director of the graduate certificate in postsecondary developmental education in the General College.

Martha Casazza is the dean of the College of Arts and Sciences at National-Louis University in Chicago, Illinois. She has served as president of the National College Learning Center Association, president of the National Association for Developmental Education, Co-Editor of the *Learning Assistance Review,* and co-editor for the National Association for Developmental Education newsletter. She is currently on the editorial board for the *Journal of Developmental Education* as well as the advisory board for the Center for Research on Developmental Education and Urban Literacy. She received the Hunter R. Boylan Outstanding Research/Publication Award in 2004. Dr. Casazza was awarded a Fulbright Scholarship to South Africa in 2000, where she worked with faculty and students at the University of Port Elizabeth. She has presented faculty workshops and speeches in Scotland, England, Spain, and Poland. Dr. Casazza has co-authored two books with Dr. Sharon Silverman: *Learning Assistance and Developmental Education: A Guide for Effective Practice* (1996) and *Learning and Development* (2000). She currently has a book in press, *Access, Opportunity and Success: Keeping the Promise of Higher Education.*

Carl J. Chung earned an A.B. in Philosophy from Occidental College in 1986 and a Ph.D. in philosophy from the University of Minnesota in 2000. He has worked at the General College since 1995, first as a graduate teaching assistant, then as a graduate teaching specialist, and finally as an assistant professor of humanities. He has served on the Center for Research on Developmental Education and Urban Literacy's Advisory Board since its inception.

Laurene Christensen earned her B.A. in English in 1993 from the University of North Dakota. She earned her M.A. in English from Portland State University in 2000 and her M.A. in teaching English to speakers of other languages (TESOL) from Portland State in 2002. She is currently pursuing a doctorate in education policy and administration with a focus on comparative and international development education at the University of Minnesota. In the General College she teaches reading and composition in the Commanding English program.

Daniel Detzner received a B.A. from the University of Notre Dame (IN), an M.A. from Georgetown University (DC), and a Ph.D. from the University of Minnesota in American studies. He began his career in General College, served as head of the social and behavioral sciences division, and won the Morse Award for Outstanding Contributions to Undergraduate Education. He moved to the University of Minnesota's family social sciences department, where he later became associate dean and interim dean in the College of Human Ecology. He currently serves as professor and associate dean for Academic Affairs in General College and is a member of the University of Minnesota's Academy of Distinguished Teachers.

Irene M. Duranczyk earned her B.A. in 1971 in Chemistry from Oakland University (MI), her M.Ed. in 1990 in educational leadership from Wayne State

University (MI), and her Ed.D. in 2002 in developmental education: higher education administration and management from Grambling State University (LA). In the General College she currently serves as associate professor in developmental mathematics and co-editor of the annual monographs of the Center for Research on Developmental Education and Urban Literacy (CRDEUL). She is co-editor of the *The Learning Assistance Review*. Previously she was the program administrator of developmental mathematics in the department of mathematics at Eastern Michigan University for 10 years.

Renata Fitzpatrick earned her B.A. in English literature and M.A. in teaching English as a second language from the University of Minnesota in 1998 and 2001 respectively. Currently Renata teaches four courses per year in the Commanding English program and serves as an English as a second language (ESL) specialist in the General College Writing Center.

David L. Ghere is an associate professor of history at the General College, University of Minnesota, where he has taught American History and World History for 14 years. He has a variety of publications on Native American history particularly focusing on northern New England during the colonial period. He also has created 15 classroom simulations and published articles on developmental education and teaching methods. He received his B.S. in secondary education and M.Ed. in social studies from the University of Illinois, and M.A. and Ph.D. in history from the University of Maine at Orono.

Emily Goff earned her B.A. in Portuguese and certificate in teaching English to speakers of other languages (TESOL) from the University of Wisconsin-Madison in 1998. She is currently pursuing a Ph.D. in adult education at the University of Minnesota. In the General College she works as the associate editor for *The Learning Assistance Review* and editorial assistant for numerous Center for Research on Developmental Education and Urban Literacy projects.

Katy Gray Brown has degrees in peace studies (B.A. from Manchester College (IN), 1991; M.A. from the University of Notre Dame (IN), 1992, and philosophy (M.A. and Ph.D. from the University of Minnesota, 1994 and 2000). She is an assistant professor in the General College.

Ian S. Haberman is currently a junior majoring in philosophy with an ethics and civic life emphasis and a minor in economics. He is an undergraduate teaching assistant at General College and a member of the Pre-Law Society, with plans to attend law school after graduation. Ian also spends his spare time as a volunteer with Habitat for Humanity.

Debra A. Hartley earned her B.A. in English in 1973 from Gustavus Adolphus College (MN), her Master of library science degree from Indiana University in 1975, and her M.A. and Ph.D. in English from the University of Iowa in 1988 and 1992 respectively. In the General College she currently serves as coordinator of the Writing Center and Academic Resource Center (ARC) Computer Center and teaching specialist in writing. Previously she tutored writing and taught English for 6 years at Augustana College in Rock Island, IL.

Leon Hsu received a B.A. in physics from Harvard University (MA) in 1991 and a Ph.D. in physics from the University of California in 1997. He is an assistant professor in the General College. Previously, he held a National Science Foundation postdoctoral fellowship in science, mathematics, engineering, and technology education at the Center for Innovation in Learning at Carnegie Mellon University (PA).

Patricia A. James earned her B.F.A. in painting from the University of Illinois in 1970, her M.F.A. in sculpture from Bradley University (IL) in 1985, and her Ph.D. in curriculum and instruction from the University of Minnesota in 1993. She has taught art in the General College since 1993 and is currently an associate professor. Before moving to Minnesota, she was an assistant professor of art at Wesleyan College in Macon, GA.

Allen B. Johnson earned a B.S. in education (secondary school science teaching) at Wisconsin State College-Superior in 1960. In 1963 he earned an M.A. at Drake University (IA), in 1968 he earned an M.S., and in 1974, he earned a Ph.D. with a major in soil science and minor in higher education, both from the University of Minnesota. He has taught the earth sciences, physical sciences, and developmental mathematics at the General College since March 1963. In 1982 he was a recipient of the Alfred L. Vaughan Award for Outstanding Service in the General College and in 1985 he received the H.T. Morse-Alumni Award for Outstanding Contributions to Undergraduate Education at the University of Minnesota. He retired in May 2004 at the rank of associate professor.

D. Patrick Kinney earned his B.S. in mathematics in 1984 from the University of Wisconsin-Superior, and his Ph.D. in mathematics education from the University of Minnesota in 1997. He taught mathematics at the General College as a teaching specialist and as an assistant professor for 5 years. Currently, he is a mathematics instructor at the Wisconsin Indianhead Technical College in New Richmond, WI.

Laura Smith Kinney earned her B.S. in mathematics from the University of Minnesota-Morris in 1985, M.S. in mathematics from Iowa State University in 1988, and Ph.D. in mathematics education from the University of Minnesota in 1997. She taught mathematics as a graduate teaching assistant at the General College for 6 years. Currently she is an assistant professor of mathematics at Northland College in Ashland, WI.

Randy Moore earned his B.S. in biology in 1975 from Texas A&M University, his M.S. in botany from the University of Georgia in 1977, and his Ph.D. in biology from the University of California at Los Angeles in 1980. Randy is professor of biology in General College.

Robin Murie has her B.A. in German and history from the University of Wisconsin-Madison and M.A. in English as a second language (ESL) from the University of Minnesota. In the General College she has been director of the Commanding English program for the past 12 years. Previously, she directed writing programs for non-native speakers of English at the University of California at Berkeley and in the College of Liberal Arts at the University of Minnesota.

Patricia J. Neiman earned her B.A.S. degree from General College and her M.A. in counseling and student personnel psychology from the University of Minnesota in 1983 and 1988 respectively. In the General College she currently serves as coordinator of the Transfer and Career Center and a counselor advocate in Student Services.

Donald L. Opitz earned his B.S. in physics and mathematics in 1991 from DePaul University in Chicago and his M.A. and Ph.D. in history of science and technology from the University of Minnesota in 1998 and 2004, respectively. In the General College he currently serves as coordinator of the Math Center and teaching specialist in mathematics. Previously he taught in Upward Bound and at Minneapolis Community and Technical College.

Robert Poch earned B.A. and M.A. degrees in history from Virginia Tech and a Ph.D. in higher education administration from the University of Virginia. He is assistant dean and director of Student Services at General College. Prior to coming to General College, he served as director of the Minnesota Higher Education Services Office (1996–2004) and as associate commissioner for access and equity and external affairs at the South Carolina Commission on Higher Education (1991–1996).

Thomas Reynolds earned his B.A. in English from the University of Notre Dame (IN) and his M.A. and Ph.D. in English from the University of Minnesota. In General College he is currently an assistant professor of writing and co-director of the Writing Program.

Douglas F. Robertson earned his B.S. in physics from Purdue University (IN) in 1968 and his Ph.D. in mathematics education from the University of Minnesota in 1979. He currently is a mathematics professor in the General College, where he has taught mathematics and computer applications since 1974.

Joshua G. Schmitt is from Edina, MN. He is currently a junior completing dual degrees in both scientific and technical communication, B.S., and political science, B.A. He also serves on the University of Minnesota's Institutional Review Board, Medical Group Four.

Mary Ellen Shaw earned her B.A. in English in 1973 from Macalester College in St. Paul, her M.A. in religious studies in 1978 from United Theological Seminary (MN), and her Ph.D. in American studies in 2001 from the University of Minnesota. She has served in a variety of roles in General College Student Services since 1985, including academic advising and coordination of advising programs.

Kwabena Siaka earned his B.B.A. in Management from the University of Alaska and his master's degree in education from the University of Minnesota. He is currently pursuing his Ph.D. in educational policy and administration. As a cultural diversity consultant, he provides expertise to student governments, higher education institutions, and corporations.

Susan K. Staats is a mathematics educator and cultural anthropologist with field experience in Guyana, South America. She earned her B.S. and M.S degrees in mathematics from the Ohio State University and a Ph.D. in cultural anthropology from Indiana University. She is an assistant professor in General College with research interests in socially-based mathematics curricula and sociolinguistic methods for assessing math classroom interactions.

David V. Taylor holds an M.A. from the University of Nebraska, and both his B.A. and Ph.D. (history of African people) from the University of Minnesota. He is a native of Minnesota, born and raised in St. Paul, where he graduated from Central High School. He was formerly associate vice chancellor for Academic Affairs at the Minnesota State University System from February 1986 to February 1989. David Taylor has been dean of the General

College at the University of Minnesota since 1989. As chief academic officer, he has provided leadership and supervision to the faculty, academic professionals, civil service employees, and graduate teaching assistants who provide instruction and academic counseling services to 1800 students. In August 2005 he will become provost and president of Academic Affairs at Morehouse College in Atlanta, GA.

Cathrine Wambach is an associate professor in General College. She earned a Ph.D. in counseling psychology from the University of Minnesota in 1981. Her interest in the process of change has led her to study the effects of computer-mediated pedagogy on students in introductory psychology, students' beliefs about their academic development, and the relationship between habits, such as procrastination, personality traits, such as conscientiousness, and academic success.

Amanda M. Wigfield is a native of St. Paul, MN, and a graduate of DeLaSalle High School in Minneapolis. She distinguishes herself through involvement in numerous volunteer activities, serving youth, the aged, and the underprivileged. She is currently completing her freshman year at the University of Minnesota and is on the Dean's List.

Leah A. Woodstrom is a junior from Minneapolis, MN. She designed her own major through the Inter-College Program and will be completing a Bachelor of Arts degree with concentrations in political science, sociology, and family social science. Leah currently is working in the General College Transfer and Career Center and with General College admissions. She is a huge advocate for General College and its services and programs!

Khong Meng Xiong is from La Crosse, WI. He is currently a freshman majoring in psychology, with a minor in Spanish. He serves as the co-chairman of the General College Student Board and is actively involved with the General College Multicultural Concerns Committee and Alumni Association Advisory Committee. Khong is also engaged in many diversity issues on campus that deal with Gay, Lesbian, Bisexual, and Transgender (GLBT) issues, violence prevention, and multicultural awareness.

Xu Zhang is teaching reading in the content area and grammar workshop in the Commanding English program in General College. She is currently a Ph.D. candidate in curriculum and instruction at the University of Minnesota, majoring in second languages and cultures education. Her research interests include content-based second language instruction, educational technology, and international teaching assistant training.

Bibliography of Developmental Education Publications by General College Authors

Compiled by Emily Goff

Adler-Kassner, L., Reynolds, T., & delMas, R. (1999). Studying a basic writing program: Problems and possibilities. *Research & Teaching in Developmental Education, 16*(1), 33–40.

Arendale, D., & Martin, D. C. (2001). Introduction to special issue on Supplemental Instruction for at-risk student populations. *Journal of Developmental Education, 24*(2), 1, 40.

Arendale, D., & Martin, D. C. (Eds.). (2001). Use of Supplemental Instruction for at-risk student populations. *Journal of Developmental Education, 24*(2).

Arendale, D. (1993a). Foundation and theoretical framework for Supplemental Instruction. In D. C. Martin & D. Arendale (Eds.), *Supplemental Instruction: Improving first-year student success in high-risk courses* (2nd ed.; pp. 19–26). Columbia, SC: National Resource Center for The First-Year Experience & Students in Transition, University of South Carolina.

Arendale, D. (1993b). Review of research on Supplemental Instruction. In D. C. Martin & D. Arendale (Eds.), *Supplemental Instruction: Improving first-year student success in high-risk courses* (2nd ed.; pp. 19–26). Columbia, SC: National Resource Center for The First-Year Experience & Students in Transition, University of South Carolina.

Arendale, D. (1993c). Supplemental Instruction in the first college year. In D. C. Martin & D. Arendale (Eds.), *Supplemental Instruction: Improving first-year student success in high-risk courses* (2nd ed.; pp. 11–18). Columbia, SC: National Resource Center for The First-Year Experience & Students in Transition, University of South Carolina.

Arendale, D. (1993d). Understanding the Supplemental Instruction model. In D. C. Martin & D. Arendale (Eds.), *Supplemental Instruction: Improving first-year student success in high-risk courses* (2nd ed.; pp. 3–10). Columbia, SC: National Resource Center for The First-Year Experience & Students in Transition, University of South Carolina.

Arendale, D. (1994). Understanding the Supplemental Instruction model. In D. C. Martin & D. Arendale (Eds.), *Supplemental Instruction: Increasing student achievement and retention* (pp. 11–21). (New Directions in Teaching and Learning, No. 60). San Francisco: Jossey-Bass.

Arendale, D. (1995). Self-assessment for adjunct instructional programs. In S. Clark-Thayer (Ed.), *National Association for Developmental Education self-evaluation guides: Models for assessing learning assistance/developmental education programs* (pp. 49–87). Clearwater, FL: H & H.

Arendale, D. (1996). Serving as enrollment management experts. *Journal of Developmental Education, 20*(1), 20.

Arendale, D. (1997). Learning centers for the 21st century. *Journal of Developmental Education, 20*(2), 16.

Arendale, D. (1998). Increasing the efficiency and effectiveness of learning for first year students through Supplemental Instruction. In J. L. Higbee & P. L. Dwinell (Eds.), *Developmental education: Preparing successful college students* (pp. 185–197). Columbia, SC: National Association for Developmental Education and National Center for the First-Year Experience & Students in Transition, University of South Carolina.

Arendale, D. (2000). Strategic plan of the National Association for Developmental Education. *Journal of Developmental Education, 33*(3), 2–4, 6, 8, 10.

Arendale, D. (2001). Effect of administrative placement and fidelity of implementation of the model on effectiveness of Supplemental Instruction programs. (Doctoral dissertation, University of Missouri-Kansas City, 2000) *Dissertation Abstracts International, 62*, 93.

Arendale, D. (2002). A memory sometimes ignored: The history of developmental education. *The Learning Assistance Review, 7*(1), 5–13.

Arendale, D. (2002). History of Supplemental Instruction (SI): Mainstreaming of developmental education. In D. B. Lundell & J. L. Higbee (Eds.), *Histories of developmental education* (pp. 15–28). Minneapolis, MN: Center for Research on Developmental Education and Urban Literacy, General College, University of Minnesota.

Arendale, D. (2002). Then and now: The early history of developmental education: Past events and future trends. *Research & Teaching in Developmental Education, 18*(2), 3–26.

Arendale, D. (2004). Pathways of persistence: A review of postsecondary peer cooperative learning programs. In J. L. Higbee, D. B. Lundell, & I. M. Duranczyk (Eds.), *Best practices for access and retention in higher education* (pp. 27–42). Minneapolis, MN: Center for Research on Developmental Education and Urban Literacy, General College, University of Minnesota.

Arendale, D. (in press-a). Mainstreamed academic assistance and enrichment for all students: The historical origins of learning assistance centers. *Research for Education Reform.*

Arendale, D. (in press-b). Terms of endearment: Words that help define our profession. *Journal of Teaching and Learning.*

Arendale, D., & Fitch, D. (1990). *Student Opportunity System (S.O.S.): A systematic plan for student retention.* (MRADE Monograph Series, #104). Warrensburg, MO: Central Missouri State University, Educational Development Center.

Barajas, H. L., & Higbee, J. L. (2003). Where do we go from here? Universal Design as a model for multicultural education. In J. L. Higbee (Ed.), *Curriculum transformation and disability: Implementing Universal Design in higher education* (pp.

285–290). Minneapolis, MN: Center for Research on Developmental Education and Urban Literacy, General College, University of Minnesota.

Barajas, H. L., Bruch, P., Choy, G., Chung, C., Hsu, L., Jacobs, W., et al. (2002). Interdisciplining pedagogy: A roundtable. *Symploke, 10*(1–2), 118–132.

Black, S., Moore, R., & Haugen, H. (2000). *Biology labs that work: The best of how-to-do-its, Part II.* Reston, VA: National Association of Biology Teachers.

Brothen, T., & Wambach, C. (1999a). An analysis of non-performers in a computer-assisted mastery learning course for developmental students. *Research & Teaching in Developmental Education, 16*(1), 41–47.

Brothen, T., & Wambach, C. (1999b). An evaluation of lectures in a computer-based, PSI introductory psychology course. *Journal of Educational Technology Systems, 27*(2), 147–155.

Brothen, T., & Wambach, C. (2000a). A beneficial self-monitoring activity for developmental students. *Research & Teaching in Developmental Education, 17*(1), 31–38.

Brothen, T., & Wambach, C. (2000b). A research based approach to developing a computer-assisted course for developmental students. In J. L. Higbee & P. L. Dwinell (Eds.), *The many faces of developmental education* (pp. 59–72). Warrensburg, MO: National Association for Developmental Education.

Brothen, T., & Wambach, C. (2000c). Using factual study questions to guide reading and promote mastery learning by developmental students in an introductory psychology course. *Journal of College Reading and Learning, 30*(1), 158–166.

Brothen, T., & Wambach, C. (2001). The relationship of conscientiousness to metacognitive study strategy use by developmental students. *Research & Teaching in Developmental Education, 18*(1), 25–31.

Bruch, P. L. (2000). Critical literacy and basic writing textbooks. *Basic Writing e-Journal, 2*(1).

Bruch, P. L. (2001). Democratic theory and developmental education. In D. B. Lundell & J. L. Higbee (Eds.), *Theoretical perspectives for developmental education* (pp. 39–50). Minneapolis, MN: Center for Research on Developmental Education and Urban Literacy, General College, University of Minnesota.

Bruch, P. L. (2002). Toward a new conversation: Multiculturalism for developmental educators. In J. L. Higbee, D. B. Lundell, & I. M. Duranczyk (Eds.), *Developmental education: Policy and practice.* Warrensburg, MO: National Association for Developmental Education.

Bruch, P. L. (2003a). Interpreting and implementing Universal Instructional Design in basic writing. In J. L. Higbee (Ed.), *Curriculum transformation and disability: Implementing Universal Design in higher education* (pp. 93–103). Minneapolis, MN: Center for Research on Developmental Education and Urban Literacy, General College, University of Minnesota.

Bruch, P. L. (2003b). Moving to the city: Redefining literacy in the post-civil rights era. In B. McComiskey & C. Ryan (Eds.), *CityComp: Identities, spaces, practices* (pp. 216–233). Albany, NY: State University of New York Press.

Bruch, P. L. (2004). Universality in basic writing: Connecting multicultural justice, Universal Instructional Design, and classroom practices. *Basic Writing e-Journal,*

5(1). Retrieved December 28, 2004, from http://www.asu.edu/clas/english/compo-sition/cbw/BWEspring2004.html

Bruch, P. L. (in press). Breaking the silenced dialogue. In P. L. Bruch & R. Marback (Eds.), *The hope and the legacy: The past, present, and future of "students' right to their own language."* Cresskill, NJ: Hampton Press.

Bruch, P. L., & Higbee, J. L. (2002). Reflections on multiculturalism in developmental education. *Journal of College Reading and Learning, 33*(1), 77–90.

Bruch, P. L., & Marback, R. (Eds.). (in press). *The hope and the legacy: The past, present, and future of "students' right to their own language."* Cresskill, NJ: Hampton Press.

Bruch, P. L., & Marback, R. (in press). Critical hope, "students' right," and the work of composition studies. In P. L. Bruch & R. Marback (Eds.), *The hope and the legacy: The past, present, and future of "students' right to their own language."* Cresskill, NJ: Hampton Press.

Bruch, P. L., Higbee, J. L., & Lundell, D. B. (2003). Multicultural legacies for the 21st century: A conversation with James A. Banks. In J. L. Higbee, D. B. Lundell, & I. M. Duranczyk (Eds.), *Multiculturalism in developmental education* (pp. 35–42). Minneapolis, MN: Center for Research on Developmental Education and Urban Literacy, General College, University of Minnesota.

Bruch, P. L., Higbee, J. L., & Lundell, D. B. (2004). Multicultural education and developmental education: A conversation about principles and connections with Dr. James A. Banks. *Research & Teaching in Developmental Education, 20*(2), 77–90.

Bruch, P. L., Jehangir, R. R., Jacobs, W. R., & Ghere, D. L. (2004). Enabling access: Toward multicultural developmental curricula. *Journal of Developmental Education, 27*(3), 12–14, 16, 18–19.

Bruch, P. L., Jehangir, R. R., Lundell, D. B., Higbee, J. L., & Miksch, K. L. (2005). Communicating across differences: Toward a multicultural approach to institutional transformation. *Innovative Higher Education, 29*(3), 195–208.

Bruch, P. L., Kinloch, V., & Marback, R. (2004). Neither distant privilege nor privileging distance: Literacies and the lessons of the Heidelberg Project. In B. Huot, B. Stroble, & C. Bazerman (Eds.), *Multiple literacies for the twenty-first century* (pp. 277–293). Cresskill, NJ: Hampton Press.

Bruch, P., & Marback R. (2002). Race, literacy, and the value of rights rhetoric in composition studies. *College Composition and Communication, 53*, 651–674.

Caniglia, J., & Duranczyk, I. M. (1999). Understanding math backwards. In J. L. Higbee & P. L. Dwinell (Eds.), *The expanding role of developmental education* (pp. 43–55). Morrow, GA: National Association for Developmental Education.

Chung, C. J. (2001). Approaching theory in developmental education. In D. B. Lundell & J. L. Higbee (Eds.), *Theoretical perspectives for developmental education* (pp. 21–27). Minneapolis, MN: Center for Research on Developmental Education and Urban Literacy, General College, University of Minnesota.

Chung, C. J. (2004a). Enhancing introductory symbolic logic with student-centered discussion projects. *Teaching Philosophy, 27*(1), 45–59.

Chung, C. J. (2004b). The impact of attendance, instructor contact, and homework completion on achievement in a developmental logic course. *Research & Teaching in Developmental Education, 20*(2), 48–57.

Chung, C. J. (2004c). Slipping through the cracks. In L. Flowers (Ed.), *Diversity issues in American colleges and universities: Case studies for higher education and student affairs professionals* (pp. 194–197). Springfield, IL: Charles C. Thomas.

Chung, C. J. (2005). Theory, practice, and the future of developmental education: Toward a pedagogy of caring. *Journal of Developmental Education, 28*(3), 2–4, 6, 8, 10, 32–33.

Chung, C. J., & Brothen, T. (2002). Some final thoughts on theoretical perspectives— Over lunch. In D. B. Lundell & J. L. Higbee (Eds.), *Proceedings of the second meeting on future directions in developmental education* (pp. 39–43). Minneapolis, MN: Center for Research on Developmental Education and Urban Literacy, General College, University of Minnesota.

Collins, M. (2001). The multicultural classroom: Immigrants reading the immigrant experience. *MinneTESOL/WITESOL Journal, 18*, 13–22.

delMas, R. (in press). Teaching statistics to underprepared college students. In J. Garfield (Ed.), *Innovations in Teaching Statistics.* Washington, DC: Mathematical Association of America.

Duranczyk, I. M., & Caniglia, J. (1998). Student belief, learning theories, and developmental mathematics: New challenges in preparing successful college students. In J. L. Higbee & P. L. Dwinell (Eds.), *Developmental education: Preparing successful college students* (pp. 123–138). Columbia, SC: National Resource Center for the First-Year Experience & Students in Transition, University of South Carolina.

Duranczyk, I. M. (1998). Unanticipated outcomes of developmental math education–A qualitative study. In D. C. Mollise & C. T. Matthews (Eds.), *NADE Selected Conference Papers, Vol. 3.* (pp. 19–21). Carol Stream, IL: National Association for Developmental Education.

Duranczyk, I. M. (2002). *Voices of underprepared university students: Outcomes of developmental mathematics education.* Unpublished doctoral dissertation, Grambling State University, LA.

Duranczyk, I. M., & White, W. G. (Eds.). (2003). *Developmental education: Pathways to excellence.* Findlay, OH: National Association for Developmental Education.

Duranczyk, I. M., Higbee, J. L., & Lundell, D. B. (Eds.). (2004). *Best practices for access and retention in higher education.* Minneapolis, MN: Center for Research on Developmental Education and Urban Literacy, General College, University of Minnesota.

Duranczyk, I. M., Leapard, B., Richards, E., & Caniglia, J. (2003). Rising stars. In T. Armington (Ed.), *Best practices in developmental education, Vol. 2.* (pp. 41–43). Findlay, OH: National Association for Developmental Education.

Duranczyk, I. M., Staats, S., Moore, R., Hatch, J., Jensen, M., & Somdahl, C. (2004). Developmental mathematics explored through a sociocultural lens. In I. M. Duranczyk, J. L. Higbee, & D. B. Lundell (Eds.), *Best practices for access and retention in higher education* (pp. 43–53). Minneapolis, MN: Center for Research on Developmental Education and Urban Literacy, General College, University of Minnesota.

Dwinell, P. L., & Higbee, J. L. (1990a). The role of assessment in predicting achievement among high risk freshmen: A bibliographic essay. *Journal of Educational Opportunity, 5*(1), 29–34.

Dwinell, P. L., & Higbee, J. L. (1990b). The Student Developmental Task and Lifestyle Inventory (SDTLI): Relationship to performance among developmental freshmen. *Georgia Journal of College Student Affairs, 5*, 29–34.

Dwinell, P. L., & Higbee, J. L. (1991a). Affective variables related to mathematics achievement among high risk college freshmen. *Psychological Reports, 69*, 399–403.

Dwinell, P. L., & Higbee, J. L. (1991b). The relationship between developmental tasks and academic success among high risk freshmen. *College Student Affairs Journal, 11*(1), 37–44.

Dwinell, P. L., & Higbee, J. L. (1993). Students' perceptions of the value of teaching evaluations. *Perceptual and Motor Skills, 76*, 995–1000.

Dwinell, P. L., & Higbee, J. L. (Eds.). (1997). *Developmental education: Enhancing student retention.* Carol Stream, IL: National Association for Developmental Education.

Dwinell, P. L., & Higbee, J. L. (Eds.). (1998). *Developmental education: Meeting diverse student needs.* Morrow, GA: National Association for Developmental Education.

Fox, J. A., & Higbee, J. L. (2002). Enhancing literacy through the application of Universal Instructional Design: The Curriculum Transformation and Disability (CTAD) project. In D. B. Lundell & J. L. Higbee (Eds.), *Exploring urban literacy and developmental education* (pp. 59–65). Minneapolis, MN: Center for Research on Developmental Education and Urban Literacy, General College, University of Minnesota.

Ghere, D. L. (2000). Teaching American history in a developmental education context. In J. L. Higbee & P. L. Dwinell (Eds.), *The many faces of developmental education* (pp. 39–46). Warrensburg, MO: National Association for Developmental Education.

Ghere, D. L. (2001). Constructivist perspectives and classroom simulations in developmental education. In D. B. Lundell & J. L. Higbee (Eds.). *Theoretical perspectives for developmental education* (pp. 101–108). Minneapolis, MN: Center for Research on Developmental Education and Urban Literacy, General College, University of Minnesota.

Ghere, D. L. (2003). Best practices with students in a college history course. In J. L. Higbee (Ed.), *Curriculum transformation and disability: Implementing Universal Design in higher education* (pp. 149–161). Minneapolis, MN: Center for Research on Developmental Education and Urban Literacy, General College, University of Minnesota.

Goolsby, C. B., Dwinell, P. L., Higbee, J. L., & Bretscher, A. S. (1994). Factors affecting mathematics achievement in high risk college students. In M. Maxwell (Ed.), *From access to success: What works best in college learning assistance* (pp. 253–259). Clearwater, FL: H & H. [Reprinted from *Research & Teaching in Developmental Education*]

Grier, T. (2004). Supplemental Instruction and noncognitive factors: Self-efficacy, outcome expectations, and effort regulation. *The Learning Assistance Review, 9*(2), 17–28.

Hare, S. C., Jacobs, W. R., & Shin, J. H. (1999). Entering the classroom from the other side: The life and times of graduate associate instructors. In B. Pescosolido & R. Aminzade (Eds.), *The social worlds of higher education: Handbook for teaching in a new century* (pp. 507–516). Thousand Oaks, CA: Pine Forge Press.

Higbee, J. L. (1988). Student development theory: A foundation for the individualized instruction of high risk freshmen. *Journal of Educational Opportunity, 3*, 42–47.

Higbee, J. L. (1989). Affective variables and success in mathematics: The counselor's role. *College Student Affairs Journal, 9*, 44–50.

Higbee, J. L. (1991). The role of developmental education in promoting pluralism. In H. E. Cheatham (Ed.), *Cultural pluralism on campus* (pp. 73–87). Alexandria, VA: American College Personnel Association.

Higbee, J. L. (1993). Developmental versus remedial: More than semantics. *Research & Teaching in Developmental Education, 9*(2), 99–105.

Higbee, J. L. (1995). Misplaced priorities or alternative developmental opportunities: A case study. *Research & Teaching in Developmental Education, 11*(2), 79–84.

Higbee, J. L. (1996a). Ability, preparation, or motivation? *Research & Teaching in Developmental Education, 13*(1), 93–96.

Higbee, J. L. (1996b). Defining developmental education: A commentary. In J. L. Higbee & P. L. Dwinell (Eds.), *Defining developmental education: Theory, research, and pedagogy* (pp. 63–66). Carol Stream, IL: National Association for Developmental Education.

Higbee, J. L. (1996c). "Who belongs" versus "Who gets to stay." *Research & Teaching in Developmental Education, 12*(2), 81–86.

Higbee, J. L. (1997). Barry: A case study on social adjustment. In B. Hodge & J. Preston-Sabin (Eds.), *Accommodations—Or just good teaching?* (pp. 100–103). Westport, CT: Praeger.

Higbee, J. L. (1999a). Can we teach responsibility? *Research & Teaching in Developmental Education, 15*(2), 81–84.

Higbee, J. L. (1999b). New directions for developmental reading programs: Meeting diverse student needs. In J. R. Dugan, P. E. Linder, W. M. Linek, & E. G. Sturtevant (Eds.), *Advancing the world of literacy: Moving into the 21st century* (pp. 172–181). Commerce, TX: College Reading Association.

Higbee, J. L. (2000). Commentary: Who is the developmental student? *The Learning Assistance Review, 5*(1), 41–50.

Higbee, J. L. (2001a). Implications of Universal Instructional Design for developmental education. *Research & Teaching in Developmental Education, 17*(2), 67–70.

Higbee, J. L. (2001b). Promoting multiculturalism in developmental education. *Research & Teaching in Developmental Education, 18*(1), 51–57.

Higbee, J. L. (2001c). The Student Personnel Point of View. In D. B. Lundell & J. L. Higbee (Eds.), *Theoretical perspectives for developmental education* (pp. 27–35). Minneapolis, MN: Center for Research on Developmental Education and Urban Literacy, General College, University of Minnesota.

Higbee, J. L. (Ed.). (2001d). *2001: A developmental odyssey*. Warrensburg, MO: National Association for Developmental Education.

Higbee, J. L. (2002a). Addressing current events in classroom discussions. *Research & Teaching in Developmental Education, 18*(2), 85–90.

Higbee, J. L. (2002b). The application of Chickering's theory of student development to student success in the sixties and beyond. *Research & Teaching in Developmental Education, 18*(2), 24–36.

Higbee, J. L., (2002c). The course syllabus: Communication tool or contract? *Research & Teaching in Developmental Education, 18*(1), 62–65.

Higbee, J. L. (2003a). Critical thinking and college success. *Research & Teaching in Developmental Education, 20*(1), 77–82.

Higbee, J. L. (Ed.). (2003b). *Curriculum transformation and disability: Implementing Universal Design in higher education*. Minneapolis, MN: Center for Research on Developmental Education and Urban Literacy, General College, University of Minnesota.

Higbee, J. L. (2003c). Response commentary: Math: Who needs it? *Journal of College Reading and Learning, 33*(2), 224–227.

Higbee, J. L. (2005). Developmental education. In M. L. Upcraft, J. N. Gardner, & B. O. Barefoot, & Associates, *Challenging and supporting the first-year student: A handbook for improving the first year of college* (pp. 292–307). San Francisco: Jossey-Bass.

Higbee, J. L., Arendale, D., & Lundell, D. B. (2005). Using theory and research to improve access and retention in developmental education. In C. Kozeracki (Ed.), *Increasing student success in developmental education.* (pp. 5–15). (New Directions for Community Colleges.) San Francisco: Jossey-Bass.

Higbee, J. L., Bruch, P. L., Jehangir, R. R., Lundell, D. B., & Miksch, K. L. (2003). The multicultural mission of developmental education: A starting point. *Research & Teaching in Developmental Education, 19*(2), 47–51.

Higbee, J. L., Chung, C. J., & Hsu, L. (2004). Enhancing the inclusiveness of first-year courses through Universal Instructional Design. In I. M. Duranczyk, J. L. Higbee, & D. B. Lundell (Eds.), *Best practices for access and retention in higher education* (pp. 13–25). Minneapolis, MN: Center for Research on Developmental Education and Urban Literacy, General College, University of Minnesota.

Higbee, J. L., & Dwinell, P. L. (1990a). Factors related to the academic success of high risk freshmen: Three case studies. *College Student Journal, 24*, 380–386.

Higbee, J. L., & Dwinell, P. L. (1990b). The high risk student profile. *Research & Teaching in Developmental Education, 7*(1), 55–64.

Higbee, J. L., & Dwinell, P. L. (1990c). Sources of stress and academic performance among high risk female and male college freshmen. *Georgia Journal of College Student Affairs, 5*, 30–33.

Higbee, J. L., & Dwinell, P. L. (1992a). The development of underprepared freshmen enrolled in a self-awareness course. *Journal of College Student Development, 33*, 26–33.

Higbee, J. L., & Dwinell, P. L. (1992b). The Developmental Inventory of Sources of Stress. *Research & Teaching in Developmental Education, 8*(2), 27–40.

Higbee, J. L., & Dwinell, P. L. (1993). A new role for counselors in academic affairs. *College Student Affairs Journal, 13*(1), 37–43.

Higbee, J. L., & Dwinell, P. L. (Eds.). (1994a). *Proceedings of the 18th annual conference of the National Association for Developmental Education: Fountains of opportunity.* Carol Stream, IL: National Association for Developmental Education.

Higbee, J. L., & Dwinell, P. L. (1994b). Salubrious lifestyle and academic achievement. *Research & Teaching in Developmental Education, 11*(1), 97–100.

Higbee, J. L., & Dwinell, P. L. (1994c). Student evaluations of part-time and full-time faculty in a developmental education program. *Research & Teaching in Developmental Education, 10*(2), 109–118.

Higbee, J. L., & Dwinell, P. L. (1995a). Affect: How important is it? *Research & Teaching in Developmental Education, 12*(1), 71–74.

Higbee, J. L., & Dwinell, P. L. (Eds.). (1995b). *Selected conference papers, Volume 1: Architects of the future.* Carol Stream, IL: National Association for Developmental Education.

Higbee, J. L., & Dwinell, P. L. (1996a). Correlates of self-esteem among high risk students. *Research & Teaching in Developmental Education, 12*(2), 41–50.

Higbee, J. L., & Dwinell, P. L. (Eds.) (1996b). *Defining developmental education: Theory, research, and pedagogy.* Carol Stream, IL: National Association for Developmental Education.

Higbee, J. L., & Dwinell, P. L. (1997a). Do developmental education programs really enhance retention? A commentary. In P. L. Dwinell & J. L. Higbee (Eds.), *Developmental education: Enhancing student retention* (pp. 55–60). Carol Stream, IL: National Association for Developmental Education.

Higbee, J. L., & Dwinell, P. L. (1997b). Educating students about the purpose of higher education. *Research & Teaching in Developmental Education, 14*(1), 75–80.

Higbee, J. L., & Dwinell, P. L. (Eds.). (1998a). *Developmental education: Preparing successful college students.* Columbia, SC: National Resource Center for The First-Year Experience & Students in Transition, University of South Carolina.

Higbee, J. L., & Dwinell, P. L. (1998b). The relationship between student development and the ability to think critically. *Research & Teaching Developmental Education, 14* (2), 93–97.

Higbee, J. L., & Dwinell, P. L. (1998c). Transitions in developmental education at the University of Georgia. In J. L. Higbee & P. L. Dwinell (Eds.), *Developmental education: Preparing successful college students* (pp. 55–61). Columbia, SC: National Resource Center for The First-Year Experience & Students in Transition, University of South Carolina.

Higbee, J. L., & Dwinell, P. L. (1999a). Depression and suicide among traditional age college students. *Research & Teaching in Developmental Education, 16*(1), 89–92.

Higbee, J. L., & Dwinell, P.L. (Eds.). (1999b). *The expanding role of developmental education.* Morrow, GA: National Association for Developmental Education.

Higbee, J. L., & Dwinell, P.L. (Eds.). (2000). *The many faces of developmental education.* Warrensburg, MO: National Association for Developmental Education.

Higbee, J. L., Dwinell, P. L., McAdams, C. R., GoldbergBelle, E., & Tardola, M. E. (1991). Serving underprepared students in institutions of higher education. *Journal of Humanistic Education and Development, 30*, 73–80.

Higbee, J. L., Dwinell, P. L., & Thomas, P. V. (2002). Beyond University 101: Elective courses to enhance retention. *Journal of College Student Retention: Research, Theory, and Practice, 3*, 311–318.

Higbee, J. L., & Eaton, S. B. (2003). Implementing Universal Design in learning centers. In J. L. Higbee (Ed.), *Curriculum transformation and disability: Implementing Universal Design in higher education* (pp. 231–239). Minneapolis, MN: Center for Research on Developmental Education and Urban Literacy, General College, University of Minnesota.

Higbee, J. L., Ginter, E. J., & Taylor, W. D. (1991). Enhancing academic performance: Seven perceptual styles of learning. *Research & Teaching in Developmental Education, 7*(2), 5–10.

Higbee, J. L., & Kalivoda, K. S. (2003). The first-year experience. In J. L. Higbee (Ed.), *Curriculum transformation and disability: Implementing Universal Design in higher education* (pp. 203–213). Minneapolis, MN: Center for Research on Developmental Education and Urban Literacy, General College, University of Minnesota.

Higbee, J. L., Kalivoda, K. S., & Hunt, P. (1993). Serving students with psychological disabilities. In P. Malinowski (Ed.), *Perspectives in practice in developmental education* (pp. 90–92). Canandaigua, NY: New York College Learning Skills Association.

Higbee, J. L., Lundell, D. B., & Duranczyk, I. M. (Eds.). (2002). *Developmental education: Policy and practice.* Auburn, CA: National Association for Developmental Education.

Higbee, J. L., Lundell, D. B., & Duranczyk, I. M. (Eds.). (2003). *Multiculturalism in developmental education.* Minneapolis, MN: Center for Research on Developmental Education and Urban Literacy, General College, University of Minnesota.

Higbee, J. L., Miksch, K. L., Jehangir, R. R., Lundell. D. B., Bruch, P. L., & Jiang, F. (2004). Assessing our commitment to providing a multicultural learning experience. *Journal of College Reading and Learning, 34*(2), 61–74.

Higbee, J. L., & Pettman, H. C. H. (2003). Report of the Future Directions Meeting multicultural theme track. In J. L. Higbee, D. B. Lundell, & I. M. Duranczyk (Eds.), *Multiculturalism in developmental education* (pp. 69–74). Minneapolis, MN: Center for Research on Developmental Education and Urban Literacy, General College, University of Minnesota.

Higbee, J. L., & Thomas, P. V. (1998). Daily brain teasers: Promoting collaboration, persistence, and critical and creative thinking. *Academic Exchange Quarterly, 2* (4), 20–23.

Higbee, J. L., & Thomas, P. V. (1999). Affective and cognitive factors related to mathematics achievement. *Journal of Developmental Education, 23*(1), 8–10, 12, 14, 16, 32.

Higbee, J. L., & Thomas, P. V. (2000a). Creating assessment tools to determine student needs. *Research & Teaching in Developmental Education, 16*(2), 83–87.

Higbee, J. L., & Thomas, P. V. (2002). Student and faculty perceptions of behaviors that constitute cheating. *NASPA Journal, 40*(1), 39–52.

Higbee, J. L., Thomas, P. V., Hayes, C. G., Glauser, A. S., & Hynd, C. R. (1998). Expanding developmental education services: Seeking faculty input. *The Learning Assistance Review, 3*(1), 20–31.

Hsu, L., Moore, R., Jensen, M., & Hatch, J. (in press). The role of science courses in developmental education. *Journal of Developmental Education.*

Jacobs, W. R. (1998). The teacher as text: Using personal experience to stimulate the sociological imagination. *Teaching Sociology, 26*(3), 222–228.

Jacobs, W. R. (2002a). Learning and living difference that makes a difference: Postmodern theory and multicultural education. *Multicultural Education, 9*(4), 2–10.

Jacobs, W. R. (2002b). Using lower-division developmental education students as teaching assistants. *Research & Teaching in Developmental Education, 19*(1), 41–48.

Jacobs, W. R., Reynolds, T. J., & Choy, G. P. (2004). The Educational Storytelling Project: Three approaches to cross-curricular learning. *Journal of College Reading and Learning, 35*(1), 50–66.

James, P. (1999). Ideas in practice: The arts as a path for developmental student learning. *Journal of Developmental Education, 22*(3), 22–28.

James, P. (2000a). Blocks and bridges: Learning artistic creativity. *Arts and Learning Research Journal, 16*(1), 110–133.

James, P. (2000b). "I am the dark forest:" Personal analogy as a way to understand metaphor. *Art Education, 53*(5), 6–11.

James, P. (2000c). Strategies for using the arts in developmental education. In M. R. Hay & N. L. Ludman (Eds.), *NADE Selected Conference Papers, Vol. 5* (pp. 16–19). Detroit, MI: National Association for Developmental Education.

James, P. (2000d). Working toward meaning: The evolution of an assignment. *Studies in Art Education, 41*(2), 146–163.

James, P. (2002a). Ideas in practice: Fostering metaphoric thinking. *Journal of Developmental Education, 25*(3), 26–28, 30, 32–33.

James, P. (2002b). Images, movements, and sounds: Working toward meaning. In E. Mirochnik & D. Sherman (Eds.), *Passion and pedagogy: Relation, creation, and transformation in teaching* (pp. 233–242). New York: Peter Lang.

James, P. (2002–2003). Between the ideal and the real: A reflective study of teaching art to young adults. *Arts & Learning Research Journal, 19*(1), 1–22.

James, P. (2004). Beyond her own boundaries: A portrait of creative work. *Studies in Art Education, 45*(4), 359–373.

James, P., & Haselbeck, B. (1998). The arts as a bridge to understanding identity and diversity. In P. L. Dwinell & J. L. Higbee (Eds.), *Developmental education: Meeting diverse student needs* (pp. 3–20). Morrow, GA: National Association for Developmental Education.

Jehangir, R. R. (2002). Higher education for whom? The battle to include developmental education in the four-year university. In J. L. Higbee, D. B. Lundell, & I. M. Duranczyk (Eds.), *Developmental education: Policy and practice* (pp. 17–34). Auburn, CA: National Association for Developmental Education.

Jehangir, R., Yamasaki, M., Ghere, D., Hugg, N., Williams, L., & Higbee, J. (2002). Creating welcoming spaces. In R. Bashaw & A. Rios (Eds.), *Symposium Proceedings of Keeping Our Faculties of Color: Addressing the recruitment and retention of faculty of color.* Minneapolis, MN: University of Minnesota.

Jensen, M., Moore, R., & Hatch, J. (2002a). Cooperative learning: Part I. Cooperative quizzes. *The American Biology Teacher, 64*(1), 29–34.

Jensen, M., Moore, R., & Hatch, J. (2002b). Cooperative learning: Part II. Setting the tone with group Web pages. *The American Biology Teacher, 64*(2), 118–120.

Jensen, M., Moore, R., & Hatch, J. (2002c). Cooperative learning: Part III. Electronic cooperative quizzes. *The American Biology Teacher, 64*(3), 29–34.

Jensen, M., Moore, R., & Hatch, J. (2002d). Cooperative learning: Part IV. Group Web projects for freshman anatomy and physiology students. *The American Biology Teacher, 64*(4), 206–209.

Jensen, M., Moore, R., Hatch, J., & Hsu, L. (2003). Ideas in practice: A novel, "cool" assignment to engage science students. *Journal of Developmental Education, 27*(2), 28–30, 32–33.

Jensen, M., & Rush, R. (2000). Teaching a human anatomy and physiology course within the context of developmental education. In J. L. Higbee & P. L. Dwinell (Eds.), *The many faces of developmental education* (pp. 47–57). Warrensburg, MO: National Association for Developmental Education

Johnson, A. B. (1993). Enhancing general education science courses. *College Teaching, 41*(2), 55–58.

Johnson, A. B. (2001). Theoretical views and practices supporting in-context developmental strategies in the physical sciences. In D. B. Lundell & J. L. Higbee (Eds.), *Theoretical perspectives for developmental education* (pp. 153–161). Minneapolis, MN: Center for Research on Developmental Education and Urban Literacy, General College, University of Minnesota.

Jones, G. C., Kalivoda, K. S., & Higbee, J. L. (1997). College students with Attention Deficit Disorder. *NASPA Journal, 34*, 262–274.

Kalivoda, K. S., & Higbee, J. L. (1989). Students with disabilities in higher education: Redefining access. *Journal of Educational Opportunity, 4*, 14–21.

Kalivoda, K. S., & Higbee, J. L. (1994). Implementing the Americans with Disabilities Act. *Journal of Humanistic Education and Development, 32*, 133–137.

Kalivoda, K. S., & Higbee, J. L. (1995). A theoretical model for the prediction of faculty intention to accommodate disabled students. *Journal of the Mid-American Association of Educational Opportunity Program Personnel, 7*(1), 7–22.

Kalivoda, K. S., & Higbee, J. L. (1998). Influencing faculty attitudes toward accommodating students with disabilities: A theoretical approach. *The Learning Assistance Review, 3*(2), 12–25.

Kalivoda, K. S., & Higbee, J. L. (1999). Serving college students with disabilities: Application of the theory of planned behavior. *Academic Exchange Quarterly, 3*(2), 6–16.

Kalivoda, K. S.. Higbee, J. L., & Brenner, D. C. (2003). Teaching students with hearing impairments. In N. A. Stahl & H. Boylan (Eds.), *Teaching developmental read-*

ing: Historical, theoretical, and practical background readings. Boston: Bedford/St. Martin's. [Reprinted from the *Journal of Developmental Education.*]

Kinney, D. P. (2001a). The American Mathematical Association of Two-Year College Standards and mediated learning. In D. B. Lundell & J. L. Higbee (Eds.), *Theoretical perspectives for developmental education* (pp. 173–82). Minneapolis, MN: Center for Research in Developmental Education and Urban Literacy, General College, University of Minnesota.

Kinney, D. P. (2001b). An application of developmental theory in a developmental mathematics program. *Journal of Developmental Education, 25*(2), 10–18.

Kinney, D. P. (2001c). A comparison of computer-mediated and lecture classes in developmental mathematics. *Research & Teaching in Developmental Education, 18*(1), 32–40.

Kinney, D. P. (2002a). Implementation models for interactive multimedia software in developmental mathematics. In M. R. Hay & N. L. Ludman (Eds.), *2001 Selected Conference Papers* (pp. 35–40). Dowagiac, MI: National Association for Developmental Education..

Kinney, D. P. (2002b). Students with disabilities in mathematics: Barriers and recommendations. *The AMATYC Review, 23*(1), 13–23.

Kinney, D. P., & Kinney, L. S. (2002). Instructors' perspectives of instruction in computer-mediated and lecture developmental mathematics classes. In J. L. Higbee, I. M. Duranczyk, & D. B. Lundell (Eds.), *Developmental education: Policy and practice* (pp. 127–138). Warrensburg, MO: National Association for Developmental Education

Kinney, D. P., & Robertson, D. F. (2003). Technology makes possible new models for delivering developmental mathematics instruction. *Mathematics and Computer Education, 37*(3), 315–328.

Kinney, D. P., Stottlemyer, J., Hatfield, J., & Robertson, D. F. (2004). Comparison of the characteristics of computer-mediated and lecture students in developmental mathematics. *Research & Teaching in Developmental Education, 21,* 14–28.

Knox, D. K., Higbee, J. L., Kalivoda, K. S., & Totty, M. C. (2000). Serving the diverse needs of students with disabilities through technology. *Journal of College Reading and Learning, 30*(2), 144–157.

Lee, A. (2000). *Composing critical pedagogies: Teaching writing as revision.* Urbana, IL: National Council of Teachers of English.

Lee, A. (2001). Getting basic: Exposing a teacher's deficiencies. In D. B. Lundell & J. L. Higbee (Eds.), *Theoretical perspectives for developmental education* (pp. 111–120). Minneapolis, MN: Center for Research in Developmental Education and Urban Literacy, General College, University of Minnesota.

Lee, A. (2002). Developing pedagogies: Learning the teaching of English. *College English, 64,* 326–347.

Lundell, D. B., & Beach, R. (2002). Dissertation writers' negotiations with competing activity systems. In C. Bazerman & D. Russell (Eds.), *Writing selves/writing societies: Research from activity perspectives. Perspectives on writing.* Fort Collins, CO: The WAC Clearinghouse.

Lundell, D. B., Chung, C., Ghere, D., Higbee, J., & Kinney, P. (2003). Setting the pace: Theoretical perspectives for developmental education. In M. R. Hay & N. Ludman (Eds.), *2001 Selected Conference Papers* (pp. 45–49). Dowagiac, MI: National Association for Developmental Education.

Lundell, D. B., & Collins, T. C. (2001). Toward a theory of developmental education: The centrality of "Discourse." In D. B. Lundell & J. L. Higbee (Eds.), *Theoretical perspectives in developmental education* (pp. 49–61). Minneapolis, MN: Center for Research on Developmental Education and Urban Literacy, General College, University of Minnesota.

Lundell, D. B., & Higbee, J. L. (Eds.). (2000). *Proceedings of the First Intentional Meeting on Future Directions in Developmental Education.* Minneapolis, MN: Center for Research on Developmental Education and Urban Literacy, General College, University of Minnesota.

Lundell, D. B., & Higbee, J. L. (Eds.). (2001). *Theoretical perspectives for developmental education.* Minneapolis, MN: Center for Research on Developmental Education and Urban Literacy, General College, University of Minnesota.

Lundell, D. B., & Higbee, J. L. (Eds.). (2002a). *Exploring urban literacy and developmental education.* Minneapolis, MN: Center for Research on Developmental Education and Urban Literacy, General College, University of Minnesota.

Lundell, D. B., & Higbee, J. L. (Eds.). (2002b). *Histories of developmental education.* Minneapolis, MN: Center for Research on Developmental Education and Urban Literacy, General College, University of Minnesota.

Lundell, D. B., & Higbee, J. L. (Eds.). (2002c). *Proceedings of the Second Meeting on Future Directions in Developmental Education.* Minneapolis, MN: Center for Research on Developmental Education and Urban Literacy, General College, University of Minnesota.

Madyun, N., Grier, T., Brothen, T., & Wambach, C. (2004). Supplemental Instruction in a Personalized System of Instruction general psychology course. *The Learning Assistance Review, 9*(1), 7–16.

Martin, D. C., & Arendale, D. (Eds.). (1993). *Supplemental Instruction: Improving first-year student success in high risk courses* (2nd ed.). Columbia, SC: National Resource Center for The First-Year Experience, University of South Carolina.

Martin, D. C., & Arendale, D. (Eds.). (1994). *Supplemental Instruction: Increasing student achievement and retention.* (New Directions in Teaching and Learning, No. 60). San Francisco: Jossey-Bass

Martin, D. C., Arendale, D., & Widmar, G. E. (1998). Creating communities for learning. In L. Hardge (Ed.), *Bridges to student success: Exemplary programs 1998* (pp. 27–33). Washington, D.C.: National Association for Student Personnel Administrators.

Martin, D. C., Blanc, R., & Arendale, D. (1996). Supplemental Instruction: Supporting the classroom experience. In J. N. Hankin (Ed.), *The community college: Opportunity and access for America's first-year students* (pp. 123–133). Columbia, SC: National Resource Center for the First-Year Experience & Students in Transition.

Martin, D. C., Hall, P. T., & Arendale, D. (1993). Use of Supplemental Instruction at an urban high school. In D. C. Martin & D. Arendale (Eds.), *Supplemental Instruction:*

Improving first-year student success in high-risk courses (2nd ed.; pp. 38–39). Columbia, SC: National Resource Center for The First-Year Experience & Students in Transition, University of South Carolina.

Miksch, K. L. (2002a). Education law and student access: Why isn't education a fundamental right? In J. L. Higbee, D. B. Lundell, & I. M. Duranczyk (Eds.), *Developmental education: Policy and practice* (pp. 65–76). Auburn, CA: National Association for Developmental Education.

Miksch, K. L. (2002b). Legal issues in developmental education: Diversity as a key element. *Research & Teaching in Developmental Education, 19*(1), 55–61.

Miksch, K. L. (2003a). Legal issues in developmental education: Affirmative action, race, and critical mass. *Research & Teaching in Developmental Education, 20* (1), 69–76.

Miksch, K. L. (2003b). Legal issues in developmental education: The impact of high-stakes testing. *Research & Teaching in Developmental Education, 19* (2), 53–59.

Miksch, K. L. (2003c). Universal Instructional Design in a legal studies classroom. In J. L. Higbee (Ed.), *Curriculum transformation and disability: Implementing Universal Design in higher education* (pp. 163–170). Minneapolis, MN: Center for Research on Developmental Education and Urban Literacy, General College, University of Minnesota.

Miksch, K. L (2004). Legal issues in developmental education: Merit-based vs. need-based financial aid. *Research & Teaching in Developmental Education, 21*(1), 78–84.

Miksch, K. L., Bruch, P. L., Higbee, J. L., Jehangir, R. R., & Lundell, D. B. (2003). The centrality of multiculturalism in developmental education. In J. L. Higbee, D. B. Lundell, & I. M. Duranczyk (Eds.), *Multiculturalism in developmental education* (pp. 5–13). Minneapolis, MN: Center for Research on Developmental Education and Urban Literacy, General College, University of Minnesota.

Miksch, K. L., & Ghere, D. (2004). Teaching Japanese incarceration. *The History Teacher, 37* (2), 211–227.

Miksch, K. L., Higbee, J. L., Jehangir, R. R., Lundell, D. B., Bruch, P. L. & Jiang, F. (2002*). Multicultural Awareness Project for Institutional Transformation (MAP-IT) pilot study.* Unpublished manuscript. Minneapolis, MN: Center for Research on Developmental Education and Urban Literacy and the Multicultural Concerns Committee, General College, University of Minnesota.

Miksch, K. L., Higbee, J. L., Jehangir, R. R., Lundell, D. B., Bruch, P. L., Siaka, K., & Dotson, M. V. (2003). *Multicultural Awareness Project for Institutional Transformation: MAP IT.* Minneapolis, MN: Multicultural Concerns Committee and Center for Research on Developmental Education and Urban Literacy, General College, University of Minnesota.

Moore, R. (1990). What's wrong with science education and how can we fix it? *The American Biology Teacher, 52,* 330–337.

Moore, R. (1991). Critical thinking in biology classes. *Strategies for Success in Anatomy & Physiology and Life Science, 5,* 1–3.

Moore, R. (1992a). How should we mark students' essays? *Journal of College Biology Teaching, 18,* 3–9.

Moore, R. (1992b). *Instructor's manual to accompany Writing to Learn Biology.* Philadelphia, PA: Saunders.

Moore, R. (1992c). *Writing to learn biology.* Philadelphia, PA: Saunders.

Moore, R. (1993). Does writing about science enhance learning about science? *Journal of College Science Teaching, 22,* 212–217.

Moore, R. (1994). Writing to learn biology. *Journal of College Science Teaching, 23,* 289–295.

Moore, R. (1995). *Biology labs that work: The best of how-to-do-its.* Reston, VA: National Association of Biology Teachers.

Moore, R. (1997). *Writing to learn science.* Philadelphia, PA: Saunders.

Moore, R. (2001). Administering science education: Expanding the pool of the "best and brightest." *Review of Human Factor Studies, 7*(1), 44–60.

Moore, R. (2002a). Do state standards matter? How the quality of state standards relates to evolution instruction. *The Science Teacher, 69*(1), 49–51.

Moore, R. (2002b). *Evolution in the courtroom: A reference guide.* Santa Barbara, CA: ABC-CLIO.

Moore, R. (2002c). The fates of developmental education students at two-year and four-year colleges. In J. L. Higbee, D. B. Lundell, & I. M. Duranczyk (Eds), *Developmental education: Policy and practice* (pp. 55–64). Auburn, CA: National Association for Developmental Education.

Moore, R. (2002d). The lessons of history: Transforming science to include developmental education. In D. B. Lundell & J. L. Higbee (Eds.), *Theoretical perspectives for developmental education* (pp. 83–92). Minneapolis, MN: Center for Research on Developmental Education and Urban Literacy, General College, University of Minnesota.

Moore, R. (2002e). Science education and the urban achievement gap. In D. B. Lundell & J. L. Higbee (Eds.), *Exploring urban literacy and developmental education* (pp. 33–45). Minneapolis, MN: Center for Research on Developmental Education and Urban Literacy, General College, University of Minnesota.

Moore, R. (2003a). Attendance and performance: How important is it for students to attend class? *Journal of College Science Teaching, 33,* 367–371.

Moore, R. (2003b). Do standards-based reforms penalize developmental education students? In I. M. Duranczyk & W. G. White (Eds.), *Developmental education: Pathways to excellence* (pp. 1–12). Findlay, OH: National Association for Developmental Education.

Moore, R. (2003c). Helping students succeed in introductory biology classes: Does improving students' attendance also improve their grades? *Bioscene, 29*(3), 17–25.

Moore, R. (2003d). Students' choices in developmental education: Is it really important to attend class? *Research & Teaching in Developmental Education, 20*(1), 42–52.

Moore, R. (2004a). Do colleges identify or develop intelligence? *Journal of Developmental Education, 28*(1), 28–30, 32.

Moore, R. (2004b). Does improving developmental education students' understanding of the importance of class attendance improve students' attendance and academic performance? *Research & Teaching in Developmental Education, 20*(2), 24–39.

Moore, R., Jensen, M., & Hatch, J. (2001). Bad teaching: It's not just for the classroom anymore. *The American Biology Teacher, 63*(6), 389–391.

Moore, R., Jensen, M., & Hatch, J. (2002). The retention of developmental education students at four-year and two-year institutions. *Research & Teaching in Developmental Education, 19*, 5–13.

Moore, R., Jensen, M., Hatch, J., Duranczyk, I., Staats, S., & Koch, L. (2003). Showing up: The importance of class attendance for academic success in introductory science courses. *The American Biology Teacher, 65*, 325–329.

Moore, R., Jensen, M., Hsu, L., & Hatch, J. (2002). Saving the "false negatives": Intelligence tests, the SAT, and developmental education. In D. B. Lundell & J. L. Higbee (Eds.), *Exploring urban literacy and developmental education* (pp. 47–57). Minneapolis, MN: Center for Research on Developmental Education and Urban Literacy, General College, University of Minnesota.

Moore, R., & Miksch, K. L. (2003). Evolution, creationism, and the courts: 20 questions. *The Science Education Review, 2*(1), 1–15.

Moore, R., & Miller, I. (1996). How the use of multimedia affects student retention and learning. *Journal of College Science Teaching, 26*, 289–293.

Opitz, D. L. (2004b). Storyteller. *Access: The General College Magazine, 3*(3), 8–9.

Pedelty, M.(2001a). The Cultural Dialogue Project (CDP): Approaching ethnographic texts through playwriting and performance. In P. Rice & D. McCurdy (Eds.), *Strategies for teaching Anthropology: Vol. 3* (pp. 128–134). Upper Saddle River, NJ: Prentice Hall.

Pedelty, M. (2001b). Jenny's painting: Multiple forms of communication in the classroom. In B. L. Smith & J. McCann (Eds.), *Reinventing ourselves: Interdisciplinary education, collaborative learning and experimentation in higher education* (pp. 230–252). Boston: Anker.

Pedelty, M. (2001c). Stigma. In J. L. Higbee (Ed.), *2001: A developmental odyssey* (pp. 53–70). Warrensburg, MO: National Association for Developmental Education.

Pedelty, M. (2001d). Teaching anthropology through performance. *Anthropology and Education Quarterly, 32*(2), 244–253.

Pedelty, M. (2002). Collaborative education and democracy. *Journal of Curriculum Theorizing, 18*(4), 127–141.

Pedelty, M. (2003a). Between many masks: Teaching stigmatized students. In K. C. MacKinnon (Ed.), *Behind many masks: Gerald Berreman and Berkeley anthropology, 1959–2001* (pp. 287–303). Berkeley, CA: Kroeber Society Papers.

Pedelty, M. (2003b). Making a statement. In J. L. Higbee (Ed.), *Curriculum transform and disability: Implementing Universal Design in higher education* (pp. 71–78). Minneapolis, MN: Center for Research on Developmental Education and Urban Literacy, General College, University of Minnesota.

Pedelty, M. (2004). Ritual and performance. In P. Rice & D. McCurdy (Eds.), *Strategies for teaching anthropology: Vol. 2* (pp.150–154). Upper Saddle River, NJ: Prentice Hall.

Pedelty, M. H., & Jacobs W. R. (2001). The place of "culture" in developmental education's social sciences. In D. B. Lundell & J. L. Higbee (Eds.), *Theoretical perspectives in developmental education* (pp. 75–90). Minneapolis, MN: Center for Research on Developmental Education and Urban Literacy, General College, University of Minnesota.

Peterson, S., & delMas, R. (1998). The component structure of career decision-making self-efficacy for underprepared college students. *Journal of Career Development, 24*(3), 209–255.

Reynolds, T. J., & Bruch, P. L. (2002). Curriculum and affect: A participatory developmental writing approach. *Journal of Developmental Education, 26*(2), 12–14, 16, 18, 20.

Schmitz, C. C., & delMas, R. C. (1991). Determining the validity of placement exams for developmental college curricula. *Applied Measurement in Education, 4*(1), 37–52.

Steel, P., Brothen, T., & Wambach, C. (2000). Procrastination, personality, performance and mood. *Personality and Individual Differences, 30,* 95–106.

Thomas, P. V., & Higbee, J. L. (1996). Enhancing mathematics achievement through collaborative problem solving. *The Learning Assistance Review, 1*(1), 38–46.

Thomas, P. V., & Higbee, J. L. (2000a). Preventing academic dishonesty. *Research & Teaching in Developmental Education, 17*(1), 63–66.

Thomas, P. V., & Higbee, J. L. (2000b). The relationship between involvement and success in developmental algebra. *Journal of College Reading and Learning, 30*(2), 222–232.

Thomas, P. V., & Higbee, J. L. (2001). Teaching mathematics on television: Perks and pitfalls. In L. S. Hagedorn (Ed.), *Sound instruction: Ready to use classroom practice* (pp. 67–70). Chattanooga, TN: Rapid Intellect. [Reprinted from *Academic Exchange Quarterly*]

Vodopich, D., & Moore, R. (2002). *Biology laboratory manual* (6th ed.). Dubuque, IA: McGraw-Hill.

Voge, D. J., & Higbee, J. L. (2004). A "grade A" controversy: A dialogue on grading policies and related issues in higher education. *Research & Teaching in Developmental Education, 21*(1), 63–77.

Wambach, C. (1992). Study questions vs. journals for underprepared freshmen. In P. A. Malinowshi & S. D. Huard (Eds.), *Perspectives on practice in developmental education* (pp. 43–44). Canandaigua, NY: New York College Learning Skills Association.

Wambach, C. (1993) Motivational themes and academic success of at-risk freshmen. *Journal of Developmental Education, 16*(3), 8–10, 12, 37.

Wambach, C. (1998). Reading and writing expectations at a research university. *Journal of Developmental Education, 22*(2), 22–26.

Wambach, C., & Brothen, T. (1990). A criterion model for developmental students. *Journal of Developmental Education, 13*(3), 14–15, 24–26.

Wambach, C., & Brothen, T. (1997). Teacher self-disclosure and student classroom participation: Effect or artifact? *Teaching of Psychology, 24,* 262–263.

Wambach, C., & Brothen, T. (2000). Content area reading tests are not a solution to reading test validity problems. *Journal of Developmental Education, 24*(2), 42–43.

Wambach, C., & Brothen, T. (2001). A case study of procrastination in a computer assisted introductory psychology course. *Research & Teaching in Developmental Education,17*(2), 41–52.

Wambach, C., Brothen, T., & Dikel, T. (2000). Toward a developmental theory for developmental educators. *Journal of Developmental Education, 24*(1), 2–4, 6, 8, 10, 29.

Wambach, C., & delMas, R. (1998). Developmental education at a public research university. In J. L. Higbee & P. L. Dwinell (Eds.), *Developmental education: Preparing successful college students* (pp. 63–77). Columbia, SC: National Resource Center for The First-Year Experience & Students in Transition, University of South Carolina.

Warner, J. F., Duranczyk, I. M., & Richards, E. (2000). Developmental math students meet success in a cooperative program emphasizing concepts. In J. L. Higbee & P L. Dwinell (Eds.), *The many faces of developmental education* (pp. 73–84). Warrensburg, MO: National Association for Developmental Education.

Wilcox, K., delMas, R., Stewart, B., Johnson, A., & Ghere, D. (1997). The "package course" experience and developmental education at the General College, University of Minnesota. *Journal of Developmental Education, 20*(3), 18–26.